For Charles Reynolds
with warm regards
Per Brinch Hansen

CLASSIC OPERATING SYSTEMS

From Batch Processing To Distributed Systems

Springer
New York
Berlin
Heidelberg
Barcelona
Hong Kong
London
Milan
Paris
Singapore
Tokyo

CLASSIC OPERATING SYSTEMS

From Batch Processing To Distributed Systems

Selected by PER BRINCH HANSEN

Springer

Per Brinch Hansen
Center for Science and Technology
Syracuse University
Syracuse, NY 13244
USA
pbh@top.cis.syr.edu

Library of Congress Cataloging-in-Publication Data

Brinch Hansen, Per, 1938–
Classic operating systems: from batch processing to distributed systems/Per Brinch Hansen.
p. cm.
Includes bibliographical references.
ISBN 0-387-95113-X (alk. paper)
1. Operating systems (Computers) I. Title.
QA76.76.O63 B7425 2000
004'.3–dc21
00-045036

Printed on acid-free paper.

Production managed by Frank McGuckin; manufacturing supervised by Erica Bresler.
Camera-ready copy prepared from the author's LaTeX 2_ε files.
Printed and bound by Hamilton Printing Co., Rensselaer, NY.
Printed in the United States of America.

9 8 7 6 5 4 3 2 1

ISBN 0-387-95113-X SPIN 10777099

Springer-Verlag New York Berlin Heidelberg
A member of BertelsmannSpringer Science+Business Media GmbH

FOR MILENA

PREFACE

In operating systems courses you learn useful *principles*, but very little about the difficult art of *software design*. So I decided to go back to the masters who made the major discoveries in operating systems and put some of their best papers together in a book and call it *Classic Operating Systems: From Batch Processing to Distributed Systems.*

Well, here is that book. The papers illustrate *the major breakthroughs in operating system technology from the 1950s to the 1990s.* All of them are written by the pioneers who designed these systems. I have added an introduction that summarizes the papers and puts them in perspective.

The book is for professional programmers and students of electrical engineering and computer science. I assume you are familiar with operating system principles. From this book you will learn something else: *How do operating system designers think?*

I hope you will enjoy reading these classic papers as much as I did.

I thank the copyright owners for permission to reprint these papers. A footnote on the title page of each paper gives full credit to the publication in which the work first appeared, including the name of the copyright holder.

PER BRINCH HANSEN
Syracuse University

CONTENTS

THE EVOLUTION OF OPERATING SYSTEMS*

PER BRINCH HANSEN

(2000)

The author looks back on the first half century of operating systems and selects his favorite papers on classic operating systems. These papers span the entire history of the field from the batch processing systems of the 1950s to the distributed systems of the 1990s. Each paper describes an operating system that combines significant ideas in an elegant way. Most of them were written by the pioneers who had the visions and the drive to make them work. The author summarizes each paper and concludes that operating systems are based on a surprisingly small number of ideas of permanent interest.

INTRODUCTION

The year 2000 marks the first half century of computer operating systems. To learn from the pioneers of the field, I have selected *my favorite papers on classic operating systems.* These papers span the entire history of the field from the batch processing systems of the 1950s to the distributed systems of the 1990s. I assume that you already know how operating systems work, but not necessarily how they were invented.

The widespread use of certain operating systems is of no interest to me, since it often has no obvious relationship to the merits (or flaws) of these systems. To paraphrase G. H. Hardy (1969), *Beauty is the first test: there is no permanent place in the world for ugly ideas.*

Let me explain how I made my choices:

---

*P. Brinch Hansen, The evolution of operating systems. In *Classic Operating Systems: From Batch Processing to Distributed Systems*, P. Brinch Hansen, Ed. Copyright © 2000, Springer-Verlag, New York.

- *Each paper describes an operating system that combines significant ideas in an elegant way.*
- I picked mostly papers written by the pioneers who had the visions and the drive to make them work. I also included a few elegant systems that broke no new ground, but convincingly demonstrated the best ideas known at the time.
- I would have preferred short papers that were a pleasure to read. However, as Peter Medawar (1979) truthfully has said, "Most scientists do *not* know how to write." In some cases, I had to settle for papers in which "clarity has been achieved and the style, if not graceful, is at least not raw and angular."

The evolution of operating systems went through seven *major phases* (Table 1). Six of them significantly changed the ways in which users accessed computers through the open shop, batch processing, multiprogramming, timesharing, personal computing, and distributed systems. In the seventh phase the foundations of concurrent programming were developed and demonstrated in model operating systems.

Table 1 Classic Operating Systems

	Major Phases		*Operating Systems*
I	Open Shop	1	IBM 701 open shop (1954)
II	Batch Processing	2	BKS system (1961)
III	Multiprogramming	3	Atlas supervisor (1961)
		4	B5000 system (1964)
		5	Exec II system (1966)
		6	Egdon system (1966)
IV	Timesharing	7	CTSS (1962)
		8	Multics file system (1965)
		9	Titan file system (1972)
		10	Unix (1974)
V	Concurrent Programming	11	THE system (1968)
		12	RC 4000 system (1969)
		13	Venus system (1972)
		14	Boss 2 system (1975)
		15	Solo system (1976)
		16	Solo program text (1976)
VI	Personal Computing	17	OS 6 (1972)
		18	Alto system (1979)
		19	Pilot system (1980)
		20	Star user interface (1982)
VII	Distributed Systems	21	WFS file server (1979)
		22	Unix United RPC (1982)
		23	Unix United system (1982)
		24	Amoeba system (1990)

I chose 24 papers on *classic operating systems* with reasonable confidence. With so many contenders for a place in operating systems history, you will probably disagree with some of my choices. For each phase, I attempted to include a couple of early *pioneering* systems followed by a few of the later systems. Some of the latter could undoubtedly have been replaced by other equally *representative* systems. Although I left out a few *dinosaurs*, I hope that there are no *missing links.*

The publication dates reveal that the 1960s and 1970s were the vintage years of operating systems; by comparison, the 1980s and 1990s seem to have yielded less. This is to be expected since the early pioneers entered the field *before* the best ideas had been invented.

The selected papers show that operating systems are based on a surprisingly small number of *ideas of permanent interest* (Table 2). The rest strike me as a fairly obvious consequence of the main themes.

Table 2 Fundamental Ideas

	Major Phases	*Technical Innovations*
I	Open Shop	The idea of operating systems
II	Batch Processing	Tape batching First-in, first-out scheduling
III	Multiprogramming	Processor multiplexing Indivisible operations Demand paging Input/output spooling Priority scheduling Remote job entry
IV	Timesharing	Simultaneous user interaction On-line file systems
V	Concurrent Programming	Hierarchical systems Extensible kernels Parallel programming concepts Secure parallel languages
VI	Personal Computing	Graphic user interfaces
VII	Distributed Systems	Remote servers

The following is a brief resume of the selected papers with some background information. Throughout I attempt to balance my own views by quoting both critical and complimentary comments of other researchers.

PART I OPEN SHOP

1 IBM 701 Open Shop

We begin the story of operating systems in 1954 when computers had *no operating systems* but were operated manually by their users:

> *The IBM 701 computer at the General Motors Research Laboratories.*
> George F. Ryckman (1983)

George Ryckman remembered the gross inefficiency of the *open shop* operation of IBM's first computer, the famous 701:

> Each user was allocated a minimum 15-minute slot, of which time he usually spent 10 minutes in setting up the equipment to do his computation ... By the time he got his calculation going, he may have had only 5 minutes or less of actual computation completed—wasting two thirds of his time slot.

The cost of the wasted computer time was $146,000 per month—in 1954 dollars!

John McCarthy (1962) made a similar remark about the TX-0 computer used in open shop mode at MIT. He added:

> If the TX-0 were a much larger computer, and if it were operated in the same manner as at present, the number of users who could be accommodated would still be about the same.

PART II BATCH PROCESSING

Surely, the greatest leap of imagination in the history of operating systems was the idea that computers might be able to schedule their own workload by means of software.

The early operating systems took drastic measures to reduce idle computer time: the users were simply removed from the computer room! They were now asked to prepare their programs and data on punched cards and submit them to a computing center for execution. The open shop had become a *closed shop*.

Now, card readers and line printers were too slow to keep up with fast computers. This bottleneck was removed by using fast tape stations and small satellite computers to perform *batch processing*.

Operators collected decks of punched cards from users and used a satellite computer to input a batch of jobs from punched cards to a magnetic tape. This tape was then mounted on a tape station connected to a main computer. The jobs were now input and run one at a time in their order of appearance on the tape. The running jobs output data on another tape. Finally, the output tape was moved to a satellite computer and printed on a line printer. While the main computer executed a batch of jobs, the satellite computers simultaneously printed a previous output tape and produced the next input tape.

Batch processing was severely limited by the sequential nature of magnetic tapes and early computers. Although tapes could be rewound, they were only efficient when accessed sequentially. And the first computers could only execute one program at a time. It was therefore necessary to run a complete batch of jobs at a time and print the output in *first-come, first-served* order.

To reduce the overhead of tape changing, it was essential to batch many jobs on the same tape. Unfortunately, large batches greatly increased service times from the users' point of view. It would typically take hours (or even a day or two) before you received the output of a single job. If the job involved a program compilation, the only output for that day might be an error message caused by a misplaced semicolon!

The *SHARE operating system* for the IBM 709 was an early batch processing system described by Bratman (1959).[1] Unfortunately, this short paper does not explain the basic idea succinctly, concentrating instead on the finer points of different job types.

2 BKS System

Much to my surprise, it was difficult to find a well-written paper about any early batch processor. Bob Rosin (2000) explained why such papers were rare:

> First, these systems were "obvious" and could be understood in minutes from reading a manual. Second, there were very few different kinds of computers, and the community of system programmers was similarly small. At least in the United States, almost everyone who wanted to know about these systems could and did communicate directly with their authors.

[1]The SHARE system is briefly mentioned at the end of Article 1.

The paper I chose describes the *BKS system* which occupied 2,688 words only out of a 32,768-word memory. In comparison to this system, later operating system designers have mostly failed in their search for simplicity!

> *The BKS system for the Philco-2000.*
> Richard B. Smith (1961)

PART III MULTIPROGRAMMING

In the 1960s large core memories, secondary storage with random access, data channels, and hardware interrupts changed operating systems radically. Interrupts enabled a processor to simulate concurrent execution of multiple programs and control simultaneous input/output operations. This form of concurrency became known as *multiprogramming.*

Christopher Strachey (1959) wrote the first seminal paper on multiprogramming. Fifteen years later, Strachey (1974) wrote to Donald Knuth:

> The paper I wrote called "Time-sharing in Large Fast Computers" was read at the first (pre IFIP) conference in 1960 [sic]. It was mainly about multiprogramming (to avoid waiting for peripherals) ... I did not envisage the sort of console system which is now so confusingly called time-sharing.

Multiprogramming and secondary storage made it possible to build operating systems that handled a continuous stream of input, computation, and output on a single computer using drums (or disks) to hold large buffers. This arrangement was called *spooling.*[2]

Since spooling required no tapes, there was no longer any overhead of tape mounting (unless user programs processed their own data tapes). Large random access buffers made it feasible to use *priority scheduling* of jobs, such as shortest-job-next (instead of first-come, first-served).

Incidentally, time-sharing may have made input spooling obsolete, but many organizations still use output spooling for printers shared by clusters of personal computers.

The term *batch processing* is now often used as a synonym for spooling. This is somewhat misleading since jobs are no longer grouped into batches. In 2000 this form of "batch processing" was still being used to run jobs through the Cray machines at the Pittsburgh Supercomputing Center.[3]

---

[2] *Spooling* is an acronym for "Simultaneous Peripheral Operation On-Line."

[3] See the Web site at http://www.psc.edu/machines/cray/j90/access/batch.html.

3 Atlas Supervisor

The use of multiprogramming for spooling was pioneered on the *Atlas* computer at Manchester University in the early 1960s:

> *The Atlas supervisor.*
> Tom Kilburn, R. Bruce Payne and David J. Howarth (1961)

Tom Kilburn felt that "No other single paper on the Atlas System would be a better choice" (Rosen 1967). This amazing paper explains completely new ideas in readable prose without the use of a single figure!

Atlas also introduced the concept of *demand paging* between a core memory of 16 K and a drum of 96 K words:

> The core store is divided into 512 word "pages"; this is also the size of the fixed blocks on drums and magnetic tapes. The core store and drum store are addressed identically, and drum transfers are performed automatically.
>
> A program addresses the combined "one-level store" and the supervisor transfers blocks of information between the core and drum store as required; the physical location of each block of information is not specified by the program, but is controlled by the supervisor.

Finally, Atlas was the first system to exploit *supervisor calls* known as "extracodes":

> Extracode routines form simple extensions of the basic order code, and also provide specific entry to supervisor routines.

The concepts of spooling, demand paging, and supervisor calls have influenced operating systems to this day. The Atlas supervisor has been called "the first recognisable modern operating system" (Lavington 1980). It is, I believe, the most significant breakthrough in the history of operating systems.

The virtual machine described in most published papers on Atlas is the one that runs user programs. The chief designer of the supervisor, David Howarth (1972a), pointed out that this virtual machine "differs in many important respects from the 'virtual machine' used by the supervisor itself." These differences complicated the design and maintenance of the system.

The later RC 4000 multiprogramming system had the same weakness (Brinch Hansen 1973).

By 1960 high-level programming languages, such as Fortran, Algol 60 and Cobol, were already being used for user programming. However, operating systems, such as the Atlas supervisor, were still programmed in machine language which was both difficult to understand and error-prone.

4 B5000 Master Control Program

The *Burroughs B5000* computer had *stack instructions* for efficient execution of sequential programs written in Algol 60 (Barton 1961). For this purpose the B5000 was truly a revolutionary architecture. The Burroughs group published only a handful of papers about the B5000 system, including

> *Operating system for the B5000.*
> Clark Oliphint (1964)

Admittedly, this brief paper does not do justice to the significant accomplishments of this pioneering effort. Organick (1973) and McKeag (1976a) provide an abundance of detailed information.

Burroughs used its own variants of Algol to program the *B5000 Master Control Program*, which supported both *multiprogramming* and *multiprocessing* of user programs.

The system used *virtual memory* with automatic transfers of data and program segments between primary and secondary storage (MacKenzie 1965). A typical system could run on the order of 10 user jobs at a time. About once a day, *thrashing* would occur. This was not detected by the system. The operator was expected to notice any serious degradation of performance and restart the system (McKeag 1976a).

Unfortunately the programming languages of the early 1960s offered no support for concurrent programming of operating systems. High-level languages for concurrent programming were only invented in the 1970s.

At the time the only option open to Burroughs was to adopt an extremely dangerous short-cut: The B5000 operating system (and its successors) were written in *extended Algol* that permitted systems programs to access the whole memory as an array of (unprotected) machine words.[4] This programming trick effectively turned extended Algol into an assembly language with

[4]It was sometimes referred to as "Burroughs overextended Algol."

an algorithmic notation. The dangers of using such an implementation language were very real.

Roche (1972) made the following comment about a B5500 installation in which the user was permitted to program in extended Algol:

> This allows the use of stream procedures, a means of addressing, without checks, an absolute offset from his data area. Mis-use and abuse of these facilities by ill-informed or over-ambitious users could, and often did, wreck the system.

Organick (1973) pointed out that the termination of a task in the B6700 operating system might cause its offspring tasks to lose their stack space! The possibility of a program being able to delete part of its own stack is, of course, completely at variance with our normal expectations of high-level languages, such as Fortran, Algol, or Pascal.

According to Rosin (1987), "High-level languages were used exclusively for both customer programming and systems programming" of the B5000. Similar claims would be made for later operating systems programmed in intermediate-level languages, including Multics (Corbató 1965), OS 6 (Stoy 1972), and Unix (Ritchie 1974). However, in each case, system programmers had extended sequential programming languages with unsafe features for low-level programming.

There is no doubt about the practical advantages of being able to program an operating system in a language that is at least partly high-level. However, a programming notation that includes machine language features is, per definition, *not* a *high-level* language.

Since nobody could expect Burroughs to use concepts that had not yet been invented, the above criticism does not in any way diminish the contribution of a bold experiment: the first tentative step towards writing operating systems in a high-level language.

5 Exec II System

The operation of early batch processing systems as closed shops set a precedence that continued after the invention of multiprogramming. The only system that boldly challenged the prevailing wisdom was the *Exec II* operating system for the Univac 1107 computer at Case Western Reserve University:

> *Description of a high capacity, fast turnaround*
> *university computing center.*
> William C. Lynch (1966)

Bill Lynch writes that

> The [Case Computing] Center employs an open-shop type philosophy that appears to be unique among large scale installations. This philosophy leads to turnaround times which are better by an order of magnitude than those commonly being obtained with comparable scale equipment.

Exec II was designed to run one job at a time using two fast drums for input/output spooling. The system was connected to several card reader/line printer groups. When a user inserted a deck in any reader, the cards were immediately input. The user would then remove her cards and proceed to the line printer where the output of the job would appear shortly.

85% of the jobs required less than a minute of computer time. A student was often able to run a small job, repunch a few cards, and run the job again in less than five minutes. The system typically ran 800 jobs a day with a processor utilization of 90%. Less than 5% of the jobs used magnetic tapes. Users were also responsible for mounting and identifying their own tapes.

Occasionally, the phenomenal success of Exec II was limited by its policy of selecting the shortest job and running it to completion (or time limit):

> when a long running program is once started, no other main program is processed until the long running job is finished. Fortunately this does not happen often but when it does, it ruins the turnaround time. It appears to be desirable to have ... an allocation philosophy which would not allow the entire machine to be clogged with one run, but would allow short jobs to pass the longer ones. Such a philosophy, implemented with conventional multiprogramming techniques, should remove this difficulty.
>
> The scheduling algorithm currently being used leaves something to be desired. It selects jobs (within classes) strictly on the basis of shortest time limit. No account is taken of waiting time. As a result, a user with a longer run can be completely frozen out by a group of users with shorter runs.

The system also supported *remote job entry* through modems and telephone lines. Exec II came remarkably close to realizing the main advantages of time-sharing (which was still in the future): remote access to a shared computer with fast response at reasonable cost.

Did I forget to mention that Exec II did all of that in a memory of 64 K words?

Exec II demonstrated that the most important ingredient of radically new ideas is often the rare intellectual ability to look at existing technology from a new point of view. (That would also be true of the first timesharing systems.)

6 Egdon System

The Egdon system deserves to be recognized as a classic operating system:

> *The Egdon system for the KDF9.*
> David Burns, E. Neville Hawkins, D. Robin Judd and John L. Venn (1966)

It ran on a KDF computer with 32 K words of core memory, eight tape units and a disk of 4 M words. The disk was mainly used to hold library routines, system programs and work space for the current user program.

The system combined traditional tape batching with spooling of tape input/output. The system automatically switched between two input tapes. Jobs were copied from a card reader onto one of the tapes. When that tape was full, the system rewound it and executed one job at a time. At the same time, the system started filling the second input tape. In a slightly more complicated way, the system switched between a third tape that received output from the running program and a fourth one that was being printed.

The Egdon system was completed on time in 15 months with a total effort of 20 person-years. The authors attribute their sense of urgency to the existence of clear objectives from the start and a stiff penalty clause for late delivery. This "meant that a clear definition was arrived at quickly and changes were kept to a minimum."

PART IV TIMESHARING

John McCarthy proposed the original idea of timesharing at MIT in an unpublished memorandum dated January 1, 1959:

> I want to propose an operating system for [the IBM 709] that will substantially reduce the time required to get a problem solved on the machine ... The only way quick response can be provided at bearable cost is by time-sharing. That is, the computer must attend to other customers while one customer is reacting to some output.

> I think the proposal points to the way all computers will be operated in the future, and we have a chance to pioneer a big step forward in the way computers are used.

In the spring of 1961 he explained his visionary thinking further (McCarthy 1962):

> By a time-sharing computer system I shall mean one that interacts with many simultaneous users through a number of remote consoles. Such a system will look to each user like a large private computer...When the user wants service, he simply starts typing in a message requesting the service. The computer is always ready to pay attention to any key that he may strike.
>
> Because programs may ... do only relatively short pieces of work between human interactions, it is uneconomical to have to shuttle them back and forth continually to and from secondary storage. Therefore, there is a requirement for a large primary memory ... The final requirement is for secondary storage large enough to maintain the users' files so that users need not have separate card or tape input-output units.

It would be difficult to summarize the essence of timesharing more concisely. But to really appreciate McCarthy's achievement, we need to remind ourselves that when he outlined his vision nobody had ever seen a timesharing system. A truly remarkable and revolutionary breakthrough in computing!

7 CTSS

Fernando Corbató at MIT is generally credited with the first demonstration of timesharing:

> *An experimental time-sharing system.*
> Fernando Corbató, Marjorie Merwin-Daggett and Robert C. Daley (1962)

A quarter of a century later, Rosin and Lee (1992) interviewed Corbató about this system, known as *CTSS*:

> By November 1961 we were able to demonstrate a really crude prototype of the system [on the IBM 709]. What we had done was [that]

> we had wedged out 5K words of the user address space and inserted a little operating system that was going to manage the four typewriters. We did not have any disk storage, so we took advantage of the fact that it was a large machine and we had a lot of tape drives. We assigned one tape drive per typewriter.
>
> The paper said we were running on the [IBM] 7090, but we in fact had not got it running yet.

Corbató agreed that

> the person who deserves the most credit for having focussed on the vision of timesharing is John McCarthy ... [He] wrote a very important memo where he outlined the idea of trying to develop a timesharing system.

In September 1962 McCarthy working with Bolt Beranek and Newman demonstrated a well-engineered small timesharing system on a PDP 1 computer with a swapping drum (McCarthy 1963). However, by then the prototype of CTSS running on inadequate hardware had already claimed priority as the *first* demonstration of timesharing.

In the summer of 1963 CTSS was still in the final stages of being tested on a more appropriate IBM 7090 computer equipped with a disk (Wilkes 1985). Eventually this version of CTSS became recognized as the first large-scale timesharing system to be offered to a wide and varied group of users (Crisman 1965).

8 Multics File System

In 1964 MIT started the design of a much larger timesharing system named *Multics.* According to Corbató (1965):

> The overall design goal of the Multics system is to create a computing system which is capable of comprehensively meeting almost all of the present and near-future requirements of a large computer service installation.

By the fall of 1969 Multics was available for general use at MIT. The same year, Bell Labs withdrew from the project (Ritchie 1984):

> To the Labs computing community as a whole, the problem was the increasing obviousness of the failure of Multics to deliver promptly any sort of usable system, let alone the panacea envisioned earlier.

Multics was never widely used outside MIT. In hindsight, this huge system was an overambitious dead end in the history of operating systems. It is a prime example of the *second-system effect*—the temptation to follow a simple, first system with a much more complicated second effort (Brooks 1975).

However, CTSS and Multics made at least one lasting contribution to operating system technology by introducing the first *hierarchical file systems*, which gave all users instant access to both private and shared files:

> *A general-purpose file system for secondary storage.*
> Robert C. Daley and Peter G. Neumann (1965)

Note that this paper was a *proposal* only published several years before the completion of Multics.

9 Titan File System

The *Titan system* was developed and used at Cambridge University (Wilson 1976). It supported timesharing from 26 terminals simultaneously and was noteworthy for its simple and reliable file system:

> *File integrity in a disc-based multi-access system.*
> A. G. Fraser (1972)

A 128 M byte disk held about 10,000 files belonging to some 700 users. It was the first file system to keep passwords in scrambled form to prevent unauthorized retrieval and misuse of them. Users were able to list the actions that they wished to authorize for each file (*execute, read, update,* and *delete.*) The system automatically made copies of files on magnetic tape as an insurance against hardware or software errors.

According to A. G. Fraser (Discussion 1972):

> The file system was designed in 1966 and brought into service in March 1967. At that time there were very few file systems designed for on-line use available, the most influential at the time being the Multics proposal.

J. Warne added that "This is a very thorough paper, so precise in detail that it is almost a guide to implementation" (Discussion 1972). Fraser's paper makes it clear that it is a nontrivial problem to ensure the integrity of user files in a timesharing system.

File integrity continues to be of vital importance in *distributed systems* with shared file servers.

10 Unix

In 1969 Dennis Ritchie and Ken Thompson at Bell Labs began trying to find an alternative to Multics. By the end of 1971, their *Unix* system was able to support three users on a PDP 11 minicomputer. Few people outside Bell Labs knew of its existence until 1973 when the Unix kernel was rewritten in the *C* language. Nothing was published about Unix until 1974:

> *The Unix time-sharing system.*
> Dennis M. Ritchie and Ken Thompson (1974)

Unix appeared at the right time (Slater 1987):

> The advent of the smaller computers, the minis—especially the PDP-11—had spawned a whole new group of computer users who were disappointed with existing operating software. They were ready for Unix. Most of Unix was not new, but rather what Ritchie calls "a good engineering application of ideas that had been around in some form and [were now] made convenient to use."

By the mid-1980s Unix had become the leading standard for timesharing systems (Aho 1984):

> In the commercial world there are 100,000 Unix systems in operation ... Virtually every major university throughout the world now uses the Unix system.

A superior tool like Unix often feels so natural that there is no incentive for programmers to look for a better one. Still, after three decades, it can be argued that the widespread acceptance of Unix has become an obstacle to further progress. Stonebraker (1981), for example, describes the problems that Unix creates for database systems.

PART V CONCURRENT PROGRAMMING

By the mid-1960s operating systems had already reached a level of complexity that was beyond human comprehension. In looking back Bill Lynch (1972) observed that:

> Several problems remained unsolved within the Exec II operating system and had to be avoided by one *ad hoc* means or another. The problem of deadlocks was not at all understood in 1962 when the system was designed. As a result several annoying deadlocks were programmed into the system.

From the mid-1960s to the mid-1970s computer scientists developed a conceptual basis that would make operating systems more understandable. This pioneering effort led to the discovery of *fundamental principles of concurrent programming.* The power of these ideas was demonstrated in a handful of influential *model operating systems.*

11 THE Multiprogramming System

The conceptual innovation began with Edsger Dijkstra's famous *THE system*:

> *The structure of the THE multiprogramming system.*
> Edsger W. Dijkstra (1968a)

This was a spooling system that compiled and executed a stream of Algol 60 programs with paper tape input and printer output. It used software-implemented demand paging between a 512 K-word drum and a 32 K-word memory. There were five user processes and 10 input/output processes, one for each peripheral device. The system used *semaphores* for process synchronization and communication.

This short paper concentrates on Dijkstra's most startling claim:

> We have found that it is possible to design a refined multiprogramming system in such a way that its logical soundness can be proved a priori and its implementation can admit exhaustive testing. The only errors that showed up during testing were trivial coding errors ... the resulting system is guaranteed to be flawless.

In Brinch Hansen (1979) I wrote:

> Dijkstra's multiprogramming system also illustrated the conceptual clarity of *hierarchical structure.* His system consisted of several program layers which gradually transform the physical machine into a more pleasant abstract machine that simulates several processes which share a large, homogeneous store and several virtual devices. These program layers can be designed and studied one at a time.

The system was described in more detail by Habermann (1967), Dijkstra (1968b, 1971), Bron (1972) and McKeag (1976b).

Software managers continue to believe that software design is based on a magical discipline, called "software engineering," which can be mastered by average programmers. Dijkstra explained that the truth of the matter is simply that

> the intellectual level needed for system design is in general grossly underestimated. I am convinced more than ever that this type of work is very difficult, and that every effort to do it with other than the best people is doomed to either failure or moderate success at enormous expense.

In my opinion, the continued neglect of this unpopular truth explains the appalling failure of most software which continues to be inflicted on computer users to this day.

12 RC 4000 Multiprogramming System

In 1974 Alan Shaw wrote:

> There exist many approaches to multiprogramming system design, but we are aware of only two that are *systematic* and *manageable* and at the same time have been *validated* by producing real working operating systems. These are the hierarchical abstract machine approach developed by Dijkstra (1968a) and the nucleus methods of Brinch Hansen (1969) ... The nucleus and basic multiprogramming system for the RC 4000 is one of the most elegant existing systems.

The *RC 4000 multiprogramming system* was not a complete operating system, but a small *kernel* upon which operating systems for different purposes could be built in an orderly manner:

> *RC 4000 Software: Multiprogramming System.*
> Per Brinch Hansen (1969)

The kernel provided the basic mechanisms for creating a *tree of parallel processes* that communicated by messages. It was designed for the RC 4000 computer manufactured by Regnecentralen in Denmark. Work on the system began in the fall of 1967, and a well-documented reliable version was running in the spring of 1969.

Before the RC 4000 multiprogramming system was programmed, I described the design philosophy which drastically generalized the concept of an operating system (Brinch Hansen 1968):

> The system has no built-in assumptions about program scheduling and resource allocation; it allows any program to initiate other programs in a hierarchal manner.[5] Thus, the system provides a general frame[work] for different scheduling strategies, such as batch processing, multiple console conversation, real-time scheduling, etc.

In retrospect, this radical idea was probably the most important contribution of the RC 4000 system to operating system technology. If the kernel concept seems obvious today, it is only because it has passed into the general stock of knowledge about system design. It is now commonly referred to as the principle of *separation of mechanism and policy* (Wulf 1974).

The RC 4000 system was also noteworthy for its *message communication.* Every communication consisted of an exchange of a message and an answer between two processes. This protocol was inspired by an early decision to treat peripheral devices as processes, which receive input/output commands as messages and return acknowledgements as answers. In distributed systems, this form of communication is now known as *remote procedure calls.*

The system also supported *nondeterministic communication* which enabled processes to inspect and receive messages in arbitrary (instead of first-come, first-served) order. This flexibility is necessary to program a process that implements priority scheduling of a shared resource. In hindsight, such a process was equivalent to the "secretary" outlined by Dijkstra (1975). In RC 4000 terminology it was known as a *conversational process.*

Initially the RC 4000 computer had only an extremely *basic operating system* running on top of the kernel. According to Lauesen (1975):

[5] Here I obviously meant "processes" rather than "programs."

> The RC 4000 software was extremely reliable. In a university environment, the system typically ran under the simple operating system for three months without crashes ... The crashes present were possibly due to transient hardware errors.

When the RC 4000 system was finished I described it in a 5-page journal paper (Brinch Hansen 1970). I then used this paper as an outline of the 160-page system manual (Brinch Hansen 1969) by expanding each section of the paper. Article 12 is a reprint of the most important part of the original manual, which has been out of print for decades.[6]

13 Venus System

The Venus system was a small timesharing system serving five or six users at a time:

> *The design of the Venus operating system.*
> Barbara H. Liskov (1972)

Although it broke no new ground, the Venus system was another convincing demonstration of Dijkstra's concepts of *semaphores* and *layers of abstraction.*

14 Boss 2 System

The *Boss 2 system* was an intellectual and engineering achievement of the highest order:

> *A large semaphore based operating system.*
> Søren Lauesen (1975)

It was an ambitious operating system that ran on top of an extended version of the RC 4000 kernel. According to its chief designer, Søren Lauesen:

> Boss 2 is a general purpose operating system offering the following types of service simultaneously: batch jobs, remote job entry, time sharing (conversational jobs), jobs generated internally by other jobs, process control jobs.

[6] My operating systems book (Brinch Hansen 1973) included a slightly different version of the original manual supplemented with abstract Pascal algorithms.

The system used over a hundred parallel activities, one for every peripheral device and job process. These activities were implemented as *coroutines* within a single system process. The coroutines communicated by means of semaphores and message queues, which potentially were accessible to all coroutines. These message queues were called "queue semaphores" to distinguish them from the message queues in the RC 4000 kernel.

Dijkstra (1968a) and Habermann (1967) were able to prove by induction that the THE system was *deadlock-free.* Lauesen used a similar argument to prove that the coroutines of Boss 2 eventually would process any request for service.

Boss 2 was implemented and tested by four to six people over a period of two years:

> During the six busiest hours, the cpu-utilization is 40–50 pct used by jobs, 10–20 pct by the operating system and the monitor.[7] The average operating system overhead per job is 3 sec.
>
> During the first year of operation, the system typically ran for weeks without crashes. Today it seems to be error free.

15 Solo System

Concurrent Pascal was the first high-level language for concurrent programming (Brinch Hansen 1975). Since synchronization errors can be extremely difficult to locate by program testing, the language was designed to permit the detection of many of these obscure errors by means of compilation checks. The language used the *scope rules* of *processes* and *monitors* to enforce security from race conditions (Brinch Hansen 1973, Hoare 1974).

By January 1975 Concurrent Pascal was running on a PDP 11/45 minicomputer with a removable disk pack. The portable compiler (written in Pascal) generated *platform-independent concurrent code*, which was executed by a small kernel written in assembly language.

The first operating system written in Concurrent Pascal was the *portable Solo* system which was running in May 1975:

> *The Solo operating system: a Concurrent Pascal program.*
> Per Brinch Hansen (1976a)

---

[7]The RC 4000 kernel was also known as the "monitor."

It was a single-user operating system for the development of Pascal programs. Every user disk was organized as a single-level file system. The heart of Solo was a job process that compiled and ran programs stored on the disk. Two additional processes performed input/output spooling simultaneously.

The Solo system demonstrated that it is possible to write small operating systems in a secure programming language without machine-dependent features. The programming tricks of assembly language were impossible in Concurrent Pascal: there were no typeless memory words, registers, and addresses in the language. The programmer was not even aware of the existence of physical processors and interrupts. *The language was so secure that concurrent processes ran without any form of memory protection.*[8]

16 Solo Program Text

Solo was the first major example of a modular concurrent program implemented in terms of abstract data types (classes, monitors and processes) with *compile-time checking of access rights.* The most significant contribution of Solo was undoubtedly that the program text was short enough to be published in its entirety in a computer journal:

> *The Solo operating system: processes, monitors and classes.*
> Per Brinch Hansen (1976b)

Harlan Mills had this to say about the Solo program text (Maddux 1979):

> Here, an entire operating system is visible, with every line of program open to scrutiny. There is no hidden mystery, and after studying such extensive examples, the reader feels that he could tackle similar jobs and that he could change the system at will. Never before have we seen an operating system shown in such detail and in a manner so amenable to modification.

PART VI PERSONAL COMPUTING

In the 1970s microprocessors and semiconductor memories made it feasible to build powerful personal computers. Reduced hardware cost eventually allowed people to own such computers. Xerox PARC was the leader in the

[8]Twenty years later, the designers of the *Java* language resurrected the idea of platform-independent parallel programming (Gosling 1996). Unfortunately they replaced the secure monitor concept of Concurrent Pascal with inferior insecure ideas (Brinch Hansen 1999).

development of much of the technology which is now taken for granted: bit-mapped displays, the mouse, laser printers and the Ethernet (Hiltzik 1999).

In Brinch Hansen (1982) I made two predictions about the future of software for personal computing:

> For a brief period, personal computers have offered programmers a chance to build small software systems of outstanding quality using the best available programming languages and design methods...The simple operating procedures and small stores of personal computers make it both possible and essential to limit the complexity of software.
>
> The recent development of the complicated programming language Ada combined with new microprocessors with large stores will soon make the development of incomprehensible, unreliable software inevitable even for personal computers.

Both predictions turned out to be true (although Ada was not to blame).

17 OS 6

The *OS 6 system* was a simple single-user system developed at Oxford University for a Modular One computer with 32 K of core memory and a 1 M word disk:

> *OS 6—an experimental operating system for a small computer: input/output and filing system.*
> Joe E. Stoy and Christopher Strachey (1972)

The system ran one program at a time without multiprogramming. The paper describes the implementation of the file system and input/output streams in some detail.

The operating system and user programs were written in the typeless language *BCPL*, which permitted unrestricted manipulation of bits and addresses (Richards 1969). BCPL was the precursor of the C language (Kernighan 1978).

18 Alto System

The Alto was the first personal computer developed by Xerox PARC. Initially it had 64 K words of memory and a 2.5 M-byte removable disk pack.

It also had a bit-mapped display, a mouse and an Ethernet interface. Over a thousand Altos were eventually built (Smith 1982).

The *Alto operating system* was developed from 1973 to 1976 (Lampson 1988):

> *An open operating system for a single-user machine.*
> Butler W. Lampson and Robert F. Sproul (1979)

This paper describes the use of known techniques in a small, single-user operating system. The authors acknowledge that "The streams are copied wholesale from Stoy and Strachey's OS 6 system, as are many aspects of the file system." A notable feature of the Alto system was that applications could select the system components they needed and omit the rest. The most revolutionary aspect of the system, its graphic user interface, was application-dependent and was *not* part of the operating system (Lampson 2000).

In some ways, the Alto system was even simpler than *Solo*. It was a strictly sequential single-user system. Apart from keyboard input, there was no concurrent input/output. The system executed only one process at a time.

It did, however, have an extremely robust file system that could be reconstructed in about one minute from "whatever fragmented state it may have fallen into."

A "world-swap" mechanism enabled a running program to replace itself with any other program (or an already preempted program). Swapped programs communicated through files with standard names. This slow form of context switching was used to simulate coroutines, among other things for a printer server that alternated strictly between input and printing of files received from the local network.

The Alto system was written almost entirely in BCPL. The use of a low-level implementation language provided many opportunities for obscure errors (Swinehart 1985):

> In the Alto system, it was possible to free the memory occupied by unneeded higher-level layers for other uses; inadvertent upward calls had disastrous results.

19 Pilot System

Pilot was another single-user operating system from Xerox:

Pilot: an operating system for a personal computer.
David D. Redell, Yogen K. Dalal, Thomas R. Horsley,
Hugh C. Lauer, William C. Lynch, Paul R. McJones,
Hal G. Murray and Stephen C. Purcell (1980)

It was written in the high-level language Mesa (Lampson 1980). From Concurrent Pascal and Solo, Mesa and Pilot borrowed the idea of writing a modular operating system in a concurrent programming language as a collection of processes and monitors with compile-time checking as the only form of memory protection.

Mesa relaxed the most severe restriction of Concurrent Pascal by supporting a variable number of user processes. However, the number of system processes remained fixed. Mesa inherited some of BCPL's problems with invalid pointers, but was otherwise fairly secure (Swinehart 1985).

Pilot adapted several features of the Alto system, including its graphic user interface and streams for reliable network communication. Pilot supported a "flat" file system. As in the Alto system, redundant data stored in each page permitted recovery of files and directories after system failure. A file could only be accessed by mapping its pages temporarily to a region of virtual memory. This unusual mechanism was removed in the subsequent Cedar system (Swinehart 1985).

Ten years after the completion of the Alto system, operating systems for personal computing were already quite large. Pilot was a Mesa program of 24,000 lines. It was succeeded by the much larger *Cedar* system (Swinehart 1985).

Solo, Pilot, Cedar and a handful of other systems demonstrated that operating systems can be written in secure high-level languages. However, most operating system designers have abandoned secure languages in favor of the low-level language C.

20 Star User Interface

Graphic user interfaces, pioneered by Doug Englebart (1968), Alan Kay (1977) and others, had been used in various experimental Alto systems (Lampson 1988). The *Xerox Star* was the first commercial computer with a *mouse* and *windows* interface. It was based on the Alto, but ran three times as fast and had 512 K bytes of memory:

The Star user interface: an overview.
David C. Smith, Charles Irby, Ralph Kimball and Eric Harslem (1982)

This wonderful paper was written when these ideas were still unfamiliar to most computer users. Before writing any software, the Star designers spent two years combining the different Alto interfaces into a single, uniform interface. Their work was guided by a brilliant vision of an *electronic office*:

> We decided to create electronic counterparts to the objects in an office: paper, folders, file cabinets, mail boxes, calculators, and so on—an electronic metaphor for the physical office. We hoped that this would make the electronic world seem more familiar and require less training.
>
> Star documents are represented, not as file names on a disk, but as pictures on the display screen. They may be selected by pointing to them with the mouse and clicking one of the mouse buttons ... When opened, documents are always rendered on the display exactly as they print on paper.

These concepts are now so familiar to every computer user in the world that it is difficult to appreciate just how revolutionary they were at the time. I view graphic interfaces as one of the most important innovations in operating system technology.

The *Macintosh* system was a direct descendant of the Star system (Poole 1984, Hiltzik 1999). In the 1990s the mouse and screen windows turned the *Internet* into a global communication medium.

PART VII DISTRIBUTED SYSTEMS

In the late 1970s Xerox PARC was already using Alto computers on Ethernets as *servers* providing printing and file services (Lampson 1988). In the 1980s universities also developed experimental systems for distributed personal computing. It is difficult to evaluate the significance of this recent work:

- By 1980 the major concepts of operating systems had already been discovered.
- Many distributed systems were built on top of the old time-sharing system *Unix*, which was designed for central rather than distributed computing (Pike 1995).
- In most distributed systems, process communication was based on a complicated, unreliable programming technique, known as *remote procedure calls*.

- Only a handful of distributed systems, including Locus (Popek 1981) and the Apollo Domain (Leach 1983), were developed into commercial products.
- There seems to be no consensus in the literature about the fundamental contributions and relative merits of these systems.

Under these circumstances, the best I could do was to select a handful of *readable* papers that I hope are *representative* of early and more recent distributed systems.

21 WFS File Server

The *WFS* system was the first *file server* that ran on an Alto computer:

> *WFS: a simple shared file system for a distributed environment.*
> Daniel Swinehart, Gene McDaniel and David R. Boggs (1979)

The WFS system behaved like a remote disk providing random access to individual pages. To perform a disk operation, a client sent a *request* packet to the WFS host, which completed the operation before returning a *response* packet to the sender. The Ethernet software did not guarantee reliable delivery of every packet. However, since the server attempted to reply after every operation, the absence of a reply implied that a request had failed. It usually sufficed to retransmit a request after a time-out period.

There was no directory structure within the system. Clients had to provide their own file naming and directories. Any host had full access to all WFS files. The lack of file security imposed further responsibility on the clients.

In spite of its limitations, WFS was an admirable example of utter simplicity. (One of the authors implemented it in BCPL in less than two months.)

The idea of controlling peripheral devices by means of request and response messages goes back to the RC 4000 system. In distributed systems, it has become the universal method of implementing remote procedure calls.

22 Unix United RPC

Remote procedure calls (RPC) were proposed as a *programming style* by James White (1976) and as a *programming language concept* by me (Brinch

Hansen 1978). Since then, system designers have turned it into an unreliable mechanism of surprising complexity.

In their present form, remote procedure calls are an attempt to use *unreliable message passing* to invoke procedures through local area networks. Many complications arise because system designers attempt to trade reliability for speed by accepting the premise that users are prepared to accept unreliable systems provided they are fast. This doubtful assumption has been used to justify distributed systems in which user programs must cope with lost and duplicate messages.

Much ingenuity has been spent attempting to limit the possible ways in which remote procedure calls can fail. To make extraneous complexity more palatable, the various *failure modes* are referred to as different forms of "semantics" (Tay 1990). Thus we have the intriguing concepts of "at-most-once" and "at-least-once" semantics. My personal favorite is the "maybe" semantics of a channel that gives no guarantee whatsoever that it will deliver any message. We are back where we started in the 1950s when unreliable computers supported "maybe" memory (Ryckman 1983).

Tay (1990) admits that "Currently, there are [*sic*] no agreed definition on the semantics of RPC." Leach (1983) goes one step further and advocates that "each remote operation implements a protocol tailored to its need." Since it can be both *system-dependent* and *application-dependent*, a remote procedure call is no longer an abstract concept.

From the extensive literature on remote procedure calls, I have chosen a well-written paper that clearly explains the various complications of the idea:

> *The design of a reliable remote procedure call mechanism.*
> Santosh Shrivastava and Fabio Panzieri (1982)

The authors describe the implementation used in the *Unix United* system. They correctly point out that:

> At a superficial level it would seem that to design a program that provides a remote procedure call abstraction would be a straightforward exercise. Surprisingly, this is not so. We have found the problem of the design of the RPC to be rather intricate.

Lost and duplicate messages may be unavoidable in the presence of hardware failures. But they should be handled *below* the user level. As an example, the *Pilot* system included a "network stream" protocol by which clients could communicate reliably between any two network addresses (Redell 1980).

23 Unix United System

By adding another software layer on top of the Unix kernel, the University of Newcastle was able to make five PDP11 computers act like a single Unix system, called *Unix United*. This was achieved without modifying standard Unix or any user programs:

> *The Newcastle Connection or Unixes of the World unite.*
> David R. Brownbridge, Lindsay F. Marshall and Brian Randell (1982)

Unix United combined the local file systems into a global file system with a common root directory. This *distributed file system* made it possible for any user to access remote directories and files, regardless of which systems they were stored on. In this homogeneous system, every computer was both a user machine and a file server providing access to local files. The most heavily used services were file transfers, line printing, network mail, and file dumping on magnetic tape.

The idea of making separate systems act like a single system seems simple and "obvious"—as elegant design always does. The authors wisely remind us that

> The additional problems and opportunities that face the designer of homogeneous distributed systems should not be allowed to obscure the continued relevance of much established practice regarding the design of multiprogramming systems.

Unix United was a predecessor of the *Sun Network File System* (Sandberg 1985).

24 Amoeba System

Amoeba is an ambitious distributed system developed by computer scientists in the Netherlands:

> *Experiences with the Amoeba distributed operating system.*
> Andrew S. Tanenbaum, Robbert van Renesse, Hans van Staveren,
> Gregory J. Sharp, Sape J. Mullender, Jack Jansen and
> Guido van Rossum (1990)

An Amoeba system consists of diskless *single-user workstations* and a pool of *single-board processors* connected by a *local area network*. *Servers* provide directory, file, and replication services. *Gateways* link Amoeba systems to wide area networks.

A *microkernel* handles low-level memory allocation and input/output, process and thread scheduling, as well as remote procedure calls. All other services are provided by system processes. Like the RC 4000 multiprogramming system, Amoeba creates a dynamic tree of processes. Each process is a cluster of non-preemptible threads that communicate by means of shared memory and semaphores.

The system is programmed as a collection of *objects*, each of which implements a set of operations. Access rights, called *capabilities*, provide a uniform mechanism for naming, accessing and protecting objects (Dennis 1966). Each object is managed by a *server process* that responds to *remote procedure calls* from user processes (using "at-most-once" semantics).

The file system is reported to be twice as fast as the Sun Network File System (Sandberg 1985). Since files can be created, but not changed, it is practical to store them contiguously on disks. The system uses fault-tolerant *broadcasting* to replicate directories and files on multiple disks.

Nothing is said about the size of the system. Amoeba has been used for parallel scientific computing. It was also used in a project involving connecting sites in several European countries.

This ends our journey through half a century of operating systems development. The first 50 years of operating systems led to the discovery of fundamental concepts of hierarchical software design, concurrent programming, graphic user interfaces, file systems, personal computing, and distributed systems.

The history of operating systems illustrates an eternal truth about human nature: *we just can't resist the temptation to do the impossible.* This is as true today as it was 30 years ago, when David Howarth (1972b) wrote:

> Our problem is that we never do the same thing again. We get a lot of experience on our first simple system, and then when it comes to doing the same thing again with a better designed hardware, with all the tools we know we need, we try and produce something which is ten times more complicated and fall into exactly the same trap. We do

> not stabilise on something nice and simple and say "let's do it again, but do it very well this time."

Acknowledgements

I thank Jonathan Greenfield, Butler Lampson, Mike McKeag, Peter O'Hearn and Bob Rosin for their helpful comments on this essay.

References

1. A. V. Aho 1984. Foreword. *Bell Laboratories Technical Journal 63*, 8, Part 2 (October), 1573–1576.
2. R. S. Barton 1961. A new approach to the functional design of a digital computer. *Joint Computer Conference 19*, 393–396.
3. H. Bratman and I. V. Boldt, Jr. 1959. The SHARE 709 system: supervisory control. *Journal of the ACM 6*, 2 (April), 152–155.
4. P. Brinch Hansen 1968. *The Structure of the RC 4000 Monitor.* Regnecentralen, Copenhagen, Denmark (February).
5. P. Brinch Hansen 1969. *RC 4000 Software: Multiprogramming System.* Regnecentralen, Copenhagen, Denmark, (April). *Article 12.*
6. P. Brinch Hansen 1970. The nucleus of a multiprogramming system. *Communications of the ACM 13*, 4 (April), 238–241, 250.
7. P. Brinch Hansen 1973. *Operating System Principles.* Prentice-Hall, Englewood Cliffs, NJ.
8. P. Brinch Hansen 1975. The programming language Concurrent Pascal. *IEEE Transactions on Software Engineering 1*, 2 (June), 199–207.
9. P. Brinch Hansen, 1976a. The Solo operating system: a Concurrent Pascal program. *Software—Practice and Experience 6*, 2 (April–June), 141–149. *Article 15.*
10. P. Brinch Hansen, 1976b. The Solo operating system: processes, monitors and classes. *Software—Practice and Experience 6*, 2 (April–June), 165–200. *Article 16.*
11. P. Brinch Hansen 1978. Distributed Processes: a concurrent programming concept. *Communications of the ACM 21*, 11 (November), 934–941.
12. P. Brinch Hansen 1979. A keynote address on concurrent programming. *Computer 12* , 5 (May), 50–56.
13. P. Brinch Hansen 1982. *Programming a Personal Computer.* Prentice-Hall, Englewood Cliffs, NJ.
14. P. Brinch Hansen 1993. Monitors and Concurrent Pascal: a personal history. *SIGPLAN Notices 28*, 3 (March), 1–35.
15. P. Brinch Hansen 1999. Java's insecure parallelism. *SIGPLAN Notices 34*, 4 (April), 38–45.

16. C. Bron 1972. Allocation of virtual store in the THE multiprogramming system. In *Operating Systems Techniques*, C. A. R. Hoare and R. H. Perrott Eds., Academic Press, New York, 168–184.

17. F. P. Brooks, Jr. 1975. *The Mythical Man-Month: Essays on Software Engineering.* Addison-Wesley, Reading, MA.

18. D. R. Brownbridge, L. F. Marshall and B. Randell 1982. The Newcastle Connection or Unixes of the World Unite! *Software—Practice and Experience 12*, 12 (December), 1147–1162. *Article 23.*

19. D. Burns, E. N. Hawkins, D. R. Judd and J. L. Venn 1966. The Egdon system for the KDF9. *The Computer Journal 8*, 4 (January), 297–302. *Article 6.*

20. F. J. Corbató, M. Merwin-Daggett and R. C. Daley 1962. An experimental time-sharing system. *Spring Joint Computer Conference 21*, 335–344.

21. F. J. Corbató and V. A. Vyssotsky 1965. Introduction and overview of the Multics system. *Fall Joint Computer Conference 27*, 185–196.

22. P. A. Crisman Ed. 1965. *The Compatible Time-Sharing System: A Programmer's Guide.* Second Edition, The MIT Press, Cambridge, MA.

23. R. C. Daley and P. G. Neumann 1965. A general-purpose file system for secondary storage. *Fall Joint Computer Conference 27*, 213–229. *Article 8.*

24. J. B. Dennis and E. C. van Horn 1966. Programming semantics for multiprogrammed computations. *Communications of the ACM 9*, 3 (March), 143–155.

25. E. W. Dijkstra 1968a. The structure of the THE multiprogramming system. *Communications of the ACM 11*, 5 (May), 341–346. *Article 11.*

26. E. W. Dijkstra 1968b. Cooperating sequential processes. In *Programming Languages*, F. Genuys Ed., Academic Press, New York, 43–112.

27. E. W. Dijkstra 1971. Hierarchical ordering of sequential processes. *Acta Informatica 1*, 2, 115–138.

28. D. C. Englebart and W. K. English 1968. A research center for augmenting human intellect. *Fall Joint Computer Conference 33*, 395–410.

29. A. G. Fraser 1972. File integrity in a disc-based multi-access system. In *Operating Systems Techniques*, C. A. R. Hoare and R. H. Perrott Eds., Academic Press, New York, 227–248. *Article 9.*

30. J. Gosling, B. Joy and G. Steele 1996. *The Java Language Specification.* Addison-Wesley, Reading, MA.

31. A. N. Habermann 1967. On the harmonious cooperation of abstract machines. Ph.D. thesis. Technological University, Eindhoven, The Netherlands.

32. G. H. Hardy 1969. *A Mathematician's Apology.* Foreword by C. P. Snow. Cambridge University Press, New York.

33. M. Hiltzik 1999. *Dealers of Lightning: Xerox PARC and the Dawn of the Computer Age.* Harper Business, New York.

34. C. A. R. Hoare 1974. Monitors: an operating system structuring concept. *Communications of the ACM 17*, 10 (October), 549–557.

35. D. J. Howarth 1972a. A re-appraisal of certain design features of the Atlas I supervisory system. In *Operating Systems Techniques*, C. A. R. Hoare and R. H. Perrott Eds., Academic Press, New York, 371–377.
36. D. J. Howarth 1972b. Quoted in *Studies in Operating Systems*, R. M. McKeag and R. Wilson Eds., Academic Press, New York, 390.
37. A. C. Kay and A. Goldberg 1977. Personal dynamic media. *IEEE Computer 10*, 3 (March), 31–41.
38. B. W. Kernighan and D. M. Richie 1978. *The C Programming Language*. Prentice-Hall, Englewood Cliffs, NJ.
39. T. Kilburn, R. B. Payne and D. J. Howarth 1961. The Atlas supervisor. *National Computer Conference 20*, 279–294. *Article 3.*
40. B. W. Lampson and R. F. Sproull 1979. An open operating system for a single-user machine. *Operating Systems Review 13*, 5 (November), 98–105. *Article 18.*
41. B. W. Lampson and D. D. Redell 1980. Experience with processes and monitors in Mesa. *Communications of the ACM 23*, 2 (February), 105–117.
42. B. W. Lampson 1988. Personal distributed computing: The Alto and Ethernet software. In *A History of Personal Workstations*, A. Goldberg Ed., Addison-Wesley, Reading, MA, 291–344.
43. B. W. Lampson 2000. Personal communication, March 20.
44. S. Lauesen 1975. A large semaphore based operating system. *Communications of the ACM 18*, 7 (July), 377–389. *Article 14.*
45. S. Lavington 1980. *Early British Computers*. Digital Press, Bedford, MA.
46. P. J. Leach, P. H. Levine, B. P. Douros, J. A. Hamilton, D. L. Nelson and B. L. Stumpf 1983. The architecture of an integrated local network. *IEEE Journal on Selected Areas in Communications 1*, 5, 842–856.
47. J. A. N. Lee 1992. Claims to the term "time-sharing." *IEEE Annals of the History of Computing 14*, 1, 16–17.
48. B. H. Liskov 1972. The design of the Venus operating system. *Communications of the ACM 15*, 3 (March), 144–149.
49. W. C. Lynch 1966. Description of a high capacity fast turnaround university computing center. *Communications of the ACM 9*, 2 (February), 117–123. *Article 5.*
50. W. C. Lynch 1972. An operating system designed for the computer utility environment. In *Operating Systems Techniques*, C. A. R. Hoare and R. H. Perrott Eds., Academic Press, New York, 341–350.
51. R. A. Maddux and H. D. Mills 1979. Review of "The Architecture of Concurrent Programs." *IEEE Computer 12*, (May), 102–103.
52. J. McCarthy 1959. A time-sharing operator program for our projected IBM 709. Unpublished memorandum to Professor P. M. Morse, MIT, January 1. Reprinted in *IEEE Annals of the History of Computing 14*, 1, 1992, 20–23.
53. J. McCarthy 1962. Time-sharing computer systems. In *Computers and the World of the Future*, M. Greenberger Ed., The MIT Press, Cambridge, MA, 221–248.

54. J. McCarthy, S. Boilen, E. Fredkin and J. C. R. Licklider 1963. A time-sharing debugging system for a small computer. *Spring Joint Computer Conference 23*, 51–57.

55. R. M. McKeag 1976a. Burroughs B5500 Master Control Program. In *Studies in Operating Systems*, R. M. McKeag and R. Wilson Eds., Academic Press, New York, 1–66.

56. R. M. McKeag 1976b. THE multiprogramming system. In *Studies in Operating Systems*, R. M. McKeag and R. Wilson Eds., Academic Press, New York, 145–184.

57. F. B. MacKenzie 1965. Automated secondary storage management. *Datamation 11*, 11 (November), 24–28.

58. P. B. Medawar 1979. *Advice to a Young Scientist.* Harper & Row, New York.

59. C. Oliphint 1964. Operating system for the B 5000. *Datamation 10*, 5 (May), 42–54. *Article 4.*

60. E. I. Organick 1973. *Computer System Organization: The B5700/B6700 Series.* Academic Press, New York.

61. R. Pike, D. Presotto, S. Dorward, B. Flandrena, K. Thompson, H. Trickey and P. Winterbottom 1995. *Plan 9 from Bell Labs.* Lucent Technologies.

62. L. Poole 1984. A tour of the Mac desktop. *Macworld 1*, (May–June), 19–26.

63. G. Popek, B. Walter, J. Chow, D. Edwards, C. Kline, G. Rudison and G. Thiel 1981. Locus: a network transparent, high reliability distributed system. *ACM Symposium on Operating Systems Principles*, Pacific Grove, CA, 169–177.

64. D. D. Redell, Y. K. Dalal, T. R. Horsley, H. C. Lauer, W. C. Lynch, P. R. McJones, H. G. Murray and S. C. Purcell 1980. Pilot: an operating system for a personal computer. *Communications of the ACM 23*, 2 (February), 81–92. *Article 19.*

65. M. Richards 1969. BCPL: a tool for compiler writing and system programming. *Spring Joint Computer Conference 34*, 557–566..

66. D. M. Ritchie and K. Thompson 1974. The Unix time-sharing system. *Communications of the ACM 17*, 7 (July), 365–375. *Article 10.*

67. D. M. Ritchie 1984. The evolution of the Unix time-sharing system. *Bell Laboratories Technical Journal 63*, 8, Part 2 (October), 1577–1593.

68. D. J. Roche 1972. Burroughs B5500 MCP and time-sharing MCP. In *Operating Systems Techniques*, C. A. R. Hoare and R. H. Perrott Eds., Academic Press, New York, 307–320.

69. S. Rosen Ed. 1967. *Programming Systems and Languages.* McGraw-Hill, New York.

70. R. F. Rosin Ed. 1987. Prologue: the Burroughs B 5000. *Annals of the History of Computing 9*, 1, 6–7.

71. R. F. Rosin and J. A. N. Lee Eds. 1992. The CTSS interviews. *Annals of the History of Computing 14*, 1, 33–51.

72. R. F. Rosin 2000. Personal communication, March 20.

73. G. F. Ryckman 1983. The IBM 701 computer at the General Motors Research Laboratories. *IEEE Annals of the History of Computing 5*, 2 (April), 210–212. *Article 1.*

74. R. Sandberg, D. Goldberg, S. Kleiman, D. Walsh and B. Lyon 1985. Design and implementation of the Sun Network Filesystem. *Usenix Conference*, (June), 119–130.

75. A. C. Shaw 1974. *The Logical Design of Operating Systems.* Prentice-Hall, Englewood Cliffs, NJ.

76. S. K. Shrivastava and F. Panzieri 1982. The design of a reliable remote procedure call mechanism. *IEEE Transactions on Computers 31*, 7 (July), 692–697. *Article 22.*

77. R. Slater 1987. *Portraits in Silicon.* The MIT Press, Cambridge, MA, 273–283.

78. D. C. Smith, C. Irby, R. Kimball and Eric Harslem 1982. The Star user interface: an overview. *National Computer Conference*, 515–528. *Article 20.*

79. R. B. Smith 1961. The BKS system for the Philco-2000. *Communications of the ACM 4*, 2 (February), 104 and 109. *Article 2.*

80. M. Stonebraker 1981. Operating system support for database management. *Communications of the ACM 24*, 7 (July), 412–418.

81. J. E. Stoy and C. Strachey 1972. OS6—an experimental operating system for a small computer. *The Computer Journal 15*, 2 & 3, 117–124 & 195–203. *Article 17.*

82. C. Strachey 1959. Time sharing in large fast computers. *Information Processing*, (June), UNESCO, 336–341.

83. C. Strachey 1974. Letter to Donald Knuth, May 1. Quoted in Lee (1992).

84. D. Swinehart, G. McDaniel and D. R. Boggs 1979. WFS: a simple shared file system for a distributed environment. *ACM Symposium on Operating Systems Principles*, Pacific Grove, CA, (December), 9–17. *Article 21.*

85. D. C. Swinehart, P. T. Zellweger and R. B. Hagmann 1985. The structure of Cedar. *SIGPLAN Notices 20*, 7 (July), 230–244.

86. A. S. Tanenbaum, R. van Renesse, H. van Staveren, G. J. Sharp, S. J. Mullender, J. Jansen and G. van Rossum 1990. Experiences with the Amoeba distributed operating system, *Communications of the ACM 33*, 12 (December), 46–63.

87. B. H. Tay and A. L. Ananda 1990. A survey of remote procedure calls. *Operating Systems Review 24*, 3 (July), 68–79.

88. J. E. White 1976. A high-level framework for network-based resource sharing. *National Computer Conference*, (June), 561–570.

89. M. V. Wilkes 1985. *Memoirs of a Computer Pioneer.* The MIT Press, Cambridge, MA.

90. R. Wilson 1976. The Titan supervisor. In *Studies in Operating Systems*, R. M. McKeag and R. Wilson Eds., Academic Press, New York, 185–263.

91. W. A. Wulf, E. S. Cohen, W. M. Corwin, A. K. Jones, R. Levin, C. Pierson and F. J. Pollack 1974. Hydra: the kernel of a multiprocessor operating system. *Communications of the ACM 17*, 6 (June), 337–345.

PART I

OPEN SHOP

1

THE IBM 701 COMPUTER AT THE GENERAL MOTORS RESEARCH LABORATORIES*

GEORGE F. RYCKMAN

(1983)

The author remembers 3.5 hours mean time between failures for the 701—an excellent record. He recalls the beginning of SHARE and also what many regard as the first monitor on the 704 or on any IBM computer. Michael Chancellor was the Applied Science representative, and Warren Hume was the branch manager.

In the summer of 1952 the General Motors Research (GMR) staff (now the GM Research Laboratories) installed an IBM Card Programmed Calculator (CPC). It cost a modest $1800/month, and it carried out design and data-reduction calculations at the rate of 150 three-address instructions per minute. It was used for torsional vibration analyses, gas turbine engine data reduction, engine bearing-load calculations, an information-retrieval project, and many other computations.

Within a year it became apparent that it could not cope with the more advanced design evaluation and data-reduction calculations required by GMR and the Allison Division of GM. At the same time IBM had announced a new, advanced stored-program machine, called the 701 Electronic Data Processing Machine operating at-least 100 times faster than the CPC and costing about 10 times as much.

---

*G. F. Ryckman, The IBM 701 computer at the General Motors Research Laboratories. *IEEE Annals of the History of Computing* 5, 2 (April 1983), 210–212. Copyright © 1983, Institute of Electrical and Electronics Engineers, Inc. Reprinted by permission.

With the help of the Allison Division, GMR ordered one of these new machines on the basis of our vice-president's approval.

The IBM 701 computer installed at General Motors Research Laboratories in 1954–56. Seated is James J. Fishman, Research Engineer. Standing at the printer is George F. Ryckman, Sr. Research Engineer. (Courtesy George F. Ryckman.)

Never again would such a computer be approved in GM at such a low level! It was the first stored-program machine installed in GM. It arrived in April 1954, and it proved its worth for a number of applications—mostly in the engineering area, but also in one important commercial application.

Following are some of the applications: torsional, vibration studies, advanced bearing-load calculations, propeller design and data reduction, harmonic analysis with feedback checking, automatic-advance cams on distributors, pump pressure-wave analysis, turbine blade properties, fatigue-data analysis, hypoid gear design.

GMR also took on a task for the GM Personnel staff involving an actuarial and statistical study of GMs some 750,000 hourly employment force. It was highly confidential, strained the 701's ability to operate on a sustained basis, and taught us engineers much about programming controls and checks on data. We knew about energy balancing, but had to apply it to counts, making sure that subcounts totaled to grand totals. This was compounded by the fact that the 701's mean time between failures (MTBF) was approximately 3.5 hours (mostly due to its cathode-ray-tube electrostatic main memory). As a result of this failure frequency, our program was designed to check itself every 5 minutes to make sure it was still intact. Whenever this so-called Project X was running in the computer room, only Joseph T. Olstzyn, M. Elizabeth Kerr, a few computer operators, and I were allowed in the area.

Imagine a machine that took only 12 microseconds for its cycle time, and an instruction required as many as five of these cycles to complete its operation. A few of us programmed the 701 in what was called the Regional Assembly Language as taught by Marie Clark in a course offered by IBM in New York City. Four or five of us took this course in the fall of 1953 in preparation for our giant computer. Most applications however were programmed in SPEEDCODE or ACOM—two programming systems that transformed the single-adddress fixed-point arithmetic machine into a stream-lined three-address floating-point system. SPEEDCODE was authored by Walter A. Ramshaw and his people at the United Aircraft Corporation. ACOM was written by Jack Horner and others at the Allison Division of GM. Both of these systems used subroutines to perform the float-point arithmetic, which in turn slowed the 701 from its basic speed of 15,000 single-address fixed-point instructions per second to about 150 three-address floating-point instructions per second.

Prior to the advent of Project X, Don F. Harroff, James J. Fishman, and I wrote a pair of "compilers" (now called macroprocessors) that turned out to be instrumental in implementing that project in a timely manner. My compiler, simply called READ, accepted specifications on the several data items in a record in decimal or alphabetical form and converted them to an appropriate internal binary form. The compiled program read data from the card reader and recorded them on magnetic tape at the fantastic density of 100 bits per inch! The mountains of input cards for Project X required only about 20 reels of magnetic tape. Harroff and Fishman's compiler (called PRINT) did the inverse, converting data from binary to decimal or alphabetical form. The compiled program read data from magnetic tape and recorded it on the printer. Special programs had to be written to perform any given analysis of this "huge" data base, but needless to say it was very impressive to get an answer to a question in hours versus the days it took to do the same task on tabulating equipment.

During this same period, both IBM and the Curtiss-Wright Corporation purchased some of GMR's computer time on the 701. Since computer time was at a premium then, we charged $300 per hour around the clock—and they were glad to pay in view of the scarcity of this resource. At that time there were only nineteen 701s in the world, and they were all taxed to the limit, even though IBM at one time thought "it was more computing power than would be needed for decades to come." We were running around the clock.

Scheduling computer time was sloppy on the 701. Each user was allocated a minimum 15-minute slot, of which time he usually spent 10 minutes in setting up the equipment to do his computation. He mounted his own tapes and set up the card reader, card punch, and printer to carry out his computation. By the time he got his calculation going, he may have had only 5 minutes or less of actual computation completed—wasting two thirds of his time slot. Standard cardreader and printer "boards" helped this situation, but the wasted time was still exorbitant. Then came the idea of streamlining the operation.

Other ideas arose among the other 701 users, and in late summer of 1955 a meeting was called in Santa Monica, California. As a result of that meeting of 701 users, SHARE was born. "GM" became the code of GMR, and it still is. North American Aviation and GM Research conceived and implemented the "Input/Output System," the first monitor or operating system. Aimed at the IBM 704 computer, it was in operation that computer when it was installed in May 1956. By the fall of 1956, all 701 programs had been converted to the 704, and GMR's first large-scale computer was released. So passed an exciting era.

PART II

BATCH PROCESSING

2

THE BKS SYSTEM FOR THE PHILCO-2000*

RICHARD B. SMITH

(1961)

The BKS System is a program sequencing system designed for the Philco-2000 computer to meet operational requirements of the Bettis and Knolls Atomic Power Laboratories. The Philco-2000 on which this system is being used has a 32,768-word memory, 16 tape transports on-line, and an electric typewriter on-line. The card-to-tape, card-to-printer, tape-to-card, tape-to-printer, and routine tape-to-tape operations are performed with off-line equipment.

The BKS System controls loading of independent programs from either cards or the master system tape, provides common functions required by most programs, assigns all logical tapes to available physical tape transports, and directs the mounting and removal of all file tapes. Some uniformity is imposed on individual programs by the system, especially in regard to operating characteristics. Established standards require that programs should *not*

(a) contain machine halts,
(b) rewind the input, output, or program tapes,
(e) require special toggle or sense switch settings, or
(d) utilize memory assigned for the system.

The system requires 2560 locations and uses an additional 128 locations as temporary storage.

All tapes are assigned by a set of established locations within the area assigned to the system. From these locations, tape subroutines may obtain

---

*R. B. Smith, The BKS System for the Philco-2000. *Communications of the ACM 4*, 2 (February 1961), 104 and 109.

the physical tape transport assignments for the program being executed. The sign bit of each tape assignment location is used to indicate tapes assigned to a program. A positive sign signifies the assignment of a tape and a negative sign signifies that the tape has not been assigned. Tape logics may be changed by interchanging the contents of two or more tape assignment locations.

Eight categories classify the general use of all tapes. The categories are as follows:

(a) A scratch or blank tape designation identifies a tape to be used for the temporary storage of data.

(b) A program tape is required of all segmented programs and identifies the tape from which the program segments may be obtained.

(c) An input tape designation is required of all programs and determines which tape logic or location should be assigned to the common input tape.

(d) An output tape designation is similarly required and specifies the tape logic on which all normal output should be written for off-line processing.

(e) A library tape classification is used to specify tapes which are always required for the execution of a program.

(f) An input file tape is similar to a library tape except that input files may or may not he required for the execution of a program.

(g) An output file tape designates a scratch tape which may be labeled during the execution of a program and removed when the program is terminated.

(h) All other tapes are unassigned and no attempt should be made to use them. No provision is made for changing the classification of a tape at execution time except for the special case of output files.

Any library or input file tape required for several jobs is retained by the system and released only when no further job calls for the specific tape. However, an output file tape may not be used by more than one job nor may it be used as an immediate input file.

All input is collected or batched and an input tape is prepared periodically with the off-line card-to-tape equipment. The arrangement of cards for each job is in the following order. An accounting card is the first card of every job and is used for recording the machine time to process the job. The system control card is the second card of a job and is inserted for the first job in a sequence of jobs for a given program. The control card identifies the source of the program, the category of all tapes, and the identification of library tapes when required. The control card may indicate that the program is on the master system tape or on cards. If the program is on cards, the card program must follow the control card and terminate with a blank card after the last program segment. Subsequent jobs in sequence for the same program must not contain the program control card or (when applicable) the binary card program. Input file tape identification or call cards follow the accounting card except when the control card and possibly the binary program are required. Punch cards are required of all programs and form the last set of cards for each job. Each job may contain several cases or sets of data. Each case must be terminated with a blank card and the last case is determined when the card following a blank is an accounting card. A special set of stop eards is written on tape following the last job.

The system initially processes each tape prepared off-line and writes a new tape which is arranged in a more convenient form for program execution. During the preparation of the modified input tape, the system extracts necessary information to prepare a directory of all jobs to be executed and all tape requirements. Furthermore, the card information is translated during this preliminary phase to the normal six-bit code representation.

The initial segment of the first program is loaded from the modified input tape and given control. Operation at this time becomes single phase. That is, each program processes all necessary input data, performs the necessary calculations, prepares all desired output, and then returns control to the system to initiate preparation of file tapes and loading of the next program in sequence.

There are 24 system entries available to every program. Twelve of the entries are for initialization and execution of general subroutine operations required by most programs. Three entries are for testing specific toggle conditions established by the operator. Two entries are for manual execution by the operator. The seven remaining entries are included to accommodate conditions necessary for system operation.

PART III

MULTIPROGRAMMING

3

THE ATLAS SUPERVISOR*

TOM KILBURN, R. BRUCE PAYNE
AND DAVID J. HOWARTH

(1961)

1 INTRODUCTION

This paper gives a brief description of work originating in the Computer Group at Manchester University. Atlas is the name given to a large computing system which can include a variety of peripheral equipments, and an extensive store. All the activities of the system are controlled by a program called the supervisor. Several types of store are used, and the addressing system enables a virtually unlimited amount of each to be included. The primary store consists of magnetic cores with a cycletime of under two microseconds, which is effectively reduced by multiple selection mechanisms. The core store is divided into 512 word "pages"; this is also the size of the fixed blocks on drums and magnetic tapes. The core store and drum store are addressed identically, and drum transfers are performed automatically as described in Section 3. There is a fixed store which consists of a wire mesh into which ferrite slugs are inserted; it has a fast read-out time, and is used to hold common routines including routines of the supervisor. A subsidiary core store is used as working space for the supervisor. The V-store is a collective name given to various flip-flops throughout the computer, which can be read, set, and re-set by reading from or writing to particular store addresses.

The accumulator performs floating point arithmetic on 48-bit numbers, of which 8 bits are the exponent. There are 128 index registers, or B-lines, each 24 bits long; in the instruction code, which is of the one address type,

*T. Kilburn, R. B. Payne and D. J. Howarth, The Atlas supervisor. *AFIPS Computer Conference 20*, (1961), 279–294.

each instruction refers to two B-lines which may modify the address and the average instruction time is between one and two microseconds. There are three control registers, referred to as "main control", "extra-code control", and "interrupt control", which are also B-lines 127, 126 and 125. Main control is used by object programs. When main control is active, access to the subsidiary store and V-store is prevented by hardware, and this makes it possible to ensure that object programs cannot interfere with the supervisor. The fixed store contains about 250 subroutines which can be called in from an object program by single instructions called extracodes. When these routines are being obeyed, extracode control is used: extracode control is also used by the supervisor, which requires access to the "private" stores. Interrupt control is used in short routines within the supervisor which deal with peripheral equipment. These routines are entered at times dictated by the peripheral equipments; the program using main or extracode control is interrupted, and continues when the peripheral equipment routine is completed.

The first Atlas installation at Manchester University will include:

16,384	words of core store
8,192	words of fixed store
1,024	words of subsidiary store
98,304	words on drums
8	magnetic tape mechanisms
4	paper tape readers
4	paper tape punches
2	teleprinters
1	line printer
1	card reader
1	card punch

Other Atlas installations will include different amounts of store and peripheral equipments, but the supervisor program herein described is of sufficient generality to handle any configuration through the minor adjustment of parameters.

2 THE CO-ORDINATION OF ROUTINES

The Structure of the Supervisor

The supervisor program controls all those functions of the system that are not obtained merely by allowing the central computer to proceed with obeying an object program, or by allowing peripheral equipments to carry out their built-in operations. The supervisor therefore becomes active on frequent occasions and for a variety of reasons—in fact, whenever any part of the system requires attention from it. It becomes activated in several different ways. Firstly, it can be entered as a direct result of obeying an object program. Thus, a problem being executed calls for the supervisor whenever it requests an action that is subject to control by the supervisor, such as a request for transfer to or from peripheral equipments or the initiation of transfers between core store and magnetic drums; the supervisor is also activated when an object program requires monitoring for any reason such as exponent or division overflow, or exceeding store or time allocation. Secondly, the supervisor may be activated by various items of hardware which have completed their assigned tasks and require further attention. Thus, for example, drums and magnetic tapes call the supervisor into action whenever the transfer of a 512 word block to or from core store is completed; other peripheral equipments require attention whenever the one character or row buffer has been filled or emptied by the equipment. Lastly, certain failures of the central computer store, and peripheral equipments call the supervisor into action.

The central computer thus shares its time between these supervisor activities and the execution of object programs, and the design of Atlas and of the supervisor programs is such that there is mutual protection between object programs and all parts of the supervisor. The supervisor program consists of many branches which are normally dormant but which can be activated whenever required. The sequence in which the branches are activated is essentially random, being dictated by the course of an object program and the functioning of the peripheral equipments.

Interrupt Routines

The most frequent and rapidly activated parts of the supervisor are the interrupt routines. When a peripheral equipment requires attention, for example, an interrupt flip-flop is set which is available to the central computer as a digit in the V-store; a separate interrupt flip-flop is provided for each reason for interruption. If an interrupt flip-flop is set and interruptions are not inhibited, then before the next instruction is started, the address 2048 of the fixed store is written to the interrupt control register, B125, and control is switched to interrupt control. Further interruptions are inhibited until control reverts to main or extracode control. Under interrupt control, the fixed store program which is held at address 2048 onwards detects which interrupt flip-flop has been set and enters an appropriate interrupt routine in the fixed store. If more than one flip-flop is set, that of highest priority is dealt with first, the priority being built-in corresponding to the urgency of action required. By the use of special hardware attached to one of the B register, B123, the source of any interruption may be determined as a result of obeying between two and six instructions.

The interrupt routines so entered deal with the immediate cause of the particular interrupt. For example, when the one-character buffer associated with a paper tape reader has been filled, the appropriate interrupt flip-flop is set and the "Paper tape reader interrupt routine" is entered. This transfers the character to the required location in store after checking parity where appropriate. The paper tape reader meanwhile proceeds to read the next character to the buffer. Separate interrupt routines in the fixed store control each type of peripheral equipment, magnetic tapes and drums. The interrupt technique is also employed to deal with certain exceptional situations which occur when the central computer cannot itself deal adequately with a problem under execution, for example, when there is an overflow or when a required block is not currently available in the core store. There are therefore interrupt flip-flops and interrupt routines to deal with such cases. Further routines are provided to deal with interruptions due to detected computer faults.

During the course of an interrupt routine further interruptions are inhibited, and the interrupt flip-flops remain set in the V-store. On resumption of main or extracode control, interruptions are again permitted. If one or more interrupt flip-flops have been set in the meantime, the relevant interrupt routines are obeyed in the sequence determined by their relative priority. In order to avoid interference with object programs or supervisory programs, interrupt routines use only restricted parts of the central computer, namely, the interrupt control register, B-lines 123 and 111 to 118 inclusive, private registers in subsidiary store and the V-store and locked out pages in core store (see Section 3). With the exception of the B-lines, no object program is permitted to use these registers. No lock out is imposed on the B-lines, but interrupt routines make no assumptions concerning the original contents of the B-lines and hence, at worst, erroneous use of interrupt B-lines by an object program can only result in erroneous functioning of that particular program. Switching of control to and from an interrupt routine is rapid, since no preservation of resetting of working registers is required.

The interrupt routines are designed to handle calls for action with the minimum delay and in the shortest time; the character-by-character transfers to and from peripheral equipments, for example, occur at high frequency and it is essential that the transfers be carried out with the minimum possible use of the central computer and within the time limit allowed by the peripheral equipment for filling or emptying the buffer. Since several interrupt flip-flops can become set simultaneously, but cannot be acted upon while another interrupt routine is still in progress, it is essential that a short time limit be observed by each interrupt routine. The majority of calls for interrupt routines involve only a few instructions, such as the transfer of a character, stepping of counts, etc., and on conclusion the interrupt routine returns to the former control, either main or extracode. On some occasions, however, longer sequences are required; for example, on completion of the input of a paper tape or deck of cards, routines must be entered to deal with the characters collected in the store, writing them to magnetic tape where appropriate, decoding and listing titles and so on. In such cases, the interrupt routine initiates a routine to be obeyed under extracode control, known as a supervisor extracode routine.

Supervisor Extracode Routines

Supervisor extracode routines (S.E.R.'s) form the principal "branches" of the supervisor program. They are activated either by interrupt routines or by extracode instructions occurring in an object program. They are protected from interference by object programs by using subsidiary store as working space, together with areas of core and drum store which are locked out in the usual way whilst an object program is being executed (see Section 3). They operate under extracode control, the extracode control register of any current object program being preserved and subsequently restored. Like the interrupt routines, they use private B-lines, in this case B-lines 100 to 110 inclusive; if any other working registers are required, the supervisory routines themselves preserve and subsequently restore the contents of such registers. The S.E.R.'s thus apply mutual protection between themselves and an object program.

These branches of the supervisor program may be activated at random intervals. They can moreover be interrupted by interrupt routines, which may in turn initiate other S.E.R's. It is thus possible for several S.E.R.'s to be activated at the same time, in the same way as it is possible for several interrupt flip-flops to be set at the same time. Although several S.E.R.'s may be activated, obviously not more than one can be obeyed at any one moment;

the rest are either halted or held awaiting execution. This matter is organized by a part of the supervisor called the "co-ordinator routine" which is held in fixed store. Activation of an S.E.R. always occurs via the co-ordinator routine, which arranges that any S.E.R. in progress is not interrupted by other S.E.R.'s. As these are activated, they are recorded in subsidary store in lists and an entry is extracted from one of these lists whenever an S.E.R. ends or halts itself. Once started, an S.E.R. is always allowed to continue if it can; a high priority S.E.R. does not "interrupt" a low priority S.E.R. but is entered only on conclusion or halting of the current S.E.R. The co-ordinator has the role of the program equivalent of the "inhibit interrupt flip-flop", the lists of activated S.E.R.'s being the equivalent of the setting of several interrupt flip-flops. The two major differences are that no time limit is placed on an S.E.R., and that an S.E.R. may halt itself for various reasons; this is in contrast to interrupt routines, which observe a time limit and are never halted.

In order that the activity of each branch of the computing system be maintained at the highest possible level, the S.E.R.'s awaiting execution are recorded in four distinct lists. Within each list, the routines are obeyed in the order in which they were activated, but the lists are assigned priorities, so that the top priority list is emptied before entries are extracted from the next list. The top priority list holds routines initiated by completion of drum transfers, and also routines entered as a result of computer failures such as core store parity. The second list holds routines arising from magnetic tape interruptions and the third holds routines arising from peripheral interruptions. The lowest priority list contains one entry for each object program currently under execution, and entry to an S.E.R. through an extracode instruction in an object program is recorded in this list. On completion of an S.E.R., the co-ordinator routine selects for execution the first activated S.E.R. in the highest priority list.

The central computer is not necessarily fully occupied during the course of an S.E.R. The routine may, for example, require the transfer of a block of information from the drum to the core store, in which case it is halted until the drum transfer is completed. Furthermore, the queue of requests for drum transfers (see Section 3), is maintained in the subsidiary store, may be full, in which case the S.E.R. making the request must be halted. When an S.E.R.is halted for this or similar reasons, it is returned to the relevant list as halted, and the next activated S.E.R.is entered by the co-ordinator routine. Before an S.E.R. is halted, a restart point is specified. A halted routine is made free to proceed when the cause of the halt has been removed—for example, by the S.E.R. which controls drum transfers and the extraction of entries from the crum queue. The S.E.R. lists can therefore hold at any one time routines awaiting execution and halted routines; interrupt routines are written in such a way that the number of such S.E.R.'s activated at any one time is limited to one per object program, and one or two per interrupt flip-flop, depending upon the particular features of each interrupt routine. When an S.E.R. is finally concluded, as distinct from halted, it is removed from the S.E.R. lists and becomes dormant again.

Although S.E.R.'s originate in many cases as routines to control peripheral equipment, magnetic tapes and drums, it should not be supposed that this is the sole function of these routines. Entrances to S.E.R.'s from interrupt routines or from extracode instructions in an object program initiate routines which control the entire operation of the computing system, including the transfer of information between store and peripherals, communication with the operators and engineers, the initiation, termination and, where necessary, monitoring of object programs, the monitoring of central computer and peripheral failures, the execution of test programs and the accumulation of logging information. Each branch of supervisory activity is composed of a series of S.E.R.'s, each one activated by an object program or an interrupt routine and terminated usually by initiating a peripheral or magnetic tape transfer or by changing the status of an S.E.R. list or object program list. The most frequently used routines are held in the fixed store; routines required less frequently are held on the magnetic drum and are transferred to core store when required. Supervisor routines in core and drum store are protected from interference by object programs by use of hardware lock-out and the basic store organization routines in the fixed store.

Object Programs

The function of all supervisor activity is, of course, to organize the progress of problems through the computer with the minimum possible delay. Object programs are initiated by S.E.R.'s, which insert them into the object program list; they are subsequently entered by the co-ordinator routine effectively as branches of lower priority than any S.E.R. Although object programs are logically subprograms of the supervisor, they may function for long periods using the computer facilities to the full without reference to the supervisor. For this reason, the supervisor program may be regarded as normally dormant, activated and using the central computer for only a small proportion of the available time.

In order to allow object programs to function with the minimum of program supervision, they are not permitted to use extracode control or interrupt control directly, enabling protection of main programs and supervisor programs to be enforced by hardware. Object programs use the main control register, B127, and are therefore forbidden access to the V-store and subsidiary store. Reference to either of these stores causes the setting of an interrupt flip-flop and hence entrance to the supervisor program.

Access to private stores is only obtained indirectly by use of extracode functions, which switch the program to extracode control and enter one of a possible maximum of 512 routines in the fixed store. These extracode routines form simple extensions of the basic order code, and also provide specific entry to supervisor routines to control the transfer of information to and from the core store and to carry out necessary organization. Such specific entrances to the supervisor program maintain complete protection of the object programs. Protection of magnetic tapes and peripheral input and output data is obtained by the use, in extracode functions, of logical tape and data numbers which the supervisor identifies within each program with the titles of the tapes or information. Blocks of core and drum store are protected by hardware and by the supervisor routines in fixed store as described in Section 3.

An object program is halted (by S.E.R.'s) whenever access is required to a block of information not immediately available in the core store. The block may be on the drums, in which case a drum transfer routine is entered, or it may be involved in a magnetic tape transfer. In both cases the program is halted until the block becomes available in core store. In the case of information involved in peripheral transfers, such as input data or output results, the supervisor buffers the information in core and drum store, and "direct" control of a peripheral equipment by an object program is not allowed. In this way, immobilization of large sections of store whilst a program awaits a peripheral transfer can be avoided. A program may however call directly for transfers involving drums or magnetic tapes by use of extracode functions, which cause entrance to the relevant supervisor routines. Queues of instructions are held in subsidiary store by these routines, in order to allow the object program to continue and to achieve the fullest possible overlap between tape and drum transfers and the execution of an object program.

While one program is halted, awaiting completion of a magnetic tape transfer for instance, the co-ordinator routine switches control to the next program in the object program list which is free to proceed. In order to maintain full protection, it is necessary to preserve and recove the contents of working registers common to all programs such as the B-lines, accumulator, and control registers, and to protect blocks in use in core store. The S.E.R. to perform this switching from one object program to another occupies the central computer for around 750 + 12p μsecs, where p is the number of pages, or 512 word blocks in core store. On the Manchester University Atlas, which has 32 pages of core store, the computing time for the round trip to switch from one program to another and to return subsequently is around 2.5 msecs. This is in contrast to the time of around 60 μsecs to enter and return from an S.E.R. and even less to switch to and from an interrupt routine. It is therefore obvious that the most efficient method of obtaining the maximum overlap between input and output, magnetic tape transfers, and computing is to reduce to a minimum the number of changes between object programs and to utilize to the full the rapid switching to and from interrupt and supervisor routines. The method of achieving this in practice is described in Section 6.

Compilation of programs is treated by the supervisor as a special case of the execution of an object program, the compiler comprising an object program which treats the source language program as input data. Special facilities are allowed to compilers in order that their allocation of storage space may be increased as need arises, and to allow exit to the supervisor before the execution of a problem or the recording of a compiled object program.

Error Conditions

In addition to programmed entrances to the supervisor, entrance may also be made in the event of certain detectable errors arising during the course of execution of a problem. A variety of program faults may occur and be detected by hardware, by programmed checks in extracodes, and in the supervisor. Hardware causes entry to the supervisor by the setting of interrupt flip-flops in the event of overflow of the accumulator, use of an unassigned instruction, and reference to the subsidiary store or V-store. Extracode routines detect errors in the range of the argument in square root, logarithm, and arcsin instructions. In the extracodes referring to peripheral equipment or magnetic tapes, a check is included that the logical number of the equipment has been previously defined. In extracodes for data translation, errors in the data may be detected. The supervisor detects errors in connection with the use of the store. All problems must supply information to the supervisor on the amount of store required, the amount of output, and the expected duration of execution. This information is supplied before the program is compiled, or may be deduced after compilation. The supervisor maintains a record of store blocks used, and can prevent the program exceeding the preset limit. In addition, an interrupt flip-flop is set by a clock at intervals of 0.1 secs, and another flip-flop is set whenever 1024 instructions have been obeyed using main or extracode control. These cause entrances to the supervisor which enable a program to be "monitored" to ensure that the preset time limit has not expired, and which are also instrumental in initiating routines to carry out regular timed operations such as logging of computer performance and initiation of routine test programs.

The action taken by the supervisor when a program "error" is detected depends upon the conditions previously set up by the program. Certain errors may be individually trapped, causing return of control to a preset address; a private monitor sequence may be entered if required enabling a program or a compiler to obtain diagnostic printing; failing specification of these actions, some information is printed by the supervisor and the program is suspended, and usually dumped to magnetic tape to allow storage space for another program.

The following sections describe in detail the action of certain supervisor routines, namely, those controlling drums, magnetic tapes, and peripheral equipment and those controlling the flow of information in the computer.

3 STORE ORGANIZATION

Indirect addressing and the One-Level Store

The core store of Atlas is provided with a form of indirect addressing which enables the supervisor to re-allocate areas of store and to alter their physical addresses, and which is also used to implement automatic drum transfers. With each page, or 512 word block, of core store there is associated a "page address register" which contains the most significant address bits of the block of information contained in the page. Every time access is required to a word of information in the core store, the page containing the word is located by hardware. This tests for equivalence between the requested "block address", or most significant address bits, and the contents of each of the page address registers in parallel. Failure to find equivalence results in a "non-equivalence" interruption. The page address registers are themselves addressable in the V-store and can thus be set appropriately by the supervisor whenever information is transferred to or from core store.

One of the most important consequences of this arrangement is that it enables the supervisor to implement automatic drum transfers. The address in an instruction refers to the combined core and drum store of the computer, and the supervisor records in subsidiary store the location of each block of information; only one copy of each block is kept, and the location is either a page of core store or a sector of the drum store. At any moment, only some of the blocks comprising a particular program may be in the core store and if only these blocks are required, the program can run at full speed. When a block is called for which is not in the core store, a non-equivalence interruption occurs, which enters the supervisor to transfer the new block from a sector of the drum to a page of the core store. During this operation the program that was interrupted is halted by the supervisor.

The block directory in subsidiary store contains one entry for each block in the combined core and drum store. It is divided into areas for each object program which is in the store; a separate program directory defines the area of the block directory occupied by each program. The size of this area, or the number of blocks used by a program, is specified before the program is obeyed in the job description (see Section 6). The entry for block n contains the block number n together with the number of the page or sector occupied by the block, and, if possible, is made in the nth position in the area; otherwise the area is filled working backwards from the end. In this way, blocks used by different object programs are always kept distinct, regardless of the addresses that are used in each program. A program addresses the combined "one-level store"[1] and the supervisor transfers blocks of information between the core and drum store as required; the physical location of each block of information is not specified by the program, but is controlled by the supervisor.

There are occasions when an object program must be prevented from obtaining access to a page of the core store such as one involved in a drum or tape transfer. To ensure complete protection of such pages, an additional bit, known as a lock out bit, is provided with each page address register. This prevents access to that page by the central computer, except when on interrupt control, and any reference to the page causes a non-equivalence interruption. By setting and resetting the lock out bits, the supervisor has complete control over the use of core store; it can allow independent object

[1]A paper on the one-level store has been written, and will, it is hoped, be published by the Institute of Radio Engineers.

programs to share the core store, it can reserve pages for peripheral transfers and can itself use parts of the core store occasionally for routines or working space, without any risk of interference. This is done by arranging that, whenever control is returned to an object program, pages that are not available to it are locked out.

A block of information forming part of an object program may also be locked out from use by that program because an operation on that information, controlled by the supervisor, is not complete. A drum, magnetic tape, or peripheral equipment transfer involving this block may have been requested. The reason for the lock out of such a block is recorded in the block directory, and if the block is in the core store, the lock out digit is also set. If reference is made to such a block by the object program, a non-equivalence interruption occurs and a supervisor extracode routine halts the program. This S.E.R. is restarted by the co-ordinator routine when the block becomes "unlocked", and the object program is re-entered when the block is available in core store.

The Drum Transfer Routine

The drum transfer routine is a group of S.E.R.s which are concerned with organizing drum transfers, and updating page address registers and the block directory. Once initiated, the transfer of a complete block to or from the drum proceeds under hardware control; the drum transfer routine initiates the transfer and identifies the required drum sector by setting appropriate bits in the V-store. It also identifies the core store page involved by setting a particular "dummy" block address, recognized by the drum control hardware, in the page address register; at the same time, this page is locked out to prevent interference from object programs while the transfer is in progress.

On completion of a transfer, an interruption occurs which enters the drum transfer routine. The routine can also be entered from the non-equivalence interrupt routine, which detects the number of the block requested but not found in the page address registers. Finally, the drum transfer routine can be activated by other parts of the supervisor which require drum transfers, and by extracode instructions which provide a means whereby object programs can if they wish exert some control over the movement of blocks to and from the drum store. A queue of requests for drum transfers, which can hold up to 64 requests, is stored in the subsidiary store; when the drum transfer routine is entered on completion of a transfer, the next transfer in the queue is initiated.

Whenever the supervisor wishes to enter another request for a drum transfer, three possible situations arise. Firstly, the queue is empty and the drum transfer can be started immediately. Secondly, the queue is already partly filled and the request is entered in the next position in the queue. Thirdly, the queue is full. In this case the routine making the request is halted by the co-ordinator routine, and is resumed when the queue can receive another entry. In the first two cases the supervisor routine is concluded when the request reaches the queue.

A non-equivalence interruption, which implies a drum transfer is required, is dealt with as follows. The core store is arranged to always hold an empty page with no useful information in it, and when required, a transfer of a block of information from the drum to this empty page is initiated. While this drum transfer is proceeding, preparation is made to write up the contents of another page of core store to the drum to maintain an empty page. The choice of this page is the task of the "learning program" which keeps details of the use made of blocks of information. This learning program will be described in detail elsewhere; it predicts the page which will not be required for the largest time, and is arranged with a feed-back so that if it writes up a block which is almost immediately required again, it only does this once. The number of the chosen page is converted to a request to write this page to the drum. This supervisor routine is now concluded and returns control to the co-ordinator routine.

When the drum transfer is completed, the drum transfer routine is again entered. This updates the block directory and page address register, makes the object program free to proceed and initiates the next drum request, which is to write the chosen page to the drum. This routine is now concluded and the co-ordinator is re-entered. The supervisor is finally entered when the write to drum transfer is complete. The block directory is updated, a note is made of the empty page, and the next drum request is initiated.

The Use of Main Store by the Supervisor

Some routines of the supervisor are obeyed in the main store, and these and others use working space in the main store. Since the supervisor is entered without a complete program change, special care must be taken to keep these blocks of store distinct and protected from interference. The active supervisor blocks of main store are recorded in the area for program 0 in the block directory. There are also some blocks of the supervisor program which are stored permanently on the drum; when one of these permanent blocks is required, it is duplicated to form an active block of the supervisor or, as in the case of a compiler, to become part of an object program.

Of the possible 2048 block numbers, 256 are "reserved" block numbers which are used exclusively by the supervisor and are not available to object program; object programs are restricted to using the remaining "non-reserved" block numbers. Blocks with reserved block numbers may be used in the core store at any time by the supervisor, and the co-ordinator routine locks out these pages of core store before returning control to an object program. The supervisor also uses some blocks having non-reserved block numbers to keep a record of sequence of blocks of information such as input and output streams. When a non-reserved supervisor block is called to the core store, the page address register is not set, since there may be a block of an object program which has the same block number already in the core store. Instead, the page address register is set to a fixed reserved block number while it is in use, and is cleared and locked out before control passes to another routine.

Not all the reserved block numbers are available to the supervisor for general use, since certain block numbers are temporarily used when drum, tape, and peripheral transfers are proceeding. These block numbers do not appear in the block directory. For example, when a magnetic tape transfer is taking place, the page of core store is temporarily given a block number which is recognized by the hardware associated with that tape channel. When the transfer is complete, the appropriate block number is restored. During a peripheral transfer, and also on other occasions, it is necessary that a block should be retained in the core store and should not be transferred to the drum. The relevant page of core store is "locked down" by setting a digit in the subsidiary store; the learning program never selects for transfer to the drum a page for which this lock-down digit is set.

4 MAGNETIC TAPE SUPERVISOR ROUTINES

The Magnetic Tape Facilities

The tape mechanism used on Atlas is the Ampex TM2 (improved FR 300) using one inch wide magnetic tape. There are sixteen tracks across the tape—twelve information tracks, two clock tracks, and two tracks used for reference purposes. The tapes are used in a fixed-block, pre-addressed mode. Information is stored on tape in blocks of 512 forty-eight bit words, together with a twenty-four bit checksum with end around carry. Each block is preceded by a block address and block marker and terminated by a block marker; the leading block address is sequential along the tape, and what is effectively the trailing block address is always zero. Tapes are tested and pre-addressed by special routines before being put into use, and the fixed position of the addresses permits selective overwriting and simple omission of faulty patches on the tape. Blocks can be read when the tape is moving either in the forward or reverse direction, but writing is only possible when the tape is moving forward. The double read and write head is used to check read when writing on the tape. When not operating the tape stops with the read head midway between blocks.

Atlas may control a maximum of 32 magnetic tape mechanisms. Each mechanism is connected to the central computer via one of eight channels, all of which can operate simultaneously, each controlling one read, write or positioning operation. It is possible for each tape mechanism to be attached to either one of a pair of channels, the switching being under the control of supervisory program through digits in the V-store. Fast wind and rewind operations are autonomous and only need the channel to initiate and, if required, terminate them. Transfer of a 512-word block of information between core store and tape is effected via a one-wordbuffer, the central computer hesitating for about 1/2 μsec, on average, each time a word is transferred to or from the core store. During a transfer the page of core store is given a particular reserved block number and the contents of the page address register are restored at the end of the transfer.

Supervisory programs are only entered when the block addresses are read before and after each block, and when the tape stops. As each block address is read, it is recorded in the V-store and an interrupt flip-flop is set, causing entrance to the block address interrupt routine.

The Block Address Interrupt Routine

This routine is responsible for initiating and checking the transfer of a single block between tape and core store, and searching along the tape for a specified block address. Digits are available in the V-store to control the speed and direction of motion of the tape and the starting and termination of read or write transfers. The block addresses are checked throughout and, in particular, a write transfer is not started until the leading block address of the tape block involved has been a read and checked. Hardware checking is provided on all transfers, and is acted upon by supervisor routines. A 24-bit check sum is formed and checked as each block is transferred to or from a tape, and a digit is set in a the V-store if any failure is detected. Similarly a digit is set in the event of failure to transfer a full block of 512 words. These digits are tested by the block address interrupt routine on the conclusion of each transfer. Parity failure either on reading from core store or on formation of the parity during a transfer to core store causes the setting of interrupt flip-flops. If a tape fails to stop, this is detected by the block address interrupt routine as a particular case of block address failure. Failure to enter the block address routine (for example, through failure to read block markers) is detected by the timed interrupt routine at intervals of 100 milliseconds. Finally, failures of the tape mechanism, such as vacuum failure, set a separate interrupt flip-flop. The detection of any of these errors causes entry to tape monitor routines, whose action will be described later.

Organization of Tape Operations

Magnetic tape operations are initiated by entrance to the tape supervisor routines in the fixed store from extracode instructions in an object program or, if the supervisor requires the tape operation for its own purposes, from supervisor extracode routines. From a table in subsidiary store, the logical tape number used in a program is converted to the actual mechanism number, and the tape "order" is entered to a queue of such orders, in subsidiary store, awaiting execution. A tape order may consist of the transfer of several blocks and any store blocks involved are "locked out" to prevent subsequent use before completion of the transfers; if any block is already involved in a transfer, the program initiating the request is halted. Similarly, the program is halted if the queue of tape instructions is already full. If the channels to which the deck can be connected are already occupied in a transfer or positioning, the tape supervisor returns control to the object program, which is then free to proceed. A program may thus request a number of tape transfers without being halted, allowing virtually the maximum possible overlap between the central computer and the tape mechanisms during execution of a program. Should a channel be available at the time a tape order is entered to the queue, the order is initiated at once by writing appropriate digits to the V-store, and by writing reserved tape transfer block numbers to the appropriate page address registers if the order involves a read or write transfer. The tape supervisor then returns control to the object program or supervisor routine.

One composite queue of tape orders is used for orders relating to all tape mechanisms and orders are extracted from the queue by S.E.R.'s entered from the block address interrupt routine. On reading the penultimate block address involved in an operation (for example, the last leading block address in a forward transfer) the next operation for the channel is located, and if it involves the same mechanism as the current order, and tape motion in the same direction, the operation is "prepared" by calling any store block involved to core store. On reading the final block address and successfully concluding checks, the block address interrupt routine initiates the next operation immediately if one has been prepared, thus avoiding stopping the tape if possible. If no operation has been prepared, the interrupt routine stops the tape by setting a digit in the V-store, and a further "block address interruption" occurs when the tape is stopped and the channel can accept further orders. This interruption enters an S.E.R. which extracts the next order for the channel from the tape queue, and the cycle of events is repeated until no further order for this channel remains. As each transfer is concluded, any object program halted through reference to the store block is made free to proceed.

An exception to the above process is when a long movement (over 200 blocks) or a rewind is required. In this case, the movement is carried out at fast speed, with block address interruptions inhibited, and the channel may meanwhile be used to control another tape mechanism. The long movement is terminated by checking the elapsed time and at the appropriate moment, entering the tape supervisor from the timed interrupt routine. The mechanism is then brought back "on channel" and the speed is returned to normal. When reading of block addresses is correctly resumed, the search is continued in the normal manner.

The Title Block

The first block on each magnetic tape is reserved for use by the supervisor, and access to information in this block by an object program is through special instructions only. This block contains the title of the tape, or an indication that the tape is free. When magnetic tapes are required by the supervisor or by an object program, the supervisor prints instructions to the operator to load the named tape and to engage the mechanism on which it is loaded. The engage button of each mechanism (see Section 5) is attached to a digit in the V-store, and these digits are scanned by the supervisor every one second. When a change to "engaged" status has been detected, the tape supervisor is entered to read the first block from the tape. The title is then checked against the expected title. In this way, the presence of the correct tape is verified, and furthermore the tape bearing the title becomes associated with a particular mechanism. Since the programmer assigns a logical tape number to the tape bearing a given title, this logical tape number used in extracode instructions can be converted by the supervisor to the actual mechanism number. Other supervisory information is included in the first block on each tape, including a system tape number and the number of blocks on the tape. Special supervisory routines allow Atlas to read tapes produced on the Ferranti Orion computer, which used the same tape mechanisms but can write blocks of varying lengths on the tape. These tapes are distinguished on Atlas by a marker written in the title block.

Magnetic Tape Failures

All failures detected by the interrupt routines cause the block address interrupt routine to stop the tape at the end of the current block when possible, and then to enter tape monitor supervisory routines; if the tape cannot be stopped, it is disengaged and the tape monitor routines entered. These routines are S.E.R.'s designed to minimize the immediate effect on the central computer of isolated errors in the tape system, to inform maintenance engineers of any faults, and to diagnose as far as possible the source of a failure. As an example of the actions taken by monitor routines, suppose a check sum failure has been detected while reading a block from tape to core store. The tape monitor routines make up to two further attempts to read the block; if either succeeds, the normal tape supervisor is re-entered after informing the engineers. Repeated failure may be caused by the tape or the tape mechanism; to distinguish these, the tape is rewound and an attempt is made to read the first block. If this is successful, a tape error is indicated, and an attempt is made to read the suspect block with reduced bias level. Failure causes the mechanism to be disengaged and the program using the tape to be suspended. If the "recover read" is successful, the tape is copied to a free tape and the operators instructed to re-address the faulty tape, omitting the particular block which failed. If on rewinding the tape, the first block cannot be read successfully, failure in the tape mechanism is suspected and the operator is instructed to remount the tape on another mechanism. Other faults are monitored in a similar manner, and throughout, the operator and engineers are informed of any detected faults. Provision is made for the program using the tape to "trap" persistent tape errors and thereby to take action suitable to the particular problem, which may be more straight-forward and efficient than the standard supervisory action.

Addressing of new tapes and re-addressing of faulty tapes are carried out on the computer by supervisory routines called in by the operator. A tape mechanism is switched to "addressing mode", which prohibits transfers to and from the core store, permits writing from the computer to the reference tracks and to the block addresses on tape, and activates a timing mechanism to space the block addresses. When a new tape is addressed, addresses are written sequentially along the tape and the area between leading and trailing block addresses is checked by writing ones to all digit positions and detecting failures on reading back. Any block causing failure is erased and the tape spaced suitably. On completion, a special block address is written to indicate "end of tape" and the entire tape is then checked by reading backwards. Any failures cause entry to the re-addressing routine. Finally, the tape mechanism is returned to "normal" mode, a little block is written containing the number of blocks on tape, a tape number, and the title "Free", and the tape is made available for use. A tape containing faulty blocks is re-addressed, omitting such blocks, by entry to the re-addressing routine with a list of faulty blocks; the faulty blocks are erased and the remaining blocks are re-labelled sequentially, the tape being checked as when addressing a new tape.

5 PERIPHERAL EQUIPMENT

Peripheral Interruptions

As mentioned in the Introduction, a large number and variety of peripheral equipments may be attached to Atlas. However, the amount of electronics associated with each equipment is kept to a minimum, and use is made of the high computing speed and interruption facilities of Atlas to provide control of these equipments and large scale buffering.

Thus the paper tape readers, which operate at 300 characters per second, set an interrupt flip-flop whenever a new character appears. Characters may be either 5 or 7 bits depending on which of two alternative widths of tape is being read. Similarly the paper tape punches, and the teleprinters which print information for the computer operators, cause an interruption whenever they are ready to receive a new character; these equipments operate at 110 and 10 characters per second respectively.

The card readers read 600 cards per minute, column by column, and interrupt the computer for every column. The card punches at 100 cards per minute, punch by rows and interrupt for each row.

The printers, which have 120 print wheels bearing 50 different characters, cause an interruption as each character approaches the printing position so that the computer may prime the hammers for those wheels where this character is to be printed. There are therefore 50 interruptions per revolution, or one every 1-1/2 millisecs.

All the information received from, or sent to, these peripheral equipments does so via particular digit positions in the V-store. For example, there are 7 such bits for each tape reader, and 120 for each printer, together with a few more bits for control signals.

The majority of interruptions can be dealt with simply by the interrupt routine for the particular type of equipment. Thus the paper tape reader interrupt routine normally has merely to refer to a table of characters to apply code conversion and parity checks, and to detect terminating characters and if all is well to store the new character in the next position in the store.

The interrupt routines for the printers and card punches are not expected to do the conversion from character coding to row binary; this is done by an S.E.R. before the card or line of print is commenced. The card routines are however complicated by the check reading stations; punching is checked one card cycle afterwards, and reading is checked 3 columns later. The interrupt routines apply these checks, and in the event of failure a monitor S.E.R. is entered.

The printer interrupt routine counts its interruptions to identify the character currently being printed; a check is provided once each revolution when a datum mark on the printer shaft causes a signal bit to appear in the V-store. This counting is maintained during the paper feed between lines, which occupies several milliseconds.

Attention by Operators

Whenever equipment needs attention it is "disengaged" from the computer. In this state, which is indicated by a light on the equipment and a corresponding bit in the V-store, it automatically stops and cannot be started by the computer.

The operator may engage or disengage an equipment by means of two buttons so labelled. The equipment may also be disengaged by the computer by writing to the appropriate V-store bit, but the computer cannot engage it.

The "engage" and "disengage" buttons do not themselves cause interruptions of the central computer. Instead, the "engaged" bits in the V-store are examined every second (this routine is activated by the clock interruption) and any change activates the appropriate S.E.R. Disengaging a device does not inhibit its interruptions, so that if the operator disengages a card machine in mid-cycle to replenish the magazine or to empty the stacker, the cycle is completed correctly.

There are also other special controls for particular equipments, e.g., a run-out key on card machines, and a 5/7-hole tape width selector switch on punched tape readers.

Most devices have detectors that indicate when cards or paper are exhausted or running low. These correspond to bits in the V-store that are read by the appropriate S.E.R. The paper tape readers however have no such detector, and the unlikely event of a punched tape passing completely through a reader (due to the absence of terminating characters) appears to the computer merely as a failure to encounter a further character within the normal time interval. This condition is detected by the one-second routine.

Store Organization of Input and Output Information

In general, input information is converted to a standard 6-bit internal character code by the interrupt routine concerned, and placed in the store 8 characters to a word. (An exception to this occurs in the case of card readers when they are reading cards not punched in a standard code, in which case the 12 bits from one column are simply copied into the store and occupy two character positions. A similar case is 7-hole punched tape, when this is used to convey 7 information bits without a parity check. Such information is distinguished by warning characters, both on the input medium and in the store.)

A certain amount of supervisor working space in the core store is set aside to receive this information from the interrupt routines, and is subdivided between the various input peripherals. The amount of this space depends on the number and type of peripherals attached; the first two Atlases will normally use one block (512 words). This block will be locked down in a page of the core store whenever any input peripheral is operating (i.e., most of the time).

As each input equipment fills its share of this block, the information is copied by an S.E.R. into another block devoted exclusively to that equipment. These copying operations are sufficiently rare that the latter block need not remain in core store in the meantime; in fact it is subject to the same treatment as object programs by the drum transfer routine, and may well be put onto a drum and brought back again for the next copying operation. Thus only one page of core store is used full time during input operations, but nevertheless each input stream finds its way into a separate set of blocks in the store.

The page that is shared between input peripherals is subdivided in such a way as to minimize the number of occasions on which information must be copied to other blocks; it turns out that the space for each equipment needs to be roughly proportional to the square root of its information rate.

Similarly, information intended for output is placed in a common output page, subdivided for the various output devices, and is taken from there by the interrupt routines as required. The interrupt routines for teleprinters and tape punches do the necessary conversion from the internal character code used by the device. As soon as the information for a particular device is exhausted, an S.E.R. is activated to copy fresh information into the common output page. Again, the page is subdivided roughly in proportion to the square roots of the information rates.

For card punches and printers, whose interrupt routines require their information arranged in rows of bits, a further stage of translation is necessary. In these cases, on completing a card or line, internal 6-bit characters are converted by an S.E.R. into a card or line image also in the output block. In fact, the desirable amount of working space for output buffering somewhat exceeds one block, and the spare capacity of the subsidiary store will be utilized to augment it.

6 THE OPERATING SYSTEM

The following is a synopsis of work explained in detail in a paper in the Computer Journal.

Input

The fast computing speed of Atlas and the use of multiple input and output peripheral equipments enable the computer to handle a large quantity and variety of problems. These will range from small jobs for which there is no data outside the program itself, to large jobs requiring several batches of data, possibly arriving on different media. Other input items may consist of amendments to programs, or requests to execute programs already supplied. Several such items may be submitted together on one deck of cards or length of punched tape. All must be properly identified for the computer.

To systematize this identification task, the concept of a "document" has been introduced. A document is a self-contained section of input information, presented to the computer consecutively through one input channel. Each document carries suitable identifying information (see below) and the supervisor keeps in the main store a list of the documents as they are accepted into the store by the input routines, and a list of jobs for which further documents are awaited.

A job may require several documents, and only when all these have been supplied can execution begin. The supervisor therefore checks the appearance of documents for each job; when they are complete the job scheduling routine is notified (see below).

Normally, the main core and drum store of the computer is unlikely to suffice to hold all the documents that are waiting to be used. The blocks of input information are therefore copied, as they are received, onto a magnetic tape belonging to the supervisor, called the "system input tape." Hence, if it becomes necessary for the supervisor to erase them from the main store, they can be recovered from the system input tape when the job is ready for execution.

The system input tape thus acts as a large scale buffer, and indeed it plays a similar part to that of the system input tape in more conventional systems. The differences here are that the tape is prepared by the computer itself instead of by off-line equipment, and that there is no tape-handling of manual supervision required after the input of the original documents—an important point in a system designed to handle many miscellaneous jobs.

This complete bufferage system for input documents is called the "input well." Documents awaiting further documents before they can be used are said to be in "input well A"; complete sets of documents for jobs from "input well B." Usually documents being accepted into input well B must be read from the system input tape back into the main store so that they are ready for execution; often however they will already be in input well A in the main store, so that only an adjustment of the block directory is required.

One result of this arrangement is that the same tape is being used both to write input blocks, in a consecutive sequence, and to read back previously written blocks to recover particular documents as they are required. The tape will therefore make frequent scans over a few feet of tape, although it will gradually progress forwards. The lengths of these scans are related to the main store space occupied by input well A. For example, so long as the scans do not exceed about 80 feet (130 blocks) the waiting time for writing fresh blocks will remain less than the time for input of three blocks from a card reader, so that comparatively little main store space need be occupied by input well A. To ensure that scans are kept down to a reasonable limit, any documents left on the system input tape for so long that they are approaching the limit of the scannable area are copied to the system dump tape (see below). If the number of these becomes large, the computer operators are warned to reduce the supply of documents through the input peripherals.

Output

The central computer can produce output at a much greater rate than the peripheral equipments can receive it, and an "output well" is used in a manner analogous to the input well. This well uses a "system output tape" to provide bulk buffering.

Output for all output peripherals is put onto the same tape, arranged in sections that are subdivided so that the contents of a section will occupy all currently operating peripherals for the same length of time. Thus if, for example, a burst of output is generated for a particular peripheral, it is spaced out on the system output tape, leaving spare blocks to be filled in later with output for other peripherals (this is possible because Atlas uses pre-addressed tape). In this way, the recovery of information from the tape into "output well B" as required by the various peripherals merely involves reading complete sections from the tape.

Again, there is a limit to the amount of information that can usefully be buffered on the output tape, due to the time required to scan back and forth between writing and reading regions, and this limit depends on the space available in the mainstore for output well B. An S.E.R. keeps a check on the amount of information remaining in output well B for each equipment, and relates this to the present scan distance to decide when to start to move the tape back for the next reading operation. If the amount of output being generated by object programs becomes too great some of it is put instead on the dump tape (see below) or a program is suspended.

The System Dump Tape

The system input and output tapes operate essentially as extensions of the main store of the computer. Broadly speaking, documents are fed into the computer, programs are executed, and output is produced. The fact that the input and output usually spends some time on magnetic tape is, in a sense, incidental. This input and output buffering is, however, a continuous and specialized requirement, so that a particular way of using these tapes has been developed and special S.E.R.'s have been written to control them.

When demands on storage exceed the capacity of the main store and input and output tapes, a separate magnetic tape, the system dump tape, is used to hold information not required immediately. This tape may be called into use for a variety of reasons. Execution of a problem may be suspended and the problem recorded temporarily on the dump tape if other problems are required to fill the output well, or alternatively if its own output cannot be accommodated in the output well. Also, as already described, the input and output wells can "overflow" to the system dump tape. This tape is not used in a systematic manner, but is used to deal with emergencies. However, the system is such that, if necessary, the system input and output tapes can be dispensed with, thereby reducing the input and output wells and increasing the load on the system dump tape. In an extreme case, the system dump tape itself can be dispensed with, implying a further reduction in the efficiency of the system.

Headings and Titles

Every input document is preceded by its identifying information, mentioned above. This consists of two lines of printing, forming the heading and the title respectively.

The heading indicates which type of document follows. The most common headings are

> COMPILER followed by the name of a program language, which means that the document is a program in the stated language;
>
> DATA which means that the document is data required by an object program; and
>
> JOB which means that the document is a request for the computer to execute a job, and gives some relevant facts about it.

The last type of document is called a "job description." It gives, for example, a list of all other documents required for the job, a list of output streams produced, any magnetic tapes required and upper limits to the storage space and computing time required. Many of these details are optional;

for example if storage space and computing time are not quoted a standard allowance will be made.

For example, if a program operates on two data documents which it refers to as data 1 and data 2, the job description would contain:

INPUT

1 followed by the title of data 1
2 followed by the title of data 2

The program would appear in this list as data 0. Alternatively, a job description may be combined with a program, forming one composite document, and this will usually happen with small jobs.

Each output stream may be assigned to a particular peripheral or type of peripheral, or may be allowed to appear on any output equipment. The amount of output in each stream may also be specified. For example, a job description may include:

OUTPUT

1 LINE PRINTER 20 BLOCKS
2 CARDS
3 ANY

Each magnetic tape used by a program is identified by a number within the program, and the job description contains a list of these numbers with the title that appears in block 0 of each tape to identify it; for example:

TAPE

1 POTENTIAL FIELD CYLIND/204-TPU5.

If a new tape is required, a free tape must be loaded, which the program may then adopt and give a new title. This is indicated thus:

TAPE FREE

2 MONTE CARLO RESULTS K49-REAC-OR4.

The loading of tapes by operators is requested by the supervisor acting on the information in job descriptions.

Finally, the end of a document is indicated by

* * *

and if this is also the end of the punched tape or deck of cards it is followed by the letter Z. On reading this the computer disengages the equipment.

Logging and Charging for Machine Time

As problems are completed, various items of information on the performance of the computing system are accumulated by the supervisor. Items such as the number of program changes and the number of drum transfers are accumulated and also, for each job, the number of instructions obeyed, the time spent on input and output, and the use made of magnetic tapes. These items are printed in batches to provide the operators with a record of computer performance, and they are also needed for assessing machine charges.

The method of calculating charges may well vary between different installations, but one desirable feature of any method is that the charge for running a program should not vary significantly from one run to another. One difficulty is that the number of drum transfers required in a program may vary considerably with the amount of core store which is being used at the same time for magnetic tape and peripheral transfers. One method of calculating the charge so as not to reflect this variation is to make no charge for drum transfers, but to base the charge for computing time on the number of instructions obeyed in a program. This, however, gives no incentive to a programmer to arrange a program so as to reduce its drum transfers, and more elaborate schemes may eventually be devised. The charge for using peripherals for input and output can be calculated from the amount of input and output. For magnetic tapes, the charge can be based on the length of time for which the tape mechanism is engaged, allowance being made for the time when the program is free to proceed but is held up by a program of higher priority. All this information is made available to the S.E.R. responsible for the costing of jobs.

Methods of Using the Operating System

The normal method of operating the computer is for documents to be loaded on any peripheral equipment in any order, although usually related documents will be loaded around the same time. The titles and job descriptions enable the supervisor program to assemble and execute complete programs, and the output is distributed on all the available peripherals. Usually programs are compiled and executed in the same order as the input is completed, but the supervisor may vary this depending on the load on different parts of the system. For example, a problem requiring magnetic tape mechanisms which are already in use may be by-passed in favour of a problem using an idle output peripheral; a problem which computes for a long time may be temporarily suspended in order to increase the load on the output peripherals. By these and similar methods, the S.E.R. responsible for scheduling attempts to maintain the fullest possible activity of the output peripherals, the magnetic tape mechanisms and the central computer.

Documents may also be supplied to the computer from magnetic tapes; these tapes may be either previous system input tapes or library tapes or tapes on which "standard", frequently used, programs are stored. Such documents are regarded as forming part of Input Well B and are read into main store when required. An alternative method of operating may be to use the computer to copy documents to a "private" magnetic tape, rather than to use the system input tape, and at a later time to supply the computer with a succession of jobs from this tape. Similarly, output may be accumulated on a private magnetic tape and later passed through the computer to one or more peripheral equipments. Routines forming part of the supervisor are available to carry out such standard "copying operations."

Provision is also made for the chief operator to modify the system in various ways; for example, priority may be given to a particular job, or a peripheral equipment may be removed from general use and allocated a particular task. An "isolated" operating station may, for example, be established by reserving a particular output equipment for use by problems loaded on a particular input equipment.

7 CONCLUSION

The Atlas supervisor program is perhaps the most advanced example so far encountered of a program involving many parallel activities, all closely interconnected. Although a great deal of it has already been coded at the time of writing, there are still a few details to be thrashed out, and no doubt many changes will have to be made to suit conditions existing at various installations. The overall structure of the program is therefore of prime importance: only if this structure is adequate, sound and systematic will it be possible to complete the coding satisfactorily and to make the necessary changes as they arise.

The structure described in this paper, involving interrupt routines and "supervisory extracode routines" controlled by a co-ordinating routine, has proved eminently satisfactory as a basis for every supervisory task that has so far been envisaged, and it is expected that all variations that might be called for will fit into this structure.

There is no doubt that its success as a supervisory scheme for a very fast computer is due largely to certain features of the Atlas hardware, in particular the provisions for protecting programs from interference, and the page address registers. The way in which the latter permit information to be moved around at run time without the need to recompile programs gives the supervisor an entirely new degree of freedom. The possible uses of this facility have turned out to be so extensive that the task of utilizing such a large computer effectively without it seems by comparison to be almost impossible.

Acknowledgements

The work described in this paper forms part of the Atlas project by a joint team of Manchester University and Ferranti Ltd., whose permission to publish is acknowledged. The authors wish to express their appreciation of the assistance given by the other members of the Atlas team.

4

OPERATING SYSTEM FOR THE B 5000*

CLARK OLIPHINT

(1964)

Two of the major B 5000 design objectives were (1) that all programming was to be done in ALGOL and COBOL, and (2) that the operation of the system was to be directed by a Master Control Program (MCP) which would relieve the operator and—especially—the programmer of virtually all the inefficient and error-causing details of peripheral unit designation, memory area assignment, and so on. The simultaneous and coordinated design of the computer and the programming system has produced a hardware-software system so well integrated that all B 5000 users employ the standard programming system (with minor modifications for special applications in a few cases). It has been the experience of B 5000 users that the exclusive use of compiler languages in programming gives advantages in documentation, program preparation, and debugging which cannot be over emphasized.

Another major design objective was that processor time unused by one program during input-output operations was to be used to process other programs, and that the availability of this feature was to have no effect on program preparation. In other words, the system was to operate in such a way that the programmer need have no concern about relative processor-I/O times. This objective has far-reaching implications. For example, if one program is to be run while another is waiting on input or output, then both must be in memory at the same time. Since the system was designed to free the programmer from housekeeping chores, and to allow any simultaneous mix of ALGOL and COBOL compilation and execution, all allocation of memory and peripheral units must be done at the time the programs are executed.

---

*C. Oliphint, Operating system for the B 5000. *Datamation 10*, 5 (May 1964), 42–54.

Operation of the Hardware

One would expect that this approach to computer design would result in a different breed of computer, and this has indeed been the case. For example, one of the unusual features of the B 5000 is the "stack," which is used to store operands, subroutine return information, subroutine parameters, and temporary values used by subroutines. Each program has its own stack in memory. As operands are brought from memory they are placed at the top of the stack, pushing down all other items in the stack. Arithmetic operators use the top two values in the stack as operands, remove them from the stack, and leave the result in the top of the stack.

The stack actually consists of two arithmetic registers, A and B, in the processor, and consecutive cells in core storage. The S register in the processor is initially set to the first address of a group of words to be used for the stack. If A and B are both full and an operator is executed which causes an operand to be added to the stack, then (as part of the execution of the syllable) S is increased by one, the contents of B are stored in the word now addressed by S, and the contents of A are transferred to B. The A register is then free to receive the operand being added to the stack. If B is empty and an operator is executed which requires two operands, then the reverse action occurs: the contents of the word addressed by S are brought to the empty register, and S is decreased by one. Analogous operations take place if A or both A and B are empty. This technique achieves the effect of a push-down stack, and makes it unnecessary to move any word in the stack from one memory cell to another. Except for the arithmetic registers A and B, which are shared by all programs, each program has its own stack. Thus, in generating programs to do series of arithmetic operations, the compiler does not have to make provision for storing temporary values; they simply remain in the appropriate stack until they are needed. Since all parameters for subroutines, including the return address, are in the stack rather than in the body of the subroutine, recursive subroutines are executed as easily as nonrecursive subroutines. It has proved to be truly gratifying, in our experience, how this implementation of the stack concept has made recursion almost trivially simple.

Since a program and its data may be anywhere in memory when the program is executed, it is useful to have an easily accessible table into which the MCP may place absolute addresses for those segments of the program or its data which are in core storage. Such a table, called the Program Reference Table (PRT), is created for each program. The R register in the processor unit is set to the base of the PRT, and all memory references in the program are relative to the R register. Operands, descriptors of data segments, and descriptors of program segments are in the PRT.

If a segment is in core storage, its descriptor contains the base address of the segment. The program may read or store any element of a data segment by using the data descriptor and an index of the element. Branches from one program segment to another, or subroutine entries, are performed by using a program descriptor. If a segment is not in core storage, a bit in its descriptor is set to zero; any reference to that segment then causes the program to be interrupted so that the MCP can bring the segment from a drum[1] into core storage.

When an input or output operation is executed by the B 5000, an input-output descriptor containing the peripheral unit number, the type of operation to be performed, and a base address in core storage, are sent to an I/O channel. The I/O channel then executes the operation independently recording errors if they occur. When the operation is completed, the I/O channel sets a bit to interrupt the processor and stores a result descriptor in memory.

There may be as many as four I/O channels in a B 5000 system. No extra complication arises, however, from the presence of multiple channels; neither memory modules nor I/O units are permanently connected to any specific channel, nor is the programmer concerned in any way. The connection is made when an I/O descriptor is sent to an I/O channel, the first channel available receives the descriptor and executes it, regardless of which memory module or peripheral unit is involved.

Two important MCP functions are made possible by the timer, which is an integral part of the B 5000: to enable log-keeping, and to prevent a program from getting caught in a loop and staying there until the operator recognizes the fact and stops the program. The timer is a six-bit counter which is incremented by 1 every 60th of a second; after 64 counts, overflow occurs and causes an interrupt. After four such interrupts, the MCP compares the elapsed processor and I/O time with the (optional) estimate supplied by the programmer. If the running time exceeds the estimate, the program is removed from memory and the operator is notified. As implied above by the word "optional" in parentheses, the programmer may omit the estimated processor and/or I/O times; in this event, the MCP inserts a time

[1]One drum is required in a minimal B 5000; a second is optional, even in a two-processor system.

"estimate." As of this writing, the MCP word reserved for this estimate is then arbitrarily filled with 1s, yielding an "estimate" of approximately 9.7 hours. Naturally, if one wishes to employ the time-keeping abilities of the MCP, he begins with a pessimistic estimate and refines it as he gains experience.

A program being executed will be interrupted when any one of 40 conditions occurs; some of these have been described above. When a program is interrupted, the contents of all the pertinent registers are stored in the upper part of that program's stack, and control is transferred to a location associated with the condition causing the interrupt. At that location is the beginning of an MCP routine which will take the proper action.

Operation of the Standard Programming System

The standard programming system, including the MCP and the ALGOL and COBOL compilers, is sent to users on magnetic tape. A small card deck is used to load the MCP on a drum. Either compiler, or both, may also be loaded on a drum. If a compiler is not in drum storage, the MCP will find it on the tape and read it in when it is required. The MCP and ALGOL compiler together require about half of one drum; if the COBOL compiler is included, about one-and-a-half drums are needed. Each drum contains 32,768 words.

The MCP uses one magnetic tape, called the Program Collection Tape (PCT), to store programs scheduled to run but not yet brought into memory. All other tapes are available for programmer use, but are individually recognized (if labeled) and selected by the MCP as required by various programs. The programmer need not (and indeed cannot) designate specific magnetic tape units, although the operator can. The operator is notified when a reel is to be removed or put on a given unit; the message also gives the name of the file and of the program.

The MCP allocates core storage for a program as the program requires it. If the storage requirements of the program exceed the available amount of core storage, the MCP automatically overlays segments of the program or its data to make room for other segments. Because of this feature, programs can be executed on the B 5000 even though they apparently require more core storage than is available.

Obviously, any program—and a compiler is no exception—requires some minimal amount of core storage for its execution. In order to execute the MCP, the compilers, and most object programs, three out of a possible eight memory modules are required on a B 5000. However, overlaying program segments and retrieving them later will require processor and I/O time, thus adding to the time required to execute a program. Considerable increases in program speeds can be achieved by simply adding one memory module. No program changes are required for adding or deleting memory modules or peripheral units, unless a drastic deletion results in an unworkable situation (e.g., attempting a three-tape sort with but two magnetic tape units on line).

MCP Functions

The major functions of the MCP are listed below in the order in which they are usually invoked.

1. Scheduling and loading programs
2. Reading program and data segments from a drum when required by a program
3. Allocating and overlaying core storage
4. Assigning peripheral units and input or output buffer areas for each program
5. Initiating input and output operations, and recognizing the completion of these operations
6. Removing a program from memory when it is finished or when certain error conditions occur
7. Adding programs to or deleting programs from a library
8. Maintaining a log of system operation, which is written on any unit when requested.

The MCP is composed of 31 segments, some of which are discussed below. Depression of the LOAD button on the B 5000 console reads 512 words of the MCP from a drum into core and transfers control to the initial portion of the MCP. The Initialization Routine in the MCP then reads into core those MCP segments which are to remain permanently in core, and initializes all MCP tables.

Four segments of the MCP remain permanently situated in core: the Program Control Routine, Input-Output Initiate Routine, Input-Output Complete Routine, and Storage Allocation and Overlay Routine. All other segments are read from a drum as they are required, and remain in core until the space is needed for some other purpose.

The Program Control Routine is used to transfer control to any segment which may not be in core. If the required segment is not present, the Program Control Routine will obtain space for it and read it from the drum. The Program Control Routine also has the function of deciding which program is to be executed if more than one is in memory ready to run. After an interrupt has been processed by an MCP routine, control is returned to the Program Control Routine, which in turn resumes (or initiates) processing of one of the programs in memory. The Program Control Routine chooses the highest priority program that is ready to run. (A program is not "ready to run" if it is waiting on an I/O operation.)

Program Scheduling and Loading

Programs are scheduled and loaded by two segments of the MCP called Collection and Selection. Collection adds programs to the schedule as they are specified by program header cards. A header card may call for a program to be compiled and executed, in which case Collection will add the compiler to the schedule, and, when compilation is completed, will add the compiled program to the schedule. If a header card calls a compiled program from a library, Collection will add that program to the schedule. In every case, a program is merged into the schedule in priority order behind all programs of equal priority already in the schedule. When processor time is available, Selection is notified by the Program Control Routine, and will attempt to find a program in the schedule which can be loaded into memory and executed. It will check information collected by the compiler as to memory and peripheral unit requirements, and will choose the first program in the schedule which will run in the amount of system now available. It then loads the selected program into memory and leaves it ready to begin operation when chosen by the Program Control Routine. The entire program is written on the drum in this process, and the beginning segment is also read into core.

When space is required in core storage for any purpose, the Storage Allocation Routine is used to obtain it. All available core storage is in a linked list, with the smallest space first on the list and the largest last. When core storage is requested, the first available section of core large enough to satisfy the request is removed from the list, the required amount of space is assigned in that section of core, and the remaining amount is linked into the available storage list. If there is not enough core storage available, the Overlay Routine is called to make more storage available. Since there is a copy of all MCP segments and program segments on a drum, it is not necessary to write these segments on the drum when they are removed from core. Data segments, however, are written on the drum if they are overlaid.

The order in which assigned memory is overlaid is: first, "overlayable" MCP segments (all segments except the four permanently in core); second, program segments of the lowest priority program; third, data segments of the lowest priority program. The second and third steps are then repeated for all remaining programs, proceeding from lowest to highest priority. The overlay operation continues until either the required space has been made available or there is nothing more which can be overlaid. In the latter case, one of the programs in memory actually requires more core storage than the compiler has estimated. It is then too late to take corrective action; an error message is typed out, and all programs in process are terminated.

When either a program segment or a data segment is overlaid, the space is linked into the available storage list, and the descriptors associated with the segment are marked absent so that any future reference to the segment will cause a "presence bit" interrupt.

As a program is executed, it may, from time to time, branch to program segments not in core, or try to refer to data not in core. In either case a presence bit interrupt occurs, and the Presence Bit Routine in the MCP must find the required segment on the drum, obtain core space for it, and read it into core. When this is completed, the segment is marked present and the program is left ready to run as soon as it is chosen by the Program Control Routine.

Input-Output

The assignment of peripheral unit numbers and buffer areas is made at the time a program first reads or writes a file. The MCP maintains a record of the file names of all input files and the units on which they are mounted, and the units on which output files are mounted. The Four-Second Routine in the MCP is responsible for maintaining this table. This routine is so called because it is normally executed on every fourth timer interrupt (approximately every four seconds). In the course of its operation, it also determines the status of all peripheral units. If the unit is a magnetic tape unit, the Four-Second Routine reads the first record on the tape and stores the name of the file mounted on the unit. Once the file name has been recorded, the tape will not be read again unless the Four-Second Routine detects a change in the status of the unit. After such a change (e.g., from ready to not ready), it is necessary to read the tape label again when the unit is returned to a ready status. If a tape is mounted with a write ring, the Four-Second Routine also checks a purge date in the label to ascertain whether the information on the tape can be destroyed. If the purge date has not been passed, a message to that effect is typed out, and the operator has a chance to correct a possible error.

When a file is opened, an input-output descriptor is created which the program then uses in the execution of any operation with that file. To perform a read or write operation, the program executes a Program Release operator, causing an interrupt which requests the MCP to perform the specified operation. After checking the availability of the requested unit and any one of up to four I/O channels, the Input-Output Initiate Routine in the MCP will either initiate the operation or put it in a waiting list of I/O operations, and then call the Program Control Routine to choose a program to run. The program requesting an I/O operation is eligible to run, since it may not need the information just requested for some time. If it tries to use the information before the operation is complete, it will be interrupted and set "not ready" until the operation is complete.

When an I/O operation is completed, it causes an interrupt. The I/O Complete Routine in the MCP then initiates a waiting operation if possible, sets the program waiting on the operation just completed "ready," and calls the Program Control Routine to choose a program to run.

When a program is finished, it executes a communicate operator, which causes an interrupt. The Communicate Routine in the MCP closes any files not closed in the program; returns all core and drum storage assigned to the program; calls the Log Routine to store information about the program; and, if the program finishing is a compiler, calls Collection to add the compiled program to the schedule. It then calls the Program Control Routine to choose another program to run.

Library Tapes

The library tape maintenance system consists of a group of routines to add or change programs on a library tape. The header card calling for compilation may specify that the program is to be added to a library or is to replace a program of the same name already on a library tape. Another control card may be used to call a program from a library, either for addition to another library or as a replacement for a program with the same name in a library. All programs to be placed in a library are written on the Program Collection Tape (PCT) when the above cards are encountered.

A library tape is created on recognition of a library tape maintenance control card. This card may either cause a specific library tape to be copied with additions and replacements as noted above, or it may cause a new library tape to be created containing only those programs previously specified to be added to a library. After the tape is created, a message on the Message Printer gives the operator the name of the library and the unit on which it was created.

Log

At any time, the operator may request that the log information be written on the peripheral unit of his choice. The first line of the log for each program shows, from left to right, the name of the program, whether the program was compiled (COM) or executed (RUN), remarks from the header card, the date, start time, finish time, number of seconds the processor was used for this program, reason for stopping the program (EOJ = normal program finish; ERR = error finish), and the number of seconds the peripheral equipment was used for this program. Each succeeding line gives information about a file declared in the program. This information, from left to right, is multifile identification, file identification, preparation date, cycle number, number of seconds this file was used by the program, number of seconds this file was assigned to the program, number of errors encountered in reading or writing this file, and, for those files actually opened, the type of peripheral unit on which the file was located. To conserve table space, peripheral unit names are abbreviated: CR means card reader, LP signifies line printer, and MT indicates magnetic tape; additions now being incorporated will include PR for paper tape reader and PP for paper tape punch. The last column is blank if the file was declared but never actually used in the program. A typical log is shown in Figure 1.

Results

As was originally planned, all programming for the B 5000 is being done in ALGOL or COBOL. Both compilers contain features which have proved to

```
 TERM14  COM COMPILATION CARD      64049 0016 0016 00023 EOJ 00024
0000000 DATA      00000 01 00004 00019 000 CR
0000000 OUTPT     00000 01 00010 00016 000 LP
MCPPCT CODEFIL    00000 01 00001 00012 000 MT
0000000 SOLT      00000 01 00000 00000 000
0000000 SOLT      00000 01 00000 00000 000
0000000 LIBRAR    00000 01 00000 00000 000
 TERM14  RUN                       64049 0016 0017 00017 EOJ 00006
0000000 TAPREC    00000 01 00002 00016 000 MT
0000000 CARDREC   00000 01 00000 00016 000 CR
```

Figure 1 Typical B 5000 log output.

be highly satisfactory in checking out programs. Estimates of increased programmer productivity resulting from the use of compiler languages indicate a manpower saving of about a factor of 10 in programming, checking out, and documenting typical programs.

In our own experience, both compilers were written in ALGOL, and we realized an increase in programmer productivity of four or five to one; i.e., if the compilers had been written in assembly language, it would have taken four or five times as many man-hours as were actually required to complete the task.

The increased productivity of the B 5000 resulting from the use of normally idle processor time is highly dependent on the type of programs being executed. If a group of programs are all processor-bound, no time can be saved by running the programs together; it is not unusual, however, to find two or three programs which run together in very little more time than that required to execute the longest program of the group.

Most cases fall between these two extremes. In the usual case, a group of programs can be executed in less time than is required for the same group if each program is run alone, but will require more time than that required for the longest program. (This should not be taken to imply that the shorter programs will not be finished before the longest one.) The actual time saved depends on the amount of idle processor time which would be available if the programs were executed serially.

5

DESCRIPTION OF A HIGH CAPACITY, FAST TURNAROUND UNIVERSITY COMPUTING CENTER*

WILLIAM C. LYNCH

(1966)

The operating system for the UNIVAC 1107 at Case Institute is reviewed. The system is of interest because of the low turnaround times achieved, the high throughput achieved and the lack of an operating staff. Turnaround times below 5 minutes and job volume above 75,000 per quarter year are reported.

1 Introduction

The purpose of this paper is to describe the performance and operation of the UNIVAC 1107 computing system installed at the Andrew R. Jennings Computing Center at the Case Institute of Technology. The Center employs an open-shop type philosophy that appears to be unique among large scale installations. This philosophy leads to turnaround times which are better by an order of magnitude than those commonly being obtained with comparable scale equipment.

A little historical review is in order. Progress in computing is marked by an attack on the apparently most crucial of nagging problems. The solution arrived at has two effects: (1) It sets a precedent which inevitably, for compatibility reasons, is very difficult to break; (2) it brings to the fore a new crucial problem. Progress, then, is a series of local optimizations which generally lead us far from a global optimum.

---

*W. C. Lynch, Description of a high capacity, fast turnaround university computing center. *Communications of the ACM 9*, 2 (February 1966), 117–123.

Let us illustrate a case in point. The users of IBM 704's (and similar machines) were quickly confronted with an input/output problem. The machine, for small to medium problems, was far too fast computationally for the limited I/O facilities and the quite slow unit record equipment available to it. The IBM 709 system represented a two-front attack on this problem. First, increased buffering capabilities were added; and second, input/output was handled by magnetic tape. Thus, the tape-oriented system was born (or reborn: recall e.g., UNIVAC I).

This arrangement, however, just deferred the input/output problems. The old philosophy of each user signing up for 10 or 15 minutes was now the crucial problem. For every minute of operation, 10 or 12 were spent changing tapes and logging on and off. This new problem was solved by software through the introduction of an executive system that scheduled the use of the machine and automatically sequenced runs through the computer. To alleviate the problem of mounting and dismounting tapes containing read and print files, several runs were batched together on system input and output tapes while system routines were collected together on a systems tape. Thus the tapes needed to be changed on a relatively infrequent basis.

With all of these improvements two solvable problems arose. First, a great deal of time was spent accessing the systems library tape. This problem was attacked head-on at the grass roots by building faster tape units. Second, since batching could not be trusted to the user, installations acquired sizeable staffs of clerks to receive the incoming jobs, pass them to the operators, and return the output. Clerks were hired to keep a set of documents to trace a deck through this process. The documents gave the clerks the capability of explaining to the user just how and why his deck had been lost.

The computers now speed on faster than ever before, with high internal computation rates coupled with fantastically fast tape rates, and problems are run in a matter of seconds. A user can submit a deck at 8:00 a.m., have it on the input tape by noon, his job completed by 12:00:35, and the output returned to him by 5:00 p.m. in the evening.

The current problem is that turnaround times do not reflect the computer's speed. Part of this problem is due to the fact that a dilemma exists concerning batch sizes—too small a batch size results in prohibitive overhead in tape changing, while too large a batch size hurts turn-around time by leaving the job idle on the tapes. Of course there are the contributions of the operators and clerical staff to consider.

2 The Case System

The UNIVAC 1107 installed at Case is a large scale binary computer with a four microsecond add time and 65,536 words of core storage. The machine has only a few unusual features:

(1) A moderately large number (16) of input/output channels.

(2) High performance drums. (The Case machine has two drums of 786,432 words each. They have a 360,000 character/second transfer rate and a 17 millisecond average access time.)

(3) A drum-oriented executive system.

All unit record equipment is online. There is no offline equipment at all (other than keypunches).

The executive system is designed to run one job at a time while copying unit record files to and from the drums. In this respect the system is similar to the SPOOL system for the IBM 7070.

A job is run by entering a deck in one of the card readers. The executive will copy this card deck to the drum where it awaits execution. When the current job is finished the executive selects a card deck from the drum and starts execution. During execution, print lines generated by the program are placed on the drum. When the printer associated with the reader in which the deck was inserted becomes available, the print lines are copied out to the printer. Since a large number of card and print files can be held on the drum at the same time, copying operations can be, and usually are, maintained on all readers and printers at the same time. Systems tape operation is eliminated by keeping all systems on the drum and punching logging information into paper tape.

From the user's point of view, he sets his cards in the read feed and presses a single button which readies the reader and signals the computer. His cards are immediately read through and completely stacked out. He then removes his cards and proceeds to the printer where his print-out appears shortly, is removed and inspected.

This operating sequence is obviously simple enough so that anyone capable of programming is capable of operating it. Since *the Computing Center employs no operators* each user runs his own program. A user may observe an error, repunch a card and return his program in a matter of seconds.

Several reader/printer groups are available, and a user is by and large free to choose which one he wishes to run on. Some reader/printer groups (UNIVAC 1004's) are connected to the machine by data-phone with their operation identical to operation on site. The salient features of the system configuration are summarized in Figure 1.

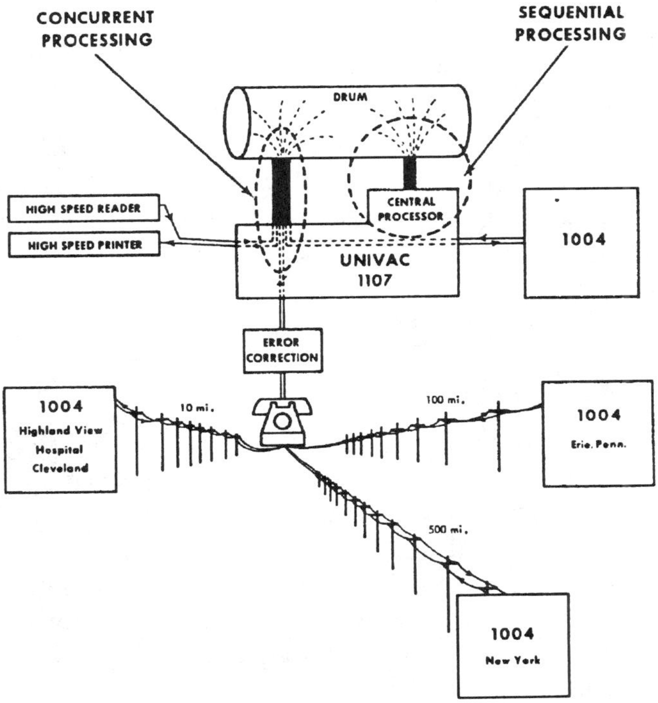

Figure 1 Case UNIVAC 1107 system configuration

3 Tape Handling

Since all systems, system scratch areas, user scratch areas and reader/printer blocking areas are on the magnetic drums, tapes are used only for true input/output of large volumes of data or program. Less than 5 percent of the runs ever cause a tape to be moved.

Ten tape units are available to the user. Users are responsible for their own tape mounting. An advanced reel hub latch and the leader on the tape make mounting a simple operation.

The logical numbering of the units is never changed. The user selects a free unit and mounts his reel. He then makes an unsolicited type-in on the keyboard indicating which reel was mounted on which unit. The system does the rest. All tapes are rewound with interlocks at the end of the run. This protects the user's tape from being inadvertently overwritten by the next user, and also identifies those units which are no longer in use. Tapes may be mounted and the identifying type-ins made well in advance of the program operation, all without penalty.

The units read and write at 25,000 characters per second. Our experience indicates that we are much better off with many slow units rather than a few fast ones. Our small data processing load is coded almost exclusively in ALGOL, and the computational processes involved are considerably more complex than found in typical data processing programs. Even with full buffering and slow 25,000 character per second tape units our data processing programs are all compute-limited.

4 Remote Computing

With the system philosophy as outlined, it should be clear that there is little need for the reader/printer groups to be near the central computer. They can be placed as far away as one wishes and connected by some communications system. At present two UNIVAC 1004 reader/printers are installed at remote locations. A 1004 was placed in operation at Highland View Hospital in Cleveland in March 1964. This location is 10 miles from Case. Another 1004 was placed in operation at Lord Manufacturing in Erie, Pennsylvania in January 1965. Erie is about 100 miles from Case. During the IFIP Conference in May 1965 a third 1004 was operated from the Univac booth at the Interdata Exhibit. All of these are connected to the 1107 via a half-duplex telephone line with 201-A MODEM units at each end (see Figure 1).

Full error detection and correction is provided. The telephone line can be severed and reattached hours later without loss of data. Our experience indicates that complete error detection and correction is essential for this type of operation. Error detection is accomplished by a horizontal and vertical parity bit scheme similar to that employed on magnetic tape. Error correction is accomplished by retransmitting a message until it is correctly received and a verification is correctly returned to the sender. Duplicate lines are deleted. Lines are alternated in direction so that, in effect, reading and printing proceed simultaneously.

At the 1107 end there is a single telephone line. To use the computer the user dials the 1107's number and the 1107 automatically answers the phone. The job is then run exactly as it would be run in the computing center. The only differences are the following:

(a) The button-pushing sequence is somewhat different although the functions are the same.

(b) The read/print speed is reduced to 60–80 lines per minute due to transmission speeds.

(c) Tape mounting (if necessary) must be accomplished by having someone at the center do the physical mounting.

The user holds the telephone line until his output is complete and then hangs up. At that time another remote 1004 can use the system. If no tape mounting is to be done, it is difficult to determine from the computing center just when the remote system is in operation. The lights on the remote I/O controller indicate use, but it is impossible to tell who is using the system. Billing information is automatically logged as usual. Specific instances of use of the remote system often go unnoticed by center personnel, as no conspicuous change of system performance is detectable.

5 System Performance

The fairly complete log punched on paper tape permits some interesting indications of system performance to be calculated. The 1107 is generally operated about 16 hours a day, 5 days a week. Often very long runs, usually of a data-proccessing nature, are made on the third (overnight) shift or on weekends. These runs naturally contribute to the total time used on the machine, but only a very little to the total number of runs. The bulk of the load consists of runs less than 5 minutes in length. Note that the times we are talking about do *not* include I/O time.

The system typically processes a large number of runs. From January 1, 1965 to March 23, 1965 a total of 78,480 runs were processed. Of these, 26,584 required less than 10 seconds of computer time and 49,238 required less than 20 seconds of computer time. A total of 66,006, or almost 85 percent, required less than 1 minute of computer time.

During the first part of April, 1965 a project was undertaken to provide more meaningful information than just these summary totals. Turnaround time is a difficult quantity to define or measure in the Case system. For example, should the turnaround interval begin when the user enters the line at the card reader, or when he puts his cards into the machine? In any case, any system which would measure and count these statistics with sufficient accuracy to be meaningful would almost certainly interfere severely with the process, and thus with the turnaround time.

To circumvent these difficulties a quantity called *circulation time* is defined. The circulation time for a program is that time interval which starts when the central processor selects that program for execution from the drum and ends when the same user is once again selected for processing. Thus the interval includes the processing time, the time to print the results, the time for the user to interpret the results and correct his deck on a keypunch, the time required to get in line, gain access to the card reader and run in his deck, and the time during which the deck resides on the drum waiting to be selected for running. In other words the circulation time is the turnaround time plus the time required for the user to interpret his results, correct his deck, and resubmit.

The circulation time is calculated in the following manner. All of the billing records for a given period are selected and sorted by user identification. (Turnaround is fast enough on the system that the tacit assumption that a user is working on but one program at a time is justified in well over 95 percent of the runs. No attempt is made to accurately estimate or control this parameter.) The log-on time for each run forms a secondary sort key. Having collected together all the run records for a given user on a given day, circulation times can now be observed. The first record for the day gives a base time, while subsequent records for the day each have a circulation time associated with them; the circulation time is thus calculated by subtracting from the current log-on time the log-on time of the previous run by the same user.

Runs are classified as to whether they were the first of the day, preceded by a run less than 5 minutes earlier, preceded by a run between 5 and 10 minutes earlier, IO to 30 minutes, 30 to 60 minutes, 1 to 2 hours, or more than 2 hours. A run must be classified in just one of these seven possible ways.

Figures 2 and 3 summarize the results of these calculations and classifications. Variations in load due to date are to be expected due to the varying academic cycle. Users are divided into two classes: (1) students who are undergraduates doing homework for computer or other courses, and (2) projects which consist of faculty and graduate students usually doing thesis research. The figures give the number of runs for each class and the average computer run length. The runs are then classified by user class and circulation time. These are further broken down by the time of day at which the run occurred ("first run" still applies on a *daily* basis).

It should be noted that only 10–15 percent of the runs are the first

PERIOD FROM 3/ 1/65 TO 5/31/65

THE NUMBER OF PROJECT RUNS DURING THIS PERIOD WAS 25036
THE AVERAGE PROJECT RUN RAN FOR 79.78 SECONDS
THE NUMBER OF STUDENT RUNS DURING THIS PERIOD WAS 31567
THE AVERAGE STUDENT RUN RAN FOR 19.70 SECONDS

BREAKDOWN OF ELAPSED TIME BETWEEN A USERS RUN AND HIS PREVIOUS RUN ON THAT DAY

	Project Runs	*Student Runs*	*Total*
FIRST RUN	4022	3723	7745
0 TO 5 MINUTES	6979	11600	18579
5 TO 10 MINUTES	4254	6200	10454
10 TO 30 MINUTES	5769	6294	12063
30 TO 60 MINUTES	1572	1345	2917
1 TO 2 HOURS	954	830	1784
GREATER THAN 2 HOURS	1486	1575	3061

STUDENT RUNS AND TIMES OF DAY WHEN RUNS OCCURRED

	Runs	*6 AM – Noon*	*Noon – 6 PM*	*6 PM – Midnight*	*Midnight – 6 AM*
FIRST RUN	3723	1367	1596	584	176
0 - 5 MINUTES	11600	2323	5150	3602	525
5 - 10 MINUTES	6200	1252	2917	1808	223
10 - 30 MINUTES	6294	1291	3002	1811	190
30 - 60 MINUTES	1345	211	699	398	37
1 - 2 HOURS	830	104	444	274	8
MORE THAN 2 HOURS	1575	58	860	653	4
TOTAL	31567	6606	14668	9130	1163

PROJECT RUNS AND TIMES OF DAY WHEN RUNS OCCURRED

	Runs	*6 AM – Noon*	*Noon – 6 M*	*6 PM – Midnight*	*Midnight – 6 AM*
FIRST RUN	4022	1779	1604	482	157
0 - 5 MINUTES	6979	1534	3285	1839	321
5 - 10 MINUTES	4254	1011	2150	922	171
10 - 30 MINUTES	5769	1440	3005	1148	176
30 - 60 MINUTES	1572	387	810	321	54
1 - 2 HOURS	954	163	593	173	25
MORE THAN 2 HOURS	1486	78	916	486	6
TOTAL	25036	6392	12363	5371	910

Figure 2 System usage (Spring 1965)

of the day, 85–90 percent are repeats, and about a third of the runs have a circulation time of less than 5 minutes. It is often possible to debug a moderate size program in less than an hour by gaining frequent access to the computer.

6 Scheduling Algorithm

It should be clear that traditional approaches to computer scheduling will not work out too well on this system. The approach currently in use is now described. A time of day clock, powered by an independent 60-cycle power supply, has been added to the computer. This allows the computer to determine at any time (except immediately following a general 60-cycle power failure) the correct time, day and month. A stencil, blocking out the general use of the machine during specific real time periods, is recorded on

PERIOD FROM 6/ 1/65 TO 8/31/65

THE NUMBER OF PROJECT RUNS DURING THIS PERIOD WAS 39411
THE AVERAGE PROJECT RUN RAN FOR 70.26 SECONDS
THE NUMBER OF STUDENT RUNS DURING THIS PERIOD WAS 3179
THE AVERAGE STUDENT RUN RAN FOR 36.75 SECONDS

BREAKDOWN OF ELAPSED TIME BETWEEN A USERS RUN AND HIS PREVIOUS RUN ON THAT DAY

	Project Runs	*Student Runs*	*Total*
FIRST RUN	4791	326	5117
0 TO 5 MINUTES	14106	948	15054
5 TO 10 MINUTES	5886	645	6531
10 TO 30 MINUTES	8395	808	9203
30 TO 60 MINUTES	2842	203	3045
1 TO 2 HOURS	1580	105	1685
GREATER THAN 2 HOURS	1811	144	1955

STUDENT RUNS AND TIMES OF DAY WHEN RUNS OCCURRED

	Runs	*6 AM – Noon*	*Noon – 6 PM*	*6 PM – Midnight*	*Midnight – 6 AM*
FIRST RUN	326	105	106	42	73
0 - 5 MINUTES	948	182	301	293	172
5 - 10 MINUTES	645	116	210	206	113
10 - 30 MINUTES	808	154	266	249	139
30 - 60 MINUTES	203	22	85	65	31
1 - 2 HOURS	105	13	39	40	13
MORE THAN 2 HOURS	144	25	56	62	1
TOTAL	3179	617	1063	957	542

PROJECT RUNS AND TIMES OF DAY WHEN RUNS OCCURRED

	Runs	*6 AM – Noon*	*Noon – 6 PM*	*6 PM – Midnight*	*Midnight – 6 AM*
FIRST RUN	4791	2317	1967	269	238
0 - 5 MINUTES	14106	2815	9195	1652	444
5 - 10 MINUTES	5886	1455	3323	803	305
10 - 30 MINUTES	8395	2126	4903	1017	349
30 - 60 MINUTES	2842	618	1697	387	140
1 - 2 HOURS	1580	264	1035	221	60
MORE THAN 2 HOURS	1811	78	1229	491	13
TOTAL	39411	9673	23349	4840	1549

Figure 3 System usage (Summer 1965)

the drum. This stencil can be updated at any time by computing center personnel. A typical stencil used during the academic year might be as follows:

From 9–10 a.m., 1–2 p.m., 4–5 p.m., and 7–8 p.m. (except Fridays), students have priority.

From 3–4 p.m. on Wednesday, project 96021 has priority.

At other times, projects have priority.

Time is classified as student time, open time and scheduled time.

During student time students have highest priority. The student with the smallest time/page limit will be selected for running. A project will be selected only if no student decks are available in the input file on the drum. In any case, no one will be allowed more than 2 minutes or 30 pages of output.

During open time the situation is reversed. The project with the smallest time/page limit will be selected. Students will be selected only if no project is available. No one is permitted more than 5 minutes or 30 pages.

Scheduled time is open time with the exception that certain designated projects (usually just one) have the highest priority. This designated project may have a time/page limit as large as he desires so long as it stays within the scheduled block. Scheduled blocks are typically an hour in length.

A complete file of all students and projects is kept on the drum. This file contains the identifying number, the user's name (e.g., MR. W. SMITH), and time/page limit information. The user may, at his option, place either his name (in any of a number of forms) of his number on his run card. Both name and number appear on the output. If a user does not wish to specify a time/page limit on his run card, one is inserted from his record in the file. Each record also contains an absolute time/page limit for each user. Students in the lower level classes, for example, are typically restricted to 30 seconds run time and/or 10 pages of output.

As a rule the 1107 can process students faster than they can load cards, while the reverse is generally true for projects. During student hours the machine will occasionally run out of student runs (due to slow loading) and be forced to select a project run. While it grinds for a minute or so the undergraduates regroup their forces and rebuild the drum input file. If during open time there are not enough projects, there are always students to take up the slack.

Scheduled time is very interesting. Typically user A will have a 20 minute run which blew up after 19 minutes on the previous day. User A has fixed "the" bug and is back. During scheduled time, A inserts his cards and gains access within 5 minutes (the maximum unscheduled run length). A is on next. His program will surely blow up during compilation. While he fixes his deck more unscheduled users run. On the next attempt, user A will typically get an early run-time abort. While he repairs this trivial error, more users run. On his third attempt A will usually run 19 minutes again before aborting. At this point he may or may not have enough of his scheduled hour left to try again. If not he will retreat home to lick his wounds and plot for his scheduled time the next day.

Almost all input/output is routed through the drums, and that is moved in large blocks. As the result the central processor is rarely idle when work is available. There is no waiting to get at the next job, and almost no waiting for input/output.

It is our observation that many installations with computers comparable to the 1107 have a run-length distribution similar to that at Case. It is also our impression that the number of runs processed on these systems in three-shift, seven-day-a-week operation is the same as, or somewhat less than, the number processed at Case on a two-shift, five-day-a-week basis. We would be sincerely interested in seeing data from other installations to either verify or contradict this impression. In any case, the time utilization on the Case system appears to be about 50 percent better than comparable tape-oriented systems.

Another interesting facet of the system is the available printing capacity. A total of about 1000 lines per minute of print capacity is available. Although this is usually considered a very small capacity for a machine of the size of the 1107, the central computer rarely must wait for a printer. Most users require little more than print statements inserted in their code to debug their programs. The rapid circulation time, the fast compilation rates and the source language diagnostics do the rest. Dumps are never taken. Output listings usually contain only a copy of the source code with compiler comments and that printing called for in the users object code. This lack of great quantities of paper output further enhances the turnaround time.

7 System Liabilities

This report would not be an honest discussion of the Case system without a presentation of the system's chief liabilities.

On projects the system throughput is limited chiefly by the speed of the central processor. During student hours, the system is limited by the square feet of floor space surrounding each reader/printer group. An abundance of floor space is essential to this system. On large campuses it would pay to place reader/printer stations in various I/O centers around campus. This would not only minimize or eliminate the travel time to the computing center, but would alleviate crowding at the I/O equipment.

In a certain limited class of problems (particularly design problems) it is desirable to communicate with the running object program. This is impossible in the Case system. It appears that there is no adequate solution to this problem short of providing a full time-sharing facility complete with conversational I/O gear.

A second problem is that when a long running program is once started, no other main program is processed until the long running job is finished. Fortunately this does not happen often but when it does, it ruins the turnaround time. It appears to be desirable to have a multiprogramming facility and an allocation philosophy which would not allow the entire machine to be clogged with one run, but would allow short jobs to pass the longer ones. Such a philosophy, implemented with conventional multiprogramming techniques, should remove this difficulty.

There is no organized facility at Case for submitting runs to the computer, having them run at some later time, and receiving the output back upon command. Such a mode of operation is desirable for extremely large jobs which have low priority and which will consume hours of machine time. There is little point in having the user wait about for such a job to be completed. This problem could be solved within the framework of the present system. What is required is a system command to receive and hold the job, run it at the appropriate time, and retain the output in mass storage (our 1.5 million words of drum is a little too small for this). The user would return at some later time, drop a call card into the reader, and cause his output to be transferred from mass storage to the printer.

The scheduling algorithm currently being used leaves something to be desired. It selects jobs (within classes) strictly on the basis of shortest time limit. No account is taken of waiting time. As a result, a user with a longer run can be completely frozen out by a group of users with shorter runs. With the high speed circulation available such a group can keep the larger user from ever running his program. A revised selection algorithm is under development which will select jobs according to a complicated nonlinear function of both estimated running time and time spent waiting in the input queue. An attempt is being made to quantitatively estimate and minimize customer aggravation.

It would be extremely desirable to eliminate the tape type-in message. When a reel is mounted the computer should be able to sense the fact and automatically determine the physical reel number. With present hardware this requires that a label block be written at the front of each reel including scratch reels. This block can be made transparent to the user but presents a problem when reels must be exchanged with some installation which does not use the same convention. What is needed is for the manufacturers to develop some system whereby an external graphic label can be prepared and attached to the reel and subsequently read by the tape unit. An adhesive tape with reflective dots and dashes encoded on it would be one possibility.

8 Conclusions

It should be pointed out that by far most of the system was *not* developed at Case. The standard software supplied by Univac for the 1107 embodies most of the system concepts discussed in this paper. The system as supplied by Univac, however, is not suitable for use without an operator. Many of the peripheral file copying operation must be initiated by a central type-in. The contribution at Case is the operation of the system entirely and exclusively by the users themselves. The delays introduced by the center staff have been eliminated.

Mention should be made of an interesting open shop FORTRAN, 1107 installation at DuPont Engineering. This installation uses hardware and software supplied by Univac. Operating system and library have been somewhat modified to DuPont specifications by DuPont and Sperry Rand personnel. The basic framework of the system remains intact, however. Users leave their input decks at a table near the computer, the decks being loaded into the system as soon as there is space in the drum input queue

Computations are performed and printer listing and deck are returned by the operator to the users' pigeon hole. Turnaround time approaches that of the Case system; however, first priority is given to jobs which take no longer than one minute and require no tape mount-dismount. Hence, during heavy load periods of the day, turn around on larger jobs may suffer. An alternate method of operation is available for those who, due to the complex nature of their programs or need to interact with the computation, cannot live with the "hands off" operating policy. These people may be present at the operator's console to direct the course of their job or, if familiarity permits, physically operate the computer during their job.[1]

Human engineering is important for the Case system. The desirability of many tape units, not necessarily fast, and ease of mounting and identification have already been discussed. All card readers of Case have been modified by our maintenance staff to have a simple one-button operation. End of file stops, leaving one or more cards embedded irretrievably in the gizzard of the reader, have been removed. Several 500 card per minute readers are preferable to a few 1000 card per minute readers. File feeds and card joggling mechanisms are terrible things to unleash on a sophomore with a 50-card deck. Similar comments apply to printers and punches.

[1]The author is indebted to Mr. R. C. Haines for supplying the information concerning the DuPont system.

The system organization employed on the Case 1107 appears to give an improvement of a factor of two in throughput and an improvement of a factor of 10 to 100 in turnaround times. With such a system in operation a great deal of the luster of typewriter-driven time-sharing systems is lost. The 1107, however, will not last forever. So we are carefully watching new harduare and software developments. A new machine should perform substantially better than the current one.

A fair acceptance and evaluation test for a new system appears to be to present the vendor with 40 sophomores with program decks in hand. System performance would be measured by how long it takes them to complete and hand in the assignment. No vendor so far seems willing to discuss this proposal with us. We feel we have a problem.

6

THE EGDON SYSTEM FOR THE KDF9*

DAVID BURNS, E. NEVILLE HAWKINS,
D. ROBIN JUDD AND JOHN L. VENN

(1966)

An operating system based on the use of high-level languages and on-the use-of a discfile for program storage is described. The use of the discfile and the fact that only a small fraction of a program has to be recompiled when an error is corrected means that a very quick turnround is provided to users.

The Egdon programming and operating system is designed for a medium to large computer installation in which a large proportion of time is occupied in program testing and in which most programs are written in high-level languages.

It is currently operating on two KDF9 computers each with the following configuration of equipment:

1 central processor with 32,768 48-bit words of core store.
8 English Electric-Leo-Marconi tape units.
1 Ampex TM4 (IBM-compatible) tape unit.
1 Data Products discfile (capacity 3.9 million words).
1 line printer.
1 card reader.
1 card punch.
1 paper tape reader.

*D. Burns, E. N. Hawkins, D. R. Judd and J. L. Venn, The Egdon system for the KDF9. *The Computer Journal 8*, 4 (January 1966), 297–302.

1 paper tape punch.
1 monitor typewriter.

It can, however, be adapted to work with variations of this configuration.

The system is of a general type which though common in the U.S., is almost unknown to British manufacturers. Its main features may be summarized as follows:

1. Its unit of compilation is not the complete program but the routine.
2. It deals with a mixture of source languages.
3. It makes extensive use of a discfile for program storage.
4. Although it does not use conventional time-sharing it buffers input and output by the use of "pseudo-off-line" card reading, card punching, and printing.

The first of these features, the independent compilation of routines, is of great value in handling large programs. Each individual routine is compiled, not to its final absolute binary" form but to "relocatable binary" (RLB), a partially compiled form in which the addresses of core locations have not yet been filled in and which can therefore be adapted to be obeyed from any position in the core store. Before a program is executed, the routines which compose it are assembled together and "relocated," i.e. their absolute addresses are filled in. The advantage of doing things this way is that if a small amendment is to be made to a program, only the routine which is to be amended has to be recompiled from the source language. The routines which have not changed are merely "relocated" as usual, which is much quicker than compilation.

Independent compilation is intimately associated with card input because if paper tape is the basic input medium, it is almost essential (because of the difficulty of amending paper tape) to hold a copy of the program in the system so that it can be updated regularly. Since it is undesirable to hold a program in both source language and RLB, the RLB is usually omitted and programs are compiled completely from source language each time they are executed. With cards no such difficulty exists. It is a simple matter to amend card packs, so the source language exists only on cards and the system merely holds the RLB form of a program. When an amendment is made a complete routine is input afresh from cards.

With regard to point 2, the mixing of source languages, these are at the moment EGTRAN (a dialect of FORTRAN II) and KDF9 User-code. ALGOL may be added later. Any given routine must be written in one and only one of the source languages, but EGTRAN routines may be freely interspersed with User-code routines. Both source languages are compiled to RLB, which serves as an interface language.

The use of the discfile for program storage as well as data is a central feature of the system. Not only are system programs and library subroutines held on the disc, which has been done before, but also some problem programs. We believe that in this respect Egdon is unique amongst conventional operating systems, although it is of course usual in multi-console systems.

The effect of using the disc, together with a fairly large core store and single-pass compilers, is to avoid completely the necessity for batch processing. This is usually necessary with non-disc systems, to avoid excessive searching time on magnetic tape. The Egdon system is a straight-through system, and jobs can be loaded into the card hopper one after the other, each with its data with a minimum of operator intervention. The flow of information through the system is shown in Fig. 1.

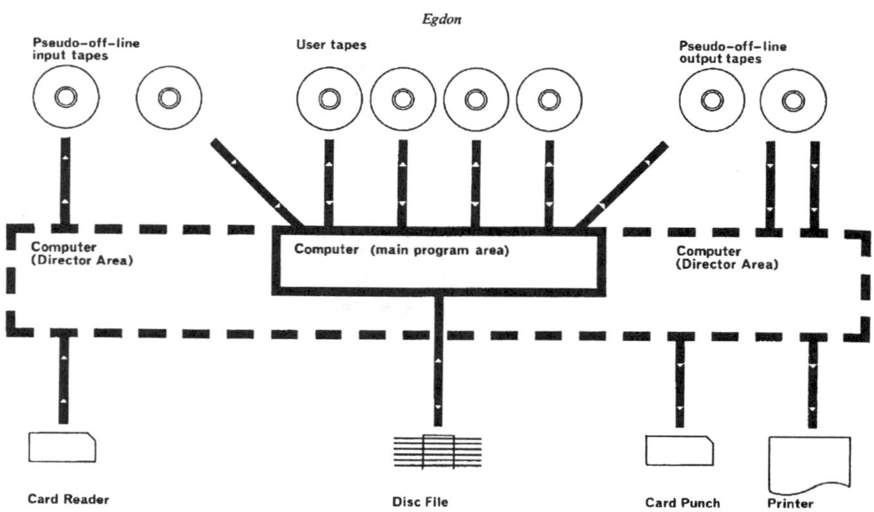

Figure 1 The flow of information through the Egdon system.

The fourth distinctive feature, "pseudo-off-line" input and output, speeds input and output up considerably without affecting the "straight-through", nature of the system. Cards are read by the supervisory program (the Director) and the information they contain is copied on to magnetic tape quite independently of the job which is actually being run. The card images are read back from tape when the job they refer to is compiled or executed in its turn, so that all the information concerned with jobs that are currently being compiled or executed is read from magnetic tape, not from physical cards. Through-put speed is thereby increased, and if a card jam should occur time is not usually lost because the transscription process, not the running of jobs, is held up. The converse happens on output, information being written on tape at the time the job is executed and sequently read back and printed or punched under Director control. These facilities are more fully described below under "Operating features".

The working of the system

The organization of the compilation and assembly of problem programs is done by a system program called Job Organizer, which is called into store by the supervisory program (Director) when work is to begin.

Let us consider first the case in which a card pack consists entirely of routines in source language (EGTRAN or User-code), together with control cards. The pack begins with control cards identifying the job and the segment and serving certain other special functions. (N.B. A *segment* is defined as the largest subdivision of a program held in core store at any one time during execution.) Job Organizer reads these control cards (or rather card images from magnetic tape) until it reaches the control card which immediately precedes the first routine. This card specifies which of the source languages the first routine is written in. Job Organizer then brings down from the disc the appropriate compiler for that language and transfers control to the compiler.

The compiler then reads the cards or images of the routine itself, and compiles the routine into RLB which it stores in the core store. Eventually a card is read which signifies the end of the routine. Control is then handed back to Job Organizer, which writes the RLB to an area of the disc called Job Assembly 1.

Job Organizer then deals with subsequent routines in the same way, except that if a routine is in the same language as the preceding routine, the compiler is not brought down from the disc because it is already in the core store.

When a complete segment has been compiled, Job Organizer automatically fetches from the disc all the library subroutines which are required, and copies them into the Job Assembly 1 area after the routines supplied by the user. If there are more segments, these are dealt with in the same way and stacked, each with its library subroutines, one after the other in the Job Assembly 1 area. All of these segments and their constituent routines are in RLB form, i.e. they have not yet been bound into a single program by having their absolute addresses filled in.

When the complete program has been written to the Job Assembly 1 area, Job Organizer calls a system program called *Relocator* which brings each segment in turn back into core store, "relocates" it, and writes it to another area of the disc called the Job Assembly 2 area. Each segment is now in absolute binary form ready to be obeyed. It is from the Job Assembly 2 area of the disc that segments are brought down during execution.

Assuming that execution is required, the first segment of the program is now brought down and entered. If, the program uses card data, this will have been fed in on cards immediately after the program, and so will follow it immediately on the input tape. If magnetic tapes are required, details of these will have been given to the system by means of control cards in the job pack. If the right tapes have been loaded, the system will find them and allocate them to the program. If they have not been loaded, a message stating which tapes are required will be typed for the operator as soon as the program tries to use that tape. The program will be executed until failure occurs, until it terminates normally, or until it is terminated by the operator.

On termination, Job Organizer is brought down again and the whole cycle of events is repeated. If the previous job has failed to read all its data, this is read and ignored until a beginning-of-job card is found, so jobs may be loaded into the hopper one after another with no fear that one will interfere with another.

All cards except data cards are listed as processing takes place, via the pseudo-off-line output tape. Failure diagnostics are output in the same way, as of course are the user's results. There is also a facility for obtaining RLB versions of routines on punched cards, by preceding the routine by a special control card.

The above is the simplest pattern of the flow of jobs through the system. There are, however, variations on this. For example, routines may be presented to Job Organizer not in source language form but in the form of RLB cards. In this case Job Organizer does not, of course, have to bring down a compiler, but merely copies the RLB from the cards straight to the Job Assembly 1 area.

Alternatively, the program or part of it may be stored in the problem program area of the discfile. In this case a special control card is included in the job pack, and Job Organizer automatically brings down the program, which will already be in RLB form. A program segment may be composed of some routines from the disc and some from cards. If all the routine names are different, all the routines will be included. If a routine from cards has the same name as a routine from the disc, the one from cards has precedence. Thus it is possible to include modified versions of disc routines in the job pack. They will override the disc versions, without actually altering what is stored in the problem program area of the disc.

A further facility is that special control cards can be introduced in the job pack which cause a number of card images stored on the disc to be inserted into the input stream as though they had been read from the card reader. This is known as "data substitution". The card images which are inserted may be stored semi-permanently on the disc in the manner of library subroutines, or they may be put there temporarily during the assembly of a particular job by including them (with special control cards) near the beginning of the job pack itself. The latter method is only useful, of course, if the same sequence of cards has to be read several times in the course of a job,

The information which is stored semi-permanently on the disc (problem programs, library subroutines, library data substition blocks) is put there in a special disc updating session which does not form part of normal running. The actual updating is done on magnetic tape. A copy of the contents of the disc is always held on magnetic tape for back-up purposes. In fact three separate tapes are used, part of the information being on each tape. The updating process is combined with copying—either tape-to-tape copying or disc-to-tape (not tape-to-disc). The updated version of the information then exists on magnetic tape. The disc itself is loaded from magnetic tape by a special loading program.

The three magnetic tapes used as a back-up can be used in an emergency as a disc simulator. The system is then considerably less efficient, but not absurdly so. The simulator also simulates the part of the disc which is available to the user, special overwriting techniques being used. Since there is no control over the way the user uses the disc, however, simulation of the user's area may be very inefficient.

Operating features

As has already been mentioned, both card input and card and printer output are normally done "pseudo-off-line," i.e. on input, cards are transcribed to magnetic tape by the Director quite independently of the problem program which is actually running, and the converse happens on output. Alternative modes of operation are available with direct input and output.

Basically two tape decks are needed for input and two for output. Taking input first, cards are read and a binary copy of the information they contain is written on to magnetic tape (each card being represented by a physical block on tape). "Binary" in this sense means that the exact pattern of holes is copied, each column being represented by 12 bits on tape. No processing at all is done at this stage. Apart from being inspected for certain patterns which indicate that the card is a directive to the pseudo-off-line process itself, the information on the cards is for the time being irrelevant. A tape that is being copied on to in this way is called a tape u.

While this is going on, a tape that has previously been produced in this way is being read back and is acting as an input to the central part of the system, i.e. the Job Organizer, compilers or problem programs. A tape that is being read in this way is called a tape v.

A switch of functions between the two input tapes occurs when a tape v is exhausted. The tape u is then rewound and becomes a tape v, and tape v likewise is rewound and becomes a tape u. To avoid holding up calculation while tape u rewinds, a special control card can be inserted anywhere in the input pack which causes it to rewind and wait, so that reading can start as soon as the switch takes place.

At the beginning of a work session, there is of course no tape v. Reading takes place to tape u until 600 cards have been read, and a switch then takes place.

A further mode of operation is available in which no automatic switching takes place, to deal with the case where it is required to build up a stock of transcribed tapes for a run which reads large numbers of cards very quickly.

Pseudo-off-line output is a slightly more complicated feature. It deals not only with printer output but also with punched card output. Two tape decks are used, one on which information from the job which is currently running is being written (known as tape x), and one from which a tape which has previously been written in this way is being read back by Director and printed (known as tape y). Blocks are variable in size, each one normally representing the output of a single EGTRAN statement.

Items of information to be printed are mingled on magnetic tape with items to be punched on cards, the kind of information being indicated by a control word at the beginning of the tape block.

Items for output are also classified in other ways, according to whether they originate from the system itself (e.g. compiler diagnostics) or from the problem program, and, if it is problem program output, according to priority, i.e. whether it is "immediate" or "delayed" output (this facility is described in more detail later). When a tape y is "played back", the operator is able to indicate which classes of output are to be dealt with in this pass of the tape (except in "rush-hour" mode—see below). A special record written on the tape itself records which items have already been printed or punched, and which still remain to be done.

At the beginning of a pass of tape y, the operator might, for example, indicate that all "immediate" printer output should be produced, but nothing else. On a subsequent pass he might indicate that all previously unprinted printer output, and all card output, should be produced, and so on. A combination of options is available which enables the operator to print or punch all information which has not been printed or punched before.

Because a tape y may need more than one pass before all its information is printed and punched, it is not possible to switch tapes automatically as is done on input. The operating procedure varies slightly according to whether "rush-hour" or "production" mode is in operation, but the operator always has to unload the tape y and save it, and load a scratch tape for the new tape x.

In order to ensure quick turnround of results to user a maximum running time and maximum amount printing are fixed for each program. If the time limit is exceeded, the program is terminated (normal wind-up procedures of course being allowed). If the print limit is exceeded, all subsequent items sent to the pseudo-off-line tape are classified as "delayed", rather than "immediate" which is the normal classification.

Besides the normal "production" mode of operation in which time and print limits are fairly generous, there is also a mode called "rush-hour", designed to provide an extra rapid turnround on short jobs, in which time and print limits are small. In rush-hour mode, operators are allowed less freedom in the handling of pseudo-off-line print tapes than in production mode. For example, no printing other than immediate printing which has not been done before is allowed, and each y tape *must* be the previous x tape (i.e. an x tape cannot but put aside and printed later).

Apart from loading cards in the hopper and handling pseudo-off-line output, almost the only thing the operator has to do is the loading and unloading of magnetic tapes. He is aided in this by a tape control scheme incorporated in Director, which locates the correct reel no matter which deck it is loaded on, checks labels, takes automatic corrective action in the case of parity failure, and produces statistics of tape usage a performance. An interesting feature is that label blocks are accessible only to Director—they cannot be overwritten by problem programs.

The discfile

The use of the discfile has certain interesting features. Like most discfiles, the KDF9 disc has the characteristic that the time taken to switch from one track to an adjacent track is, because of the time taken to move the positioner arm, considerably more than the time taken to switch to a totally different surface, assuming that no arm movement has to take place to bring the head into position on the new surface. The addressing of the disc is therefore arranged "cylindrically", i.e. so that sequential addresses, having passed along all the tracks accessible to one positioner, pass to the corresponding tracks on the next disc and thence to the corresponding tracks on other discs of the file, instead of passing to adjacent tracks on the same surface. Sequential addresses are thus arranged spatially along concentric "cylinders" rather than along plane surfaces. In fact, for a reason given below, the cylindrical addressing is not continued through all sixteen discs which compose the file, but stops short at the eighth disc. The file is thus divided into two halves, eaeh half having cylindrical addressing within itself. No address in the first half of the numerical range of addresses will lie on the same disc as any address in the second half of the range. Since the positioner arms of the KDF9 can move independently (*not* all together like a comb) any area of consecutive addresses of less than a certain size (in fact 30,720 words) within each half of the addressing scheme will be "movement-independent", i.e. once the arms have settled into position for accessing this area, any part of the area may be referred to without necessitating further arm-movement.

A further feature of the addressing scheme is that it optimizes as far as possible the use of fast and slow zones of the discfile. (Again like most discs, the KDF9 disc packs twice as much information in the outer tracks as in the inner ones, hence the transfer rate is twice as great.) To the programmer, an address consists of two parts, a "logical disc number" and a "sector number". Logical discs always begin at the beginning of a series of fast zone addresses, so that if a unit of information does not exceed a certain size (actually 2560 words) it can be stored entirely in a fast zone.

Disc storage is allocated in the following way at the time of writing, though this allocation may well be changed in the future. Areas are named in the order in which they occur.

AREA	APPROXIMATE SIZE (THOUSANDS OF WORDS)
Subroutine library	131
Library data substitution	131
Temporary data substitution	80
System programs	77
Job Assembly 2	230
Problem Programs	1317
User's area (also Job Assembly 1)	1966
	3932

It will be noticed that the user's area (the beginning of which is used between jobs for the Job Assembly 1 area) occupies the second half of the disc while everything else is in the first half. This means that no positioner arm which is used to access the Job Assembly 1 area is used for any other area used by the system. The reason for this is that during job organization, Job Assembly 1 is constantly being referred to. in the first place various items (e.g. library subroutines) are brought down from the first half of the disc and packed into Job Assembly 1. Later, at the relocation stage, chunks of programs are brought down from Job Assembly 1 and sent to Job Assembly 2. Access to the first half of the disc takes place over a wide area and in a fairly random fashion, but access to Job Assembly 1 is localized to a small area. Thus Job Assembly 1, unless it exceeds 30,720 words, becomes a "movement-independent" area as described above. This has a significant reducing effect on job organization time.

The compilers

Two compilers were written specially for the Egdon system, a FORTRAN (EGTRAN) compiler and a User-code compiler. Both operate entirely in the core store, i.e. they are one-pass compilers, and both compile one routine at a time. The routines are subsequently read back and bound into a complete program by a system program called the *Relocator*. Relocator also carries out some optimization of FORTRAN routines in the light of extra information which is available at relocate time which was not available at compile time.

The FORTRAN compiler compiles from a dialect of FORTRAN II called EGTRAN which is not appropriate to discuss at length here. All the usual facilities of FORTRAN II are included, together with certain additional facilities peculiar to EGTRAN. In particular the following may be noted:

(1) A facility for varying the dimensions of arrays at run time without sacrificing the optimization of subscripts.

(2) Recursive funcions and subroutines, with preservation of the values of variables between recursions if required.

(3) Some additional statements for transferring whole arrays to or from disc or magnetic tape, rather than the normal FORTRAN "list" of variables. This makes it possible to make transfers proceed simultaneusly with each other and with central processor calculations, which cannot be done (except to a very limited extent) with "list" type statements because of the need for store protection.

The User-code compiler or assembler accepts a punched card version of ordinary KDF9 User-code. Its output takes the form of relocatable binary routines which are completely interchangeable with those produced by the EGTRAN compiler.

Operational experience

Some seven months operational experience has now been gained on the Egdon system. It has behaved substantially as expected, being an efficient job-shop operating system capable of reducing the time between the submission of a job and the printing of results to a minimum.

The combination of in-core compiler and independent compilation of routines means that large jobs can be amended and made ready for execution in a very short time. For example, a particular multi-segment program comprising 26,000 words of instruction in all (say 8000 EGTRAN statements) takes about $2\frac{1}{2}$ minutes to organize and relocate. This means that this is the time it takes to make a trivial amendment to the program and to start to execute it. This time will be significantly reduced when certain improvements which are being made to reduce the number of disc accesses are completed.

The compiler itself compiles 300 to 350 EGTRAN statements per minute. Object program efficiency is not as high as can be achieved with a multi-pass compiler, but is typically 1.5 to 4 times slower than hand-coded program.

There are some points on which it can now be seen that the system is inconvenient, the most important being pseudo-off-line output. The volume of printed output has been less than was expected, and the facilities for coping with large volumes have therefore been largely redundant. "Rush-hour" mode is currently not being used at all, production mode with a small print limit being used instead. Modifications will probably be made to simplify the system.

A number of program errors have, of course, been found after the passing of the acceptance tests. The majority of these have been in the Director area, which is not surprising because supervisory programs, being dependent on real-time events, are notoriously difficult to debug. No run has ever failed, however, for a reason that was not fairly easily circumvented, and there has never been a complete stoppage of work because of errors in the software.

Implementation

One of the more unusual features of the Egdon system is that it was completed on time and passed two stringent series of acceptance tests. Since this cannot be entirely explained by the brilliance of those who have worked on it, it is worth while examining other factors which may have contributed.

First, there are political factors. Since the customers for whom the system was written had previously suffered from a late delivery of software from an American manufacturer, a stiff penalty clause was built into the contract. This in itself did not ensure success, but it led to an attitude of urgency on the part of all concerned which was a major contributory factor. For example, it made the customer particularly careful to fulfil his obligations to us, such as providing us with information by a given date, and to avoid too-frequent changes of mind.

Secondly, PERT critical path scheduling was carried out regularly. The writing of software is not an ideal activity for this kind of control because there are so many possible ways of achieving the final object. This meant that the network underwent several major revisions during the course of the project. But in spite of this and of the large amount of unproductive clerical effort involved in preparing data, the existence of the PERT caused a kind of planning-consciousness to be created which had an important bearing on success.

Thirdly, and perhaps most important of all, was the existence of clear objectives from the start. The fact that there was a formal customer-supplier relationship, and that the customer was already an experienced computer user, meant that decisions were arrived at by controlled discussion, and properly documented. This does not mean that every detail was worked out in advance and that nothing was changed—in fact only a general outline existed at first, the details were worked out progressively over a period of several months, and decisions were reversed on several occasions. But the existence of a formal relationship, and the knowledge that a penalty clause existed, damped down the oscillations that this kind of discussion often gives rise to, and meant that a clear definition was arrived at quickly and changes were kept to a minimum.

Implementation from the first planning meeting to the beginning of the acceptance tests, took about 15 months. A total of 20 man-years' programming work was involved altogether, split roughly as follows:

	Man years
EGTRAN and required library	7
User-code Assembler	4
Director	$3\frac{1}{2}$
Relocator	1
Disc Update	1
Job Organizer	$\frac{1}{2}$
Auxiliary programs	3
	20

Acknowledgements

Dr. L. H. Underhill and Mr. I. C. Pull of A.E.E. Winfrith, and Dr. K. V. Roberts and Mr. L. A. J. Verra of Culham Laboratory played a major part in defining the system and made many valuable suggestions concerning implementation. The following, of English Electric-Leo-Marconi Computers Ltd. unless otherwise stated, helped to implement it:

J. W. Adams, G. M. A. Bernau (Culham Laboratory), D. C. Bindon (A.E.E. Winfrith), T. R. Clayton, J. K. Ebbutt, R. Godfrey, A. J. Harding, J. E. Hartley, P. L. Havard, A. J. Heyes, Miss P. Higson, E. F. Hill, G. H. Johnston, F. D. McIntosh, D. G. Manns, B. F. J. Manly, J. O'Brien, A. C. Peters, A. J. Robbins, A. Sutcliffe, J. G. Walker, P. J. L. Wallis, B. C. Warboys, A. M. Yates.

PART IV

TIMESHARING

7

AN EXPERIMENTAL TIME-SHARING SYSTEM*

FERNANDO J. CORBATÓ,
MARJORIE MERWIN-DAGGETT
AND ROBERT C. DALEY

(1962)

It is the purpose of this paper to discuss briefly the need for time-sharing, some of the implementation problems, an experimental time-sharing system which has been developed for the contemporary IBM 7090, and finally a scheduling algorithm of one of us (FJC) that illustrates some of the techniques which may be employed to enhance and be analyzed for the performance limits of such a time-sharing system.

INTRODUCTION

The last dozen years of computer usage have seen great strides. In the early 1950's, the problems solved were largely in the construction and maintenance of hardware; in the mid-1950's, the usage languages were greatly improved with the advent of compilers; now in the early 1960's, we are in the midst of a third major modification to computer usage: the improvement of man-machine interaction by a process called time-sharing.

Much of the time-sharing philosophy, expressed in this paper, has been developed in conjunction with the work of an MIT preliminary study committee, chaired by H. Teager, which examined the long range computational needs of the Institute, and a subsequent MIT computer working committee,

---

*F. J. Corbató, M. Merwin-Daggett and R. C. Daley, An experimental time-sharing system. *Spring Joint Computer Conference 21*, 1962, 335–344.

chaired by J. McCarthy. However, the views and conclusions expressed in this paper should be taken as solely those of the present authors.

Before proceeding further, it is best to give a more precise interpretation to time-sharing. One can mean using different parts of the hardware at the same time for different tasks, or one can mean several persons making use of the computer at the same time. The first meaning, often called multiprogramming, is oriented towards hardware efficiency in the sense of attempting to attain complete utilization of all components [5,6,7,8]. The second meaning of time-sharing, which is meant here, is primarily concerned with the efficiency of persons trying to use a computer [1,2,3,4]. Computer efficiency should still be considered but only in the perspective of the total system utility.

The motivation for time-shared computer usage arises out of the slow man-computer interaction rate presently possible with the bigger, more advanced computers. This rate has changed little (and has become worse in some cases) in the last decade of widespread computer use [10]. In part, this effect has been due to the fact that as elementary problems become mastered on the computer, more complex problems immediately become of interest. As a result, larger and more complicated programs are written to take advantage of larger and faster computers.

This process inevitably leads to more programming errors and a longer period of time required for debugging. Using current batch monitor techniques, as is done on most large computers, each program bug usually requires several hours to eliminate, if not a complete day. The only alternative presently available is for the programmer to attempt to debug directly at the computer, a process which is grossly wasteful of computer time and hampered seriously by the poor console communication usually available. Even if a typewriter is the console, there are usually lacking the sophisticated query and response programs which are vitally necessary to allow effective interaction. Thus, what is desired is to drastically increase the rate of interaction between the programmer and the computer without large economic loss and also to make each interaction more meaningful by extensive and complex system programming to assist in the man-computer communication.

To solve these interaction problems we would like to have a computer made simultaneously available to many users in a manner somewhat like a telephone exchange. Each user would be able to use a console at his own pace and without concern for the activity of others using the system. This console could as a minimum be merely a typewriter but more ideally would contain an incrementally modifiable self-sustaining display. In any case, data transmission requirements should be such that it would be no major obstacle to have remote installation from the computer proper.

The basic technique for a time-sharing system is to have many persons simultaneously using the computer through typewriter consoles with a time-sharing supervisor program sequentially running each user program in a short burst or quantum of computation. This sequence, which in the most straightforward case is a simple round-robin, should occur often enough so that each user program which is kept in the high-speed memory is run for a quantum at least once during each approximate human reaction time ($\sim$ 0.2 seconds). In this way, each user sees a computer fully responsive to even single key strokes each of which may require only trivial computation; in the non-trivial cases, the user sees a gradual reduction of the response time which is proportional to the complexity of the response calculation, the slowness of the computer, and the total number of active users. It should be clear, however, that if there are n users actively requesting service at one time, each user will only see on the average 1/n of the effective computer speed. During the period of high interaction rates while debugging programs, this should not be a hindrance since ordinarily the required amount of computation needed for each debugging computer response is small compared to the ultimate production need.

Not only would such a time-sharing system improve the ability to program in the conventional manner by one or two orders of magnitude, but there would be opened up several new forms of computer usage. There would be a gradual reformulation of many scientific and engineering applications so that programs containing decision trees which currently must be specified in advance would be eliminated and instead the particular decision branches would be specified only as needed. Another important area is that of teaching machines which, although frequently trivial computationally, could naturally exploit the consoles of a time-sharing system with the additional bonus that more elaborate and adaptive teaching programs could be used. Finally, as attested by the many small business computers, there are numerous applications in business and in industry where it would be advantageous to have powerful computing facilities available at isolated locations with only the incremental capital investment of each console. But it is important to realize that even without the above and other new applications, the major advance in programming intimacy available from time-sharing would be of immediate value to computer installations in universities, research laboratorics, and engineering firms where program debugging is a major problem.

Implementation Problems

As indicated, a straightforward plan for time-sharing is to execute user programs for small quantums of computation without priority in a simple round-robin; the strategy of time-sharing can be more complex as will be shown later, but the above simple scheme is an adequate solution. There are still many problems, however, some best solved by hardware, others affecting the programming conventions and practices. A few of the more obvious problems are summarized:

Hardware Problems:

1. Different user programs if simultaneously in core memory may interfere with each other or the supervisor program so some form of memory protection mode should be available when operating user programs.

2. The time-sharing supervisor may need at different times to run a particular program from several locations. (Loading relocation bits are no help since the supervisor does not know how to relocate the accumulator, etc.) Dynamic relocation of *all* memory accesses that pick up instructions or data words is one effective solution.

3. Input-output equipment may be initiated by a user and read words in on another user program. A way to avoid this is to trap all input-output instructions issued by a user's program when operated in the memory protection mode.

4. A large random-access back-up storage is desirable for general program storage files for all users. Present large capacity disc units appear to be adequate.

5. The time-sharing supervisor must be able to interrupt a user's program after a quantum of computation. A program-initiated one-shot multivibrator which generates an interrupt a fixed time later is adequate.

6. Large core memories (e.g. a million words) would ease the system programming complications immensely since the different active user programs as well as the frequently used system programs such as compilers, query programs, etc. could remain in core memory at all times.

Programming Problems:

1. The supervisor program must do automatic user usage charge accounting. In general, the user should be charged on the basis of a system usage formula or algorithm which should include such factors as computation time, amount of high-speed memory required, rent of secondary memory storage, etc.

2. The supervisor program should coordinate all user input-output since it is not desirable to require a user program to remain constantly in memory during input-output limited operations. In addition, the supervisor must coordinate all usage of the central, shared high-speed input-output units serving all users as well as the clocks, disc units, etc.

3. The system programs available must be potent enough so that the user can think about his problem and not be hampered by coding details or typographical mistakes. Thus, compilers, query programs, postmortem programs, loaders, and good editing programs are essential.

4. As much as possible, the users should be allowed the maximum programming flexibility both in choices of language and in the absence of restrictions.

Usage Problems:

1. Too large a computation or excessive typewriter output may be inadvertently requested so that a special termination signal should be available to the user.

2. Since real-time is not computer usage-time, the supervisor must keep each user informed so that he can use his judgment regarding loops, etc.

3. Computer processor, memory and tape malfunctions must be expected. Basic operational questions such as "Which program is running?" must be answerable and recovery procedures fully anticipated.

An Experimental Time-Sharing System for the IBM 7090

Having briefly stated a desirable time-sharing performance, it is pertinent to ask what level of performance can be achieved with existant equipment.

To begin to answer this question and to explore all the programming and operational aspects, an experimental time-sharing system has been developed. This system was originally written for the IBM 709 but has since been converted for use with the 7090 computer.

The 7090 of the MIT Computation Center has, in addition to three channels with 19 tape units, a fourth channel with the standard Direct Data Connection. Attached to the Direct Data Connection is a real-time equipment buffer and control rack designed and built under the direction of H. Teager and his group[1]. This rack has a variety of devices attached but the only ones required by the present systems are three flexowriter typewriters. Also installed on the 7090 are two special modifications (i.e. RPQ's): a standard 60 cycle accounting and interrupt clock, and a special mode which allows memory protection, dynamic relocation and trapping of all user attempts to initiate input-output instructions.

In the present system the time-sharing occurs between four users, three of whom are on-line each at a typewriter in a foreground system, and a fourth passive user of the background Fap-Mad-Madtran-BSS Monitor System similar to the Fortran-Fap-BSS Monitor System (FMS) used by most of the Center programmers and by many other 7090 installations.

Significant design features of the foreground system are:

1. It allows the user to develop programs in languages compatible with the background system,
2. Develop a private file of programs,
3. Start debugging sessions at the state of the previous session, and
4. Set his own pace with little waste of computer time.

Core storage is allocated such that all users operate in the upper 27,000 words with the time-sharing supervisor (TSS) permanently in the lower 5,000 words. To avoid memory allocation clashes, protect users from one another, and simplify the initial 709 system organization, only one user was kept in core memory at a time. However, with the special memory protection and relocation feature of the 7090, more sophisticated storage allocation procedures are being implemented. In any case, user swaps are minimized

[1]This group is presently using another approach [9] in developing a time-sharing system for the MIT 7090.

by using 2-channel overlapped magnetic tape reading and writing of the pertinent locations in the two user programs.

The foreground system is organized around commands that each user can give on his typewriter and the user's private program files which presently (for want of a disc unit) are kept on a separate magnetic tape for each user.

For convenience the format of the private tape files is such that they are card images, have title cards with name and class designators and can be written or punched using the off-line equipment. (The latter feature also offers a crude form of large-scale input-output.) The magnetic tape requirements of the system are the seven tapes required for the normal functions of the background system, a system tape for the time-sharing supervisor that contains most of the command programs, and a private file tape and dump tape for each of the three foreground users.

The commands are typed by the user to the time-sharing supervisor (not to his own program) and thus can be initiated at any time regardless of the particular user program in memory. For similar coordination reasons, the supervisor handles all input-output of the foreground system typewriters. Commands are composed of segments separated by vertical strokes; the first segment is the command name and the remaining segments are parameters pertinent to the command. Each segment consists of the last 6 characters typed (starting with an implicit 6 blanks) so that spacing is an easy way to correct a typing mistake. A carriage return is the signal which initiates action on the command. Whenever a command is received by the supervisor, "WAIT," is typed back followed by "READY." when the command is completed. (The computer responses are always in the opposite color from the user's typing.) While typing, an incomplete command line may be ignored by the "quit" sequence of a code delete signal followed by a carriage return. Similarly after a command is initiated, it may be abandoned if a "quit" sequence is given. In addition, during unwanted command typeouts, the command and output may be terminated by pushing a special "stop output" button.

The use of the foreground system is initiated whenever a typewriter user completes a command line and is placed in a waiting command queue. Upon completion of each quantum, the time-sharing supervisor gives top priority to initiating any waiting commands. The system programs corresponding to most of the commands are kept on the special supervisor command system tape so that to avoid waste of computer time, the supervisor continues to operate the last user program until the desired command program on tape is positioned for reading. At this point, the last user is read out on his dump tape, the command program read in, placed in a working status and initiated as a new user program. However, before starting the new user for a quantum of computation, the supervisor again checks for any waiting command of another user and if necessary begins the look-ahead positioning of the command system tape while operating the new user.

Whenever the waiting command queue is empty, the supervisor proceeds to execute a simple round-robin of those foreground user programs in the working status queue. Finally, if both these queues are empty, the background user program is brought in and run a quantum at a time until further foreground system actively develops.

Foreground user programs leave the working status queue by two means. If the program proceeds to completion, it can reenter the supervisor in a way which eliminates itself and places the user in dead status; alternatively, by a different entry the program can be placed in a dormant status (or be manually placed by the user executing a quit sequence). The dormant status differs from the dead status in that the user may still restart or examine his program.

User input-output is through each typewriter, and even though the supervisor has a few lines of buffer space available, it is possible to become input-output limited. Consequently, there is an additional input-output wait status, similar to the dormant, which the user is automatically placed in by the supervisor program whenever input-output delays develop. When buffers become near empty on output or near full on input, the user program is automatically returned to the working status; thus waste of computer time is avoided.

Commands

To clarify the scope of the foreground system and to indicate the basic tools available to the user, a list of the important commands follows along with brief summaries of their operations:

1. $\mid \alpha$

   $\alpha =$ arbitrary text treated as a comment.

2. login $\mid \alpha \mid \beta$

   $\alpha =$ user problem number

β = user programmer number

Should be given at beginning of each user's session. Rewinds user's private file tape; clears time accounting records.

3. logout

   Should be given at end of each user's session. Rewinds user's private file tape; punches on-line time accounting cards.

4. input

   Sets user in input mode and initiates automatic generation of line numbers. The user types a card image per line according to a format appropriate for the programming language. (The supervisor collects these card images at the end of the user's private file tape.) When in the automatic input mode, the manual mode may be entered by giving an initial carriage return and typing the appropriate line number followed by | and line for as many lines as desired. To reenter the automatic mode, an initial carriage return is given.

   The manual mode allows the user to overwrite previous lines and to insert lines. (cf. File Command.)

5. edit | α | β

   α = title of file

   β = class of file

   The user is set in the automatic input mode with the designated file treated as initial input lines. The same conventions apply as to the input command.

6. file | α | β

   α = title to be given to file

   β = class of language used during input

   The created file will consist of the numbered input lines (i.e. those at the end of the user's private file tape) in *sequence*; in the case of duplicate line numbers, the last version will be used. The line numbers will be written as sequence numbers in the corresponding card images of the file. For convenience the following editing conventions apply to input lines:

a. an underline signifies the deletion of the previous characters of the line.
b. a backspace signifies the deletion of the previous character in the field.

The following formats apply:

a. FAP: symbol, tab, operation, tab, variable field and comment.
b. MAD, MADTRAN, FORTRAN: statement label, tab, statement. To place a character in the continuation column: statement label, tab, backspace, character, statement.
c. DATA: cols. 1–72.

7. fap | α

Causes the file designated as α,fap to be translated by the FAP translator (assembler). Files α,symtb and α,bss are added to the user's private file tape giving the symbol table and the relocatable binary BSS form of the file.

8. mad | α

Causes file α,mad to be translated by the MAD translator (compiler). File α,bss is created.

9. madtrn | α

Causes file α,madtrn (i.e. a pseudo-Fortran language file) to be edited into an equivalent file α,mad (added to the user's file) and translation occurs as if the command mad|α had been given.

10. load | α_1 | α_2 ... | α_n

Causes the consecutive loading of files α_i,bss (i = 1, 2, ..., n). An exception occurs if α_i = (libe), in which case file α_{i+1},bss is searched as a library file for all subprograms still missing. (There can be further library files.)

11. use | α_1 | α_2 | ... | α_n

This command is used whenever a load or previous use command notifies the user of an incomplete set of subprograms. Same α_i conventions as for load.

12. start | α | β

    Starts the program setup by the load and use commands (or a dormant program) after first positioning the user private file tape in front of the title card for file α,β. (If β is not given, a class of data is assumed; if both α and β are not given, no tape movement occurs and the program is started.)

13. pm | α

    α = "lights", "stomap", or the usual format of the standard Center post-mortem (F2PM) request: subprogram name | loc_1 | loc_2 | mode | direction where mode and direction are optional.

    Produces post-mortem of user's dormant program according to request specified by α. (E.g. matrix | 5 | 209 | flo | rev will cause to be printed on the user's typewriter the contents of subprogram "matrix" from relative locations 5 to 209 in floating point form and in reverse sequence.)

14. skippm

    Used if a pm command is "quit" during output and the previous program interruption is to be restarted.

15. listf

    Types out list of all file titles on user's private file tape.

16. printf | α | β | γ

    Types out file α, β starting at line number γ. If γ is omitted, the initial line is assumed. Whenever the user's output buffer fills, the command program goes into an I/O wait status allowing other users to time-share until the buffer needs refilling.

17. xdump | α | β

    Creates file α, β (if β omitted, xdump is assumed) on user's private file tape consisting of the complete state of the user's last dormant program.

18. xundmp | α | β

    Inverse of xdump command in that it resets file α, β as the user's program, starting it where it last left off.

Although experience with the system to date is quite limited, first indications are that programmers would readily use such a system if it were generally available. It is useful to ask, now that there is some operating experience with the 7090 system, what observations can be made. An immediate comment is that once a user gets accustomed to computer response, delays of even a fraction of a minute are exasperatingly long, an effect analogous to conversing with a slow-speaking person. Similarly, the requirement that a complete typewritten line rather than each character be the minimum unit of man-computer communication is an inhibiting factor in the sense that a press-to-talk radio-telephone conversation is more stilted than that of an ordinary telephone. Since maintaining a rapid computer response on a character by character basis requires at least a vestigial response program in core memory at all times, the straight-forward solution within the present system is to have more core memory available. At the very least, an extra bank of memory for the time-sharing supervisor would ease compatibility problems with programs already written for 32,000 word 7090's.

For reasons of expediency, the weakest portions of the present system are the conventions for input, editing of user files, and the degree of rapid interaction and intimacy possible while debugging. Since to a large extent these areas involve the taste, habits, and psychology of the users, it is felt that proper solutions will require considerable experimentation and pragmatic evaluation; it is also clear that these areas cannot be treated in the abstract for the programming languages used will influence greatly the appropriate techniques. A greater use of symbolic referencing for locations, program names and variables is certainly desired; symbolic post-mortem programs, trace programs, and before-and-after differential dump programs should play useful roles in the debugging procedures.

In the design of the present system, great care went into making each user independent oi the other users. However, it would be a useful extension of the system if this were not always the case. In particular, when several consoles are used in a computer controlled group such as in management or war games, in group behavior studies, or possibly in teaching machines, it would be desirable to have all the consoles communicating with a single program.

Another area for further improvement within the present system is that of file maintenance, since the presently used tape units are a hindrance to the easy deletion of user program files. Disc units will be of help in this area as well as with the problem of consolidating and scheduling large-scale central input-output generated by the many console users.

Finally, it is felt that it would be desirable to have the distinction between the foreground and background systems eliminated. The present-day computer operator would assume the role of a stand-in for the background users, using an operator console much like the other user consoles in the system, mounting and demounting magnetic tapes as requested by the supervisor, receiving instructions to read card decks into the central disc unit, etc. Similarly the foreground user, when satisfied with his program, would by means of his console and the supervisor program enter his program into the queue of production background work to be performed. With these procedures implemented the distinction of whether one is time-sharing or not would vanish and the computer user would be free to choose in an interchangable way that mode of operation which he found more suitable at a particular time.

A Multi-Level Scheduling Algorithm

Regardless of whether one has a million word core memory or a 32,000 word memory as currently exists on the 7090, one is inevitably faced with the problem of system saturation where the total size of active user programs exceeds that of the high-speed memory or there are too many active user programs to maintain an adequate response at each user console. These conditions can easily arise with even a few users if some of the user programs are excessive in size or in time requirements. The predicament can be alleviated if it is assumed that a good design for the system is to have a saturation procedure which gives graceful degradation of the response time and effective real-time computation speed of the large and long-running users.

To show the general problem, Figure 1 qualitatively gives the user service as a function of n, the number of active users. This service parameter might be either of the two key factors; computer response time or n times the real-time computation speed. In either case there is some critical number of active users, N, representing the effective user capacity, which causes saturation. If the strategy near saturation is to execute the simple round-robin of all users, then there is an abrupt collapse of service due to the sudden onset of the large amount of time required to swap programs in-and-out of the secondary memory such as a disc or drum unit. Of course, Figure 1 is quite qualitative since it depends critically on the spectrum of user program sizes as well as the spectrum of user operating times.

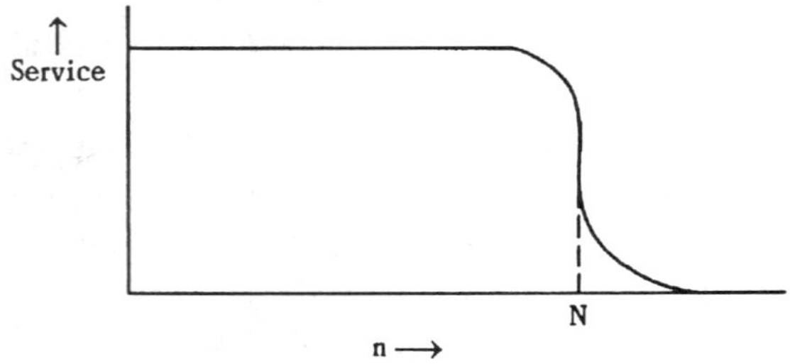

Figure 1 Service vs. number of active users.

To illustrate the strategy that can be employed to improve the saturation performance of a time-sharing system, a multi-level scheduling algorithm is presented. This algorithm also can be analyzed to give broad bounds on the system performance.

The basis of the multi-level scheduling algorithm is to assign each user program as it enters the system to be run (or completes a response to a user) to an lth level priority queue. Programs are initially entered into a level l_0, corresponding to their size such that

$$l_0 = \left[\log_2 \left(\left[\frac{w_p}{w_q} \right] + 1 \right) \right] \quad (1)$$

where w_p is the number of words in the program, w_q is the number of words which can be transmitted in *and* out of the high-speed memory from the secondary memory in the time of one quantum, q, and the bracket indicates "the integral part of." Ordinarily the time of a quantum, being the basic time unit, should be as small as possible without excessive overhead losses when the supervisor switches from one program in high-speed memory to another The process starts with the time-sharing supervisor operating the program at the head of the lowest level occupied queue, l, for up to 2^l quanta of time and then if the program is not completed (i.e. has not made a response to the user) placing it at the end of the l+1 level queue. If there are no programs entering the system at levels lower than l, this process proceeds until the queue at level l is exhausted; the process is then iteratively begun again at level l+1, where now each program is run for 2^{l+1} quanta of time.

If during the execution of the 2^l quanta of a program at level l, a lower level , l', becomes occupied , the current user is replaced at the head of the lth queue and the process is reinitiated at level l'.

Similarly, if a program of size w_p at level l, during operation requests a change in memory size from the time-sharing supervisor, then the enlarged (or reduced) version of the program should be placed at the end of the l'' queue where

$$l'' = l + \left[\log_2 \left(\left[\frac{w_p''}{w_p} \right] + 1 \right) \right] \tag{2}$$

Again the process is re-initiated with the head-of-the-queue user at the lowest occupied level of l'.

Several important conclusions can be drawn from the above algorithm which allow the performance of the system to be bounded.

Computational Efficiency

1. Because a program is always operated for a time greater than or equal to the swap time (i.e. the time required to move the program in and out of secondary memory), it follows that the computational efficiency never falls below one-half. (Clearly, this fraction is adjustable in the formula for the initial level, l_0.) An alternative way of viewing this bound is to say that the real-time computing speed available to one out of n active users is no worse than if there were 2n active users all of whose programs were in the high-speed memory.

Response Time

2. If the maximum number of active users is N, then an individual user of a given program size can be guaranteed a response time

$$t_r \leq 2Nq \left(\left[\frac{w_p}{w_q} \right] + 1 \right) \tag{3}$$

since the worst case occurs when all competing user programs are at the same level. Conversely, if t_r is a guaranteed response of arbitrary value and the largest size of program is assumed, then the maximum permissible number of active users is bounded.

Long Runs

3. The relative swap time on long runs can be made vanishingly small. This conclusion follows since the longer a program is run, the higher the level number it cascades to with a correspondingly smaller relative swap time. It is an important feature of the algorithm that long runs must in effect prove they are long so that programs which have an unexpected demise are detected quickly. In order that there be a finite number of levels, a maximum level number, L, can be established such that the asymptotic swap overhead is some arbitrarily small percentage, p:

$$L = \left[\log_2 \left(\left[\frac{w_{pmax}}{pw_q} \right] + 1 \right) \right] \tag{4}$$

where w_{pmax} is the size of the largest possible program.

Multi-level vs. Single-level Response Times

4. The response time for programs of equal size, entering the system at the same time, and being run for multiple quanta, is no worse than approximately twice the response-time occurring in a single quanta round-robin procedure. If there are n equal sized programs started in a queue at level l, then the worst case is that of the end-of-the-queue program which is ready to respond at the very first quantum run at the l+j level. Using the multi-level algorithm, the total delay for the end-of-the-queue program is by virtue of the geometric series of quanta:

$$T_m \sim q2^l \left\{ n(2^j - 1) + (n-1)2^j \right\} \tag{5}$$

Since the end-of-the-queue user has computed for a time of $2^l(2^j - 1)$ quanta, the equivalent single-level round-robin delay before a response is:

$$T_s \sim q2^l \left\{ n(2^j - 1) \right\} \tag{6}$$

Hence

$$\frac{T_m}{T_s} \sim 1 + \left(\frac{n-1}{n}\right)\left(\frac{2^j}{2^j-1}\right) \sim 2 \tag{7}$$

and the assertion is shown. It should be noted that the above conditions, where program swap times are omitted, which are pertinent when all programs remain in high-speed memory, are the least favorable for the multi-level algorithm; if swap times are included in the above analysis, the ratio of T_m/T_s can only become smaller and may become much less than unity. By a similar analysis it is easy to show that even in the unfavorable case where there are no program swaps, head-of-the-queue programs that terminate just as the 2^{l+j} quanta are completed receive under the multi-level algorithm a response which is twice as fast as that under the single-level round-robin (i.e. $T_m/T_s = 1/2$).

Highest Serviced Level

5. In the multi-level algorithm the level classification procedure for programs is entirely automatic, depending on performance and program size rather than on the declarations (or hopes) of each user. As a user taxes the system, the degradation of service occurs progressively starting with the higher level users of either large or long-running programs; however, at some level no user programs may be run because of too many active users at lower levels. To determine a bound on this cut-off point we consider N active users at level l each running 2^l quanta, terminating, and reentering the system again at level l at a user response time, t_u, later, If there is to be no service at level $l+1$, then the computing time, $Nq2^l$, must be greater than or equal to t_u. Thus the guaranteed active levels, l_a, are given by the relation:

$$l_a \leq \left[\log_2 \left(\left[\frac{t_u}{Nq} \right] \right) \right] \tag{8}$$

In the limit, t_u could be as small as a minimum user reaction time ($\sim$ 0.2 sec.), but the expected value would be several orders of magnitude greater as a result of the statistics of a large number of users.

The multi-level algorithm as formulated above makes no explicit consideration of the seek or latency time required before transmission of programs to and from disc or drum units when they are used as the secondary memory, (although formally the factor w_q could contain an average figure for these times). One simple modification to the algorithm which usually avoids wasting the seek or latency time is to continue to operate the last user program for as many quanta as are required to ready the swap of the new user with the least priority user; since ordinarily only the higher level number programs would be forced out into the secondary memory, the extended quanta of operation of the old user while seeking the new user should be but a minor distortion of the basic algorithm.

Further complexities are possible when the hardware is appropriate. In computers with input-output channels and low transmission rates to and from secondary memory, it is possible to overlap the reading and writing of the new and old users in and out of high-speed memory while operating the current user. The effect is equivalent to using a drum giving 100% multiplexor usage but there are two liabilities, namely, no individual user can utilize all the available user memory space and the look-ahead procedure breaks down whenever an unanticipated scheduling change occurs (e.g. a program terminates or a higher-priority user program is initiated).

Complexity is also possible in storage allocation but certainly an elementary procedure and a desirable one with a low-transmission rate secondary memory is to consolidate in a single block all high-priority user programs whenever sufficient fragmentary unused memory space is available to read in a new user program. Such a procedure is indicated in the flow diagram of the multi-level scheduling algorithm which is given as Figure 2.

It should also be noted that Figure 2 only accounts for the scheduling of programs in a working status and still does not take into account the storage allocation of programs which are in a dormant (or input-output wait status). One systematic method of handling this case is to modify the scheduling algorithm so that programs which become dormant at level l are entered into the queue at level l+1. The scheduling algorithm proceeds as before with the dormant programs continuing to cascade but not operating when they reached the head of a queue. Whenever a program must be removed from high-speed memory, a program is selected from the end-of-the-queue of the highest occupied level number.

Finally, it is illuminating to apply the multi-level scheduling algorithm bounds to the contemporary IBM 7090. The following approximate values are obtained:

$q =$ 16 m.s. (based on 1% switching overhead)
$w_q =$ 120 words (based on one IBM 1301 model 2 disc unit without seek or latency times included)
$t_r \leq$ $8Nf_{sec}$ (based on programs of (32k)f words)
$l_a \leq$ $\log_2(1000/N)$ (based on $t_u = 16$ sec.)
$l_0 \leq$ 8 (based on a maximum program size of 32K words)

Using the arbitrary criteria that programs up to the maximum size of 32,000 words should always get some service, which is to say that max $l_a =$

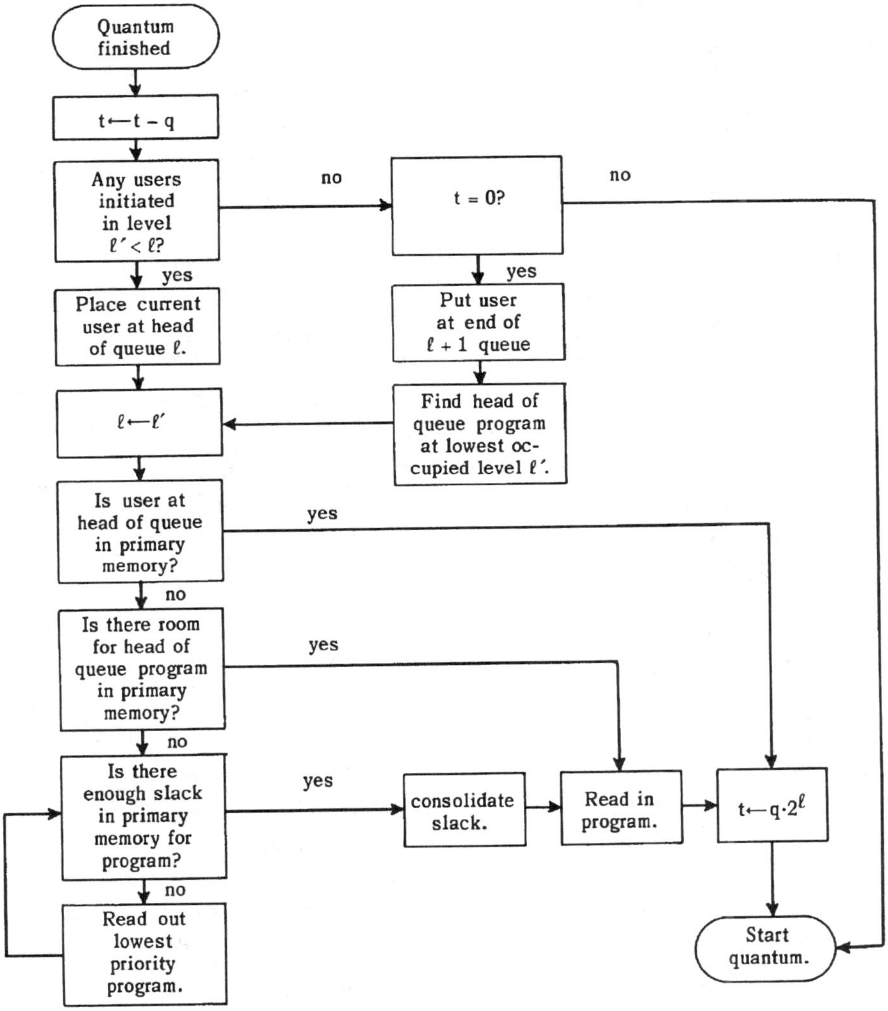

Figure 2 Flow chart of multi-level scheduling algorithm.

max l_0, we deduce as a conservative estimate that N can be 4 and that at worst the response time for a trivial reply will be 32 seconds.

The small value of N arrived at is a direct consequence of the small value of w_q that results from the slow disc word transmission rate. This rate is only 3.3% of the maximum core memory multiplexor rate. It is of interest that using high-capacity high-speed drums of current design such as in the Sage System or in the IBM Sabre System it would be possible to attain nearly 100% multiplexor utilization and thus multiply w_q by a factor of 30. It immediately follows that user response times equivalent to those given above with the disc unit would be given to 30 times as many persons or to 120 users; the total computational capacity, however, would not change.

In any case, considerable caution should be used with capacity and computer response time estimates since they are critically dependent upon the distribution functions for the user response time, t_u, and the user program size, w_p, and the computational capacity requested by each user. Past experience using conventional programming systems is of little assistance because these distribution functions will depend very strongly upon the programming systems made available to the time-sharing users as well as upon the user habit patterns which will gradually evolve.

Conclusions

In conclusion, it is clear that contemporary computers and hardware are sufficient to allow moderate performance time-sharing for a limited number of users. There are several problems which can be solved by careful hardware design, but there are also a large number of intricate system programs which must be written before one has an adequate time-sharing system. An important aspect of any future time-shared computer is that until the system programming is completed, especially the critical time-sharing supervisor, the computer is completely worthless. Thus, it is essential for future system design and implementation that all aspects of time-sharing system problems be explored and understood in prototype form on present computers so that major advances in computer organization and usage can be made.

Acknowledgements

The authors wish to thank Bernard Galler, Robert Graham and Bruce Arden, of the University of Michigan, for making the MAD compiler available and for their advice with regard to its adaption into the present time-sharing system. The version of the Madtran Fortran-to-Mad editor program was generously supplied by Robert Rosin of the University of Michigan. Of the MIT Computation Center staff, Robert Creasy was of assistance in the evaluation of time-sharing performance, Lynda Korn is to be credited for her contributions to the pm and madtran commands, and Evelyn Dow for her work on the fap command.

References

1. Strachey, C., "Time Sharing in Large Fast Computers," *Proceedings of the International Conference on Information Processing, UNESCO* (June, 1959), Paper B.2.19.
2. Licklider, J. C. R., "Man-Computer Symbiosis," *IRE Transactions on Human Factors in Electronics, HFE-1*, No. 1 (March, 1960), 4-11.
3. Brown, G., Licklider, J. C. R., McCarthy, J., and Perlis, A., Lectures given spring, 1961, *Management and the Computer of the Future*, (to be published by the M.I.T. Press, March, 1962).
4. Corbató, F. J., "An Experimental Time-Sharing System," *Proceedings of the IBM University Director's Conference*, July, 1961 (to be published).
5. Schmitt, W. F., Tonik, A. B., "Sympathetically Programmed Computers," *Proceedings of the International Conference on Information Procesing, UNESCO*, (June, 1959) Paper B.2.18.
6. Codd, E. F., "Multiprogram Scheduling," *Communications of the ACM, 3*, 6 (June, 1960), 347-350.
7. Heller, J., "Sequencing Aspects of Multiprogramming," *Journal of the ACM, 8*, 3 (Juy, 1961), 426-439.
8. Leeds, H. D., Weinberg, G. M., "Multi-programming," *Computer Programming Fundamentals*, 356-359, McGraw-Hill (1961).
9. Teager, H. M., "Real-Time Time-Shared Computer Project," *Communications of the ACM, 5*, 1 (January, 1962) Research Summaries, 62.
10. Teager, H. M., McCarthy, J., "Time-Shared Program Testing," paper delivered at the *14th National Meeting of the ACM* (not published).

8

A GENERAL-PURPOSE FILE SYSTEM FOR SECONDARY STORAGE*

ROBERT C. DALEY AND PETER G. NEUMANN

(1965)

1 INTRODUCTION

The need for a versatile on-line secondary storage complex in a multiprogramming environment is immense. During on-line interaction, user owned off-line detachable storage media such as cards and tape become highly undesirable. On the other hand, if all users are to be able to retain as much information as they wish in machine-accessible secondary storage, various needs become crucial: Little-used information must percolate to devices with longer access times, to allow ample space on faster devices for more frequently used files. Furthermore, information must be easy to access when required, it must be safe from accidents and maliciousness, and it should be accessible to other users on an easily controllable basis when desired. Finally, any consideration which is not basic to a user's ability to manipulate this information should be invisible to him unless he specifies otherwise.

The basic formulation of a file system designed to meet these needs is presented here. This formulation provides the user with a simple means of addressing an essentially infinite amount of secondary storage in a machine-independent and device independent fashion. The basic structure of the file system is independent of machine considerations. Within a hierarchy of files, the user is aware only of symbolic addresses. All physical addressing of a multilevel complex of secondary storage devices is done by the file system, and is not seen by the user.

---

*R. C. Daley and P. G. Neumann, A general-purpose file system for secondary storage. *Fall Joint Computer Conference 27*, 1965, 213–229.

Section 2 of the paper presents the hierarchical structure of files, which permits flexible use of the system. This structure contains sufficient capabilities to assure versatility. A set of representative control features is presented. Typical commands to the file system are also indicated, but are not elaborated upon; although the existence of these commands is crucial, the actual details of their specific implementations may vary without affecting the design of the basic file structure and of the access control.

Section 3 discusses the file backup system, which makes secondary storage appear to the user as a single essentially infinite storage medium. The backup system also provides for salvage and catastrophe reload procedures in the event of machine or system failure. Finally, Section 4 presents a summary of the file system program modules and their interrelationship with one another. The modularity of design enables modules affecting secondary storage device usage to be altered without changing other modules. Similarly, the files are formatless at the level of the file system, so that any changes in format do not affect the basic structure of the file system. Machine independence is attempted wherever it is meaningful.

Sections 2 and 3 are essentially self-contained, and may be read independently of the companion papers (see references 1–5). Section 4 requires a knowledge of the first three papers.

2 THE FILE STRUCTURE AND ACCESS CONTROL

In this section of the paper, the logical organization of the file structure is presented. The file structure consists of a basic tree hierarchy of files, across which links may be added to facilitate simple access to files elsewhere in the hierarchy. Each file has an independent means for controlling the way in which it may be used. If files are to be shared among various users in a way which can be flexibly controlled, various forms of safeguards are desirable. These include:

- S1. Safety from someone masquerading as someone else;
- S2. Safety from accidents or maliciousness by someone specifically permitted controlled access;
- S3. Safety from accidents or maliciousness by someone specifically denied access;
- S4. Safety from accidents self-inflicted;

S5. Total privacy, if needed, with access only by one user or a set of users;

S6. Safety from hardware or system software failures;

S7. Security of system safeguards themselves from tampering by non-authorized users;

S8. Safeguard against overzealous application of other safeguards.

These safeguards recur in the subsequent discussion. The various features of the file system presented below are summarized in Section 2.4, along with the way in which these features help to provide the above safeguards.

2.1 Basic Concepts

In the context of this paper, the word "user" refers to a person, or to a process, or possibly to a class of persons and/or processes. The concept of the user is rigorously defined in terms of a fixed number of *components*, such as an accounting number, a project number, and a name. (Classes of users may be defined by leaving certain components unspecified.) For present purposes, the only users considered are those who employ the file system by means of its normal calls.

A *file* is simply an ordered sequence of *elements*, where an element could be a machine word, a character, or a bit, depending upon the implementation. A user may create, modify or delete files only through the use of the file system. At the level of the file system, a file is formatless. All formatting is done by higher-level modules or by user-supplied programs, if desired. As far as a particular user is concerned, a file has one name, and that name is symbolic. (Symbolic names may be arbitrarily long, and may have syntax of their own. For example, they may consist of several parts, some of which are relevant to the nature of the file, e.g., ALPHA FAP DEBUG.) The user may reference an element in the file by specifying the symbolic file name and the linear index of the element within the file. By using higher-level modules, a user may also be able to reference suitably defined sequences of elements directly by context.

A *directory* is a special file which is maintained by the file system, and which contains a list of *entries*. To a user, an entry appears to be a file and is accessed in terms of its symbolic *entry name*, which is the user's file name. An entry name need be unique only within the directory in which it occurs. In reality, each entry is a pointer of one of two kinds. The entry may point directly to a file (which may itself be a directory) which is stored in secondary storage, or else it may point to another entry in the same or another directory. An entry which points directly to a file is called a *branch*, while an entry which points to another directory entry is called a *link*. Except for a pathological case mentioned below, a link always eventually points to a branch (although possibly via a chain of links to the branch), and thence to a file. Thus the link and the branch both *effectively point* to the file. (In general, a user will usually not need to know whether a given entry is a branch or a link, but he easily may find out.)

Each branch contains a description of the way in which it may be used and of the way in which it is being used. This description includes information such as the actual physical address of the file, the time this file was created or last modified, the time the file was last referred to, and access control information for the branch (see below). The description also includes the current state of the file (open for reading by N users, open for reading and writing by one user, open for data sharing by N users, or inactive), discussed in Section 4. Some of this information is unavailable to the user.

The only information associated with a link is the pointer to the entry to which it links. This pointer is specified in terms of a symbolic name which uniquely identifies the linked entry within the hierarchy. A link derives its access control information from the branch to which it effectively points.

2.2 The Hierarchy of the File Structure

The hierarchical file structure is discussed here. The discussion of access control features for selected privacy and controlled sharing are deferred until Section 2.3. For ease of understanding, the file structure may be thought of as a tree of files, some of which are directories. That is, with one exception, each file (e.g., each directory) finds itself directly pointed to by exactly one branch in exactly one directory. The exception is the root directory, or *root*, at the root of the tree. Although it is not explicitly pointed to from any directory, the root is implicitly pointed to by a fictitious branch which is known to the file system.

A file directly pointed to in some directory is *immediately inferior* to that directory (and the directory is *immediately superior* to the file). A file which is immediately inferior to a directory which is itself immediately inferior to a second directory is *inferior* to the second directory (and similarly the second directory is *superior* to the file). The root has level zero, and files immediately inferior to it have level one. By extension, inferiority (or superiority) is defined for any number of levels of separation via a chain of immediately inferior (superior) files. (The reader who is disturbed by the level numbers increasing with inferiority may pretend that level numbers have negative signs.) Links are then considered to be superimposed upon, but independent of, the tree structure. Note that the notions of inferiority and superiority are not concerned with links, but only with branches.

In a tree hierarchy of this kind, it seems desirable that a user be able to work in one or a few directories, rather than having to move about continually. It is thus natural for the hierarchy to be so arranged that users with similar interests can share common files and yet have private files when desired. At any one time, a user is considered to be operating in some one directory, called his *working directory.* He may access a file effectively pointed to by an entry in his working directory simply by specifying the entry name. More than one user may have the same working directory at one time.

An example of a simple tree hierarchy without links is shown in Fig. 1. Nonterminal nodes, which are shown as circles, indicate files which are directories, while the lines downward from each such node indicate the entries (i.e., branches) in the directory corresponding to that node. The terminal nodes, which are shown as squares, indicate files other than directories. Letters indicate entry names, while numbers are used for descriptive purposes only, to identify directories in the figure. For example, the letter "J" is the entry name of various entries in different directories in the figure, while the number "0" refers to the root.

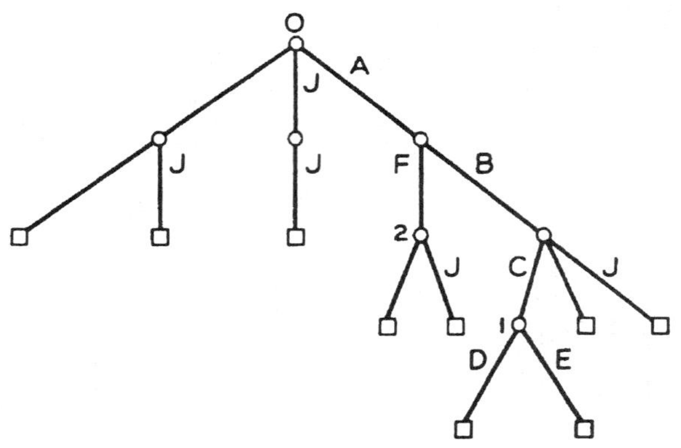

Figure 1 An example of a hierarchy without links.

An entry name is meaningful only with respect to the directory in which it occurs, and may or may not be unique outside of that directory. For various reasons, it is desirable to have a symbolic name which does uniquely define an entry in the hierarchy as a whole. Such a name is obtained relative to the root, and is called the *tree name.* It consists of the chain of entry names required to reach the entry via a chain of branches from the root. For example, the tree name of the directory corresponding to the node marked 1 in Fig. 1 is A:B:C, where a colon is used to separate entry names. (The two files with entry names D and E shown in this directory have tree names A:B:C:D and A:B:C:E, respectively.) In most cases, the user will not need to know the tree name of an entry.

Unless specifically stated otherwise, the tree name of a file is defined relative to the root. However, a file may also be named uniquely relative to an arbitrary directory, as follows. If a file X is inferior to a directory Y, the tree name of X relative to Y is the chain of entry names required to reach X from Y. If X is superior to Y. the tree name of X relative to Y consists of a chain of asterisks, one for each level of immediate superiority. (Note that since only the tree structure is being considered, each file other than the root has exactly one immediately superior file.) If the file is neither inferior nor superior to the directory, first find the directory Z with the maximum level which is superior to both X and Y. Then the tree name of X relative to Y consists of the tree name of Z relative to X (a chain of asterisks) followed by the tree name of Y relative to Z (a chain of entry names). For the example of Fig. 1, consider the two directories marked 1 and 2. The tree name of 1 relative to 2 is :*:B:C, while the tree name of 2 relative to 1 is :*:*:F. An initial colon is used to indicate a name which is relative to the working directory. A link with an arbitrary name (LINKNAME) may be established to an entry in another directory by means of a command

```
LINK LINKNAME, PATHNAME.
```

(A command is merely a subroutine call.) The name of the entry to be linked to (PATHNAME) may be specified as a tree name relative to the working directory or to the root, or more generally as a path name (defined below). Note that a file may thus have different names to different users, depending on how it is accessed. A link serves as a shortcut to a branch somewhere else in the hierarchy, and gives the user the illusion that the link is actually a branch pointing directly to the desired file. Although the links add no basic capabilities to those already present within the tree structure of branches, they greatly facilitate the ease with which the file system may be used.

Links also help to eliminate the need for duplicate copies of sharable files. The superimposing of links upon the tree structure of Fig. 1 is illustrated in Fig. 2. The dashed lines downward from a node show entries which are links to other entries. When the links are added to the tree structure, the result is a directed graph. (The direction is of course downward from each node.)

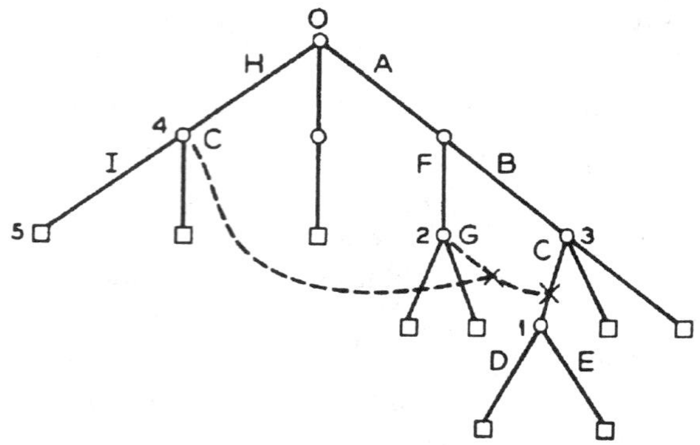

Figure 2 The example of Fig. 1 with links added.

In the example of Fig 2, the entry named G in directory 2 is a link to the branch named C in directory 3. The entry named C in directory 4 (recall that entry names need not be unique except within a directory) is a link to the entry G in directory 2, and thus acts as a link to C in directory 3. Both of these links effectively point to the directory 1.

It is desirable to have a name analogous to the tree name which includes links. Such a name is the *path name*, and is assumed to be relative to the root unless specifically stated otherwise. The path name of a file (relative to the root) is the chain of entry names used to name the file, relative to the root. (For example, the directory 1 in Fig. 2 may have path name A:B:C;D, A:F:G or H:C, depending on its usage.) The working directory is always established in terms of a path name. A user may change his working directory by means of a command such as

```
CHANGEDIRECTORY PATHNAME,
```

where the path name may be relative to the (old) working directory or to the root. The definition of a path name relative to a directory other than the root is similar to the definition of a tree name, with the following exceptions:

the concept of a file immediately inferior to a directory is replaced by the concept of a file effectively pointed to by the entry. The concept of a directory immediately superior to a file is replaced by a concept which is well defined only as the inverse of the above effective pointer, that is, dependent on what entry in which directory was previously used to reach the file.

In general, any file may be specified by a path name (which may in fact be a tree name, or an entry name) relative to the current working directory. A file may also be specified by a path name relative to the root. In the former case, the path name begins with a colon, in the latter case it does not.

To illustrate these somewhat elusive concepts, consider the example of Fig. 2. Suppose that the working directory has the path name H (i.e., directory 4). The command

```
CHANGEDIRECTORY :C
```

results in the working directory with path name H:C (i.e., directory 1). Subsequent reference to a file with path name : * :1 (relative to the working directory with path name H:C) refers to the file 5 in the figure. The command

```
CHANGEDIRECTORY :*
```

results in restoring the original working directory with path name H. (With this interpretation of *, the user believes he is working in a tree. Note that the design could be modified so that a path other than the one used on the way down could be used on the way back up toward the root, but not without adding considerable complexity to the design.)

The pathological case referred to above with respect to a link effectively pointing to a file arises as follows. Consider again Fig. 2. Suppose that the branch C in directory 3 is deleted from this directory; suppose also that in the same directory a link with name C is then established to the entry C in directory 4, e.g., by means of the command

```
LINK C,H:C.
```

Access to entry C in directory 3 (or to entry G in 2, or C in 4, for that matter) then results in a loop in which no branch is ever found. This and similar loops in which no branch is found may be broken in various ways, for example, by observing whether an entry is used twice on the same access. Note that much more devious loops may arise, as for example that resulting from the establishment of a link (named K) from directory 1 to entry H in the root. Then the path name :C:K relative to directory 4 refers to directory 4 itself. This and similar loops which involve chains of directories are inherent in the use of links, and may in fact be used constructively.

2.3 Access Control

An initial sign-on procedure is normally desirable in order to establish the identity of the user for accounting purposes. It may also be necessary to control the way in which the user may use the system. There are two basic approaches to using the hierarchy of files described here. First, the file structure may be *essentially open*, with initial access unrestricted and with subsequent access permitted to all other directories unless specifically denied. On the other hand, the file structure may be *essentially closed*, with initial access restricted for any user to a particular initial directory (assuming his ability to give a password, for example) and with subsequent access to other directories denied unless specifically permitted. There are in fact arguments for each extreme. The essentially open scheme implies that locks need be placed only where they are essential (and most effective). The essentially closed scheme provides well-defined working areas, frees the user from worrying about other users, and helps prevent the user's files from being accidentally altered. It may be observed that the scope of capabilities of the file structure described here does not depend on whether the structure is essentially open or closed. In practice, a position somewhere in between the two extremes is likely to result.

In attempting to access a file, a user may or may not be successful, depending upon what he is trying to do. The basic framework within which permissions are granted is now considered. This framework is independent of the file structure described above. Although the exact set of permissions may therefore vary from system to system, a flexible set adequate for normal usage is given here as an illustration. All permissions are logically on the branches which point to files. (In actual implementation, however, there may in some cases be permissions associated with a directory rather than repeated for each entry in that directory.)

The set of permissions with which a given user may access a particular branch is called the *mode* of the branch for that user. Associated with each branch is an *access control list*, which contains the list of users (or sets of users) along with the corresponding mode associated with each user. The permissions for any users on the list may be overridden (assuming permission to do so—see below) by adding subsequent users and modes to the list. The list is scanned in order of recency, and thus the addition acts as an override. (Each time the access control list is changed, a garbage collection is performed in order to keep the list nonredundant.) All access control information required for the use of a given file is contained in the list on the branch pointing to that file, and is thus independent of the way in which the file was accessed.

The mode consists of five *attributes*, named TRAP, READ, EXECUTE, WRITE and APPEND, each of which is either ON or OFF. In performing access control, the TRAP attribute is examined first. It is by itself powerful enough to accomplish the roles of the other four attributes, which are called *usage attributes*. However, the four usage attributes are included here for ease of description, as well as for ease of use of the system. The four usage attributes indicate permission to perform the given activity on the branch by the particular user only if the corresponding attribute is ON. The function of each attribute is now defined.

TRAP. When a branch has the TRAP attribute ON for a given user, a trap occurs on any reference by that user which affects the contents of the file to which that branch points. In this case, the access control module calls a procedure whose name is given as the first entry of a *trap list*. A trap list may be associated with each user in the access control list. Additional parameters may be defined in the trap list, and are passed as constants to the called procedure. Furthermore, all pertinent information regarding the branch as well as the calling sequence which caused the trap are passed to the called procedure. The traps are processed in the order specified by the trap list. The return to the access control module specifies the effective values of the four usage attributes which are to govern the access. The returned value may override the initial values of these attributes.

The user of a branch may inhibit the trap process. In this case, all references to an entry with the TRAP attribute ON cause an error return to the calling procedure. The TRAP attribute is extremely useful for monitoring of file usage, for placing additional restrictions on access (e.g., user-applied locks), for obtaining subroutines only if and when they are actually referenced, etc. A pair of commands such as LOCK and UNLOCK provide the user with a standard way of applying locks on an entry.

```
LOCK FILENAME,KEY

UNLOCK FILENAME
```

(FILENAME is the name of a branch given as a path name.) The command LOCK inserts a trap which on each attempted access may request the user to supply the designated key, and permit access only if the key is correctly supplied. UNLOCK removes the lock. (A timelock command might also be desirable, for example, to make a given branch available to a particular user only between certain times on certain days.) These commands are available to a user only if the branch pointing to the directory which contains the entry FILENAME has the WRITE attribute ON for that user (see below).

The Usage Attributes. The READ, EXECUTE, WRITE and APPEND attributes govern permission to perform operations upon files with certain intents, with an intent corresponding to each attribute. Every operation on a given branch implies one of the four intents, namely *read, execute, write or append.* The interpretation of the intent depends upon whether the accessed branch points to a directory (a *directory branch*) or to a nondirectory (a *nondirectory branch*), as seen below.

If a branch is a nondirectory branch, the meaning of each intent is quite simple. The read intent is the desire to read the contents of the file. The execute intent is the desire to execute the contents of the file as a procedure. The write intent is the desire to alter the contents of the file without adding to the end of it. The append intent is the desire to add to the end of the file without altering its original contents. The attribute on a nondirectory branch which corresponds to the particular intent of an operation on that branch indicates permission to carry out that operation only if that attribute is ON.

If a branch is a directory branch, the meaning of each intent is different. The read intent is the desire to read those contents of the directory which may be available to the user, i.e., to obtain an itemization of the directory entries. The execute intent is the desire to search the directory. The write intent is the desire to alter existing entries in the directory without adding new ones. This includes renaming entries, deleting entries, and changing the access control list for branches in that directory. The last of these includes adding traps to the trap list and changing the usage attributes. The append intent is the desire to add new entries without altering the original entries. The attribute on a directory branch which corresponds to the particular intent of an operation on that branch indicates permission to carry out that operation only if that attribute is ON.

Several additional examples of system commands are now given. Assuming the necessary WRITE attributes are ON for the appropriate directory branches, a user may by use of suitable commands change the access control list of entries or delete entries in various ways. For example, he may change (wherever permitted by the WRITE attribute of an inferior branch) the list for all inferior directory branches, or for all inferior nondirectory branches, or for all inferior nondirectory branches whose names include the parts FAP DEBUG, or for all directory branches not more than some number of levels inferior. Similarly, an elaborate delete command may be constructed. (The possibility of no one having the WRITE attribute ON for a given directory branch can be combated in various ways. One way is not to permit a change in the list to occur which brings about this circumstance, another way is to make this condition imply no restriction.)

Assuming that the necessary READ attributes are ON for the appropriate directory branches, a user may obtain an itemization of desired portions of desired inferior directories, possibly obtaining a graphical picture of the hierarchy.

2.4 Summary of File System Features

At this point, it is desirable to summarize the various features of the file system, and to state which of these contribute to which of the safeguards S1 through S8 mentioned above. The basic features of the file system may be stated as follows:

F1. The inherent hierarchical structure of the file system itself;

F2. The access control which may be associated with a directory branch;

F3. The backup procedures (discussed in the next section).

In addition, certain aspects of the hardware and of the central software also contribute to providing these safeguards:

F4. The hardware, and central software system [2, 3].

The ways in which the safeguards S1–S8 interact with the features F1–F4 are summarized in Table 1.

3 SECONDARY STORAGE BACKUP AND RETRIEVAL

One important aspect of the file system is that the user is given the illusion that the capacity of file storage is infinite. This concept is felt to be extremely important, as it gives all responsibility for remembering files to the system rather than to the individual user. Many computer installations already find

Table 1 The features of the file system and which safeguards they assist in providing.

Safeguards	MASQ	PERM	DENY	SELF	PRIV	BUGS	TAMP	ZEAL
Features	S1	S2	S3	S4	S5	S6	S7	S8
F1. Hierarchy	Y		Y	Y	Y	Y		
F2. Attributes	Y	Y	Y	Y	Y	Y	Y	Y
F3. Backup	Y	Y		Y		Y		
F4. System			Y		Y	Y	Y	

Note: Y = YES, the feature does exist. Blank = NO, it does not.

themselves in the business of providing tape and card-file storage for their users. It is intended that most of this need will be replaced by the file system in a more general and orderly manner.

That portion of the file system storage complex which is immediately accessible to the file system, i.e. disks and drums, is called the *on-line storage system.* Devices which are removable from the storage complex, such as tapes, data cells and disk packs which are used by the file system as an extension of the on-line facilities, are called the *file backup storage system.* To the user, all files appear to be on line, although access to some files may be somewhat delayed. For the purpose of discussion, a backup system consisting only of magnetic tape is considered. However, the system presented here is readily adaptable to other devices.

Incremental Dumping of New Files

Whenever a user signs off, additional copies of all files created or modified by that user are made in duplicate on a pair of magnetic tapes. At the end of every N hour period, any newly created or modified files which have not previously been dumped are also copied to these tapes. When this is done, the tapes are removed from the machine and replaced by a fresh set of tapes for the next N hour period. Typically N would be a period of between 2 and 4 hours. This procedure has the advantage that the effects of the most catastrophic machine or system failure can be confined to the N hour dumping period.

Weekly Dumping of Frequently Used Files

In the event of a catastrophe, the on-line storage system could be reloaded from these incremental dump tapes. However, since many valuable files, including system programs, may not have been modified for a year or over, this method of reloading is far too impractical. In order to minimize the time necessary to recover after a catastrophe, a weekly dump is prepared of all files which have been used within the last M weeks. This dump is also made on duplicate tapes for reliability.

Actually this weekly dump is taken in two parts. The first part consists of all files which must be present in order to start and run the basic system. The second part consists of all other files which have been used within the last M week period. Typically M would be a period of about three to five weeks. The weekly dump tapes may be released for other use after a period of about two or three months. The incremental dump tapes must be kept indefinitely. However, it may be advantageous to consolidate these tapes periodically by deleting obsolete files.

Catastrophe Reload Procedure

Should a catastrophe occur in which the entire contents of the on-line storage system is lost, the following reload procedure can be used. First reload a copy of the system files from the most recent weekly dump tapes. When this has been done the system may be started, with the rest of the reloading process continuing under the control of the system. Note that this does not necessarily represent the most recent copy of the system. If an important system change has been made since the weekly dump was taken, it may be necessary to reload the incremental tapes before starting the system.

After the system files are reloaded, the incremental dump tapes are reloaded in reverse chronological order, starting with the most recent set of incremental tapes. This process is continued until the time of the last weekly dump is reached. At this time, the second part of the weekly dump tapes is reloaded. During this process all redundant or obsolete files are ignored. The date and time a file is created or last modified is used to insure that only the most recent copy of a file remains in the on-line storage system. Since directories are dumped and reloaded in the same manner as ordinary files, the contents of the on-line storage system can be accurately restored.

It is possible to continue to load the older weekly tapes until the on-line system is totally reloaded. However, the amount of new information picked up from these tapes becomes increasingly small as one goes further back in time. In view of this, files which do not appear on the most recent set of weekly dump tapes, due to inactivity, are not reloaded at this time. Instead, a trap is added to the Appropriate directory branch so that a retrieval procedure is called when the file is first referenced. This allows these files to be reloaded as needed by the retrieval mechanism which is discussed later in this paper.

On-Line Storage Salvage Procedure

Although the catastrophe reload procedure can accurately reconstruct the contents of the on-line storage system, it is normally used only as a backstop against the most catastrophic of machine or system failures. When the milder and more common failures occur, it is often possible to salvage the contents of secondary storage without having to resort to the reload procedure. If this can be done, many files which have been created or modified since the end of the last incremental dump period can be saved. In addition, much of the time necessary to run the reload procedure can also be saved.

The usual result of a machine or system failure is that the contents of secondary storage are left in a state which is inconsistent. For example, two completely unrelated directory entries may end up pointing to the same physical location in secondary storage, while the storage assignment tables indicate that this area of storage is unused. If the system were restarted at this time, the situation might never be resolved. The usual effect is that any information subsequently assigned to that area of secondary storage is likely to be overwritten.

This situation arises when the system goes down before the file system has updated its assignment tables and directories on secondary storage. What has probably happened is that some user has deleted a file and another user created a new file which was assigned to the area of storage just vacated by the previous file. When the system goes down, the changes have not been recorded in secondary storage. This is only one example of the type of trouble which occurs when the system fails unexpectedly.

The salvage procedure is designed to read through all the directories in the hierarchy and correct inconsistent information wherever possible. The remaining erroneous files and directory entries are deleted or truncated at the point at which the error was found. Storage assignment tables are corrected so that only one branch points to the same area of secondary storage. Since it is necessary to read only the directories and the storage assignment tables, the salvage procedure can be run in a small percentage of the time necessary to run a complete reload procedure.

The salvage procedure also serves as a useful diagnostic tool, since it provides a printout of every error found and the action taken. This program can also be run in a mode in which it only detects errors but does not try to correct them.

Retrieval of Files from Backup Storage

Unless a file has been explicitly deleted by a user, the directory entry for that file remains in the file system indefinitely. If, for some reason, the file associated with this entry does not currently reside on an on-line storage device, the corresponding branch for that file contains a trap to a file retrieval procedure. When a user references a file which is in this condition, his process traps to the retrieval procedure. At this time the user may elect to wait until the file is retrieved from the backup system, to request that the file be retrieved while he works on something else, to abort the process that requested the files or to delete the directory entry.

If the user elects to retrieve the file, the date and time the file was created or last modified (which are available from the directory entry) are used to select the correct set of incremental dump tapes. The retrieval procedure requests the tape operator to find and mount these tapes. These tapes are then searched until the precise copy of the requested file is found and reloaded. At this time the original access control list of the branch is restored, and the file is now ready to be used by the user.

If a user deletes a file, both the file and the corresponding directory entry are deleted. However, if a copy of this file appears on a set of incremental dump tapes, this copy is not deleted at this time. This file can still be retrieved if the user specifies the approximate date and time when the file was created or last modified. To help the user in this situation, the incremental dump procedure provides a listing for the operations staff of the contents of each set of incremental tapes. These listings are kept in a log book which may be consulted by the operators in situations such as the above. Selected portions of this listing may be made available to the user.

The user is able to declare that he wishes a certain file to be removed from the on-line storage system without deleting the corresponding directory entry. This may be accomplished by using a system procedure which places the file in a state where it can be retrieved by the normal retrieval procedure.

General Reliability

Since the file system is designed to provide the principal information storage facility for all users of the system, the full responsibility for all considerations of reliability rests with the file system. For this reason all dumping, retrieval and reloading procedures use duplicate sets of tapes. These tapes are formatted in such a manner as to minimize the possibility of unrecoverable error conditions. When reading from these tapes during a reload or retrieval process, multiple errors on both sets of tapes can be corrected as long as the errors do not occur in the same physical record of both tapes. If an error occurs which cannot be corrected, only the information which was in error is lost. If the error is a simple parity error, the information is accepted as if no error occurred. When a user first attempts to use a file in which a parity or other error was found, he is notified of this condition through a system procedure using the trap mechanism.

Secondary Storage Allotments

The file system assigns all secondary storage dynamically as needed. In general, no areas of the on-line storage system are permanently assigned to a user. A user may keep an essentially infinite amount of information within the file system. However, it is necessary to control the amount of information which can be kept in the on-line storage system at a time.

When a user first signs on, the file system is given an account name or number. All files subsequently created by this user are labeled with his account name. When the user wishes to increase his usage of secondary storage, the file system calls upon a secondary storage accounting procedure giving the user's account name and the amount and class of storage requested.

The accounting procedure maintains records of all secondary storage usage and allotments. A storage allotment is defined as the amount of information which a particular account is allowed to keep in the on-line storage system at one time. Normally the accounting procedure allows a process to exceed the allotment after informing the file system that the account is overdrawn. However, the accounting procedure may decide to interrupt the user's process if the amount of online storage already used seems unreasonable.

Multilevel Nature of Secondary Storage

In most cases a user does not need to know how or where a file is stored by the file system. A user's primary concern is that the file be readily available to him when he needs it. In general, only the file system knows on which device a file resides.

The file system is designed to accommodate any configuration of secondary storage devices. These devices may cover a wide range of speeds and capacities. All considerations of speed and efficiency of storage devices are left to the file system. Thus all user programs and all other system programs are independent of the particular configuration of secondary storage.

All permanent secondary storage devices are assigned a level number according to the relative speed of the device. The devices which have the highest transmission and access rates are assigned the highest level numbers. As files become active, they are automatically moved to the highest-level storage device available. This process is tempered by considerations such as the size of the file and the frequency of use.

As more space is needed on a particular storage device, the least active files are moved to a lower-level storage device. Files which belong to overdrawn accounts are moved first. Files continue to be moved to lower-level storage until the desired amount of higher-level storage is freed. If a file must be moved from the lowest-level on-line storage device, the file is removed and the branch for this file is set to trap to the retrieval procedure.

4 FILE SYSTEM PROGRAM STRUCTURE

This section describes the basic program structure of the file system presented in the preceding sections, as implemented in the Multics system [1]. (It is assumed here that the reader is familiar with the papers referred to in references 1, 2 and 3.)

A user may reference data elements in a file explicitly through read and write statements, or implicitly by means of segment addressing. It should be noted here that the word "file" is not being used in the traditional sense (i.e., to specify any input or output device). In the Multics system a file is a linear array of data which is referenced by means of a symbolic name or segment number and a linear index. In general, a user will not know how or on what device a file is stored.

A Multics file is a segment, and all segments are files [1, 3]. Although a file may sometimes be referenced as an input or an output device, only a file can be referenced through segment addressing. For example, a tape or a teletype cannot be referenced as a segment, and therefore cannot be regarded as a file by this definition.

Input or output requests which are directed to I/O devices other than files (i.e. tapes, teletypes, printers, card readers, etc.) will be processed directly by a Device Interface Module (see reference 4) which is designed to handle I/O requests for that device. However, I/O requests which are directed to a file will be processed by a special procedure known as the File System Interface Module (see reference 4). This module acts as a device interface module for files within the file system. Unlike other device interface modules, this procedure does not explicitly issue I/O requests. Instead, the file system interface module accomplishes its I/O implicitly by means of segment addressing and by issuing declarative calls to the basic file system indicating how certain areas of a segment are to be overlayed.

4.1 The Basic File System

Whether a user refers to a file through the use of read and write statements or by means of segment addressing, ultimately a segment must be made available to his process. The basic file system may now be defined as that part of the central software which manages segments. In general this package performs the following basic functions.

1. Maintain directories of existing segments (files)
2. Make segments available to a process upon request.
3. Create new segments.
4. Delete existing segments.

Figure 3 is a rough block diagram of the modules which make up the basic file system. This diagram is by no means complete but is used here to give the reader an overall view of the basic flow. The directional lines indicate the flow of control through the use of formal calling sequences, with formal return implied. Lines with double arrowheads are used to indicate possible flow of control in either direction. The circles in the diagram indicate some of the data bases which are common to the modules indicated. The modules and data bases drawn below the dotted line must at least partially reside in core memory at all times since they will be invoked during a missing-page fault (see reference 3).

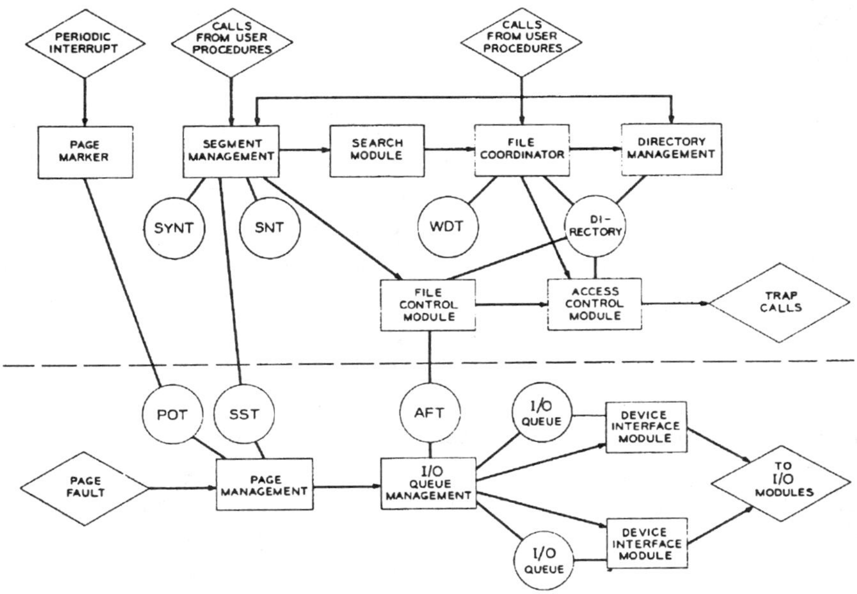

Figure 3 The basic file system.

Segment Management Module

The segment management module maintains records of all segments which are known to the current process. A segment is *known to a process* once a segment number has been assigned to that segment for this process. A segment which is known to a process is *active* if the page table for that segment is currently in core. If the page table is not currently in core, that segment is *inactive.*

If a segment is known to a process, an entry will exist for that segment in the Segment Name Table (SNT). This entry contains the call name, the tree name and the segment number of the segment (file) along with other information pertinent to the segment as used by this process. The *call name* is a symbolic name used by the user to reference a segment. This name normally corresponds to an entry in the user's directory hierarchy which effectively points to the desired file. It should be noted that a different copy of the segment name table exists for each individual process.

If a segment is active, an entry for that segment exists in the Segment Status Table (SST). This table is common to all processes and contains an entry for each active segment. If a segment is inactive (no page table is in core), no entry exists for that segment in this table. Each entry in the segment status table contains information such as the number of processes to which this segment is known and a pointer which may be used to reference the file or files which are to receive all I/O resulting from paging this segment in and out of core [3]. When a user references a segment for the first time, a directed fault will occur. At this time control is passed to a procedure known as the linker [3]. This procedure picks up the symbolic segment call name from a pointer contained in the machine word causing the fault. The linker must now establish a segment number from this symbolic name. An entry to the segment management module is provided for precisely this purpose. When a call is made to the segment management module to establish a segment number from a call name, the segment name table is searched for that call name. If the call name is found in the segment name table, the segment number from this table is returned immediately to the calling procedure. However, if this is not the case, the segment management module must take the following steps.

1. Locate the segment (file) in the user's directory hierarchy via a call to the search module.

2. Assign a segment number for this segment.

3. Update the segment name table indicating that this segment is now known to this process.

4. Open the file or files which are to receive I/O resulting from paging.

5. Create or update the appropriate entry in the segment status table.

6. Establish a page table and segment descriptor for this segment if the segment was not already active for some other process.

7. Return the segment number to the calling procedure.

If a segment is known to a process but is not currently active, the descriptor for that segment will indicate a fault condition. If and when this fault occurs, the segment can be reactivated by locating the approve private entry in the segment name table and repeating steps 4 through 7. Note that the segment does not have to be located again in the directory hierarchy since the tree name is retained in the segment name table.

If a segment is to be modified during its use in a process, the user may elect to modify a copy of that segment rather than the original. When this is the case, the copying of this segment is done dynamically as a by-product of paging. However, if the copying is not complete at the time the segment becomes inactive, the copying must be completed at this time.

If a segment is to be copied, there are actually two open files involved, the original file and the copy or *execution file*. When a page table is initially constructed by the segment management module, each entry in that page table will contain a fault indication and a flag indicating what action should be taken if and when that fault occurs. This flag may indicate one of the following actions:

1. Assign a blank page.
2. Retrieve the missing page from the original file.
3. Retrieve the missing page from the execution file.

Once a page has been paged out (written) into the execution file, it must be retrieved from that file.

An entry to the segment management module is provided by which a user may declare a synonym or list of synonyms for a segment name. For example, a user may have a certain procedure which references a segment called "Gamma" and another procedure which references a segment called "Alpha." If the user wishes to operate both procedures as part of the same process using a segment called "Data" he may do so by declaring Alpha and Gamma to be synonyms for Data. This association is kept by the segment management module in a Synonym Table (SYNT). Whenever the segment management module is presented with a call name which has been defined as a synonym, the appropriate name is substituted before any further processing takes place.

In addition to the functions described above, the segment management module provides entries through which the user may ask questions or make declarations involving the use of segments known to his process. Some of these functions are listed below.

1. Declare that a segment or some specific locations within a segment are no longer needed at this time.
2. Declare that a segment or some specific locations within a segment are to be reassigned rather than paged in as needed. (The user is about to overwrite these locations.)

3. Ask if a segment or some specific locations within a segment are currently in core.

4. Declare that a certain segment is to be created when first referenced.

5. Terminate a segment, indicating that this segment is no longer to be considered as known to this process.

Search Module

The search module is called by the segment management module to find a particular segment (file) in the user's directory hierarchy. The search module directs the search of individual directories in the user's hierarchy in a predetermined pattern until the requested branch is found or the algorithm is exhausted. This module calls the file coordinator to search particular directories and to move to other directories in the hierarchy. The user is able to override this search procedure by providing his own search procedure at the initiation or during the execution of his process.

The File Coordinator

The file coordinator provides all the basic tools for manipulating entries within the user's current working directory. The functions provided by this module perform only the most primitive operations and are usually augmented by more elaborate system library procedures. The following is a list (of some of these operations.

1. Create a new directory entry.

2. Delete an existing entry.

3. Rename an entry.

4. Return status information concerning a particular entry.

5. Change the access control list for a particular branch.

6. Change working directory.

Whenever a user wishes to perform any operation through the use of the file coordinator, the access control module is consulted to determine if the operation is to be permitted.

Since most calls to the file coordinator refer to entries contained in the user's working directory, the file coordinator must maintain a pointer to this directory. This is done by keeping the tree name of the working directory in a Working Directory Table (WDT) for this process.

Directory Management Module

When the file coordinator wishes to search the user's working directory, the actual search is accomplished by use of the directory management module. This module searches a single directory specified by a tree name for a particular entry or group of entries. The actual directory search is confined to this module to isolate the recursion process which may be required to search a given directory.

The directory management module issues calls to the segment management module to obtain a segment number for the directory for which it has only a tree name. When the directory management module obtains this segment number and references the directory by means of segment addressing, a descriptor fault may occur indicating that this segment is no longer active. If this happens, the segment management module will try to reactivate this segment by attempting to find this directory in the next superior directory by means of the tree name in the segment name table. To do this the segment management module issues a direct call to the directory management module to search the next superior directory for the missing directory. After obtaining a segment number for the superior directory, the directory management module may cause another descriptor fault to occur when attempting to search this directory. This process may continue until a directory is found to be an active segment or until the root of the directory hierarchy is reached. Since the root is always known to the directory management module, the depth of recursion is finite.

File Control Module

The file control module is provided to open and close files for the segment management module. A file is said to be open, or active, if it has a corresponding entry in the Active File Table (AFT). If a file is active, the corresponding entry in the active file table provides sufficient information to control subsequent I/O requests for that file.

If the file is inactive, the open procedure needs only to open the file to the requested state and make the corresponding entry in the active file table. If the file is active, it may have N users reading, or 1 user reading and writing, or N users data sharing (using file as a common data base). If the requested state is incompatible with the current state of the file, the current process must be blocked [3]. For example, if the current user wishes to read a stable copy of the file and there is currently a user writing into that file, the requested state (reading) and the current state (reading and writing) are said to be incompatible.

If the requested state and the current state of the file are found to be compatible, the number of users using the file in that state is increased by one. When a file has been successfully opened by the file control module (with the permission of the access control module), the pointer to the corresponding entry in the active file table is returned to the calling procedure. This pointer is used to direct requests for subsequent input or output to the correct file.

Access Control Module

The access control module is called to evaluate the access control information for a particular branch, as defined in Section 2. This module is given a pointer to the directory entry for the branch in question and a code indicating the type of operation which is being attempted. The access control module returns a single effective mode to the calling procedure. The effective mode is the mode which governs the use of a file with respect to the current user or process. The calling procedure uses this mode to determine if the requested operation is to be permitted.

If the access control information indicates that a trap is to be effected, the procedure to which the trap is directed is passed the entry for the branch in question and the operation code. The procedure which processes the trap must return to the access control module, specifying the effective mode to be returned by the access control module to its calling procedure. The procedure which processes the trap may choose to strengthen, weaken or leave unchanged the usage attributes which define the effective mode for the branch.

Page Marker Module

The page marker periodically interrupts the current process and takes note of page usage, and resets the page use bits [2] of all pages involved in the current process. Pages which fall below a dynamically set activity threshold are listed in the Page Out Table (POT) as likely candidates for removal when space becomes needed.

Page Management Module

Control passes to the page management module by means of a missing-page fault in a page table in use by the current process. This fault may indicate that a new page should be assigned from free storage or that an existing page should be retrieved from an active file. In either case a free page must be assigned before anything else can happen. If no pages are currently available, the first page listed in the page out table is paged out. If no pages are listed in the page out table, a random page of appropriate size is removed.

If a new page is to be read in, the page table entry for the missing page contains a pointer to the appropriate entry in the segment status table and a flag indicating whether this page is to be read from the original file or the execution file. In either case a pointer to the appropriate active file may be obtained from the segment status table. This pointer is passed as a parameter to the I/O queue management module with a read request to restore the correct page to core memory.

I/O Queue Management Module

The I/O queue management module processes input and output requests for a particular active file. The calling procedure specifies a read or a write request and a pointer to an entry in the active file table which corresponds to the desired file. This request is placed on the appropriate queue for the particular device interface module which will process the request. The queue management module then calls that device interface module indicating that a new request has been placed on its queue. When this is done, the queue management module returns to the calling procedure which must decide whether or not to block itself until the I/O request or requests are completed.

Device Interface Modules

For each type of secondary storage device used by the basic file system, a device interface module will be provided. A device interface module has the sole responsibility for the strategy to be used in dealing with the particular device for which it was written. Any special considerations pertaining to a particular storage device are invisible to all modules except the interface module for that device.

A device interface module is also responsible for assigning physical storage areas, as needed, on the device for which it was written. To accomplish this function, the interface module must maintain records of all storage already assigned on that device. These records are kept in *storage assignment tables* which reside on the device to which they refer.

4.2 Other File System Modules

The modules described below are not considered part of the basic file system and are not indicated in Fig. 3. However, these modules are considered to be a necessary and integral part of the file system as a whole.

Multilevel Storage Management Module

The multilevel storage management module operates as an independent process within the Multics system. This module collects information concerning the frequency of use of files currently active in the system. In addition, this module collects information concerning overdrawn accounts from the secondary storage accounting module.

The storage management module insures that an adequate amount of secondary storage is available to the basic file system at all times. This is accomplished by moving infrequently used files downward in the multilevel storage complex. This module also moves the most frequently used files to the highest-level secondary storage device available.

Storage Backup System Modules

The storage backup system consists of five modules which operate as independent processes. These modules perform the functions described in Section 3.

1. Incremental Dump Module—The sole responsibility of this module is to prepare incremental dump tapes of all new or recently modified files.

2. Weekly Dump Module—This module is run once a week to prepare the weekly dump tapes.

3. Retrieval Module—This module retrieves files which have been removed from the on-line storage system.

4. Salvage Module—This module is run after a machine or system failure to correct any inconsistencies which may have resulted in the on-line storage system. Since the Multics system cannot safely be run until these inconsistencies are corrected, the salvage module must be capable of running on a raw machine.

5. Catastrophe Reload Module—This module is used to reload the contents of the on-line storage system from the incremental and weekly dump tapes after a machine or system failure. Normally, this module is run only when all attempts to salvage the contents of the on-line storage system have failed. This module must be capable of running on a raw machine or under the control of the Multics system.

Utility and Service Modules

A large library of utility modules is provided as part of the file system. These modules provide all the necessary functions for manipulating links, and branches using the more primitive functions provided by the file coordinator. A special group of utility modules is provided to copy information currently stored as a file to other input or output media, and vice versa. The following functions are provided as a bare minimum:

1. File to printer
2. File to cards
3. Cards to file
4. Tape to file
5. File to tape

Actually these modules merely place the user's request on a queue for subsequent processing by the appropriate service module. The service module executes the requests in its queue as an independent process. As soon as the user's request has been placed on an appropriate queue, control is returned to the calling procedure although the request has not yet been executed.

5 CONCLUSIONS

In this paper, a versatile secondary storage file system is presented. Various goals which such a system should attain have been set, and the system designed in such a way as to achieve these goals. Such a system is felt to be an essential part of an effective on-line interactive computing system.

Acknowledgements

The file system presented here is the result of a series of contributions by numerous people, beginning with the MIT Computation Center, continuing with Project MAC, and culminating in the present effort. Work reported herein was supported (in part) by Project MAC, an M.I.T. research program sponsored by the Advanced Research Projects Agency, Department of Defense, under Office of Naval Research Contract Number Nonr-4102(01).

References

1. F. J. Corbató and V. A. Vyssotsky, "Introduction and Overview of the Multics System," this volume.
2. E. L. Glaser, J. F. Couleur and G. A. Oliver, "System Design of a Computer for Time-Sharing Applications," this volume.
3. V. A. Vyssotsky, F. J. Corbató and R. M. Graham, "Structure of the Multics Supervisor," this volume.
4. J. F. Ossanna, L. E. Mikus and S. D. Dunten, "Communications and Input-Output Switching in a Multiplex Computing System," this volume.
5. E. E. David, Jr., and R. M. Fano, "Some Thoughts About the Social Implications of Accessible Computing," this volume.

Additional References

- C. W. Bachman and S. B. Williams, "A General Purpose Programming System for Random Access Memories," Proceedings of the Fall Joint Computer Conference 26, Spartan Books, Baltimore, 1964.
- J. B. Dennis and E. C. Van Horn, "Programming Semantics for Multiprogrammed Computations," *ACM Conference on Programming Languages*, San Dimas, Calif., Aug. 1965. To be published in *Comm. ACM*.
- A. W. Holt, "Program Organization and Record Keeping for Dynamic Storage Allocation," *Comm. ACM* 4, pp. 422–431, Oct. 1961.
- T. H. Nelson, "A File Structure for the Complex, the Changing and the Indeterminate," *ACM National Conference*, Aug. 1965.
- M. V. Wilkes, "A Programmer's Utility Filing System," *Computer Journal* 7, pp. 180–184, Oct. 1964.

9

FILE INTEGRITY IN A DISC-BASED MULTI-ACCESS SYSTEM*

A. G. FRASER

(1972)

INTRODUCTION

The operating system that is used on the Titan computer at Cambridge University includes procedures for the organization and maintenance of file storage. About 10,000 files, belonging to some 700 users, are held on a magnetic disc that has a total capacity of 128 million characters. For the past 4 1/2 years this system has been used on a scheduled 20-hour day to provide job-shop and multiple-access facilities to a total user population of about 1500 persons. The file management software is described here in some detail. An overview of the system will be found in reference [1], and further details will be found in references [2] and [3]. Under the heading of file management we include these procedures which are a concerned with file identification, file privacy, space allocation and file integrity. In this context a file may be any ordered string of data and it is of no interest to the file management software to know what that data represents. In practice each file is held as a string of blocks (one block can accommodate 4096 characters). A quite distinct set of data handling routines provide the user with convenient means of processing the contents of a file. The file management software consists of complete programs that operate under supervisor control in the manner normally associated with other users of the system. One of these programs, the File Master, receives special recognition

*A. G. Fraser, File integrity in a disc-based multi-access system. In *Operating Systems Techniques*, C. A. R. Hoare and R. H. Perrott, Eds., Academic Press, New York, 1972, 227–248.

from the supervisor and it is around this program that the file management system revolves. The File Master contains five main functional parts.

1. Routines that service calls made by the supervisor itself.
2. Routines that service enquiries and demands that come direct from a user program.
3. Routines that provide special functions for the other programs in the set of file management software.
4. A routine that is entered at the start of day and after a system failure.
5. Routines that investigate or alter a user's entitlement to perform a requested activity.

The special status of the File Master stems from two facts.

1. The supervisor knows about and relies upon the File Master to provide it with certain services.
2. The File Master uses information on disc to decide what disc accesses the supervisor should allow and determines which area of the disc it should access.

The File Master program is set in operation before any other program is allowed to run and it does not terminate itself until the operating system closes itself down. The program is activated whenever its services are requested and each activation services just one request; a queue of outstanding requests is held by the supervisor. The File Master is the only program that has direct access to the disc and it has certain other special privileges that allow it to communicate with the supervisor in order to obtain a few specialized services.

There is a substantial number of distinct programs in the total set of file management software and they fall into the following five categories.

A. Programs that use magnetic tape as additional file storage space and as an insurance against loss of filed data.

B. Programs that provide the user with convenient facilities connected with file management, such as printing a list of file titles.

C. Programs that provide the installation management with necessary statistics and allows him to exercise necessary control over the use of various file system resources and functions.

D. Programs that facilitate inspection and maintenance of the file system data base both on disc and magnetic tape.

E. Programs that provide an artificial environment in which to test new versions of the file system.

In this paper I deal only with the operations of the File Master and the programs in category A. Programs falling into the other four categories represent a substantial part of the whole but are often somewhat parochial in nature.

THE FILE DIRECTORIES

Lists of file titles and related information are maintained on disc. The lists, known as file directories, are maintained by the File Master and are the key to its operation.

Each file is a separate entity. Although some files may have similar titles, they are each preserved and protected separately. For administrative purposes we form collections of files, and one directory contains the names of all the files in one collection. In many cases the file directory bears the name of one user and the collection of files will usually be his own private property. Other directories contain collections of more general interest. A group of users may choose to share together and the library of publically available programs provides an extreme example of the communal use of a file directory.

Certain administrative controls are linked to the file directory. Space accounting is an example. Each directory is given an allocation that is an upper limit to the volume of filed information that is permitted on disc. There are three classes of file and for each class there is a separate allocation. The classes are:

1 Permanent

Files in this class reside permanently on disc. The file support software automatically makes spare copies of these files on magnetic tape so that there is some protection against loss.

2 Temporary

Files in this class reside on disc during the day on which they are created; temporary files are flushed out at the start of each day. No spare copies are made on magnetic tape.

3 Archive

Files in this class reside permanently on magnetic tape and are not available for processing until they have been re-classified as permanent. The file space allocations are checked by the File Master whenever it services a request to change a file or create a new one. Before a file can be processed, the user must OPEN it, and when he has finished it must be CLOSED. When opening a file the user must specify the way in which he intends to use it and, once access has been granted, the program will be held to its stated intention. The actions which take place when a user opens or closes a file are two-fold.

1. The supervisor calls upon the File Master to check the validity of the requested action, to verify that no privacy restrictions are being violated and, in the case of file access, to obtain the disc address of the file.
2. The data handling routines that will be used to manipulate the content of the file are initiated, or terminated, as appropriate.

The three recognized modes of file use are READ, EXECUTE and UPDATE.

File creation is treated specially but for most practical purposes is rather like updating a previously null file. We allow any number of users to use one file simultaneously providing that none of them wishes to update it; only one user is allowed access to a file if it is being updated. In consequence, one of the reasons that a request to open a file may fail is that someone else is using it. A request to open a file may also fail because the specified file title is not listed in the file directory, because there is a privacy restriction on the file in question or because the file is in archive storage and not on disc.

FILE DIRECTORY STRUCTURE

The file directory serves three main purposes.

(*a*) To contain a list of file titles with some information about each.

(*b*) To contain a list of privacy arrangements.

(*c*) To contain certain administrative data that affects all the files collected into the one directory.

Each file has a name, such as /x/mk.1, which contains two components separated by solidus. Each component is the arbitrary choice of the author but no component may contain more than 8 characters. A file directory also has a name, such as D, which prefixes the file name to give the full file title, D/x/mk.1. For convenience, the user may omit the directory name if the default setting will suffice. The default value may be set arbitrarily by the user but it is normally set to his own name.

With the name of each file, the directory contains the disc address of the data that is the file. The disc address of the directory is itself held in another list, the MASTER FILE DIRECTORY (see figure 1).

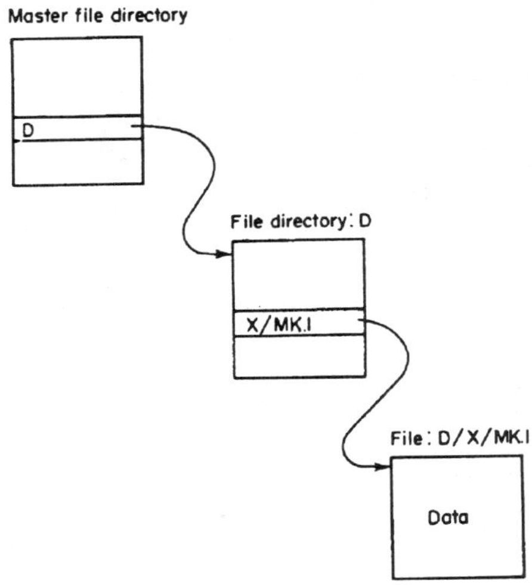

Figure 1 File directory hierarchy.

The directories are all held as files in their own right and in this capacity they are associated with a file directory named SYSTEM (figure 2). By this means we have arranged that all of the standard data handling facilities provided by the supervisory software are available to the system programs that manipulate the file directories themselves. In consequence we have made an important contribution towards simplicity in the file management software.

In principle it would have been possible to make the file directory SYSTEM serve a dual role and thereby avoid a separate main file directory. But, by using a separate main file directory with a compact internal structure, we have been able to reduce directory search time appreciably.

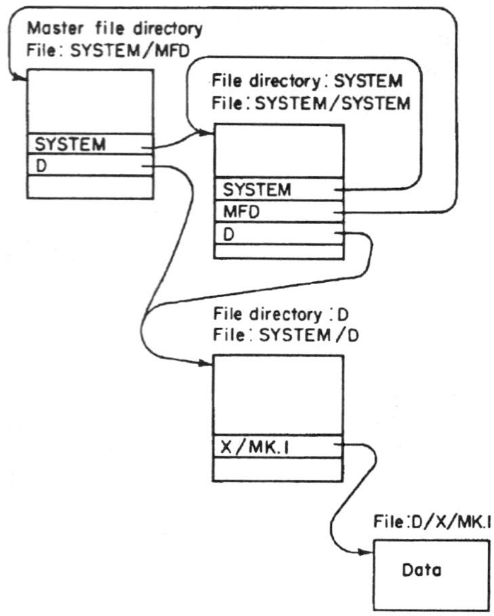

Figure 2 File directory structure.

STORE SPACE MAP

A file may occupy more than one block and these will not usually be located in consecutive positions on the disc. To link the several blocks of one file together we use a store space map in which there is one entry for each block position on disc (figure 3). Each entry contains two fields.

(*a*) The block address of the next block in the file.

(*b*) A flag to identify the first block of a completed file.

The unused blocks are linked together as if they formed two large files; the significance of using two rather than one free store list is discussed later in this paper.

PRIVACY

The control system that safeguards the privacy of filed material operates, for the most part, on the basis that nothing is permitted unless it has been

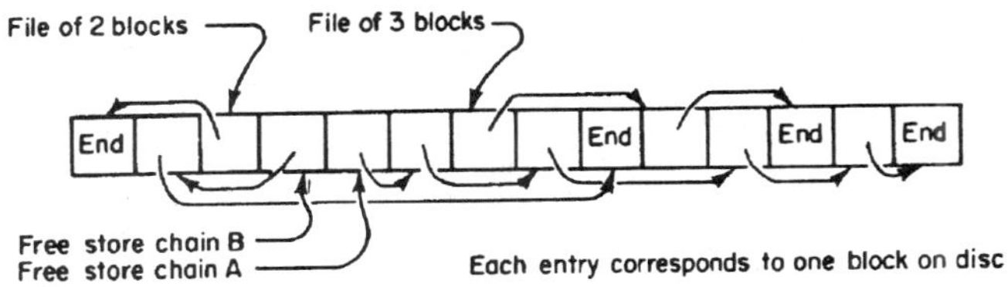

Figure 3 Disc space map.

authorized. For convenience, of course, default settings exist for most controls so that it is usually unnecessary for a user to be continuously aware of these controls. There are two distinct mechanisms. One mechanism exists to prevent one user from masquerading as another (without, at least, the co-operation of the other). The second mechanism concerns the right of access to filed data and the use of special file system functions.

USER IDENTITY CHECK

As a means of preventing one user from masquerading as another, each person has a password which is chosen by him and can be changed by him whenever he chooses. The user must quote his password when seeking access to the system through an on-line console and he may optionally quote it from within a program that is run through the job-shop system.

The passwords are held in scrambled form. The mechanics of the process used to scramble a password are not kept a secret since there is no known economic way of performing the reverse operation. Whenever a user attempts to quote his password, the quoted word is first scrambled and then compared with the stored original. If the scrambled forms are identical then it is assumed that he has quoted correctly.

From time to time a user will forget his password and appeal to the administration for help. For this reason there is a privileged system function that allows a password to be set to a new value by someone other than its proper owner. It would also be necessary to use this device if, through some system malfunction, the password file becomes corrupt.

It is assumed that each user keeps his password secret. As a means of policing this arrangement the system records the date and time whenever a password is changed or quoted correctly. When a user successfully quotes his password he is told the date and time of the previous occasion on which this was done. By this means a user can detect an infringement although the evidence may not always be sufficient to identify the offender. Of course, the user can choose a new password immediately after detecting an infringement.

RESTRAINT ON USER ACTIVITY

The controls that prevent unauthorized access to data can also give protection against accidental misuse. In a university environment it is the latter that is the more common requirement although privacy controls are essential for the accounting files and other central facilities. Control over user activity is exercised in two stages.

1. The authority of the user is calculated. This is, in effect, a list of the activities that he is entitled to perform.
2. The authority is compared with the requested activity and, where an existing file is involved, it is also compared with the particular restrictions associated with that file.

Before it is possible to describe either of these two steps it is necessary to explain the method by which activities are identified for control purposes.

For control purposes, activities fall into two distinct classes. They are as follows:

1. Activities that involve existing files. These are: EXECUTE, READ, DELETE, UPDATE and CHANGE STATUS.
2. Activities that do not involve existing files. These fall into two groups for efficiency reasons only. In group A are those that are more generally useful: FILE CREATION, and CREATION or DELETION OF A PRIVACY ARRANGEMENT.

In group B are special activities reserved, usually, for system programs and the administration. Some of these are:

(*a*) Creation or deletion of a privacy arrangement that authorizes a special activity.

(*b*) The use of system calls that are ordinarily reserved for use by dump system programs.

(*c*) The act of overriding all file access controls.

(*d*) The use of a system call that permits one person to masquerade as another.

(*e*) The act of reloading a file from a system dump tape.

(*f*) Creation of a new file directory.

(*g*) Interference with the schedule of dump and reload activities.

(*h*) Alteration to file space accounting controls.

In order to be able to perform calculations about activities and the authorities that are necessarily associated with them, we use the following internal representation.

1 Activities that involve existing files

Each activity in this class is represented by a 4 by 5 array of one-bit elements. For the ith activity the ith column of the array contains non-zero elements whereas all other columns contain zero elements. For example, READ, which is the second activity, is represented by the following array:

$$\begin{matrix} 0 & 1 & 0 & 0 & 0 \\ 0 & 1 & 0 & 0 & 0 \\ 0 & 1 & 0 & 0 & 0 \\ 0 & 1 & 0 & 0 & 0 \end{matrix}$$

The reason for adopting this particular representation will become apparent in due course.

2 Activities that do not involve existing files

Each activity in this class is represented by a 26 element vector of one-bit elements. The ith activity is represented by a vector that has zero elements in all but the ith position. Thus, file creation, which is the first activity in this class, is represented by

1000000000...000

It will be immediately apparent that we are able to represent composite activities by the logical sum of the representations of the separate activities involved.

RESTRAINTS ON FILE USE

It has already been stated that, where a requested activity involves an existing file, the authority of the user is compared with the specific act requested and with the particular restrictions associated with the file involved. Whenever a file is created, the creator must specify a list of the actions that are to be permitted for that file. The internal representation of this list is the 4 by 5 array that is the logical sum of the representations for the permitted activities. Thus, for a file that is generally available for reading (activity 2) and execution (activity 1) the representation would be

$$\begin{matrix} 1 & 1 & 0 & 0 & 0 \\ 1 & 1 & 0 & 0 & 0 \\ 1 & 1 & 0 & 0 & 0 \\ 1 & 1 & 0 & 0 & 0 \end{matrix}$$

Now, it is convenient to be selective in the issue of permits to act on a file. For example, the owner will usually wish to retain the right to delete the file whereas he may not usually wish others to be able to do the same. This facility is provided by identifying four categories of file use.

The activity READ, is subdivided into four component activities:

READ in category 1
READ in category 2
READ in category 3
READ in category 4

The representation for READ in category 1 is a 4 by 5 array with zeros in all elements except the ith row of the second column (READ is activity number 2). Thus the total action called READ is a composition of four primitives and the representation of the composite activity is the logical sum of the representations of the primitives.

We allow a file creator to list the primitive actions that he wishes to authorize for his file and we represent this list by the logical sum of the representations of each of of the primitives. Thus, for example, a file may be available to every possible category 1 activity, it may be restricted to reading and execution in category 2, and not available at all in the other two categories. The representation for this would be:

$$\begin{matrix} 1 & 1 & 1 & 1 & 1 \\ 1 & 1 & 0 & 0 & 0 \\ 0 & 0 & 0 & 0 & 0 \\ 0 & 0 & 0 & 0 & 0 \end{matrix}$$

In practice, the user describes his privacy requirements by quoting four letters, one for each category. The situation described in the above example would ordinarily be described by the four letters

F R N N

Each letter specifies the set of actions permitted in one category and a sequence of four letters completely describes the total permitted activity. Each letter must be chosen from the following list:

- F Free access. Allow all activities including UPDATE.
- D Allow DELETE, READ, EXECUTE and CHANGE STATUS.
- C Allow READ, EXECUTE and CHANGE STATUS.
- R Allow READ and EXECUTE.
- L Allow EXECUTE only.
- N No access.

The default value, which is used if the creater does not specify any privacy requirement, is

F F R R

That is, free access in categories 1 and 2, and read or execute in categories 3 and 4. As will be seen later, category 1 activities are normally only authorized to the file owner and category 4 activities are available to all users without restriction. The default value, FFRR, therefore gives free access to the file owner whereas members of the general public are restricted to reading and execution.

AUTHORITY TO ACT

A user's total authority is a list of all the activities in which he is entitled to indulge. The representation for this authority is the logical sum of the representations of the individual actions that are allowed. This is computed in two parts which correspond to the two classes of activity identified earlier. For example, the file access authority for a user who is allowed to perform all actions in categories 2 and 4, and is allowed to read or execute in category 3, is represented as

```
0 0 0 0 0
1 1 1 1 1
1 1 0 0 0
1 1 1 1 1
```

The same user may be able to create new files and his authority for class 2 activities would be represented as

1000000...000

To discover whether a user may create files we need only check that the first element in his class 2 authority is non-zero. In general, if we need to decide whether he can perform some class 2 action, r, we need compare the representation for r with the class 2 authority of the user and if these two have a non-zero element in common the requested action is allowed. In practice, this means that we require the logical product of r and the user's class 2 authority to be non-zero.

When reference to a file is requested, we also need to check the privacy arrangements for the particular file in question. The request is allowed if the logical product of r, the file privacy and the user's class 1 authority yields a non-zero result.

CALCULATION OF USER AUTHORITY

A user's total authority is made up of his basic entitlement together with any additional authority that has been vested in him by explicit statements made to that effect.

Every user has a basic entitlement that allows him to perform all category 4 actions when referencing a file. This will be his total basic entitlement unless his name is the same as that of the file directory being used.

The file directory contains two marker digits that determine the basic entitlement of a user whose name is the same as that of the directory. The presence of either of these markers places an additional requirement on this user. If the additional requirement is met, or if the marker digits are not set, then his basic entitlement will allow all activities in classes 1 and 4, and in addition he will be permitted to create new files or privacy arrangements. The extra requirements that may be made are:

(*a*) The user must have quoted his own password correctly, and

(*b*) The user must be sitting at an on-line console.

The user's additional authority is determined by scanning the list of statements of authority held within each file directory. Each entry in this list contains a condition and an authority. The authority, which may be a composite activity, is given to any user that satisfies the specified condition. To compute the total additional authority we look for conditions that are met by the user in question and we accumulate the logical sum of the associated authorities. Where the requested activity involves a particular file, we scan the directory in which that file is listed. Where the activity does not involve any particular file, we scan the one particular file directory that is set aside just for this purpose.

In the interests of speed and space economy, the condition contained in one directory entry has a rather limited structure. There are four parts to this condition all of which must be satisfied (or null) before the condition is said to have been satisfied. The four parts are as follows.

Part 1	If not null, this requires that the user be sitting at an on-line console.
Part 2	If not null, this requires that the user should have quoted his own password correctly.
Parts 3 and 4	Each contain expressions of the form F(X) which must either be null or true. The choice of function F is as follows:

(i) User name is X.
(ii) User has quoted key X.
(iii) User is obeying command program X.
(iv) User is using a file in group X.

Typically, a file owner will create a number of partners each of which is allowed to indulge in some category 2 activity and create new files. To do this he creates a a directory entry with the associated condition:

User name is FRED

The authority that he gives to FRED is specified in the same notation as is the privacy requirement for a file. Thus, the authority to act freely in category 2 is written as NFNN and represented within the machine as

```
0 0 0 0 0
1 1 1 1 1
0 0 0 0 0
0 0 0 0 0
```

ARCHIVES

It is convenient to use magnetic tape to provide storage space for files that are not in regular use. There are at least two attitudes that one can adopt towards the use of this second level of file storage.

(*a*) One can attempt to integrate the two storage levels so that the user is unaware of the division and one can seek to find an operating strategy that minimizes the overheads involved in the management of the slower store. To do this one needs to find an effective means of deciding which material to keep in the faster store. This approach is analogous to the use of a paging technique between core and drum.

(*b*) One can seek to use the slower store in a way that does not conceal its existence from the user yet gives him convenient means of exploiting its extra capacity. In this case the user's view of the system is more elaborate but the onus of deciding which material to keep in the faster store is left in the hands of the user, who is better placed to make the necessary assessment of relative priorities.

It is the latter approach that has been adopted at Cambridge, and the second level store is known to the user as the archive store.

The user is required to assign each of his files to one of three classes: Permanent, Temporary, and Archive. Material with long-term value will be classified as Permanent if it is to be held on disc, and as Archive if it should be held on tape. It is by classification and re-classification of filed data that the user makes use of the archive store. However, he is subject to certain restraints that make him aware of the different characteristics of the storage media involved.

(*a*) Files must normally be transferred from archive store to permanent store before they can be used and this operation takes time (there is a delay of up to one hour). The user is thus aware that re-classification involves substantial system overheads and should not be undertaken without due consideration.

(*b*) Each file directory has associated with it a space account in which Permanent, Temporary and Archive files are each accounted for separately. Within each class, there is an upper limit on the permitted volume of filed material and this limit is set individually for each directory.

(*c*) The maximum number of file directory entries that can be accommodated in one file directory is set individually for each directory by the installation management. This reflects the fact that system overheads increase with the number of files handled as well as the volume of material filed.

ARCHIVE TAPE SYSTEM

For the purposes of tape management, file directories are assembled into archive groups; each directory is assigned to one group. For each group there is a distinct set of magnetic tapes that provide secondary storage for filed material.

The groups are chosen such that the total of the Permanent and Archive space allocations is not greater than the capacity of one magnetic tape. All files in these two classes and belonging to one archive group can therefore be accommodated on one magnetic tape. A set of tapes (usually four) is assigned to each group and these are used in rotation. At each update, one tape is completely re-written to contain the up-to-date material for all members of one archive group (figure 4). The three previous generations are kept for back-up purposes and to allow limited facilities for retrieval of 'deleted' files. The tapes are used and re-used on a cyclic basis so that, for a cycle of four tapes, the father and grandfather are always available. The fourth tape, the great grandfather, will also be available until the start of the next update run. Under normal circumstances there is one update for each group each week but a user may request an unscheduled archive update when necessary in order to clear a backlog of material from the disc.

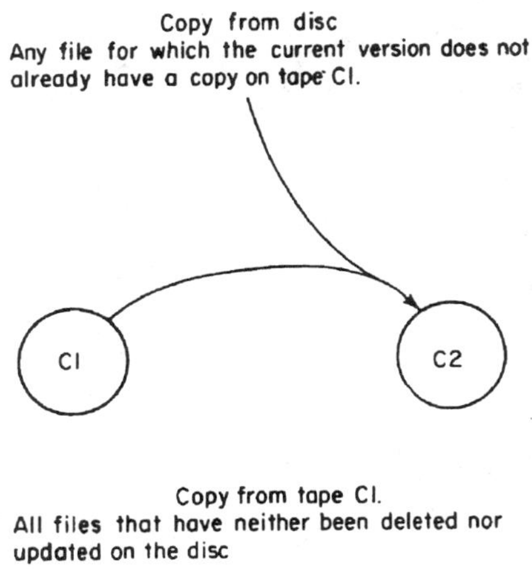

Figure 4 Archive update.

Archive files are held on disc until they have been transferred to the archive tapes. Once an archive file has been preserved in this way it is removed from the disc leaving only the file directory entry as a link with the copy on magnetic tape. In view of the fact that permanent files are also copied on to archive tapes, it will usually be the case that there is little or no delay between the change to archive status and the subsequent release of disc space. If subsequently a file is re-classified as permanent, the copy on archive tape continues to be maintained so that further disc to tape transfers are avoided.

File recovery is initiated by re-classifying an archive file as permanent. When this act takes place a flag is set in the directory entry for the file in question. At hourly intervals, the directory is scanned and a batch of reload jobs is initiated. The directory entry contains enough information to allow the system to identify the magnetic tape from which the file may be reloaded. This operation together with the mechanics of the archive tape update program are discussed in greater detail later in this article.

INTEGRITY

The integrity of a disc-based file system is put at risk by the possibility of hardware failure, software malfunction, mismanagement by the operating staff and misplaced user activity. To minimise loss and corruption in the face of these hazards, we have taken some trouble to incorporate error detection and correction procedures at a number of levels throughout the file management software. In practice these procedures account for a very substantial part of the software involved.

It is convenient to describe the system in two parts. First, there are those actions that are taken in order to detect, prevent or repair file corruption within the confines of the disc store itself. Secondly, there are the procedures that use magnetic tape to hold redundant copies of filed data.

FILE INTEGRITY ON DISC

Error detection relies upon the existence of redundancy in the data base. However, it may be noted that this is not the only function of redundancy and, in particular, we use redundancy in a number of ways to obtain increased operating speed. In the first instance we sought a basic data structure that was simple in the sense that it contained little redundancy. The file management process was then defined in terms of manipulations upon this structure and it was this process and this structure that were used to assess the effects of hardware malfunction. Using this as a design base, we have added redundancy both as a means of enhancing the error detection capability and as a means of increasing run-time speed.

We have found that it is possible to obtain a high level of integrity and yet retain simplicity of design by persistent and meticulous attention to detail during the early design stage. There are three questions which must be asked when evaluating a design proposal.

1. How would the data base look after a system failure? To answer this question one must have a knowledge of hardware (and low-level software) failure characteristics. With this knowledge one can determine the effect of a failure at critical points in the run-time process.
2. Is it possible to deduce a valid and self-consistent data base from that which is left after a failure? It is quite possible to produce a system that fails in such a way that it is not possible to decide upon a data configuration that can be reliably used as the basis for a system restart. It is desirable to design the system so that the more likely configurations into which it falls after system failure are those from which a satisfactory restart configuration can most readily be obtained.
3. What is the cost of the search for inconsistency within the data base? Since the search must usually be conducted on every restart, it is desirable to avoid data base designs for which a thorough check is ruled out on economic grounds.

This method of evaluation can be applied to some advantage even at the earliest design stages. I shall give two examples.

It is necessary to choose some means of associating the several blocks of a file with the file directory entry for that file. One way of doing this is to link each block to the next by a pointer contained in the block itself. The file directory entry would point to the first block and the last block would contain a null pointer. But consider the effect of a central processor stop while a file is being copied to the disc. It is most likely that some, but not all, of the data will actually have reached the disc. As a result the chain of pointers that link these blocks will end by pointing to a block with arbitrary content. A loop may result or two files may appear to have some data in common. The restart program must therefore be able to detect this type of corruption in the data base and it is more than likely that the most effective solution to this and allied problems would be to make a full check of all inter-block links. But this would involve reading every block of disc store and could be prohibitively expensive in consequence. At Cambridge we use a map of disc space, as described earlier, and this particular aspect of the restart process is consequently a thoroughly practical proposition.

One of the possible erroneous configurations that could result from an untimely central processor stop results in one, apparently legitimate file obtaining data that belonged to a file that was deleted just before the system failed. This effect is one consequence of the fact that file directories and the disc map are updated in core store and then transferred to disc separately. It is the information on disc that forms the basis for restart. Rather than try to make it possible for the restart program to detect erroneous configurations of this type, we chose to adopt a run-time procedure that minimizes the likelihood of the error occurring in a not-easily identifiable form. Three actions are required.

1. We use two free store chains (see figure 3). When a file is deleted the space that it used is added to free store chain B but when a file is created it uses space from free store chain A. Only when the disc map has been safely written on to disc does the free space in chain B become part of that on chain A.
2. When a file has been deleted we refuse to construct the directory entry for a new file until the directory entry for the deleted file has been successfully written to disc.
3. The last act taken on behalf of a newly created file is to set a marker in the disc map entry for the first block of the file. When a file is deleted this marker is removed. On restart, we discard any filed data for which the disc map entry is unmarked.

RESTART FROM DISC

The operating system must be restarted after any serious failure and after a period of scheduled down-time. When this happens, the system calls the file restart program. It is the task of this program to make maximum use of information held on disc, to check it as thoroughly as possible and to re-establish the file management system with a sound data base. There is no attempt to utilize information left in the core store at the end of the previous session.

The checks made by the restart program are as thorough as we can make them in the direction of ensuring that there is no inconsistency within the file control information. We emphasize the need for consistency in this area because it is a property of this type of system that minor errors in the control information can provoke wholesale corruption throughout the data base. For this reason we read and check the disc map and every file directory.

Whenever errors are found we chose to abandon data on disc rather than risk an apparent comption to the content of a file. For example, we abandon any file that is in the course of being created since we are uncertain whether it actually reached the disc before the system failed.

When all checks have been made and when corruptions have been cut out, the redundant control information is re-computed; totals of space used, the free space chains and the cross-reference from file directory to master file directory, are all re-set to their correct values. The entire restart process takes about one minute and part of this is time-shared with the normal computing load.

Finally, the restart program notes the absence of any file directory. If one or more directories are missing a suitable directory reload job is automatically inserted in the job queue and this job is run before any other jobs are permitted to proceed. The job obtains copies of the missing directories from the magnetic tape most recently written by the incremental file dumper.

THE INCREMENTAL DUMPER

At regular intervals new and recently updated files are copied from disc on to magnetic tape. This is a purely precautionary measure that avoids complete dependence upon the integrity of the disc system. The material copied on to the dump tapes is only used when the original is lost or corrupted.

The dumper is a program that is automatically inserted into the job queue at regular intervals. The appropriate choice of interval depends upon the reliability of the disc hardware and on the overhead involved in running the program. In practice the interval has been as short as 20 minutes but is currently set at 3 hours.

The dumper uses a set of about 15 magnetic tapes in rotation (see figure 5). At any instant one of these tapes is known as the current dump tape. When the dumper runs it copies material on to this tape starting at the position reached at the end of the previous dump run. Gradually the tape is filled and when a tape is full the next in the cycle is used. We count the number of reels of tape that have been filled and this number, the series number, is used to identify the content of the current dump tape. When a file is dumped the series number and tape position are written into the file directory. The combination of series number and tape position is known as the dump name. The dump name uniquely identifies a dumped version of a file and serves to distinguish between successive sets of data to which the user has assigned identical file titles. It is relevant to note that the dump name increases in numeric value with each successive dump activity. The significance of this becomes clear when one considers the controls that are required in order to ensure integrity within the dump system itself.

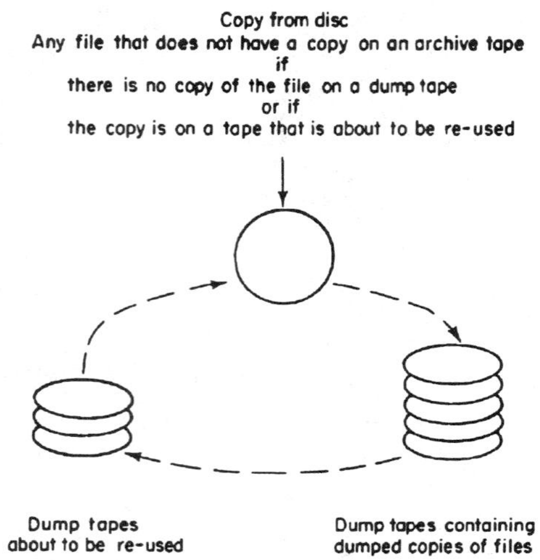

Figure 5 Incremental dump.

From time to time it is necessary to re-dump a file. The fact that the dump tapes are used in rotation implies that we risk over-writing a valuable copy of a file when the tape containing it is re-used. To avoid this, we automatically request a re-dump of a file that is threatened in this way. We periodically compare the dump name of every file with the series number of the current dump tape. If the difference between these two values exceeds a preset limit, the dumper is asked to re-dump the file in question. A similar problem arises if the system fails while dumper is running. After restart we need to compare the dump name of every file with the position and series number of the current dump tape. It is necessary to re-dump any file with dump name that is beyond the point from which dumper will resume operations.

When dumper finds a file that needs dumping, it copies the file on to tape and then writes the dump name into the file directory. The directory itself is also copied on to magnetic tape when a file is dumped or when the directory contains a marker indicating that a significant change has been made to its content. We also dump one copy of every file directory on to the beginning of every dump tape in order to facilitate restart when a directory has been lost from the disc.

TWO TIER DUMP SYSTEM

Two systems which copy files on to magnetic tape have now been described. The archive system maintains copies of all permanent and archive files on magnetic tape in an orderly fashion and this is done on a weekly basis. The dump system, on the other hand, writes material to tape in no particular order but with minimum delay. In practice, the two systems are made to work together to provide a uniform system providing magnetic tape back-up as well as archive storage. The archive system provides long-term storage in an efficient and orderly fashion, and the incremental dumper gives protection between the time of file creation and the next archive update. In consequence of its dual role, the archive system is also known as the secondary dump system.

Coordination of dumping is effected by a subroutine that is entered whenever a a new file is created, an existing one is altered or when a dumper requests access to a file directory. The routine checks and, if necessary, resets a number of flags which in turn control dumper action. The five flags and two dump names, which are held in the file directory entry for each file, are used as follows:

1. Incremental dump name.
This is the series number and tape position of the file on the incremental dump tape. It is re-set only when the file is copied from disc on to tape.
2. Archive dump name.
This is the series number and archive group for the archive tape on which the file is held. It is re-set only when the file is copied from disc on to tape.
3. Incremental dump request.
If this flag is set the incremental dumper will copy the file at the earliest opportunity. It is set when a file is created or updated. It is also set when the "archive current" flag is not set but the "Incremental dump name" is less than the series number of the current tape minus some constant (5 at present).
4. Incremental dump made.
This flag indicates that the current version of the file is also to be found on an incremental dump tape.

5. Archive dump request.
If this flag is set the file will be copied from disc to the appropriate archive tape at the next update. It is set whenever "Incremental dump made" is set and "Archive dump made" is not set.
6. Archive dump made.
This flag indicates that the current version of the file is also to be found on the latest tape of the appropriate archive group.
7. Archive dump in trouble.
This flag is set when magnetic tape failure or some other hazard leads to abandonment of the archive copy of a file.

The overheads of file dumping are reduced substantially by keeping, in core store, a vector in which there is one element for each file directory. One flag per directory signals the need for attention by the incremental dumper. By this means we can avoid reading every directory from disc.

MANAGEMENT OF MAGNETIC TAPES

It is desirable to take whatever steps one can to ensure continuity of file dumping in in spite of hardware failure or injudicious operator action; the dump system will be expected to run automatically and unattended. Thus, for example, a bad patch on one magnetic tape should not be allowed to bring all progress to a halt. Another consequence of the absence of supervision is that there will be no frequent check on the integrity of the dump process. Errors in this part of the system will only be found when attempting to restart the file management system after some failure and on these occasions one is rarely equipped to deal with unwanted complications. To avoid this, it is necessary to incorporate consistency checks into the dump system itself. Time spent in this way will rarely be wasted. In addition to the usual device of checking tape identity by program, we include identity and consistency checks on each section of dumped material. If bad sections of tape are found we ignore them, and if corruptions are detected the system automatically backs up to the last good position. However, we have found it essential to make sure that all errors and corrective actions are reported on paper so that events can be traced manually should the system knot itself.

As added protection against loss, we write all incremental dump tapes in duplicate. The duplicate copy is written at the same time as the original. This system has the disadvantage that both copies are on the machine and being written at the same time. In an earlier system the copy was made after the original was written but the need to skip over bad sections of tape is then inconsistent with the almost essential aim of obtaining exact duplication. Without exact duplication, errors encountered during the recovery process become more complex to handle.

FILE RECOVERY

Permanent files that are not on disc will be reloaded automatically from magnetic tape. At regular intervals (currently once per hour) the file directories are inspected and a list of missing files is assembled. Each entry in this list contains a file title together with a dump name or archive name. When the list has been completed file reload jobs are inserted into the job queue; each job uses one dump or archive tape. When a reload job reaches the execution stage it scans the list of missing files and copies to disc as many of the missing files as it can.

The effect of this strategy is to batch file reloads and so avoid excessive tape handling. However, it does mean that a user may have to wait for some time before a missing file is replaced. The list of missing files is not strictly necessary but it does serve to reduce system overheads. Without it, each reload program would need to search the file directories and this would involve a substantial number of disc transfers. System overheads are further reduced by holding in core store, a vector in which there is one entry per file directory. A single flag per directory signals the need to search that directory for missing files.

It is essential to arrange that failure to reload one file does not halt progress with other reload activity. If magnetic tape or other failure means that a file cannot be reloaded the system sets a flag in the file directory, prints a warning message, and then proceeds to reload other files. The flag is inspected by several system programs which issue warning messages to both management and the user.

There is usually more than one copy of a file on magnetic tape; dump tapes are written in duplicate and it is a property of the archive system that a new copy of a file is made each week. During its first week, a file is held by the incremental dump system and on one archive tape. Thereafter there will be copies on at least two archive tapes. At present, there is no automatic mechanism that makes the system try to find the second copy of a file when reload fails. Such a mechanism would make a worthwhile improvement if it could be designed to distinguish sensibly between transient, avoidable and intransient failures since it would further reduce the need for human supervision.

The mechanics of file reload are very similar to file creation. There are two main differences. When a file is reloaded we insist on using an existing file directory entry for the file instead of creating a new entry. If the reload fails the file directory entry is not deleted, as could be the case when file creation fails, but is reset to its initial state. We take particular notice of failures that result when the file space allocation is exceeded. Reload tasks for such files will not be scheduled until the necessary space becomes available.

APPENDIX

Information held in a file directory

1 The directory heading

1.1 The name of the directory.

1.2 The size of the directory.

1.3 The total volume of disc space occupied by files associated with this directory. There are separate totals of space occupied by Permanent, Temporary and Archive files respectively.

1.4 The maximum volume of disc space allowed to files associated with this directory. There are separate allocations of space for Permanent, Temporary and Archive files respectively.

1.5 The name of the archive group to which the directory is assigned.

1.6 The total volume of space occupied on the latest archive tape.

1.7 The position of the master file directory entry that contains the name of this directory.

1.8 Dump control markers. There are three flags.

(*a*) Indicates that the directory should be written to tape as soon as possible.

(*b*) Indicates that incremental dumping has started and has not been interrupted by a further change to the directory.

(*c*) Indicates that this directory should be deleted from the disc. Deletion actually takes place when a final copy of the directory has been dumped.

1.9 A flag to indicate that files associated with this directory can be read or executed but new information may not be added. This flag will usually be set prior to final deletion.

1.10 Conditions for directory ownership. If a user should have the same name as the directory itself then he will be treated as the "owner" if he satisfies the conditions demanded by the following two flags.

(*a*) If this flag is set the user must have quoted his password correctly.

(*b*) If this flag is set the user must be sitting at an on-line console.

2 A file description entry

2.1 The name of the file.

2.2 The size of the file.

2.3 The access status. This is a 4 by 5 array of one-bit entries. Each of the four rows describes permitted activity for one category of user. Associated with each column is one possible activity and a one-bit indicates that the activity is permitted.

2.4 An interlock that indicates the number of people using the file and the manner of use. If positive, it is the number of people reading the file and, if negative, the file is being written.

2.5 The position of the file on disc. Zero if there is no copy of the file on disc.

2.6 The class of the file. Files are classed as Permanent, Temporary or Archive.

2.7 A flag to identify a file that forms an essential part of the system software and which should therefore be present on disc before normal service jobs can be expected to run properly.

2.8 A flag to identify the "preferred" version of a group of files that all have similar names. This flag is consulted whenever the user asks to use the "preferred" version and it is this version of a system program that is normally used.

2.9 Control information for the incremental dumper.

(*a*) A flag to indicate that a copy of the latest version is held on the incremental dump tape.

(*b*) A flag to indicate the file should be copied on to an incremental dump tape.

(*c*) A flag to indicate that dumping has started. This flag is cleared if the file is updated during the dump process.

(*d*) The dump name. This is the series number and position of the dump tape when the file was dumped.

2.10 Control information for the archive dumper.

(*a*) A flag to indicate that a copy of the latest version of the file is held on the latest archive tape.

(*b*) A flag to indicate that the file should be copied on to the archive tape.

(*c*) A flag to indicate that an archive update has started. This flag is cleared if the file is updated while the update is proceeding.

(*d*) The archive name. This is the name of the archive group and the series number of the tape on to which the file was first copied.

(*e*) A flag to indicate that, through some system malfunction, the copy held on tape may have been corrupted.

2.11 Control information for the file reloader. This consists of three flags.

(*a*) A flag to indicate that the file should be reloaded from an archive tape.

(*b*) A flag to indicate that the file should be reloaded from an incremental dump tape.

(*c*) A flag to indicate that the reload system failed to recover the file from tape. This was probably due to a system malfunction.

2.12 The date and time of file creation.

3 An authority description entry

3.1 An integer that uniquely identifies the directory entry.

3.2 A marker to distinguish the type of activity that is authorized. There are two types:

(*a*) File access (see 3.3 below).

(*b*) Special file system function (see 3.4 below).

3.3 A description of authorized file system actions:

(*a*) A flag to indicate that file creation is permitted.

(*b*) A flag to indicate that new statements of authority can be created.

(*c*) A 4 by 5 array of one-bit entries.

The four rows correspond to the four categories of file use. The five columns refer to the five ways of using a file. If the entry is non-zero then the activity is permitted.

3.4 A description of authorized special file system activities. This is a 24-bit array in which each one-bit entry denotes permission to perfomm one special activity Some of these are:

(*a*) Ability to use the system calls that create and destroy statements of authority that allow special file system activities.

(*b*) Ability to use the system calls that are normally reserved only for dump system programs.

(*c*) Ability to override all file access controls.

(*d*) Ability to use a system call that permits one person to masquerade as another.

(*e*) Ability to reload a file from a system dump tape.

(*f*) Ability to create a new file directory entry.

(*g*) Ability to interfere with the schedule of dump and reload activities.

3.5 A description of the conditions under which authority is granted. There are four parts to the condition all of which must be satisfied before the condition is said to have been satisfied:

(*a*) A flag to indicate that the user must have quoted his own password correctly.

(*b*) A flag to indicate that the user must be sitting at an on-line console.

(*c*) A function F(X). The function F must be chosen from the following list:

User name is X.

User has quoted key X.

User is executing the command program X.

User is using a file from group X.

(*d*) A second function plus parameter chosen from the same list as for *c*.

3.6 The date and time when the statement of authority was added to the file directory.

Acknowledgements

The work described in this paper is part of the program of research and development being carried out at the University Mathematical Laboratory, Cambridge, under the direction of Professor M. V. Wilkes. The entire operating system has been the co-operative effort of many people but is mainly due to Professor D. W. Barron, Dr. D. F. Hartley, Mr. B. Landy, Dr. R. M. Needham and the author. The early stage of the basic supervisor work were carried out in collaboration with International Computers and Tabulators Ltd., and subsequently the project has been supported by the Science Research Council.

References

1. Barron *et al*,, "File Handling at Cambridge University". *AFIPS Conf: Proc.* **30** (SJCC 1967), 163.
2. "An introduction to the Cambridge multiple-access system". University Mathematical Laboratory, Cambridge (1968).
3. "Cambridge multiaccess system manual". University Mathematical Laboratory, Cambridge (1968).

10

THE UNIX TIME-SHARING SYSTEM*

DENNIS M. RITCHIE AND KEN THOMPSON

(1974)

UNIX is a general-purpose, multi-user, interactive operating system for the Digital Equipment Corporation PDP-11/40 and 11/45 computers. It offers a number of features seldom found even in larger operating systems, including: (1) a hierarchical file system incorporating demountable volumes; (2) compatible file, device, and inter-process I/O; (3) the ability to initiate asynchronous processes; (4) system command language selectable on a per-user basis; and (5) over 100 subsystems including a dozen languages. This paper discusses the nature and implementation of the file system and of the user command interface.

1. Introduction

There have been three versions of UNIX. The earliest version (circa 1969–70) ran on the Digital Equipment Corporation PDP-7 and -9 computers. The second version ran on the unprotected PDP-11/20 computer. This paper describes only the PDP-11/40 and /45 [1] system since it is more modern and many of the differences between it and older UNIX systems result from redesign of features found to be deficient or lacking.

Since PDP-11 UNIX became operational in February 1971, about 40 installations have been put into service; they are generally smaller than the system described here. Most of them are engaged in applications such as the preparation and formatting of patent applications and other textual material, the collection and processing of trouble data from various switching machines within the Bell System, and recording and checking telephone service orders. Our own installation is used mainly for research in operating

*D. M. Ritchie and K. Thompson, The Unix time-sharing system. *Communications of the ACM 17*, 7 (July 1974), 365–375.

systems, languages, computer networks, and other topics in computer science, and also for document preparation.

Perhaps the most important achievement of UNIX is to demonstrate that a powerful operating system for interactive use need not be expensive either in equipment or in human effort: UNIX can run on hardware costing as little as $40,000, and less than two man-years were spent on the main system software. Yet UNIX contains a number of features seldom offered even in much larger systems. It is hoped, however, the users of UNIX will find that the most important characteristics of the system are its simplicity, elegance, and ease of use. Besides the system proper, the major programs available under UNIX are: assembler, text editor based on QED [2], linking loader, symbolic debugger, compiler for a language resembling BCPL [3] with types and structures (C), interpreter for a dialect of BASIC, text formatting program, Fortran compiler, Snobol interpreter, top-down compiler-compiler (TMG) [4], bottom-up compiler-compiler (YACC), form letter generator, macro processor (M6) [5], and permuted index program.

There is also a host of maintenance, utility, recreation, and novelty programs. All of these programs were written locally. It is worth noting that the system is totally self-supporting. All UNIX software is maintained under UNIX; likewise, UNIX documents are generated and formatted by the UNIX editor and text formatting program.

2. Hardware and Software Environment

The PDP-11/45 on which our UNIX installation is implemented is a 16-bit word (8-bit byte) computer with 144K bytes of core memory; UNIX occupies 42K bytes. This system, however, includes a very large number of device drivers and enjoys a generous allotment of space I/O buffers and system tables; a minimal system capable of running the software mentioned above can require as little as 50K bytes of core altogether.

The PDP-11 has a 1M byte fixed-head disk, used for file system storage and swapping, four moving-head disk drives which each provide 2.5M bytes on removable disk cartridges, and a single moving-head disk drive which uses removable 40M byte disk packs. There are also a high-speed paper tape reader-punch, nine-track magnetic tape, and DECtape (a variety of magnetic tape facility in which individual records may be addressed and rewritten). Besides the console typewriter, there are 14 variable-speed communications interfaces attached to 100-series datasets and a 201 dataset interface used primarily for spooling printout to a communal line printer.

There are also several one-of-a-kind devices including a Picturephone interface, a voice response unit, a voice synthesizer, a phototypesetter, a digital switching network, and a satellite PDP-11/20 which generates vectors, curves, and characters on a Tektronix 611 storage-tube display.

The greater part of UNIX software is written in the above-mentioned C language [6]. Early versions of the operating system were written in assembly language, but during the summer of 1973, it was rewritten in C. The size of the new system is about one third greater than the old. Since the new system is not only much easier to understand and to modify but also includes many functional improvements, including multiprogramming and the ability to share reentrant code among several user programs, we considered this increase in size quite acceptable.

3. The File System

The most important role of UNIX is to provide a file system. From the point of view of the user, there are three kinds of files: ordinary disk files, directories, and special files.

3.1 Ordinary Files

A file contains whatever information the user places on it, for example symbolic or binary (object) programs. No particular structuring is expected by the system. Files of text consist simply of a string of characters, with lines demarcated by the new-line character. Binary programs are sequences of words as they will appear in core memory when the program starts executing. A few user programs manipulate files with more structure: the assembler generates and the loader expects an object file in a particular format. However, the structure of files is controlled by the programs which use them, not by the system.

3.2 Directories

Directories provide the mapping between the names of files and the files themselves, and thus induce a structure on the file system as a whole. Each user has a directory of his own files; he may also create subdirectories to contain groups of files conveniently treated together. A directory behaves exactly like an ordinary file except that it cannot be written on by unprivileged programs, so that the system controls the contents of directories.

However, anyone with appropriate permission may read a directory just like any other file.

The system maintains several directories for its own use. One of these is the *root* directory. All files in the system can be found by tracing a path through a chain of directories until the desired file is reached. The starting point for such searches is often the root. Another system directory contains all the programs provided for general use; that is, all the *commands*. As will be seen, however, it is by no means necessary that a program reside in this directory for it to be executed.

Files are named by sequences of 14 or fewer characters. When the name of a file is specified to the system, it may be in the form of a *path name*, which is a sequence of directory names separated by slashes "/" and ending in a file name. If the sequence begins with a slash, the search begins in the root directory. The name */alpha/beta/gamma* causes the system to search the root for directory *alpha*, then to search *alpha* for *beta*, finally to find *gamma* in *beta*. *Gamma* may be an ordinary file, a directory, or a special file. As a limiting case, the name "/" refers to the root itself.

A path name not starting with "/" causes the system to begin the search in the user's current directory. Thus, the name *alpha/beta* specifies the file named *beta* in subdirectory *alpha* of the current directory. The simplest kind of name, for example *alpha*, refers to a file which itself is found in the current directory. As another limiting case, the null file name refers to the current directory.

The same nondirectory file may appear in several directories under possibly different names. This feature is called *linking*; a directory entry for a file is sometimes called a link. UNIX differs from other systems in which linking is permitted in that all links to a file have equal status. That is, a file does not exist within a particular directory; the directory entry for a file consists merely of its name and a pointer to the information actually describing the file. Thus a file exists independently of any directory entry, although in practice a file is made to disappear along with the last link to it.

Each directory always has at least two entries. The name "." in each directory refers to the directory itself. Thus a program may read the current directory under the name "." without knowing its complete path name. The name ".." by convention refers to the parent of the directory in which it appears, that is, to the directory in which it was created.

The directory structure is constrained to have the form of a rooted tree.

Except for the special entries "." and "..", each directory must appear as an entry in exactly one other, which is its parent. The reason for this is to simplify the writing of programs which visit subtrees of the directory structure, and more important to avoid the separation of portions of the hierarchy. If arbitrary links to directories were permitted, it would be quite difficult to detect when the last connection from the root to a directory was severed.

3.3 Special Files

Special files constitute the most unusual feature of the UNIX file system. Each I/O device supported by UNIX is associated with at least one such file. Special files are read and written just like ordinary disk files, but requests to read or write result in activation of the associated device. An entry for each special file resides in directory, */dev*, although a link may be made to one of these files just like an ordinary file. Thus, for example, to punch paper tape, one may write on the file */dev/ppt*. Special files exist for each communication line, each disk, each tape drive, and for physical core memory. Of course, the active disks and the core special file are protected from indiscriminate access.

There is a threefold advantage in treating I/O devices this way: file and device I/O are as similar as possible; file and device names have the same syntax and meaning, so that a program expecting a file name as a parameter can be passed a device name; finally, special files are subject to the same protection mechanism as regular files.

3.4 Removable File Systems

Although the root of the file system is always stored on the same device, it is not necessary that the entire file system hierarchy reside on this device. There is a *mount* system request which has two arguments: the name of an existing ordinary file, and the name of a direct-access special file whose associated storage volume (e.g. disk pack) should have the structure of an independent file system containing its own directory hierarchy. The effect of *mount* is to cause references to the heretofore ordinary file to refer instead to the root directory of the file system on the removable volume. In effect, *mount* replaces a leaf of the hierarchy tree (the ordinary file) by a whole new subtree (the hierarchy stored on the removable volume). After the *mount*, there is virtually no distinction between files on the removable volume and those in the permanent file system. In our installation, for example, the root directory resides on the fixed-head disk, and the large disk drive, which contains user's files, is mounted by the system initialization program; the four smaller disk drives are available to users for mounting their own disk packs. A mountable file system is generated by writing on its corresponding special file. A utility program is available to create an empty file system, or one may simply copy an existing file system.

There is only one exception to the rule of identical treatment of files on different devices: no link may exist between one file system hierarchy and another. This restriction is enforced so as to avoid the elaborate bookkeeping which would otherwise be required to assure removal of the links when the removable volume is finally dismounted. In particular, in the root directories of all file systems, removable or not, the name ".." refers to the directory itself instead of to its parent.

3.5 Protection

Although the access control scheme in UNIX is quite simple, it has some unusual features. Each user of the system is assigned a unique user identification number. When a file is created, it is marked with the user ID of its owner. Also given for new files is a set of seven protection bits. Six of these specify independently read, write, and execute permission for the owner of the file and for all other users.

If the seventh bit is on, the system will temporarily change the user identification of the current user to that of the creator of the file whenever the file is executed as a program. This change in user iD is effective only during the execution of the program which calls for it. The set-user-ID feature provides for privileged programs which may use files inaccessible to other users. For example, a program may keep an accounting file which should neither be read nor changed except by the program itself. If the set-user-identification bit is on for the program, it may access the file although this access might be forbidden to other programs invoked by the given program's user. Since the actual user ID of the invoker of any program is always available, set-user-ID programs may take any measures desired to satisfy themselves as to their invoker's credentials. This mechanism is used to allow users to execute the carefully written commands which call privileged system entries. For example, there is a system entry invokable only by the "super-user" (below) which creates an empty directory. As indicated above, directories are expected to have entries for "." and "..". The command which creates a directory is owned by the super-user and has the set-user-ID bit set. After it checks its invoker's authorization to create the specified directory, it creates it and makes the entries for "." and "..".

Since anyone may set the set-user-ID bit on one of his own files, this mechanism is generally available without administrative intervention. For example, this protection scheme easily solves the MOO accounting problem posed in [7]. The system recognizes one particular user ID (that of the "super-user") as exempt from the usual constraints on file access; thus (for example) programs may be written to dump and reload the file system without unwanted interference from the protection system.

3.6 I/O Calls

The system calls to do I/O are designed to eliminate the differences between the various devices and styles of access. There is no distinction between "random" and "sequential" I/O, nor is any logical record size imposed by the system. The size of an ordinary file is determined by the highest byte written on it; no predetermination of the size of a file is necessary or possible.

To illustrate the essentials of I/O in UNIX, some of the basic calls are summarized below in an anonymous language which will indicate the required parameters without getting into the complexities of machine language programming. Each call to the system may potentially result in an error return, which for simplicity is not represented in the calling sequence.

To read or write a file assumed to exist already, it must be opened by the following call:

filep = open(name, flag)

Name indicates the name of the file. An arbitrary path name may be given. The *flag* argument indicates whether the file is to be read, written, or "updated," that is read and written simultaneously.

The returned value *filep* is called a *file descriptor*. It is a small integer used to identify the file in subsequent calls to read, write, or otherwise manipulate it.

To create a new file or completely rewrite an old one, there is a *create* system call which creates the given file if it does not exist, or truncates it to zero length if it does exist. *Create* also opens the new file for writing and, like *open*, returns a file descriptor.

There are no user-visible locks in the file system, nor is there any restriction on the number of users who may have a file open for reading or writing. Although it is possible for the contents of a file to become scrambled when two users write on it simultaneously, in practice, difficulties do not arise. We take the view that locks are neither necessary nor sufficient, in our environment to prevent interference between users of the same file. They are unnecessary because we are not faced with large, single-file data bases maintained by independent processes. They are insufficient because locks in the ordinary sense, whereby one user is prevented from writing on a file which another user is reading, cannot prevent confusion when, for example, both users are editing a file with an editor which makes a copy of the file being edited.

It should be said that the system has sufficient internal interlocks to maintain the logical consistency of the file system when two users engage simultaneously in such inconvenient activities as writing on the same file, creating files in the same directory, or deleting each other's open files.

Except as indicated below, reading and writing are sequential. This means that if a particular byte in the file was the last byte written (or read), the next I/O call implicitly refers to the first following byte. For each open file there is a pointer, maintained by the system, which indicates the next byte to be read or written. If n bytes are read or written, the pointer advances by n bytes. Once a file is open, the following calls may be used:

n = read(filep, buffer, count)
n = write(filep, buffer, count)

Up to *count* bytes are transmitted between the file specified by *filep* and the byte array specified by *buffer*. The returned value n is the number of bytes actually transmitted. In the *write* case, n is the same as *count* except under exceptional conditions like I/O errors or end of physical medium on special files; in a *read*, however, n may without error be less than *count*. If the read pointer is so near the end of the file that reading *count* characters would cause reading beyond the end, only sufficient bytes are transmitted to reach the end of the file; also, typewriter-like devices never return more than one line of input. When a *read* call returns with n equal to zero, it indicates the end of the file. For disk files this occurs when the read pointer becomes equal to the current size of the file. It is possible to generate an end-of-file from a typewriter by use of an escape sequence which depends on the device used.

Bytes written on a file affect only those implied by the position of the write pointer and the count; no other part of the file is changed. If the last byte lies beyond the end of the file, the file is grown as needed.

To do random (direct access) I/O, it is only necessary to move the read or write pointer to the appropriate location in the file.

location = seek(filep, base, offset)

The pointer associated with *filep* is moved to a position *offset* bytes from the beginning of the file, from the current position of the pointer, or from the end of the file, depending on *base*. *Offset* may be negative. For some devices (e.g. paper tape and typewriters) seek calls are ignored. The actual offset from the beginning of the file to which the pointer was moved is returned in *location*.

3.6.1 Other I/O Calls

There are several additional system entries having to do with I/O and with the file system which will not be discussed. For example: close a file, get the status of a file, change the protection mode or the owner of a file, create a directory, make a link to an existing file, delete a file.

4. Implementation of the File System

As mentioned in §3.2 above, a directory entry contains only a name for the associated file and a pointer to the file itself. This pointer is an integer called the *i-number* (for index number) of the file. When the file is accessed, its i-number is used as an index into a system table (the *i-list*) stored in a known part of the device on which the directory resides. The entry thereby found (the file's *i-node*) contains the description of the file as follows.

1. Its owner.
2. Its protection bits.
3. The physical disk or tape addresses for the file contents.
4. Its size.
5. Time of last modification.
6. The number of links to the file, that is, the number of times it appears in a directory.
7. A bit indicating whether the file is a directory.
8. A bit indicating whether the file is a special file.
9. A bit indicating whether the file is "large" or "small."

The purpose of an *open* or *create* system call is to turn the path name given by the user into an i-number by searching the explicitly or implicitly named directories. Once a file is open, its device, i-number, and read/write pointer are stored in a system table indexed by the file descriptor returned by the *open* or *create*. Thus the file descriptor supplied during a subsequent call to read or write the file may be easily related to the information necessary to access the file.

When a new file is created, an i-node is allocated for it and a directory entry is made which contains the name of the file and the i-node number. Making a link to an existing file involves creating a directory entry with the new name, copying the i-number from the original file entry, and incrementing the link-count field of the i-node. Removing (deleting) a file is done by decrementing the link-count of the i-node specified by its directory entry and erasing the directory entry. If the link-count drops to 0, any disk blocks in the file are freed and the i-node is deallocated.

The space on all fixed or removable disks which contain a file system is divided into a number of 512-byte blocks logically addressed from 0 up to a limit which depends on the device. There is space in the i-node of each file for eight device addresses. A *small* (nonspecial) file fits into eight or fewer blocks; in this case the addresses of the blocks themselves are stored. For *large* (nonspecial) files, each of the eight device addresses may point to an indirect block of 256 addresses of blocks constituting the file itself. Thus files may be as large as $8 \cdot 256 \cdot 512$, or 1,048,576 (2^{20}) bytes.

The foregoing discussion applies to ordinary files. When an I/O request is made to a file whose i-node indicates that it is special, the last seven device address words are immaterial, and the first is interpreted as a pair of bytes which constitute an internal *device name*. These bytes specify respectively a device type and subdevice number. The device type indicates which system routine will deal with I/O on that device; the subdevice number selects, for example, a disk drive attached to a particular controller or one of several similar typewriter interfaces.

In this environment, the implementation of the *mount* system call (§3.4) is quite straightforward. *Mount* maintains a system table whose argument is the i-number and device name of the ordinary file specified during the *mount*, and whose corresponding value is the device name of the indicated special file. This table is searched for each (i-number, device)-pair which turns up while a path name is being scanned during an *open* or *create*; if a match is found, the i-number is replaced by 1 (which is the i-number of the root directory on all file systems), and the device name is replaced by the table value.

To the user, both reading and writing of files appear to be synchronous and unbuffered. That is, immediately after return from a *read* call the data are available, and conversely after a *write* the user's workspace may be reused. In fact the system maintains a rather complicated buffering mechanism which reduces greatly the number of I/O operations required to access a file. Suppose a *write* call is made specifying transmission of a single byte.

UNIX will search its buffers to see whether the affected disk block currently resides in core memory; if not, it will be read in from the device. Then the affected byte is replaced in the buffer, and an entry is made in a list of blocks to be written. The return from the *write* call may then take place, although the actual I/O may not be completed until a later time. Conversely, if a single byte is read, the system determines whether the secondary storage block in which the byte is located is already in one of the system's buffers; if so, the byte can be returned immediately. If not, the block is read into a buffer and the byte picked out.

A program which reads or writes files in units of 512 bytes has an advantage over a program which reads or writes a single byte at a time, but the gain is not immense; it comes mainly from the avoidance of system overhead. A program which is used rarely or which does no great volume of I/O may quite reasonably read and write in units as small as it wishes.

The notion of the i-list is an unusual feature of UNIX. In practice, this method of organizing the file system has proved quite reliable and easy to deal with. To the system itself, one of its strengths is the fact that each file has a short, unambiguous name which is related in a simple way to the protection, addressing, and other information needed to access the file. It also permits a quite simple and rapid algorithm for checking the consistency of a file system, for example verification that the portions of each device containing useful information and those free to be allocated are disjoint and together exhaust the space on the device. This algorithm is independent of the directory hierarchy, since it need only scan the linearly-organized i-list. At the same time the notion of the i-list induces certain peculiarities not found in other file system organizations. For example, there is the question of who is to be charged for the space a file occupies, since all directory entries for a file have equal status. Charging the owner of a file is unfair, in general, since one user may create a file, another may link to it, and the first user may delete the file. The first user is still the owner of the file, but it should be charged to the second user. The simplest reasonably fair algorithm seems to be to spread the charges equally among users who have links to a file. The current version of UNIX avoids the issue by not charging any fees at all.

4.1 Efficiency of the File System

To provide an indication of the overall efficiency of UNIX and of the file system in particular, timings were made of the assembly of a 7621-line program. The assembly was run alone on the machine; the total clock time was 35.9 sec, for a rate of 212 lines per sec. The time was divided as follows: 63.5 percent assembler execution time, 16.5 percent system overhead, 20.0 percent disk wait time. We will not attempt any interpretation of these figures nor any comparison with other systems, but merely note that we are generally satisfied with the overall performance of the system.

5. Processes and Images

An *image* is a computer execution environment. It includes a core image, general register values, status of open files, current directory, and the like. An image is the current state of a pseudo computer.

A *process* is the execution of an image. While the processor is executing on behalf of a process, the image must reside in core; during the execution of other processes it remains in core unless the appearance of an active, higher-priority process forces it to be swapped out to the fixed-head disk.

The user-core part of an image is divided into three logical segments. The program text segment begins at location 0 in the virtual address space. During execution this segment is write-protected and a single copy of it is shared among all processes executing the same program. At the first 8K byte boundary above the program text segment in the virtual address space begins a non-shared, writable data segment, the size of which may be extended by a system call. Starting at the highest address in the virtual address space is a stack segment, which automatically grows downward as the hardware's stack pointer fluctuates.

5.1 Processes

Except while UNIX is bootstrapping itself into operation, a new process can come into existence only by use of the *fork* system call:

processid = fork(label)

When *fork* is executed by a process, it splits into two independently executing processes. The two processes have independent copies of the original core image, and share any open files. The new processes differ only in that one is considered the parent process: in the parent control returns directly from the *fork*, while in the child, control is passed to location *label.* The *processid* returned by the *fork* call is the identification of the other process.

Because the return points in the parent and child process are not the same, each image existing after a *fork* may determine whether it is the parent or child process.

5.2 Pipes

Processes may communicate with related processes using the same system *read* and *write* calls that are used for file system I/O. The call

filep = pipe()

returns a file descriptor *filep* and creates an interprocess channel called a *pipe.* This channel, like other open files, is passed from parent to child process in the image by the *fork* call. A *read* using a pipe file descriptor waits until another process writes using the file descriptor for the same pipe. At this point, data are passed between the images of the two processes. Neither process need know that a pipe, rather than an ordinary file, is involved.

Although interprocess communication via pipes is a quite valuable tool (see §6.2), it is not a completely general mechanism since the pipe must be set up by a common ancestor of the processes involved.

5.3 Execution of Programs

Another major system primitive is invoked by

execute(file, arg_1, arg_2, ..., arg_n)

which requests the system to read in and execute the program named by *file*, passing it string arguments arg_1, arg_2, ..., arg_n. Ordinarily, arg_1 should be the same string as *file*, so that the program may determine the name by which it was invoked. All the code and data in the process using *execute* is replaced from the *file*, but open files, current directory, and interprocess relationships are unaltered. Only if the call fails, for example because *file* could not be found or because its execute-permission bit was not set, does a return take place from the *execute* primitive; it resembles a "jump" machine instruction rather than a subroutine call.

5.4 Process Synchronization

Another process control system call

processid = wait()

causes its caller to suspend execution until one of its children has completed execution. Then *wait* returns the *processid* of the terminated process. An error return is taken if the calling process has no descendants. Certain status from the child process is also available. *Wait* may also present status from a grandchild or more distant ancestor; see §5.5.

5.5 Termination

Lastly,

exit(status)

terminates a process, destroys its image, closes its open files, and generally obliterates it. When the parent is notified through the *wait* primitive, the indicated *status* is available to the parent; if the parent has already terminated, the status is available to the grandparent, and so on. Processes may also terminate as a result of various illegal actions or user-generated signals (§7 below).

6. The Shell

For most users, communication with UNIX is carried on with the aid of a program called the Shell. The Shell is a command line interpreter: it reads lines typed by the user and interprets them as requests to execute other programs. In simplest form, a command line consists of the command name followed by arguments to the command, all separated by spaces:

command arg_1 arg_2 ... arg_n

The Shell splits up the command name and the arguments into separate strings. Then a file with name *command* is sought; *command* may be a path name including the "/" character to specify any file in the system. If *command* is found, it is brought into core and executed. The arguments collected by the Shell are accessible to the command. When the command is finished, the Shell resumes its own execution, and indicates its readiness to accept another command by typing a prompt character.

If file *command* cannot be found, the Shell prefixes the string */bin/* to *command* and attempts again to find the file. Directory */bin* contains all the commands intended to be generally used.

6.1 Standard I/O

The discussion of I/O in §3 above seems to imply that every file used by a program must be opened or created by the program in order to get a file descriptor for the file. Programs executed by the Shell, however, start off with two open files which have file descriptors 0 and 1. As such a program begins execution, file 1 is open for writing, and is best understood as the standard output file. Except under circumstances indicated below, this file is the user's typewriter. Thus programs which wish to write informative or diagnostic information ordinarily use file descriptor 1. Conversely, file 0 starts off open for reading, and programs which wish to read messages typed by the user usually read this file.

The Shell is able to change the standard assignments of these file descriptors from the user's typewriter printer and keyboard. If one of the arguments to a command is prefixed by ">", file descriptor 1 will, for the duration of the command, refer to the file named after the ">". For example,

ls

ordinarily lists, on the typewriter, the names of the files in the current directory. The command

ls >there

creates a file called *there* and places the listing there. Thus the argument ">there" means, "place output on *there*." On the other hand,

ed

ordinarily enters the editor, which takes requests from the user via his typewriter. The command

ed <script

interprets *script* as a file of editor commands; thus "<script" means, "take input from *script*."

Although the file name following "<" or ">" appears to be an argument to the command, in fact it is interpreted completely by the Shell and is not passed to the command at all. Thus no special coding to handle I/O redirection is needed within each command; the command need merely use the standard file descriptors 0 and 1 where appropriate.

6.2 Filters

An extension of the standard I/O notion is used to direct output from one command to the input of another. A sequence of commands separated by vertical bars causes the Shell to execute all the commands simultaneously and to arrange that the standard output of each command be delivered to the standard input of the next command in the sequence. Thus in the command line

```
ls | pr –2 | opr
```

ls lists the names of the files in the current directory; its output is passed to *pr*, which paginates its input with dated headings. The argument "–2" means double column. Likewise the output from *pr* is input to *opr*. This command spools its input onto a file for off-line printing.

This process could have been carried out more clumsily by

```
ls >temp1
pr –2 <temp1 >temp2
opr <temp2
```

followed by removal of the temporary files. In the absence of the ability to redirect output and input, a still clumsier method would have been to require the *ls* command to accept user requests to paginate its output, to print in multi-column format, and to arrange that its output be delivered off-line. Actually it would be surprising, and in fact unwise for efficiency reasons, to expect authors of commands such as *ls* to provide such a wide variety of output options.

A program such as *pr* which copies its standard input to its standard output (with processing) is called a *filter*. Some filters which we have found useful perform character transliteration, sorting of the input, and encryption and decryption.

6.3 Command Separators: Multitasking

Another feature provided by the Shell is relatively straightforward. Commands need not be on different lines; instead they may be separated by semicolons.

```
ls; ed
```

will first list the contents of the current directory, then enter the editor.

A related feature is more interesting. If a command is followed by "&", the Shell will not wait for the command to finish before prompting again; instead, it is ready immediately to accept a new command. For example,

as source >output & ls> files &

causes *source* to be assembled, with diagnostic output going to *output*; no matter how long the assembly takes, the Shell returns immediately. When the Shell does not wait for the completion of a command, the identification of the process running that command is printed. This identification may be used to wait for the completion of the command or to terminate it. The "&" may be used several times in a line:

as source >output & ls >files &

does both the assembly and the listing in the background. In the examples above using "&", an output file other than the typewriter was provided; if this had not been done, the outputs of the various commands would have been intermingled.

The Shell also allows parentheses in the above operations. For example

(date; ls) > x &

prints the current date and time followed by a list of the current directory onto the file x. The Shell also returns immediately for another request.

6.4 The Shell as a Command: Command files

The Shell is itself a command, and may be called recursively. Suppose file *tryout* contains the lines

as source
mv a.out testprog
testprog

The *mv* command causes the file *a.out* to be renamed *testprog*. *a.out* is the (binary) output of the assembler, ready to be executed. Thus if the three lines above were typed on the console, *source* would be assembled, the resulting program named *testprog*, and *testprog* executed. When the lines are in *tryout*, the command

sh <tryout

would cause the Shell *sh* to execute the commands sequentially.

The Shell has further capabilities, including the ability to substitute parameters and to construct argument lists from a specified subset of the file names in a directory. It is also possible to execute commands conditionally on character string comparisons or on existence of given files and to perform transfers of control within filed command sequences.

6.5 Implementation of the Shell

The outline of the operation of the Shell can now be understood. Most of the time, the Shell is waiting for the user to type a command. When the new-line character ending the line is typed, the Shell's *read* call returns. The Shell analyzes the command line, putting the arguments in a form appropriate for *execute*. Then *fork* is called. The child process, whose code of course is still that of the Shell, attempts to perform an *execute* with the appropriate arguments. If successful, this will bring in and start execution of the program whose name was given. Meanwhile, the other process resulting from the *fork*, which is the parent process, *waits* for the child process to die. When this happens, the Shell knows the command is finished, so it types its prompt and reads the typewriter to obtain another command.

Given this framework, the implementation of background processes is trivial; whenever a command line contains "&", the Shell merely refrains from waiting for the process which it created to execute the command.

Happily, all of this mechanism meshes very nicely with the notion of standard input and output files. When a process is created by the *fork* primitive, it inherits not only the core image of its parent but also all the files currently open in its parent, including those with file descriptors 0 and 1. The Shell, of course, uses these files to read command lines and to write its prompts and diagnostics, and in the ordinary case its children—the command programs—inherit them automatically. When an argument with "<" or ">" is given however, the offspring process, just before it performs *execute*, makes the standard I/O file descriptor 0 or 1 respectively refer to the named file. This is easy because, by agreement, the smallest unused file descriptor is assigned when a new file is *open*ed (or *create*d); it is only necessary to close file 0 (or 1) and open the named file. Because the process in which the command program runs simply terminates when it is through, the association between a file specified after "<" or ">" and file descriptor 0 or 1 is ended automatically when the process dies. Therefore the Shell need not know the actual names of the files which are its own standard input and output since it need never reopen them.

Filters are straightforward extensions of standard I/O redirection with pipes used instead of files.

In ordinary circumstances, the main loop of the Shell never terminates. (The main loop includes that branch of the return from *fork* belonging to the parent process; that is, the branch which does a *wait*, then reads another command line.) The one thing which causes the Shell to terminate is discovering an end-of-file a condition on its input file. Thus, when the Shell is executed as a command with a given input file, as in

sh <comfile

the commands in *comfile* will be executed until the end of *comfile* is reached; then the instance of the Shell invoked by *sh* will terminate. Since this Shell process is the child of another instance of the Shell, the *wait* executed in the latter will return, and another command may be processed.

6.6 Initialization

The instances of the Shell to which users type commands are themselves children of another process. The last step in the initialization of UNIX is the creation of a single process and the invocation (via *execute*) of a program called *init.* The role of *init* is to create one process for each typewriter channel which may be dialed up by a user. The various subinstances of *init* open the appropriate typewriters for input and output. Since when *init* was invoked there were no files open, in each process the typewriter keyboard will receive file descriptor 0 and the printer file descriptor 1. Each process types out a message requesting that the user log in and waits, reading the typewriter, for a reply. At the outset, no one is logged in, so each process simply hangs. Finally someone types his name or other identification. The appropriate instance of *init* wakes up, receives the log-in line, and reads a password file. If the user name is found, and if he is able to supply the correct password, *init* changes to the user's default current directory, sets the process's user ID to that of the person logging in, and performs an *execute* of the Shell. At this point the Shell is ready to receive commands and the logging-in protocol is complete.

Meanwhile, the mainstream path of *init* (the parent of all the subinstances of itself which will later become Shells) does a *wait.* If one of the child processes terminates, either because a Shell found an end of file or because a user typed an incorrect name or password, this path of *init* simply recreates the defunct process, which in turn reopens the appropriate input and output files and types another login message. Thus a user may log out simply by typing the end-of-file sequence in place of a command to the Shell.

6.7 Other Programs as Shell

The Shell as described above is designed to allow users full access to the facilities of the system since it will invoke the execution of any program with appropriate protection mode. Sometimes, however, a different interface to the system is desirable, and this feature is easily arranged.

Recall that after a user has successfully logged in by supplying his name and password, *init* ordinarily invokes the Shell to interpret command lines. The user's entry in the password file may contain the name of a program to be invoked after login instead of the Shell. This program is free to interpret the user's messages in any way it wishes.

For example, the password file entries for users of a secretarial editing system specify that the editor *ed* is to be used instead of the Shell. Thus when editing system users log in, they are inside the editor and can begin work immediately; also, they can be prevented from invoking UNIX programs not intended for their use. In practice, it has proved desirable to allow a temporary escape from the editor to execute the formatting program and other utilities.

Several of the games (e.g. chess, blackjack, 3D tic-tac-toe) available on UNIX illustrate a much more severely restricted environment. For each of these an entry exists in the password file specifying that the appropriate game-playing program is to be invoked instead of the Shell. People who log in as a player of one of the games find themselves limited to the game and unable to investigate the presumably more interesting offerings of UNIX as a whole.

7. Traps

The PDP-11 hardware detects a number of program faults, such as references to nonexistent memory, unimplemented instructions, and odd addresses used where an even address is required. Such faults cause the processor to trap to a system routine. When an illegal action is caught, unless other arrangements have been made, the system terminates the process and writes the user's image on file *core* in the current directory. A debugger can be used to determine the state of the program at the time of the fault.

Programs which are looping, which produce unwanted output, or about which the user has second thoughts may be halted by the use of the *interrupt* signal, which is generated by typing the "delete" character. Unless special action has been taken, this signal simply causes the program to cease execution without producing a core image file.

There is also a *quit* signal which is used to force a core image to be produced. Thus programs which loop unexpectedly may be halted and the core image examined without prearrangement.

The hardware-generated faults and the interrupt and quit signals can, by request, be either ignored or caught by the process. For example, the Shell ignores quits to prevent a quit from logging the user out. The editor catches interrupts and returns to its command level. This is useful for stopping long printouts without losing work in progress (the editor manipulates a copy of the file it is editing). In systems without floating point hardware, unimplemented instructions are caught, and floating point instructions are interpreted.

8. Perspective

Perhaps paradoxically, the success of UNIX is largely due to the fact that it was not designed to meet any predefined objectives. The first version was written when one of us (Thompson), dissatisfied with the available computer facilities discovered a little-used PDP-7 and set out to create a more hospitable environment. This essentially personal effort was sufficiently successful to gain the interest of the remaining author and others, and later to justify the acquisition of the PDP-11/20, specifically to support a text editing and formatting system. When in turn the 11/20 was outgrown, UNIX had proved useful enough to persuade management to invest in the PDP-11/45. Our goals throughout the effort, when articulated at all, have always concerned themselves with building a comfortable relationship with the machine and with exploring ideas and inventions in operating systems. We have not been faced with the need to satisfy someone else's requirements, and for this freedom we are grateful.

Three considerations which influenced the design of UNIX are visible in retrospect.

First, since we are programmers, we naturally designed the system to make it easy to write, test, and run programs. The most important expression of our desire for programming convenience was that the system was arranged for interactive use, even though the original version only supported one user. We believe that a properly-designed interactive system is much more productive and satisfying to use than a "batch" system. Moreover such a system is rather easily adaptable to noninteractive use, while the converse is not true.

Second, there have always been fairly severe size constraints on the system and its software. Given the partially antagonistic desires for reasonable efficiency and expressive power, the size constraint has encouraged not only economy but a certain elegance of design. This may be a thinly disguised version of the "salvation through suffering" philosophy, but in our case it worked.

Third, nearly from the start, the system was able to, and did, maintain itself. This fact is more important than it might seem. If designers of a system are forced to use that system, they quickly become aware of its functional and superficial deficiencies and are strongly motivated to correct them before it is too late. Since all source programs were always available and easily modified on-line, we were willing to revise and rewrite the system and its software when new ideas were invented, discovered, or suggested by others.

The aspects of UNIX discussed in this paper exhibit clearly at least the first two of these design considerations. The interface to the file system, for example, is extremely convenient from a programming standpoint. The lowest possible interface level is designed to eliminate distinctions between the various devices and files and between direct and sequential access. No large "access method" routines are required to insulate the programmer from the system calls; in fact, all user programs either call the system directly or use a small library program, only tens of instructions long, which buffers a number of characters and reads or writes them all at once.

Another important aspect of programming convenience is that there are no "control blocks" with a complicated structure partially maintained by and depended on by the file system or other system calls. Generally speaking, the contents of a program's address space are the property of the program, and we have tried to avoid placing restrictions on the data structures within that address space.

Given the requirement that all programs should be usable with any file or device as input or output, it is also desirable from a space-efficiency standpoint to push device-dependent considerations into the operating system itself. The only alternatives seem to be to load routines for dealing with each device with all programs, which is expensive in space, or to depend on some means of dynamically linking to thc routine appropriate to each device when it is actually needed, which is expensive either in overhead or in hardware.

Likewise, the process control scheme and command interface have proved both convenient and efficient. Since the Shell operates as an ordinary, swappable user program, it consumes no wired-down space in the system proper, and it may be made as powerful as desired at little cost. In particular, given the framework in which the Shell executes as a process which spawns other processes to perform commands, the notions of I/O redirection, background processes, command files, and user-selectable system interfaces all become essentially trivial to implement.

8.1 Influences

The success of UNIX lies not so much in new inventions but rather in the full exploitation of a carefully selected set of fertile ideas, and especially in showing that they can be keys to the implementation of a small yet powerful operating system.

The *fork* operation, essentially as we implemented it,was present in the Berkeley time-sharing system [8]. On a number of points we were influenced by Multics, which suggested the particular form of the I/O system calls [9] and both the name of the Shell and its general functions. The notion that the Shell should create a process for each command was also suggested to us by the early design of Multics, although in that system it was later dropped for efficiency reasons. A similar scheme is used by TENEX [10].

9. Statistics

The following statistics from UNIX are presented to show the scale of the system and to show how a system of this scale is used. Those of our users not involved in document preparation tend to use the system for program development, especially language work. There are few important "applications" programs.

9.1 Overall

72	user population
14	maximum simultaneous users
300	directories
4400	files
34000	512-byte secondary storage blocks used

9.2 Per day (24-hour day, 7-day week basis)

There is a "background" process that runs at the Iowest possible priority; it is used to soak up any idle CPU time. It has been used to produce a million-digit approximation to the constant e–2, and is now generating composite pseudoprimes (base 2).

1800	commands
4.3	CPU hours (aside from background)
70	connect hours
30	different users
75	logins

9.3 Command CPU Usage (cut off at 1 %)

15.7%	C compiler
15.2%	users' programs
11.7%	editor
5.8%	Shell (used as a command, including command times)
5.3%	chess
3.3%	list directory
3.1%	document formatter
1.6%	backup dumper
1.8%	assembler
1.7%	Fortran compiler
1.6%	remove file
1.6%	tape archive
1.6%	file system consistency check
1.4%	library maintainer
1.3%	concatenate/print files
1.3%	paginate and print file
1.1%	print disk usage
1.0%	copy file

9.4 Command Accesses (cut off at 1%)

15.3%	editor
9.6%	list directory
6.3%	remove file
6.3%	C compiler
6.0%	concatenate/print file
6.0%	users' programs
3.3%	list people logged on system
3.2%	rename/move file
3.1%	file status
1.8%	library maintainer
1.8%	document formatter
1.6%	execute another command conditionally
1.6%	debugger
1.6%	Shell (used as a command)
1.5%	print disk availability
1.4%	list processes executing
1.4%	assembler
1.4%	print arguments
1.2%	copy file
1.1%	paginate and print file
1.1%	print current date/time
1.1%	file system consistency check
1.0%	tape archive

9.5 Reliability

Our statistics on reliability are much more subjective than the others. The following results are true to the best of our combined recollections. The time span is over one year with a very early vintage 11/45.

There has been one loss of a file system (one disk out of five) caused by software inability to cope with a hardware problem causing repeated power fail traps. Files on that disk were backed up three days.

A "crash" is an unscheduled system reboot or halt. There is about one crash every other day; about two-thirds of them are caused by hardware-related difficulties such as power dips and inexplicable processor interrupts to random locations. The remainder are software failures. The longest uninterrupted up time was about two weeks. Service calls average one every three weeks, but are heavily clustered. Total up time has been about 98 percent of our 24-hour, 365-day schedule.

Acknowledgments. We are grateful to R.H. Canaday, L.L. Cherry, and L.E. McMahon for their contributions to UNIX. We are particularly appreciative of the inventiveness, thoughtful criticism, and constant support of R. Morris, M.D. McIlroy, and J.F. Ossanna.

References

1. Digital Equipment Corporation. PDP-11/40 Processor Handbook, 1972, and PDP-11/45 Processor Handbook, 1971.
2. Deutsch, L.P., and Lampson, B.W. An online editor. *Comm. ACM 10*, 12 (Dec. 1967), 793–799, 803.
3. Richards, M. BCPL: A tool for compiler writing and system programming. Proc. AFIPS 1969 SJCC, Vol. 34, AFIPS Press, Montvale, N.J., pp. 557-566.
4. McClure, R.M. TMG—A syntax directed compiler. Proc. ACM 20th Nat. Conf., ACM, 1965, New York, pp. 262-274.
5. Hall, A.D. The M6 macroprocessor. Computing Science Tech. Rep.#2, Bell Telephone Laboratories, 1969.
6. Ritchie, D.M. C reference manual. Unpublished memorandum, Bell Teiephone Laboratories, 1973.
7. Aleph-null. Computer Recreations. *Software Practice and Experience 1*, 2 (Apr.–June 1971), 201–204.
8. Deutsch, L.P., and Lampson, B.W. SDS 930 time-sharing system preliminary reference manual. Doc. 30.10.10, Project GENIE, U of California at Berkeley, Apr. 1965.
9. Feiertag, R.J., and Organick, E.I. The Multics input-output system. Proc. Third Symp. on Oper. Syst. Princ., Oct. 18–20, 1971, ACM, New York, pp. 35–41.

10. Bobrow, D.G., Burchfiel, J.D., Murphy, D.L., and Tomlinson, R.S. TENEX, a paged time sharing system for the PDP-10. *Comm. ACM 15*, 3 (Mar. 1972), 135–143.

PART V

CONCURRENT PROGRAMMING

11

THE STRUCTURE OF THE "THE" MULTIPROGRAMMING SYSTEM*

EDSGER W. DIJKSTRA

(1968)

A multiprogramming system is described in which all activities are divided over a number of sequential processes. These sequential processes are placed at various hierarchical levels, in each of which one or more independent abstractions have been implemented. The hierarchical structure proved to be vital for the verification of the logical soundness of the design and the correctness of its implementation.

Introduction

In response to a call explicitly asking for papers "on timely research and development efforts," I present a progress report on the multiprogramming effort at the Department of Mathematics at the Technological University in Eindhoven.

Having very limited resources (viz. a group of six people of, on the average, half-time availability) and wishing to contribute to the art of system design—including all the stages of conception, construction, and verification, we were faced with the problem of how to get the necessary experience. To solve this problem we adopted the following three guiding principles:

(1) Select a project as advanced as you can conceive, as ambitious as you can justify, in the hope that routine work can be kept to a minimum; hold out against all pressure to incorporate such system expansions that would

---

*E. W. Dijkstra, The structure of the "THE" multiprogramming system. *Communications of the ACM 11*, 5 (May 1968), 341–346.

only result into a purely quantitative increase of the total amount of work to be done.

(2) Select a machine with sound basic characteristics (e.g. an interrupt system to fall in love with is certainly an inspiring feature); from then on try to keep the specific properties of the configuration for which you are preparing the system out of your considerations as long as possible.

(3) Be aware of the fact that experience does by no means automatically lead to wisdom and understanding; in other words, make a conscious effort to learn as much as it possible from your previous experiences.

Accordingly, I shall try to go beyond just reporting what we have done and how, and I shall try to formulate as well what we have learned.

I should like to end the introduction with two short remarks on working conditions, which I make for the sake of completeness. I shall not stress these points any further.

One remark is that production speed is severely slowed down if one works with half-time people who have other obligations as well. This is at least a factor of four; probably it is worse. The people themselves lose time and energy in switching over; the group as a whole loses decision speed as discussions, when needed, have often to be postponed until all people concerned are available.

The other remark is that the members of the group (mostly mathematicians) have previously enjoyed as good students a university training of five to eight years and are of Master's or Ph.D. level. I mention this explicitly because at least in my country the intellectual level needed for system design is in general grossly underestimated. I am convinced more than ever that this type of work is very difficult, and that every effort to do it with other than the best people is doomed to either failure or moderate success at enormous expense.

The Tool and the Goal

The system has been designed for a Dutch machine, the EL XS (N.V. Electrologica, Rijswijk (ZH)). Characteristics of our configuration are:

(1) core memory cycle time 2.5 μsec, 27 bits; at present 32K;

(2) drum of 512K words, 1024 words per track, rev. time 40 msec;

(3) an indirect addressing mechanism very well suited for stack implementation;

(4) a sound system for commanding peripherals and controlling of interrupts;

(5) a potentially great number of low capacity channels; ten of them are used (3 paper tape readers at 1000 char/sec; 3 paper tape punches at 150 char/sec; 2 teleprinters; a plotter; a line printer);

(6) absence of a number of not unusual, awkward features.

The primary goal of the system is to process smoothly a continuous flow of user programs as a service to the university. A multiprogramming system has been chosen with the following objectives in mind: (1) a reduction of turn-around time for programs of short duration, (2) economic use of peripheral devices, (3) automatic control of backing store to be combined with economic use of the central processor, and (4) the economic feasibility to use the machine for those applications for which only the flexibility of a general purpose computer is needed, but (as a rule) not the capacity nor the processing power.

The system is not intended as a multiaccess system. There is no common data base via which independent users can communicate with each other: they only share the configuration and a procedure library (that includes a translator for Algol 60 extended with complex numbers). The system does not cater for user programs written in machine language.

Compared with larger efforts one can state that quantitatively speaking the goals have been set as modest as the equipment and our other resources. Qualitatively speaking, I am afraid, we became more and more immodest as the work progressed.

A Progress Report

We have made some minor mistakes of the usual type (such as paying too much attention to eliminating what was not the real bottleneck) and two major ones.

Our first major mistake was that for too long a time we confined our attention to "a perfect installation"; by the time we considered how to make the best of it, one of the peripherals broke down, we were faced with nasty problems. Taking care of the "pathology" took more energy than we had expected, and some of our troubles were a direct consequence of our earlier ingenuity, i.e. the complexity of the situation into which the system could have maneuvered itself. Had we paid attention to the pathology at an earlier stage of the design, our management rules would certainly have been less refined.

The second major mistake has been that we conceived and programmed the major part of the system without giving more than scanty thought to the problem of debugging it. I must decline all credit for the fact that this mistake had no serious consequences—on the contrary! one might argue as an afterthought.

As captain of the crew I had had extensive experience (dating back to 1958) in making basic software dealing with real-time interrupts, and I knew by bitter experience that as a result of the irreproducibility of the interrupt moments a program error could present itself misleadingly like an occasional machine malfunctioning. As a result I was terribly afraid. Having fears regarding the possibility of debugging, we decided to be as careful as possible and, prevention being better than cure, to try to prevent nasty bugs from entering the construction.

This decision, inspired by fear, is at the bottom of what I regard as the group's main contribution to the art of system design. We have found that it is possible to design a refined multiprogramming system in such a way that its logical soundness can be proved a priori and its implementation can admit exhaustive testing. The only errors that showed up during testing were trivial coding error (occurring with a density of one error per 500 instructions) each of them located within 10 minutes (classical) inspection by the machine and each of them correspondingly easy to remedy. At the time this was written the testing had not yet been completed, but the resulting system is guaranteed to be flawless. When the system is delivered we shall not live in the perpetual fear that a system derailment may still occur in an unlikely situation, such as might result from an unhappy "coincidence" of two or more critical occurrences, for we shall have proved the correctness of the system with a rigor and explicitness that is unusual for the great majority of mathematical proofs.

A Survey of the System Structure

Storage Allocation. In the classical von Neumann machine, information is identified by the address of the memory location containing the information. When we started to think about the automatic control of secondary storage we were familiar with a system (viz. GIER ALGOL) in which all information was identified by its drum address (as in the classical von Neumann machine) and in which the function of the core memory was nothing more than to make the information "page-wise" accessible.

We have followed another approach and, as it turned out, to great advantage. In our terminology we made a strict distinction between memory units (we called them "pages" and had "core pages" and "drum pages") and corresponding information units (for lack of a better word we called them "segments"), a segment just fitting in a page. For segments we created a completely independent identification mechanism in which the number of possible segment identifiers is much larger than the total number of pages in primary and secondary store. The segment identifier gives fast access to a so-called "segment variable" in core whose value denotes whether the segment is still empty or not, and if not empty, in which page (or pages) it can be found.

As a consequence of this approach, if a segment of information, residing in a core page, has to be dumped onto the drum in order to make the core page available for other use, there is no need to return the segment to the same drum page from which it originally came. In fact, this freedom is exploited: among the free drum pages the one with minimum latency time is selected.

A next consequence is the total absence of a drum allocation problem: there is not the slightest reason why, say, a program should occupy consecutive drum pages. In a multiprogramming environment this is very convenient.

Processor Allocation. We have given full recognition to the fact that in a single sequential process (such as can be performed by a sequential automaton) only the time succession of the various states has a logical meaning, but not the actual speed with which the sequential process is performed. Therefore we have arranged the whole system as a society of sequential processes, progressing with undefined speed ratios. To each user program accepted by the system corresponds a sequential process, to each input peripheral corresponds a sequential process (buffering input streams in synchronism with the execution of the input commands), to each output peripheral corresponds a sequential process (unbuffering output streams in synchronism with the execution of the output commands); furthermore, we have the "segment controller" associated with the drum and the "message interpreter" associated with the console keyboard.

This enabled us to design the whole system in terms of these abstract "sequential processes." Their harmonious cooperation is regulated by means of explicit mutual synchronization statements. On the one hand, this explicit mutual synchronization is necessary, as we do not make any assumption about speed ratios; on the other hand, this mutual synchronization is possible because "delaying the progress of a process temporarily" can never be harmful to the interior logic of the process delayed. The fundamental consequence of this approach—viz. the explicit mutual synchronization—is that the harmonious cooperation of a set of such sequential processes can be established by discrete reasoning; as a further consequence the whole harmonious society of cooperating sequential processes is independent of the actual number of processors available to carry out these processes, provided the processors available can switch from process to process.

System Hierarchy. The total system admits a strict hierarchical structure.

At level 0 we find the responsibility for processor allocation to one of the processes whose dynamic progress is logically permissible (i.e. in view of the explicit mutual synchronization). At this level the interrupt of the real-time clock is processed and introduced to prevent any process to monopolize processing power. At this level a priority rule is incorporated to achieve quick response of the system where this is needed. Our first abstraction has been achieved; above level 0 the number of processors actually shared is no longer relevant. At higher levels we find the activity of the different sequential processes, the actual processor that had lost its identity having disappeared from the picture.

At level 1 we have the so-called "segment controller," a sequential process synchronized with respect to the drum interrupt and the sequential processes on higher levels. At level 1 we find the responsibility to cater to the bookkeeping resulting from the automatic backing store. At this level our next abstraction has been achieved; at all higher levels identification of information takes place in terms of segments, the actual storage pages that had lost their identity having disappeared from the picture.

At level 2 we find the "message interpreter" taking care of the allocation of the console keyboard via which conversations between the operator and any of the higher level processes can be carried out. The message interpreter works in close synchronism with the operator. When the operator presses a key, a character is sent to the machine together with an interrupt signal to announce the next keyboard character, whereas the actual printing is done through an output command generated by the machine under control of the message interpreter. (As far as the hardware is concerned the console teleprinter is regarded as two independent peripherals: an input keyboard and an output printer.) If one of the processes opens a conversation, it identifies itself in the opening sentence of the conversation for the benefit of the operator. If, however, the operator opens a conversation, he must identify the process he is addressing, in the opening sentence of the conversation, i.e.

this opening sentence must be interpreted before it is known to which of the processes the conversation is addressed! Here lies the logical reason for the introduction of a separate sequential process for the console teleprinter, a reason that is reflected in its name, "message interpreter."

Above level 2 it is as if each process had its private conversational console. The fact that they share the same physical console is translated into a resource restriction of the form "only one conversation at a time," a restriction that is satisfied via mutual synchronization. At this level the next abstraction has been implemented; at higher levels the actual console teleprinter loses its identity. (If the message interpreter had not been on a higher level than the segment controller, then the only way to implement it would have been to make a permanent reservation in core for it; as the conversational vocabulary might become large (as soon as our operators wish to be addressed in fancy messages), this would result in too heavy a permanent demand upon core storage. Therefore, the vocabulary in which the messages are expressed is stored on segments, i.e. as information units that can reside on the drum as well. For this reason the message interpreter is one level higher than the segment controller.)

At level 3 we find the sequential processes associated with buffering of input streams and unbuffering of output streams. At this level the next abstraction is effected, viz. the abstraction of the actual peripherals used that are allocated at this level to the "logical communication units" in terms of which are worked in the still higher levels. The sequential processes associated with the peripherals are of a level above the message interpreter, because they must be able to converse with the operator (e.g. in the case of detected malfunctioning). The limited number of peripherals again acts as a resource restriction for the processes at higher levels to be satisfied by mutual synchronization between them.

At level 4 we find the independent user programs and at level 5 the operator (not implemented by us).

The system structure has been described at length in order to make the next section intelligible.

Design Experience

The conception stage took a long time. During that period of time the concepts have been born in terms of which we sketched the system in the previous section. Furthermore, we learned the art of reasoning by which we could deduce from our requirements the way in which the processes should influence each other by their mutual synchronization so that these requirements would be met. (The requirements being that no information can be used before it has been produced, that no peripheral can be set to two tasks simultaneously, etc.). Finally we learned the art of reasoning by which ve could prove that the society composed of processes thus mutually synchronized by each other would indeed in its time behavior satisfy all requirements.

The construction stage has been rather traditional, perhaps even old-fashioned, that is, plain machine code. Reprogramming on account of a change of specifications has been rare, a circumstance that must have contributed greatly to the feasibility of the "steam method." That the first two stages took more time than planned was somewhat compensated by a delay in the delivery of the machine.

In the verification stage we had the machine, during short shots, completely at our disposal; these were shots during which we worked with a virgin machine without any software aids for debugging. Starting at level 0 the system was tested, each time adding (a portion of) the next level only after the previous level had been thoroughly tested. Each test shot itself contained, on top of the (partial) system to be tested, a number of testing processes with a double function. First, they had to force the system into all different relevant states; second, they had to verify that the system continued to react according to specification.

I shall not deny that the construction of these testing programs has been a major intellectual effort: to convince oneself that one has not overlooked "a relevant state" and to convince oneself that the testing programs generate them all is no simple matter. The encouraging thing is that (as far as we know) it could be done.

This fact was one of the happy consequences of the hierarchical structure.

Testing level 0 (the real-time clock and processor allocation) implied a number of testing sequential processes on top of it, inspecting together that under all circumstances processor time was divided among them according to the rules. This being established, sequential processes as such were implemented.

Testing the segment controller at level 1 meant that all "relevant states" could be formulated in terms of sequential processes making (in various combinations) demands on core pages, situations that could be provoked by explicit synchronization among the testing programs. At this stage the existence of the real-time clock—although interrupting all the time—was so immaterial that one of the testers indeed forgot its existence!

By that time we had implemented the correct reaction upon the (mutually unsynchronized) interrupts from the real-time clock and the drum. If we had not introduced the separate levels 0 and 1, and if we had not created a terminology (viz. that of the rather abstract sequential processes) in which the existence of the clock interrupt could be discarded, but had instead tried in a nonhierarchical construction, to make the central processor react directly upon any weird time succession of these two interrupts, the number of "relevant states" would have exploded to such a height that exhaustive testing would have been an illusion. (Apart from that it is doubtful whether we would have had the means to generate them all, drum and clock speed being outside our control.)

For the sake of completeness I must mention a further happy consequence. As stated before, above level 1, core and drum pages have lost their identity, and buffering of input and output streams (at level 3) therefore occurs in terms of segments. While testing at level 2 or 3 the drum channel hardware broke down for some time, but testing proceeded by restricting the number of segments to the number that could be held in core. If building up the line printer output streams had been implemented as "dumping onto the drum" and the actual printing as "printing from the drum," this advantage would have been denied to us.

Conclusion

As far as program verification is concerned I present nothing essentially new. In testing a general purpose object (be it a piece of hardware, a program, a machine, or a system), one cannot subject it to all possible cases: for a computer this would imply that one feeds it with all possible programs! Therefore one must test it with a set of relevant test cases. What is, or is not, relevant cannot be decided as long as one regards the mechanism as a black box; in other words, the decision has to be based upon the internal structure of the mechanism to be tested. It seems to be the designer's responsibility to construct his mechanism in such a way—i.e. so effectively structured—that at each stage of the testing procedure the number of relevant test cases will be so small that he can try them all and that what is being tested will be so perspicuous that he will not have overlooked any situation. I have presented a survey of our system because I think it a nice example of the form that such a structure might take.

In my experience, I am sorry to say, industrial software makers tend to react to the system with mixed feelings. On the one hand, they are inclined to think that we have done a kind of model job; on the other hand, they express doubts whether the techniques used are applicable outside the sheltered atmosphere of a University and express the opinion that we were successful only because of the modest scope of the whole project. It is not my intention to underestimate the organizing ability needed to handle a much bigger job, with a lot more people, but I should like to venture the opinion that the larger the project the more essential the structuring! A hierarchy of five logical levels might then very well turn out to be of modest depth. especially when one designs the system more consciously than we have done, with the aim that the software can be smoothly adapted to (perhaps drastic) configuration expansions.

Acknowledgments. I express my indebtedness to my five collaborators, C. Bron, A. N. Habermann, F. J. Hendriks, C. Ligtmans, and P. A. Voorhoeve. They have contributed to all stages of the design, and together we learned the art of reasoning needed. The construction and verification was entirely their effort; if my dreams have come true, it is due to their faith, their talents, and their persistent loyalty to the whole project.

Finally I should like to thank: the members of the program committee, who asked for more information on the synchronizing primitives and some justification of my claim to be able to prove logical soundness a priori. In answer to this request an appendix has been added, which I hope will give the desired information and justification.

APPENDIX

Synchronizing Primitives

Explicit mutual synchronization of parallel sequential processes is implemented via so-called "semaphores." They are special purpose integer variables allocated in the universe in which the processes are embedded; they are initialized (with the value 0 or 1) before the parallel processes themselves are started. After this initialization the parallel processes will access the semaphores only via two very specific operations, the so-called synchronizing primitives. For historical reasons they are called the P-operation and the V-operation.

A process, "Q" say, that performs the operation "P(sem)" decreases the value of the semaphore called "sem" by 1. If the resulting value of the semaphore concerned is nonnegative, process Q can continue with the execution of its next statement; if, however, the resulting value is negative, process Q is stopped and booked on a waiting list associated with the semaphore concerned. Until further notice (i.e. a V-operation on this very same semaphore), dynamic progress of process Q is not logically permissible and no processor will be allocated to it (see above "System Hierarchy," at level 0).

A process, "R" say, that performs the operation "V(sem)" increases the value of the semaphore called "sem" by 1. If the resulting value of the semaphore concerned is positive, the V-operation in question has no further effect; if, however, the resulting value of the semaphore concerned is nonpositive, one of the processes booked on its waiting list is removed from this waiting list, i.e. its dynamic progress is again logically permissible and in due time a processor will be allocated to it (again, see above "System Hierarchy," at level 0).

COROLLARY 1. *If a semaphore value is nonpositive its absolute value equals the number of processes booked on its waiting list.*

COROLLARY 2. *The P-operation represents the potential delay, the complementary V-operation represents the removal of a barrier.*

Note 1. P- and V-operations are "indivisible actions"; i.e. if they occur "simultaneously" in parallel processes they are noninterfering in the sense that they can be regarded as being performed one after the other.

Note 2. If the semaphore value resulting from a V-operation is negative, its waiting list originally contained more than one process. It is undefined—i.e. logically immaterial–which of the waiting processes is then removed from the waiting list.

Note 3. A consequence of the mechanisms described above is that a process whose dynamic progress is permissible can only loose this status by actually progressing, i.e. by performance of a P-operation on a semaphore with a value that is initially nonpositive.

During system conception it transpired that we used the semaphores in two completely different ways. The difference is so marked that, looking back, one wonders whether it was really fair to present the two ways as uses of the very same primitives. On the one hand, we have the semaphores used for mutual exclusion, on the other hand, the private semaphores.

Mutual Exclusion

In the following program we indicate two parallel, cyclic processes (between the brackets "parbegin" and "parend") that come into action after the surrounding universe has been introduced and initialized.

```
begin semaphore mutex; mutex := 1;
  parbegin
    begin L1: P(mutex); critical section 1; V(mutex);
      remainder of cycle 1; go to L1
    end;
    begin L2: P(mutex); critical section 2; V(mutex);
      remainder of cycle 2; go to L2
    end
  parend
end
```

As a result of the P- and V-operations on "mutex" the actions, marked as "critical sections" exclude each other mutually in time; the scheme given allows straightforward extension to more than two parallel processes, the maximum value of mutex equals 1, the minimum value equals $-(n - 1)$ if we have n parallel processes.

Critical sections are used always, and only for the purpose of unambiguous inspection and modification of the state variables (allocated in the surrounding universe) that describe the current state of the system (as far as needed for the regulation of the harmonious cooperation between the various processes).

Private Semaphores

Each sequential process has associated with it a number of private semaphores and no other process will ever perform a P-operation on them. The universe initializes them with the value equal to 0, their maximum value equals 1, and their minimum value equals –1.

Whenever a process reaches a stage where the permission for dynamic progress depends on current values of state variables, it follows the pattern:

```
P(mutex);
"inspection and modification of state variables including
  a conditional V(private semaphore)";
V(mutex);
P(private semaphore)
```

If the inspection learns that the process in question should continue, it performs the operation "V(private semaphore)"—the semaphore value then changes from 0 to 1—otherwise, this V-operation is skipped, leaving to the other processes the obligation to perform this V-operation at a suitable moment. The absence or presence of this obligation is reflected in the final values of the state variables upon leaving the critical section.

Whenever a process reaches a stage where as a result of its progress possibly one (or more) blocked processes should now get permission to continue, it follows the pattern:

P(mutex);
"modification and inspection of state variables including
  zero or more V-operations on private semaphores
  of other processes";
V(mutex)

By the introduction of suitable state variables and appropriate programming of the critical sections any strategy assigning peripherals, buffer areas, etc. can be implemented.

The amount of coding and reasoning can be greatly reduced by the observation that in the two complementary critical sections sketched above the same inspection can be performed by the introduction of the notion of "an unstable situation," such as a free reader and a process needing a reader. Whenever an unstable situation emerges it is removed (including one or more V-operations on private semaphores) in the very same critical section in which it has been created.

Proving the Harmonious Cooperation

The sequential processes in the system can all be regarded as cyclic processes in which a certain neutral point can be marked, the so-called "homing position," in which all processes are when the system is at rest.

When a cyclic process leaves its homing position "it accepts a task"; when the task has been performed and not earlier, the process returns to its homing position. Each cyclic process has a specific task processing power (e.g. the execution of a user program or unbuffering a portion of printer output, etc.).

The harmonious cooperation is mainly proved in roughly three stages.

(1) It is proved that although a process performing a task may in so doing generate a finite number of tasks for other processes, a single initial task cannot give rise to an infinite number of task generations. The proof is simple as processes can only generate tasks for processes at lower levels of the hierarchy so that circularity is excluded. (If a process needing a segment from the drum has generated a task for the segment controller,

special precautions have been taken to ensure that the segment asked for remains in core at least until the requesting process has effectively accessed the segment concerned. Without this precaution finite tasks could be forced to generate an infinite number of tasks for the segment controller, and the system could get stuck in an unproductive page flutter.)

(2) It is proved that it is impossible that all processes have returned to their homing position while somewhere in the system there is still pending a generated but unaccepted task. (This is proved via instability of the situation just described.)

(3) It is proved that after the acceptance of an initial task all processes eventually will be (again) in their homing position. Each process blocked in the course of task execution relies on the other processes for removal of the barrier. Essentially, the proof in question is a demonstration of the absence of "circular waits": process P waiting for process Q waiting for process R waiting for process P. (Our usual term for the circular wait is "the Deadly Embrace.") In a more general society than our system this proof turned out to be a proof by induction (on the level of hierarchy, starting at the lowest level), as A. N. Habermann has shown in his doctoral thesis.

12

RC 4000 SOFTWARE: MULTIPROGRAMMING SYSTEM*

PER BRINCH HANSEN

(1969)

The RC 4000 multiprogramming system consists of a monitor program that can be extended with a hierarchy of operating systems to suit diverse requirements of program scheduling and resource allocation. This manual defines the functions of the monitor and the basic operating system, which allows users to initiate and control parallel program execution from typewriter consoles. The excerpt reprinted here is the general description of the philosophy and structure of the system. This part will be of interest to anyone wishing an understanding of the system in order to evaluate its possibilities and limitations without going into details about exact conventions. The discussion treats the hardware structure of the RC 4000 only in passing.

1 SYSTEM OBJECTIVES

This chapter outlines the philosophy that guided the design of the RC 4000 multiprogramming system. It emphasizes the need for different operating systems to suit different applications.

The primary goal of *multiprogramming* is to share a central processor and its peripheral equipment among a number of programs loaded in the internal store. This is a meaningful objective if single programs only use a fraction of the system resources and if the speed of the machine is so fast, compared to that of peripherals, that idle time within one program can be utilized by other programs.

---

*P. Brinch Hansen, *RC 4000 Software: Multiprogramming System*, Part I General Description. Regnecentralen, Copenhagen, Denmark, April 1969, 13–52.

The present system is implemented on the RC 4000 computer, a 24-bit, binary computer with typical instruction execution times of 4 microseconds. It permits practically unlimited expansion of the internal store and standardized connection of all kinds of peripherals. Multiprogramming is facilitated by concurrency of program execution and input/output, program interruption, and storage protection.

The aim has been to make multiprogramming feasible on a machine with a minimum internal store of 16 k words backed by a fast drum or disk. Programs can be written in any of the available programming languages and contain programming errors. The storage protection system guarantees non-interference among 8 parallel programs, but it is possible to start up to 23 programs provided some of them are error free.

The system uses standard multiprogramming techniques: the central processor is shared between loaded programs. Automatic swapping of programs in and out of the store is possible but not enforced by the system. Backing storage is organized as a *common data bank*, in which users can retain named files in a semi-permanent manner. The system allows a *conversational mode* of access from typewriter consoles.

An essential part of any multiprogramming system is an *operating system*, a program that coordinates all computational activities and input/output. An operating system must be in complete control of the strategy of program execution, and assist the users with such functions as operator communication, interpretation of job control statements, allocation of resources, and application of execution time limits.

For the designer of advanced information systems, a vital requirement of any operating system is that it allows him to change the mode of operation it controls; otherwise his freedom of design can be seriously limited. Unfortunately this is precisely what present operating systems do not allow. Most of them are based exclusively on a single mode of operation, such as batch processing, priority scheduling, real-time scheduling, or time-sharing.

When the need arises, the user often finds it hopeless to modify an operating system that has made rigid assumptions in its basic design about a specific mode of operation. The alternative—to replace the original operating system with a new one—is in most computers a serious, if not impossible, matter, the reason being that the rest of the software is intimately bound to the conventions required by the original system.

This unfortunate situation indicates that the main problem in the design of a multiprogramming system is not to define functions that satisfy specific operating needs, but rather to supply a system nucleus that can be extended with new operating systems in an orderly manner. This is the primary objective of the RC 4000 system.

The nucleus of the RC 4000 multiprogramming system is a *monitor* program with complete control of storage protection, input/output, and interrupts. Essentially the monitor is a software extension of the hardware structure, which makes the RC 4000 more attractive for multiprogramming. The following elementary functions are implemented in the monitor:

> scheduling of time slices among programs executed in parallel by means of a digital clock,
>
> initiation and control of program execution at the request of other running programs,
>
> transfer of messages among running programs,
>
> initiation of data transfers to or from peripherals.

The monitor has no built-in strategy of program execution and resource allocation; it allows any program to initiate other programs in a hierarchal manner and to execute them according to any strategy desired. In this *hierarchy of programs* an operating system is simply a program that controls the execution of other programs. Thus operating systems can be introduced in the system as other programs without modification of the monitor. Furthermore operating systems can be replaced dynamically, enabling each installation to switch among various modes of operation; several operating systems can, in fact, be active simultaneously.

In the following chapters we shall explain this dynamic operating system concept in detail. In accordance with our philosophy all questions about particular strategies of program scheduling will be postponed, and the discussion will concentrate on the fundamental aspects of the control of an environment of parallel processes.

2 ELEMENTARY MULTIPROGRAMMING PROBLEMS

This chapter introduces the elementary multiprogramming problems of mutual exclusion and synchronization of parallel processes. The discussion is restricted to the logical problems that arise when independent processes try to access common variables and shared resources. An understanding of these concepts is indispensable to the uninitiated reader, who wants to appreciate the difficulties of switching from uniprogramming to multiprogramming.

2.1 Multiprogramming

In multiprogramming the sharing of computing time among programs is controlled by a *clock*, which interrupts program execution frequently and activates a *monitor program*. The monitor saves the registers of the interrupted program and allocates the next slice of computing time to another program and so on. Switching from one program to another is also performed whenever a program must wait for the completion of input/output.

Thus although the computer is only able to execute one instruction at a time, multiprogramming creates the illusion that programs are being executed simultaneously, mainly because peripherals assigned to different programs indeed operate in parallel.

2.2 Parallel Processes

Most of the elementary problems in multiprogramming arise from the fact that one *process* (e.g. an executed program) cannot make any assumptions about the relative speed and progress of other processes. This is a potential source of conflict whenever two processes try to access a common variable or a shared resource.

It is evident that this problem will exist in a truly parallel system, in which programs are executed simultaneously on several central processors. It should be realized, however, that the problem will also appear in a quasi-parallel system based on the sharing of a single processor by means of interrupts; since a program cannot detect when it has been interrupted, it does not know how far other programs have progressed.

Another way of stating this is that if one considers the system as seen from within a program, it is irrelevant whether multiprogramming is implemented on one or more central processors—the logical problems are the same.

Consequently a multiprogramming system must in general be viewed as an environment with a number of truly *parallel processes*. Having reached this conclusion, a natural generalization is to treat not only program execution but input/output also as independent, parallel processes. This point will be illustrated abundantly in the following chapters.

2.3 Mutual Exclusion

The idea of multiprogramming is to share the computing equipment among a number of parallel programs. At any moment, however, a given resource must belong to one program only. In order to ensure this it is necessary to introduce global variables, which programs can inspect to decide whether a given resource is available or not.

As an example consider a typewriter used by all programs for messages to the operator. To control access to this device we might introduce a global boolean *typewriter available*. When a program p wishes to output a message, it must examine and set this boolean by means of the following instructions:

```
wait:  load       typewriter available
       skip if    true
       jump to    wait
       load       false
       store      typewriter available
```

While this is taking place the program may be interrupted after the loading of the boolean, but before inspection and assignment to it. The register containing the value of the boolean is then stored within the monitor, and program q is started. Q may load the same boolean and find that the typewriter is available. Q accordingly assigns the value false to the boolean and starts using the typewriter. After a while q is interrupted, and at some later time p is restarted with the original contents of the register reestablished by the monitor. Program p continues the inspection of the original value of the boolean and concludes erroneously that the typewriter is available.

This conflict arises because programs have no control over the interrupt system. Thus the only indivisible operations available to programs are single instructions such as load, compare, and store. This example shows that one cannot implement a multiprogramming system without ensuring a *mutual exclusion* of programs during the inspection of global variables. Evidently the entire reservation sequence must be executed as an *indivisible function.* One of the purposes of a monitor program is to execute indivisible functions in the disabled mode.

In the use of reservation primitives one must be aware of the problem of "the *deadly embrace*" between two processes, p and q, which attempt to share the resources r and s as follows:

```
process p: wait and reserve(r) ... wait and reserve(s) ...
process q: wait and reserve(s) ... wait and reserve(r) ...
```

This can cause both processes to wait forever, since neither is aware of that it wants what the other one has.

To avoid this problem we need a third process (an *operating system*) that controls the allocation of shared resources between p and q in a manner that guarantees that both will be able to proceed to completion (if necessary by delaying the other until resources become available).

2.4 Mutual Synchronization

In a multiprogramming system parallel processes must be able to *cooperate* in the sense that they can activate one another and exchange information. One example of a process activating another process is the initiation of input/output by a program. Another example is that of an operating system that schedules a number of programs. The exchange of information between two processes can also be regarded as a problem of mutual exclusion, in which the receiver must be prevented from inspecting the information until the sender has delivered it in a common storage area.

Since the two processes are independent with respect to speed, it is not certain that the receiver is ready to accept the information at the very moment the sender wishes to deliver it, or conversely the receiver can become idle at a time when there is no further information for it to process.

This problem of the *synchronization* of two processes during a transfer of information must be solved by indivisible monitor functions, which allow a process to be *delayed* on its own request and *activated* on request from another process.

For a more extensive analysis of multiprogramming fundamentals, the reader should consult E. W. Dijkstra's monograph: *Cooperating Sequential Processes.* Math. Dep. Technological University, Eindhoven, (Sep. 1965).

3 BASIC MONITOR CONCEPTS

This chapter opens a detailled description of the RC 4000 monitor. A multiprogramming system is viewed as an environment in which program execution and input/output are handled uniformly as cooperating, parallel processes. The need for an exact definition of the process concept is stressed. The purpose of the monitor is to bridge the gap between the actual hardware and the abstract concept of multiprogramming.

3.1 Introduction

The aim has been to implement a multiprogramming system that can be extended with new operating systems in a well-defined manner. In order to do this a sharp distinction must be made between the *control* and the *strategy* of program execution.

The mechanisms provided by the monitor solve the logical problems of the control of parallel processes. They also solve the safety problems that arise when erroneous or malicious processes try to interfere with other processes. They do, however, leave the choice of particular strategies of program scheduling to the processes themselves.

With this objective in mind we have implemented the following fundamental mechanisms within the monitor:

simulation of parallel processes,
communication among processes,
creation, control, and removal of processes.

3.2 Programs and Internal Processes

As a first step we shall assign a precise meaning to the process concept, i.e. introduce an unambiguous terminology for what a process is and how it is implemented on the RC 4000.

We distinguish between internal and external processes, roughly corresponding to program execution and input/output.

More precisely: an *internal process* is the execution of one or more interruptable programs in a given storage area. An internal process is identified by a unique *process name*. Thus other processes need not be aware of the actual location of an internal process in the store, but can refer to it by name.

The following figure illustrates a division of the internal store among the monitor and three internal processes, p, q, and r.

Later it will be explained how internal processes are created and how programs are loaded into them. At this point it should only be noted that an internal process occupies a fixed, contiguous storage area during its whole lifetime. The monitor has a *process description* of each internal process; this table defines the name, storage area, and current state of the process.

Computing time is shared cyclically among all active internal processes; as a standard the monitor allocates a maximum time slice of 25 milliseconds to each internal process in turn; after the elapse of this interval the process is interrupted and its registers are stored in the process description; following this the monitor allocates 25 milliseconds to the next internal process, and so on. The cyclic queue of active internal processes is called the *time slice queue*.

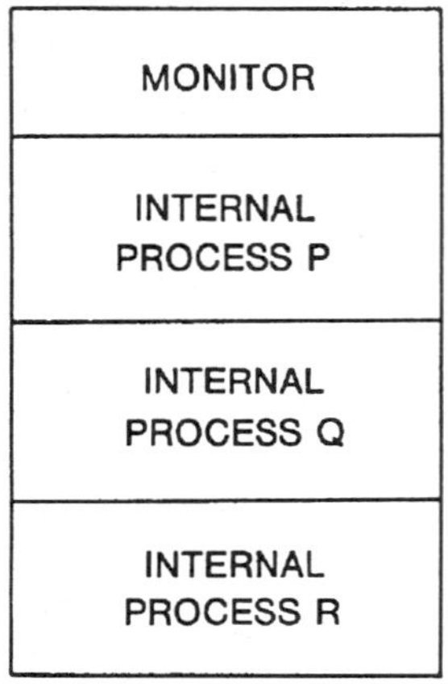

A sharp distinction is made between the concepts program and internal process. A *program* is a collection of instructions describing a computational process, whereas an internal process is the execution of these instructions in a given storage area.

An internal process like p can involve the execution of a sequence of programs, for example, editing followed by translation and execution of an object program. It is also possible that copies of the same program (e.g. the Algol compiler) can be executed simultaneously in two processes q and r. These examples illustrate the need for a distinction between programs and processes.

3.3 Documents and External Processes

In connection with input/output the monitor distinguishes between peripheral devices, documents, and external processes.

A *peripheral device* is an item of hardware connected to the data channel and identified by a device number.

A *document* is a collection of data stored on a physical medium. Examples of documents are:

a roll of paper tape,
a deck of punched cards,
a printer form,
a reel of magnetic tape,
a data area on the backing store.

By the expression *external process* we refer to the input/output of a given document identified by a unique process name. This concept implies that once a document has been mounted, internal processes can refer to it by name without knowing the actual device it uses.

For each external process the monitor keeps a process description defining its name, kind, device number, and current state. The *process kind* is an integer defining the kind of peripheral device on which the document is mounted.

For each kind of external process the monitor contains an interrupt procedure that can initiate and terminate input/output on request from internal processes.

3.4 Monitor

The monitor is a program activated by means of interrupts. It can execute privileged instructions in the disabled mode, meaning that (1) it is in complete control of input/output, storage protection, and the interrupt system, and that (2) it can execute a sequence of instructions as an indivisible entity.

After initial system loading the monitor resides permanently in the internal store. We do not regard the monitor as an independent process, but rather as a software extension of the hardware structure, which makes the computer more attractive for multiprogramming. Its function is to (1) keep descriptions of all processes; (2) share computing time among internal and external processes; and (3) implement procedures that processes can call in order to create and control other processes and communicate with them.

So far we have described the multiprogramming system as a set of independent, parallel processes identified by names. The emphasis has been on a clear understanding of relationships among resources (store and peripherals), data (programs and documents), and processes (internal and external).

4 PROCESS COMMUNICATION

This chapter deals with the monitor procedures for the exchange of information between two parallel processes. The mechanism of message buffering is defended on the grounds of safety and efficiency.

4.1 Message Buffers and Queues

Two parallel processes can cooperate by sending messages to each other. A *message* consists of eight words. Messages are transmitted from one process to another by means of *message buffers* selected from a common *pool* within the monitor.

The monitor administers a *message queue* for each process. Messages are linked to this queue when they arrive from other processes. The message queue is a part of the process description.

Normally a process serves its queue on a first-come, first-served basis. After the processing of a message, the receiving process returns an *answer* of eight words to the sending process in the same buffer.

As described in Section 2.4, communication between two independent processes requires a synchronization of the processes during a transfer of information. A process requests synchronization by executing a wait operation; this causes a delay of the process until another process executes a send operation.

The term *delay* means that the internal process is removed temporarily from the time slice queue; the process is said to be *activated* when it is again linked to the time slice queue.

4.2 Send and Wait Procedures

The following monitor procedures are available for communication among internal processes:

```
send message(receiver, message, buffer)
wait message(sender, message, buffer)
send answer(result, answer, buffer)
wait answer (result,answer, buffer)
```

Send message copies a message into the first available buffer within the pool and delivers it in the queue of a named receiver. The receiver is activated if it is waiting for a message. The sender continues after being informed of the address of the message buffer.

Wait message delays the calling process until a message arrives in its queue. When the process is allowed to proceed, it is supplied with the name of the sender, the contents of the message, and the address of the message buffer. The buffer is removed from the queue and is now ready to transmit an answer.

Send answer copies an answer into a buffer in which a message has been received and delivers it in the queue of the original sender. The sender of the message is activated if it is waiting for the answer. The answering process continues immediately.

Wait answer delays the calling process until an answer arrives in a given buffer. On arrival, the answer is copied into the process and the buffer is returned to the pool. The result specifies whether the answer is a response from another process, or a dummy answer generated by the monitor in response to a message addressed to a non-existing process.

The use of these procedures can be illustrated by the following example of a conversational process. The figure below shows one of several user processes, which deliver their output on the backing store. After completion of its output a user process sends a message to a converter process requesting it to print the output. The converter process receives and serves these requests one by one, thus ensuring that the line printer is shared by all user processes with a minimum delay.

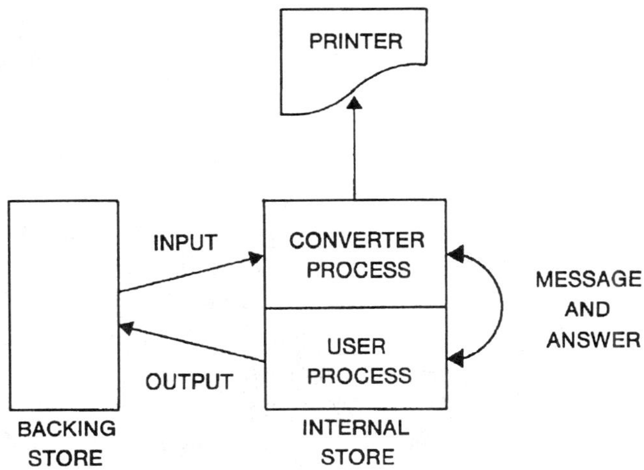

The algorithms of the converter and the user are as follows:

```
converter process:
   wait message(sender, message, buffer);
   print from backing store(message);
   send answer(result, answer, buffer);
   goto converter process;
```

```
user process:
   ...
   output on backing store;
   send message(converter, message, buffer);
   wait answer(result, answer, buffer);
```

4.3 General Event Procedures

The communication procedures enable a conversational process to receive messages simultaneously from several other processes. To avoid becoming a bottleneck in the system, however, a conversational process must be prepared to be actively engaged in more than one conversation at a time. As an example think of a conversational process that engages itself, on request from another process, in a conversation with one of several human operators in order to perform some manual operation (mounting of a tape etc.). If one restricts a conversational process to only accepting one request (i.e. a message) at a time, and to completing the requested action before receiving the next request, the unacceptable consequence of this is that other processes (including human operators at consoles) can have their requests for response delayed for a long or even undefined time.

As soon as a conversational process has started a lengthy action, by sending a message to some other process, it must receive further messages and initiate other actions. It will then be reminded later of the completion of earlier actions by means of normal answers. In general a conversational process is now engaged in several requests at one time. This introduces a scheduling and resource problem: when the process receives a request, some of its resources (storage or peripheral devices) can be tied up by already initiated actions; thus in some cases the process will not be able to honor new requests before old ones are completed. In this case the process wants to postpone the reception of some requests and leave them pending in the queue, while examining others.

The procedures *wait message* and *wait answer*, which force a process to serve its queue in a strict sequential order and delay itself while its own requests to other processes are completed, do not fulfill the above requirements.

Consequently we have introduced two more general communication procedures, which enable a process to wait for the arrival of the next message or answer and serve its queue in any order:

wait event(last buffer, next buffer, result)
get event(buffer)

The term *event* denotes a message or an answer. In accordance with this the queue of a process from now on will be called the *event queue.*

Wait event delays the calling process until either a message or an answer arrives in its queue after a given last buffer. The process is supplied with the address of the next buffer and a result indicating whether it contains a message or an answer. If the last buffer address is zero, the queue is examined from the start. The procedure does not remove the next buffer from the queue or in any other way change its status.

As an example, consider an event queue with two pending buffers A and B:

queue = buffer A, buffer B

The monitor calls: wait event(0, buffer) and wait event(A, buffer) will cause immediate return to the process with *buffer* equal to A and B, respectively; while the call: wait event(B, buffer) will delay the process until another message or answer arrives in the queue after buffer B.

Get event removes a given buffer from the queue of the calling process. If the buffer contains a message, it is made ready for the sending of an answer. If the buffer contains an answer, it is returned to the common pool. The copying of the message or answer from the buffer must be done by the process itself before *get event* is called.

The following algorithm illustrates the use of these procedures within a conversational process:

```
first event:    buffer:=0;
next event:     last buffer:=buffer;
                wait event(last buffer, buffer, result);
                if result = message then
                begin
exam request:   if resources not available then go to next event;
init action:    get event(buffer);
                reserve resources;
                ...
                send message to some other process;
                save state of action;
                end else
                begin comment: result = answer;
term action:    restore state of action,
                get event(buffer);
                release resources,
                send answer to original sender;
                end;
                go to first event;
```

The process starts by examining its queue; if empty, it awaits the arrival of the next event. If it finds a message, it checks whether it has the necessary resources to perform the requested action; if not, it leaves the message in the queue and examines the next event. Otherwise it accepts the message, reserves resources, and initiates an action. As soon as this involves the sending of a message to some other process, the conversational process saves information about the state of the incomplete action and proceeds to examine its queue from the start in order to engage itself in another action.

Whenever the process finds an answer in its queue, it immediately accepts it and completes the corresponding action. It can now release the resources used and send an answer to the original sender that made the request. After this it examines the entire queue again to see whether the release of resources has made it possible to accept pending messages.

One example of a process operating in accordance with this scheme is the basic operating system s, which creates internal processes on request from typewriter consoles. S can be engaged in conversations with several consoles at the same time. It will only postpone an operator request if its storage is occupied by other requests, or if it is already in the middle of an action requested from the same console.

4.4 Advantages of Message Buffering

In the design of the communication scheme we have given full recognition to the fact that the multiprogramming system is a dynamic environment, in which some of the processes may turn out to be black sheep.

The system is dynamic in the sense that processes can appear and disappear at any time. Therefore a process does not in general have a complete knowledge about the existence of other processes. This is reflected in the procedure *wait message*, which makes it possible for a process to be unaware of the existence of other processes until it receives messages from them.

On the other hand once a communication has been established between two processes (e.g. by means of a message), they need a common identification of it in order to agree on when it is terminated (e.g. by means of an answer). Thus we can properly regard the selection of a buffer as the creation of an identification of a conversation.

A happy consequence of this is that it enables two processes to exchange more than one message at a time. We must be prepared for the occurence of erroneous or malicious processes in the system (e.g. undebugged programs). This is tolerable only if the monitor ensures that no process can interfere with a conversation between two other processes. This is done by storing information about the sender and receiver in each buffer, and checking it whenever a process attempts to send or wait for an answer in a given buffer.

Efficiency is obtained by the queuing of buffers, which enables a sending process to continue immediately after delivery of a message or an answer regardless of whether the receiver is ready to process it or not.

In order to make the system dynamic it is vital that a process can be removed at any time, even if it is engaged in one or more conversations. In the previous example of user processes that deliver their output on the backing store and ask a converter process to print it, it would be sensible to remove a user process that has completed its task and is now only waiting for an answer from the converter process. In this case the monitor leaves all messages from the removed process undisturbed in the queues of other processes. When these processes terminate their actions by sending answers, the monitor simply returns the buffers to the common pool.

The reverse situation is also possible: during the removal of a process, the monitor finds unanswered messages sent to the process. These are returned as dummy answers to the senders. A special instance of this is the generation of a dummy answer to a message addressed to a process that does not exist.

The main drawback of message buffering is that it introduces yet another resource problem, since the common pool contains a finite number of buffers. If a process was allowed to empty the pool by sending messages to ignorant processes, which do not respond with answers, further communication within the system would be blocked. We have consequently set a limit to the number of messages a process can send simultaneously. By doing this, and by allowing a process to transmit an answer in a received buffer, we have placed the entire risk of a conversation on the process that opens it (see Section 7.4).

5 EXTERNAL PROCESSES

This chapter clarifies the meaning of the external process concept. It explains initiation of input/output by means of messages from internal processes, dynamic creation and removal of external processes, and exclusive access to documents by means of reservation. The similarity of internal and external processes is stressed.

5.1 Initiation of Input/Output

Consider the following situation, in which an internal process, p, inputs a block from an external process, q (say, a magnetic tape):

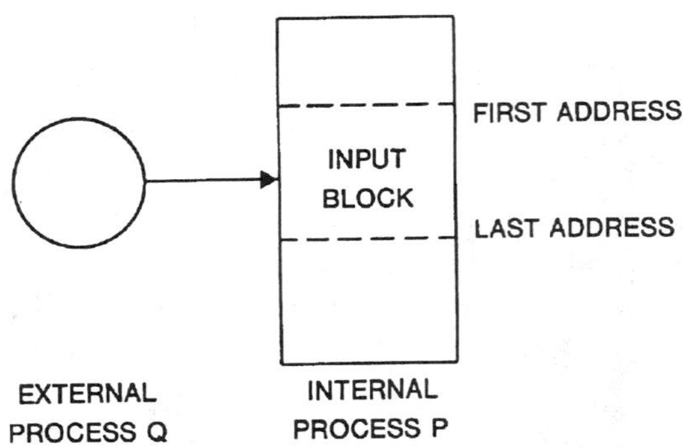

P initiates input by sending a message to q:

send message(q, message, buffer)

The message consists of eight words defining an input/output operation and the first and last addresses of a storage area within process p:

message: operation
first storage address
last storage address
(five irrelevant words)

The monitor copies the message into a buffer and delivers it in the queue of process q. Following this it uses the kind parameter in the process description of process q to switch to a piece of code common to all magnetic tapes. If the tape station is busy, the message is merely left in its queue; otherwise input is initiated to the given storage area. On return, program execution continues in process p.

When the tape station completes input by means of an interrupt, the monitor generates an answer and delivers it in the queue of p, which in turn receives it by calling *wait answer*:

wait answer(result, answer, buffer)

The answer contains status bits sensed from the device and the actual block length expressed as the number of bytes and characters input:

answer: status bits
number of bytes
number of characters
(five irrelevant words)

After delivery of the answer, the monitor examines the queue of the external process q and initiates its next operation (unless the queue is empty).

Essentially all external processes follow this scheme, which can be defined by the following algorithm:

```
external process: wait message;
                  analyse and check message;
                  initiate input/output;
                  wait interrupt;
                  generate answer;
                  send answer;
                  goto external process;
```

With low-speed, character-oriented devices, the monitor repeats input/output and the interrupt response for each character until a complete block has been transferred; (while this is taking place, the time between interrupts is of course shared among internal processes). Internal processes can therefore regard all input/output as block oriented.

5.2 Reservation and Release

The use of message buffering provides a direct way of sharing an external process among a number of internal processes: an external process can simply accept messages from any internal process and serve them in their order of arrival. An example of this is the use of a single typewriter for output of messages to a main operator. This method of sharing a device ensures that a block of data is input or output as an indivisible entity. When sequential media such as paper tape, punched cards, or magnetic tape are used, however, an internal process must have exclusive access to the entire document. This is obtained by calling the following monitor procedure:

reserve process(name, result)

The result indicates whether the reservation has been accepted or not. An external process that handles sequential documents of this kind rejects messages from all internal processes except the one that has reserved it. Rejection is indicated by the result of the procedure *wait answer.*

During the removal of an internal process, the monitor removes all reservations made by it. Internal processes can, however, also do this explicitly by means of the monitor procedure:

release process(name)

5.3 Creation and Removal

From the operator's point of view an external process is created when he mounts a document on a device and names it. The name must, however, be communicated to the monitor by means of an operating system, i.e. an internal process that controls the execution of programs. Thus it is more correct to say that external processes are created when internal processes assign names to peripheral devices. This is done by means of the monitor procedure:

create peripheral process(name, device number, result)

The monitor has, in fact, no way of ensuring whether a given document is mounted on a device. Furthermore, there are some devices which operate without documents, e.g. the real-time clock.

The name of an external process can be explicitly removed by a call of the monitor procedure:

remove process(name, result)

It is also possible to implement an automatic removal of the process name when the monitor detects operator intervention in a device. At present, this is done only in connection with magnetic tapes (see Section 10.1).

5.4 Replacement of External Processes

The decision to control input/output by means of interrupt procedures within the monitor, instead of using dedicated internal processes for each kind of peripheral device, was made to obtain immediate initiation of input/output after the sending of messages. In contrast the activation of an internal process merely implies that it is linked to the time slice queue; after activation several time slices can elapse before the internal process actually starts to execute instructions.

The price paid for the present implementation of external processes is a prolongation of the time spent in the disabled mode within the monitor. This limits the system's ability to cope with real-time events, i.e. data that are lost unless they are input and processed within a certain time.

An important consequence of the uniform handling of internal and external processes is that it allows us to replace any external process by an internal process of the same name; other processes that communicate with it are quite unaware of this replacement.

Thus it is possible to improve the response time of the system by replacing a time-consuming external process, such as the paper tape reader, by a somewhat slower internal process, which executes privileged instructions in the enabled mode.

This type of replacement also makes it possible to enforce more complex rules of access to a document. In the interests of security, for example, one might want to limit the access of an internal process to one of several files recorded on a particular magnetic tape. This can be ensured by an internal process that traps all messages to the tape and decides whether they should be passed on to it.

As a final example let us consider the problem of debugging a process control system before it is connected to an industrial plant. A convenient way of doing this is to replace analog inputs with an internal process that simulates relevant values of actual measuring instruments.

We conclude that the ability to replace any process in the system with another process is a very useful tool. This can now be seen as a practical result of the general, but somewhat vague idea (expressed in Section 2.2) that internal and external processes are independent processes, which differ only in their processing capability.

6 INTERNAL PROCESSES

This chapter explains the creation and control of internal processes. The emphasis is on the hierarchal structuring of internal processes, which makes it possible to extend the system with new operating systems. The dynamic behaviour of the system is explained in terms of process states and the transition between these.

6.1 Creation, Control, and Removal

Internal processes are *created* on request from other internal processes by means of the monitor procedure:

create internal process(name, parameters, result)

The monitor initializes the process description of the new internal process with its name and storage area selected by the *parent process*. The storage area must be within the parent's own area. Also specified by the parent is a protection key, which must be set in all storage words of the *child process* before it is started.

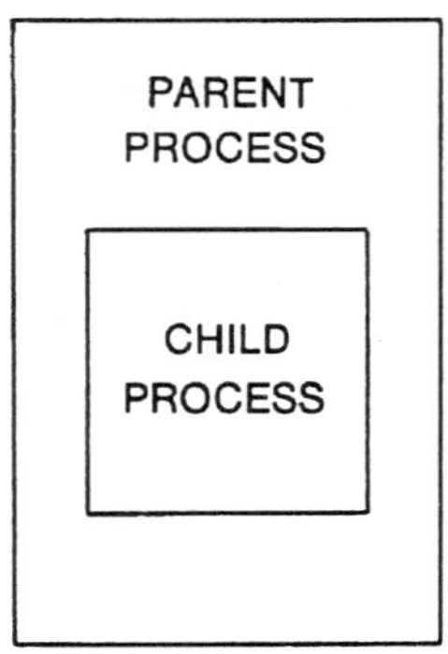

After creation the child process is simply a named storage area, which is described within the monitor. It has not yet been linked to the time slice queue.

The parent process can now *load* a program into the child process by means of an input operation. Following this the parent can *initialize* the *registers* of its child using the monitor procedure:

modify internal process(name, registers, result)

The register values are stored in the process description until the child process is started. As a standard convention adopted by parent processes (but not enforced by the monitor), the registers inform the child about the process descriptions of itself, its parent, and the typewriter console it can use for operator communication.

Finally the parent can *start* program execution within the child by calling:

start internal process(name, result)

which sets the protection keys within the child and links it to the time slice queue. The child now shares time slices with other active processes including the parent.

On request from a parent process, the monitor waits for the completion of all input/output initiated by a child process and *stops* it, i.e. removes it from the time slice queue:

stop internal process(name, buffer, result)

The meaning of the message buffer will be made clear in Section 6.3.

In the stopped state a child process can be modified and started again, or it can be completely *removed* by the parent process:

remove process(name, result)

During removal, the monitor generates dummy answers to all messages sent to the child and releases all external processes used by it. Finally the protection keys are reset to the value used within the parent process. The parent can now use the storage area to create other child processes.

6.2 Process Hierarchy

The idea of the *monitor* has been described as the simulation of an environment in which program execution and input/output are handled uniformly as parallel, cooperating processes. A fundamental set of procedures allows the dynamic creation and control of processes as well as communication among them.

For a given installation we still need, as part of the system, programs that control strategies for operator communication, program scheduling, and resource allocation. But it is essential for the orderly growth of the systems that these *operating systems* be implemented as other programs. Since the difference between operating systems and production programs is one of jurisdiction only, this problem is solved by arranging the internal processes in a *hierarchy* in which parent processes have complete control over child processes.

After initial loading the internal store contains the monitor and an internal process, s, which is the *basic operating system.* S can create parallel processes, a, b, c, etc., on request from consoles. These processes can in turn create other processes, d, e, f, etc. Thus while s acts as a primitive operating system for a, b, and c, these in turn act as operating systems for their children, d, e, f, etc. This is illustrated by the following figure, which shows a *family tree* of processes on the left and the corresponding storage allocation on the right:

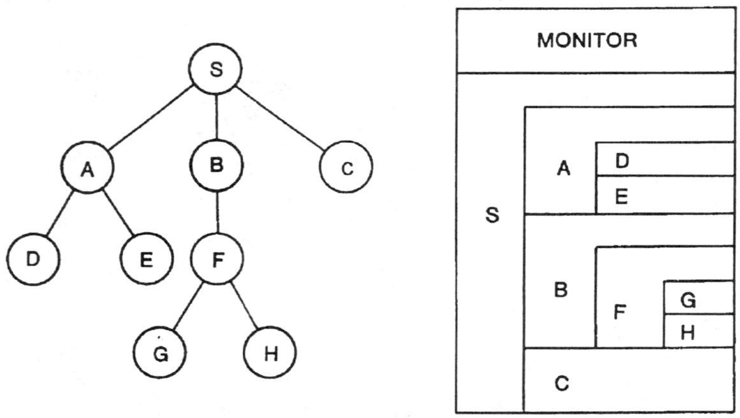

This family tree of processes can be extended to any level, subject only to a limitation of the total number or processes. At present the maximum number of internal processes is 23 including the basic operating system s. It must, however, be remembered that the storage protection system only provides mutual protection of 8 independent processes. When this number is exceeded, one must rely on some of the processes being error free.

In this multiprogramming system all privileged functions are implemented in the monitor, which has no built-in strategy. Strategies can be introduced at the various higher levels, where each process has the power to control the scheduling and resource allocation of its own children. The only rules enforced by the monitor are the following: a process can only allocate a subset of its own resources (including storage) to its children; a process can only modify, start, stop, and remove its own children.

The structure of the family tree is defined in the process descriptions within the monitor. We emphasize that the only function of the tree is to define the basic rules of process control and resource allocation. Time slices are shared evenly among active processes regardless of their position in the hierarchy, and each process can communicate with all other processes.

As regards the future development of operating systems, the most important characteristics can now be seen as the following:

1. *New operating systems can be implemented as other programs* without modification of the monitor. In this connection we should mention that the Algol and Fortran languages for the RC 4000 contain facilities for calling the monitor and initiating parallel processes. Thus it is possible to write operating systems in high-level languages.

2. *Operating systems can be replaced dynamically*, thus enabling an installation to switch among various modes of operation; several operating systems can, in fact, be active simultaneously,

3. *Standard programs and user programs can be executed under different operating systems* without modification; this is ensured by a standardization of communication between parents and children.

6.3 Process States

We are now in a position to define the possible states of an internal process as described within the monitor. An understanding of the transition from one state to the other is vital as a key to the dynamic behaviour of the system.

An internal process is either *running* (executing instructions or ready to do so) or *waiting* (for an event outside the process). In the running state the process is linked to the time slice queue; in the waiting state it is temporarily removed from this queue.

A process can either be *waiting* for a *message*, an *answer*, or an *event*, as explained in Chapter 4.

Of a more complex nature are the situations in which a process is *waiting* to be *stopped* or *started* by another process. In order to explain this we shall once more refer to the family tree shown in the previous section.

Let us say that process b wants to stop its child f. The purpose of doing this is to ensure that all program execution and input/output within the storage area of process f is stopped. Since a part of the storage area has been allocated to children of f, it is obviously necessary to stop not only the *child* f but also all *descendants* of f. This is complicated by the fact that some of these descendants may already have been stopped by their own parents. In the present example process g may still be running, while process h may have been stopped by its parent f. Consequently the monitor should only stop processes f and g.

Consider now the reverse situation, in which process b starts its child f again. Now the purpose is to reestablish the situation exactly as it was before process f was stopped. Thus the monitor must be very careful only to start those descendants of f that were stopped along with f. In our example the monitor must start processes f and g but not h. Otherwise we confuse f, which still relies on its child h being stopped.

Obviously, then, the monitor must distinguish between processes that are stopped by their *parents* and by their *ancestors*.

The possible *states* of an internal process are the following:

running
running after error
waiting for message
waiting for answer
waiting for event
waiting for start by parent
waiting for stop by parent
waiting for start by ancestor
waiting for stop by ancestor
waiting for process function

A process is created in the state *waiting for start by parent*. When it is started, its state becomes *running*. The meaning of the state *running after error* is explained in Section 8.1.

When a parent wants to stop a child, the state of the child is changed to *waiting for stop by parent*, and all running descendants of the child are described as *waiting for stop by ancestor*. At the same time these processes are removed from the time slice queue.

What remains to be done is to ensure that all input/output initiated by these processes is terminated. In order to control this each internal process description contains an integer called the *stop count.* The stop count is increased by one each time the internal process initiates input/output from an external process. On arrival of an answer from an external process, the monitor decreases the stop count by one and examines the state of the internal process. If the stop count becomes zero and the process is *waiting for stop by parent* (or *ancestor*), its state is changed to *waiting for start by parent* (or *ancestor*).

Only when all involved processes are waiting for start is the stop operation finished. This can last some time, and it may not be acceptable to the parent (being an operating system with many other duties) to be inactive for so long. For this reason the stop operation is split into two parts. The stop procedure:

stop internal process(name, buffer, result)

only initializes the stopping of a child and selects a message buffer for the parent. When the child and its running descendants are completely stopped, the monitor delivers an answer to the parent in this buffer. Thus the parent can use the procedures *wait answer* or *wait event* to wait for the completion of the stop.

A process can be in any state when a stop is initiated. If it is waiting for a message, answer, or an event, its state will be changed to waiting for stop, as explained above, but at the same time its instruction counter is decreased by two in order that it can, repeat the call of *wait message*, *wait answer*, or *wait event* when it is started again.

It should be noted that a process can receive messages and answers in its queue in any state. This ensures that a process does not loose contact with its surroundings while stopped.

The meaning of the state *waiting for process function* is explained in Section 9.1.

7 RESOURCE CONTROL

This chapter describes a set of monitor rules that enables a parent process to control the allocation of resources to its children.

7.1 Introduction

In the multiprogramming system the internal processes compete for the following limited resources:

computing time
storage and protection keys
message buffers
process descriptions
peripheral devices
backing storage

Initially all resources are owned by the basic operating system s. As a basic principle enforced by the monitor a process can only allocate a subset of its own resources to a child process. These are returned to the parent process when the child is removed.

7.2 Time Slice Scheduling

All running processes are allocated *time slices* in a cyclical manner. Depending on the interrupt frequency of the hardware interval timer, the length of a time slice can vary between 1.6 and 1638.4 milliseconds. A reasonable time slice is 25.6 milliseconds; with shorter intervals the percentage of computing time consumed by timer interrupts grows drastically; with longer intervals the delay between activation and execution of an internal process increases.

In practice internal processes often initiate input/output and wait for it in the middle of a time slice. This creates a scheduling problem when internal processes are activated by answers: Should the monitor link processes to the beginning or to the end of the time slice queue? The first possibility ensures that processes can use peripherals with maximum speed, but there is the danger that a process can monopolize computing time by communicating frequently with fast devices. The second choice prevents this, but introduces a delay in the time slice queue, which slows down peripherals.

We have introduced a modified form of round-robin scheduling to solve this dilemma. As soon as a process is removed from the time slice queue, the monitor stores the actual value of the *time quantum* used by it. When the process is activated again, the monitor compares this quantum with the maximum time slice. As long as this limit is not exceeded, the process is linked to the beginning of the queue; otherwise it is linked to the end of the queue and its time quantum is reset to zero. The same test is applied when the interval timer interrups an internal process.

This scheduling attempts to share computing time evenly among active internal processes regardless of their position in the hierarchy. It permits a process to be activated immediately until it threatens to monopolize the central processor, only then is it pushed into the background to give other processes a chance. This is admittedly a built-in strategy at the microlevel. Parent processes can in fact only control the allocation of computing time to their children in larger portions (on the order of seconds) by means of the procedures *start* and *stop internal process.*

For accounting purposes the monitor retains the following information for each internal process: the time at which the process was created and the sum of time quantums used by it; these quantities are denoted *start time* and *run time.*

7.3 Storage Allocation and Protection

An internal process can only create child processes within its own storage area. The monitor does not check whether storage areas of child processes overlap each other. This freedom can be used to implement time-sharing of a common storage area among several processes as described in Sections 10.2 and 10.4.

During creation of an internal process the parent must specify the values of the *protection register* and the *protection key* used by the child. In the protection register each bit corresponds to one of the eight possible protection keys; if a bit is zero the process can change or execute storage words with the corresponding key.

The protection key is the key that is set in all storage words of the child process itself. A parent process can only allocate a subset of its own protection keys to a child. It has complete freedom to allocate identical or different keys to its children. The keys remain accessible to the parent after creation of a child.

7.4 Message Buffers and Process Descriptions

The monitor only has room for a finite number of message buffers and tables describing internal processes and the so-called area processes (files on the backing store used as external processes). A message buffer is selected when a message is sent to another process; it is released when the sending process receives an answer. A process description is selected when an internal process creates another internal process or an area process, and released when the process is removed.

Thus it is clear that message buffers and process descriptions only assume an identity when they are actually used. As long as they are unused, they can be regarded as anonymous pools of resources. Consequently it is sufficient to specify the maximum number of each resource an internal process can use. These so-called *buffer claim*, *internal claim*, and *area claim* are defined by the parent when a child process is created. The claims must be a subset of the parent's own claims, which are diminished accordingly, they are returned to the parent when the child is removed.

The buffer claim defines the maximum number of messages an internal process can exchange simultaneously with other internal and external processes. The internal claim limits the number of children an internal process can have at the same time. The area claim defines how many backing store areas an internal process can access simultaneously.

The monitor decreases a claim by one each time a process actually uses one of its resources, and increases it by one when the resource is released again. Thus at a moment the claims define the number of resources that can still be used by the process.

7.5 Peripheral Devices

A distinction has been made between peripheral devices and external processes. An external process is created when a name is assigned to a device.

Thus it is also true of peripheral devices that they only assume an identity when they are actually used for input/output. Indeed the whole idea of identification by name is to give the operator complete freedom in allocation of devices. It would therefore seem natural to control the allocation of devices to internal processes by a complete set of claims—one for each kind of device.

In a system with remote peripherals, however, it is unrealistic to treat all devices of a given kind as a single, anonymous pool. An operating system must be able to force its children and their human operators to remain within a certain geographical *configuration* of devices. It should be noted that the concept of configuration must be defined in terms of physical devices and not in terms of external processes, since a parent generally speaking does not know in advance which documents its children are going to use.

Configuration control is exercised as follows. From the point of view of other processes an internal process is identified by a name. Within the monitor, however, internal process can also be identified by a single bit in a machine word. The process descriptions of peripheral devices include a word in which each bit indicates whether the corresponding internal process is a *potential user* of the device. Another word indicates the *current user* that has reserved the device in order to obtain exclusive access to a document.

Initially the basic operating system s is a potential user of all peripherals. A parent process can *include* or *exclude* a child as a user of any device, provided the parent is also a user of it:

include user(child, device number, result)
exclude user(child, device number, result)

During removal of a child, the monitor excludes it as a user of all devices.

All in all three conditions must be fulfilled before an internal process can initiate input/output:

The device must be an external process with a unique name.

The internal process must be a user of the device.

The internal process must reserve the external process if it controls a sequential document.

7.6 Privileged Functions

Files on the backing store are described in a catalog, which is also kept on the backing store. Clearly there is a need to be able to prevent an internal process from reserving an excessive amount of space in the catalog or on the backing store as such. It seems difficult, however, to specify a reasonable rule in the form of a claim that is defined once and for all when a child process is created. The main difficulty is that catalog entries and data areas can survive the removal of the process that created them; in other words backing storage is a resource a parent process can loose permanently by allocating it to its children.

As a half-hearted solution we have introduced the concept of *privileged monitor procedures*. A parent process must supply each of its children with a *function mask*, in which each bit specifies whether the child is allowed to perform a certain monitor function. The mask must be a subset of the parent's own mask.

At present the privileged functions include all monitor procedures that:

change the catalog on the backing store,
create and remove names of peripheral devices,
change the real-time clock.

8 MONITOR FEATURES

This chapter is a survey of specific monitor features such as internal interruption, the real-time clock, conversational access from consoles, and permanent storage of files on the backing store. Although these are not essential primitive concepts, they are indispensable features of practical multiprogramming systems.

8.1 Internal Interruption

The monitor can assist internal processes with the detection of infrequent events such as violation of storage protection or arithmetic overflow. This causes an interruption of the internal process followed by a jump to an *interrupt procedure* within the process.

The interrupt procedure is defined by calling the monitor procedure:

set interrupt(interrupt address, interrupt mask)

When an internal interrupt occurs, the monitor stores the values of registers at the head of the interrupt procedure and continues execution of the internal process in the body of the procedure:

interrupt address: working registers
instruction counter
interrupt cause
(execution continues here)

The system distinguishes between the following *causes* of internal interruption:

protection violation
integer overflow
floating-point overflow or underflow
parameter error in monitor call
breakpoint forced by parent

The *interrupt mask* specifies whether arithmetic overflow should cause internal interruption. Other kinds of internal interrupts cannot be masked off.

If an internal process provokes an interrupt without having defined an interrupt procedure after its creation, the monitor removes the process from the time slice queue and changes its state to *running after error*. The process does not receive any more computing time in this state, but from the point of view of other processes it is still an existing process. The parent of the erroneous process can, however, reactivate it by means of stop and start.

A parent can force a *breakpoint* in a child process as follows: first, stop the child; second, fetch the registers and interrupt address from the process description of the child and store the registers in the interrupt area together with the cause; third, modify the registers of the child to ensure that program execution continues in the interrupt procedure; fourth, start the child again.

8.2 Real-Time Clock

Real time is measured by means of a hardware interval timer, which counts modulo 16384 in units of 0.1 msec and interrupts the computer regularly (normally every 25.6 msec).

The monitor uses this timer to update a programmed *real-time clock* of 48 bits. This clock can be initialized and sensed by means of the procedures:

set clock(clock)
get clock(clock)

The setting of the clock is a privileged function. A standard convention adopted by operating systems (but not enforced by the monitor) is to let the clock express the time interval elapsed since midnight 31 December 1967 in units of 0.1 msec.

The interval timer is also used to implement an external process that permits the synchronization of internal processes with real time. All internal processes can send messages to this *clock process*. After the elapse of a time interval specified in the message, the clock process returns an answer to the sender. In order to avoid a heavy overhead time of clock administration, the clock process only examines its queue every second.

8.3 Console Communication

A multiprogramming system encourages a conversational mode of operation, in which users interact directly with internal processes from typewriter consoles. The external processes for consoles clearly reflect this objective.

Initially all program execution is ordered by human operators who communicate with the basic operating system. It would be very wasteful if the operating system had to examine all consoles regularly for possible operator requests. Therefore our first requirement is that consoles be able to activate internal processes by sending messages to them. Note that other external processes are only able to receive messages.

Second, it must of course be possible for an internal process to open a conversation with any console.

Third, a console should accept messages simultaneously from several internal processes. This will enable us to control more than one internal process from the same console, which is valuable in a small installation.

In short, consoles should be independent processes that can open conversations with any internal process and vice versa. The console should assist the operator with the identification of the internal processes using it.

An operator opens a conversation by depressing an interrupt key on the console. This causes the monitor to select a line buffer and connect it to the console. The operator must now identify the internal process to which his message is addressed. Following this he can input a message of one line, which is delivered in the queue of the receiving process.

A message to the basic operating system s can, for example, look like this (the word in italics is output by the console process in response to the key interrupt):

to s
new pbh run

An internal process opens a conversation with a console by sending a message to it. Before the input/output operation is initiated, the console identifies the internal process to the operator. This identification is suppressed after the first of a series of messages from the same process.

In the following example internal processes a and b share the same console for input/output. Process identifications are in italics:

to a
first input line to a
second input line to a
from b
first output line from b
second output line from b
from a
first output line from a
etc.

Note that these processes are unaware of their sharing the same console. From the point of view of internal processes the identification of user processes makes it irrelevant whether the system contains one or more consoles. (Of course one cannot expect operators to feel the same way about it).

8.4 Files on Backing Store

8.4.1 Introduction

The monitor permits semi-permanent storage of files on a backing store consisting of one or more drums and disks. The monitor makes these appear as a single backing store with a number of segments of 256 words each. This *logical backing store* is organized as a collection of named *data areas.* Each area occupies a consecutive number of segments on a single backing store device. A fixed part of the backing store is reserved for a *catalog* describing the names and locations of data areas.

Data areas are treated as external processes by the internal processes; input/output is initiated by sending messages to the areas specifying input/output operations, storage areas, and relative segment numbers within the areas. The identification of a data area requires a catalog search. In order to reduce the number of searches, input/output must be preceded by an explicit creation of an *area process* description within the monitor.

8.4.2 Catalog Entries

The catalog is a fixed area on the backing store divided into a number of *entries* identified by unique *names.* Each entry is of fixed length and consists of a *head,* which identifies the entry, and a *tail,* which contains the rest of the information. The monitor distinguishes between entries describing data areas on the backing store and entries describing other things.

An entry is *created* by calling the monitor procedure:

create entry(name, tail, result)

The first word of the *tail* defines the *size* of an area to be reserved and described in the entry; if the size is negative or zero, no area is reserved. The rest of the tail contains nine *optional parameters*, which can be selected freely by the internal process.

Internal processes can *look up*, *change*, *rename*, or *remove* existing entries by means of the procedures:

look up entry(name, tail, result)
change entry(name, tail, result)
rename entry(name, new name, result)
remove entry(name, result)

The catalog describes itself in an entry named *catalog*.

The search for catalog entries is minimized by using a hashed value of names to define the first segment to be examined. Each segment contains 15 entries; thus most catalog searches only require the input of a single segment unless the catalog is filled to the brim. The allocation of data areas is speeded up by keeping a bit table of available segments within the monitor. In practice the creation or modification of an entry therefore requires only the input and output of a single catalog segment.

8.4.3 Catalog Protection

Since many users share the backing store as a common data base, it is vital that they have a means of protecting their files gainst unintentional modification or complete removal. The protection system used is similar to the storage protection system: each catalog entry is supplied with a *catalog key* in its head; the rules of access within an internal process are defined by a *catalog mask* set by the parent of the internal process. Each bit in this mask corresponds to one of 24 possible catalog keys; if a bit is one, the internal process can modify or remove entries with the corresponding key; otherwise it can only look up these entries. A parent can only allocate a subset of its own catalog keys to a child process. Initially the basic operating system owns all keys.

In order to prevent the catalog and the rest of the backing store from being filled with irrelevant data, the concept of *temporary entry* is introduced.

This is an entry that can be removed by another internal process as soon as the internal process that created the entry has been removed. Typical examples are working areas used during program compilation and data areas created, but not removed, by faulty programs.

This concept is implemented as follows. After creation of an internal process, the monitor increases an integer *creation number* by one and stores it within the new process description. Each time an internal process creates a catalog entry, the monitor includes its creation number in the entry head indicating that it is temporary. Internal processes can at any time scan the catalog and remove all temporary entries provided the corresponding creators no longer exist within the monitor. Thus in accordance with our basic philosophy the monitor only provides the necessary mechanism for the handling of temporary entries, but leaves the actual strategy of removal to the hierarchy of processes.

In order to ensure the survival of a catalog entry, an internal process must call the privileged monitor function:

permanent entry(name, catalog key, result)

to replace the creation number with a catalog key. A process can of course only set one of its own keys in the catalog; otherwise it might fill the catalog with highly protected entries, which could be difficult to detect and remove.

8.4.3 Area Processes

In order to be used for input/output a data area must be looked up in the catalog and described as an external process within the monitor:

create area process(name, result)

The area process is created with the same name as the catalog entry.

Following this internal processes can send messages with the following format to the area process:

message: input/output operation
first storage address
last storage address
first relative segment

The reader is reminded that the tables used to describe area processes within the monitor are a limited resource, which is controlled by means of area claims defined by parent processes (Section 7.4).

The backing store is a random access medium that serves as a common data base. In order to utilize this property fully internal processes should be able to input simultaneously from the same area (e.g. when several copies of the Algol compiler are executed in parallel). On the other hand access to an area should be exclusive during output, because its content is undefined from the point of view of other processes.

Consequently we distinguish between internal processes that are *potential users* of an area process and the single process that may have *reserved* the area exclusively. This distinction was also made for peripheral devices (Section 5.2), but the rules of access are different here: An internal process is a user of an area after the creation of it. This enables the internal process to perform input as long as no other process reserves it. An internal process can reserve an area process if its catalog mask permits modification of the corresponding catalog entry. After reservation the internal process can perform both input and output.

Finally we should mention that the catalog is described permanently as an area process within the monitor. This enables internal processes to input and scan the catalog sequentially, for instance, during the detection and removal of temporary entries. Only the monitor itself, however, can perform output to the catalog.

9 SYSTEM IMPLEMENTATION

This chapter gives important details about the implementation as well as figures about the size and performance of the system.

9.1 Interruptable Monitor Functions

Some of the monitor functions are too long to be executed entirely in the disabled mode, e.g. updating of the catalog on the backing store and creation, start, stop, and removal of processes. These so-called *process functions* are called as other monitor procedures, but behind the scenes they are executed by an anonymous internal process, which only operates in disabled mode for short intervals while updating monitor tables, otherwise the anonymous process shares computing time with other internal processes.

When an internal process calls a process function, the following takes place: the calling process is removed from the time slice queue and its state is changed to *waiting for process function.* At the same time the process description is linked to the event queue of the anonymous process that is activated. The anonymous process serves the calling processes one by one and returns them to the time slice queue after completion of each function.

Process functions are interruptable like other internal processes. From the point of view of calling processes, however, process functions are indivisible, since (1) they are executed only by the anonymous process one at a time in their order of request, and (2) calling processes are delayed until the functions are completed.

The following monitor procedures are implemented as interruptable functions:

create entry
look up entry
change entry
rename entry
remove entry
permanent entry
create area process
create peripheral process
create internal process
start internal process
stop internal process
modify internal process
remove process

9.2 Stopping Processes

According to theory an internal process cannot be stopped while input/output is in progress within its storage area (Section 6.3). This requirement is inevitable in the case of high-speed devices such as a drum or a magnetic tape station, which are beyond program control during input/output. On the other hand it is not strictly necessary to enforce this for low-speed devices controlled by the monitor on a character-by-character basis.

In practice the monitor handles the stop situation as follows:

Before an external process initiates *high-speed input/output*, it examines the state of the sending process. If the sender is stopped (or waiting to be stopped), input/output is not initiated, but the external process immediately returns an answer with block length zero; the sender must then repeat input/output after restart. If the sender is not stopped, its stop count is increased and input/output is initiated. Note that if the stop count was increased immediately after the sending of a message, the sending process could only be stopped after completion of all previous operations pending in the external queue. By increasing the stop count as late as possible, we ensure that high-speed peripherals at most prevent the stopping of internal processes during a single block transfer.

Low-speed devices never increase the stop count. During output an external process fetches one word at a time from the sending process and outputs it character by character regardless of whether the sender is stopped meanwhile. Before fetching a word the external process examines the state of the sender. If it is stopped (or waiting to be stopped), output is terminated by an answer defining the actual number of characters output; otherwise output continues. During input an external process examines the state of the sender after each character. If the sender is stopped (or waiting to be stopped), input is terminated by an answer; otherwise the character is stored and input continues. Some devices, such as the typewriter, lose the last input character when stopped; others, such as the paper tape reader, do not. It can be seen that low-speed devices never delay the stopping of a process.

9.3 System Size

After initial system loading the monitor and the basic operating system s occupy a fixed part of the internal store. The size of a typical system is as follows:

		words:
monitor procedures:		2400
code for external processes:		1150
clock	50	
backing store	100	
typewriters	300	
paper tape readers	250	
paper tape punches	150	
line printers	100	
magnetic tape stations	200	
process descriptions and buffers:		1250
15 peripheral devices	350	
20 area processes	200	
6 internal processes	200	
25 message buffers	300	
6 console buffers	200	
basic operating system s		1400
total system		6200

It should be noted that the 6 internal processes include the anonymous process and the basic operating system, thus leaving room for 4 user processes. As a minimum the standard programs (editor, assembler, and compilers) require an internal process of 5–6000 words for their execution. This means that a 16 k store can only hold the system plus 1–2 standard programs, while a 32 k store enables parallel execution of 4 such programs. A small store can of course hold more programs, if these are written in machine code and executed without the assistance of standard programs.

9.4 System Performance

The following execution times of monitor procedures are conservative estimates based on a manual count of instructions. The reader should keep in mind that the basic instruction execution time of the RC 4000 computer is 4 μsec. A complete conversation between two internal processes takes about 2 milliseconds distributed as follows:

	msec
send message	0.6
wait answer	0.4
wait message	0.4
send answer	0.6

It can be seen that one internal process can activate another internal process in 0.6 msec, this is also approximately the time required to activate an external process. An analysis shows that the 2 msec required by an internal communication are used as follows:

	percent
validity checking	25
process activation	45
message buffering	30

This distribution is so even that one cannot hope to speed up the system by introducing additional, *ad hoc* machine instructions. The only realistic solution is to make the hardware faster.

The maximum time spent in the disabled mode within the monitor limits the system's response to real-time events. The monitor procedures themselves are only disabled for 0.2–1 msec. The situation is worse in the case of interrupt procedures that handle low-speed devices with hardware buffers, because the monitor empties or fills such buffers in the disabled mode after each interrupt. For the paper tape reader (flexowriter input) and the line printer, the worst-case figures are:

empty reader buffer (256 characters)	20 msec
fill printer buffer (170 characters)	7 msec

It should be noted, however, that these buffers normally only contain 64–70 characters corresponding to 4–5 msec. The worst-case situations can be remedied either by using smaller input/output areas within internal processes, or by replacing these external processes with dedicated internal processes (Section 5.4).

Finally we shall look at the interruptable monitor functions. An internal process of 5000 words can be created and controlled by a parent process with the following speed:

	msec
create internal process	3
modify internal process	2
start internal process	26
stop internal process	4
remove internal process	30

Most of the time required to start and remove an internal process is used to set storage protections keys.

Assuming that the backing store is a drum with a transfer time of 15 msec per segment, the catalog can be accessed with the following speed:

	msec
create entry	38
look up entry	20
change entry	38
rename entry	85
remove entry	38
permanent entry	38

The execution time of process functions should be taken with some reservations. First it must be remembered that process functions, like other internal processes, can be delayed for some time before they receive a time slice. In practice process functions will be activated immediately as long as they have not used a complete time slice (Section 7.2). Second one must take into consideration the fact that process function calls are queued within the monitor. Thus when a process wants to stop another process, the worst thing that can happen is that the anonymous process is engaged in updating the catalog. In this situation the stop is not initiated before the catalog has been updated. One also has to keep in mind that process functions share the drum or disk with other processes, and must wait for the completion of all input/output operations that preceed their own in the drum or disk queue. The execution times given here assume that process functions and catalog input/output are initiated instantly.

9.5 System Tape

The first version of the multiprogramming system consists of the monitor, the basic operating system s, and a program for initializing the catalog. It is programmed in the Slang 3 language. Before assembly the system is edited to include process descriptions of the peripheral devices connected to a particular installation and to define the following *options*:

number of storage bytes
number of internal processes
number of area processes
number of message buffers
number of console buffers
maximum time slice
inclusion of code for external processes
backing store configuration
size of catalog

The system is delivered in the form of a binary paper tape, which can autoload and initialize itself. After loading the system starts the basic operating system. Initially the operating system executes a program that can initialize the backing store with catalog entries and binary Slang programs input from paper tape. When this has been done, the operating system is ready to accept operator commands from consoles.

10 SYSTEM POSSIBILITIES

The strength of the monitor is the generality of its basic concepts, its weakness that it must be supported by operating systems to obtain realistic multiprogramming. We believe that the ultimate limits to the use of the system will depend on the imagination of designers of future operating systems. The purpose of this chapter is to stimulate creative thinking by pointing out a few of the possibilities inherent in the system.

10.1 Identification of Documents

In tape-oriented installations, operating systems should assist the operator with automatic identification of magnetic tapes. At present the external process concept gives the operator complete freedom to mount a magnetic tape on any station and identify it by name. When a tape station is set in the *local* mode, the monitor immediately removes its name to indicate that the operator has interfered with it. The station gives an interrupt when the operator returns it to the *remote* mode. Thus the monitor distinguishes between three states of a tape station:

document removed (after intervention)
unidentified document mounted (after remote interruption)
identified document mounted (after process creation)

It is a simple matter to introduce a *watch-dog process* in the monitor, to which internal processes can send messages in order to receive answers each time an unidentified tape is mounted somewhere. After reception of an answer, an internal process can give the actual station a temporary name, identify the tape by reading its label, and rename it accordingly.

Automatic identification requires general aggreement on the format of tape labels, at least to the extent of assigning a standard position to the names of tapes.

10.2 Temporary Removal of Programs

We have not imposed any restrictions on individual programs with respect to their demand for storage, run time, and peripherals. It is taken for granted that some programs will need most of the system resources for several hours. Such large programs must not, however, prevent other users from obtaining immediate access to the machine in order to execute more urgent programs of short duration. Thus the system must permit temporary removal of a program in order to make its storage area and peripherals available for other programs. One example, where this is absolutely necessary, is the periodic supervision of a real-time process combined with the execution of large background programs in idle intervals.

A program can be removed temporarily by stopping the corresponding internal process and dumping its storage area on the backing store by an output operation. Note that this dump automatically includes all children and descendants created within the area. The monitor is only aware of the process being stopped; it is still described within the monitor and can receive messages from other processes.

It is now possible to create and start other processes in the same storage area, since the monitor does not check whether internal processes overlap each other as long as they remain within their parent processes. Peripherals can also be taken from the dumped process and assigned to others simply by mounting new documents and renaming the peripherals.

Temporary removal makes sense only if it is possible to restart a program at a later stage. This requires reloading the program into its original storage area as well as mounting and repositioning of its documents. After restart the internal process can detect interference with its documents in one of two ways: either it finds that a document does not exist any more, whereupon it must ask the operator to mount and name it; or it discovers that an existing document no longer is reserved by it, meaning that the operator has mounted it, but that it needs to be repositioned. These cases are indicated by the result parameter after a call of *wait answer*.

The need for repositioning can also arise during normal program execution, if the operator interferes with a peripheral device (by mistake or in order to move a document to a more reliable device). Consequently all major programs should consider each input/output operation as a potential restart situation.

10.3 Batch Processing

In the design of a batch processing system the distinction between parent and child processes prevents the batch of programs from destroying the operating system. Note that in general an operating system must remove a child process (and not merely stop it) to ensure that all its resources are released again (Section 7.4). Even then, it must be remembered that messages sent by a child to other processes remain in their queues until these processes either answer them or are removed (Section 4.4).

The multiprogramming capabilities can be utilized to accept job requests in a conversational mode during execution of the batch. Thus a *batch processing* system can include facilities for *remote job entry* combined with *priority scheduling* of programs.

10.4 Time-Sharing

The basic requirement of a *time-sharing* system, in which a large number of users have conversational access to the system from consoles, is the ability to swap programs between the internal store and the backing store. A time-sharing operating system must create an internal process for each user, and make these processes share the same storage area by frequent removal and restart of programs (say, every few seconds). The problem is that stopping a process temporarily also means stopping its communication with peripherals. Thus in order to keep typewriter input/output alive while a user process is dumped, the system must include an internal process that buffers all data between programs and consoles.

10.5 Real-Time Scheduling

We conclude these hints with an example of a *real-time* system. The application we have in mind is a process control system, in which a number of programs must perform data logging, alarm scanning, trend logging, and so forth periodically under the real-time control of an operating system.

This can be organized as follows: initially all task programs send messages to the operating system and wait for answers. The operating system communicates with the clock process and is activated every second in order to scan a time table of programs. If the real time exceeds the start time of a task program, the operating system activates the program by an answer. After completion of its task, the program again sends a message to the operating system and waits for the answer. In response the operating system increases the start time of the program by the period between two successive executions of the task.

Acknowledgements

The design of the system is based on the ideas of Jørn Jensen, Søren Lauesen, and the author; Leif Svalgaard participated in its implementation.

13

THE DESIGN OF THE VENUS OPERATING SYSTEM*

BARBARA H. LISKOV

(1972)

The Venus Operating System is an experimental multiprogramming system which supports five or six concurrent users on a small computer. The system was produced to test the effect of machine architecture on complexity of software. The system is defined by a combination of microprograms and software. The microprogram defines a machine with some unusual architectural features; the software exploits these features to define the operating system as simply as possible. In this paper the development of the system is described, with particular emphasis on the principles which guided the design.

Introduction

The Venus Operating System is an experimental multiprogramming system for a small computer. It supports five or six concurrent users, who operate on-line and interactively through teletypes. It may be distinguished from other multiuser systems in that it primarily caters to users who are cooperating with each other, for example, a group of users sharing a data base or building a system composed of cooperating processes.

The operating system was produced to test the following hypothesis: the difficulties encountered in building a system can be greatly reduced if the system is built on a machine with the "correct" architecture. We had in mind a complex system whose data and processing requirements vary dynamically, for example, an operating system or an on-line data management system. We

*B. H. Liskov, The design of the Venus operating system. *Communications of the ACM 15*, 3 (March 1972), 144–149.

felt that machines available today do not support the programming of such systems very well and that considerable software complexity is introduced to cope with the inadequacies of the hardware.

First, it was necessary to build the machine with the correct architecture. This was done through microprogramming on an Interdata 3 computer; the result is called the Venus machine. The microprogram contained solutions to some of the time-consuming and complex tasks performed by such systems as well as useful mechanisms for building these systems.

Next, it was necessary to use the Venus machine for a software application. An operating system was selected as the initial effort because it was the type of system the machine was intended to support and because it would provide a facility which could support later applications.

System Design Principles

Two main principles were followed in the design of the operating system:

1. The system was built as a hierarchy of levels of abstraction, defined by Dijkstra [1]. We expected this would lead to a better design with greater clarity and fewer errors. A level is defined not only by the abstraction which it supports (for example, virtual memories) but also by the resources which it uses to realize that abstraction. Lower levels (those closer to the machine) are not aware of the resources of higher levels; higher levels may apply the resources of lower levels only by appealing to the functions of the lower level. This reduces the number of interactions among parts of a system and makes them more explicit. Examples of levels of abstraction, which occur in both the microprogram and software, are given throughout the paper.

2. The features of the Venus machine were allowed to influence the operating system design in order to evaluate the effect of the architecture on the development of the software.

Several other principles also guided the design of the system:

3. Efficiency of performance was always considered when making design choices but was not the major criterion.

4. Independent users were protected, insofar as possible, from each other's mistakes by limiting the effects of errors to the user or group of cooperating users involved.

5. Users were given as much access as possible to the features of the machine and the software mechanisms developed for the operating system.

This paper is primarily concerned with the development of the operating system according to the design principles with special emphasis on the two main principles. In the next section the Venus machine features of most influence on the operating system design are described. The following section explains how these features were extended to support the design of the operating system. Then the design of the resource management portion of the system is described. Finally, the design experience is evaluated. A user's view of the system is given in the Appendix; it is intended to clarify the abstract view of the system contained in the body of the paper by showing how the system supports the user in performing his job.

The Venus Machine

Hardware

The Venus machine was built by microprogramming an Interdata 3, a small, slow, and inexpensive computer. The microprogram is stored in a read-only memory; it is limited to 2,000 microinstructions, which imposes fairly severe restrictions on its content.

The Interdata is connected to several teletypes, a card reader, a printer, and two magnetic tapes. In addition, there is a small paging disk with a capacity of half a million bytes of storage. The disk and tapes have direct memory access through hardware selector channels; other devices transfer data a byte at a time.

The Microprogram

In addition to an ordinary instruction set, the Venus microprogram supports a number of nonstandard architectural features [2]. Those features most important to the design of the operating system are briefly described in this paper; they are: segments, multiprogramming of 16 concurrent processes, a microprogrammed multiplexed I/O channel, and procedures.

Segments. Segments are named virtual memories, as defined for Multics [3]. Each segment contains a maximum of 64 thousand bytes of data and has a 15-bit name; segments are the primary storage structure on the Venus machine. Segments and core memory are both divided into 256-byte pages. Information about the contents of each core page is kept in a single, centralized core-resident table, the core page table, which is used by the microprogram to map virtual addresses into real addresses. All references to a given virtual address will be mapped by the microprogram into the same real address, which implies that segments are physically shared among processes. In addition, there is no way for one process to protect a segment from access by other processes. This restriction makes sense only because the Venus machine was designed to support a system composed of *cooperating* processes.

Paging on the Venus machine is performed on demand. If the microprogram cannot locate the desired segment page in the core page table, it starts a software routine, the page fault routine, to fetch the page from the disk. The page fault routine acts like a subroutine of the microprogram, called by the microprogram when needed and returning, via a special instruction, to the microprogram at the point where the page fault was detected.

Multiprogramming. A process is defined to be a program in execution on a virtual machine.[1] The Venus microprogram supports 16 virtual machines, each consisting of an address space and a work area. The address space encompasses all segments and is the same for all processes, although only a few segments are of interest to a particular process. The work area is permanently located in core and contains about 150 bytes of process-related information including the general registers, program counter, and other information about the state of the process.

Scheduling of the CPU to the processes is performed by the microprogram, which enabled us to define a single uniform mechanism for passing control of the processor among the processes. This mechanism, used even for indicating the end of I/O, is provided by semaphores, first defined by Dijkstra [11]. Semaphores are used to control the sharing of resources and to synchronize processes. Two operations may be performed on semaphores: P and V. P is performed when a process wishes to wait for an event to occur or a resource to become available. A process performs a V to free a resource; either a process or the I/O channel performs a V to signal the occurrence of an event. Dijkstra defined a semaphore to be an integer variable and an associated waiting list. In Venus the waiting list is represented by a queue, and the association is made explicit by defining a semaphore to be an ordered pair (*count, link*). If *count* is negative, its absolute value equals the number of processes on the queue. In this case, *link* points to the work area of the process which most recently performed a P on the semaphore; in the work area of that process is a pointer to the work area of the next newest process on the queue, and so on. Also in the work area of each process is a priority which can be set by software. When the time comes to remove a process from the queue (because a V was performed on the semaphore), the process

[1]The reader is referred to Saltzer [4] for a more precise definition of "process." The Venus virtual machine is an instance of Saltzer's "pseudo processor."

with the highest priority is removed; if the highest priority is associated with more than one process, the one which has been on the queue the longest is selected. Process swapping in Venus only occurs as the result of P's and V's being performed by processes or by the I/O channel. All processes in Venus are in one of three states: a single *running* process, processes which are *ready* to run, or processes which are *blocked*. Ready processes are listed on a special queue, the J queue. Blocked processes are on queues associated with semaphores. If the running process performs a P, requesting a resource which is not available or waiting for an event which has not occurred, it becomes blocked; at this point, the highest priority, oldest process on the J queue is selected to be the new running i process. If a V is performed, some blocked process may become ready. If this process does not have higher priority than the running process, it is added to the J queue; otherwise, it becomes the running process, and the old running process is added to the J queue. The running process always has a priority at least as high as all ready processes.

Input/Output Channel. The microprogrammed I/O channel relieves the software from all real-time constraints associated with devices by permitting the specification of I/O transfers in increments which suit the requirement of the devices. The microprogram runs the channel between the execution of instructions; from the software point of view, the channel is running simultaneously with the execution of instructions. The channel signals the completion of I/O by performing a V on a special semaphore located in the work area of the process which started the transfer. When the process wishes to synchronize with the I/O, it performs a P on this semaphore.

Procedures. Each procedure is stored in a unique segment. Call and return instructions switch a process from the instructions in one procedure to those in another; they also save and restore part of the work area at the time of the call. Arguments and values can be passed in separate segments which are used as pushdown stacks, referenced by push and pop instructions.

Sharing procedures is desirable on the Venus machine. Of course, only reentrant procedures can be successfully shared. The primary support for reentrant procedures comes from the separate virtual machines. The call, return, push, and pop instructions provide a reentrant procedure interface. In addition, no easy way of storing into procedures is available, and segments provide private and temporary work space whenever this is needed.

Levels of Abstraction

The design principle of levels of abstraction was applied to the microprogram as well as to software. Levels supported by the microprogram and the page fault handler include the virtual memory abstraction, the virtual machine abstraction, and the I/O channel which really provides virtual devices–for example, a card reader which reads an entire card at once. Figure 1 illustrates the resources and methods of appeal associated with these levels.

ABSTRACTION	RESOURCES	METHOD OF APPEAL
SEGMENTS	CORE PAGE TABLE, DISK	SEGMENT REFERENCE, EL1 INSTRUCTION
VIRTUAL DEVICES	DEVICES, DEVICE STATUS WORD TABLE	SIO INSTRUCTION, CHANNEL COMMANDS
VIRTUAL MACHINES	J QUEUE, PROCESSOR	P AND V INSTRUCTIONS

Figure 1 Levels of abstraction supported by the Venus microprogram.

Extensions to the Venus Machine

The second main design principle was to let the features of the Venus machine influence the design of the operating system. Thus we expected the system to use segments for data and to be composed of a combination of reentrant procedures and asynchronous processes. A feeling for the usefulness of such structures can be gained by considering how they correspond to the way in which the system most conveniently performs its work.

We were interested in designing a system to support multiple users. Each user is assigned a separate virtual machine and is thus represented by an independent process. To support the users, the system must perform certain tasks. Some will most naturally be performed on the user's virtual machine by reentrant system procedures, which use segments to hold user-related data. Other system tasks are logically asynchronous with the user (for example, running I/O devices for the system as a whole). These tasks can be made physically asynchronous by assigning them to separate processes. Thus the work done by the system can be distributed among the processes so that logically concurrent and asynchronous tasks can be performed by physically concurrent and asynchronous processes. This leads to clarity in the design.

To make the features of the Venus machine more convenient to use, several levels of abstraction were defined in software. Two levels are described below: the first, dictionaries, supports the convenient use of segments; the second, queues, supports communication between processes.

Dictionaries

Building a system out of segments containing procedures and data requires cross-referencing between segments. The Venus machine supports references to segments by internal segment name, which is not a very convenient item for a programmer to use or remember. In addition, internal segment names are dynamically assigned (by the page fault handler); the programmer needs a static name. Therefore, external segment names were introduced.

To support external segment names, a mapping between external and internal names is required. This is supplied by *dictionaries*, which are stored in segments. An external segment name is actually a pair of symbolic names: the symbolic name attached to the segment and the symbolic name of the dictionary which should be used to perform the mapping. One special dictionary contains the mappings between the symbolic and internal names of all dictionaries. The two-level external name allows related segments to be grouped together (referenced through the same dictionary) and makes it easier for a user to obtain unique names.

Although dictionaries are primarily intended to support external segment names, they are actually a general mapping facility and are occasionally used as such by the system.

Queues

Processes which synchronize with each other may also need to send and receive information. P's and V's permit processes to wait for or signal the occurrence of events but do not contain any information about what the event is. A process may be waiting for several dfferent events; it must know which event occurred in order to take appropriate action. A mechanism was required which allows one process to send information and the same or another process to receive it. *Queues* were selected for this purpose because they supply a chronological ordering for their elements. All queues are held in a single "queue segment"; the location within this segment of the head of a particular queue is obtained from an associated "queue dictionary."

Resource Management

An operating system must manage the resources available on a machine in such a manner that deadlock is avoided and access to resources is distributed fairly among the users. Resource management in Venus is described here in some detail, partly because this is an interesting part of the operating system and partly as an example of the use of levels of abstraction and distribution of work among processes. Resource management is primarily provided by independent processes synchronizing and communicating with each other.

If several processes compete freely for resources, deadlock may result. The simplest example of deadlock is:

Process 1 owns Resource A and is waiting for Resource B.

Process 2 owns Resource B and is waiting for Resource A.

Neither Process 1 nor Process 2 can continue. We wanted to avoid deadlock in the Venus Operating System, which required careful design of resource management. Resources to be managed by software include segments and input/output devices; core, the paging disk, and the CPU are managed by the microprogram. Virtual machines must also be managed, but only in the sense that no more can be assigned to users than are available.

Management of Shared Data Segments

The management of shared data segments is difficult because general solutions which insure that deadlock will not occur tend to prevent users from running even when the situation is perfectly safe [5, 6, 7]. In our system, users must control the sharing of user-defined data segments. The availability of semaphores provides users with a tool for controlling sharing by means of an algorithm of their own choosing. If the algorithm does not work correctly, only the group of users would be affected.

There still remains the problem of system data structures which are also available to users, for example, the dictionaries. Dictionaries are intended to be shared and may be referenced simultaneously. While a dictionary is being changed, it does not contain consistent data; thus there is a need for mutual exclusion here. Associated with each dictionary is a semaphore which is used to control sharing. Dictionaries may be accessed only by calls to special reentrant dictionary procedures, which perform P's and V's on the associated semaphore where appropriate. Restricting dictionary access to these procedures guarantees that the semaphores will be used correctly (for example, every P will eventually be followed by a V) and that no access errors will occur.

Access to any shared system data structure (queues are another example) is always limited to a group of procedures. This group comprises a level of abstraction which owns the accessed segments as a resource.

Management of I/O Devices

All I/O devices are managed similarly. The system retains ownership of the devices; users are given access for well-defined and limited transactions, which insures that deadlock cannot occur. This section discusses how devices are managed; the next section explains how levels of abstraction were used to accomplish the management.

Teletypes. Our system is on-line and interactive; therefore every user needs a teletype. One solution is to assign each user a teletype which he alone can use. This requires one teletype to be designated the "operator's console" and to be handled differently since the system occasionally needs a teletype to announce special conditions and errors. Furthermore it would not be natural for one user to send a message to another user's teletype or for the system to do so.

The solution chosen defines the teletype on which a user starts running as his "preferred" teletype. He can reference this device symbolically and will ordinarily use it, but he is not constrained to do so and is unable to prevent others from using it. A teletype may be accessed without interruption long enough to write and then read one line. This insures that the standard use of teletypes, which is the user responding to the program (with a command) when told to do so, can occur without interference from other users.

Other Devices. The card reader, the printer, and the two magnetic tapes are all in high demand. Because the disk is small, symbolic data can be maintained in core and disk storage for only a limited time. The card reader and tapes provide the only reasonable method for entering large amounts of symbolic data; only on tape can edited symbolic data be saved and then retrieved later. The printer provides the only reasonable method for listing symbolic data. Users will probably require lengthy access to several of these devices each time they run. All users benefit when the system retains control, thus insuring that the devices will be run efficiently and kept busy as long as there is work to do. For user convenience, the devices may be accessed without interruption for a fairly long time, for example, long enough to list the assembly of a user's procedure or read the cards in a user's card deck.

Levels of Abstraction

The system performs device management by providing the user with virtual devices which are quite different from real devices. This is accomplished through several levels of abstraction, which are spread over several processes (see Figure 2).

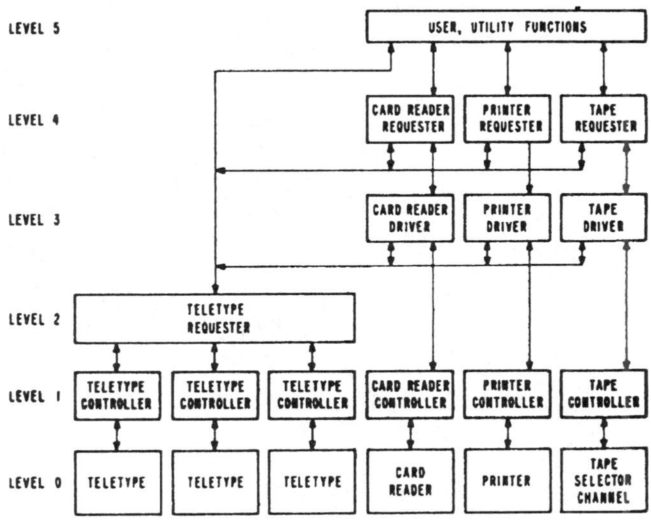

Figure 2 Levels of abstraction used in resource management.

Level 0, which the microprogram supplies, provides devices which have no real-time constraints but which require core buffers. Level 1 is made up of software Controllers, one for each device. Each Controller is an independent process (although one reentrant procedure may serve as several Controllers). The virtual devices supported by the Controllers have the following characteristics:

1. Only a few types of transfers are possible, for example, exactly one card may be read.

2. The buffers for the transfer are located in segments.

3. A transfer on the device may be requested at any time, regardless of whether the device is currently in use. It will be performed when the device is available.

4. The completion of the transfer is signalled by the performance of a V on a semaphore specified by the transfer request.

Above the Controller level, teletypes are handled quite differently from the other devices.

Teletypes. A single reentrant procedure, the Teletype Requester (level 2), handles teletypes. Primarily it provides an interface between the user and the Controllers; it runs on the user's virtual machine.

Other Devices. The card reader, printer, and tapes are accessed for much larger amounts of data than are accepted by the Controllers. The Drivers (level 3) support this abstraction. Each Driver handles one device and is an independent process. The characteristics supported are:

1. The device is accessed a segment at a time. The Driver breaks the segment into buffers acceptable to the Controller.

2. The Driver defines the type of synchronization required. The Card Reader Driver builds segments containing the images of card decks whenever there are cards in the hopper; user synchronization is required only to obtain the completed segments. The Printer Driver requires notification that a segment should be printed; no synchronization with the completion of printing is required. The Tape Driver requires notification to read or write a segment on a tape; the user must wait for completion.

Above each Driver is a Requester (level 4) which primarily provides an interface between the user and the Driver and runs on the user's virtual machine. These Requesters are more elaborate than the Teletype Requester. For example, the Printer Requester helps the user build printable segments, while the Tape Requester is an interactive procedure which reads and wntes segments on tape on user command.

Conclusions

The Venus Operating System has been supporting multiple users for several months. Two to three man-years were spent building the machine; then an estimated six man-years were required to design and implement the system (including utility functions, such as the Assembler, Editor, and debugging aids, as well as operating system functions). We feel this surprisingly brief development time indicates that the architecture of the Venus machine is suitable for supporting the programming of complex software and, in fact, reduces the difficulties encountered in building such software.

In addition, the use of levels of abstraction proved a valuable tool because it provided a way of thinking about the design with clarity and precision. Errors were uncovered while putting the system together, but the rule about ownership of resources was for the most part faithfully followed, minimizing errors resulting from interactions of parts of the system. Such errors as were discovered resulted from errors internal to some piece of the system which was not fully checked out and errors traced to breaking the rule about resources. An added benefit of levels of abstraction is the ease with which the system can be modified; its design is stratified so that the effects of proposed modifications are plainly visible.

Acknowledgments. The author wishes to thank several colleagues at The MITRE Corporation, and especially J.A. Clapp, for many helpful discussion of both the Venus Operating System and this paper, and the referee for his valid and useful criticisms.

Appendix–A User's View of the System

The user views the system in two ways. First, he must write his programs; for this he is interested in available data structures and system procedures. Then he is interested in running and debugging his programs.

Programs running under Venus use segments for all storage—procedures, data, and pushdown stacks. Because segments are available by external name through dictionaries, users can readily share data and procedures. Users may also synchronize with other users through queues and semaphores.

A user runs on-line and interactively. He starts up by typing a command on a teletype and is assigned a virtual machine under the control of an interactive system procedure called the Loader. The Loader recognizes many commands; the most important is the "E" command, which passes control to a specified system, utility, or user procedure. Important system and utility procedures are the Assembler, Editor, Tape Requester, and Debugger.

The user submits card decks to be read prior to his run; he may access all decks through a command to the Loader. The names of the segments containing the card deck images are entered in a dictionary associated with the user. The user may read segments from tape; the names of these segments are also entered into his dictionary where they may be assembled or edited on command. Binding of intersegment references occurs on completion of assembly.

The user executes procedures by giving the "E" command. Execution can occur with or without debugging; no change to the procedures being run is required. Debugging is handled by an interactive system procedure which runs before the execution of every instruction and can be used to stop execution at a specified "breakpoint." A dialogue with the user then commences in which the contents of a segment or his work area may be displayed and modified, a new breakpoint specified, and control returned to the interrupted procedure or the Loader.

The system also provides interactive interrupt procedures which run as the result of exceptional conditions, for example, a stack underflow or overflow. They make use of a subset of the debugging commands, permitting the user to discover the reason for the error, restore his data, and return to the Loader.

When the user has finished running he saves his symbolic data on tape and then informs the Loader, which releases his virtual machine and destroys his symbolic data. His checked-out programs may be entered in the system and become accessible to others through dictionaries.

References

1. Dijkstra, E.W. The structure of the 'THE' multiprogramming system. *Comm. ACM 11*, 5 (May 1968), 341-346.
2. Huberman, B.J. Principles of operation of the Venus microprogram. MTR 1843, F19(628)-71-C-0002, The MITRE Corporation, Bedford, Mass., May 1970.
3. Corbato, F.J., and Vyssotsky, V.A. Introduction and overview of the Multics system. Proc. AFIPS 1965 FJCC, Vol. 27, Pt 1, Spartan Books, New York, pp. 185-196.
4. Saltzer, J.H. Traffic control in a multiplexed computer system. Tech. Rep. TR-30, Proj. MAC, MIT, Cambridge, Mass., June, 1966.
5. Habermann, A.N. Prevention of system deadlocks. *Comm. ACM 12*, 7 (July 1969), 373-377, 385.
6. Holt, R.C. Comments on prevention of system deadlocks. *Comm. ACM 14*, 1 (Jan. 1971), 36-38.
7. Coffman, E.G. Jr., Elphick, M.J., and Shoshani, A. System deadlocks. *Computing Surveys 3*, 2 (June 1971), 67-78.

14

A LARGE SEMAPHORE BASED OPERATING SYSTEM*

SØREN LAUESEN

(1975)

The paper describes the internal structure of a large operating system as a set of cooperating sequential processes. The processes synchronize by means of semaphores and extended semaphores (queue semaphores). The number of parallel processes is carefully justified, and the various semaphore constructions are explained. The system is proved to be free of "deadly embrace" (deadlock). The design principle is an alternative to Dijkstra's hierarchical structuring of operating systems. The project management and the performance are discussed, too. The operating system is the first large one using the RC 4000 multiprogramming system.

1. Introduction

1.1 Facilities of Boss 2

The operating system Boss 2 was developed for RC 4000 in the period 1970 to 1972. Boss 2 is a general purpose operating system offering the following types of service simultaneously: batch jobs, remote job entry, time sharing (conversational jobs), jobs generated internally by other jobs, process control jobs. The system can at the same time be part of a computer network, allowing jobs to transmit files to CDC 6400 and Univac 1106/1108.

Boss 2 handles a maximum of 50 terminals, various types of backing stores and magnetic tapes, printers, the readers, punch, plotter, and various process control devices. The resources are available for all types of service.

*S. Lauesen, A large semaphore based operating system. *Communications of the ACM 18*, 7 (July 1975), 377–389.

Boss has a dynamic priority system based on swapping and updates an estimate of the job completion times taking into account all resources demanded by the jobs. This estimate is available from the terminals. All the facilities can be used with a core store from 32 k words (of 24 bits) and a disk of 2 M words.

Performance measurements have been made on a service center configuration with 20 terminals, 64 k words of core store, and a small added drum. The jobs are production runs and debugging of medium and large data processing programs. During the six busiest hours, the cpu-utilization is 40–50 pct used by jobs, 10–20 pct by the operating system and the monitor. The average operating system overhead per job is 3 sec—including nonoverlapping i/o transfers in the operating system. The response time to simple on-line commands like editing is negligible (less than 0.5 sec).

During the first year of operation, the system typically ran for weeks without crashes. Today it seems to be error free.

1.2 The RC 4000 System Without Boss 2

Boss 2 runs under an extended version of the *Monitor* (Nucleus) described in [2, 3, and 16]. The principles of the Monitor may be outlined as follows. The Monitor is a set of procedures which make the computer appear as if it were executing several programs at the same time. The sequential execution of such a program is called a *process.* Some of the processes are built-in *drivers* (external processes), some of them are *job processes* executing a sequence of user defined programs (job steps), and some of them are *operating systems.*

Any two processes can communicate and synchronize by means of *messages.* Each process owns a set of message buffers in the protected Monitor and it has a message queue in which it can receive message buffers sent to it from other processes (Figure 1). It can call a Monitor procedure asking to wait until a message buffer is in this queue, and it can return a message buffer to the sender (send answer). Two other Monitor procedures allow it to send a message to another process and wait for an answer to be returned. A further Monitor procedure—essential for implementation of operating systems—allows a process to wait for the first coming message or answer (wait event).

A process owns a set of resources like working store and message buffers. It can use a part of these resources to create another process (a child) running in parallel with the creator (the parent). Later the parent can remove the child and get the resources back. A process which is an operating system

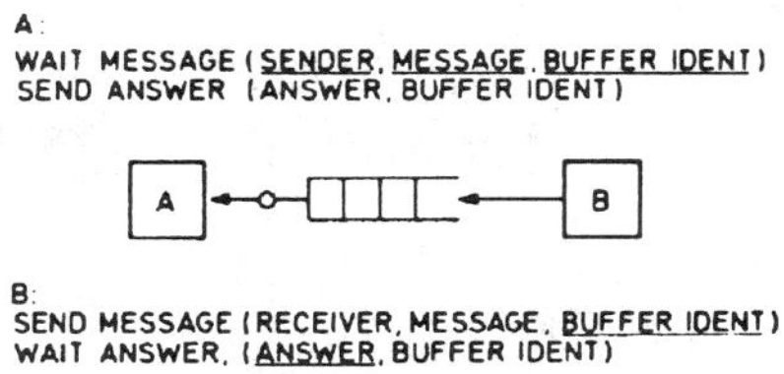

Fig. 1. Process communication by means of messages. In the example, B is the sender of a message to the receiver A. Sender and receiver are identified by a process name of at most 11 characters. Return parameters are underlined.

creates job processes in this way.

The pragmatic rules for communication job/operating system and job/drivers were developed from 1969 to 1970, that is, before any advanced operating system was planned. In this early period a lot of compilers and utility programs were developed, and for compatibility reasons Boss had to follow the old pragmatic rules.

During the period from 1969 to 1972 the computer was mostly operated with an extremely simple operating system which handled core resident job processes only. The creation and removal of job processes was always ordered manually and executed immediately or rejected (i.e. no job queue existed in the computer). A job process could send two kinds of messages: input/output messages to the drivers and parent messages to the operating system. The input/output messages asked for operations very close to the hardware, like transfer of a data block or position of a magnetic tape. Input/output strategies and error recovery were mostly handled by the user programs and the library procedures. The parent messages asked for a variety of functions like mount a magnetic tape, mount a paper tape, terminate the job, abort the job step in at most x seconds, print an operator message.

The simple operating system simply printed all parent messages on a console without trying to understand them. Although it was quite convenient to handle tape mounting and paper tapes in this way, the method was unsuited for handling files on disk (open file, create file, etc.). A major fault in the early design was that file handling was not communicated as parent messages—with automatic handling in the simple operating system. Instead a special set of monitor procedures was supplied, which did not even use the message mechanism. As a result, later operating systems could not "catch" the file handling requests, and disk allocation strategies became limited by the monitor.

1.3 The Place of Boss 2 in RC 4000

These were the conditions upon which we started the development of Boss 2. We would not change the existing software unless strictly necessary. However, we soon found it necessary to modify and extend the file handling procedures in the monitor, and this project developed in parallel with Boss 2 [16].

Figure 2 shows the process Boss which executes the Boss 2 program. The job processes are children of Boss. Boss receives messages from the job processes and sends the answer when the requested operation is completed. Of course the jobs send all parent messages to Boss, but some input/output messages are also sent to Boss, because Boss simulates some devices and behaves like a set of drivers toward the job. The devices simulated are very slow devices requiring spooling and devices difficult to share (low speed terminal, paper tape reader, printer). The job sends input/output messages directly to the drivers for fast devices like disk and magnetic tape.

Boss sends messages to various drivers either to complete the device simulation (terminal, reader printer) or to execute a parent message (reading a magnetic tape label in connection with the parent message "mount magnetic tape").

Inside Boss, a set of parallel activities is going on: one activity synchronized to each job and one synchronized to each peripheral device (i.e. to the driver). These activities will, in principle, communicate with each other as shown in Figure 2. Each activity could have been implemented as a process under the monitor, but in an unsuccessful project (Boss 1) we had learned that processes and messages were completely unsuited for the purpose.

The major problem is that each process has its own message queue. For instance it is not possible to let a message queue represent a pool of free records—common to several processes—because only one process can get messages from the queue. For the same reason, Dijkstra's semaphore construction for critical regions cannot be made directly with messages. It would be possible to solve these problems by introducing an administrator process, but its logic would be complicated.

Other problems are that RC 4000 processes are very difficult to make reentrant, and they cannot readily share code or data tables, especially when

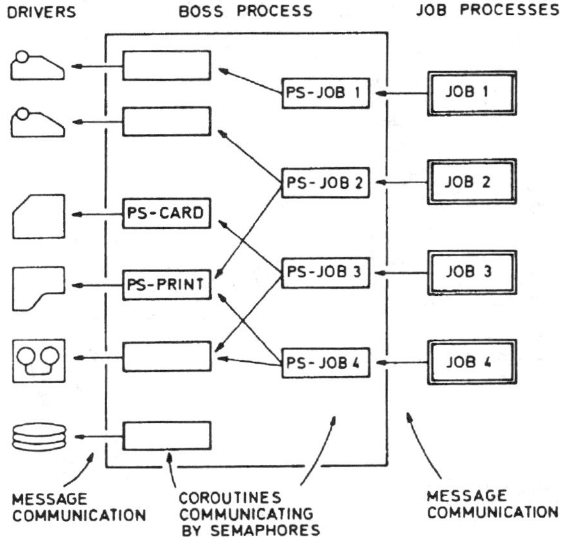

Fig. 2. Processes and coroutines. Processes are implemented by the RC 4000 Monitor. Coroutines are implemented inside the single Boss process. The set of coroutines are idealized.

swapping or paging is used.

Finally, only 23 processes plus drivers can be created in RC 4000, and we needed more than a hundred parallel activities inside Boss. So in all cases we would have to simulate more parallel activities inside one process.

The solution we chose was another level of multiprogramming running inside the single Boss process. The monitor of this "multiprogramming system" is called the Boss 2 Central Logic, the parallel activities are called coroutines, and the communication and synchronization is done by means of simple semaphores and queue semaphores as explained in the sequel. The coroutines run in a virtual memory simulated by the Central Logic and with the core store areas of the job processes considered special pages. The synchronization to the surroundings (replacing interrupts in a conventional multiprogramming system) is handled by means of the monitor procedure "wait event," which allows the Central Logic to wait for the first answer or message (the first "interrupt").

Below we will discuss the coroutines and show why the Deadlock problem changes the idealized picture of Figure 2 to the actual one in Figure 3.

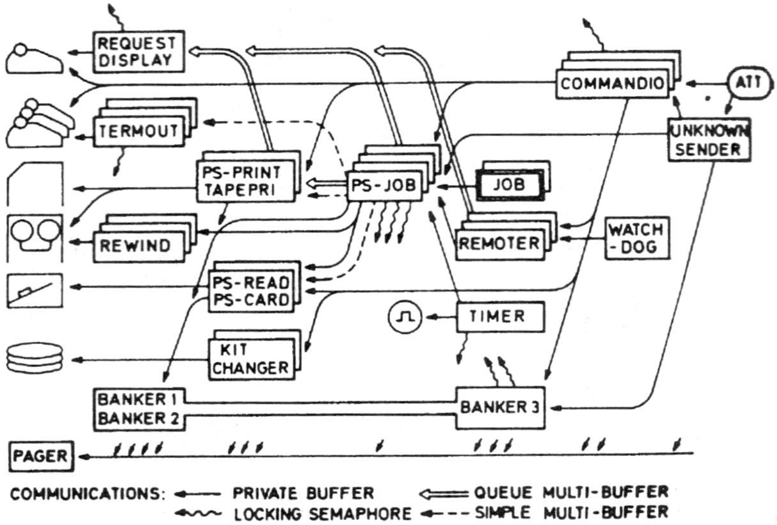

Fig. 3. All coroutines of Boss 2 and their communication. Some peripheral devices are shown, too.

The design is shown to be governed by the parallel activities (one synchronized to each job and one synchronized to each peripheral device). A hierarchical structure of the parallel activities is imposed afterward in order to prevent Deadlock.

2. Coroutines and Semaphores

2.1 Basic Coroutine Scheme

Each coroutine of Boss will perform an activity with a speed determined by a peripheral device or a job process. Typically, the following activities will be in progress simultaneously:

a. Printing data from the disk to the line printer—as fast as allowed by the printer (performed by the coroutine "ps-printer").

b. Reading data from card reader to the disk—as fast as allowed by the reader and the operator (coroutine "ps-card").

c. Communicating with a user terminal about editing, file listing, etc. (coroutine "commandio 1").

d. Communicating with a second user terminal (coroutine "commandio 2").

e. Performing a user job, i.e. handle the messages sent from the job process to Boss (coroutine "ps-job 3").

f. Performing a second user job (coroutine "ps-job 4").

The coroutines may be thought of as parallel processes, the only essential difference being the rigid scheduling of cpu-time.

The coroutines use only a little cpu-time and disk time, and as a result they need not delay each other. Of course, an activity like (a) above may run out of data to be printed, and then it will have to await the arrival of new data from activities like (e) and (f).

In general, the algorithm executed by a coroutine follows this *basic scheme*:

Step 1. Wait for a request to do some work.
Step 2. Send a finite number of requests to other coroutines or drivers.
Step 3. Answer the request of Step 1.
Step 4. Send a finite number of requests to other coroutines or drivers.
Step 5. Go to Step 1.

For a ps-printer (activity (a)), Step 1 waits for a request to print some data. The requests are sent from other coroutines by means of semaphores, and in busy periods several requests may be queued up. Step 2 sends requests to the printer driver in the form of messages and awaits the answers. When there are troubles with the printer, Step 2 may also send requests to the operator. Step 4 is blind.

For a ps-job (activity (e) and (f)), Step 1 waits for a message from the job process or a request from the operator's or user's terminal. Steps 2 and 4 depend on the actual request, and they may involve requests to a variety of coroutines and drivers.

In general, a coroutine waits for a request in Step 1 and for answers to requests in Steps 2 and 4. This is accomplished by calling the Central Logic, which returns to the coroutine in case the request or answer is ready. If it is not ready, the Central Logic returns to another coroutine which is ready to run, or it calls the monitor function "wait event." Section 4.2 elaborates on this topic and on the use of reentrant code to implement identical activities like (e) and (f).

The size of the coroutine algorithms varies considerably: "rewinder" is just 30 instructions, "ps-job" , and "commandio" are several thousand. Thus coroutines are not a partition of the code into manageable pieces. Rather they reflect the external requirements to parallel action. Notice, that if we want the basic scheme above and want to run all peripherals and all jobs in parallel, we need *at least one coroutine for each peripheral and each job.*

2.2 Queue Semaphores

The communication and synchronization between coroutines is done by means of queue semaphores and simple semaphores. A *queue semaphore* is an abstraction which represents a queue of records or a set of coroutines waiting for records to be put in the queue (Figure 4).

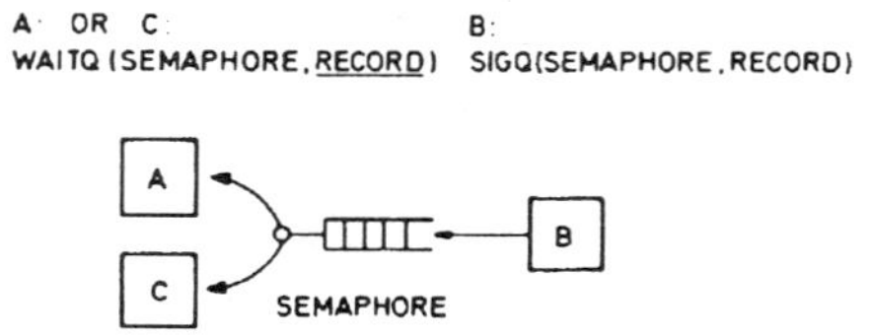

Fig. 4. Process (or coroutine) communication by means of queue semaphores. The queue semaphores have no fixed relation to the processes, and in principle, any process may wait or signal (send into) the queue. When A or C has received a record, they will later return it to a separate queue of free records (not shown). R can then get a new record from this queue.

Two procedures of the Central Logic handle the queue semaphores:

waitq(semaphore, record):

The procedure "wait queue" removes the first record from the queue represented by the semaphore. A pointer to the record is returned to the calling coroutine. If the queue is empty, the calling coroutine is suspended–waiting until a record is available in the queue.

sigq(semaphore, record):

The procedure "signal queue" inserts a record (specified by a pointer) into the queue of semaphore. If coroutines are waiting for records in the queue, one of them will be activated and it will run later.

The main difference between queue semaphores and messages is that a queue semaphore does not belong to a single process (or coroutine). In principle, any coroutine may wait for or signal any queue semaphore. Another difference is that the records may have any length, while the message buffers are restricted to eight words.

When coroutines communicate, two semaphores are involved. One semaphore holds the requests, the other the answers.

As an example, consider the communication between a ps-job and a ps-printer. The requests are queued by the semaphore "print queue," and a request record specifies that a certain file should be printed. The free records are queued by the semaphore "print free." Now the ps-job uses the basic scheme in this way:

Step 1. Wait for a request from job, operator, or user.
Step 2. **if** request is print a file **then**
        begin *waitq*(print free, record);
          store print request in record;
          sigq(print queue, record);
        end;
Step 3. ...

The ps-printer uses the basic scheme in this way:

Step 1. *waitq*(print queue, record).
Step 2. print the file using send message and wait answer.
Step 3. *sigq*(print free, record).
Step 5. **goto** step 1;

Note that these algorithms cause waiting in the proper way. When no free records are available, the ps-job will wait on "print free" in Step 2. When no requests are in the queue, the ps-printer will wait on "print queue" in Step 1.

If several printers exist, each of them is served by its own ps-printer. Any printer may print a file. This is obtained automatically if "print queue" is common to all ps-printers. As long as "print queue" is nonempty, all printers will be busy. This simple implementation of parallel request processing is difficult to obtain with most other communication methods. For instance, messages are completely unsuited for that purpose.

The communication principle corresponds to the beautiful, symmetrical producer-consumer algorithm of Dijkstra: the ps-job consumes free records and produces requests. The ps-printer consumes requests and produces free records. The principle can also be thought of as a generalization of the conventional double buffer scheme to *multi-buffers*. (A record corresponds to a buffer.) In Figure 3, 4 double arrows show such multi-buffer communication based on queue semaphores. The arrow shows the direction of the request.

2.3 Simple Semaphores

Simple semaphores were introduced by Dijkstra [5, 6]. They resemble queue semaphores, but the queue is not represented explicitly. Only a count of the records in an abstract "queue" is kept track of.

Thus, simple semaphores can be used to implement queues where the records are linked in a user defined manner or where the record does not contain essential information.

Simple semaphores are handled by the following two procedures of the Central Logic:

wait(semaphore)
sig(semaphore)

It is assumed that coroutines follow the discipline of handling a semaphore either with *waitq/sigq* exclusively or with *wait/sig*.

As an example, consider the handling of output from a job to the terminal. Each request consists of one word to be printed (3 characters), and an ordinary queue would be too cumbersome. Instead the ps-job and the "termout" agree to use a backing store area in a cyclical manner. Two simple semaphores represent the number of full and free words, and the algorithms look exactly like those originally proposed by Dijkstra. Multi-buffers implemented in this way appear as dotted arrows in Figure 3.

As another example, we will elaborate on the parallel printers of Section 2.2. In practice we want to sort the files according to paper type (one copy, two copies, special forms, etc.) in order to minimize paper changing. So we use one queue for each paper type and a common abstract queue representing the total number of print requests. The abstract queue is implemented by a simple semaphore "common print." Now the ps-job sends a print request in this way:

Step 2. *waitq*(print free, record);
  store print request in record;
  sigq(paper type queue, record);
  sig(common print);

The ps-printer proceeds like this:

```
Step 1. wait(common print);
        if queue of current paper type is empty then
        begin select a non-empty paper type queue
          (at least one exists) according to some strategy;
          current paper type := queue selected
        end
        waitq(current paper type, record);
Step 2....
```

Note that selection of current paper type is a critical region which should be executed by at most one ps-printer at a time. Otherwise two ps-printers could decide to wait for the same paper type queue, which happened to contain only one request.

2.4 Critical Regions

A critical region is a part of an algorithm which updates variables common to several processes (or coroutines). If a certain relation is to be maintained between the common variables, one process must complete the critical region before another process can enter a critical region working on the same variables.

A sound solution is to use a queue with one record which contains the common variables. When a process wants to update the variables, it gets the record by means of *waitq*. After the updating it returns the record to the same queue by means of *sigq*. If other processes want to update the variables meanwhile, they will be suspended when executing *waitq*.

Because only one record is involved, its address may be known to all processes, and a simple semaphore may replace the queue semaphore. This was the solution described by Dijkstra, and it is also used in Boss. The corresponding *locking semaphores* are shown in Figure 3 as waved arrows.

The special coroutine scheduling of cpu-time allows a simpler handling of critical regions in many cases: the Central Logic can only pass control to another coroutine when a coroutine explicitly waits. As a result, critical regions without embedded waiting can be handled without semaphores. This simplifies programming in many cases, for instance in the printer case of the preceding section.

2.5 Private Buffers and Messages

A special case of multi-buffer communication is frequently used. Each sender of a request has his own record, and he wants the answer to be returned through his private semaphore, which may be simple. The private semaphore is specified in the request. The sender uses the basic scheme in this way.

Step 2 or 4. *sigq*(request queue, private record);
wait(private answer semaphore);

Because all the algorithms are loops, you may think of the scheme in a rotated form with *wait* preceding *sigq*. Then it looks again like the producer-consumer algorithm.

The receiver uses the basic scheme in this way:

Step 1. *waitq*(request queue, record);
Step 3. *sig*(record [private answer]);

This private buffer communication corresponds exactly to the message/answer communication with the drivers. In Figure 3 they are all represented by normal arrows.

3 Deadlock and Hierarchical Structuring

3.1 Absence of Deadlock, Basic Proof

We can prove the absense of Deadlock by Boss by proving that no coroutine waits forever when it has useful work to do.

ln the basic scheme of Section 2.1 we can distinguish two kinds of waiting. Waiting in Step 1 for a request is *idle waiting*. If the coroutine waits forever here, it does no harm as it then has no work to do. Waiting in Step 2 or 4 is *answer waiting*. If the coroutine waits forever here, we have a Deadlock as it will not be able to process the requests.

In Figure 3 all requests go from right to left, and we can then prove by induction that all requests are processed in a finite time: All "coroutines" to the extreme left are drivers which by definition complete their operation in a finite time (at least if they are handled properly by the operator). Now it follows that coroutines in column 2 from the left terminate their Steps 2 and 4 in a finite time, and hence they produce the answer (Step 3) in a finite time. If the request queue is implemented as First-ln-First-Out or any other kind of fair scheduling, we have then proved that all coroutines in column 2 answer a request in a finite time. We can now proceed to column 3, and so on, until absence of Deadlock has been proved for every coroutine.

Note that data may flow in the same direction as the request (e.g. for a printer) or in the opposite direction (e.g. requests for paper tape input).

In the next section we will tackle the Deadlock problems originating from locking semaphores and other deviations from the basic coroutine scheme.

The requirement that "all requests go from right to left" is a very strong design criterion. In some cases it has caused a coroutine synchronized to a single peripheral device to be split up in two.

This has happened with terminals which have a two-way initiative: The job may request input or output from the terminal, and this is handled by the coroutine "termout." The user may also request actions from the system while his job is running. For instance he may want a print out of the job state or the job queue, or he may ask the system to kill the job. This is handled by the coroutine "commandio." As the two coroutines share the terminal, they use a locking semaphore to get exclusive terminal access during a conversation.

In Figure 2 the system is shown with only one coroutine to handle a terminal, but then we have requests in both directions to the ps-job. As a result we would risk Deadlock, because the terminal coroutine could wait for an answer from the ps-job, while the ps-job waited for an answer from the terminal coroutine. None of them would then be able to process the request from the other.

Also magnetic tape stations have a two-way initiative, because Boss may try to rewind the tape (the coroutine "rewinder") while the operator unloads it and mounts a new tape (the coroutine "remoter").

Because all communications are symmetrical producer-consumer algorithms, the direction of the request may seem rather arbitrary. However, it is well defined from a semantic point of view. For instance if the ps-printer does not get a request. it is because no printing is needed. But if it does not get an answer, printing is needed but not carried out.

In some cases we could imagine a system with a reversed request direction. For instance, we could try to construct a system where the tape reader issued a request whenever a paper tape was inserted. We could then try to prove that all tapes were loaded sooner or later. In the present system we can only prove that a job requesting a tape will be able to progress sooner or later.

3.2 Absence of Deadlock, Special Cases

The basic coroutine scheme does not explicitly mention the use of locking semaphores to control critical regions. So we will have to prove separately that no coroutine waits forever to enter a critical region.

When a coroutine has two or more nested critical regions, all other coroutines must use the same sequence of nesting. Then the entering into an inner critical region cannot be delayed endlessly by another coroutine being in the same critical region.

If a coroutine awaits an answer inside a critical region, the producer of the answer may not require entrance to the same critical region. This rule propagates recursively, as the producer of the answer may not even await an answer from another coroutine using the same critical region.

Thus the locking semaphores create two rules to be followed (and proved) in each coroutine.

Next we will discuss a more serious deviation from the basic coroutine scheme: In some cases a coroutine does not produce the answer in Step 3 until it has gotten other requests in Step 1. The proof methods used here vary from case to case.

As an example consider the coroutine "request display," which prints operator requests and maintains a list of operator requests which have not yet been completed. Operator requests are messages like "mount magnetic tape" or "change paper." The list of incompleted requests can be printed on demand.

The request display receives two kinds of requests. One is "insert," which specifies an operator request to be printed and kept in the list. This request is not answered in Step 3. The other kind is "delete," which specifies that a request should be deleted from the list–presumably because the operator action is completed. In this case Step 3 answers both the delete request and the earlier insert request.

The proof that all requests are eventually answered involves two rules. First, the operator is supposed to honor a request in a finite time and this must cause a "delete" to the request display. The second rule imposes a limit on the number of "insert" requests which a coroutine may have pending. This limit is one for each ps-printer, ps-reader, and ps-job with addition of one for each tape station (to be used either by the ps-job or the remoter). The limit is zero for all other coroutines. If these rules are followed by every coroutine, we prevent Deadlock simply by making a sufficiently large pool of free request records.

As a more important example consider the coroutine "Banker," which allocates resources to the jobs. When a coroutine wants to reserve or release resources, it sends a private buffer (Section 2.5) to the Banker stating the set of resources involved. It gets the answer to a release request immediately, and the answer to a reserve request when the resources are available. Again, the Banker may skip the answer in Step 3 until more resources have been released. The proof in this case is somewhat complicated and assumes that the maximum set of resources needed by a job is stated at job start. The allocation algorithm and details of the proof are given in [11].

We should mention that the Banker is the only coroutine not synchronized to a job or a peripheral device. In fact the Banker is superfluous as a coroutine, and it could be replaced by a reentrant procedure which is called by any coroutine wanting to reserve or release resources for a job. The solution would then become the "private semaphore" scheme described by Dijkstra [5]. Later, Dijkstra has proposed the private buffer scheme actually used in Boss (the "Secretary" of [7]).

During the debugging we met some Deadlocks caused by trivial programming errors (e.g. waiting for a wrong semaphore) and one Deadlock caused by violation of the second rule for locking semaphores (easily corrected by splitting the critical region in two).

3.3 Hierarchical Structuring and Coroutine Structuring

The basic proof of Deadlock absence is equivalent to that of Dijkstra and Habermann [5 and 9]. Especially, the idle waiting in Step 1 corresponds to their "homing position."

If we wish it, we could regard the set of coroutines as structured in a hierarchy like Dijkstra's. Each column of coroutines would then correspond to a level of the hierarchy. But this is not the way things developed.

A hierarchical structuring is usually invented during the construction process. This we have done inside each coroutine, by arranging the program in nested parts and procedures in the usual manner.

Contrary to this, the structuring into coroutines is mainly determined by the external requirements. The general rule seems to be this: *Make one coroutine (or process) for each independent stream of external events.* In our case, each job process and each peripheral device supplies an independent stream of events. Devices with a two-way initiative supply two independent streams of events and are consequently handled by two coroutines. (The only exception in Boss is the Banker, as discussed in Section 3.2.) The structuring into columns comes later and serves to guide the proof of Deadlock absence.

The author has used this structuring principle with equal success in later projects like message switching and remote process control. One additional rule has turned up; Assume that the processing of a critical event stream requires much cpu or disk time. Then two coroutines with an intermediate multi-buffer should be used in order to overlap event receiving and processing: one coroutine which receives the external events and one which spends the cpu or disk time. The latter coroutine may as well serve several coroutines of the first kind.

4. Implementation Principles

4.1 Virtual Store

The total space occupied by coroutine algorithms, records, and other variables is much too large for the core store. Instead, we implemented a virtual store based on software paging.

Each word in the virtual store is identified by a 22-bit virtual address. The lower range of addresses corresponds to resident parts of the virtual store—with the virtual address being the hardware core address. The middle range of addresses corresponds to virtual store parts on drum—which are transferred to the core store upon demand. The high range of addresses is similar, but corresponds to virtual store parts on a disk.

The virtual store is divided in *sections*, where each section is a full number of physical blocks on the device (block size equals 256 words of 24 bits). Whenever a word of the virtual store is needed and it is not in the core store, the entire section containing the word is transferred. In practice we consider the virtual store as divided in *pages* of consecutive words. A page is always allocated inside a section to allow fast addressing of the entire page after an initial page access. Several small pages can be allocated in a one block section, whereas large pages occupy a section each.

4.2 Coroutines

Each coroutine is represented by an 8-word coroutine description which is resident in the core store. One of the words is used as a link, either to a semaphore (when the coroutine waits for it), to the pager queue (when the coroutine waits for page transfers), to the active queue (when it waits for cpu-time), or to the answer queue (when it waits for a driver answer). One word is used for identifying the driver answer waited for, or for working during operations on queue semaphores. Five words contain virtual addresses, which represent pages to be held in the core store while the coroutine uses the cpu. A bit in each of these *page description* words shows whether the page is modified by the coroutine so that it should be written back. The first page description always represents the *code page* in which the current coroutine algorithm is found. The last word represents the return address to the coroutine. The address is relative to the beginning of the code page.

When a coroutine runs, the first five words of its current code page contain the absolute core addresses of the five pages of its coroutine description. In this way the code can easily access data in the five pages. Note that the page allocation can only change when the coroutine explicitly calls the Central Logic. The coroutine gets access to other pages by changing the coroutine description and then calling the Central Logic. In this case other coroutines may run during the page transfers.

Reentrant coroutines are handled by allocating all the variables in pages other than the code page. Thus, two reentrant coroutines may run with the same code page but different variable pages.

4.3 Semaphores

Each semaphore is represented by 3 core resident words. One word is a count of the number of records or—when negative—the number of coroutines waiting on the semaphore. Two words point to the beginning and the end of the record queue (or the queue of coroutine descriptions waiting on the semaphore). This semaphore representation is rather clumsy and could be replaced by a one-word representation as shown in [15].

The records of a queue are pages in the virtual store—linked together through their first word.

4.4 Paging Method

As outlined above, demand paging is used. Of particular interest is the fact that several pages may be needed simultaneously, and any page size (really section size) may be used.

The core resident pager coroutine transfers pages upon request from other coroutines. It will complete all page transfers for one coroutinc before it handles the next coroutine in its request queue. It awaits the disk and drum transfers as all other coroutines by means of an entry to the Central Logic, thereby allowing the execution of other coroutines with all their current pages in the core store.

The pager coroutine and the Central Logic maintain a priority for each page in the core store. The priority represents a least-recently-used strategy, but with regard to pages presently used as I/O buffers or job processes. The latter type of pages will have a very high priority until the answer arrives or the job process is swapped out by the Banker. The pager tries with a simple strategy to allocate all demanded pages in low priority parts of the core store.

5. Project Plan and Tlme Schedule

5.1 First Project Plan

The design of Boss 2 was started at Regnecentralen, Copenhagen, in August 1970 by Klavs Landberg, Per Mondrup, and the author. In October 1970 we completed the *project specification* as an internal report. That part of the report which specified the facilities of the first version and the possible later extensions was published in March 1971 [13]. In this section, I will give a summary of the project specification and explain the key estimates. In Section 5.4, I will compare it to the actual progress of the project.

The project specification was 25 closely written pages. the facilities were described as follows. For each type of peripheral device there was described the strategy to be used by Boss for handling it and the actions to be taken by the operator.The devices considered were: typewriter-like terminals, paper tape reader, printers, several types of magnetic tape stations, several kinds of drums and disks.

The on-line commands, the implementation, and conventions for the on-line editor were outlined. Also described were the resource allocation on backing stores, the job scheduling and swapping strategies, the user catalog, the account and statistics files.

One section estimated the storage demands and the total system overhead.

A ten-page section described 21 major extensions of the basic project to be decided before implementation started. They included things like conversational jobs (the basic version proposed only remote job entry combined with fast on-line editing), vdu-terminals, card reader, remote batch terminals, and simple facilities for process control experiments.

These parts of the report were published. The unpublished part (five pages) defined the extent of the project, the preconditions, the time schedule, the use of man-months and computer time, the cost for extensions of the basic project, and the necessary implementation group.

The extent of the project fixed the relations to other parts of the software, accounting programs, writing of manuals, transitions to maintenance, and—of course—the facilities as described above. Some facilities which were not considered, but which might be important, were pointed out.

The preconditions stated that certain other software parts should be finished at certain times, that 76 hours of computer time should be available for debugging, that the extensions had to be decided and the specification accepted within a month.

A total of four persons (the three designers and Bjørn Ørding-Thomsen) were assumed as the implementation group with a time schedule built on check points as follows:

November 1970. Final decisions on extensions.
December 1970. Detailed specification of the internal structure and the interface between all parallel activities inside Boss.
February 1971. Debugged Central Logic. All other parts punched.
May 1971. Prototype debugged.
July 1971. Installation of the prototype completed.

In view of the later facts that the prototype was completed April 1972, and the first public release was August 1972, this time schedule seems utterly ridiculous. Let us see, however, how we arrived at it.

The key point was the estimate of the total number of instructions. Our basis was the list of facilities and strategies—not horrible—which we estimated as equivalent to our Algol compiler:

First estimate: Boss is 7,000 instructions.

From this the rest was deduced. An old rule of thumb told that in a project from design to maintenance, a programmer produced an average of 200 machine instructions a month. Thus *35 man-months* were necessary. Of these 6 were spent already with design (3 persons in 2 months), so 29 were left for 4 persons. This brought us to June 1971. We specified July to be cautious.

Another rule of thumb told that a good programmer made one error or design fault for each 20 instructions and that he could find one error for each test run. With the debug technique we were accustomed to, a good test run with succeeding careful inspection of the test output could reveal about 5 errors. To be careful because of the multiprogramming, we assumed that only half an error could be found and corrected for each test run.

So the 7,000 instructions should give 350 errors and 700 test runs. The modular design of the system was estimated to be sufficiently good so that the four programmers could work nearly independently of each other, reducing the debug demand to 200 sessions at the computer. We planned the debug sessions to 15 minutes each, i.e. a total of 50 hours, and asked for 76. The main debug period should be February, March, April (80 days), so two periods of 15 minutes a day should be sufficient.

In order to utilize periods of 15 minutes, we planned the debug sessions carefully, as explained in the next section.

5.2 Planning a Debug Session

A new and extended version of the Monitor was to be used together with Boss, so that a total exchange of the software had to take place during each debug session. We devised a method for a fast exchange of the system based on exchange of disk packs and swap of drum contents to the disk.

A special autoload paper tape was used to switch at the beginning of each session, and another tape was used to switch back to the end of the session. This took a total of 5 minutes.

When we had used this system for a few weeks, we happened to load the start tape at the end of the session—and the entire standard system disappeared and had to be loaded from magnetic tape. The computer staff responded by only allowing us run time in the night after saving the standard system on tape. We responded by changing the autoload tapes to one which itself found out which of the two actions to perform. After a while we regained our short periods of day time. After reduction for the switch time, we were left with 10 minutes of which we wanted to use four times 1 minute for the planned translation and test of the four programmer's parts. The 6 minutes left were spares for rush corrections. In order to translate and generate a new version in half a minute, all files had to be on disk and only a small text file had to be translated into binary form. No linker (loader) exists in RC 4000, so we had to implement a special linker which loads the binary files into the virtual store in which Boss runs. A simulation program was also devised to feed Boss with input lines from "terminals", etc., in the 30 seconds left.

We used the well-proven technique of permanent test output [17] from all parts of Boss, so that the result of a test run was a list of test output for later inspection of what had happened. This test output is still used in the normal production run, where it is stored on disk or magnetic tape for analysis if the system breaks down [14, Chap. 9, Installation and Maintenance]. A test output record is generated by the Central Logic whenever a coroutine executes *sig, wait*, etc. Some coroutines also produce private test output records showing intermediate results.

Obviously, listing of source programs were the exception rather than the rule. With a careful marking of all corrections in the latest listing, we had no troubles finding our way in the latest version. An important point was the use of an extremely careful programmer—Isabella Carstensen—for the clerical work of keeping track of paper tape corrections, keeping track of on-line rush corrections, punching correction tapes according to pencil marks in the listings, arranging safety copies, etc. This work was drastically underestimated in the planning stage.

Finally, the system of project file directories and private file directories (planned for the extended monitor) was utilized in the debug sessions to assure that one test file could be tested together with reasonably good versions of the other files [14, Section 4.6.3, User's Manual]. The decision that a private file was reasonably good and could be made a project file had to be taken between debug sessions after careful inspection of the test output.

5.3 Choice of Programming Language, Paging

The author had previously been involved in the development of Boss 1 in Algol 5 for RC 4000. Although Algol 5 was sufficient for the purpose, the necessary use of reentrant coroutines was very cumbersome to express in Algol. Worse, however, was that the object code turned out to be 4 to 5 times longer than equivalent handwritten assembly language code. With the same overhead in page transfers this would need 4 to 5 times more core store.

It should be noted that the Algol 5 compiler generates fairly good code. For instance it is claimed that Algol W on IBM 360 generates very efficient code, but investigations have shown [1] that it is just as long as Algol 5 code.

As the long object code was prohibitive for the goals of Boss 2, assembly language was chosen.

From the beginning it was assumed that the code and variables of Boss were to be in a virtual store controlled by a software paging system. RC 4000 has no hardware for paging so software page references must be inserted where needed. We had experience with this kind of software paging from several Algol compilers. The main problem was the hand-written standard procedures which had to fit into a few of the fixed size pages. Whenever changes were needed, it caused great troubles to fit the new version into the fixed size pages. Another problem was a lot of difficult *paging bugs* caused by code which had brought a page to core and later referenced it with an absolute address when it was possibly not in core any more.

We solved the first problem by designing the paging system for variable length pages. We partially solved the second problem (paging bugs) by allowing a coroutine to specify that an entire set of pages had to reside in core simultaneously when it was running.

5.4 Actual Time Schedule

The first check point on the time schedule concerned the final decisions on extensions. They were delayed 6 weeks due to disagreements between the user groups. The extensions chosen were vdu-terminals, card reader, job controlled selection of print forms, printer back-up on magnetic tape. According to the project specification, this should delay the installation by three months (of which 6 weeks were due to the delay of the decision).

The next check point was apparently reached on schedule with release of the report "Boss 2, Internal Structure" dated January 1971. However, a close reading of the report reveals many missing details in the interface between the coroutines. The report contained a detailed version of Sections 2, 3, and 4 of this paper.

In March and April 1971 the company changed their development policy, claiming that they would neglect, somehow, the RC 4000 and try to find other areas for the development groups. The Boss 2 group was heavily involved in these discussions and a delay of one month was accepted. The new schedule looked like this:

May 1971. Debugged Central Logic. All other parts punched.
September 1971. Prototype debugged.
November 1971. Installation completed.

The Central Logic was debugged on schedule, but most other parts were still not written. A lot of detailed revisions of the schedule were made, but none of them reflected reality. Several parts were completed and debugged, and around July 1971 about half of the system was in the test phase.

A general reluctance to face the facts caused me—as a project manager—to discard all planning and just let the group implement as fast as possible. Around August 1971, the group was augmented with Bo Jacoby and Bo

Tveden Jørgensen, and the responsibilities of the group were extended to also cover some related software project excluded in the project specification.

In January 1972 everything was in the test phase, but some parts were in a preliminary version. This point most likely corresponded to the check point "All Parts Punched," but the delay was 8 months.

In January 1972 we finally detected the real reason for the delay. We had programmed *20,000 instructions* instead of the estimated 7,000. When the project entered the maintenance stage in August 1972, we had programmed *26,000 instructions* (including a few further extensions).

The prototype was put in operation in April 1972. Further extensions for conversational jobs (time sharing) and process control were implemented until August 1972, when the first public release took place. At that time 115 man-months had been used instead of the latest estimate of 55 man-months.

5.5 Conclusion

The main fault in the estimates was that the number of instructions were underestimated by a factor of 3 (excluding contributions from later extensions). A possible cause for this—pointed out by Peter Naur—is that we initially compared the project to an Algol compiler which used a very advanced table technique to bring down the program length [17]. A similar technique was not used in Boss, possibly because we concentrated too much on the structuring into coroutines and forgot to design the sequential algorithms inside each coroutine in the same careful manner. Another cause may be that each facility and strategy were conceived and implemented individually, whereas an Algol compiler benefits from the extremely homogeneous structure of Algol 60.

A secondary reason for the underestimate was the interface to the Monitor. The Monitor was extended in the same period with several facilities needed by Boss. Especially the interface concerning drum and disks was much more complicated to utilize than anticipated. This problem was felt severely during the development and caused major revisions of Boss and the Monitor.

A minor contribution to the underestimate is the late inclusion of further extensions and related projects (user catalog updating, accounting, process control, etc.).

A main fault in the project management (the author primarily) was the sticking to a time schedule instead of revising the more fundamental estimate of the number of instructions. It is typical that the main influence of the underestimate is in the programming phase. The debug phase and the installation phase were not so significantly affected.

The rule of thumb saying 200 instructions per man-month may now be checked for the actual schedule: 26,000 instructions/115 man-months = 230.

What might have helped us in the planning was a similar rule of thumb for the programming phase alone.

6. Evaluation

6.1 Performance

The facilities as originally specified were implemented, sometimes in an extended version. We dropped one extension—the vdu terminals—because the hardware was not developed. Another extension—printer back-up on magnetic tape—has not been put in operation, partially because there seems to be no serious need for it.

The backing store and core store requirements are in good agreement with the specification. However, the system overhead was somewhat underestimated. When Boss runs in the specified core area (15,000 characters), the overhead is many times more than estimated because of thrashing. When Boss uses 30,000 characters in the core store, the overhead is 1.5 times the estimate (actually 3 seconds overhead to execute a job). The larger core demand is related to the code being 3 times longer than estimated. The factor 1.5 could easily have been anticipated if a more detailed analysis was carried out in the specification phase.

6.2 Reliability, Bugs, Proof

When we started the Boss 2 design, we knew that the RC 4000 software was extremely reliable. In a university environment, the system typically ran under the simple operating system for three months without crashes. Although some errors existed in compilers and utility programs, they affected, at most, one job. The crashes present were possibly due to transient hardware errors. Errors in the peripherals were more frequent, but did not wreck the rest of the system.

From the beginning, we aimed at a similar stability for Boss six months after release. So we did not implement any restart facilities, except that the permanent files on disk were preserved by a simple strategy. We believe that this decision is a major reason for the relatively simple and stable operating system.

In fact, Boss 2 passed a 3-week delivery test in September 1972—one month after the first release. In these 3 weeks the contract allowed at most four crashes because of hardware or software. Actually four crashes occurred, three of them caused by bugs in Boss. In the period the system was heavily loaded with unrestricted user jobs: program debugging, process control jobs, and conversational jobs.

From September 1972 to March 1973, dozens of errors were reported as the users explored the corners of the system. In April 1973 all reported errors, except one, were located and corrected. Today the system seems to be error free. The corrections nearly always converged in the sense that one correction did not cause errors somewhere else.

We have collected all corrections during the development and maintenance, but we have not done statistical analysis on them. Nearly all errors are simple programming errors that occur also in uni-programming (loading a wrong register, testing a wrong condition). The most difficult bugs to find were associated with paging (paging bugs, see Section 5.3), and the correct return of borrowed resources (see below).

A few bugs were typical multiprogramming bugs: forgetting to reserve a resource which then happened to be used by another coroutine at the same time. One case of Deadlock occurred (see Section 3.2), but it was simple to correct.

The only important design faults were those associated with booking of resources on the backing store and parallel access to fies. I am afraid we still have only a superficial knowledge of these problems (see [16]).

The successful detection and correction of errors after release of the system could not have been achieved without the permanent test output (Section 5.2). If the system broke down, the computer staff would send the test output file to the project group, which then was able to find the error in most cases. As normally only a short backing store file (80,000 characters) is used for cyclical collection of test output, some errors were still difficult to find because they occurred a long time before the symptoms. For instance, if a resource is borrowed and later only a part of it is returned, it will take a long time before something wrong becomes apparent. The cause is then not available in the test output. In the cases where we have had test output on magnetic tape (one large reel every three hours), we have always been able to locate the error—possibly by means of an ad hoc program for analyzing the tapes.

The prototype was very carelessly tested, but after it had been put in operation nobody had time to make careful, systematic test programs. I believe that if the prototype had been delayed some months, we could have found most errors via systematic test programs.

The question of proving an operating system is sometimes discussed. We have proved some statements about the system, for instance the absence of Deadlock. However, in order to prove the entire system, we would have to formalize every statement in the manuals (120 pages) and prove them. Still I doubt whether a statement like "absence of Deadlock" would have emerged from the manuals. It seems to me that the only systems which can realistically be proved are those where the entire manual is below, say, 10 pages.

Acknowledgments. The design of Boss 2 is due to the exciting collaboration of Per Mondrup, Klavs Landberg, and the author. The implementation is due to the hard work of the project group consisting of Isabella Carstensen, Bo Jacoby, Bo Tveden Jørgensen, Bjørn Ørding-Thomsen, and the three designers. The author had the overall project responsibility until June 1972 when Klavs Landberg took over the job.

I would like to thank Peter Lindblad Andersen and Hans Rischel for their patient development and modifications of the Monitor and the utility programs.

An independent project run by Ole Caprani, Lise Lauesen, and Flemming Sejergård Olsen extended the system to serve also as a remote batch terminal for CDC 6400 and Univac 1106.

Finally, we are very indebted to Christian Gram, our manager, for his patience and encouragement, especially during the exhausting winter 1971–72.

References

1. Andersen, J., Møller, T., Ravn, A.P., and Stamp, S. Rapport over Effektivt Kørende Algol System (In Danish). Projekt 71-9-7. Datalogisk Institut, U of Copenhagen, 1972.
2. Brinch Hansen, P. The nucleus of a multiprogramming system. *Comm. ACM 13*, 4 (Apr. 1970), 238–250.
3. Brinch Hansen, P. RC 4000 Software, Multiprogramming System. RCSL No. 55-D140. Regnecentralen, Copenhagen, 1971.
4. Denning, P.J. Third generation computer systems.*Computing Surveys 3*, 4 (Dec. 1971), 175–216.
5. Dijkstra, E.W. The structure of the "THE" multiprogramming system. *Comm. ACM 11*, 5 (May 1968), 341–346.

6. Dijkstra, E.W. Cooperating sequential processes. In *Programming Languages*, F. Genyus (Ed.), Academic Press, New York, 1968, 43–112.

7. Dijkstra, E.W. Hierarchical ordering of sequential processes. In *Operating Systems Techniques* , C.A.R. Hoare and R.M. Perroth (Eds.), Academic Press, London 1972.

8. Habermann, A.N. Prevention of System Deadlocks. *Comm. ACM 12*, 7 (July 1969), 373–377, 385.

9. Habermann, A.N. On the harmonious cooperation of abstract machines. Technische Hogeschool, Eindhoven, 1967.

10. Horning, JJ., and Randell, B. Process structuring. *Computing Surveys 5*, 1 (Mar. 1973), 5–30.

11. Lauesen, S. Job scheduling guaranteeing reasonable turn-around times. *Acta Infor-rnatica 2* (1973), 1–11.

12. Lauesen, S. Program control of operating systems. *BIT 13 3* (1973), 323–337.

13. Lauesen, S. Foreløbig Specifikation af Operativsystemet Boss 2 (in Danish). RCSL No. 55-D153. Regnecentralen, Copenhagen, 1971.

14. Lauesen, S. Boss 2, user's manual, operator's manual, installation and maintenance. RCSL No. 31-D211, 31-D230, and 31-D191, Regnecentralen, Copenhagen, 1972.

15. Lauesen, S. Implementation of semaphores and parallel processes. NBB Doc. EC-D4, Nordisk Brown Boveri, Copenhagen, 1973.

16. Lindblad Andersen, P. Monitor 3. RCSL No. 31-D109. Regnecentralen, Copenhagen, 1972.

17. Naur, P. The design of the Gier Algol Compiler. *BIT 3* (1963), 124–140 and 145–166.

18. Baker, F.T. Chief programmer team management of production programming. *IBM Syst. J.* 1 (1972), 56–73.

Appendix A. Survey of Coroutines in Boss

The list below refers to Figure 3 and mentions all coroutines in a row by row sequence.

Request Display. Prints messages to the operator on the main console. Messages demanding action from the operator are kept until the action is completed (Section 3.2).

Commandio. One commandio to each on-line terminal and to the operator's console. Performs all conversation with the on-line user and the operator, including editing and listing of files. Some commands are passed on to other coroutines (commands like "run job," "kill job," "start printer").

Termout. One termout to each on-line terminal. Prints job output on the terminal from a multi-buffer on disk. For nonconversational jobs the progress of the job is not delayed by the slow terminal.

Ps-printer. One ps-printer to each physical printer. Prints completed files from the backing stores or job controlled output from a multi-buffer. Attempts to minimize change of paper type (see Section 2.3). Communicates with request display about change of paper, etc.

Tape Printer. May copy print files from the backing store to a magnetic tape. When the backing store is about to run full of print files, the tape printer asks the operator for a tape and copies the files.

Ps-job. One ps-job to each on-line terminal plus spares for execution of batch jobs and internally generated jobs. A ps-job interprets the job specification (the first job control command), loads possible data files from card or paper tape, reserves most of the temporary resources for the job, and creates and starts the job process.

Now the ps-job receives messages from the job process (all parent messages and some input/output messages). Some messages are checked and then passed on to other coroutines (e.g. print a backing store file, write special operator request). In the same queue the ps-job receives certain buffers from commandio ("kill job," "answer to special operator request"), from remoters (tape ready,), and from timer (time exceeded). Messages which will cause a longer waiting time cause the ps-job to ask the Banker to swap out the job meanwhile.

When the job is finished, the ps-job cleans temporary files, asks for rewind of tapes, produces account records, etc.

Job. The job process. In a given moment only some of the ps-jobs have associated job processes.

Unknown Sender. Receives messages from unlogged terminals and processes other than Boss jobs. May either pass the login request to a free commandio, or enroll an internal job (via Banker and a free ps-job), or reject the message.

Rewinder. One rewinder to each magnetic tape station. Rewinds the tape when it is released. Unloads the tape when the station is to be used for something else. A short queue of such requests may exist becausc the unload cannot be ordered until the tape is rewound.

Remoter. One remoter to each magnetic tape station. Reads the tape label when the operator sets the station in the remote state. Tells request display if the label is unreadable or if the tape is not needed now. Obeys operator commands telling the name of the tape or asking for a label to be written.

When the tape has been identified in one way or another, a possible ps-job waiting ing for the tape is activated.

Watch-dog. Detects whether a station has been set remote and activates the corresponding remoter. This coroutine is only needed because the Monitor has a special driver proces responding to any station set in remote.

Ps-reader. Loads paper tapes either via a multi-buffer as job controlled input or via a double buffer to a backing store. Tells the Banker when the reader becomes empty and available for other jobs.

Ps-card. Loads card files just like the ps-reader. Tells the Banker when a job separation card is met (this signals the presence of a new job in the reader).

Kit Changers. One kit changer to each disk drive with exchangeable kits. Clears up on the old disk pack when the operator requests a kit change, waits until the new kit is ready, reads the kit label, and adjusts the file catalog.

Timer. Supervises the run time of the jobs in the core store and tells the ps-jobs when time has expired.

Banker. The Banker receives records and handles them in one out of three rather different parts of the code with different status in the hierarchy of coroutines. Banker 1 receives requests for swap in and swap out of jobs ard performs the swapping on a priority basis. Banker 2 receives requests for reservation or relase oftemporary resources (Section 3.2). Finally Banker 3 handles the idle ps-jobs and tells them when to start running a job and the kind of the job (card job, paper tape job, internally generated job).

Pager. Handles the virtual store as described in Section 4.1.

15

THE SOLO OPERATING SYSTEM: A CONCURRENT PASCAL PROGRAM*

PER BRINCH HANSEN

(1976)

This is a description of the single-user operating system Solo written in the programming language Concurrent Pascal. It supports the development of Sequential and Concurrent Pascal programs for the PDP 11/45 computer. Input/output are handled by concurrent processes. Pascal programs can call one another recursively and pass arbitrary parameters among themselves. This makes it possible to use Pascal as a job control language. Solo is the first major example of a hierarchical concurrent program implemented in terms of abstract data types (classes, monitors and processes) with compile-time control of most access rights. It is described here from the user's point of view as an introduction to another paper describing its internal structure.

INTRODUCTION

This is a description of the first operating system *Solo* written in the programming language Concurrent Pascal (Brinch Hansen 1975). It is a simple, but useful single-user operating system for the development and distribution of Pascal programs for the PDP 11/45 computer. It has been in use since May 1975.

From the user's point of view there is nothing unusual about the system. It supports editing, compilation and storage of Sequential and Concurrent Pascal programs. These programs can access either console, cards, printer,

*P. Brinch Hansen, The Solo operating system: a Concurrent Pascal program. *Software—Practice and Experience 6*, 2 (April–June 1976), 141–149.

tape or disk at several levels (character by character, page by page, file by file, or by direct device access). Input, processing, and output of files are handled by concurrent processes. Pascal programs can call one another recursively and pass arbitrary parameters among themselves. This makes it possible to use Pascal as a job control language (Brinch Hansen 1976a).

To the system programmer, however, Solo is quite different from many other operating systems:

1. Less than 4 per cent of it is written in machine language. The rest is written in Sequential and Concurrent Pascal.

2. In contrast to machine-oriented languages, Pascal does not contain low-level programming features, such as registers, addresses and interrupts. These are all handled by the virtual machine on which compiled programs run.

3. System protection is achieved largely by means of compile-time checking of access rights. Run-time checking is minimal and is not supported by hardware mechanisms.

4. Solo is the first major example of a hierarchical concurrent program implemented by means of abstract data types (classes, monitors, and processes).

5. The complete system consisting of more than 100,000 machine words of code (including two compilers) was developed by a student and myself in less than a year.

To appreciate the usefulness of Concurrent Pascal one needs a good understanding of at least one operating system written in the language. The purpose of this description is to look at the Solo system from a user's point of view before studying its internal structure (Brinch Hansen 1976b). It tells how the user operates the system, how data flow inside it, how programs call one another and communicate, how files are stored on disk, and how well the system performs in typical tasks.

JOB CONTROL

The user controls program execution from a display (or a teletype). He calls a program by writing its name and its parameters, for example:

```
move(5)
read(maketemp, seqcode, true)
```

The first command positions a magnetic tape at file number 5. The second one inputs the file to disk and stores it as sequential code named maketemp. The boolean true protects the file against accidental deletion in the future.

Programs try to be helpful to the user when he needs it. If the user forgets which programs are available, he may for example type:

```
help
```

(or anything else). The system responds by writing:

```
not executable, try
    list(catalog, seqcode, console)
```

The suggested command lists the names of all sequential programs on the console.

If the user knows that the disk contains a certain program, but is uncertain about its parameter conventions, he can simply call it as a program without parameters, for example:

```
read
```

The program then gives the necessary information:

```
try again
    read(file: identifier; kind: filekind; protect: boolean)
using
    filekind = (scratch, ascii, seqcode, concode)
```

Still more information can be gained about a program by reading its manual:

```
copy(readman, console)
```

A user session may begin with the input of a new Pascal program from cards to disk:

```
copy(cards, sorttext)
```

followed by a compilation:

pascal(sorttext, printer, sort)

If the compiler reports errors on the program listing:

pascal:
compilation errors

the next step is usually to edit the program text:

edit(sorttext)
...

and compile it again. After a successful compilation, the user program can now be called directly:

sort(...)

The system can also read job control commands from other media, for example:

do(tape)

A task is preempted by pushing the bell key on the console. This causes the system to reload and initialize itself. The command *start* can be used to replace the Solo system with any other concurrent program stored on disk.

DATA FLOW

Figure 1 shows the data flow inside the system when the user is processing a single text file sequentially by copying, editing, or compiling it.

The input, processing, and output of text take place simultaneously. Processing is done by a *job process* that starts input by sending an argument through a buffer to an input process. The argument is the name of the input device or disk file.

The *input process* sends the data through another buffer to the job process. At the end of the file the input process sends an argument through yet another buffer to the job process indicating whether transmission errors occurred during the input.

Output is handled similarly by means of an *output process* and another set of buffers.

In a single-user operating system it is desirable to be able to process a file continuously at the highest possible speed. So the data are buffered in core instead of on disk. The capacity of each buffer is 512 characters.

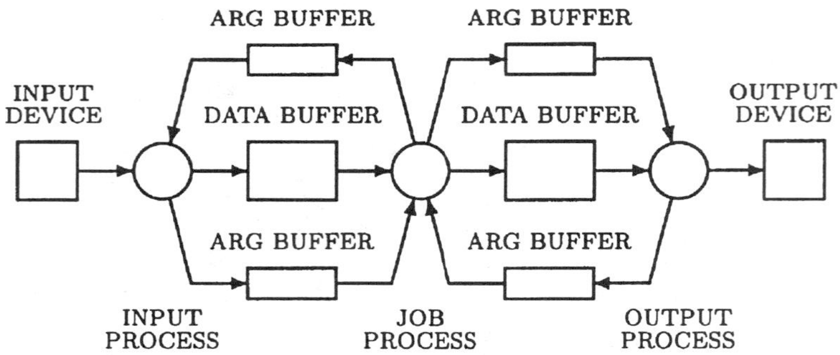

Figure 1 Processes and buffers.

CONTROL FLOW

Figure 2 shows what happens when the user types a command such as:

edit(cards, tape)

After system loading the machine executes a Concurrent Pascal program (Solo) consisting of three processes. Initially the input and output processes both load and call a sequential program *io* while the job process calls another sequential program *do*. The do program reads the user command from the console and calls the *edit* program with two parameters, *cards* and *tape*.

The editor starts its input by sending the first parameter to the io program executed by the input process. This causes the io program to call another program *cards* which then begins to read cards and send them to the job process.

The editor starts its output by sending the second parameter to the io program executed by the output process. The latter then calls a program *tape* which reads data from the job process and puts them on tape.

At the end of the file the cards and tape programs return to the io programs which then await further instructions from the job process. The editor returns to the do program which then reads and interprets the next command from the console.

It is worth observing that the operating system itself has no built-in drivers for input/output from various devices. Data are simply produced

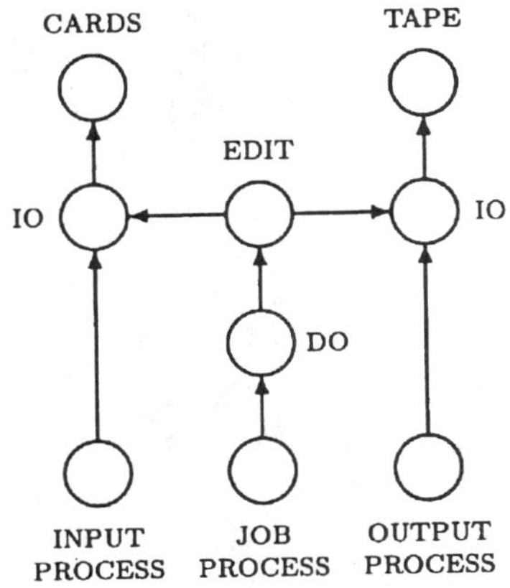

Figure 2 Concurrent processes and sequential programs.

and consumed by Sequential Pascal programs stored on disk. The operating system only contains the mechanism to call these. This gives the user complete freedom to supplement the system with new devices and simulate complicated input/output such as the merging, splitting and formatting of files without changing the job programs.

Most important is the ability of Sequential Pascal programs to call one another recursively with arbitrary parameters. In Fig. 2, for example, the do program calls the edit program with two identifiers as parameters. This removes the need for a separate (awkward) job control language. *The job control language is Pascal.*

This is illustrated more dramatically in Fig. 3 which shows how the command:

pascal(sorttext, printer, sort)

causes the do program to call the program *pascal.* The latter in turn calls seven compiler passes one at a time, and (if the compiled program is correct) *pascal* finally calls the filing system to store the generated code.

A program does not know whether it is being called by another program or directly from the console. In Fig. 3 the program *pascal* calls the filing system. The user, may, however, also call the file system directly, for example, to protect his program against accidental deletion:

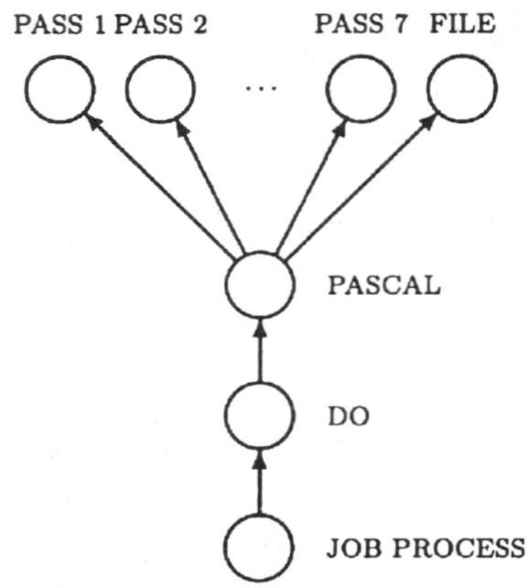

Figure 3 Compilation.

file(protect, sort, true)

The Pascal *pointer* and *heap* concepts give programs the ability to pass arbitrarily complicated data structures among each other, such as symbol tables during compilation (Jensen 1974). In most cases, however, it suffices to be able to use identifiers, integers, and booleans as program parameters.

STORE ALLOCATION

The run-time environment of Sequential and Concurrent Pascal is a kernel of 4 K words. This is the only program written in machine language. The user loads the kernel from disk into core by means of the operator's panel. The kernel then loads the Solo system and starts it. The Solo system consists of a fixed number of processes. They occupy fixed amounts of core store determined by the compiler.

All other programs are written in Sequential Pascal. Each process stores the code of the currently executed program in a fixed core segment. After termination of a program called by another, the process reloads the previous program from disk and returns to it. The data used by a process and the programs called by it are all stored in a core resident stack of fixed length.

FILE SYSTEM

The backing store is a slow *disk* with removable packs. Each user has his own disk pack containing the system and his private files. So there is no need for a hierarchical file system.

A disk pack contains a *catalog* of all files stored on it. The catalog describes itself as a file. A *file* is described by its name, type, protection and disk address. Files are looked up by hashing.

All system programs check the *types* of their input files before operating on them and associate types with their output files. The Sequential Pascal compiler, for example, will take input from an ascii file (but not from a scratch file), and will make its output a sequential code file. The possible file types are scratch, ascii, seqcode and concode.

Since each user has his own disk pack, files need only be *protected* against accidental overwriting or deletion. All files are initially unprotected. To protect one the user must call the file system from the console as described in Section 4.

To avoid compacting of files (lasting several minutes), file pages are scattered on disk and addressed indirectly through a *page map* (Fig. 4). A file is opened by looking it up in the catalog and bringing its page map into core.

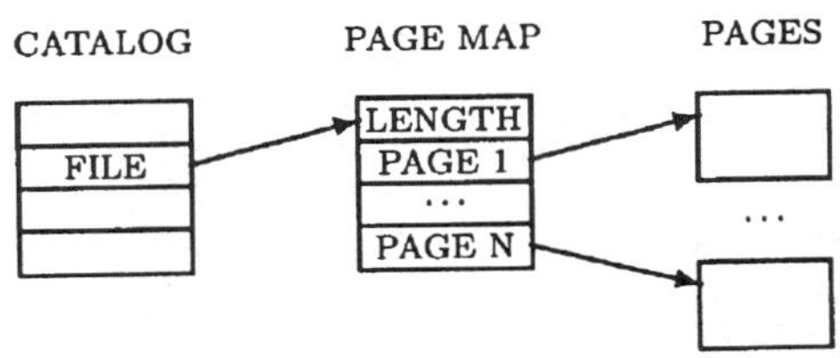

Figure 4 File system.

The resident part of the Solo system implements only the most frequently used file operations: lookup, open, close, get and put. A nonresident, sequential program, called *file*, handles the more complicated and less frequently used operations: create, replace, rename, protect, and delete file.

DISK ALLOCATION

The disk always contains a scratch file of 255 pages called *next*. A program creates a new file by outputting data to this file. It then calls the file system to associate the data with a new name, a type, and a length (≤ 255). Having done this the file system creates a new instance of *next*.

This scheme has two advantages:

1. All files are initialized with typed data.

2. A program creating a file need only call the nonresident file system once (after producing the file). Without the file *next* the file system would have to be called at least twice: before output to create the file, and after output to define its final length.

The disadvantages of having a single file *next* is that a program can only create one file at a time.

Unused disk pages are defined by a powerset of page indices stored on the disk.

On a slow disk special care must be taken to make *program loading* fast. If program pages were randomly scattered on the disk it would take 16 seconds to load the compiler and its input/output drivers. An algorithm described in Brinch Hansen (1976c) reduces this to 5 seconds. When the system creates the file *next* it tries to place it on consecutive pages within neighboring cylinders as far as possible (but will scatter the pages somewhat if it has to). It then rearranges the page indices within the page map to minimize the number of disk revolutions and cylinder movements needed to load the file. Since this is done before a program is compiled and stored on disk it is called *disk scheduling at compile time.*

The system uses a different allocation technique for the two temporary files used during compilation. Each pass of the compiler takes input from a file produced by its predecessor and delivers output to its successor on another file. A program *maketemp* creates these files and interleaves their page indices (making every second page belong to one file and every second one to the other). This makes the disk head sweep slowly across both files during a pass instead of moving wildly back and forth between them.

OPERATOR COMMUNICATION

The user communicates with the system through a console. Since a task (such as editing) usually involves several programs executed by concurrent processes these programs must identify themselves to the user before asking for input or making output:

```
do:
edit(cards, tape)
edit:
...
do:
...
```

Program identity is only displayed every time the user starts talking to a different program. A program that communicates several times with the user without interruption (such as the editor) only identifies itself once.

Normally only one program at a time tries to talk to the user (the current program executed by the job process). But an input/output error may cause a message from another process:

```
tape:
inspect
```

Since processes rarely compete for the console, it is sufficient to give a process *exclusive access* to the user for input or output of a single line. A conversation of several lines will seldom be interrupted.

A Pascal program only calls the operating system once with its identification. The system will then automatically display it when necessary.

SIZE AND PERFORMANCE

The Solo system consists of an operating system written in Concurrent Pascal and a set of system programs written in Sequential Pascal:

Program	Pascal lines	Machine words
operating system	1,300	4 K
do, io	700	4 K
file system	900	5 K
concurrent compiler	8,300	42 K
sequential compiler	8,300	42 K
editor	400	2 K
input/output programs	600	3 K
others	1,300	8 K
	21,800	110 K

(The two Pascal compilers can be used under different operating systems written in Concurrent Pascal—not just Solo.)

The amount of code written in different programming languages is:

Language	%
machine language	4
Concurrent Pascal	4
Sequential Pascal	92

This clearly shows that a good sequential programming language is more important for operating system design than a concurrent language. But although a concurrent program may be small it still seems worthwhile to write it in a high-level language that enables a compiler to do thorough checking of data types and access rights. Otherwise, it is far too easy to make time-dependent programming errors that are extremely difficult to locate.

The kernel written in machine language implements the process and monitor concepts of Concurrent Pascal and responds to interrupts. It is independent of the particular operating system running on top of it.

The Solo system requires a core store of 39 K words for programs and data:

Programs	K words
kernel	4
operating system	11
input/output programs	6
job programs	18
core store	39

This amount of space allows the Pascal compiler to compile itself.

The speed of text processing using disk input and tape output is:

Program	char/sec
copy	11,600
edit	3,300–6,200
compile	240

All these tasks are 60–100 per cent disk limited. These figures do not distinguish between time spent waiting for peripherals and time spent executing operating system or user code since this distinction is irrelevant to the user. They illustrate an overall performance of a system written in a high-level language using straightforward code generation without any optimization.

FINAL REMARKS

The compilers for Sequential and Concurrent Pascal were designed and implemented by Al Hartmann and me in half a year. I wrote the operating system and its utility programs in 3 months. In machine language this would have required 20–30 man-years and nobody would have been able to understand the system fully. The use of an efficient, abstract programming language reduced the development cost to less than 2 man-years and produced a system that is completely understood by two programmers.

The low cost of programming makes it acceptable to throw away awkward programs and rewrite them. We did this several times: An early 6-pass compiler was never released (although it worked perfectly) because we found its structure too complicated. The first operating system written in Concurrent Pascal (called *Deamy*) was used only to evaluate the expressive power of the language and was never built (Brinch Hansen 1974). The second one (called *Pilot*) was used for several months but was too slow.

From a manufacturer's point of view it is now realistic and attractive to replace a huge ineffective "general-purpose" operating system with a range of small, efficient systems for special purposes.

The kernel, the operating system, and the compilers were tested very systematically initially and appear to be correct.

Acknowledgements

The work of Bob Deverill and Al Hartmann in implementing the kernel and compiler of Concurrent Pascal has been essential for this project. I am also grateful to Gilbert McCann for his encouragement and support.

Stoy and Strachey (1972) recommend that one should learn to build good operating systems for single-users before trying to satisfy many users simultaneously. I have found this to be very good advice. I have also tried to follow the advice of Lampson (1974) and make both high- and low-level abstractions available to the user programmer.

The Concurrent Pascal project is supported by the National Science Foundation under grant number DCR74–17331.

References

1. P. Brinch Hansen 1974. Deamy—A structured operating system. Information Science, California Institute of Technology, (May), (out of print).
2. P. Brinch Hansen 1975. The programming language Concurrent Pascal. *IEEE Trans. on Software Engineering*, **1**, 2 (June).

3. P. Brinch Hansen 1976a. The Solo operating system: job interface. *Software—Practice and Experience*, **6**, 2 (April–June).

4. P. Brinch Hansen 1976b. The Solo operating system: processes, monitors and classes. *Software—Practice and Experience*, **6**, 2 (April–June).

5. P. Brinch Hansen 1976c. Disk scheduling at compile-time. *Software—Practice and Experience 6*, 2 (April–June), 201–205.

6. K. Jensen and N. Wirth 1974. Pascal–User manual and report. *Lecture Notes in Computer Science*, **18**, Springer-Verlag, New York.

7. B. W. Lampson 1974. An open operating system for a single-user machine. In *Operating Systems, Lecture Notes in Computer Science*, **16**, Springer Verlag, 208–217.

8. J. E. Stoy and C. Strachey 1972. OS6—an experimental operating system for a small computer. *Comput. J.*, **15**, 2.

16

THE SOLO OPERATING SYSTEM: PROCESSES, MONITORS AND CLASSES*

PER BRINCH HANSEN

(1976)

This paper describes the implementation of the Solo operating system written in Concurrent Pascal. It explains the overall structure and details of the system in which concurrent processes communicate by means of a hierarchy of monitors and classes. The concurrent program is a sequence of nearly independent components of less than one page of text each. The system has been operating since May 1975.

INTRODUCTION

This is a description of the program structure of the Solo operating system. Solo is a single-user operating system for the PDP 11/45 computer written in the programming language Concurrent Pascal (Brinch Hansen 1976a, 1976b).

The main idea in Concurrent Pascal is to divide the global data structures of an operating system into small parts and define the meaningful operations on each of them. In Solo, for example, there is a data structure, called a resource, that is used to give concurrent processes exclusive access to a disk. This data structure can only be accessed by means of two procedures that request and release access to the disk. The programmer specifies that these are the only operations one can perform on a resource, and the compiler

*P. Brinch Hansen, The Solo operating system: processes, monitors and classes. *Software—Practice and Experience 6*, 2 (April–June 1976), 165–200.

checks that this rule is obeyed in the rest of the system. This approach to program reliability has been called *resource protection at compile-time* (Brinch Hansen 1973). It makes programs more reliable by detecting incorrect interactions of program components before they are put into operation. It makes them more efficient by reducing the need for hardware protection mechanisms.

The combination of a data structure and the operations used to access it is called an *abstract data type.* It is abstract because the rest of the system need only know what operations one can perform on it but can ignore the details of how they are carried out. A Concurrent Pascal program is constructed from three kinds of abstract data types: processes, monitors and classes. *Processes* perform concurrent operations on data structures. They use *monitors* to synchronize themselves and exchange data. They access private data structures by means of *classes.* Brinch Hansen (1975a) is an overview of these concepts and their use in concurrent programming.

Solo is the first major example of a hierarchical concurrent program implemented in terms of abstract data types. It has been in use since May 1975. This is a complete, annotated program listing of the system. It also explains how the system was tested systematically.

PROGRAM STRUCTURE

Solo consists of a hierarchy of *program layers*, each of which controls a particular kind of computer resource, and a set of concurrent processes that use these resources (Fig. 1):

- *Resource management* controls the scheduling of the operator's console and the disk among concurrent processes.
- *Console management* lets processes communicate with the operator after they have gained access to the console.
- *Disk management* gives processes access to the disk files and a catalog describing them.
- *Program management* fetches program files from disk into core on demand from processes that wish to execute them.
- *Buffer management* transmits data among processes.

These facilities are used by seven concurrent processes:

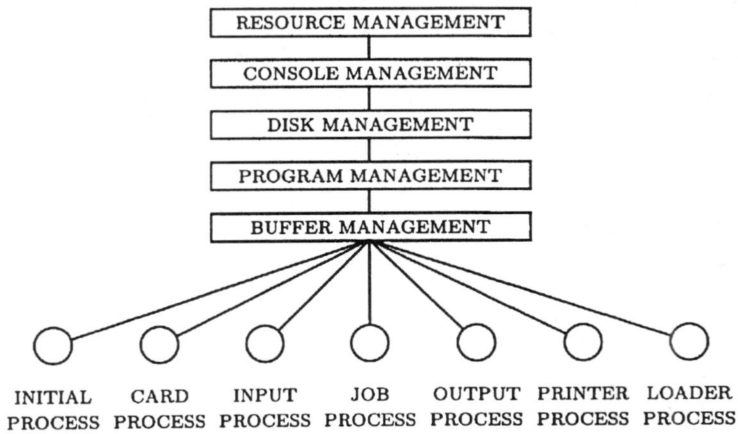

Figure 1 Program layers and processes.

- A *job process* executes Pascal programs upon request from the operator.
- Two *input/output processes* produce and consume the data of the job process.
- A *card process* feeds punched cards to the input process which then removes trailing blanks from them and packs the text into blocks.
- A *printer process* prints lines that are unpacked from blocks and sent to it by the output process.
- A *loader process* preempts and reinitializes the operating system when the operator pushes the bell key on the console.
- An *initial process* starts up the rest of the system after system loading.

The term *program layer* is only used as a convenient way of explaining the gross division of labor within the system. It cannot be represented by any language notation in Concurrent Pascal.

ABSTRACT DATA TYPES

Each program layer consists of one or more abstract data types (monitors and classes).

Resource management

A *fifo* class implements a first-in, first-out queue that is used to maintain multiprocess queues and message buffers.

A *resource* monitor gives processes exclusive access to a computer resource. It is used to control disk access.

A *typewriter resource* monitor gives processes exclusive access to a console and tells them whether they need to identify themselves to the operator.

Console management

A *typewriter* class transmits a single line between a process and a console (but does not give a process exclusive access to it).

A *terminal* class gives a process the illusion that it has its own private console by giving it exclusive access to the operator for input or output of a single line.

A *terminal stream* makes a terminal look character oriented.

Disk management

A *disk* class can access a page anywhere on disk (but does not give a process exclusive access to it). It uses a terminal to report disk failure.

A *disk file* can access any page belonging to a particular file. The file pages, which may be scattered on disk, are addressed indirectly through a page map. The disk address of the page map identifies the file. It uses a disk to access the map and its pages.

A *disk table* class makes a disk catalog of files look like an array of entries, some of which describe files, and some of which are empty. The entries are identified by numeric indices. It uses a disk file to access the catalog page by page.

A *disk catalog* monitor can look up files in a disk catalog by means of their names. It uses a resource to get exclusive acess to the disk and a disk table to scan the catalog.

A *data file* class gives a process access to a named disk file. It uses a resource, a disk catalog, and a disk file to access the disk.

Program management

A *program file* class can load a named disk file into core when a process wishes to execute it. It uses a resource, a disk catalog, and a disk file to do this.

A *program stack* monitor keeps track of nested program calls within a process.

Buffer management

The *buffer* monitors transmit various kinds of messages between processes: arguments (scalars or identifiers), lines, and pages.

The following defines the purpose, specification, and implementation of each of these abstract data types.

INPUT/OUTPUT

The following data types are used in elementary input/output operations:

```
type iodevice =
  (typedevice, diskdevice, tapedevice, printdevice, carddevice);

type iooperation = (input, output, move, control);

type ioarg = (writeeof, rewind, upspace, backspace);

type ioresult =
  (complete, intervention, transmission, failure,
  endfile, endmedium, startmedium);

type ioparam =
  record
    operation: iooperation;
    status: ioresult;
    arg: ioarg
  end;

const nl = '(:10:)'; ff = '(:12:)'; cr = '(:13:)'; em = '(:25:)';

const linelength = 132;
```

```
type line = array [1..linelength] of char;

const pagelength = 512;
type page = array [1..pagelength] of char;
```

They define the identifiers of peripheral devices, input/output operations and their results as well as the data types to be transferred (printer lines or disk pages). The details of input/output operations are explained in Brinch Hansen (1975b).

FIFO QUEUE

type fifo = class(limit: integer)

A fifo keeps track of the length and the head and tail indices of an array used as a first-in, first-out queue (but does not contain the queue elements themselves). A fifo is initialized with a constant that defines its range of queue indices 1..limit. A user of a fifo must ensure that the length of the queue remains within its physical limit:

$$0 \leq \text{arrivals} - \text{departures} \leq \text{limit}$$

The routines of a fifo are:

function arrival: integer

Returns the index of the next queue element in which an arrival can take place.

function departure: integer

Returns the index of the next queue element from which a departure can take place.

function empty: boolean

Defines whether the queue is empty (arrivals = departures).

function full: boolean

Defines whether the queue is full (arrivals = departures + limit).

Implementation:

A fifo queue is represented by its head, tail and length. The Concurrent Pascal compiler will ensure that these variables are only accessed by the routines of the class. In general, a class variable can only be accessed by calling one of the routines associated with it (Brinch Hansen 1975a). The final statement of the class is executed when an instance of a fifo queue is declared and initialized.

```
type fifo =
class(limit: integer);

var head, tail, length: integer;

function entry arrival: integer;
begin
  arrival := tail;
  tail := tail mod limit + 1;
  length := length + 1;
end;

function entry departure: integer;
begin
  departure := head;
  head := head mod limit + 1;
  length := length - 1;
end;

function entry empty: boolean;
begin empty := (length = 0) end;

function entry full: boolean;
begin full := (length = limit) end;

begin head := 1; tail := 1; length := 0 end;
```

RESOURCE

type resource = monitor

A resource gives exclusive access to a computer resource (but does not perform any operations on the resource itself). A user of a resource must request it before using it and release it afterwards. If the resource is released within a finite time it will also become available to any process requesting it within a finite time. In short, the resource scheduling is fair.

procedure request

Gives the calling process exclusive access to the resource.

procedure release

Makes the resource available for other processes.

Implementation:

A resource is represented by its state (free or used) and a queue of processes waiting for it. The multiprocess queue is represented by two data structures: an array of single-process queues and a fifo to keep track of the queue indices.

The initial statement at the end of the monitor sets the resource state to free and initializes the fifo variable with a constant defining the total number of processes that can wait in the queue.

The compiler will ensure that the monitor variables only can be accessed by calling the routine entries associated with it. The generated code will ensure that at most one process at a time is executing a monitor routine (Brinch Hansen 1975a). The monitor can delay and (later) continue the execution of a calling process.

A routine associated with a class or monitor is called by mentioning the class or monitor variable followed by the name of the routine. As an example

next.arrival

will perform an arrival operation on the fifo variable next.

```
const processcount = 7;
type processqueue = array [1..processcount] of queue;

type resource =
```

```
monitor

var free: boolean; q: processqueue; next: fifo;

procedure entry request;
begin
  if free then free := false
  else delay(q[next.arrival]);
end;

procedure entry release;
begin
  if next.empty then free := true
  else continue(q[next.departure]);
end;

begin free := true; init next(processcount) end;
```

TYPEWRITER RESOURCE

type typeresource = monitor

A typewriter resource gives processes exclusive access to a typewriter console. A calling process supplies an identification of itself and is told whether it needs to display it to the operator. The resource scheduling is fair as explained in Section 6.

procedure request(text: line; var changed: boolean)

Gives the calling process exclusive access to the resource. The process identifies itself by a text line. A boolean changed defines whether this is the same identification that was used in the last call of request (in which case there is no need to display it to the operator again).

procedure release

Makes the resource available again for other processes.

Implementation:

```
type typeresource =
monitor

var free: boolean; q: processqueue; next: fifo; header: line;

procedure entry request(text: line; var changed: boolean);
begin
  if free then free := false
  else delay(q[next.arrival]);
  changed := (header <> text);
  header := text;
end;

procedure entry release;
begin
  if next.empty then free := true
  else continue(q[next.departure]);
end;

begin
  free := true; header[1] := nl;
  init next(processcount);
end;
```

TYPEWRITER

type typewriter = class(device: iodevice)

A typewriter can transfer a text line to or from a typewriter console. It does not identify the calling process on the console or give it exclusive access to it. A typewriter is initialized with the identifier of the device it controls.

A newline character (nl) terminates the input or output of a line. A line that exceeds 73 characters is forcefully terminated by a newline character.

procedure write(text: line)

Writes a line on the typewriter.

procedure read(var text: line)

Rings the bell on the typewriter and reads a line from it. Single characters or the whole line can be erased and retyped by typing *control c* or *control l.* The typewriter responds to erasure by writing a question mark.

Implementation:

The procedure writechar is not a routine entry; it can only be called within the typewriter class. The standard procedure io delays the calling process until the transfer of a single character is completed.

```
type typewriter =
class(device: iodevice);

const linelimit = 73;
  cancelchar = '(:3:)'; "control c"
  cancelline = '(:12:)'; "control l"

procedure writechar(x: char);
var param: ioparam; c: char;
begin
  param.operation := output;
  c := x;
  io(c, param, device);
end;

procedure entry write(text: line);
var param: ioparam; i: integer; c: char;
begin
  param.operation := output;
  i := 0;
  repeat
    i := i + 1; c := text[i];
    io(c, param, device);
  until (c = nl) or (i = linelimit);
  if c <> nl then writechar(nl);
end;

procedure entry read(var text: line);
```

```
const bel = '(:7:)';
var param: ioparam; i: integer; c: char;
begin
  writechar(bel);
  param.operation := input;
  i := 0;
  repeat
    io(c, param, device);
    if c = cancelline then
      begin
        writechar(nl);
        writechar('?');
        i := 0;
      end
    else if c = cancelchar then
      begin
        if i > 0 then
          begin
            writechar('?');
            i := i - 1;
          end
      end
    else
      begin i := i + 1; text[i] := c end
  until (c = nl) or (i = linelimit);
  if c <> nl then
    begin
      writechar(nl);
      text[linelimit + 1] := nl;
    end;
end;

begin end;
```

TERMINAL

type terminal = class(access: typeresource)

A terminal gives a single process exclusive access to a typewriter, identifies the process to the operator and transfers a line to or from the device. The terminal uses a typewriter resource to get exclusive access to the device.

procedure read(header: line; var text: line)

Writes a header (if necessary) on the typewriter and reads a text line from it.

procedure write(header, text: line)

Writes a header (if necessary) followed by a text line on the typewriter.

The header identifies the calling process. It is only output if it is different from the last header output on the typewriter.

Implementation:

A class or monitor can only call other classes or monitors if they are declared as variables within it or passed as parameters during initialization (Brinch Hansen 1975a). So a terminal can only call the monitor *access* and the class *unit.* These access rights are checked during compilation.

```
type terminal =
class(access: typeresource);

var unit: typewriter;

procedure entry read(header: line; var text: line);
var changed: boolean;
begin
  access.request(header, changed);
  if changed then unit.write(header);
  unit.read(text);
  access.release;
end;

procedure entry write(header, text: line);
```

```
var changed: boolean;
begin
  access.request(header, changed);
  if changed then unit.write(header);
  unit.write(text);
  access.release;
end;

begin init unit(typedevice) end;
```

TERMINAL STREAM

type terminalstream = class(operator: terminal)

A terminal stream enables a process to identify itself once and for all and then proceed to read and write single characters on a terminal. A terminal stream uses a terminal to input or output a line at a time.

procedure read(var c: char)

Reads a character from the terminal.

procedure write(c: char)

Writes a character on the terminal.

procedure reset(text: line)

Identifies the calling process.

Implementation:

The terminal stream contains two line buffers for input and output.

```
type terminalstream =
class(operator: terminal);

const linelimit = 80;

var header: line; endinput: boolean;
  inp, out: record count: integer; text: line end;
```

```
procedure initialize(text: line);
begin
  header := text;
  endinput := true;
  out.count := 0;
end;

procedure entry read(var c: char);
begin
  with inp do
    begin
      if endinput then
        begin
          operator.read(header, text);
          count := 0;
        end;
      count := count + 1;
      c := text[count];
      endinput := (c = nl);
    end;
end;

procedure entry write(c: char);
begin
  with out do
    begin
      count := count + 1;
      text[count] := c;
      if (c = nl) or (count = linelimit) then
        begin
          operator.write(header, text);
          count := 0;
        end;
    end;
end;

procedure entry reset(text: line);
```

```
begin initialize(text) end;

begin initialize('unidentified:(:10:)') end;
```

DISK

type disk = class(typeuse: typeresource)

A disk can transfer any page to or from a disk device. A disk uses a typewriter resource to get exclusive access to a terminal to report disk failure. After a disk failure, the disk writes a message to the operator and repeats the operation when he types a newline character.

procedure read(pageaddr: integer; var block: univ page)

Reads a page identified by its absolute disk address.

procedure write(pageaddr: integer; var block: univ page)

Writes a page identified by its absolute disk address.

A page is declared as a universal type to make it possible to use the disk to transfer pages of different types (and not just text).

Implementation:

The standard procedure io delays the calling process until the disk transfer is completed (Brinch Hansen 1975b).

```
type disk =
class(typeuse: typeresource);

var operator: terminal;

procedure transfer(command: iooperation;
  pageaddr: univ ioarg; var block: page);
var param: ioparam; response: line;
begin
  with param, operator do
    begin
      operation := command;
```

```
          arg := pageaddr;
          io(block, param, diskdevice);
          while status <> complete do
            begin
              write('disk:(:10:)', 'error(:10:)');
              read('push return(:10:)', response);
              io(block, param, diskdevice);
            end;
      end;
  end;

  procedure entry read(pageaddr: integer; var block: univ page);
  begin transfer(input, pageaddr, block) end;

  procedure entry write(pageaddr: integer; var block; univ page);
  begin transfer(output, pageaddr, block) end;

  begin init operator(typeuse) end;
```

DISK FILE

type diskfile = class(typeuse: typeresource)

A disk file enables a process to access a disk file consisting of a fixed number of pages ($\leq$ 255). A disk file uses a typewriter resource to get exclusive access to the operator after a disk failure.

The disk file is identified by the absolute address of a page map that defines the length of the file and the disk addresses of its pages. To a calling process the pages of a file are numbered 1, 2, ..., length.

Initially, the file is closed (inaccessible). A user of a file must open it before using it and close it afterwards. Read and write have no effect if the file is closed or if the page number is outside the range 1..length.

procedure open(mapaddr: integer)

Makes a disk file with a given page map accessible.

procedure close

Makes the disk file inaccessible.

function length: integer

Returns the length of the disk file (in pages). The length of a closed file is zero.

procedure read(pageno: integer; **var** *block:* **univ** *page)*

Reads a page with a given number from the disk file.

procedure write(pageno: integer; **var** *block:* **univ** *page)*

Writes a page with a given number on the disk file.

Implementation:

The variable *length* is prefixed with the word *entry*. This means that its value can be used directly outside the class. It can, however, only be changed within the class. So a *variable entry* is similar to a function entry. Variable entries can only be used within classes.

```
const maplength = 255;
type filemap =
  record
    filelength: integer;
    pageset: array [1..maplength] of integer
  end;

type diskfile =
class(typeuse: typeresource);

var unit: disk; map: filemap; opened: boolean;

entry length: integer;

function includes(pageno: integer): boolean;
begin
  includes := opened &
    ( 1 <= pageno) & (pageno <= length);
end;

procedure entry open(mapaddr: integer);
```

```
begin
  unit.read(mapaddr, map);
  length := map.filelength;
  opened := true;
end;

procedure entry close;
begin
  length := 0;
  opened := false;
end;

procedure entry read(pageno: integer; var block: univ page);
begin
  if includes(pageno) then
    unit.read(map.pageset[pageno], block);
end;

procedure entry write(pageno: integer; var block: univ page);
begin
  if includes(pageno) then
    unit.write(map.pageset[pageno], block);
end;

begin
  init unit(typeuse);
  length := 0;
  opened := false;
end;
```

CATALOG STRUCTURE

The disk contains a catalog of all files. The following data types define the structure of the catalog:

```
const idlength = 12;
type identifier = array [1..idlength] of char;

type filekind = (empty, scratch, ascii, seqcode, concode);
```

```
type fileattr =
  record
    kind: filekind;
    addr: integer;
    protected: boolean;
    notused: array [1..5] of integer
  end;

type catentry =
  record
    id: identifier;
    attr: fileattr;
    key, searchlength: integer
  end;

const catpagelength = 16;
type catpage = array [1..catpagelength] of catentry;

const cataddr = 154;
```

The catalog is itself a file defined by a page map stored at the *catalog address*. Every *catalog page* contains a fixed number of catalog entries. A *catalog entry* describes a file by its identifier, attributes and hash key. The search length defines the number of files that have a hash key equal to the index of this entry. It is used to limit the search for a non-existing file name.

The *file attributes* are its kind (empty, scratch, ascii, sequential or concurrent code), the address of its page map, and a boolean defining whether it is protected against accidental deletion or overwriting. The latter is checked by all system programs operating on the disk, but not by the operating system. Solo provides a mechanism for protection, but does not enforce it.

DISK TABLE

type disktable = class(typeuse: typeresource; cataddr: integer)

A disk table makes a disk catalog look like an array of catalog entries identified by numeric indices 1, 2, ..., length. A disk table uses a typewriter resource to get exclusive access to the operator after a disk failure and a catalog address to locate a catalog on disk.

function length: integer

Defines the number of entries in the catalog.

procedure read(i: integer; var elem: catentry)

Reads entry number *i* in the catalog. If the entry number is outside the range 1..length the contents of the entry is undefined.

Implementation:

A disk table stores the most recently used catalog page to make a sequential search of the catalog fast.

```
type disktable =
class(typeuse: typeresource; cataddr: integer);

var file: diskfile; pageno: integer; block: catpage;

entry length: integer;

procedure entry read(i: integer; var elem: catentry);
var index: integer;
begin
  index := (i - 1) div catpagelength + 1;
  if pageno <> index then
    begin
      pageno := index;
      file.read(pageno, block);
    end;
  elem := block[(i - 1) mod catpagelength + 1];
end;

begin
  init file(typeuse);
  file.open(cataddr);
  length := file.length * catpagelength;
  pageno := 0;
end;
```

DISK CATALOG

type diskcatalog =
monitor(typeuse: typeresource; diskuse: resource; cataddr: integer)

The disk catalog describes all disk files by means of a set of named entries that can be looked up by processes. A disk catalog uses a resource to get exclusive access to the disk during a catalog lookup and a typewriter resource to get exclusive access to the operator after a disk failure. It uses a catalog address to locate the catalog on disk.

procedure lookup(id: identifier; var attr: fileattr; var found: boolean)

Searches for a catalog entry describing a file with a given identifier and indicates whether it found it. If so, it also returns the file attributes.

Implementation:

A disk catalog uses a disk table to make a cyclical search for an identifier. The initial catalog entry is selected by hashing. The search stops when the identifier is found or when there are no more entries with the same hash key. The disk catalog has exclusive access to the disk during the lookup to prevent competing processes from causing disk arm movement.

```
type diskcatalog =
monitor(typeuse: typeresource; diskuse: resource; cataddr: integer);

var table: disktable;

function hash(id: identifier): integer;
var key, i: integer; c: char;
begin
  key := 1; i := 0;
  repeat
    i := i + 1; c := id[i];
    if c <> ' ' then
      key := key * ord(c) mod table.length + 1;
  until (c = ' ') or (i = idlength);
  hash := key;
end;
```

```
procedure entry lookup(id: identifier;
  var attr: fileattr; var found: boolean);
var key, more, index: integer; elem: catentry;
begin
  diskuse.request;
  key := hash(id);
  table.read(key, elem);
  more := elem.searchlength;
  index := key; found := false;
  while not found & (more > 0) do
    begin
      table.read(index, elem);
      if elem.id = id then
        begin attr := elem.attr; found := true end
      else
        begin
          if elem.key = key then more := more - 1;
          index := index mod table.length + 1;
        end;
    end;
  diskuse.release;
end;

begin init table(typeuse, cataddr) end;
```

DATA FILE

type datafile =
class(typeuse: typeresource; diskuse: resource; catalog: diskcatalog)

A data file enables a process to access a disk file by means of its name in a diskcatalog. The pages of a data file are numbered 1, 2, ..., length. A data file uses a resource to get exclusive access to the disk during a page transfer and a typewriter resource to get exclusive access to the operator after disk failure. It uses a catalog to look up the the file.

Initially a data file is inaccessible (closed). A user of a data file must open it before using it and close it afterwards. If a process needs exclusive access to a data file while using it, this must be ensured at higher levels of programming.

procedure open(id: identifier; var found: boolean)

Makes a file with a given identifier accessible if it is found in the catalog.

procedure close

Makes the file inaccessible.

procedure read(pageno: integer; var block: univ page)

Reads a page with a given number from the file. It has no effect if the file is closed or if the page number is outside the range 1..length.

procedure write(pageno: integer; var block: univ page)

Writes a page with a given number on the file. It has no effect if the file is closed or if the page number is outside the range 1..length.

function length: integer

Defines the number of pages in the file. The length of a closed file is zero.

Implementation:

```
type datafile =
class(typeuse: typeresource; diskuse: resource; catalog: diskcatalog);

var file: diskfile; opened: boolean;

entry length: integer;

procedure entry open(id: identifier; var found: boolean);
var attr: fileattr;
begin
  catalog.lookup(id, attr, found);
  if found then
    begin
      diskuse.request;
      file.open(attr.addr);
      length := file.length;
```

```
        diskuse.release;
      end;
    opened := found;
  end;

  procedure entry close;
  begin
    file.close;
    length := 0;
    opened := false;
  end;

  procedure entry read(pageno: integer; var block: univ page);
  begin
    if opened then
      begin
        diskuse.request;
        file.read(pageno, block);
        diskuse.release;
      end;
  end;

  procedure entry write(pageno: integer; var block: univ page);
  begin
    if opened then
      begin
        diskuse.request;
        file.write(pageno, block);
        diskuse.release;
      end;
  end;

  begin
    init file(typeuse);
    length := 0;
    opened := false;
  end;
```

PROGRAM FILE

type progfile =
class(typeuse: typeresource; diskuse: resource; catalog: diskcatalog)

A program file can transfer a sequential program from a disk file into core. The program file is identified by its name in a disk catalog. A program file uses a resource to get exclusive access to the disk during program loading and a typewriter resource to get exclusive access to the operator after disk failure. It uses a disk catalog to look up the file.

procedure open(id: identifier; var state: progstate)

Loads a program with a given identifier from disk and returns its state. The program state is one of the following: ready for execution, not found, the disk file is not sequential code, or the file is too big to be loaded into core.

function store: progstore

Defines the variable in which the program file is stored. A program store is an array of disk pages.

Implementation:

A program file has exclusive access to the disk until it has loaded the entire program. This is to prevent competing processes from slowing down program loading by causing disk arm movement.

```
type progstate = (ready, notfound, notseq, toobig);

const storelength1 = 40;
type progstore1 = array [1..storelength1] of page;

type progfile1 =
class(typeuse: typeresource; diskuse: resource; catalog: diskcatalog);

var file: diskfile;

entry store: progstore1;

procedure entry open(id: identifier; var state: progstate);
```

```
var attr: fileattr; found: boolean; pageno: integer;
begin
  catalog.lookup(id, attr, found);
  with diskuse, file, attr do
    if not found then state := notfound
    else if kind <> seqcode then state := notseq
    else
      begin
        request;
        open(addr);
        if length <= storelength1 then
          begin
            for pageno := 1 to length do
              read(pageno, store[pageno]);
            state := ready;
          end
        else state := toobig;
        close;
        release;
      end;
end;

begin init file(typeuse) end;
```

Solo uses two kinds of program files (progfile1 and progfile2); one for large programs and another one for small ones. They differ only in the dimension of the program store used. The need to repeat the entire class definition to handle arrays of different lengths is an awkward inheritance from Pascal.

PROGRAM STACK

type progstack = monitor

A program stack maintains a last-in, first-out list of identifiers of programs that have called one another. It enables a process to keep track of nested calls of sequential programs.

For historical reasons a program stack was defined as a monitor. In the present version of the system it might as well have been a class.

function space: boolean

Tells whether there is more space in the program stack.

function any: boolean

Tells whether the stack contains any program identifiers.

procedure push(id: identifier)

Puts an identifier on top of the stack. It has no effect if the stack is full.

procedure pop(var line, result: univ integer)

Removes a program identifier from the top of the stack and defines the line number at which the program terminated as well as its result. The result either indicates normal termination or one of several run-time errors as explained in the Concurrent Pascal report (Brinch Hansen 1975b).

procedure get(var id: identifier)

Defines the identifier stored in the top of the stack (without removing it). It has no effect if the stack is empty.

Implementation:

A program stack measures the extent of the heap of the calling process before pushing an identifier on the stack. If a pop operation shows abnormal program termination, the heap is reset to its original point to prevent the calling process from crashing due to lack of data space.

The standard routines, *attribute* and *setheap*, are defined in the Concurrent Pascal report.

```
type resulttype =
  (terminated, overflow, pointererror, rangeerror, varianterror,
  heaplimit, stacklimit, codelimit, timelimit, callerror);

type attrindex =
  (caller, heaptop, progline, progresult, runtime);

type progstack =
```

```
monitor

const stacklength = 5;

var stack:
  array [1..stacklength] of
    record progid: identifier; heapaddr: integer end;
  top: 0..stacklength;

function entry space: boolean;
begin space := (top < stacklength) end;

function entry any: boolean;
begin any := (top > 0) end;

procedure entry push(id: identifier);
begin
  if top < stacklength then
    begin
      top := top + 1;
      with stack[top] do
        begin
          progid := id;
          heapaddr := attribute(heaptop);
        end;
    end;
end;

procedure entry pop(var line, result: univ integer);
const terminated = 0;
begin
  line := attribute(progline);
  result := attribute(progresult);
  if result <> terminated then
    setheap(stack[top].heapaddr);
  top := top - 1;
end;
```

```
procedure entry get(var id: identifier);
begin
  if top > 0 then id := stack[top].progid;
end;

begin top := 0 end;
```

PAGE BUFFER

type pagebuffer = monitor

A page buffer transmits a sequence of data pages from one process to another. Each sequence is terminated by an end of file mark.

procedure read(var text: page; var eof: boolean)

Receives a message consisting of a text page and an end of file indication.

procedure write(text: page; eof: boolean)

Sends a message consisting of a text page and an end of file indication.

If the end of file is true then the text page is empty.

Implementation:

A page buffer stores a single message at a time. It will delay the sending process as long as the buffer is full and the receiving process until it becomes full ($0 \leq \text{writes} - \text{reads} \leq 1$).

```
type pagebuffer =
monitor

var buffer: page; last, full: boolean;
  sender, receiver: queue;

procedure entry read(var text: page; var eof: boolean);
begin
  if not full then delay(receiver);
  text := buffer; eof := last; full := false;
  continue(sender);
```

```
end;

procedure entry write(text: page; eof: boolean);
begin;
  if full then delay(sender);
  buffer := text; last := eof; full := true;
  continue(receiver);
end;

begin full := false end;
```

Solo also implements buffers for transmission of arguments (enumerations and identifiers) and lines. They are similar to the page buffer (but use no end of file marks). The need to duplicate routines for each message type is an inconvenience caused by the fixed data types of Pascal.

CHARACTER STREAM

type charstream = class(buffer: pagebuffer)

A character stream enables a process to communicate with another process character by character. A character stream uses a page buffer to transmit one page of characters at a time from one process to another.

A sending process must open its stream for writing before using it. The last character transmitted in a sequence should be an end of medium (em).

A receiving process must open its stream for reading before using it.

procedure initread

Opens a character stream for reading.

procedure initwrite

Opens a character stream for writing.

procedure read(var c: char)

Reads the next character from the stream. The effect is undefined if the stream is not open for reading.

procedure write(c: char)

Writes the next character in the stream. The effect is undefined if the stream is not open for writing.

Implementation:

```
type charstream =
class(buffer: pagebuffer);

var text: page; count: integer; eof: boolean;

procedure entry read(var c: char);
begin
  if count = pagelength then
    begin
      buffer.read(text, eof);
      count := 0;
    end;
  count := count + 1;
  c := text[count];
  if c = em then
    begin
      while not eof do buffer.read(text, eof);
      count := pagelength;
    end;
end;

procedure entry initread;
begin count := pagelength end;

procedure entry write(c: char);
begin
  count := count + 1;
  text[count] := c;
  if (count = pagelength) or (c = em) then
    begin
      buffer.write(text, false); count := 0;
      if c = em then buffer.write(text, true);
```

```
        end;
    end;

    procedure entry initwrite;
    begin count := 0 end;

    begin end;
```

TASKS AND ARGUMENTS

The following data types are used by several processes:

```
type taskkind = (inputtask, jobtask, outputtask);

type argtag = (niltype, booltype, inttype, idtype, ptrtype);
  argtype = record tag: argtag; arg: identifier end;

const maxarg = 10;
type arglist = array [1..maxarg] of argtype;

type argseq = (inp, out);
```

The *task kind* defines whether a process is performing an input task, a job task, or an output task. It is used by sequential programs to determine whether they have been loaded by the right kind of process. As an example, a program that controls card reader input can only be called by an input process.

A process that executes a sequential program can pass a list of arguments to it. A program *argument* consists of a tag field defining its type (boolean, integer, identifier, or pointer) and another field defining its value. (Since Concurrent Pascal does not include the variant records of Sequential Pascal one can only represent a program argument by the largest one of its variants—an identifier.)

A job process is connected to two input and output processes by *argument buffers* called its input and output sequences.

JOB PROCESS

```
type jobprocess =
process
  (typeuse: typeresource; diskuse: resource;
  catalog: diskcatalog; inbuffer, outbuffer: pagebuffer;
  inrequest, inresponse, outrequest, outresponse: argbuffer;
  stack: progstack)
"program data space" +16000
```

A job process executes Sequential Pascal programs that can call one another recursively. Initially, it executes a program called *do* with console input. A job process also implements the interface between sequential programs and the Solo operating system as defined in Brinch Hansen (1976b).

A job process needs access to the operator's console, the disk, and its catalog. It is connected to an input and an output process by two page buffers and four argument buffers as explained in Brinch Hansen (1976a). It uses a program stack to handle nested calls of sequential programs.

It reserves a data space of 16,000 bytes for user programs and a code space of 20,000 bytes. This enables the Pascal compiler to compile itself.

Implementation:

The private variables of a job process give it access to a terminal stream, two character streams for input and output, and two data files. It uses a large program file to store the currently executed program. These variables are inaccessible to other processes.

The job process contains a declaration of a sequential program that defines the types of its arguments and the variable in which its code is stored (the latter is inaccessible to the program). It also defines a list of interface routines that can be called by a program. These routines are implemented within the job process. They are defined in Brinch Hansen (1976b).

Before a job process can call a sequential program it must load it from disk into a program store and push its identifier onto a program stack. After termination of the program, the job process pops its identifier, line number, and result from the program stack, reloads the previous program from disk and returns to it.

A process can only interact with other processes by calling routines within monitors that are passed as parameters to it during initialization (such as the catalog declared at the beginning of a job process). These access rights are checked at compile-time (Brinch Hansen 1975a).

```
type jobprocess =
process
  (typeuse: typeresource; diskuse: resource;
  catalog: diskcatalog; inbuffer, outbuffer: pagebuffer;
  inrequest, inresponse, outrequest, outresponse: argbuffer;
  stack: progstack);
"program data space" +16000

const maxfile = 2;
type file = 1..maxfile;

var operator: terminal; opstream: terminalstream;
  instream, outstream: charstream;
  files: array [file] of datafile;
  code: progfile1;

program job(var param: arglist; store: progstore1);
entry read, write, open, close, get, put, length,
  mark, release, identify, accept, display, readpage,
  writepage, readline, writeline, readarg, writearg,
  lookup, iotransfer, iomove, task, run;

procedure call(id: identifier; var param: arglist;
  var line: integer; var result: resulttype);
var state: progstate; lastid: identifier;
begin
  with code, stack do
    begin
      line := 0;
      open(id, state);
      if (state = ready) & space then
        begin
          push(id);
          job(param, store);
          pop(line, result);
        end
```

```
        else if state = toobig then result := codelimit
        else result := callerror;
        if any then
          begin get(lastid); open(lastid, state) end;
      end;
  end;

  procedure entry read(var c: char);
  begin instream.read(c) end;

  procedure entry write(c: char);
  begin outstream.write(c) end;

  procedure entry open(f: file; id: identifier; var found: boolean);
  begin files[f].open(id, found) end;

  procedure entry close(f: file);
  begin files[f].close end;

  procedure entry get(f: file; p: integer; var block: page);
  begin files[f].read(p, block) end;

  procedure entry put(f: file; p: integer; var block: page);
  begin files[f].write(p, block) end;

  function entry length(f: file): integer;
  begin length := files[f].length end;

  procedure entry mark(var top: integer);
  begin top := attribute(heaptop) end;

  procedure entry release(top: integer);
  begin setheap(top) end;

  procedure entry identify(header: line);
  begin opstream.reset(header) end;

  procedure entry accept(var c: char);
```

```
begin opstream.read(c) end;

procedure entry display(c: char);
begin opstream.write(c) end;

procedure entry readpage(var block: page; var eof: boolean);
begin inbuffer.read(block, eof) end;

procedure entry writepage(block: page; eof: boolean);
begin outbuffer.write(block, eof) end;

procedure entry readline(var text: line);
begin end;

procedure entry writeline(text: line);
begin end;

procedure entry readarg(s: argseq; var arg: argtype);
begin
  if s = inp then inresponse.read(arg)
  else outresponse.read(arg);
end;

procedure entry writearg(s: argseq; arg: argtype);
begin
  if s = inp then inrequest.write(arg)
  else outrequest.write(arg);
end;

procedure entry lookup(id: identifier;
  var attr: fileattr; var found: boolean);
begin catalog.lookup(id, attr, found) end;

procedure entry iotransfer(device: iodevice;
  var param: ioparam; var block: page);
begin
  if device = diskdevice then
    begin
```

```
      diskuse.request;
      io(block, param, device);
      diskuse.release;
    end
  else io(block, param, device);
end;

procedure entry iomove(device: iodevice; var param: ioparam);
begin io(param, param, device) end;

function entry task: taskkind;
begin task := jobtask end;

procedure entry run(id: identifier; var param: arglist;
  var line: integer; var result: resulttype);
begin call(id, param, line, result) end;

procedure initialize;
var i: integer; param: arglist; line: integer; result: resulttype;
begin
  init operator(typeuse), opstream(operator),
    instream(inbuffer), outstream(outbuffer);
  instream.initread; outstream.initwrite;
  for i := 1 to maxfile do
    init files[i](typeuse, diskuse, catalog);
  init code(typeuse, diskuse, catalog);
  with param[2] do
    begin tag := idtype; arg := 'console     ' end;
  call( 'do          ', param, line, result);
  operator.write('jobprocess:(:10:)', 'terminated (:10)');
end;

begin initialize end;
```

IO PROCESS

type ioprocess =
process
(typeuse: typeresource; diskuse: resource;
catalog: diskcatalog; slowio: linebuffer;
buffer: pagebuffer; request, response: argbuffer;
stack: progstack; iotask: taskkind)
"program data space" +2000

An io process executes Sequential Pascal programs that produce or consume data for a job process. It also implements the interface between these programs and the Solo operating system.

An io process needs access to the operator, the disk, and the catalog. It is connected to a card reader (or a line printer) by a line buffer and to a job process by a page buffer and two argument buffers. It uses a program stack to handle nested calls of sequential programs.

It reserves a data space of 2,000 bytes for input/output programs and a code space of 4,000 bytes.

Initially, it executes a program called *io*

Implementation:

The implementation details are similar to a job process.

```
type ioprocess =
process
  (typeuse: typeresource; diskuse: resource;
  catalog: diskcatalog; slowio: linebuffer;
  buffer: pagebuffer; request, response: argbuffer;
  stack: progstack; iotask: taskkind);
"program data space" +2000

type file = 1..1;

var operator: terminal; opstream: terminalstream;
  iostream: charstream; iofile: datafile;
  code: progfile2;

program driver(var param: arglist; store: progstore2);
```

```
entry read, write, open, close, get, put, length,
  mark, release, identify, accept, display, readpage,
  writepage, readline, writeline, readarg, writearg,
  lookup, iotransfer, iomove, task, run;

procedure call(id: identifier; var param: arglist;
  var line: integer; var result: resulttype);
var state: progstate; lastid: identifier;
begin
  with code, stack do
    begin
      line := 0;
      open(id, state);
      if (state = ready) & space then
        begin
          push(id);
          driver(param, store);
          pop(line, result);
        end
      else if state = toobig then result := codelimit
      else result := callerror;
      if any then
        begin get(lastid); open(lastid, state) end;
    end;
end;

procedure entry read(var c: char);
begin iostream.read(c) end;

procedure entry write(c: char);
begin iostream.write(c) end;

procedure entry open(f: file; id: identifier; var found: boolean);
begin iofile.open(id, found) end;

procedure entry close(f: file);
begin iofile.close end;
```

```
procedure entry get(f: file; p: integer; var block: page);
begin iofile.read(p, block) end;

procedure entry put(f: file; p: integer; var block: page);
begin iofile.write(p, block) end;

function entry length(f: file): integer;
begin length := iofile.length end;

procedure entry mark(var top: integer);
begin top := attribute(heaptop) end;

procedure entry release(top: integer);
begin setheap(top) end;

procedure entry identify(header: line);
begin opstream.reset(header) end;

procedure entry accept(var c: char);
begin opstream.read(c) end;

procedure entry display(c: char);
begin opstream.write(c) end;

procedure entry readpage(var block: page; var eof: boolean);
begin buffer.read(block, eof) end;

procedure entry writepage(block: page; eof: boolean);
begin buffer.write(block, eof) end;

procedure entry readline(var text: line);
begin slowio.read(text) end;

procedure entry writeline(text: line);
begin slowio.write(text) end;

procedure entry readarg(s: argseq; var arg: argtype);
begin request.read(arg) end;
```

```
procedure entry writearg(s: argseq; arg: argtype);
begin response.write(arg) end;

procedure entry lookup(id: identifier;
  var attr: fileattr; var found: boolean);
begin catalog.lookup(id, attr, found) end;

procedure entry iotransfer(device: iodevice;
  var param: ioparam; var block: page);
begin
  if device = diskdevice then
    begin
      diskuse.request;
      io(block, param, device);
      diskuse.release;
    end
  else io(block, param, device);
end;

procedure entry iomove(device: iodevice; var param: ioparam);
begin io(param, param, device) end;

function entry task: taskkind;
begin task := iotask end;

procedure entry run(id: identifier; var param: arglist;
  var line: integer; var result: resulttype);
begin call(id, param, line, result) end;

procedure initialize;
var param: arglist; line: integer; result: resulttype;
begin
  init operator(typeuse), opstream(operator),
    iostream(buffer), iofile(typeuse, diskuse, catalog),
    code(typeuse, diskuse, catalog);
  if iotask = inputtask then iostream.initwrite
  else iostream.initread;
```

```
    call( 'io          ', param, line, result);
    operator.write('ioprocess:(:10:)', 'terminated (:10)');
  end;

  begin initialize end;
```

CARD PROCESS

type cardprocess =
process(typeuse: typeresource; buffer: linebuffer)

A card process transmits cards from a card reader through a line buffer to an input process. The card process can access the operator to report device failure and a line buffer to transmit data. It is assumed that the card reader is controlled by a single card process. As long as the card reader is turned off or is empty the card process waits. It begins to read cards as soon as they are available in the reader. After a transmission error the card process writes a message to the operator and continues the input of cards.

Implementation:

The standard procedure *wait* delays the card process one second (Brinch Hansen 1975b). This reduces the processor time spent waiting for operator intervention.

```
type cardprocess =
process(typeuse: typeresource; buffer: linebuffer);

var operator: terminal; param: ioparam;
  text: line; ok: boolean;
begin
  init operator(typeuse);
  param.operation := input;
  cycle
    repeat
      io(text, param, carddevice);
      case param.status of
        complete:
          ok := true;
        intervention:
```

```
          begin ok := false; wait end;
        transmission, failure:
          begin
            operator.write('cards:(:10:)', 'error(:10:)');
            ok := false;
          end
      end
    until ok;
    buffer.write(text);
  end;
end;
```

PRINTER PROCESS

type printerprocess =
process(typeuse: typeresource; buffer: linebuffer)

A printer process transmits lines from an output process to a line printer. The printer process can access the operator to report device failure and a line buffer to receive data. It is assumed that the line printer is controlled only by a single printer process. After a printer failure the printer process writes a message to the operator and repeats the output of the current line until it is successful.

Implementation:

```
type printerprocess =
process(typeuse: typeresource; buffer: linebuffer);

var operator: terminal; param: ioparam; text: line;
begin
  init operator(typeuse);
  param.operation := output;
  cycle
    buffer.read(text);
    io(text, param, printdevice);
    if param.status <> complete then
      begin
        operator.write('printer:(:10:)', 'inspect(:10:)');
```

```
          repeat
            wait;
            io(text, param, printdevice);
          until param.status = complete;
        end;
    end;
  end;
```

LOADER PROCESS

type loaderprocess =
process(diskuse: resource)

A loader process preempts the operating system and reinitializes it when the operator pushes the *bell* key (*control g*) on the console. A loader process needs access to the disk to be able to reload the system.

Implementation:

A control operation on the typewriter delays the loader process until the operator pushes the bell key (Brinch Hansen 1975b).

The operating system is stored on consecutive disk pages starting at the *Solo address.* It is loaded by means of a control operation on the disk as defined in Brinch Hansen (1975b). Consecutive disk pages are used to make the system kernel of Concurrent Pascal unaware of the structure of a particular filing system (such as the one used by Solo). The disk contains a sequential program *start* that can copy the Solo system from a concurrent code file into the consecutive disk segment defined above.

```
type loaderprocess =
process(diskuse: resource);

const soloaddr = 24;
var param: ioparam;

procedure initialize(pageno: univ ioarg);
begin
  with param do
    begin
      operation := control;
```

```
        arg := pageno;
      end;
  end;

  begin
    initialize(soloaddr);
    "await bel signal"
    io(param, param, typedevice);
    "reload solo system"
    diskuse.request;
    io(param, param, diskdevice);
    diskuse.release;
  end;
```

INITIAL PROCESS

The initial process initializes all other processes and monitors and defines their access rights to one another. After initialization the operating system consists of a fixed set of components: a card process, an input process, a job process, an output process, a printer process, and a loader process. They have access to an operator, a disk, and a catalog of files. Process communication takes place by means of two page buffers, two line buffers and four argument buffers (see also Fig. 1).

Implementation:

When a process, such as the initial process, terminates its execution, its variables continue to exist (because they may be used by other processes).

```
var
  typeuse: typeresource;
  diskuse: resource; catalog: diskcatalog;
  inbuffer, outbuffer: pagebuffer;
  cardbuffer, printerbuffer: linebuffer;
  inrequest, inresponse, outrequest, outresponse: argbuffer;
  instack, outstack, jobstack: progstack;
  reader: cardprocess; writer: printerprocess;
  producer, consumer: ioprocess; master: jobprocess;
  watchdog: loaderprocess;
begin
```

```
    init
      typeuse, diskuse,
      catalog(typeuse, diskuse, cataddr),
      inbuffer, outbuffer,
      cardbuffer, printerbuffer,
      inrequest, inresponse, outrequest, outresponse,
      instack, outstack, jobstack,
      reader(typeuse, cardbuffer),
      writer(typeuse, printerbuffer),
      producer(typeuse, diskuse, catalog, cardbuffer,
        inbuffer, inrequest, inresponse, instack, inputtask),
      consumer(typeuse, diskuse, catalog, printerbuffer),
        outbuffer, outrequest, outresponse, outstack, outputtask),
      master(typeuse, diskuse, catalog, inbuffer, outbuffer,
        inrequest, inresponse, outrequest, outresponse,
        jobstack),
      watchdog(diskuse);
  end;
```

CONCLUSION

The Solo system consists of 22 line printer pages of Concurrent Pascal text divided into 23 component types (10 classes, 7 monitors, and 6 processes). A typical component is less than one page long and can be studied in isolation as an (almost) independent piece of program. All program components called by a given component are explicitly declared within that component (either as permanent variables or a parameters to it). To understand a component it is only necessary to know *what* other components called by it do, but *how* they do it is irrelevant.

The entire system can be studied component by component as one would read a book. In that sense, Concurrent Pascal supports *abstraction* and *hierarchical structuring* of concurrent programs very nicely.

It took 4 compilations to remove the formal programming errors from the Solo system. It was then tested systematically from the bottom up by adding one component type at a time and trying it by means of short test processes. The whole program was tested in 27 runs (or about 1 run per component type). This revealed 7 errors in the test processes and 2 trivial ones in the system itself. Later, about one third of it was rewritten to speed up program loading. This took about one week. It was then compiled and put into operation in one day and has worked ever since.

I can only suggest two plausible explanations for this unusual testing experience. It seems to be vital that the compiler prevents new components from destroying old ones (since old components cannot call new ones, and new ones can only call old ones through routines that have already been tested). This strict checking of hierarchical access rights makes it possible for a large system to evolve gradually through a sequence of intermediate, stable subsystems.

I am also convinced now that the use of abstract data types which hide implementation details within a fixed set of routines encourages a clarity of design that makes programs practically correct before they are even tested. The slight inconvenience of strict type checking is of minor importance compared to the advantages of instant program reliability.

Although Solo is a small concurrent program of only 1,300 lines it does implement a virtual machine that is very convenient to use for program development (Brinch Hansen 1976a). The availability of cheap microprocessors will put increasing pressure on software designers to develop special-purpose operating systems at very low cost. Concurrent Pascal is one example of a programming tool that may make this possible.

References

1. P. Brinch Hansen 1973. *Operating System Principles*, Chapter 7, Resource Protection. Prentice-Hall, Englewood Cliffs, NJ.
2. P. Brinch Hansen 1975a. The programming language Concurrent Pascal. *IEEE Trans. on Software Engineering*, **1**, 2.
3. P. Brinch Hansen 1975b. *Concurrent Pascal Report.* Information Science, California Institute of Technology, (June).
4. P. Brinch Hansen 1976a. The Solo operating system: a Concurrent Pascal program. *Software—Practice and Experience*, **6**, 2 (April–June).
5. P. Brinch Hansen 1976b. The Solo operating system: job interface. *Software—Practice and Experience*, **6**, 2 (April–June),.

Acknowledgements

The development of Concurrent Pascal and Solo has been supported by the National Science Foundation under grant number DCR74–17331.

PART VI

PERSONAL COMPUTING

17

OS 6—AN EXPERIMENTAL OPERATING SYSTEM FOR A SMALL COMPUTER: Input/Output and Filing System*

JOE E. STOY AND CHRISTOPHER STRACHEY

(1972)

This is a continuation of the description of OS6, and it covers the facilities for input/output, and the handling of files on the disc. The input/output system uses a very general form of stream; the filing system is designed to have a clear and logical structure. Both are implemented almost completely in the high-level language BCPL.

0 Introduction

In Part 1 (Stoy and Strachey, 1972) we discussed the general design of OS6, an experimental operating system running on a Modular One computer. This paper is devoted to a description of the provisions made for input/output in OS6, and a description of the disc filing system.

The input/output facilities are often the messiest parts of an operating system. The requirements are difficult to satisfy. On the one hand, the system must deal with the flow of information to and from several devices of different kinds. Some of this information may need processing—such things as character code conversion—before a program can conveniently use it; and one device may handle information of several different types. The paper tape reader, for example, handles binary code, which requires packing up

*J. E. Stoy and C. Strachey, OS 6—an experimental operating system for a small computer, Part 2. Input/output and filing system. *The Computer Journal 15*, 3 (1972), 195–203.

into words before it is supplied to the loader, and also text tapes punched in a variety of character sets. On the other hand, a program should be capable of processing information of a given type no matter where it comes from—the program should not require rewriting for each new source. Very flexible provisions are obviously required.

1 Character sets

Before we describe the general provisions for input/output, it is convenient to dispose at once of one of the difficult problems, which is that of choosing the character set and character codes for information processed in the form of text. The problem is not particularly acute if the system must cope with peripherals and data preparation devices with a variety of different character sets. A common solution is to deal systematically only with the *intersection* of the character sets in use. This leads to attempts to restrict high-level languages to, say, 48 characters. Since the purpose of a high-level language is to make programs and programming more intelligible to human beings, such a restriction is unhelpful. The elegance of BCPL programs is due a considerable extent to the extensive character set employed.

The OS6 solution to the character set problem is almost the reverse of that described above. The character set handled by most of the systems programs is practically the *union* of all the characters available on the various devices (though, for those devices which permit overprinting, only the overprinted characters meaningful in CPL and BCPL are included). This internal character set is represented by an eight bit code, known as *Internal Code*. One bit is used as an underlining indicator, and the remaining seven are based on ASCII, in the sense that the ASCII characters in the set have their ASCII values. There are a few unallocated values to allow for a limited extension, and there are also a few control characters. Although these include TAB, because it is useful when writing routines for controlling devices which use it, it is too device-dependent to be used in the system for any other purpose. To be forced to use only SPACE would be unacceptable, however, as half the characters in the average well laid out program would be spaces, and we therefore include a device-independent character, 4-SPACES.

The result of using Internal Code is that there is a unique representation inside the machine of the contents of any print position. This makes the design of input routines quite straight-forward, and it also avoids making any preconceived assumptions about the nature of the information coming in (for example, by treating '&' and '$\wedge$' as synonymous, which might be true for logical formulae, but would not do for the names of businesses). It leaves any equivalence of characters to be dealt with, in Internal Code, by the program reading the data. Of course, a program may sometimes attempt to output a character to a device on which it does not appear: in this case the output routines will do the best they can, in an *ad hoc* fashion.

2 Streams

2.1 Basic properties

The vehicles provided in OS6 for the transfer of information into and out of the system are called *streams.* Most streams are either *input streams* or *output streams*, though a few streams, such as those connected with a keyboard terminal, are capable of transfer of information in both directions, and are called *bilateral streams.* These are perfectly general objects, and their basic property is that a number of primitive functions and routines may meaningfully be applied to them. The most important primitive applicable to an input stream is the function *Next*, and for output streams the most important is the routine *Out.*

The result of applying *Next* to an input (or bilateral) stream is an object: the 'next' object in the stream. Thus, *BytesfromPT* is an input stream of bytes from the paper tape reader, and the command

$$x := Next[BytesfromPT]$$

will assign to x the value of the next row on the tape (so that $0 \leq x \leq 255$, for eight-hole tape). It will be seen that two successive applications of *Next* to a stream will not, in general, return the same result. The same function *Next* is applicable to all input streams, and there is no restriction on the type of object produced. If *Next* is applied to a character input stream the result is a character, and if to a word stream the result is a word. Character streams and word streams occur most frequently, but it is also possible to have streams of strings, or of vectors, or of any other data type.

The routine *Out* takes two parameters, an output stream and an object, and its effect is to output the object along the stream. For example, if *BytestoPT* is an output stream of bytes to the paper tape punch, the command

$$Out[BytestoPT, x]$$

will cause a tape row corresponding to x to be punched (though, because of buffering arrangements, not immediately). The command

$$Out[BytestoPT, Next[BytesfromPT]]\ \mathbf{repeat}$$

would copy paper tape indefinitely.

2.2 Stream functions

Unlike most operating systems, OS6 treats streams as 'first-class objects'. That is to say, they may be freely assigned to variables, passed as parameters, or returned as the result of a function call. New streams are created by means of stream functions, which may be provided by the system or be defined by the user. These *stream functions* usually take a stream as an argument, and give a new stream as the result.

To illustrate the use of stream functions we may consider the problem of reading, with the paper tape reader, a text tape punched on a machine such as a flexowriter. We have already mentioned the stream *BytesfromPT*, which is an input stream of raw bytes from the reader. These, however, would be in flexowriter code, and would include shift characters, erase characters, runout and so on. What we require is a stream of characters in Internal Code, and to obtain this we use the stream function *IntcodefromFlexowriter*:

$$\mathbf{let}\ S = IntcodefromFlexowriter[BytesfromPT]\ .$$

S is now defined to be an Internal Code stream, so that $Next[S]$ will produce an internal code character corresponding to one on the tape. (Since the flexowriter allows backspacing, it is in fact necessary to read raw bytes corresponding to a whole line at a time, and to form a line image in some buffer, from which characters in Internal Code are read as required: all this mechanism is specified in the definition of *IntcodefromFlexowriter*.)

If, instead of a flexowriter, the tape had been prepared on an Olivetti terminal, we could have written

$$\mathbf{let}\ S = IntcodefromOlivetti[BytesfromPT]$$

and the rest of the program using S would be unchanged. We are thus able to confine the device-dependent part of the program to where the streams are defined (usually in some kind of steering program).

A stream produced by a stream function can itself be the argument of another stream function, and the functions can perform jobs other than character conversion. As an example, suppose the tape we have been considering is an ALGOL 60 program, and we are writing an ALGOL compiler. Then the layout characters on the tape (spaces, newlines etc.) are redundant, and we could write a stream function *RemoveLayoutChs* to remove them altogether. We could write:

$$\textbf{let } S2 = RemoveLayoutChs[S]$$

or, more directly:

$$\textbf{let } S2 = RemoveLayoutChs[IntcodefromFlexowriter[BytesfromPT]].$$

$S2$ is also an Internal Code stream, but $Next[S2]$ will never produce any layout characters. (When we describe the implementation of stream functions we shall give the BCPL text of the definition of *RemoveLayoutChs*: see Section 2.5.2.)

An important property of stream functions is that streams produced by applications of one of them to two different arguments are quite independent. For example, if $S1$ and $S2$ are two Internal Code streams from different sources, we might define $S3$ and $S4$ by:

$$\begin{aligned}&\textbf{let } S3 = RemoveLayoutChs[S1]\\ &\textbf{and } S4 = RemoveLayoutChs[S2]\ .\end{aligned}$$

Calls of $Next[S3]$ and $Next[S4]$ could then be mixed in any order, and there would be no interaction between the two streams.

2.3 Errors

Problems arise when a stream has to cope with error situations: either invalid data coming in, or commands to output data unsuitable for the destination device. The difficulties are due to the wide choice of possible actions. One might abandon the program (that is, call *GiveUp*), one might simply ignore the offending item, or one might subject it to further analysis to determine what it ought to have been. It is impossible to build remedial action into a stream function sufficiently general to satisfy everybody. We therefore arrange that the majority of stream functions are available in a general form taking an extra parameter, which is an error function. E.g.:

$$\textbf{let } S = GeneralIntcodefromFlexowriter[BytesfromPT, ErrorFn]$$

The error function is called when invalid data subsequently occurs, and it decides what to do about it. The majority of programs, which do not need to take peculiar special action, use the non-general form, defined by the system:

$$\begin{aligned}&\textbf{let } IntcodefromFlexowriter[Str]\\ &\qquad = GeneralIntcodefromFlexowriter[Str, StandardErrorFn]\end{aligned}$$

The standard rule at present seems to be to produce an error report, and otherwise to ignore invalid input data, to replace valid but unprintable output characters by a space (so that they can be subsequently inserted, if required, by hand), and invalid characters, if applicable, by a blank tape row.

An exception to the standard rule occurs if a stream function is acting on the paper tape reader stream *BytesfromPT*. In that case a routine called *TryAgain* is applied. This is defined only on *BytesfromPT*, and only when nothing is 'put back' to the stream in the sense described in Section 2.4.5 below: in all other cases it leads to *GiveUp*. Since the Modular One paper tape reader can read in either direction, it is possible to move the tape back in order to have another attempt to read the offending character, and this is what *TryAgain* does. The job is only slightly complicated by the fact that input is double-buffered by *BytesfromPT*. After back-skipping, the system pauses to allow the operator to inspect the tape, and to clean up if necessary. A similar routine deals with sum-checked binary input, where it is necessary to reread a whole block.

The *TryAgain* technique is common practice in magnetic tape usage, but rare with paper tape. Particularly before the disc was delivered, however, this routine proved invaluable, as great quantity of paper tape was read and it would have been excessively timewasting if every error had been catastrophic.

We have described dealing with errors in some detail, in order to make the point that designing an operating system to be elegant and coherent does not imply that we must pretend that errors do not exist. We can deal with particular errors sensibly without obscuring the basic structure of the system.

2.4 Other primitives acting on streams

In addition to *Next* and *Out*, which may be thought of as performing the operations 'suck' and 'blow', there are a number of other primitives which operate on streams.

2.4.1 Endof

Endof is a predicate which is applicable to input streams. It produces the result **true** if there are no more objects to be input. The interpretation of this criterion depends both on the source of the information and on its nature. When the information comes from a disc file the matter is simple: the housekeeping information on the disc will contain the length of the file. With information of indefinite length, however, like input from the paper tape reader, there is a difficulty. It might be solved by reserving a particular character to signify the end of the information, but this is unsatisfactory for streams like *BytesfromPT* which may have to read a binary tape in which every bit-pattern is significant. It is because of the impossibility of having separate 'end of stream' character that a separate function *Endof* is necessary at all. In the absence of any knowledge about the structure or nature of the information we cannot tell when it ends, and we therefore make $Endof[BytesfromPT]$, for example, always **false**. Stream functions concerned with particular kinds of information decide according to their own conventions: text, for example, can be ended by a particular unusual sequence of characters, chosen *ad hoc* (we often use a full stop on a line by itself), while binary information will require more elaborate rules.

This matter is also discussed by Needham and Hartley (1969), who 'do not believe at all that this whole problem can be swept under the rug by an appeal to convention'. To surmount the difficulty of free-format binary information, they recommend the sensing by the device of the physical end of the medium–in our case, the end of the tape. We think that this is just as much a matter of *ad hoc* convention as any other action, since where the tape happens to run out or to tear has no logical connection with the information on the tape. As an approximate test of this view, we wrote one of our stream functions to end when it detected over a foot of runout. This convention was abominated by all, and has been abolished.

Our insistence that determination of the end of the stream depends on the nature of the information it contains would lead to difficulties if we were managing an input well, or 'spooling' the input, because we would then be processing information without regard to its content. It would be necessary to impose some sort of convention which could coexist with all the possible types of information—in the last resort, the operator could tell the system when the information had been completely read.

In situations where the terminating character approach is acceptable, it might waste time to be testing $Endof[S]$ between each call of $Next[S]$.

So we compromise by arranging that when *Endof*[*S*] has become **true** a subsequent call of *Next*[*S*] does not lead to failure; instead the result of *Next*[*S*] is a stream-dependent constant, usually known as *EndofStreamCh*.

2.4.2 Reset

Reset is a routine applicable both to input streams and to output streams, which restores them, in some sense which varies from stream to stream, to their initial state. In the case of output streams, any information temporarily in buffers associated with the stream is forced to its final destination, while for input streams any information in buffers is discarded, so that the next object requested will be read at that time from the input device. Other action may also be taken, such as setting an input device unready, or moving to a new page on a printer.

2.4.3 Close

Close also acts both on input and on output streams. It forces out any information in output buffers, informs the system that the stream is no longer required, and returns its storage areas.

2.4.4 State and ResetState

Usually, a stream is either an input or an output stream. Sometimes, however, an input device and an output device, although logically separate, are physically on the same chassis; then, as we have already mentioned, for administrative convenience we combine the two streams into a single bilateral stream There is another kind of information which can be obtained from a device: rather than obtaining another new object (as *Next* does), we can look at something to see whether it has changed. For example, we could look at the on-line/off-line switch on the reader. In the case of consoles, the question usually is: 'Has anyone typed anything yet, and, if so, what?' Again, this kind of information is logically separable from the stream-like kinds; but since both kinds come from the same machine, it is convenient to include it in the stream.

We therefore define two new primitives on streams. The first is a function, *State*[*S*], which produces the current state of the device. For those devices where the state is defined by asking whether some event has yet occurred, we also need a routine, *ResetState*[*S*], to reinitialise the state.

(Possibly the *Reset* routine, described above, could also do this, but it seems cleaner to have a separate routine.)

State and *ResetState* were a later addition to the scheme. and for reasons of domestic economy have so far been implemented only for bilateral streams. They are most frequently used when the machine is performing some repetitive operation, in order that the loop may be broken when the operator types a character on the console. Thus the tape-copying loop quoted ahove might be modified to read:

$$\begin{array}{l} Out[BytestoPT,\ Next[BytesfromPT]] \\ \quad \textbf{repeatwhile}\ State[Console] = NOTHINGTYPED \end{array}$$

(in fact our tape-copying program is a little more elaborate). Notice the essential difference between *State* and *Next*: if *Next* is called, the program is held up until a new object comes along, whereas *State* can return the null answer.

2.4.5 PutBack

We frequently require to perform operations like reading a multi-digit number from a character input stream. This raises the interesting question of what to do with the terminating character. It must not be simply absorbed as part of the number, for we may later require to consider it independently For example, we may be trying to parse an expression like

$$27 + a$$

and we shall obviously require to know that the character terminating the number was '+'. It would be possible to leave the character in a conventional location; but then it would be necessary to take care to remove it immediately, before the location was used by something else. The cleanest solution would be, if possible, to return the character to the stream, so that it could be produced again the next time there was any input. This is done by the routine *PutBack*, which takes two arguments, an input stream and an object; for example:

$$PutBack[Stream,\ TermCh]\ .$$

Then, the next time we call *Next*[*Stream*], the result will be *TermCh*.

PutBack is of unrestricted application. It may be used on any input stream; it may be used to put back several items *seriatim* to a stream (the last item put back will be the first to reappear); and there is no need for the items put back to have come from the stream in the first place.

2.5 *Implementation*

2.5.1 *Implementation of streams*

In principle a stream is represented by a data structure, the components of which are functions and routines for performing the primitive operations. In BCPL this is implemented as a vector. Thus if S is an input stream, the element S_0 (which in BCPL is typed as $S{\downarrow}0$, the zeroth element of S) is reserved for the function which produces the next object. Let us call the function *NextFn*. *NextFn* will require some working variables to survive from each activation to the next, in order to keep pointers, buffers and so on. In particular, if S was produced from a stream function,

$$S = StreamFn[ArgStream] \ ,$$

then *NextFn* will require to refer to *ArgStream*.

The mechanism for referring to non-local variables which is built into the BCPL language is inadequate to deal naturally with this situation. (So, for that matter, are those in ALGOL 60, ALGOL 68 and PL/I; two languages which are sufficiently powerful are PAL (Evans, 1968) and POP-2 (Burstall, Collins, and Popplestone, 1968).) This means that we must make special provisions to preserve the information ourselves, which we do by keeping it all in the vector S. The length of S may therefore vary from stream to stream, but the first few elements are always reserved for the basic functions and routines.

To obtain the next object from S, we must supply S to $NextFn$ as a parameter,

$$NextFn[S] \ ,$$

in order to allow access by $NextFn$ to elements of S. Since $NextFn$ is itself stored in S_0, we may define the general primitive function $Next$, applicable to all input streams, by writing:

$$\textbf{let } Next[S] = (S{\downarrow}0)[S] \ .$$

The other primitives are similarly defined; for example:

$$\textbf{let } Out[S, x] \textbf{ be } \S\ (S{\downarrow}1)[S, x]\ \S.$$

We arrange that in input streams the element corresponding to the *Out* routine contains an error routine, and vice versa. Note that the functions and routines which operate on streams store the information they must preserve from one call to the next in the stream vector itself; this means that they can be used on several different streams in the same program without confusion.

2.5.2 Implementation of stream functions

The result of applying a stream function is a new stream; the function must therefore claim a new vector from the storage allocator, and place in it the functions and routines to perform the standard operations, together with any other initial information that may be necessary, including, for example, the stream supplied as the parameter for the stream function.

To illustrate this, we give the BCPL text of a particularly simple example, the function *RemoveLayoutChs* described in Section 2.2 above. To simplify still further, we will ignore *State* and *ResetState*. As *PutBack* does not require a vector element (see Section 2.5.3 below), the vector has to contain five standard elements (for *Next*, *Out*, *Close*, *Endof* and *Reset*). It must also contain the argument stream, so a vector of six elements is required; its layout is shown in Fig. 1.

0	*NextRLC*
1	*(Out)* an error routine
2	*CloseRLC*
3	*Str*
4	*EndofRLC*
5	*ResetRLC*

Figure 1 Layout of the *RemoveLayoutChs* stream vector

The fact that the third element is not reserved for a standard operation, and is therefore available for *Str*, is for historical reasons. In any case, we shall ignore its embarrassing arbitrariness because, to improve readability, we shall refer to the elements by name. We therefore define the following constants (from now on in this section we will be writing BCPL; comments in this language are introduced by two vertical bars (||) and continue to the end of the line):

```
manifest §
   NEXT = 0
   OUT = 1
   CLOSE = 2
   STR = 3
   ENDOF = 4
   RESET = 5
   VECSIZE = 5
          §
```

|| The definition of *RemoveLayoutChs* is then as follows:

```
let RemoveLayoutChs[Str] = valof
    §RLC let v = NewVec[VECSIZE] || We claim a vector
         v↓NEXT,   := NextRLC,
         v↓OUT,    := StreamError,
         v↓CLOSE,  := CloseRLC,
         v↓ENDOF,  := EndofRLC,
         v↓RESET   := ResetRLC
            || and initialise the standard contents (note that
            || StreamError is a system error routine).
         v↓STR := Str
         resultis v § RLC
```

|| We must now define the subsidiary routines. The most important
|| is *NextRLC*.

```
and NextRLC[S] = valof
§N      §1 let x = Next[S↓STR] || We read a character
                               || from the argument stream.
           unless x = '*s' ∨ x = '*4' ∨ x = '*n'
                               || Unless it's a layout character,
              then resultis x  || it's the result;
        §1 repeat §N           || otherwise we repeat the process.
```

|| Note that '*s' means space, '*4' the 4-space character, and '*n' newline.
|| We next define *CloseRLC*: we close the argument stream, and
|| return the storage space.

```
and CloseRLC[S] be
   §C Close[S↓STR]
      ReturnVec[S, VECSIZE] §C
```

|| The simplest and fastest definition of *EndofRLC* is merely
|| to test the end of the argument stream:

```
and EndofRLC[S] = Endof[S↓STR]
```

```
|| This, however, would be wrong if Str ended with layout
|| characters, because our function would give the result false
|| when in fact there were no more characters to come. If this
|| were important, we would have to get more complicated:
||
|| and EndofRLC[S] = valof
||      §E let Str = S↓STR              || Str is the argument stream
||         §1 if Endof[Str] resultis true
||           § let Ch = Next[Str]        || look at the next character
||             unless Ch = '*s' ∨ Ch = '*4' ∨ Ch = '*n'
||             do § PutBack[Str,Ch]      || if it's not a layout
||                      resultis false § || character, put it back on
||         §1 repeat §E                  || Str, and the answer is
||                                       || false; otherwise, repeat.
|| || Note that although PutBack[Str,Ch] is more obvious,
|| || PutBack[S,Ch] would have been more efficient.

|| ResetRLC is, however, simple—we merely reset the argument
|| stream:

   and ResetRLC[S] be Reset[S↓STR]

|| That completes the example.
```

2.5.3 Implementation of PutBack

A call of the routine *PutBack* is of the form

$$PutBack[S, x]$$

where S is an input stream and x is an object. The routine claims a small vector from the free store and stores in it the returned object, and also the values of some of the first few elements of the stream vector, which it then overwrites with other routines. The final situation is as shown in Fig. 2. Then when *Next* is applied to S, *NextPB* is activated. This restores S to the *status quo*, and returns the *PutBack* vector to free storage; its result is then the object put back. *ClosePB* and *ResetPB* also restore the previous state and then apply the appropriate original routine; the result of *EndofPB* is always **false**. The *PutBack* vectors are chained together for a reason described below, and when a *PutBack* vector is removed, care is taken to heal the breach in the chain. Extra care has to be taken with bilateral streams, to ensure that the output part of the stream still works

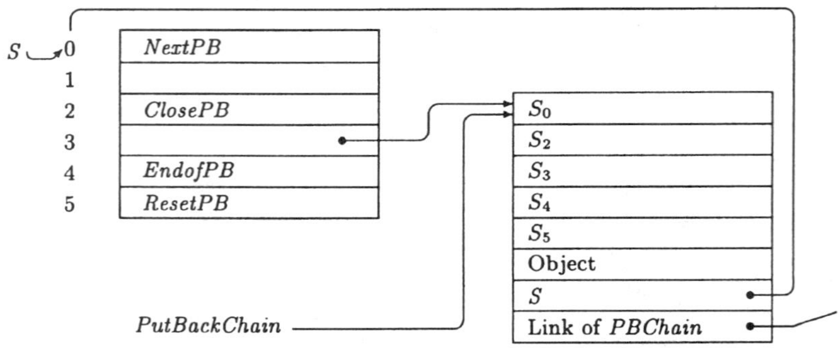

Figure 2 Implementation of *PutBack*

when an object has been put back to the input part, since some elements in the vector are thereby overwritten.

This implementation gave rise to the following difficulty. If the last action on an input stream before the end of a Run is to perform *PutBack* (after reading a number, for example), then the *PutBack* vector is returned together with the rest of the free store area, and the stream is thereafter unusable. This is of troublesome, of course, only when the stream vector itself is claimed from an earlier free store, and therefore remains in existence longer than the *PutBack* vector.

This particular problem required a special solution. The free storage system was altered, so that when it reverts to an earlier free storage area it copies into the earlier area any *PutBack* vectors still in use. This is why the *PutBackChain* is required. This is an example of the clash between the hierarchical structure of OS6 and the nature of storage mechanisms, which was discussed in the previous paper. The solution must be *ad hoc*, because in BCPL there can be no systematic way of relocating vectors of information. Fortunately, this is the only place where the system requires its use of free storage to transcend the discipline of the *Run* system, and the special solution is therefore satisfactory. The only general solution would be to alter the language to allow garbage collection, and to make all off-stack storage permanent.

2.6 Efficiency of streams

A possible objection to the use of streams might be that the overheads associated with their structure make them excessively inefficient. Certainly, when a stream is formed from a deep nest of stream functions, processing a single character can involve many function calls. To some extent a greater expenditure of time than usual is unavoidable, simply because the flexible nature of streams and the ease of nesting stream function calls lead to the possibility of specifying much more complex operations to be performed on each character. It is sometimes profitable to examine the program to ensure that some of these operations do not undo the work of others. A stream, for example, might be formed by one stream function which unpacks words into bytes, followed by another one which packs them all up again.

An improvement in speed may be made by streamlining the definition of *Next* and *Out*, by hand-coding them into machine code, and this was done from the start (that is, they were written in virtual machine code—see Part 1, Section 0.2 for a definition of 'machine code' and 'hardware' in this discussion). Further analysis was done by taking measurements of the actual usage of the operating system during the compilation of the null program, when most of the time is spent in loading the compiler. A histogram was produced showing how often each group of 10 words of code had been accessed (there are about 10,000 words of code in the operating system). The result was a startling concentration into a few peaks with virtually nothing measurable in between. Further analysis showed that most of these peaks were at pieces of program concerned with taking single items out of buffers and putting them somewhere else after testing for various conditions such as the end of the buffer.

Our system runs in a virtual machine, which is implemented by an interpreter. We can therefore easily add new instructions to our virtual hardware, merely by extending the interpreter. We have used this facility several times in order to replace frequently occurring operations by single instructions, thus increasing the efficiency of the system. This activity is quite legitimate, provided that the instructions we add are such as could reasonably be implemented in real hardware if required. The ability to proceed in this way is very liberating, and is in accord with our general philosophy of not allowing ourselves to be bullied by machines. The conclusion to be drawn from our statistical investigation was that the buffering operations were obvious candidates for such optimisation.

A new kind of data structure, called a *fast stream*, was devised. A stream is marked as being either fast or slow (in practice by using the sign bit which is not required to be part of the address). If a stream is marked as being slow, it is a normal stream of the kind we have already described. If it is a fast stream, however, we may derive from it the address of a vector, of the form shown in Fig. 3. The definitions of the primitive stream operations are extended to deal with fast streams. If *Next* is applied to a fast stream, the normal action is to return as result the object referenced by the input buffer pointer, and to increment the pointer. If the pointer has reached the limit, the appropriate routine is called in the further vector, which is very like a normal stream, to refill the buffer. It is convenient also to break out of the buffering if the item picked up is equal to the input escape item. *Out* is defined similarly. If S is a fast stream, $Endof[S]$ is **false** if the input buffer pointer is below its limit, and otherwise a function in the further vector is called. The other primitives merely activate routines in the further vector.

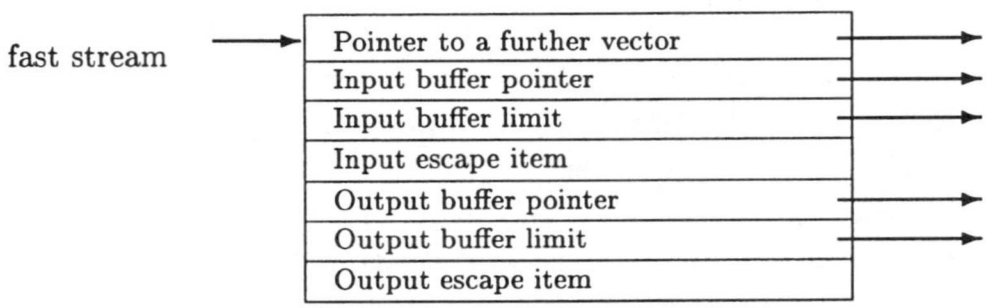

Figure 3 Form of a fast stream

Single hardware instructions corresponding to *Next*, *Out* and *Endof* were written into the interpreter; the other primitives are used less frequently, and are therefore defined in BCPL. Hardware instructions were also written to implement the routine

$$TransferIn[S, v, n]$$

where S is an input stream (slow or fast), and v is a vector of length n, in either the code area or the data area; its action is to place in the elements of v the results of n calls of $Next[S]$.

The corresponding output routine

$$TransferOut[S, v, n]$$

was implemented by hardware too.

The result of all this was to reduce the time for compiling the null program by a factor of six. We feel that this is the proper way to treat problems of efficiency. Peter Landin has remarked that most programs are designed to be as fast as possible—so that one then goes through a lengthy process (debugging) of improving the correctness to a tolerable level while preserving the speed—whereas the sensible course would be to design them to be as correct as possible, and then gradually to increase the speed till it is tolerable while preserving the accuracy. (Dijkstra (1971) suggests that this is because many programmers find debugging so much fun that they could not contemplate giving it up, because the element of black magic in it satisfies one of our most undernourished psychological needs.) Streams were designed to be elegant, because in the long run this is the best guarantee that programs using them will be correct; questions of efficiency, including the decision about which operations should be done by hardware, were attended to later.

It may be convenient in the future to modify the behaviour of fast streams. In particular, for doing more complex activities like syntax analysis, there may be advantages in replacing the escape item test by something more elaborate, such as a masked test.

2.7 System streams

OS6 contains one or two permanent streams, closely associated with particular peripheral devices. An example is $BytesfromPT$, which is the only route by which paper tape is read by the system. These streams are permanent in the sense that an attempt to close them merely resets them.

In addition to the permanent streams, OS6 has four global variables to hold streams reserved for conventional purposes. These are called variable streams, and may be freely altered by programs. Their values are preserved in the Run-blocks (see Part 1, Section 1.2.1), and they are restored to their previous values at the end of each Run. The four variables are In, the normal input stream; *Output*, for normal output; *ReportStream*, for error reports; and $Console$, for messages to or from an operator's console.

2.8 Input/output routines

Programs frequently require to print numbers, strings etc. on a character device. It would be possible to do this by stream functions: for example, one which when applied to a character output stream would provide a stream for the output of integers. However, programmers usually need finer control over the layout of their output, and prefer to work directly with characters. For this reason a set of routines is provided to output items of various types along character streams. A typical one is $OutN[S, n]$, which outputs n as a decimal integer along the stream S. As well as this set which takes the stream as a parameter, two other sets are provided to perform the same operations specifically on *Output* and *ReportStream*, Input functions are also provided for reading a similar range of items from input streams.

3 The filing system

It now remains for us to describe the outline of the filing system, the regime under which information is kept on the disc. We do not claim any great originality or sophistication in the design of the system. However, this is an area in which there tends be confusion—it is easy, for example, to muddle the name of a object with the object itself—and we have taken care that our system should be 'clean', and that its structure should be clear.

Our previous discussion on input/output in OS6 has been based on the idea of streams. These could be freely manipulated in the programming language and had the same status as any other type of object. We now extend this approach to another kind of object, called a *file*. These, like streams, may freely be assigned to variables, be passed as parameters, or be the result of function calls. This implies that each file has a unique *value* which may be stored in a single BCPL variable, and is the handle by which to access the two components of the file structure, the *heading* and the *body*.

Each file has its own unique heading. This contains various items of housekeeping information about the file, including the means by which the system can access the body. The body contains the information stored in the file, and also belongs exclusively to one file: files do not share components. A empty file has no body.

3.1 Some basic functions

As in the case of streams, the basic property of a file f is that a number of system functions may meaningfully be applied to it. One of these, *FindHeading*, produces the heading of the file as a vector in core:

$$\textbf{let } H = FindHeading[f]$$

(The contents of this vector are given in full below, in Section 3.4). One of the fields of H is called the *title* of the file. It is a BCPL string, of arbitrary length, and its sole purpose is contain a description, fit for human consumption, of the contents of the file. The properties of the file which might concern a program—such as the date it was created, its owner, or the type of information stored in it—are all kept in other fields of the heading, and it is not intended that the system should do anything with the title except print it out from time to time. In particular, the title is *not* used when the system is searching for file.

Most of the entries in the heading of a file (including all those already mentioned) are invariant: they are set when the file is created and may not subsequently be altered. Some of them such as the date the file was last changed, or its size—are updated automatically by the system. Only one field, which contains an entry stating who is allowed to overwrite the file may be altered by the programmer (by calling a special routine *UpdatePermission*.)

3.1.1 Streams from files

Other basic functions concern the file body. The commonest way of reading a file into the system is by forming an input stream from it, by the function *InfromFile*:

$$\textbf{let } S = InfromFile[f] \ .$$

S is a word input stream, so that if f is a file of packed bytes it is necessary to apply the stream function *BytesfromWords*:

$$\textbf{let } S2 = BytesfromWords[InfromFile[f]] \ .$$

S is a fast stream. If at any time it is reset, then any subsequent calls of $Next[S]$ will recommence from the beginning of the file.

The corresponding function to produce output streams to the file is also available:

$$\textbf{let } S3 = OuttoFile[f] \ .$$

Since this involves overwriting, it is designed to minimise incidents in the case of error. As output *via* $S3$ proceeds, a new body is constructed, but only when $S3$ is closed does this new body replace the old one. Thus if the program fails before $S3$ is explicitly closed, f will not be altered; instead the *new* body is abandoned.

3.1.2 Vectors from files

Instead of forming a stream from the information in a file body, it may be treated as a vector. There are two possible ways of doing this. If the body is not too large, the simplest way is to transfer it completely to a vector in core. A function is available for this:

$$\textbf{let } v = \mathit{VectorfromFile}[f] \ .$$

By convention v_0 contains n, the size of the body in words, and the body itself is in v_1 to v_n. The complementary routine is also available,

$$\mathit{VectortoFile}[f, v] \ ,$$

in which the same convention is observed.

If the body is too large to exist in core, another mechanism is needed. An object called a *disc vector* is defined, which may be produced by the function $\mathit{DiscVectorfromFile}$:

$$\textbf{let } Dv = \mathit{DiscVectorfromFile}[f] \ .$$

Then a particular element of the body may be accessed by a further function:

$$\textbf{let } El = \mathit{DiscVectorElement}[Dv, i] \ ,$$

or updated by a routine:

$$\mathit{UpdateDiscVectorElement}[Dv, i, x] \ .$$

Dv is a vector in core which contains addressing information allowing reasonably quick random access to any part of the file body. When no longer required it may be relinquished by a call of the routine $\mathit{ReturnDiscVector}[Dv]$.

3.1.3 File creation

Files are created by the function $\mathit{MakeNewFile}$. This is given the title of the file and its type as parameters:

$$\textbf{let } f = \mathit{MakeNewFile}[\text{'Line printer stream functions'}, \mathit{BCPLTEXT}] \ .$$

The result is a new empty file.

3.2 Indexes

The file f may be created and used freely within a single program with no further apparatus. 'f', however, is the name of an ordinary BCPL variable, and is governed by the usual scope rules: that is, it refers to the file only inside the block of program at the top of which its definition occurs. If the file is to be usable by other programs, we need another mechanism. This mechanism is provided by *indexes*.

An index is a file (of type $INDEX$) on which a number of special routines are defined. When a file is entered in an index, two *names* (BCPL strings) are associated with it. This is done by the routine *Enter*.

$$Enter[f,\ p,\ q,\ i]$$

means: 'associate the names p and q with the file f in the index file i.' Particular values for p and q might be, for example, '$LinePrinter$' and '$Text$'. If another file is already associated with p and q in i, the new mapping supersedes the old.

The complementary operation is provided by the function *LookUp*:

$$\textbf{let}\ f = LookUp[\text{‘}LinePrinter\text{’},\ \text{‘}Text\text{’},\ i]$$

defines f to be the file previously associated with the names '$LinePrinter$' and '$Text$' in the index i. If there is no such file, the result is the constant NIL: the request does not lead to failure. On the other hand, an attempt actually to access the components of a non-existent file, for example by setting up a stream, implies that the program has definitely gone wrong, and such an attempt leads to *GiveUp*.

A further function applicable to index files is the stream function *Entries-from*:

$$\textbf{let}\ S = Entriesfrom[i]\ .$$

The result of $Next[S]$ is then normally a vector containing the two names and the value of the file (there is also another form of index entry which we shall mention below). This enables programmers to perform operations like: 'Compile all the files with second name 'OS6' in the index.' It should be noted that the system itself attaches no semantic significance to either index name–all the information the system requires about a file is in the heading—but the fact that there are two names allows the programmer to systematise his indexes in any way convenient to himself.

3.2.1 Index structure and sharing

There is a special index, called the system index, which the system keeps in a global variable called *SystemIndex*. Each user of the system has his own index, for which there is an entry in the system index. So one may write, for example:

$$\textbf{let } i = \mathit{LookUp}[\text{`}\mathit{JES}\text{'}, \text{`}\mathit{Index}\text{'}, \mathit{SystemIndex}]$$
$$\textbf{let } f = \mathit{LookUp}[\text{`}\mathit{LinePrinter}\text{'}, \text{`}\mathit{Text}\text{'}, i]$$

or, all at once:

$$\textbf{let } f = \mathit{LookUp}[\text{`}\mathit{LinePrinter}\text{'}, \text{`}\mathit{Text}\text{'}, \mathit{LookUp}[\text{`}\mathit{JES}\text{'}, \text{`}\mathit{Index}\text{'}, \text{SystemIndex}]]\ .$$

In fact, any index may be entered in any other index, not merely in the system index.

A single file may be associated with different pairs of names in different indexes, or even in the same index. This is one form of sharing of files: two different entries point to the same file. There is another form of sharing sometimes employed, which is available in OS6. Instead of two entries pointing to the same file, one entry may point to the other entry (this is the 'special' form of index entry referred to above). Such an entry is constructed by the routine *Link*, which takes seven arguments:

$$\mathit{Link}[N1, N2, N3, N4, N5, N6, i]\ .$$

This means: 'Construct a special entry in the index i, so that the names $N1$, $N2$ refer to the entry with names $N3$, $N4$ in a second index. This second index is entered with names $N5$, $N6$ in the system index.' Then a call

$$\mathit{LookUp}[N1, N2, i]$$

will initiate a search in the second index. In principle links may occur to any depth; care is taken when setting up a link to ensure that the chain of links does not lead to a loop of references to each other.

There is a third method of sharing the information in a file, which is simply to copy the contents into a completely new file. Which of these three methods is used in any particular situation is partly a matter of personal taste. The first seems to be most popular in our group. It is possible, however, to imagine a situation in which there is a real choice between all three possibilities.

Suppose a user A keeps programs on the disc, and has the convention that when correcting a mistake he overwrites the file body, but if he alters the specification of a program he creates a new file and changes the entry in his index to point to the new program. Then a second user B who wishes to access one of A's programs can choose as follows. If he wants the program as it stands, ignoring any of A's later alterations, he copies the file. If he wants to benefit when A corrects a mistake, but not to have the specification changed, he constructs an entry pointing to A's file. If he wants to keep up with A's latest ideas on what the program ought to be doing, then he constructs an entry pointing to A's entry.

3.3 Deletion of files

There are three sorts of deleting possible in the system. One may delete the body of a file, preserving the file itself and any index entries pointing to it; one may delete the file, heading and body, but not affect any index entries; or one may delete an index entry, which will not affect the file the entry pointed to. All three kinds are separately available in OS6. Of course, an index entry pointing to a deleted file is not much use, and a file is inaccessible unless at least one entry points to it: these matters are the concern of a special housekeeping program, which performs a garbage-collection operation on the filing system.

3.4 Outline of implementation

Files on the disc are accessed through a Master File List (MFL). The value of a file is the serial number of its entry in the MFL; the MFL entry gives the disc address (page and word) of the file heading. The Burroughs disc has fixed heads, so the access time is half a revolution; moreover, the use of an interpreter slows down the rate at which the system can process information. There is therefore no advantage in optimising position of the pages in the body of a file; they are allocated in no particular order, and the pages of a body are chained together. Usually, the last body page contains a pointer indicating how much of it is occupied (thus avoiding the $Endof$ problem discussed earlier in Section 2.4.1).

A diagram of the structure is given in Fig. 4. It should be noted that the headings are kept all together in a heading file and the MFL is also a file. This implies, of course, that the heading file will have its own heading, somewhere in its own body, and the MFL will contain its own entry. It is necessary to know two quantities in order to access the structure: the address of the first page of the MFL body, and the value of the system index. The second of these is kept in a global variable, set up when the system is initiated, and is available to user programs; the former is private to the system, and is incorporated as a constant declaration at the head of the appropriate segment of the text of the system. This is a mistake: if the particular page developed a fault, it would be impossible to use the filing system until the segment had been recompiled—and the normal compiler uses the disc.

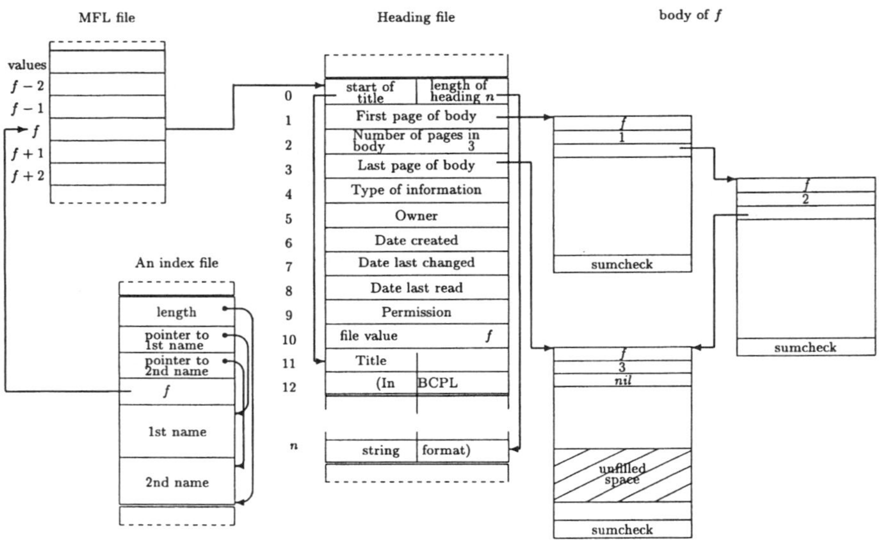

Figure 4 Structure of the filing system

3.4.1 Disc storage allocation

The addresses of all the free pages on the disc are kept in a file, the free storage file. For efficiency's sake a page of this file is kept in core, and for safety's sake this core is in the program segment. It is written back to the disc at frequent intervals (at the end of each Run, and whenever the page kept in core changes to another page).

3.4.2 User details

The system has a file of users. A user's entry contains his name (a string), the unique number by which he is known to the system (which gets entered in the owner field of his file headings), and his main index. A user may 'log in' by specifying his name on the console: the system places his personal details in various system variables ($User$, $UserIndex$). The entry also contains the size of the user's allocation of disc storage space. The system warns him when this is nearly used up, and he is presented from exceeding it.

4 3 Protection against error

Protection in the filing system is of two kinds: we try to prevent the occurrence of accidents; and we keep a certain quantity of redundant information, so that if a crash does happen we have some chance of reconstituting the system, rather than having to restart it *ab initio*.

The most important prophylactic is the permission system, governing the access programs may have to files. Since we are solely concerned to prevent accidents, and have no confidential files, we allow anybody to read anything; there are only three values for the permission field in the heading, which have the following meanings:

$UNRESTRICTED$:	anyone can write to the file
$OWNER$:	only the owner permitted to write
$INHIBITED$:	no one may write to the file.

The permission field may be changed only by the owner (or anyone masquerading as the owner).

Our present philosophy is not to be constantly checking the redundant information. Every so often we run a disc validation program which thoroughly checks everything, and we investigate any discrepancies. If there is a crash, we have an armoury of little programs to aid the system programmers in sorting out the system.

3.4.4 Garbage collection

It is probable that the filing system will contain some outdated information in inaccessible places. This may be found and removed by a garbage collection system, which operates in well defined phases. Firstly, the system index and any deeper indexes are scanned, and entries referring to deleted files are removed. Having purged these indexes, we construct a list of the files entered in them, and delete all files which do not occur in the list. At this stage the heading file may be compacted. Finally, we form a list of the disc pages used by the files which remain, and ensure that all other pages are entered in the free storage file.

3.5 Extensions to the filing system

We may require to extend the filing system to deal with a more sophisticated system, in particular (a) automatic incremental dumping, if suitable extra equipment becomes available, and (b) the possibility of several users using files simultaneously through a console system. This will probably require new fields in the heading of a file, to contain new items like its current status, for interlocking purposes. None of this will require changes to the basic principles of the system.

4 Recapitulation

In any description of an input/output system it is only too easy to lose sight of the basic outline. Although we wanted to include some merely corroborative detail intended to give artistic verisimilitude to an otherwise bald and unconvincing narrative (Gilbert, 1885), it may be worth while repeating the principles which we hope underlie our system.

The main objects manipulated in the system are *streams* and *files*. Both may be handled freely by all the facilities in the programming language. In particular, new streams may be created by *streamfunctions*, which may be written by the user, and which usually take a previously defined stream as argument, returning a new stream as the result. (A new file cannot be created by a user-defined function because the medium in which they are stored is administered solely by the system.)

Streams and files are characterised by the basic functions and routines which act on them. For streams, the most important of these are *Next* and *Out*, which respectively obtain an object from an input stream and consign one to an output stream (the type of the object depends on the stream, and the same basic routines can be applied to all streams).

The basic functions on files allow the information in the file to be accessed in various ways (random, serial or all at once), and allow a file to become the subject of an entry in an *index*. The index entry, however, is not part of the file itself.

Acknowledgements

The work on streams has been going on for some years, and began long before we had a computer or operating system of our own. Several people have helped in the implementation of the system described in these two papers. Our thanks are due particularly to Julia Bayman, B. N. Biswas, M. K. Harper, C. Hones and P. D. Mosses.

The work described in Section 2.6 was performed by P. H. F. McGregor.

References

1. BURSTALL, R. M., COLLINS, J. S., and POPPLESTONE, R. J. (1968). *POP-2 Papers*, Edinburgh & London: Oliver & Boyd.
2. DIJKSTRA, E. W. (1971). Concern for correctness as a guiding principle for program composition, *The Fourth Generation, International Computer State of the Art Report*, pp. 357–367. Maidenhead: Infotech.
3. EVANS, A., Jr. (1968). PAL—a language for teaching programming linguistics, *Proc. ACM 23rd National Conf.* Princeton, N.J.: Brandon/Systems Press.
4. GILBERT, W. S. (1885). *The Mikado* or *The Town of Titipu*, Act II, London: Chappell & Co.
5. NEEDHAM, R. M., and HARTLEY, D. F. (1969). Theory and Practice in Operating System Design, *Second Symposium on Operating Systems Principles*, pp. 8–12. Princeton, N.J.: ACM.
6. STOY, J. E., and STRACHEY, C. (1972). OS6—an experimental operating system for a small computer. Part 1: general principles and structure, *The Computer Journal*, Vol. 15, pp. 117–124.

18

AN OPEN OPERATING SYSTEM FOR A SINGLE-USER MACHINE*

BUTLER W. LAMPSON AND ROBERT F. SPROULL

(1979)

The file system and modularization of a single-user operating system are described. The main points of interest are the openness of the system, which establishes no sharp boundary between itself and the users programs, and the techniques used to make the system robust.

1 Introduction

In the last few years a certain way of thinking about operating systems has come to be widely accepted. According to this view, the function of an operating system is to provide a kind of womb (or, if you like, a virtual machine) within which the user or her program can live and develop, safely insulated from the harsh realities of the outside world [2, 5, 13]. One of the authors, in fact, was an early advocate of such "closed" systems [12]. They have a number of attractive features:

- When the hardware is too dreadful for ordinary mortals to look upon, concealment is a kindness, if not a necessity.
- Useful and popular facilities can be made available in a uniform manner, with the name binding and storage allocation required to implement them kept out of the way.
- The system can protect itself from the users without having to make any assumptions about what they do (aside from those implicit in the definition of the virtual machine).

*B. W. Lampson and R. F. Sproull, An open operating system for a single-user machine. *Operating Systems Review 13*, 5 (November 1979), 98–105.

- A more robust facility can perhaps be provided if all of the underlying structure is concealed.

On the other hand, a good deal may be lost by putting too much distance between the user and the hardware [4], especially if she needs to deal with unconventional input-output devices. Furthermore, a lot of flexibility is given up by the flat, all-or-nothing style of these systems, and it is extremely difficult for a user to extend or modify the system because of the sharp line which is drawn between the two.

In this paper we explore a different, more "open" approach: the system is thought of as offering a variety of facilities, any of which the user may reject, accept, modify or extend. In many cases a facility may become a component out of which other facilities are built up: for example, files are built out of disk pages. When this happens, we try as far as possible to make the small components accessible to the user as well as the large ones. The success of such a design depends on the extent to which we can exploit the flexibility of the small components without destroying the larger ones. In particular, we must pay a great deal of attention to the robustness of the system, i.e., recovery from crashes and resistance to misuse.

Another aspect of our system is that the file system and communications are standardized at a level below any of the software in the operating system. In fact, it is the representation of files on the disk and of packets on the network that are standardized. This has permitted programs written in radically different languages (BCPL [4], Mesa [8], Lisp [7] and Smalltalk [10]; the former came first, and is the host language of the software described in this paper) and executed using radically different instruction sets (implemented in writeable microcode) to share the same file system and remote facilities. In doing so, they do not give up any storage to an operating system written in a foreign language, or any cycles in switching from one programming environment and instruction set to another at every access to disk storage or communications.

The price paid for this flexibility is that any change in these representations requires changing several pieces of code, written in several languages and maintained by several different people; the cost of this rewriting is so high that it is effectively impossible to make such changes. Thus the approach cannot be recommended when processor speed and memory are ample; standardization at a higher level is preferable in this case. In our situation, however, the policy has made many major applications of the machine possible which would otherwise have been completely infeasible.

Furthermore, we have found that these restrictions have caused few practical problems, in spite of the fact that the range of uses of the system has been far greater than was initially anticipated.

In a multi-user system, of course, there must be compulsory protection mechanisms that ensure equitable and safe sharing of the hardware resources, and this consideration sets limits to the openness that can be achieved. Within these limits, however, much can be done, and indeed the facilities discussed below can be provided in a protected way without any great changes, although this paper avoids an explicit analysis of the problem by confining itself to a single-user system. To describe an entire system in this way would be a substantial undertaking. We will confine ourselves here to the disk file system, the method of doing world swapping, and the way in which the system is constructed out of packages.

2 Background

The operating system from which the examples in this paper are drawn was written for a small computer called the Alto [16], which has a 16-bit processor, 64k words of 800 ns memory, and one or two moving-head disk drives, each of which can store 2.5 megabytes on a single removable pack and can transfer 64k words in about one second. The machine and system can also support another disk with about twice the size and performance. The machine has no virtual memory hardware. The processor executes an instruction set that supports BCPL, including special instructions for procedure calls and returns.

The system is written almost entirely in BCPL, and in fact this language is considered to be one of the standard ways of programming the machine. The compiler generates ordinary machine instructions, and uses no runtime support routines except for a small body of code that extends the instruction set slightly.

Only one user at a time is supported, and peripheral equipment other than the disk and terminal is infrequently used. As a result, the current version of the system has only two processes, one of which puts keyboard input characters into a buffer, while the other does all the interesting work. The keyboard process is interrupt-driven and has no critical sections; hence there are no synchronization primitives and no scheduler other than the hardware interrupt system. As a result, the system does not control processor allocation, and in fact gets control only when a user program calls some system facility. The system does control storage allocation to some extent, both in main memory and on the disk, in order to make it possible for the users programs to coexist and to call each other.

Thus the system can reasonably be viewed as a collection of procedures which implement various potentially useful abstract objects. There is no significant difference between these system procedures and a set of procedures that the user might write to implement his own abstract objects. In fact, the system code is made available as a set of independent subroutine packages, each implementing one of the objects, and these packages have received a great deal of independent use, in applications which do not need all the services of the system and cannot afford its costs.

There are several kinds of abstract object: input-output streams, files, storage zones, physical disks. All of these objects are implemented in such a way that they can be values of ordinary variables; since BCPL is a typeless language this means that each object can be represented by a 16-bit machine word. In many cases, of course, this word will be a pointer to something bigger. The streams are copied wholesale from Stoy and Strachey's OS6 system [15], as are many aspects of the file system. We give a summary description here for completeness. A stream is an object that can produce or consume items. Items can be arbitrary BCPL objects: bytes, words, vectors, other streams etc. There is a standard set of operations defined on every stream:

> Get an item from the stream;
>
> Put an item into the stream (normally only one of these is defined);
>
> Reset, which puts the stream into some standard initial state (the exact meaning of this operation depends on the type of the stream);
>
> Test for end of input;

and a few others. These operations are invoked by ordinary BCPL procedure calls.

A stream is thus something like a Simula class [6]. It differs from a class in that the procedures that implement the operations are not the same for all streams, and indeed can change from time to time, even for a particular stream. A stream is represented by a record (actually a BCPL vector) whose first few components contain procedures that provide that streams implementation of the standard operations. The rest of the record holds state information, which may vary from stream to stream (e.g. word counts, pointers to buffers, disk addresses, or whatever is appropriate). The size of the record is not fixed, but rather is determined entirely by the procedure that creates the stream.

It is also possible for the record to contain procedures that implement non-standard operations (e.g. set buffer size, read position in a disk file, etc.). Alternatively, arbitrary procedures can be written which perform such operations on certain types of stream. In both cases the procedure receives the record which represents the stream as an argument, and can store any permanent state information in that record. Of course, a program that uses a non-standard operation sacrifices compatibility, since it will only work with streams for which that operation is implemented.

This scheme for providing abstract objects with multiple implementations is used throughout the system. Each abstract object is defined by the operations that can be invoked on it; the semantics of each operation are defined (more or less rigorously). Any number of concrete implementations are possible, each providing a concrete procedure for each of the abstract operations. Hierarchical structures can be built up in this way. For instance, the procedure to create a stream object of concrete type "disk file stream" takes as parameters two other objects: a disk object which implements operations to access the storage on which the file resides, and a zone object which is used to acquire and release working storage for the stream.

3 Pages and files

The system organizes long-term storage (on disk) into files, each of which is a sequence of fixed-size pages; every page is represented by a single disk sector. Although a file is sufficient unto itself, one normally wants to be able to attach a string name to it, and for this purpose an auxiliary directory facility is provided. Since the integrity of long-term storage is of paramount importance to the user, a scavenging procedure is provided to reconstruct the state of the file system from whatever fragmented state it may have fallen into. The requirements of this procedure govern much of the system design. The remainder of this section expands on the outline just given.

3.1 Pages

The simplest object that can be used for long-term storage is a page. It consists of:

an *address*—one word which uniquely specifies a physical disk location (H);

a *label*, which consists of:

F: a file identifier—two words (A);

V: a version number—one word (A);

PN: a page number—one word (A);

L: a length (the number of bytes in this page that contain data)—one word (A);

NL: a next link—one word (H);

PL: a previous link—one word (H);

a *value*—256 data words (A).

The information that makes up a page is of two kinds: *absolutes* (A) and *hints* (H). The page is completely defined by the absolutes. The hints, therefore, are present solely to improve the efficiency of the implementation. Whenever a hint is used, it is checked against some absolute to confirm its continued validity. Furthermore, there is a recovery operation that reconstructs all the hints from the absolutes.

Thus a page has a unique absolute name, which is the file identifier, version number and page number (represented by (FV, n), where n is the page number and FV is the file identifier and version), and it has a *hint name*, which is the address. The *full name* (FN) of a page is the pair (absolute name, hint name). The links of the page (FV, n) are the addresses of the pages whose absolute names are (FV, $n-1$) and (FV, $n+1$), or NIL if no such pages exist. The basic operations on a page are to read and write the data, and to read the links, given the full name. Note that it is easy to go from the full name of a page to the full names of the next and previous pages.

3.2 Files

A file is a set of pages with absolute names (FV, 0), (FV, 1) (FV, n). The name of page (FV, 0) is also the name of the file. The basic operations on files are

create a new, empty file;

add a page to the end of a file;
delete one or more pages from the end;
delete the entire file.

Thus, if page (FV, n) exists, pages (FV, i) exist for all i between 0 and n. Hence, if the address of one page of a file is known, every page can be found by following the links. If (FV, n) is the last page of the file, then pages (FV, i) for $i < n$ have L=512 (i.e., they are full of data), and the last page has L<512.

The data bytes of the file are contained in pages 1 through n. Page 0 is called the *leader* page, and contains all the properties of the file other than its length and its data:

dates of creation, last write, and last read (A);
a string called the *leader name*, discussed in Section 3.5 (A);
the page number and disk address of the last page (H);
a *maybe consecutive* flag (H).

3.3 Representation of pages

The physical representation of a page on the disk is called a sector, and consists of three parts:

a *header*, which contains the disk pack number (different for each removable pack) and the disk address;

a label, which contains the seven words specified in Section 3.1;

a value, which contains the 256 data words.

A single disk operation can perform read, check or write actions independently on each of these parts, with the restriction that once a write is begun, it must continue through the rest of the sector. A check action compares data on the disk with corresponding data taken from memory, word by word, and aborts the entire operation if they don't match. If a memory word is 0, however, it is replaced by the corresponding disk word, so that a check action is a simple kind of pattern match.

The system uses these facilities to make the disk a rather robust storage medium. Disk pages are always accessed by their full names. The label of a sector is always checked before it is written, and is written on only three occasions:

When the page is freed—its full name must be given, and the check is that the label is the right one. Then ones are written into label and value, to ensure that any attempt to treat the page as part of a file will fail with a label check error.

The first time the page is written after it has been allocated—the check is that the page is free. Then the proper label for the page is written.

In order to change the length of the file—the label of the last page is read and checked. Then it is rewritten, possibly with new values of L and NL.

This scheme costs a disk revolution each time a page is allocated or freed, but it makes accidental overwriting of a page quite unlikely. On any other write the label is checked, at no cost in time. The check action is distinguished from a read so that a subsequent write operation can be aborted before anything is written, without taking an extra revolution. The label is also checked on reads, of course. If the checks succeed, it is certain that the hint (address) used to access a disk page actually leads to the page specified by the absolute part of the full name. As we shall see below, it is also possible to find a page from the absolute name alone (though not very efficiently) and to reconstruct all the hint names from the absolute names.

A disk contains a file called the *disk descriptor* with a standard name and disk address. In it are:

the *allocation map*, a bit table indicating which pages are free (H);

the disk *shape*, i.e., number of tracks, surfaces, and other information needed to parameterize the disk routines for a particular model of disk (A);

the name of the root directory (H).

Note that the allocation map is a hint because the absolute information about which pages are free is contained in the labels. If the map says that a page is free, the allocator marks it busy when allocating it, and when the label check described above fails, the allocator is called again to obtain another page. Thus a page improperly marked free in the map results in a little extra one-time disk activity. A page improperly marked busy will never be allocated; such lost pages are recovered by the Scavenger described in Section 3.5.

Our implementation of the disk descriptor is slightly different from the description above. The main directory has a standard name and disk address, and points to the disk descriptor file. This scheme arose because the disk descriptor was added to the file system data structure when it became apparent that the disk shape must be recorded in some way. The description given above reflects the logical relationship between the disk descriptor and the main directory (i.e., thats how we should have done it).

3.4 Directories

So far we have constructed a data storage facility based on pages, and an allocation facility based on files. Allocation is not provided at the page level because losing track of pages is too easy, which in turn is because a page, being of fixed size, cannot be a logical unit of storage. A file, on the other hand, can be of arbitrary size and hence is a suitable receptacle for a collection of data that the user views as a unit (as long as it isn't too small). Since a file is a logical unit, moreover, it should have a logical name, i.e., a string name, as well as its unique file identifier, and the name should be interpreted in some context, so that names can be assigned independently without fear of conflict.

This is the familiar line of reasoning which leads to a tree-structured directory hierarchy [5]. Our system takes a somewhat different tack (following OS6) because of our desire to treat files as independent objects in their own right. We take the view that any operation on a file can be performed with no more than a knowledge of its full name (which is the full name of its first page), and that a separate mechanism exists for associating names with files. This is done by a file called a *directory*, which contains a set of pairs (string, full name). A file may appear in any number of directories. Since there is nothing special about a directory from the point of view of the file system, it is possible to have a tree, or indeed an arbitrary directed graph, of directories. We do need to be able to identify all the directories for the scavenging procedure described below, and to this end we reserve a subset of the file identifiers for directory files.

A further implication (and here we part company with OS6) is that it must be possible to recover some logical name from the file itself, so that the file can survive even if the directory entries for it are lost or scrambled. This is the purpose of the leader name in the leader page; its significance should be apparent from the roles that it plays in scavenging. The information in the leader page is considered to be absolute, since this is a name by which the file can be located even if all the directory entries for it are destroyed. Directory entries, by contrast, are taken less seriously, although they are not entirely redundant and hence cannot be treated as pure hints. If a directory is destroyed, we don't lose any files, but we do lose some information, namely the information that a certain set of files was referenced from that directory by a certain set of names.

3.5 Scavenging

By reading all the labels on the disk, we can check that all the links are correct (reconstructing any that prove faulty), obtain full names for all existing files, and produce a list of free pages. To do this, all we have to do is create a list of all the labels not marked free and sort it by absolute name. If there is enough main storage to hold a table with 48 bits per sector, a suitable choice of data structure allows this processing to be done without any auxiliary storage. This is in fact the case for the machines standard disks. Larger disks require this list to be written on a specially reserved section of the disk.

We can then read all the directories and verify that each entry points to page 0 of an existing file, fixing up the address if necessary and detecting entries which point elsewhere. If any file remains unaccounted for by directory entries, we can make a new entry for it in the mail directory, using its leader name. This is the sole function of the leader name.

This entire process is called scavenging, and it takes about a minute for a 2.5 megabyte disk. When it is complete, all hints have been recomputed from absolutes, and any inconsistencies (incomplete files, null directory entries, nameless files, etc.) have been detected. The question of what to do with the inconsistencies is beyond the scope of this paper. During scavenging any permanently bad pages are marked in the label with a special value so that they will never be used again.

As we have noted, scavenging cannot fully reconstruct lost directories. This could be accomplished by writing a journal of all changes to directories and taking an occasional snapshot of all the directories. By applying the changes in the journal to the snapshot we would get back the current state. This is of course a standard technique by which the integrity of any database may be safeguarded. For the reasons already mentioned, we do not consider our directories important enough to warrant such attentions. If the user disagrees, he is free to modify the system-provided procedures for managing directories, or to write his own.

We have also written a more elaborate scavenger that does an in-place permutation of the file pages on the disk so that the pages of each file are in consecutive sectors. This arrangement typically increases the speed with which the files can he read sequentially by an order of magnitude over what is possible if the pages have become scattered.

3.6 Using hints

The purpose of hints is to increase performance. For example, if a program possesses the full name (FV, i) of a file page and the hint address, it can access the page directly without going through a directory lookup and without scanning down the chain of data blocks. If this direct access fails (i.e., the page at that hint address turns out not to be (FV, i)), the program has several options:

> It may have a full name for some other portion of the file (typically, the leader page) which is correct. Then it can follow links from that page, still avoiding the directory lookup. Hint addresses can also be kept for every k-th page of the file to reduce the number of links that must be followed.
>
> If this fails, it may look up the FV in a directory to obtain the proper disk address.
>
> If this fails, it may look up the string name of the file in a directory to obtain a new FV and disk address.
>
> Finally, it may invoke the Scavenger to reconstruct the entire file system and all the directories, and then retry one of the earlier steps.

Note that such a hint can be expanded to name a particular byte within the file system, simply by augmenting a full name with a byte position within the page.

The hint mechanism can also be used advantageously for files that are thought to be allocated consecutively. A program is free to assume that a file is consecutive and, knowing the address a_i of page i, to compute the address of page j as $a_i + j - i$. The label check will prevent any incorrect overwriting of data, and will inform the program whether the disk access succeeds.

Many programs use a collection of auxiliary files to which they need rapid access. The editor, for example, uses two scratch files, a journal file, a file of messages etc. When these programs are "installed", they create the necessary files and store hints for them in a data structure that is then written onto a *state file*. Subsequently the program can start up, read the state file, and access all its auxiliary files at maximum disk speed. If a hint fails, e.g. because a scratch file got deleted or moved, the program must repeat the installation phase. It doesnt matter where hints are stored, and the system makes no effort to keep them up to date. It simply insures that when a hint fails, no damage is done, and the program using the hint is informed so that it can take corrective action.

4 Communication between programs

A key objective of most operating systems is to foster communication between separate programs, often written in different programming languages or environments. But how can communication be provided by an open operating system that allows the programmer to reject all facilities of the system? The most conservative solution is to allow communication only through disk files, since the file structure must be observed by all programs. For example, a command scanner may write the command string typed by the user on a file with a standard name, and may then invoke a program that will execute the command. Ordinary disk files can be used in this way to pass data from one program to another. The disk file structure must also serve as a way to invoke an arbitrary program, that is, to "transfer control" from one program to another. Because of the openness of the operating system, the called and calling programs may have little or nothing in common.

These transfers of control are achieved by defining a convention for restoring the entire state of the machine from a disk file; this allows an arbitrary program to take control of the machine. The files that describe the machine state can be used to implement several control disciplines. A coroutine structure is commonly used: a program first records its state on one disk file, and then restores the machine state from a second file. The original program resumes execution when the machine state is restored from the first file.

The interprogram communication mechanism has found many uses. Examples are:

— Bootstrapping. A hardware bootstrap button causes the state of the machine to be restored from a disk file whose first page is kept at a fixed location on the disk. This *boot* file may be written by a linker that writes programs and data in the file, arranged so that they will constitute a running program when the machine state is restored from the file. Alternatively, the file may have been written by saving the state of a running program that will be resumed each time the machine is bootstrapped.

— Debugging. When a breakpoint is encountered or when the user strikes a special DEBUG key on the keyboard, the state of the machine is written on a disk file, and the machine state is restored from a file that contains the debugger. The debugging program may examine or alter the state of the faulty program by reading or writing portions of the file that was written as a result of the breakpoint. The debugger can later resume execution of the original program by restoring the machine state from the file. The original program and the debugger thus operate as coroutines.

— Checkpointing. A program may occasionally save its state on a disk file. It may then be interrupted, either by a processor malfunction or by user action (e.g., bootstrapping the machine). The computation may be resumed later by restoring the machine state from the checkpoint file.

— Activity switching. The coroutine structure is used to switch between several tasks that are part of a single application. One example is a *printing server*, a program that accepts files from a local communications network and prints them. The program is divided into two tasks: a *spooler* that reads files from the network and queues them in a disk file, and a *printer* that removes entries from the queue and controls the hardware that prints them. Because each of these tasks has considerable internal state and operates in a different environment, they communicate using the state save/restore mechanism. Whenever the spooler is idle but the queue is not empty, it saves its state and calls the printer. Whenever the printer is finished or detects incoming network traffic, it stops the printer hardware, saves its state, and invokes the spooler. This scheme easily allows printing to be interrupted in order to respond quickly to incoming files.

In many systems, state-restoring mechanisms would be extremely dangerous, as they could lead to severely damaged disk file structures. This may happen if a program is saved when it contains copies in memory of parts of the disk data structure (e.g., parts of a directory, or an allocation map that indicates free blocks) and it is never restored, or fails to update this information to reflect the actual disk state after it is restored. The label-checking machinery described in section 3.3 prevents catastrophic damage if the information is incorrectly updated. Moreover, hints that are saved and restored are usually still valid, and can be used to re-read quickly whatever disk data may have been cached in main memory.

4.1 InLoad and OutLoad

Two procedures, *InLoad* and *OutLoad*, are the ones most commonly used to operate on disk files containing machine states. Each routine takes as argument the full name of a disk file, and requires about a second to complete its operation:

$$(written,\ message) := OutLoad(OutFN)$$
$$InLoad(InFN,\ message)$$

OutLoad writes the current machine state on the file, and returns with the *written* flag true. Note that the program counter saved on the output file is inside the *OutLoad* procedure itself. The *InLoad* procedure restores the state of the machine from the given file, and passes a message (about 20 words) to the restored program. The effect is that *OutLoad* returns again, this time with *written* false and with the message that was provided in the *InLoad* call. Code for a coroutine linkage thus looks like:

```
. . .
messageToPartner = parameters to pass in coroutine call;
(written, messageFromPartner) := OutLoad(myStateFN);
if written then InLoad(partnerStateFN, messageToPartner);
messageFromPartner contains parameters passed to me;
. . .
```

If the parameters in the coroutine call will not fit in the small message vector, the vector is used to pass the full name of a place on the disk where the parameters have been written. Often the message contains a *return address*, that is, the full name of a file to restore upon return. In the example above, a return address can be provided by copying *myStateFN* into *messageToPartner* before the *InLoad* call.

The *InLoad* and *OutLoad* procedures, although quite small (about 900 words), are nevertheless subject to obliteration by a sufficiently errant program. For linkage to debuggers, it would be preferable if these routines were protected in some way. Machines without memory protection hardware should probably implement the procedures in read-only memory (or in processor microcode that cannot be damaged). We fashioned a partial solution to this problem with a special emergency bootstrap program, containing only the *OutLoad* procedure, that writes most of the machine state onto a disk file. Unfortunately, this method could not preserve some of the most vital state (e.g., processor registers).

5 Organization of the open system

The operating system is a collection of commonly used subroutine packages that are normally present in memory for the convenience of user programs. The system provides streams for disk files, keyboard input and display output; routines for reading and writing disk pages directly; the *OutLoad* and *InLoad* procedures; a free storage allocator; BCPL runtime routines; and storage for a good deal of handy data, such as hints for frequently-used files, the users name and password, etc. The subroutine packages are written almost entirely in BCPL, with consistent conventions for storage allocation and for object invocation.

5.1 Invoking programs

The system includes a procedure for invoking BCPL programs that execute under the operating system. Code for the program is read from a disk stream and loaded into low memory addresses. All references to operating system procedures are bound, using a fixup table contained in the code file. Finally, the program is invoked by calling a single entry routine. The program may terminate either by calling the program loader to read in another program and thus overlay the first program, or by returning from the main procedure. If the program returns, the system loads and runs a standard Executive program. The Executive accepts user commands from the keyboard and executes them, often by calling the loader to invoke a program the user has requested.

Programs that run under the operating system may also be invoked from an entirely different programming environment. The *InLoad* procedure is invoked on the file that contains the operating system state, which causes the system to be loaded and initialized. The message vector passed to *InLoad* may contain the name of a file containing the program to be invoked. A stream is opened on this file, and the program is loaded and run.

5.2 *Junta*

The packages that form the operating system are organized to support its openness. A program that prefers not to use the standard procedures provided by the system, or that needs to use the memory space occupied by them, may request that some or all system procedures be deleted from memory. The procedure that removes procedures is called *Junta* because it forcibly takes over the machine. When a program terminates, a *CounterJunta* procedure is called to restore the standard procedures from the *InLoad/OutLoad* context for the operating system.

The system is organized into several levels of services, so that a program may select the procedures it wishes to retain. Procedures are arranged so that the lowest level, which contains the most commonly used services, is at the very top of memory. Less ubiquitous services are in levels with higher numbers, located lower in memory. The highest level number to be retained is passed as an argument to *Junta*, which removes all higher-numbered levels and frees the storage they occupy. The *CounterJunta* procedure restores all levels that were removed, and reinitializes any data structures they contain.

The facilities in each level are summarized below:

1 *OutLoad/InLoad*, *CounterJunta*

2 Keyboard input buffer.

3 Hints for important files.

4 BCPL runtime procedures (e.g., stack frame allocator).

5,6 Disks (code and data for the disk object for the standard disk).

7 Zones (code for the standard free-storage object).

8 Disk streams (code for standard disk stream objects).

9 Disk directories.

10 Keyboard streams (code for standard keyboard stream object).

11 Display streams (code for standard display stream objects).

12 The program loader and Junta procedure.

13 System free storage, including room for default display stream, disk streams, etc.

The keyboard input buffer is present nearly always, so that any characters typed ahead by the user when running one program are saved for interpretation by the next.

The *Junta* and *CounterJunta* procedures give the programmer simple but precise control over the operating system facilities retained in memory. Unlike more elaborate mechanisms such as swapping code segments, this scheme guarantees the performance of the resident system. There is no distinction between procedures and data of the user and those of the system. The storage allocator, for example, will build zone objects to allocate any part of memory, whether in the system free storage region or not. The routine that creates a disk stream object requires two other objects as parameters: a zone to allocate space for the stream data structure (defaulted to the system free storage zone), and a disk object used to invoke disk transfers (defaulted to the "standard disk"). It is common for a program using a large non-standard disk to include a package that implements only the disk object for the special disk hardware, and to open streams on files using the standard operating system disk stream implementation.

A programmer desiring even more flexibility is encouraged to remove most of the system with *Junta* and to incorporate copies of the standard packages in his own program, placed wherever he wants. A common reason for this approach is that scarce memory space forces the programmer to overlay program structures. For example, a file server program that uses only the non-standard big disk nevertheless uses the standard disk stream package, organized in overlays. The display, keyboard, and storage-allocation packages have been assembled to form an operating system for use without a disk, used to support diagnostics or other programs that depend on network communications rather than on local disk storage.

The success of the operating system as a collection of subroutine packages depends primarily on the design of the packages. Retaining common procedures in memory simply saves disk space by reducing the size of many programs. Retaining common data structures in memory saves initialization time. The *Junta* procedure is a convenience, but not a necessity. It is the considerable effort that was devoted to refining the subroutine packages that makes them useful both as a cohesive operating system and as separate packages. Like any language design, this is a non-trivial undertaking whose difficulty is belied by the apparent simplicity of the result.

6 Conclusion

We have described the design of three major parts of a small operating system. In each case considerable trouble has been taken to make all the facilities accessible to users, in the sense that they can build up their own macro-operations from the primitives in the system if those provided by the system prove unsatisfactory. In the treatment of files we emphasized the methods used to minimize the probability that data will be destroyed. and to permit full automatic recovery after a crash. The program communication facilities emphasize reasonable communication between programs that take over the entire machine and organize it in different ways. The organization into levels accommodates programs which don't go quite so far, but still need a great deal of control over their own destiny; here proper design of the packages which make up the system to permit stand-alone operation is crucial.

The measures taken to make the file system robust, in which the label checking is crucial, have worked extremely well. Many thousands of file systems currently exist, running on hundreds of machines without any centralized maintenance. The incidence of complaints about lost information is negligible. The hint schemes have also worked well in making it possible to obtain high performance from the system. Because of inadequate explanation of the proper use of hints, however, many programmers did not understand exactly what was a hint and what was absolute, or how to recover properly from failure of a hint. As a result, it is more common than it should be for a program to crash with the message "Hint failed, please reinstall," rather than automatically invoking the proper recovery procedure.

The open character of the system has also been successful, and has fostered a large number of different programming environments that work together quite harmoniously. The Junta has been used frequently to remove standard handlers for human input/output that simulate a teletype terminal, so that experimental programs can control interaction very carefully, or in novel ways.

The disadvantages of openness are about what one would expect. Since it is not possible to virtualize the system, there is no practical way to change the representation or functionality of the file system or communications. Furthermore, there is no way to intercept all accesses to the file system, display, or whatever and direct them to some other device, such as a remote file system. This could be done only by changing the machines microcode.

Acknowledgements

Many of the facilities described above were first implemented by Gene McDaniel. The current implementation was done by the authors, and has since been improved by David Boggs. The original implementations of *InLoad/OutLoad* and of the Scavenger are due to Jim Morris.

References

1. Bensoussan, A., et al., "The Multics virtual memory," *Comm. ACM* **15**, 5 (May 1972).
2. Bobrow, D. G. et al., "Tenex, a paged time sharing system for the PDP-10," *Comm. ACM* **15**, 3 (March 1972).
3. Bobrow, D. G. and B. Wegbreit, "A model and stack implementation of multiple environments," *Comm. ACM* **16**, 10 (Oct 1973).
4. Brinch Hansen, P., *Operating Systems Principles*, Prentice-Hall, New York, 1973.
5. Corbato, F. J. et al., "An introduction and overview of the Multics system," *Proc. AFIPS Conf.* **27** (1965 FJCC).
6. Dahl, O-J. and C. A. R. Hoare, "Hierarchical program structures," in *Structured Programming*, Academic Press, New York, 1972.
7. Deutsch, L. P., "Experience with a microprogrammed Interlisp system," *IEEE Trans. Computers* **C-28**, 10 (Oct 1979).
8. Geschke, C. M., J. H. Morris Jr., and E. H. Satterthwaite, "Early experience with Mesa," *Comm. ACM* **20**, 8 (Aug 1977).
9. Hoare, C. A. R. and R. M. McKeag, "A survey of store management techniques," in *Operating Systems Techniques*, Academic Press, New York, 1972.
10. Ingalls, D., "The Smalltalk-76 programming system: Design and implementation," *Fifth ACM Symposium on Principles of Programming Languages*, Tucson, Arizona, Jan 1978.
11. Knuth, D. E. *The Art of Computer Programming*, vol. 1, Addison-Wesley, Reading, Mass., 1968.
12. Lampson, B. W. et al, "A user machine in a time-sharing system," *Proc IEEE* **54**, 12 (Dec 1966).
13. Meyer, P. A. and L. H. Seawright, "A virtual machine time-sharing system," *IBM Systems Journal* **9**, 3 (July 1970).
14. Richards, M., "BCPL: A tool for compiler writing and system programming," *Proc. AFIPS Conf.* **35** (1969 SJCC).
15. Stoy, J. E. and C. Strachey, "OS6—An experimental operating system for a small computer," *Computer Journal* **15**, 2 and 3.
16. Thacker, C.P. et. al., "Alto: A personal computer," to appear in *Computer Structures: Readings and Examples*, Sieworek, Bell and Newell, eds., McGraw-Hill, 1979.

19

PILOT: AN OPERATING SYSTEM FOR A PERSONAL COMPUTER*

DAVID D. REDELL, YOGEN K. DALAL, THOMAS R. HORSLEY, HUGH C. LAUER, WILLIAM C. LYNCH, PAUL R. McJONES, HAL G. MURRAY AND STEPHEN C. PURCELL

(1980)

The Pilot operating system provides a single-user, single language environment for higher level software on a powerful personal computer. Its features include virtual memory, a large "flat" file system, streams, network communication facilities, and concurrent programming support. Pilot thus provides rather more powerful facilities than are normally associated with personal computers. The exact facilities provided display interesting similarities to and differences from corresponding facilities provided in large multi-user systems. Pilot is implemented entirely in Mesa, a high-level system programming language. The modularization of the implementation displays some interesting aspects in terms of both the static structure and dynamic interactions of the various components.

1 Introduction

As digital hardware becomes less expensive, more resources can be devoted to providing a very high grade of interactive service to computer users. One important expression of this trend is the personal computer. The dedication of a substantial computer to each individual user suggests an operating

*D. D. Redell, Y. K. Dalal, T. R. Horseley, H. C. Lauer, W. C. Lynch, P. R. McJones, H. G. Murray and S. C. Purcell, Pilot: an operating system for a personal computer. *Communications of the ACM 23*, 2 (February 1980), 81–92.

system design emphasizing close user/system cooperation, allowing full exploitation of a resource-rich environment. Such a system can also function as its user's representative in a larger community of autonomous personal computers and other information resources, but tends to deemphasize the largely ajudicatory role of a monolithic time-sharing system.

The Pilot operating system is designed for the personal computing environment. It provides a basic set of services within which higher level programs can more easily serve the user and/or communicate with other programs on other machines. Pilot omits certain functions that have been integrated into some other operating systems, such as character-string naming and user-command interpretation; such facilities are provided by higher level software, as needed. On the other hand, Pilot provides a more complete set of services than is normally associated with the "kernel" or "nucleus" of an operating system. Pilot is closely coupled to the Mesa programming language [16] and runs on a rather powerful personal computer, which would have been thought sufficient to support a substantial time-sharing system of a few years ago. The primary user interface is a high resolution bit-map display, with a keyboard and a pointing device. Secondary storage is provided by a sizable moving-arm disk. A local packet network provides a high bandwidth connection to other personal computers and to server systems offering such remote services as printing and shared file storage.

Much of the design of Pilot stems from an initial set of assumptions and goals rather different from those underlying most time-sharing systems. Pilot is a single-language, single-user system, with only limited features for protection and resource allocation. Pilot's protection mechanisms are *defensive*, rather than *absolute* [9], since in a single-user system, errors are a more serious problem than maliciousness. All protection in Pilot ultimately depends on the type-checking provided by Mesa, which is extremely reliable but by no means impenetrable. We have chosen to ignore such problems as "Trojan Horse" programs [20], not because they are unimportant, but because our environment allows such threats to be coped with adequately from outside the system. Similarly, Pilot's resource allocation features are not oriented toward enforcing fair distribution of scarce resources among contending parties. In traditional multi-user systems, most resources tend to be in short supply, and prevention of inequitable distribution is a serious problem. In a single-user system like Pilot, shortage of some resource must generally be dealt with either through more effective utilization or by adding more of the resource.

The close coupling between Pilot and Mesa is based on mutual interdependence; Pilot is written in Mesa, and Mesa depends on Pilot for much of its runtime support. Since other languages are not supported, many of the language-independence arguments that tend to maintain distance between an operating system and a programming language are not relevant. In a sense, all of Pilot can be thought of as a very powerful runtime support package for the Mesa language, Naturally, none of these considerations eliminates the need for careful structuring of the combined Pilot/Mesa system to avoid accidental circular dependencies.

Since the Mesa programming language formalizes and emphasizes the distinction between an *interface* and its *implementation*, it is particularly appropriate to split the description of Pilot along these lines. As an environment for its client programs, Pilot consists of a set of Mesa interfaces, each defining a group of related types, operations, and error signals. Section 2 enumerates the major interfaces of Pilot and describes their semantics, in terms of both the formal interface and the intended behavior of the system as a whole. As a Mesa program, Pilot consists of a large collection of modules supporting clients. Section 3 describes the interior structure of the Pilot implementation and mentions a few of the lessons learned in implementing an operating system in Mesa.

2 Pilot Interfaces

In Mesa, a large software system is constructed from two kinds of modules: *program* modules specify the algorithms and the actual data structures comprising the *implementation* of the system, while *definitions* modules formally specify the *interfaces* between program modules. Generally, a given interface, defined in a definitions module, is *exported* by one program module (its *implementor*) and *imported* by one or more other program modules (its *clients*). Both program and definitions modules are written in the Mesa source language and are compiled to produce binary object modules. The object form of a program module contains the actual code to be executed; the object form of a definitions module contains detailed specifications controlling the binding together of program modules. Modular programming in Mesa is discussed in more detail by Lauer and Satterthwaite [13].

Pilot contains two kinds of interfaces.

(1) *Public* interfaces defining the services provided by Pilot to its clients (i.e., higher level Mesa programs);

(2) *Private* interfaces, which form the connective tissue binding the implementation together.

This section describes the major features supported by the public interfaces of Pilot, including files, virtual memory, streams, network communication, and concurrent programming support. Each interface defines some number of named items, which are denoted *Interface.Item*. There are four kinds of items in interfaces: types, procedures, constants, and error signals. (For example, the interface *File* defines the type *File.Capability*, the procedure *File.Create*, the constant *file.maxPagesPerFile*, and the error signal *File.Unknown*.) The discussion that follows makes no attempt at complete enumeration of the items in each interface, but focuses instead on the overall facility provided, emphasizing the more important and unusual features of Pilot.

2.1 Files

The Pilot interfaces *File* and *Volume* define the basic facilities for permanent storage of data. Files are the standard containers for information storage; volumes represent the media on which files are stored (e.g., magnetic disks). Higher level software is expected to superimpose further structure on files and volumes as necessary (e.g., an executable subsystem on a file, or a detachable directory subtree on a removable volume). The emphasis at the Pilot level is on simple but powerful primitives for accessing large bodies of information. Pilot can handle files containing up to about a million pages of English text, and volumes larger than any currently available storage device ($\sim 10^{13}$ bits). The total number of files and volumes that can exist is essentially unbounded (2^{64}). The space of files provided is "flat," in the sense that files have no recognized relationships among them (e.g., no directory hierarchy). The size of a file is adjustable in units of pages. As discussed below, the contents of a file are accessed by mapping one or more of its pages into a section of virtual memory.

The *File.Create* operation creates a new file and returns a capability for it. Pilot file capabilities are intended for *defensive* protection against errors [9]; they are mechanically similar to capabilities used in other systems for absolute protection, but are not designed to withstand determined attack by a malicious programmer. More significant than the protection aspect of capabilities is the fact that files and volumes are named by 64-bit universal identifiers (uids) which are guaranteed unique in both space and time. This means that distinct files, created anywhere at any time by any incarnation of Pilot, will always have distinct uids. This guarantee is crucial, since removable volumes are expected to be a standard method of transporting information from one Pilot system to another. If uid ambiguity were allowed (e.g., different files on the same machine with the same uid), Pilot's life would become more difficult, and uids would be much less useful to clients. To guarantee uniqueness, Pilot essentially concatenates the machine serial number with the real time clock to produce each new uid.

Pilot attaches only a small fixed set of attributes to each file, with the expectation that a higher level directory facility will provide an extendible mechanism for associating with a file more general properties unknown to Pilot (e.g., length in bytes, date of creation, etc.). Pilot recognizes only four attributes: size, type, permanence, and immutability.

The *size* of a file is adjustable from 0 pages to 2^{23} pages, each containing 512 bytes. When the size of a file is increased, Pilot attempts to avoid fragmentation of storage on the physical device so that sequential or otherwise clustered accesses can exploit physical contiguity. On the other hand, random probes into a file are handled as efficiently as possible, by minimizing file system mapping overhead.

The *type* of a file is a 16-bit tag which is essentially uninterpreted, but is implemented at the Pilot level to aid in type-dependent recovery of the file system (e.g., after a system failure). Such recovery is discussed further in Section 3.4.

Permanence is an attribute attached to Pilot files that are intended to hold valuable permanent information. The intent is that creation of such a file proceed in four steps:

(1) The file is created using *File.Create* and has temporary status.

(2) A capability for the file is stored in some permanent directory structure.

(3) The file is made permanent using the *File.MakePermanent* operation.

(4) The valuable contents are placed in the file.

If a system failure occurs before step 3, the file will be automatically deleted (by the scavenger; see Section 3.4) when the system restarts; if a system failure occurs after step 2, the file is registered in the directory structure and is thereby accessible. (In particular, a failure between steps 2 and 3 produces a registered but nonexistent file, an eventuality which any robust directory system must be prepared to cope with.) This simple mechanism solves the "lost object problem" [25] in which inaccessible files take up space but cannot be deleted. Temporary files are also useful as scratch storage which will be reclaimed automatically in case of system failure.

A Pilot file may be made *immutable*. This means that it is permanently read-only and may never be modified again under any circumstances. The intent is that multiple physical copies of an immutable file, all sharing the *same* universal identifier, may be replicated at many physical sites to improve accessibility without danger of ambiguity concerning the contents of the file. For example, a higher level "linkage editor" program might wish to link a pair of object-code files by embedding the uid of one in the other. This would be efficient and unambiguous, but would fail if the contents were copied into a new pair of files, since they would have different uids. Making such files immutable and using a special operation (*File.ReplicateImmutable*) allows propagation of physical copies to other volumes without changing the uids, thus preserving any direct uid-level bindings.

As with files, Pilot treats volumes in a straightforward fashion, while at the same time avoiding oversimplifications that would render its facilities inadequate for demanding clients. Several different sizes and types of storage devices are supported as Pilot volumes. (All are varieties of moving-arm disk, removable or nonremovable; other nonvolatile random access storage devices could be supported.) The simplest notion of a volume would correspond one to one with a physical storage medium. This is too restrictive, and hence the abstraction presented at the *Volume* interface is actually a *logical volume*; Pilot is fairly flexible about the correspondence between logical volumes and *physical volumes* (e.g., disk packs, diskettes, etc.). On the one hand, it is possible to have a large logical volume which spans several physical volumes. Conversely, it is possible to put several small logical volumes on the same physical volume. In all cases, Pilot recognizes the comings and goings of physical volumes (e.g., mounting a disk pack) and makes accessible to client programs those logical volumes all of whose pages are on-line.

Two examples which originally motivated the flexibility of the volume machinery were database applications, in which a very large database could be cast as a multi-disk-pack volume, and the CoPilot debugger, which requires its own separate logical volume (see Section 2.5), but must be usable on a single-disk machine.

2.2 Virtual Memory

The machine architecture on which Pilot runs defines a simple linear virtual memory of up to 2^{32} 16-bit words. All computations on the machine (including Pilot itself) run in the same address space, which is unadorned with any noteworthy features, save a set of three flags attached to each page: *referenced*, *written*, and *write-protected.* Pilot structures this homogenous address space into contiguous runs of page called *spaces*, accessed through the interface *Space*. Above the level of Pilot, client software superimposes still further structure upon the contents of spaces, casting them as client-defined data structures within the Mesa language.

While the underlying linear virtual memory is conventional and fairly straightforward, the space machinery superimposed by Pilot is somewhat novel in its design, and rather more powerful than one would expect given the simplicity of the *Space* interface. A space is capable of playing three fundamental roles:

Allocation Entity. To allocate a region of virtual memory, a client creates a space of appropriate size.

Mapping Entity. To associate information content and backing store with a region of virtual memory, a client maps a space to a region of some file.

Swapping Entity. The transfer of pages between primary memory and backing store is performed in units of spaces.

Any given space may play any or all of these roles. Largely because of their multifunctional nature, it is often useful to nest spaces. A new space is always created as a subspace of some previously existing space, so that the set of all spaces forms a tree by containment, the root of which is a predetermined space covering all of virtual memory.

Spaces function as allocation entities in two senses: when a space is created, by calling *Space.Create*, it is serving as the unit of allocation; if it is later broken into subspaces, it is serving as an allocation subpool within which smaller units are allocated and freed [19]. Such suballocation may be nested to several levels; at some level (typically fairly quickly) the page granularity of the space mechanism becomes too coarse, at which point finer grained allocation must be performed by higher level software.

Spaces function as mapping entities when the operation *Space.Map* is applied to them. This operation associates the space with a run of pages in a file, thus defining the content of each page of the space as the content of its associated file page, and propagating the write-protection status of the file capability to the space. At any given time, a page in virtual memory may be accessed only if its content is well-defined, i.e., if *exactly one* of the nested spaces containing it is mapped. If none of the containing spaces is mapped, the fatal error *AddressFault* is signaled. (The situation in which more than one containing space is mapped cannot arise, since the *Space.Map* operation checks that none of the ancestors or descendents of a space being mapped are themselves already mapped.) The decision to cast *AddressFault* and *WriteProtectFault* (i.e., storing into a write-protected space) as fatal errors is based on the judgment that any program which has incurred such a fault is misusing the virtual memory facilities and should be debugged; to this end, Pilot unconditionally activates the CoPilot debugger (see Section 2.5).

Spaces function as swapping entities when a page of a mapped space is found to be missing from primary memory. The swapping strategy followed is essentially to swap in the lowest level (i.e., smallest) space containing the page (see Section 3.2). A client program can thus optimize its swapping behavior by subdividing its mapped spaces into subspaces containing items whose access patterns are known to be strongly correlated. In the absence of such subdivision, the entire mapped space is swapped in. Note that while the client can always opt for demand paging (by breaking a space up into one-page subspaces), this is *not* the default, since it tends to promote thrashing. Further optimization is possible using the *Space.Activate* operation. This operation advises Pilot that a space will be used soon and should be swapped in as soon as possible. The inverse operation, *Space.Deactivate*, advises Pilot that a space is no longer needed in primary memory. The *Space.Kill* operation advises Pilot that the current contents of a space are of no further interest (i.e., will be completely overwritten before next being read) so that useless swapping of the data may be suppressed. These forms of optional advice are intended to allow tuning of heavy traffic periods by eliminating unnecessary transfers, by scheduling the disk arm efficiently, and by ensuring that during the visit to a given arm position all of the appropriate transfers take place. Such advice-taking is a good example of a feature which has been deemed undesirable by most designers of timesharing systems, but which can be very useful in the context of a dedicated personal computer.

There is an intrinsic close coupling between Pilot's file and virtual memory features: virtual memory is the only access path to the contents of files, and files are the only backing store for virtual memory. An alternative would have been to provide a separate backing store for virtual memory and require that clients transfer data between virtual memory and files using explicit read/write operations. There are several reasons for preferring the mapping approach, including the following.

(1) Separating the operations of mapping and swapping decouples buffer allocation from disk scheduling, as compared with explicit file read/write operations.

(2) When a space is mapped, the read/write privileges of the file capability can propagate automatically to the space by setting a simple read/write lock in the hardware memory map, allowing illegitimate stores to be caught immediately.

(3) In either approach, there are certain cases that generate extra unnecessary disk transfers; extra "advice-taking" operations like *Space.Kill* can eliminate the extra disk transfers in the mapping approach; this does not seem to apply to the read/write approach.

(4) It is relatively easy to simulate a read/write interface given a mapping interface, and with appropriate use of advice, the efficiency can be essentially the same. The converse appears to be false.

The Pilot virtual memory also provides an advice-like operation called *Space.ForceOut*, which is designed as an underpinning for client crash-recovery algorithms. (It is advice-like in that its effect is invisible in normal operation, but becomes visible if the system crashes.) *ForceOut* causes a space's contents to be written to its backing file and does not return until the write is completed. This means that the contents will survive a subsequent system crash. Since Pilot's page replacement algorithm is also free to write the pages to the file at any time (e.g., between *ForceOuts*), this facility by itself does not constitute even a minimal crash recovery mechanism; it is intended only as a "toehold" for higher level software to use in providing transactional atomicity in the face of system crashes.

2.3 Streams and I/0 Devices

A Pilot client can access an I/O device in three different ways:

(1) *implicitly*, via some feature of Pilot (e.g., a Pilot file accessed via virtual memory);

(2) *directly*, via a low-level device driver interface exported from Pilot;

(3) *indirectly*, via the Pilot stream facility.

In keeping with the objectives of Pilot as an operating system for a personal computer, most I/O devices are made directly available to clients through low-level procedural interfaces. These interfaces generally do little more than convert device-specific I/O operations into appropriate procedure calls. The emphasis is on providing maximum flexibility to client programs; protection is not required. The only exception to this policy is for devices accessed implicitly by Pilot itself (e.g., disks used for files), since chaos would ensue if clients also tried to access them directly.

For most applications, direct device access via the device driver interface is rather inconvenient, since all the details of the device are exposed to view. Furthermore, many applications tend to reference devices in a basically sequential fashion, with only occasional, and usually very stylized, control or repositioning operations. For these reasons, the Pilot *stream* facility is provided, comprising the following components:

(1) The *stream* interface, which defines device independent operations for full-duplex sequential access to a source/sink of data. This is very similar in spirit to the stream facilities of other operating systems, such as OS6 [23] and UNIX [18].

(2) A standard for *stream components*, which connect streams to various devices and/or implement "on-the-fly" transformations of the data flowing through them.

(3) A means for cascading a number of primitive stream components to provide a compound stream.

There are two kinds of stream components defined by Pilot: the transducer and the filter. A *transducer* is a module which imports a device driver interface and exports an instance of the Pilot *Stream* interface. The transducer is thus the implementation of the basic sequential access facility for that device. Pilot provides standard transducers for a variety of supported devices. A *filter* is a module which imports one instance of the Pilot standard *Stream* interface and exports another. Its purpose is to transform a stream of data "on the fly" (e.g., to do code or format conversion). Naturally, clients can augment the standard set of stream components provided with Pilot by writing filters and transducers of their own. The *Stream* interface provides for dynamic binding of stream components at runtime, so that a transducer and a set of filters can be cascaded to provide a *pipeline*, as shown in Figure 1.

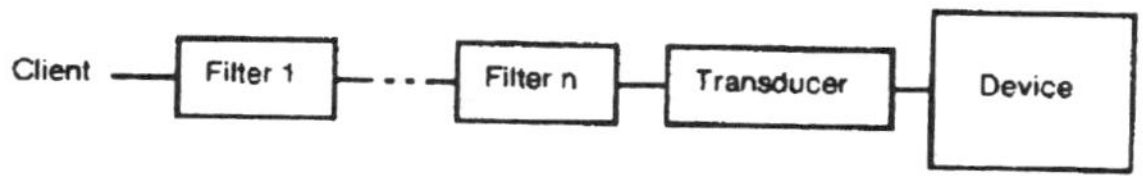

Figure 1 A pipeline of cascaded stream components.

The transducer occupies the lowest position in the pipeline (i.e., nearest the device) while the client program accesses the highest position. Each filter accesses the next lower filter (or transducer) via the *Stream* interface, just as if it were a client program, so that no component need be aware of its position in the pipeline, or of the nature of the device at the end. This facility resembles the UNIX pipe and filter facility, except that it is implemented at the module level within the Pilot virtual memory, rather than as a separate system task with its own address space.

2.4 Communications

Mesa supports a shared-memory style of interprocess communication for *tightly coupled* processes [11]. Interaction between *loosely coupled* processes (e.g. suitable to reside on different machines) is provided by the Pilot *communications* facility. This facility allows client processes in different machines to communicate with each other via a hierarchically structured family of packet communication protocols. Communication software is an integral part of Pilot, rather than an optional addition, because Pilot is intended to be a suitable foundation for network-based distributed systems.

The protocols are designed to provide communication across multiple interconnected networks. An interconnection of networks is referred to as an *internet*. A Pilot internet typically consists of local, high bandwidth Ethernet broadcast networks [15], and public and private long-distance data networks like SBS, TELENET, TYMNET, DDS, and ACS. Constituent networks are interconnected by *internetwork routers* (often referred to as *gateways* in the literature) which store and forward packets to their destination using distributed routing algorithms [2, 4]. The constituent networks of an internet are used only as a transmission medium. The source, destination, and internetwork router computers are *all* Pilot machines. Pilot provides software drivers for a variety of networks; a given machine may connect directly to one or several networks of the same or different kinds.

Pilot clients identify one another by means of *network addresses* when they wish to communicate and need not know anything about the internet topology or each other's locations or even the structure of a network address. In particular, it is not necessary that the two communicators be on different computers. If they are on the same computer, Pilot will optimize the transmission of data between them and will avoid use of the physical network resources. This implies that an isolated computer (i.e. one which is not connected to any network) may still contain the communications facilities of Pilot. Pilot clients on the same computer should communicate with one another using Pilot's communications facilities, as opposed to the tightly coupled mechanisms of Mesa, if the communicators are loosely coupled subsystems that could some day be reconfigured to execute on different machines on the network. For example, printing and file storage server programs written to communicate in the loosely coupled mode could share the same machine if the combined load were light, yet be easily moved to separate machines if increased load justified the extra cost.

A network address is a resource assigned to clients by Pilot and identifies a specific *socket* on a specific machine. A socket is simply a site from which packets are transmitted and at which packets are received; it is rather like a post office box, in the sense that there is no assumed relationship among the packets being sent and received via a given socket. The identity of a socket is unique only at a given point in time; it *may* be reused, since there is no long-term static association between the socket and any other resources. Protection against dangling references (e.g., delivery of packets intended for a previous instance of a given socket) is guaranteed by higher level protocols.

A network address is, in reality, a triple consisting of a 16-bit network number, a 32-bit processor ID, and a 16-bit socket number, represented by a system-wide Mesa data type *System.NetworkAddress*. The internal structure of a network address is not used by clients, but by the communications facilities of Pilot and the internetwork routers to deliver a packet to its destination. The administrative procedures for the assignment of network numbers and processor IDs to networks and computers, respectively, are outside the scope of this paper, as are the mechanisms by which clients find out each others' network addresses.

The family of packet protocols by which Pilot provides communication is based on our experiences with the Pup Protocols [2]. The Arpa Internetwork Protocol family [8] resemble our protocols in spirit. The protocols fall naturally into three levels:

Level 0: Every packet must be encapsulated for transmission over a particular communication medium, according to the network-specific rules for that communication medium. This has been termed level 0 in our protocol hierarchy, since its definition is of no concern to the typical Pilot client.

Level 1: Level 1 defines the format of the *internetwork packet*, which specifies among other things the source and destination network addresses, a checksum field, the length of the entire packet, a transport control field that is used by internetwork routers, and a packet type field that indicates the kind of packet defined at level 2.

Level 2: A number of level 2 packet formats exist, such as error packet, connection-oriented sequenced packet, routing table update packet, and so on. Various level 2 protocols are defined according to the kinds of level 2 packets they use, and the rules governing their interaction.

The *Socket* interface provides level 1 access to the communication facilities, including the ability to create a socket at a (local) network address, and to transmit and receive internetwork packets. In the terms of Section 2.3, sockets can be thought of as *virtual devices*, accessed directly via the *Socket* (virtual driver) interface. The protocol defining the format of the internetwork packet provides end-to-end communication at the packet level. The internet is required only to be able to transport independently addressed packets from source to destination network addresses. As a consequence, packets transmitted over a socket may be expected to arrive at their destination only with *high probability* and not necessarily in the order they were transmitted. It is the responsibility of the communicating end processes to agree upon higher level protocols that provide the appropriate level of reliable communication. The *Socket* interface, therefore, provides service similar to that provided by networks that offer *datagram* services [171 and is most useful for connectionless protocols.

The interface *NetworkStream* defines the principal means by which Pilot clients can communicate reliably between any two network addresses. It provides access to the implementation of the *sequenced packet protocol*—a level 2 protocol. This protocol provides sequenced, duplicate-suppressed, error-free, flow-controlled packet communication over arbitrarily interconnected communication networks and is similar in philosophy to the Pup Byte Stream Protocol [2l or the Arpa Transmission Control Protocol [3, 24]. This protocol is implemented as a transducer, which converts the device-like *Socket* interface into a Pilot stream. Thus all data transmission via a network stream is invoked by means of the operations defined in the standard *Stream* interface.

Network streams provide reliable communication, in the sense that the data is reliably sent from the source transducer's packet buffer to the destination transducer's packet buffer. No guarantees can be made as to whether the data was successfully received by the destination client or that the data was appropriately processed. This final degree of reliability must lie with the clients of network streams, since they alone know the higher level protocol governing the data transfer. Pilot provides communication with varying degrees of reliability, since the communicating clients will, in general, have differing needs for it. This is in keeping with the design goals of Pilot, much like the provision of defensive rather than absolute protection.

A network stream can be set up between two communicators in many ways. The most typical case, in a network-based distributed system, involves a *server* (a supplier of a service) at one end and a *client* of the service at the other. Creation of such a network stream is inherently asymmetric. At one end is the server which advertises a network address to which clients can connect to obtain its services. Clients do this by calling *NetworkStream.Create*, specifying the address of the server as parameter. It is important that concurrent requests from clients not conflict over the server's network address; to avoid this, some additional machinery is provided at the server end of the connection. When a server is operational, one of its processes *listens* for requests on its advertised network address. This is done by calling *NetworkStream.Listen*, which automatically creates a new network stream each time a request arrives at the specified network address. The newly created network stream connects the client to *another* unique network address on the server machine, leaving the server's advertised network address free for the reception of additional requests.

The switchover from one network address to another is transparent to the client, and is part of the definition of the sequenced packet protocol. At the server end, the *Stream.Handle* for the newly created stream is typically passed to an *agent*, a subsidiary process or subsystem which gives its full attention to performing the service for that particular client. These two then communicate by means of the new network stream set up between them for the duration of the service. Of course, the *NetworkStream* interface also provides mechanisms for creating connections between arbitrary network addresses, where the relationship between the processes is more general than that of server and client.

The mechanisms for establishing and deleting a connection between any two communicators and for guarding against old duplicate packets are a departure from the mechanisms used by the Pup Byte Stream Protocol [2] or the Transmission Control Protocol [22], although our protocol embodies similar principles. A network stream is terminated by calling *NetworkStream.Delete*. This call initiates no network traffic and simply deletes all the data structures associated with the network stream. It is the responsibility of the communicating processes to have decided *a priori* that they wish to terminate the stream. This is in keeping with the decision that the reliable processing of the transmitted data ultimately rests with the clients of network streams.

The manner in which server addresses are advertised by servers and discovered by clients is not defined by Pilot; this facility must be provided by the architecture of a particular distributed system built on Pilot. Generally, the binding of names of resources to their addresses is accomplished by means of a network-based database referred to as a *clearinghouse*. The manner in which the binding is structured and the way in which clearinghouses are located and accessed are outside the scope of this paper.

The communication facilities of Pilot provide clients various interfaces, which provide varying degrees of service at the internetworking level. In keeping with the overall design of Pilot, the communication facility attempts to provide a standard set of features which capture the most common needs, while still allowing clients to custom tailor their own solutions to their communications requirements if that proves necessary.

2.5 Mesa Language Support

The Mesa language provides a number of features which require a nontrivial amount of runtime support [16]. These are primarily involved with the control structure of the language [10, 11] which allow not only recursive procedure calls, but also coroutines, concurrent processes, and signals (a specialized form of dynamically bound procedure call used primarily for exception handling). The runtime support facilities are invoked in three ways:

(1) explicitly, via normal Mesa interfaces exported by Pilot (e.g., the *Process* interface);

(2) implicitly, via compiler-generated calls on built-in procedures;

(3) via traps, when machine-level op-codes encounter exceptional conditions.

Pilot's involvement in client procedure calls is limited to trap handling when the supply of activation record storage is exhausted. To support the full generality of the Mesa control structures, activation records are allocated from a heap, even when a strict LIFO usage pattern is in force. This heap is replenished and maintained by Pilot.

Coroutine calls also proceed without intervention by Pilot, except during initialization when a trap handler is provided to aid in the original setup of the coroutine linkage.

Pilot's involvement with concurrent processes is somewhat more substantial. Mesa casts process creation as a variant of a procedure call, but unlike a normal procedure call, such a FORK statement *always* invokes Pilot to create the new process. Similarly, termination of a process also involves substantial participation by Pilot. Mesa also provides monitors and condition variables for synchronized interprocess communication via shared memory; these facilities are supported directly by the machine and thus require less direct involvement of Pilot.

The Mesa control structure facilities, including concurrent processes, are light weight enough to be used in the fine-scale structuring of normal Mesa programs. A typical Pilot client program consists of some number of processes, any of which may at any time invoke Pilot facilities through the various public interfaces. It is Pilot's responsibility to maintain the semantic integrity of its interfaces in the face of such client-level concurrency (see Section 3.3). Naturally, any higher level consistency constraints invented by the client must be guaranteed by client-level synchronization, using monitors and condition variables as provided in the Mesa language.

Another important Mesa-support facility which is provided as an integral part of Pilot is a "world-swap" facility to allow a graceful exit to CoPilot, the Pilot/Mesa interactive debugger. The world-swap facility saves the contents of memory and the total machine state and then starts CoPilot from a *boot-file*, just as if the machine's bootstrap-load button had been pressed. The original state is saved on a second boot-file so that execution can be resumed by doing a second world-swap. The state is saved with sufficient care that it is virtually always possible to resume execution without any detectable perturbation of the program being debugged. The world-swap approach to debugging yields strong isolation between the debugger and the program under test. Not only the contents of main memory, but the version of Pilot, the accessible volume(s), and even the microcode can be different in the two worlds. This is especially useful when debugging a new version of Pilot, since CoPilot can run on the old, stable version until the new version becomes trustworthy. Needless to say, this approach is not directly applicable to conventional multi-user time-sharing systems.

3 Implementation

The implementation of Pilot consists of a large number of Mesa modules which collectively provide the client environment as decribed above. The modules are grouped into larger *components*, each of which is responsible for implementing some coherent subset of the overall Pilot functionality. The relationships among the major components are illustrated in Figure 2.

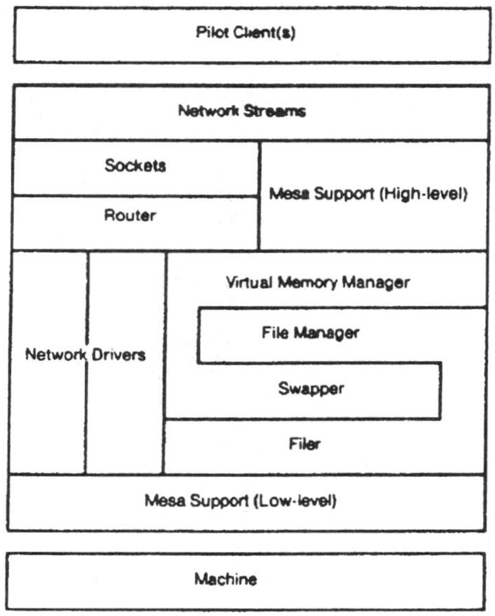

Figure 2 Major components of Pilot.

Of particular interest is the interlocking structure of the four components of the *storage system* which together implement files and virtual memory. This is an example of what we call the *manager/kernel* pattern, in which a given facility is implemented in two stages: a low-level kernel provides a basic core of function, which is extended by the higher level manager. Layers interposed between the kernel and the manager can make use of the kernel and can in turn be used by the manager. The same basic technique has been used before in other systems to good effect, as discussed by Habermann et al. [6], who refer to it as "functional hierarchy." It is also quite similar to the familiar "policy/mechanism" pattern [1, 25]. The main difference is that we place no emphasis on the possibility of using the same kernel with a variety of managers (or without any manager at all). In Pilot, the manager/kernel pattern is intended only as a fruitful decomposition tool for the design of integrated mechanisms.

3.1 Layering of the Storage System Implementation

The kernel/manager pattern can be motivated by noting that since the purpose of Pilot is to provide a more hospitable environment than the bare machine, it would clearly be more pleasant for the code implementing Pilot if it could use the facilities of Pilot in getting its job done. In particular, both components of the *storage system* (the file and virtual memory implementations) maintain internal databases which are too large to fit in primary memory, but only parts of which are needed at any one time. A client-level program would simply place such a database in a file and access it via virtual memory, but if Pilot itself did so, the resulting circular dependencies would tie the system in knots, making it unreliable and difficult to understand. One alternative would be the invention of a special separate mechanism for low-level disk access and main memory buffering, used only by the storage system to access its internal databases. This would eliminate the danger of circular dependency but would introduce more machinery, making the system bulkier and harder to understand in a different sense. A more attractive alternative is the extraction of a streamlined kernel of the storage system functionality with the following properties:

(1) It can be implemented by a small body of code which resides permanently in primary memory.

(2) It provides a powerful enough storage facility to significantly ease the implementation of the remainder of the full-fledged storage system.

(3) It can handle the majority of the "fast cases" of client-level use of the storage system.

Figure 2 shows the implementation of such a kernel storage facility by the swapper and the filer. These two subcomponents are the kernels of the virtual memory and file components, respectively, and provide a reasonably powerful environment for the nonresident subcomponents, the virtual memory manager, and the file manager, whose code and data are both swappable. The kernel environment provides somewhat restricted virtual memory access to a small number of special files and to preexisting normal files of fixed size.

The managers implement the more powerful operations, such as file creation and deletion, and the more complex virtual memory operations, such as those that traverse subtrees of the hierarchy of nested spaces. The most frequent operations, however, are handled by the kernels essentially on their own. For example, a page fault is handled by code in the swapper, which calls the filer to read the appropriate page(s) into memory, adjusts the hardware memory map, and restarts the faulting process.

The resident data structures of the kernels serve as caches on the swappable databases maintained by the managers. Whenever a kernel finds that it cannot perform an operation using only the data in its cache, it conceptually "passes the buck" to its manager, retaining no state information about the failed operation. In this way, a circular dependency is avoided, since such failed operations become the total responsibility of the manager. The typical response of a manager in such a situation is to consult its swappable database, call the resident subcomponent to update its cache, and then retry the failed operation.

The intended dynamics of the storage system implementation described above are based on the expectation that Pilot will experience three quite different kinds of load.

(1) For short periods of time, client programs will have their essentially static working sets in primary memory and the storage system will not be needed.

(2) Most of the time, the client working set will be changing slowly, but the description of it will fit in the swapper/filer caches, so that swapping can take place with little or no extra disk activity to access the storage system databases.

(3) Periodically, the client working set will change drastically, requiring extensive reloading of the caches as well as heavy swapping.

It is intended that the Pilot storage system be able to respond reasonably to all three situations: In case (1), it should assume a low profile by allowing its swappable components (e.g., the managers) to swap out. In case (2), it should be as efficient as possible, using its caches to avoid causing spurious disk activity. In case (3), it should do the best it can, with the understanding that while continuous operation in this mode is probably not viable, short periods of heavy traffic can and must be optimized, largely via the advice-taking operations discussed in Section 2.2.

3.2 Cached Databases of the Virtual Memory Implementation

The virtual memory manager implements the client visible operations on spaces and is thus primarily concerned with checking validity and maintaining the database constituting the fundamental representation behind the *Space* interface. This database, called the *hierarchy*, represents the tree of nested spaces defined in Section 2.2. For each space, it contains a record whose fields hold attributes such as size, base page number, and mapping information.

The swapper, or virtual memory kernel, manages primary memory and supervises the swapping of data between mapped memory and files. For this purpose it needs access to information in the hierarchy. Since the hierarchy is swappable and thus off limits to the swapper, the swapper maintains a resident space cache which is loaded from the hierarchy in the manner described in Section 3.1.

There are several other data structures maintained by the swapper. One is a bit-table describing the allocation status of each page of primary memory. Most of the bookkeeping performed by the swapper, however, is on the basis of the *swap unit*, or smallest set of pages transferred between primary memory and file backing storage. A swap unit generally corresponds to a "leaf" space; however, if a space is only partially covered with subspaces, each maximal run of pages not containing any subspaces is also a swap unit. The swapper keeps a *swap unit cache* containing information about swap units such as extent (first page and length), containing mapped space, and state (mapped or not, swapped in or out, replacement algorithm data).

The swap unit cache is addressed by page rather than by space; for example, it is used by the page fault handler to find the swap unit in which a page fault occurred. The content of an entry in this cache is logically derived from a sequence of entries in the hierarchy, but direct implementation of this would require several file accesses to construct a single cache entry. To avoid this, we have chosen to maintain another database: the *projection*. This is a second swappable database maintained by the virtual memory manager, containing descriptions of all existing swap units, and is used to update the swap unit cache. The existence of the projection speeds up page faults which cannot be handled from the swap unit cache; it slows down space creation/deletion since then the projection must be updated. We expect this to be a useful optimization based on our assumptions about the relative frequencies and CPU times of these events; detailed measurements of a fully loaded system will be needed to evaluate the actual effectiveness of the projection.

An important detail regarding the relationship between the manager and kernel components has been ignored up to this point. That detail is avoiding "recursive" cache faults; when a manager is attempting to supply a missing cache entry, it will often incur a page fault of its own; the handling of that page fault must *not* incur a second cache fault or the fault episode will never terminate. Basically the answer is to make certain key records in the cache ineligible for replacement. This pertains to the space and swap unit caches and to the caches maintained by the filer as well.

3.3 Process Implementation

The implementation of processes and monitors in Pilot/Mesa is summarized here; more detail can be found in [11].

The task of implementing the concurrency facilities is split roughly equally among Pilot, the Mesa compiler, and the underlying machine. The basic primitives are defined as language constructs (e.g., entering a MONITOR, WAITing on a CONDITION variable, FORKING a new PROCESS) and are implemented either by machine op-codes (for heavily used constructs, e.g., WAIT) or by calls on Pilot (for less heavily used constructs, e.g., FOR). The constructs supported by the machine and the low-level Mesa support component provide procedure calls and synchronization among existing processes, allowing the remainder of Pilot to be implemented as a collection of monitors, which carefully synchronize the multiple processes executing concurrently inside them. These processes comprise a variable number of client processes (e.g., which have called into Pilot through some public interface) plus a fixed number of dedicated system processes (about a dozen) which are created specially at system initialization time. The machinery for creating and deleting processes is a monitor within the high-level Mesa support component; this places it above the virtual memory implementation; this means that it is swappable, but also means that the rest of Pilot (with the exception of network streams) cannot make use of dynamic process creation. The process implementation is thus another example of the manager/kernel pattern, in which the manager is implemented at a very high level and the kernel is pushed down to a very low level (in this case, largely into the underlying machine). To the Pilot client, the split implementation appears as a unified mechanism comprising the Mesa language features and the operations defined by the Pilot *Process* interface.

3.4 File System Robustness

One of the most important properties of the Pilot file system is robustness. This is achieved primarily through the use of *reconstructable maps.* Many previous systems have demonstrated the value of a *file scavenger*, a utility program which can repair a damaged file system, often on a more or less *ad hoc* basis [5, 12, 14, 21]. In Pilot, the scavenger is given first-class citizenship, in the sense that the file structures were all designed from the beginning with the scavenger in mind. Each file page is self-identifying by virtue of its *label*, written as a separate physical record adjacent to the one holding the actual contents of the page. (Again, this is not a new idea, but is the crucial foundation on which the file system's robustness is based.) Conceptually, one can think of a file page access proceeding by scanning all known volumes, checking the label of each page encountered until the desired one is found. In practice, this scan is performed only once by the scavenger, which leaves behind maps on each volume describing what it found there; Pilot then uses the maps and incrementally updates them as file pages are created and deleted. The logical redundancy of the maps does not, of course, imply lack of importance, since the system would be not be viable without them; the point is that since they contain *only* redundant information, they can be completely reconstructed should they be lost. In particular, this means that damage to any page on the disk can compromise only data on that page.

The primary map structure is the volume file map, a B-tree keyed on (file-uid, page-number) which returns the device address of the page. All file storage devices check the label of the page and abort the I/O operation in case of a mismatch; this does not occur in normal operation and generally indicates the need to scavenge the volume. The volume file map uses extensive compression of uids and run-encoding of page numbers to maximize the out-degree of the internal nodes of the B-tree and thus minimize its depth.

Equally important but much simpler is the volume allocation map, a table which describes the allocation status of each page on the disk. Each free page is a self-identifying member of a hypothetical file of free pages, allowing reconstruction of the volume allocation map.

The robustness provided by the scavenger can only guarantee the integrity of files as defined by Pilot. If a database defined by client software becomes inconsistent due to a system crash, a software bug, or some other unfortunate event, it is little comfort to know that the underlying file has been declared healthy by the scavenger. An "escape-hatch" is therefore provided to allow client software to be invoked when a file is scavenged. This is the main use of the file-type attribute mentioned in Section 2.1. After the Pilot scavenger has restored the low-level integrity of the file system, Pilot is restarted; before resuming normal processing, Pilot first invokes all client-level scavenging routines (if any) to reestablish any higher level consistency constraints that may have been violated. File types are used to determine which files should be processed by which client-level scavengers.

An interesting example of the first-class status of the scavenger is its routine use in transporting volumes between versions of Pilot. The freedom to redesign the complex map structures stored on volumes represents a crucial opportunity for continuing file system performance improvement, but this means that one version of Pilot may find the maps left by another version totally inscrutable. Since such incompatibility is just a particular form of "damage," however, the scavenger can be invoked to reconstruct the maps in the proper format, after which the corresponding version of Pilot will recognize the volume as its own.

3.5 Communication Implementation

The software that implements the packet communication protocols consists of a set of network-specific drivers, modules that implement sockets, network stream transducers, and at the heart of it all, a *router*. The router is a software switch. It routes packets among sockets, sockets and networks, and networks themselves. A router is present on every Pilot machine. On personal machines, the router handles only incoming, outgoing, and intra-machine packet traffic. On internetwork router machines, the router acts as a service to other machines by transporting internetwork packets across network boundaries. The router's data structures include a list of all active sockets and networks on the local computer. The router is designed so that network drivers may easily be added to or removed from new configurations of Pilot; this can even be done dynamically during execution. Sockets come and go as clients create and delete them. Each router maintains a routing table indicating, for a given remote network, the best internetwork router to use as the next "hop" toward the final destination. Thus, the two kinds of machines are essentially special cases of the same program. An internetwork router is simply a router that spends most of its time forwarding packets between networks and exchanging routing tables with other internetwork routers. On personal machines the router updates its routing table by querying internet-work routers or by overhearing their exchanges over broadcast networks.

Pilot has taken the approach of connecting a network much like any other input/output device, so that the packet communication protocol software becomes part of the operating system and operates in the same personal computer. In particular, Pilot does *not* employ a dedicated front-end communications processor connected to the Pilot machine via a secondary interface.

Network-oriented communication differs from conventional input/output in that packets arrive at a computer *unsolicited*, implying that the intended recipient is unknown until the packet is examined. As a consequence, each incoming packet must be buffered initially in router-supplied storage for examination. The router, therefore, maintains a buffer pool shared by all the network drivers. If a packet is undamaged and its destination socket exists, then the packet is copied into a buffer associated with the socket and provided by the socket's client.

The architecture of the communication software permits the computer supporting Pilot to behave as a user's personal computer, a supplier of information, or as a dedicated internetwork router.

3.6 The Implementation Experience

The initial construction of Pilot was accomplished by a fairly small group of people (averaging about 6 to 8) in a fairly short period of time (about 18 months). We feel this is largely due to the use of Mesa. Pilot consists of approximately 24,000 lines of Mesa, broken into about 160 modules (programs and interfaces), yielding an average module size of roughly 150 lines. The use of small modules and minimal intermodule connectivity, combined with the strongly typed interface facilities of Mesa, aided in the creation of an implementation which avoided many common kinds of errors and which is relatively rugged in the face of modification. These issues are discussed in more detail in [7] and [13].

4 Conclusion

The context of a large personal computer has motivated us to reevaluate many design decisions which characterize systems designed for more familiar situations (e.g., large shared machines or small personal computers). This has resulted in a somewhat novel system which, for example, provides sophisticated features but only minimal protection, accepts advice from client programs, and even boot-loads the machine periodically in the normal course of execution.

Aside from its novel aspects, however, Pilot's real significance is its careful integration, in a single relatively compact system, of a number of good ideas which have previously tended to appear individually, often in systems which were demonstration vehicles not intended to support serious client programs. The combination of streams, packet communications, a hierarchical virtual memory mapped to a large file space, concurrent programming support and a modular high-level language, provides an environment with relatively few artificial limitations on the size and complexity of the client programs which can be supported.

Acknowledgements

The primary design and implementation of Pilot were done by the authors. Some of the earliest ideas were contributed by D. Gifford, R. Metcalfe, W. Shultz, and D. Stottlemyre. More recent contributions have been made by C. Fay, R. Gobbel, F. Howard, C. Jose, and D. Knutsen. Since the inception of the project, we have had continuous fruitful interaction with all the members of the Mesa language group; in particular, R. Johnsson, J. Sandman, and J. Wick have provided much of the software that stands on the border between Pilot and Mesa. We are also indebted to P. Jarvis and V. Schwartz, who designed and implemented some of the low-level input/output drivers. The success of the close integration of Mesa and Pilot with the machine architecture is largely due to the talent and energy of the people who designed and built the hardware and microcode for our personal computer.

References

1. Brinch-Hansen, P. The nucleus of a multiprogramming system. *Comm. ACM 13*, 4 (April 1970), 238–241.

2. Boggs, D.R., Shoch, J.F., Taft, E., and Metcalfe, R.M. Pup: An internetwork architecture. To appear in *IEEE Trans. Commun.* (Special Issue on Computer Network Architecture and Protocols).

3. Cerf, V.G., and Kahn, R.E. A protocol for packet network interconnection. *IEEE Trans. Commun. COM-22*, 5 (May 1974), 637–641.

4. Cerf, V.G., and Kirstein, P.T. Issues in packet-network interconnection. *Proc. IEEE 66*, 11 (Nov. 1978), 1386–1408.

5. Farber, D.J. and Heinrich, F.R. The structure of a distributed computer system: The distributed file system. In Proc. 1st Int. Conf. Computer Communication, 1972, 364–370.

6. Habermann, A.N., Flon, L., and Cooprider, L. Modularization and hierarchy in a family of operating systems. *Comm. ACM 19*, 5 (May 1976), 266–272.

7. Horsley, T.R., and Lynch, W.C. Pilot: A software engineering case history. In Proc. 4th Int. Conf. Software Engineering, Munich, Germany, Sept. 1979, 999.

8. Internet Datagram Protocol Version 4. Prepared by USC/Information Sciences Institute, for the Defense Advanced Research Projects Agency, Information Processing Techniques Office, Feb. 1979

9. Lampson, B.W. Redundancy and robustness in memory protection. *Proc. IFIP 1974*, North Holland, Amsterdam, 128–132.

10. Lampson, B.W., Mitchell, J.G., and Satterthwaite, E.H. On the transfer of control between contexts. In *Lecture Notes in Computer Science 19*, Springer-Verlag, New York, 1974, 181–203.

11. Lampson, B.W., and Redell, D.D. Experience with processes and monitors in Mesa. *Comm. ACM 23*, 2 (Feb. 1980), 105–117.

12. Lampson, B.W., and Sproull, R.F. An open operating system for a single user machine. Presented at the ACM 7th Symp. Operating System Principles (*Operating Syst. Rev. 13*, 5), Dec. 1979, 98–105.

13. Lauer, H.C., and Satterthwaite, E.H. The impact of Mesa on system design. In Proc. 4th Int. Conf. Software Engineering, Munich, Germany, Sept. 1979, 174–182.

14. Lockemann, P.C., and Knutsen, W.D. Recovery of disk contents after system failure. *Comm. ACM 11*, 8 (Aug. 1968), 542.

15. Metcalfe, R.M., and Boggs, D.R. Ethernet: Distributed packet switching for local computer networks. *Comm. ACM 19*, 7 (July 1976), 395–404.

16. Mitchell, J.G., Maybury, W., and Sweet, R. Mesa Language Manual. Tech. Rep., Xerox Palo Alto Res. Ctr., 1979.

17. Pouzin, L. Virtual circuits vs. datagrams—technical and political problems. Proc. 1976 NCC, AFIPS Press, Arlington, Va., 483–494.

18. Ritchie, D.M., and Thompson, K. The UNIX time-sharing system. *Comm. ACM 17*, 7 (July 1974), 365–375.

19. Ross, D.T. The AED free storage package. *Comm. ACM 10*, 8 (Aug. 1967), 481–492.

20. Rotenberg, Leo J. Making computers keep secrets. Tech. Rep. MAC-TR-115, MIT Lab. for Computer Science.

21. Stern, J.A. Backup and recovery of on-line information in a computer utility. Tech. Rep. MAC-TR-116 (thesis), MIT Lab. for Computer Science, 1974.

22. Sunshine, C.A., and Dalal, Y.K. Connection management in transport protocol. *Comput. Networks 2*, 6 (Dec. 1978), 454–473.

23. Stoy, J.E., and Strachey, C. OS6—An experimental operating system for a small computer. *Comput. J. 15*, 2 and 3 (May, Aug. 1972).

24. Transmission Control Protocol, TCP, Version 4. Prepared by USC/Information Sciences Institute, for the Defense Advanced Research Projects Agency, Information Processing Techniques Office, Feb. 1979.

25. Wulf, W., et. al. HYDRA: The kernel of a multiprocessor operating system. *Comm. ACM 17*, 6 (June 1974), 337–345.

20

THE STAR USER INTERFACE: AN OVERVIEW*

DAVID C. SMITH, CHARLES IRBY, RALPH KIMBALL AND ERIC HARSLEM

(1982)

In April 1981 Xerox announced the 8010 Star Information System, a new personal computer designed for office professionals who create, analyze, and distribute information. The Star user interface differs from that of other office computer systems by its emphasis on graphics, its adherence to a metaphor of a physical office, and its rigorous application of a small set of design principles. The graphic imagery reduces the amount of typing and remembering required to operate the system. The office metaphor makes the system seem familiar and friendly; it reduces the alien feel that many computer systems have. The design principles unify the nearly two dozen functional areas of Star, increasing the coherence of the system and allowing user experience in one area to apply in others.

INTRODUCTION

In this paper we present the features in the Star system without justifying them in detail. In a companion paper [1], we discuss the rationale for the design decisions made in Star. We assume that the reader has a general familiarity with computer text editors, but no familiarity with Star.

The Star hardware consists of a processor, a two-page-wide bit-mapped display, a keyboard, and a cursor control device. The Star software addresses about two dozen functional areas of the office, encompassing document creation; data processing; and electronic filing, mailing, and printing.

---

*D. C. Smith, C. Irby, R. Kimball and E. Harslem, The Star user interface: an overview. *National Computer Conference*, (1982), 515–528.

Document creation includes text editing and formatting, graphics editing, mathematical formula editing, and page layout. Data processing deals with homogeneous databases that can be sorted, filtered, and formatted under user control. Filing is an example of a network service using the Ethernet local area network [2, 3]. Files may be stored on a work station's disk (Figure 1), on a file server on the work station's network, or on a file server on a different network. Mailing permits users of work stations to communicate with one another. Printing uses laser-driven xerographic printers capable of printing both text and graphics. The term *Star* refers to the total system, hardware plus software.

Figure 1 A Star workstation showing the processor, display, keyboard and mouse.

As Jonathan Seybold has written, "This is a very different product: Different because it truly bridges word processing and typesetting functions; different because it has a broader range of capabilities than anything which has preceded it; and different because it introduces to the commercial market radically new concepts in human engineering" [4].

The Star hardware was modeled after the experimental Alto computer developed at the Xerox Palo Alto Research Center [5]. Like Alto, Star consists of a Xerox-developed high-bandwidth MSI processor, local disk storage, a bit-mapped display screen having a 72-dot-per-inch resolution, a pointing device called the mouse, and a connection to the Ethernet. Stars are higher-performance machines than Altos, being about three times as fast, having 512K bytes of main memory (vs. 256K bytes on most Altos), 10 or 29M bytes of disk memory (vs. 2.5M bytes), a 10 1/2-by-13 1/2-inch display screen (vs. a 10 1/2-by-82-inch one), 1024 × 808 addressable screen dots (vs. 606 × 808), and a 10M bits-per-second Ethernet (vs. 3M bits). Typically, Stars, like Altos, are linked via Ethernets to each other and to shared file, mail, and print servers. Communication servers connect Ethernets to one another either directly or over phone lines, enabling internetwork communication to take place. This means, for example, that from the user's perspective it is no harder to retrieve a file from a file server across the country than from a local one.

Unlike the Alto, however, the Star user interface was designed before the hardware or software was built. Alto software, of which there was eventually a large amount, was developed by independent research teams and individuals. There was little or no coordination among projects as each pursued its own goals. This was acceptable and even desirable in a research environment producing experimental software. But it presented the Star designers with the challenge of synthesizing the various interfaces into a single, coherent, uniform one.

ESSENTIAL HARDWARE

Before describing Star's user interface, we should point out that there are several aspects of the Star (and Alto) architecture that are essential to it. Without these elements, it would have been impossible to design a user interface anything like the present one.

Display

Both Star and Alto devote a portion of main memory to the bit-mapped display screen: 100K bytes in Star, 50K bytes (usually) in Alto. Every screen dot can be individually turned on or off by setting or resetting the corresponding bit in memory. This gives both systems substantial ability to portray graphic images.

Memory Bandwidth

Both Star and Alto have a high memory bandwidth—about 50 MHz, in Star. The entire Star screen is repainted from memory 39 times per second. This 50-MHz video rate would swamp most computer memories, and in fact refreshing the screen takes about 60% of the Alto's memory bandwidth. However, Star's memory is double-ported; therefore, refreshing the display does not appreciably slow down CPU memory access. Star also has separate logic devoted solely to refreshing the display.

Microcoded Personal Computer

Both Star and Alto are personal computers, one user per machine. Therefore the needed memory access and CPU cycles are consistently available. Special microcode has been written to assist in changing the contents of memory quickly, permitting a variety of screen processing that would otherwise not be practical [6].

Mouse

Both Star and the Alto use a pointing device called the mouse (Figure 2). First developed at SRI [7], Xerox's version has a ball on the bottom that turns as the mouse slides over a flat surface such as a table. Electronics sense the ball rotation and guide a cursor on the screen in corresponding motions. The mouse is a "Fitts's law" device: that is, after some practice you can point with a mouse as quickly and easily as you can with the tip of your finger. The limitations on pointing speed are those inherent in the human nervous system [8, 9]. The mouse has buttons on top that can be sensed under program control. The buttons let you point to and interact with objects on the screen in a variety of ways.

Local Disk

Every Star and Alto has its own rigid disk for local storage of programs and data. Editing does not require using the network. This enhances the personal nature of the machines, resulting in consistent behavior regardless of how many other machines there are on the network or what anyone else is doing. Large programs can be written, using the disk for swapping.

Network

The Ethernet lets both Stars and Altos have a distributed architecture. Each machine is connected to an Ethernet. Other machines on the Ethernet are dedicated as servers, machines that are attached to a resource and that provide access to that resource. Typical servers are these:

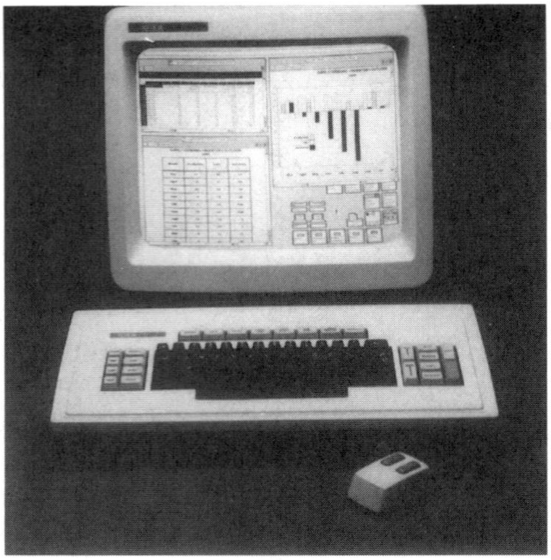

Figure 2 **The Star keyboard and mouse.** *The keyboard has 24 easy-to-understand function keys. The mouse has two buttons on top.*

1. *File server*—Sends and receives files over the network, storing them on its disks. A file server improves on a work station's rigid disk in several ways: (a) Its capacity is greater—up to 1.2 billion bytes. (b) It provides backup facilities. (c) It allows files to be shared among users. Files on a work station's disk are inaccessible to anyone else on the network.

2. *Mail server*—Accepts files over the network and distributes them to other machines on behalf of users, employing the Clearinghouse's database of names and addresses (see below).

3. *Print server*—Accepts print-format files over the network and prints them on the printer connected to it.

4. *Communication server*—Provides several services: The *Clearinghouse service* resolves symbolic names into network addresses [10]. The *Internetwork Routing service* manages the routing of information between networks over phone lines. The *Gateway service* allows word processors and dumb terminals to access network resources.

A network-based server architecture is economical, since many machines can share the resources. And it frees work stations for other tasks, since most server actions happen in the background. For example, while a print server is printing your document, you can edit another document or read your mail.

PHYSICAL OFFICE METAPHOR

We will briefly describe one of the most important principles that influenced the form of the Star user interface. The reader is referred to Smith et al. [1] for a detailed discussion of all the principles behind the Star design. The principle is to apply users' existing knowledge to the new situation of the computer. We decided to create electronic counterparts to the objects in an office: paper, folders, file cabinets, mail boxes, calculators, and so on—an electronic metaphor for the physical office. We hoped that this would make the electronic world seem more familiar and require less training. (Our initial experiences with users have confirmed this.) We further decided to make the electronic analogues be *concrete objects*.

Star documents are represented, not as file names on a disk, but as pictures on the display screen. They may be selected by pointing to them with the mouse and clicking one of the mouse buttons. Once selected, documents may be moved, copied, or deleted by pushing the MOVE, COPY, or DELETE key on the keyboard. Moving a document is the electronic equivalent of picking up a piece of paper and walking somewhere with it. To file a document, you move it to a picture of a file drawer, just as you take a piece of paper to a physical filing cabinet. To print a document, you move it to a picture of a printer, just as you take a piece of paper to a copying machine.

Though we want an analogy with the physical world for familiarity, we don't want to limit ourselves to its capabilities. One of the *raisons d'être* for Star is that physical objects do not provide people with enough power to manage the increasing complexity of their information. For example, we can take advantage of the computer's ability to search rapidly by providing a search function for its electronic file drawers, thus helping to solve the problem of lost files.

THE DESKTOP

Every user's initial view of Star is the Desktop, which resembles the top of an office desk, together with surrounding furniture and equipment. It represents a working environment, where current projects and accessible resources reside. On the screen (Figure 3) are displayed pictures of familiar office objects, such as documents, folders, file drawers, in-baskets, and out-baskets. These objects are displayed as small pictures, or *icons.*

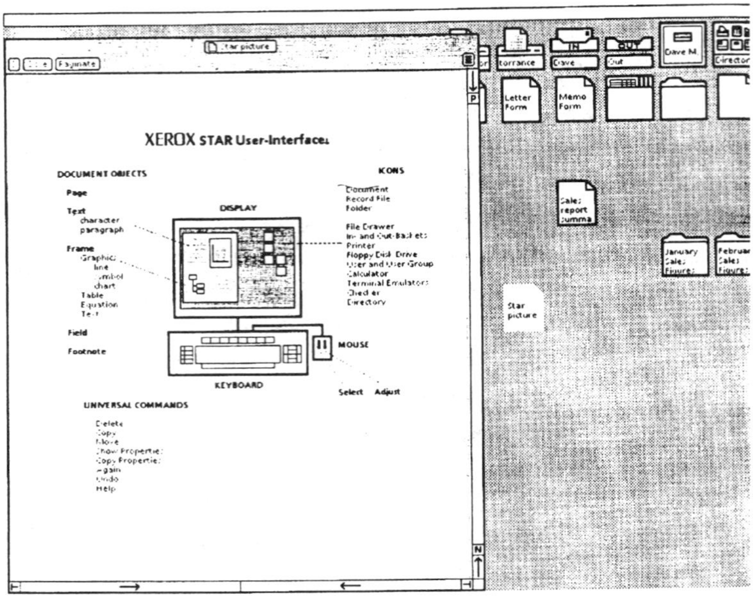

Figure 3 A "Desktop" as it appears on the Star screen. *This one has several commonly used icons along the top, including documents to serve as "form pad" sources for letters, memos and blank paper. There is also an open window displaying a document.*

You can "open" an icon by selecting it and pushing the OPEN key on the keyboard. When opened, an icon expands into a larger form called a *window*, which displays the icon's contents. This enables you to read documents, inspect the contents of folders and file drawers, see what mail has arrived, and perform other activities. Windows are the principal mechanism for displaying and manipulating information.

The Desktop surface is displayed as a distinctive grey pattern. This is restful and makes the icons and windows on it stand out crisply, minimizing eye strain. The surface is organized as an array of 1-inch squares, 14 wide by 11 high. An icon may be placed in any square, giving a maximum of 154 icons. Star centers an icon in its square, making it easy to line up icons neatly. The Desktop always occupies the entire display screen; even when windows appear on the screen, the Desktop continues to exist "beneath" them.

The Desktop is the principal Star technique for realizing the physical office metaphor. The icons on it are visible, concrete embodiments of the corresponding physical objects. Star users are encouraged to think of the objects on the Desktop in physical terms. You can move the icons around to arrange your Desktop as you wish. (Messy Desktops are certainly possible, just as in real life.) You can leave documents on your Desktop indefinitely, just as on a real desk, or you can file them away.

ICONS

An icon is a pictorial representation of a Star object that can exist on the Desktop. On the Desktop, the size of an icon is approximately 1 inch square. Inside a window such as a folder window, the size of an icon is approximately 1/4-inch square. Iconic images have played a role in human communication from cave paintings in prehistoric times to Egyptian hieroglyphics to religious symbols to modern corporate logos. Computer science has been slow to exploit the potential of visual imagery for presenting information, particularly abstract information. "Among [the] reasons are the lack of development of appropriate hardware and software for producing visual imagery easily and inexpensively; computer technology has been dominated by persons who seem to be happy with a simple, very limited alphabet of characters used to produce linear strings of symbols" [11]. One of the authors has applied icons to an environment for writing programs; he found that they greatly facilitated human-computer communication [12]. Negroponte's Spatial Data Management system has effectively used iconic images in a research setting [13]. And there have been other efforts [14, 15, 16]. But Star is the first computer system designed for a mass market to employ icons methodically in its user interface. We do not claim that Star exploits visual communication to the ultimate extent; we do claim that Star's use of imagery is a significant improvement over traditional human-machine interfaces.

At the highest level the Star world is divided into two classes of icons, (1) data and (2) function icons:

Data Icons

Data icons (Figure 4) represent objects on which actions are performed. All data icons can be moved, copied, deleted, filed, mailed, printed, opened, closed, and have a variety of other operations performed on them. The three types of data icons are document, folder, and record file.

Figure 4 The "data" icons: document, folder and record file

Document

A document is the fundamental object in Star. It corresponds to the standard notion of what a document should be. It most often contains text, but it may also include illustrations, mathematical formulas, tables, fields, footnotes, and formatting information. Like all data icons, documents can be shown on the screen, rendered on paper, sent to other people, stored on a file server or floppy disk, etc. When opened, documents are always rendered on the display screen exactly as they print on paper (informally called "what you see is what you get"), including displaying the correct type fonts, multiple columns, headings and footings, illustration placement, etc. Documents can reside in the system in a variety of formats (e.g., Xerox 860, IBM OS6), but they can be edited only in Star format. Conversion operations are provided to translate between the various formats.

Folder

A folder is used to group data icons together. It can contain documents, record files, and other folders. Folders can be nested inside folders to any level. Like file drawers (see below), folders can be sorted and searched.

Record file

A record file is a collection of information organized as a set of records. Frequently this information will be the variable data from forms. These records may be sorted, subset via pattern matching, and formatted into reports. Record files provide a rich set of information storage and retrieval functions.

Function Icons

Function icons represent objects that perform actions. Most function icons will operate on any data icon. There are many kinds of function icons, with more being added as the system evolves:

File drawer

A file drawer (Figure 5) is a place to store data icons. It is modeled after the drawers in office filing cabinets. The organization of a file drawer is up to you; it can vary from a simple list of documents to a multilevel hierarchy of folders containing other folders. File drawers are distinguished from other storage places (folders, floppy disks, and the Desktop) in that (1) icons placed in a file drawer are physically stored on a file server, and (2) the contents of file drawers can be shared by multiple users. File drawers have associated access rights to control the ability of people to look at and modify their contents (Figure 6).

Figure 5 A file drawer icon

Although the design of file drawers was motivated by their physical counterparts, they are a good example of why it is neither necessary nor desirable to stop with just duplicating real-world behavior. People have a lot of trouble finding things in filing cabinets. Their categorization schemes are frequently ad hoc and idiosyncratic. If the person who did the categorizing

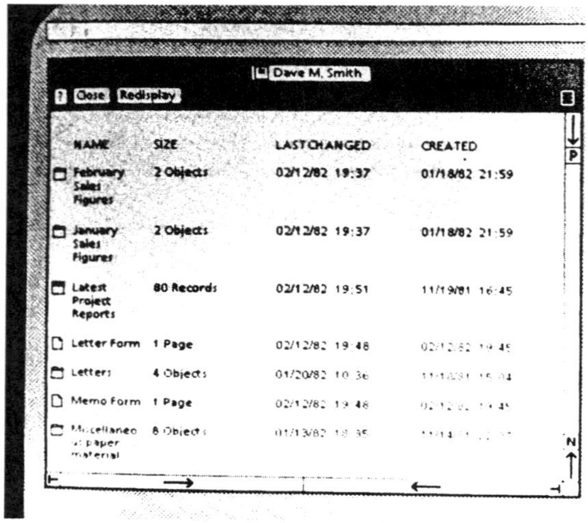

Figure 6 An open file drawer window. *Note that there is a miniature icon for each object inside the file drawer.*

leaves the company, information may be permanently lost. Star improves on physical filing cabinets by taking advantage of the computer's ability to *search rapidly.* You can search the contents of a file drawer for an object having a certain name, or author, or creation date, or size, or a variety of other attributes. The search criteria can use fuzzy patterns containing match-anything symbols, ranges, and other predicates. You can also sort the contents on the basis of those criteria. The point is that whatever information retrieval facilities are available in a system should be applied to the information in files. Any system that does not do so is not exploiting the full potential of the computer.

In basket and Out basket

These provide the principal mechanism for sending data icons to other people (Figure 7). A data icon placed in the Out basket will be sent over the Ethernet to a mail server (usually the same machine as a file server), thence to the mail servers of the recipients (which may be the same as the sender's), and thence to the In baskets of the recipients. When you have mail waiting for you, an envelope appears in your In basket icon. When you open your In basket, you can display and read the mail in the window.

Figure 7 In and Out basket icons

Any document, record file, or folder can be mailed. Documents need not be limited to plain text, but can contain illustrations, mathematical formulas, and other nontext material. Folders can contain any number of items. Record files can be arbitrarily large and complex.

Printer

Printer icons (Figure 8) provide access to printing services. The actual printer may be directly connected to your work station, or it may be attached to a print server connected to an Ethernet. You can have more than one printer icon on your Desktop, providing access to a variety of printing resources. Most printers are expected to be laser-driven raster-scan xerographic machines; these can render on paper anything that can be created on the screen. Low-cost typewriter-based printers are also available; these can render only text.

Figure 8 A printer icon

As with filing and mailing, the existence of the Ethernet greatly enhances the power of printing. The printer represented by an icon on your Desktop can be in the same room as your work station, in a different room, in a different building, in a different city, even in a different country. You perform exactly the same actions to print on any of them: Select a data icon, push the MOVE key, and indicate the printer icon as the destination.

Floppy disk drive

The floppy disk drive icon (Figure 9) allows you to move data icons to and from a floppy disk inserted in the machine. This provides a way to store documents, record files and folders off line. When you open the floppy disk drive icon, Star reads the floppy disk and displays its contents in the window. Its window looks and acts just like a folder window: icons may be moved or copied in or out, or deleted. The only difference is the physical location of the data.

Figure 9 A floppy disk drive icon

User

The user icon (Figure 10) displays the information that the system knows about each user: name, location, password (invisible, of course), aliases if any, home file and mail servers, access level (ordinary user, system administrator, help/training writer), and so on. We expect the information stored for each user to increase as Star adds new functionality. User icons may be placed in address fields for electronic mail.

User icons are Star's solution to the naming problem. There is a crisis in computer naming of people, particularly in electronic mail addressing. The convention in most systems is to use last names for user identification. Anyone named Smith, as is one of the authors, knows that this doesn't

Figure 10 A user icon

work. When he first became a user on such a system, *Smith* had long ago been taken. In fact, "D. Smith" and even "D. C. Smith" had been taken. He finally settled on "DaveSmith", all one word, with which he has been stuck to this day. Needless to say, that is not how he identifies himself to people. In the future, people will not tolerate this kind of antihumanism from computers. Star already does better: it follows society's conventions. User icons provide unambiguous unique references to individual people, using their normal names. The information about users, and indeed about all network resources, is physically stored in the Clearinghouse, a distributed database of names. In addition to a person's name in the ordinary sense, this information includes the name of the organization (e.g., Xerox, General Motors) and the name of the user's division within the organization. A person's linear name need be unique only within his division. It can he fully spelled out if necessary, including spaces and punctuation. Aliases can be defined. User icons are references to this information. You need not even know, let alone type, the unique linear representation for a user; you need only have the icon.

User group

User group icons (Figure 11) contain individual users and/or other user groups. They allow you to organize people according to various criteria. User groups serve both to control access to information such as file drawers (access control lists) and to make it easy to send mail to a large number of people (distribution lists). The latter is becoming increasingly important as more and more people start to take advantage of computer-assisted communication. At Xerox we have found that as soon as there were more than a thousand Alto users, there were almost always enough people interested in any topic whatsoever to form a distribution list for it. These user groups have broken the bonds of geographical proximity that have historically limited group membership and communication. They have begun to turn Xerox into a nationwide "village," just as the Arpanet has brought computer science researchers around the world closer together. This may be the most profound impact that computers have on society.

Figure 11 A user group icon

Calculator

A variety of styles of calculators (Figure 12) let you perform arithmetic calculations. Numbers can be moved between Star documents and calculators, thereby reducing the amount of typing and the possibility of errors. Rows or columns of tables can be summed. The calculators are user-tailorable and extensible. Most are modeled after pocket calculators—business, scientific, four-function—but one is a tabular calculator similar to the popular Visicalc program.

Terminal emulators

The terminal emulators permit you to communicate with existing mainframe computers using existing protocols. Initially, teletype and 3270 terminals are emulated, with additional ones later (Figure 13). You open one of the terminal icons and type into its window; the contents of the window behave exactly as if you were typing at the corresponding terminal. Text in

Figure 12 A calculator icon

Figure 13 3270 and TTY emulation icons

the window can be copied to and from Star documents, which makes Star's rich environment available to them.

Directory

The Directory provides access to network resources. It serves as the source for icons representing those resources; the Directory contains one icon for each resource available (Figure 14). When you are first registered in a Star network, your Desktop contains nothing but a Directory icon. From this initial state, you access resources such as file drawers, printers, and mail baskets by opening the Directory and copying out their icons. You can also get blank data icons out of the Directory. You can retrieve other data icons from file drawers. Star places no limits on the complexity of your Desktop except the limitation imposed by physical screen area (Figure 15). The Directory also contains Remote Directories representing resources available on other networks. These can be opened, recursively, and their resource icons copied out, just as with the local Directory. You deal with local and remote resources in exactly the same way.

Figure 14 A Directory icon

The important thing to observe is that although the functions performed by the various icons differ, the way you interact with them is the same. You select them with the mouse. You push the MOVE, COPY, or DELETE key. You push the OPEN key to see their contents, the PROPERTIES key to see their properties, and the SAME key to copy their properties. This is the result of rigorously applying the principle of uniformity to the design of icons. We have applied it to other areas of Star as well, as will be seen.

WINDOWS

Windows are rectangular areas that display the contents of icons on the screen. Much of the inspiration for Star's design came from Alan Kay's Flex machine [17] and his later Smalltalk programming environment on the Alto [18]. The Officetalk treatment of windows was also influential; in fact, Officetalk, an experimental office-forms-processing system on the Alto, provided ideas in a variety of areas [19]. Windows greatly increase the amount of information that can be manipulated on a display screen. Up to six windows at a time can be open in Star. Each window has a header containing the name of the icon and a menu of commands. The commands consist of a stan-

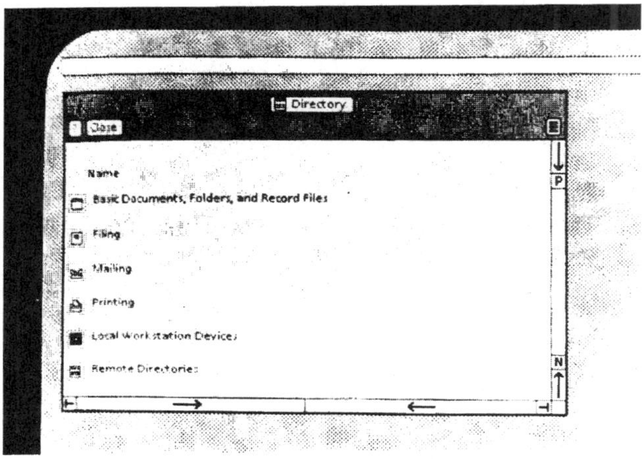

Figure 15 The Directory window showing the categories of resources available

dard set present in all windows ("?", CLOSE, SET WINDOW) and others that depend on the type of icon. For example, the window for a record file contains commands tailored to information retrieval. CLOSE removes the window from the display screen, returning the icon to its tiny size. The "?" command displays the online documentation describing the type of window and its applications.

Each window has two scroll bars for scrolling the contents vertically and horizontally. The scroll bars have jump-to-end areas for quickly going to the top, bottom, left, or right end of the contents. The vertical scroll bar also has areas labeled N and P for quickly getting the next or previous screenful of the contents; in the case of a document window, they go to the next or previous page. Finally, the vertical scroll bar has a jumping area for going to a particular part of the contents, such as to a particular page in a document.

Unlike the windows in some Alto programs, Star windows do not overlap. This is a deliberate decision, based on our observation that many Alto users were spending an inordinate amount of time manipulating windows themselves rather than their contents. This manipulation of the medium is overhead, and we want to reduce it. Star automatically partitions the display space among the currently open windows. You can control on which side of the screen a window appears and its height.

PROPERTY SHEETS

At a finer grain, the Star world is organized in terms of *objects* that have *properties* and upon which *actions* are performed. A few examples of objects in Star are text characters, text paragraphs, graphic lines, graphic illustrations, mathematical summation signs, mathematical formulas, and icons. Every object has properties. Properties of text characters include type style, size, face, and posture (e.g., bold, italic). Properties of paragraphs include indentation, leading, and alignment. Properties of graphic lines include thickness and structure (e.g., solid, dashed, dotted). Properties of document icons include name, size, creator, and creation date. So the properties of an object depend on the type of the object. These ideas are similar to the notions of classes, objects, and messages in Simula [20] and Smalltalk. Among the editors that use these ideas are the experimental text editor Bravo [21] and the experimental graphics editor Draw [22], both developed at the Xerox Palo Alto Research Center. These all supplied valuable knowledge and insight to Star. In fact, the text editor aspects of Star were derived from Bravo.

In order to make properties visible, we invented the notion of a property sheet (Figure 16). A property sheet is a two-dimensional formlike environment which shows the properties of an object. To display one, you select the object of interest using the mouse and push the PROPERTIES key on the keyboard. Property sheets may contain three types of parameters:

1. *State*—State parameters display an independent property, which may be either on or off. You turn it on or off by pointing to it with the mouse and clicking a mouse button. When on, the parameter is shown video reversed. In general, any combination of state parameters in a property sheet can be on. If several state parameters are logically related, they are shown on the same line with space between them. (See "Face" in Figure 16.)

2. *Choice*—Choice parameters display a set of mutually exclusive values for a property. Exactly one value must be on at all times. As with state parameters, you turn on a choice by pointing to it with the mouse and clicking a mouse button. If you turn on a different value, the system turns off the previous one. Again the one that is on is shown video reversed. (See "Font" in Figure 16.) The motivation for state and choice parameters is the observation that it is generally easier to take

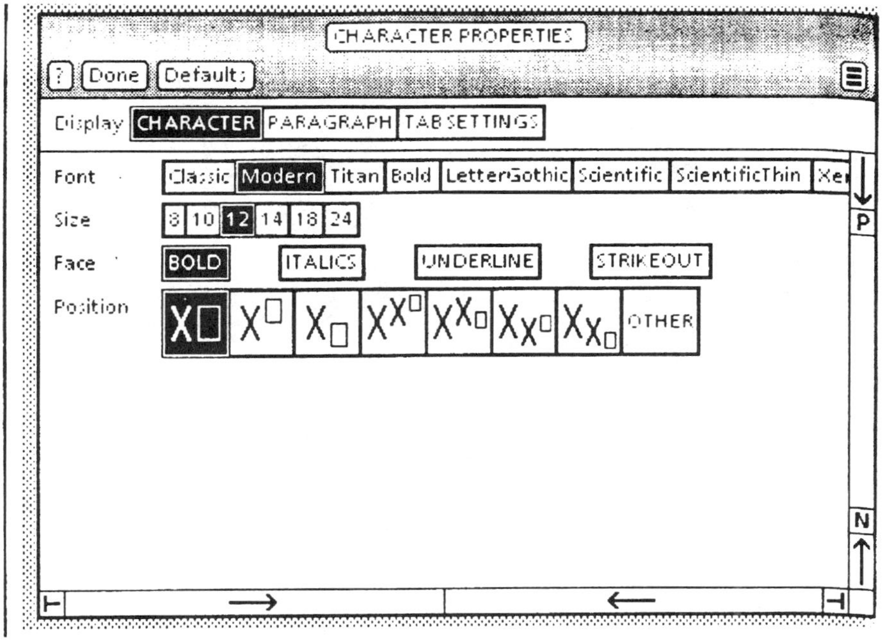

Figure 16 The property sheet for text characters

a multiple-choice test than a fill-in-the-blanks one. When options are made visible, they become easier to understand, remember, and use.

3. *Text*—Text parameters display a box into which you can type a value. This provides a (largely) unconstrained choice space; you may type any value you please, within the limits of the system. The disadvantage of this is that the set of possible values is not visible; therefore Star uses text parameters only when that set is large. (See "Search for" in Figure 17.)

Property sheets have several important attributes:

1. A small number of parameters gives you a large number of combinations of properties. They permit a rich choice space without a lot of complexity. For example, the character property sheet alone provides for 8 fonts, from 1 to 6 sizes for each (an average of about 2), 4 faces (any combination of which can be on), and 8 positions relative to the

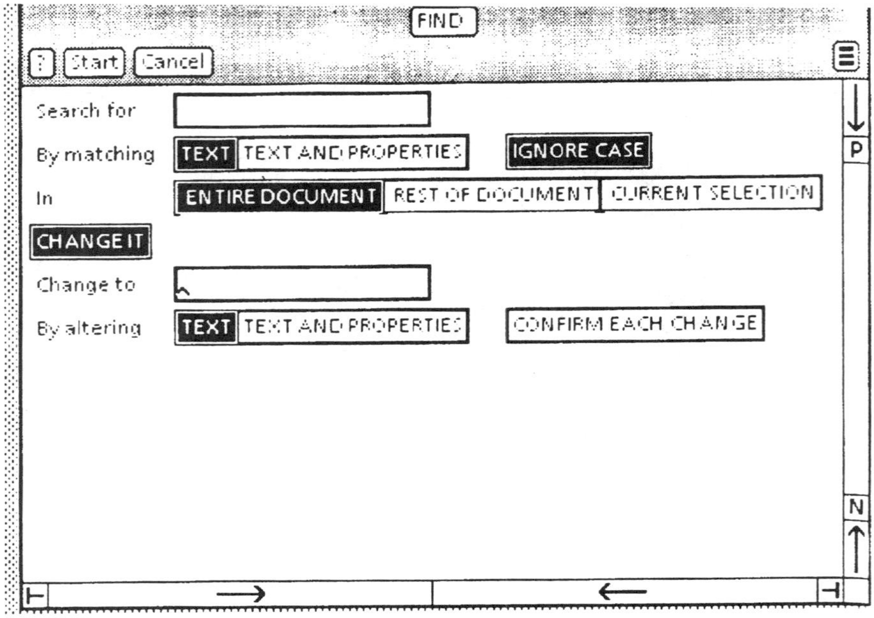

Figure 17 The option sheet for the Find command

baseline (including OTHER, which lets you type in a value). So in just four parameters, there are over $8 \times 2 \times 2^4 \times 8 = 2048$ combinations of character properties.

2. They show all of the properties of an object. None is hidden. You are constantly reminded what is available every time you display a property sheet.

3. They provide progressive disclosure. There are a large number of properties in the system as a whole, but you want to deal with only a small subset at any one time. Only the properties of the selected object are shown.

4. They provide a "bullet-proof" environment for altering the characteristics of an object. Since only the properties of the selected object are shown, you can't accidentally alter other objects. Since only valid choices are displayed, you can't specify illegal properties. This reduces errors.

Property sheets are an example of the Star design principle that *seeing* and *pointing* is preferred over *remembering* and *typing.* You don't have to remember what properties are available for an object; the property sheet will show them to you. This reduces the burden on your memory, which is particularly important in a functionally rich system. And most properties can be changed by a simple pointing action with the mouse.

The three types of parameters are also used in *option sheets* (Figure 18). Option sheets are just like property sheets, except that they provide a visual interface for *arguments to commands* instead of *properties of objects.* For example, in the Find option sheet there is a text parameter for the string to search for, a choice parameter for the range over which to search, and a state parameter (CHANGE IT) controlling whether to replace that string with another one. When CHANGE IT is turned on, an additional set of parameters appears to contain the replacement text. This technique of having some parameters appear depending on the settings of others is another part of our strategy of progressive disclosure: hiding information (and therefore complexity) until it is needed, but making it visible when it is needed. The various sheets appear simpler than if all the options were always shown.

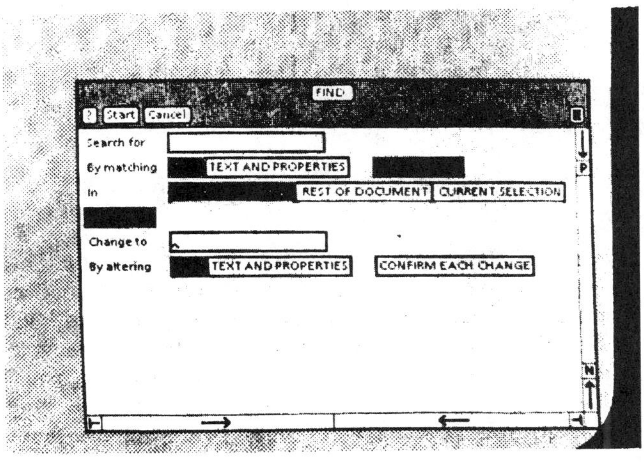

Figure 18 The Find option sheet showing Substitute options. *(The extra options appear only when CHANGE IT is turned on.)*

COMMANDS

Commands in Star take the form of noun-verb pairs. You specify the object of interest (the noun) and then invoke a command to manipulate it (the verb). Specifying an object is called *making a selection.* Star provides powerful selection mechanisms, which reduce the number and complexity of commands in the system. Typically, you exercise more dexterity and judgment in making a selection than in invoking a command. The ways to make a selection are as follows:

1. With the mouse—Place the cursor over the object on the screen you want to select and click the first (SELECT) mouse button. Additional objects can be selected by using the second (ADJUST) mouse button; it adjusts the selection to include more or fewer objects. Most selections are made in this way.

2. With the NEXT key on the keyboard—Push the NEXT key, and the system will select the contents of the next field in a document. Fields are one of the types of special higher-level objects that can be placed in documents. If the selection is currently in a table, NEXT will step through the rows and columns of the table, making it easy to fill in and modify them. If the selection is currently in a mathematical formula, NEXT will step through the various elements in the formula, making it easy to edit them. NEXT is like an intelligent step key; it moves the selection between semantically meaningful locations in a document.

3. With a command—Invoke the FIND command, and the system will select the next occurrence of the specified text, if there is one. Other commands that make a selection include OPEN (the first object in the opened window is selected) and CLOSE (the icon that was closed becomes selected). These optimize the use of the system.

The object (noun) is almost always specified before the action (verb) to be performed. This makes the command interface *modeless*; you can change your mind as to which object to affect simply by changing the selection before invoking the command [23]. No "accept" function is needed to terminate or confirm commands, since invoking the command is the last step. Inserting text does not require a command; you simply make a selection and begin typing. The text is placed after the end of the selection. A few commands require more than one operand and hence are modal. For example, the MOVE and COPY commands require a destination as well as a source.

GENERIC COMMANDS

Star has a few commands that can be used throughout the system: MOVE, COPY, DELETE, SHOW PROPERTIES, COPY PROPERTIES, AGAIN, UNDO, and HELP. Each performs the same way regardless of the type of object selected. Thus we call them generic commands. For example, you follow the same set of actions to move text in a document as to move a document in a folder or a line in an illustration: select the object, move the MOVE key, and indicate the destination. Each generic command has a key devoted to it on the keyboard. (HELP and UNDO don't use a selection.)

These commands are more basic than the ones in other computer systems. They strip away extraneous application-specific semantics to get at the underlying principles. Star's generic commands are derived from *fundamental computer science concepts* because they also underlie operations in programming languages. For example, program manipulation of data structures involves moving or copying values from one data structure to another. Since Star's generic commands embody fundamental underlying concepts, they are widely applicable. Each command fills a host of needs. Few commands are required. This simplicity is desirable in itself, but it has another subtle advantage: it makes it easy for users to form a model of the system. What people can understand, they can use. Just as progress in science derives from simple, clear theories, so progress in the usability of computers depends on simple, clear user interfaces.

Move

MOVE is the most powerful command in the system. It is used during text editing to rearrange letters in a word, words in a sentence, sentences in a paragraph, and paragraphs in a document. It is used during graphics editing to move picture elements such as lines and rectangles around in an illustration. It is used during formula editing to move mathematical structures such as summations and integrals around in an equation. It replaces the conventional "store file" and "retrieve file" commands; you simply move an icon into or out of a file drawer or folder. It eliminates the "send mail" and "receive mail" commands; you move an icon to an Out basket or from an In basket. It replaces the "print" command; you move an icon to a printer. And so on. MOVE strips away much of the historical clutter of computer commands. It is more fundamental than the myriad of commands it replaces. It is simultaneously more powerful and simpler.

MOVE also reinforces Star's physical metaphor: a moved object can be in only one place at one time. Most computer file transfer programs only make copies; they leave the originals behind. Although this is an admirable attempt to keep information from accidentally getting lost, an unfortunate side effect is that sometimes you lose track of where the most recent information is, since there are multiple copies floating around. MOVE lets you model the way you manipulate information in the real world, should you wish to. We expect that during the *creation* of information, people will primarily use MOVE; during the *dissemination* of information, people will make extensive use of COPY.

Copy

COPY is just like MOVE, except that it leaves the original object behind untouched. Star elevates the concept of copying to the level of *a paradigm for creating.* In all the various domains of Star, you *create by copying.* Creating something out of nothing is a difficult task. Everyone has observed that it is easier to modify an existing document or program than to write it originally. Picasso once said, "The most awful thing for a painter is the white canvas.... To copy others is necessary" [24]. Star makes a serious attempt to alleviate the problem of the "white canvas," to make copying a practical aid to creation. Consider:

- You create new documents by copying existing ones. Typically you set up blank documents with appropriate formatting properties (e.g., fonts, margins) and then use those documents as *form pad* sources for new documents. You select one, push COPY, and presto, you have a new document. The form pad documents need not be blank; they can contain text and graphics, along with fields for variable text such as for business forms.

- You place new network resource icons (e.g., printers, file drawers) on your Desktop by copying them out of the Directory. The icons are registered in the Directory by a system administrator working at a server. You simply copy them out; no other initialization is required.

- You create graphics by copying existing graphic images and modifying them. Star supplies an initial set of such images, called *transfer symbols.* Transfer symbols are based on the idea of dry-transfer rub-off symbols used by many secretaries and graphic artists. Unlike the physical transfer symbols, however, the computer versions can be modified: they can be moved, their sizes and proportions can be changed, and their appearance properties can be altered. Thus a single Star transfer symbol can produce a wide range of images. We will eventually supply a set of documents (transfer sheets) containing nothing but special images tailored to one application or another: people, buildings, vehicles, machinery. Having these as sources for graphics copying helps to alleviate the "white canvas" feeling.

- In a sense, you can even type characters by copying them from keyboard windows. Since there are many more characters (up to 2^{16}) in the Star character set than there are keys on the keyboard, Star provides a series of keyboard interpretation windows (Figure 19), which allow you to see and change the meanings of the keyboard keys. You are presented with the options; you look them over and choose the ones you want.

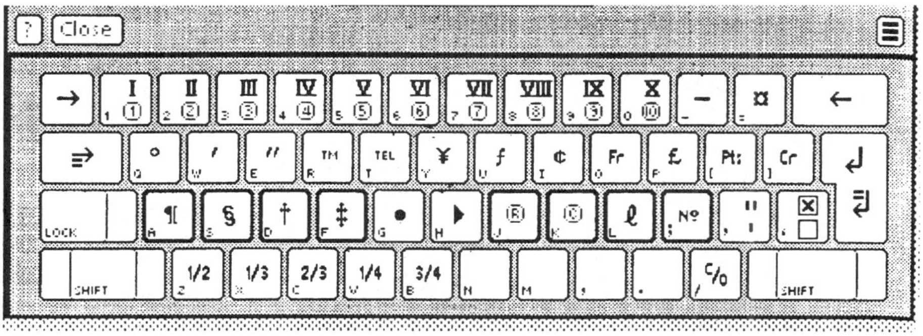

Figure 19 The Keyboard Interpretation window. *This displays other characters that may be entered from the keyboard. The character set shown here contains a variety of common office symbols.*

Delete

This deletes the selected object. If you delete something by mistake, UNDO will restore it.

Show Properties

SHOW PROPERTIES displays the properties of the selected object in a property sheet. You select the object(s) of interest, push the PROPERTIES (PROP'S) key, and the appropriate property sheet appears on the screen in such a position as to not overlie the selection, if possible. You may change as many properties as you wish, including none. When finished, you invoke the Done command in the property sheet menu. The property changes are applied to the selected objects, and the property sheet disappears. Notice that SHOW PROPERTIES is therefore used both to examine the current properties of an object and to change those properties.

Copy Properties

You need not use property sheets to alter properties if there is another object on the screen that already has the desired properties. You can select the object(s) to be changed, push the SAME key, then designate the object to use as the source. COPY PROPERTIES makes the selection look the "same" as the source. This is particularly useful in graphics editing. Frequently you will have a collection of lines and symbols whose appearance you want to be coordinated (all the same line width, shade of grey, etc.). You can select all the objects to be changed, push SAME, and select a line or symbol having the desired appearance. In fact, we find it helpful to set up a document with a variety of graphic objects in a variety of appearances to be used as sources for copying properties.

Again

AGAIN repeats the last command(s) on a new selection. All the commands done since the last time a selection was made are repeated. This is useful when a short sequence of commands needs to be done on several different selections; for example, make several scattered words bold and italic and in a larger font.

Undo

UNDO reverses the effects of the last command. It provides protection against mistakes, making the system more forgiving and user-friendly. Only a few commands cannot be repeated or undone.

Help

Our effort to make Star a personal, self-contained system goes beyond the hardware and software to the tools that Star provides to teach people how to use the system. Nearly all of its teaching and reference material is on line, stored on a file server. The Help facilities automatically retrieve the relevant material as you request it.

The HELP key on the keyboard is the primary entrance into this online information. You can push it at any time, and a window will appear on the screen displaying the Help table of contents (Figure 20). Three mechanisms make finding information easier: *context-dependent invocation*, *help references*, and a *keyword search command*. Together they make the online documentation more powerful and useful than printed documentation.

- *Context-dependent invocation*—The command menu in every window and property/option sheet contains a "?" command. Invoking it takes you to a part of the Help documentation describing the window, its commands, and its functions. The "?" command also appears in the message area at the top of the screen; invoking that one takes you to a description of the message (if any) currently in the message area. That provides more detailed explanations of system messages.

- *Help references*—These are like menu commands whose effect is to take you to a different part of the Help material. You invoke one by pointing to it with the mouse, just as you invoke a menu command. The writers of the material use the references to organize it into a network of interconnections, in a way similar to that suggested by Vannevar Bush [25] and pioneered by Doug Engelbart in his NLS system [26, 27]. The interconnections permit cross-referencing without duplication.

- The *SEARCH FOR KEYWORD command*—This command in the Help window menu lets you search the available documentation for information on a specific topic. The keywords are predefined by the writers of the Help material.

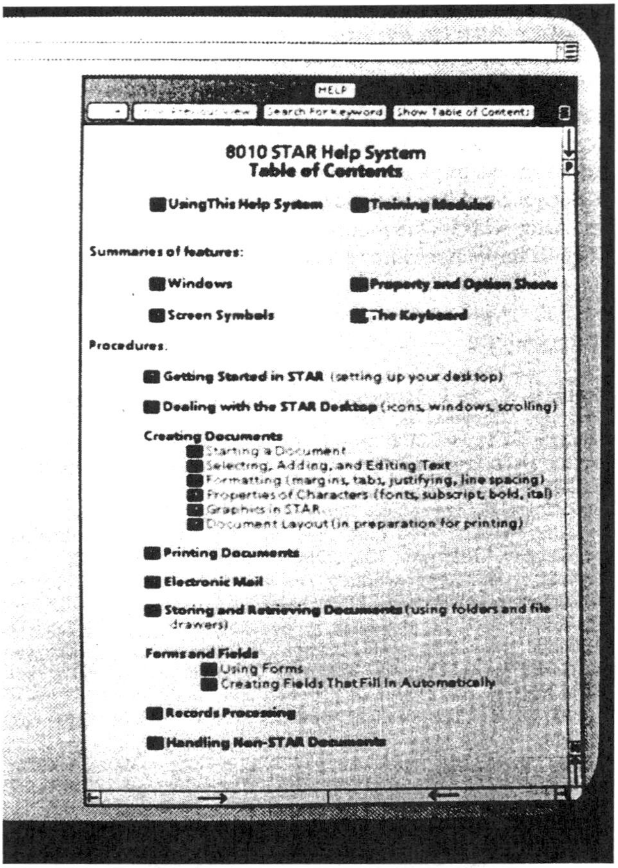

Figure 20 The Help window, showing the table of contents. *Selecting a square with a question mark in it takes you to the associated part of the Help documentation.*

SUMMARY

We have learned from Star the importance of formulating the user's conceptual model *first*, *before* software is written, rather than tacking on a user interface *afterward*. Doing good user interface design is not easy. Xerox devoted about thirty work-years to the design of the Star user interface. It was designed *before* the functionality of the system was fully decided. It was designed *before* the computer hardware was even built. We worked for two years *before* we wrote a single line of actual product software. Jonathan Seybold put it this way: "Most system design efforts start with hardware specifications, follow this with a set of functional specifications for the software, then try to figure out a logical user interface and command structure. The Star project started the other way around: the paramount concern was to define a conceptual model of how the user would relate to the system. Hardware and software followed from this" [4].

Alto served as a valuable prototype for Star. Over a thousand Altos were eventually built, and Alto users have had several thousand work-years of experience with them over a period of eight years, making Alto perhaps the largest prototyping effort in history. There were dozens of experimental programs written for the Alto by members of the Xerox Palo Alto Research Center. Without the creative ideas of the authors of those systems, Star in its present form would have been impossible. On the other hand, it was a real challenge to bring some order to the different user interfaces on the Alto. In addition, we ourselves programmed various aspects of the Star design on Alto, but every bit (sic) of it was throwaway code. Alto, with its bit-mapped display screen, was powerful enough to implement and test our ideas on visual interaction.

References

1. Smith, D. C., E. F. Harslem, C. H. Irby, R. B. Kimball, and W. L. Verplank. "Designing the Star User Interface." *Byte*, April 1982.
2. Metcalfe, R. M., and D. R. Boggs. "Ethernet: Distributed Packet Switching for Local Computer Networks." *Communications of the ACM*, 19 (1976), pp, 395-404,
3. Intel, Digital Equipment, and Xerox Corporations. "The Ethernet, A Local Area Network: Data Link Layer and Physical Layer Specifications (version 1.0)." Palo Alto: Xerox Office Products Division, 1980.
4. Seybold, J. W. "Xerox's Star." *The Seybold Report.* Media, Pennsylvania: Seybold Publications, 10 (1981), 16.
5. Thacker, C. P., E. M. McCreight, B. W. Lampson, R. F. Sproull, and D. R. Boggs. "Alto: A Personal Computer." In D. Siewiorek, C. G. Bell, and A. Newell (eds.), *Computer Structures: Principles and Examples.* New York: McGraw-Hill, 1982.
6. Ingalls, D. H. "The Smalltalk Graphics Kernel." *Byte*, 6 (1981), pp. 168-194
7. English, W. K., D. C. Engelbart, and M. L. Berman. "Display-Selection Techniques for Text Manipulation." *IEEE Transactions on Human Factors in Electronics*, HFE-8 (1967), pp. 21-31.
8. Fitts, P. M. "The Information Capacity of the Human Motor System in Controlling Amplitude of Movement." *Journal of Experimental Psychology*, 47 (1954), pp. 381-391.

9. Card, S., W. K. English, and B. Burr. "Evaluation of Mouse, Rate-Controlled Isometric Joystick, Step Keys, and Text Keys for Text Selection on a CRT." *Ergonomics*, 21 (1978), pp. 601-613.

10. Oppen, D. C., and Y. K. Dalal. "The Clearinghouse: A Decentralized Agent for Locating Named Objects in a Distributed Environment." Palo Alto: Xerox Office Products Division, OPD-T8103, 1981.

11. Huggins, W. H., and D. Entwisle. *Iconic Communication.* Baltimore and London: The Johns Hopkins University Press, 1974.

12. Smith, D. C. *Pygmalion, A Computer Program to Model and Stimulate Creative Thought.* Basel and Stuttgart: Birkhäuser Verlag, 1977.

13. Bolt, R. *Spatial Data-Management.* Cambridge, Massachusetts: Massachusetts Institute of Technology Architecture Machine Group, 1979.

14. Sutherland, I. "Sketchpad, A Man-Machine Graphical Communication System." *AFIPS, Proceedings of the Fall Joint Computer Conference* (Vol. 23), 1963, pp. 329-346.

15. Sutherland, W. "On-Line Graphical Specifications of Computer Procedures." Cambridge, Massachusetts: Massachusetts Institute of Technology, 1966.

16. Christensen, C. "An Example of the Manipulation of Directed Graphs in the AMBIT/G Programming Language." In M. Klerer and J. Reinfelds (eds.), *Interactive Systems for Experimental and Applied Mathematics.* New York: Academic Press, 1968.

17. Kay, A. C. *The Reactive Engine.* Salt Lake City: University of Utah. 1969.

18. Kay, A. C., and the Learning Research Group. "Personal Dynamic Media." Xerox Palo Alto Research Center Technical Report SSL-76-1, 1976. (A condensed version is in *IEEE Computer*, March 1977, pp. 31-41.)

19. Newman, W. M. "Officetalk-Zero: A User's Manual." Xerox Palo Alto Research Center Internal Report, 1977.

20. Dahl, O. J., and K. Nygaard. "SIMULA—An Algol-Based Simulation Language." *Communications of the ACM*, 9 (1966), pp. 671-678.

21. Lampson, B. "Bravo Manual." In *Alto User's Handbook*, Xerox Palo Alto Research Center, 1976 and 1978. (Much of the design and all of the implementation of Bravo was done by Charles Simonyi and the skilled programmers in his "software factory.")

22. Baudelaire, P., and M. Stone. "Techniques for Interactive Raster Graphics." *Proceedings of the 1980 Siggraph Conference*, 14 (1980), 3.

23. Tesler, L. "The Smalltalk Environment." *Byte*, 6 (1981), pp. 90-147.

24. Wertenbaker, L. *The World of Picasso.* New York: Time-Life Books, 1967.

25. Bush, V. "As We May Think." *Atlantic Monthly*, July 1945.

26. Engelbart, D. C. "Augmenting Human Intellect: A Conceptual Framework." Technical Report AFOSR-3223, SRI International, Menlo Park, Calif., 1962.

27. Engelbart, D. C., and W. K. English. "A Research Center for Augmenting Human Intellect." *AFIPS Proceedings of the Fall Joint Computer Conference* (Vol. 33), 1968, pp. 395-410.

PART VII

DISTRIBUTED SYSTEMS

21

WFS: A SIMPLE SHARED FILE SYSTEM FOR A DISTRIBUTED ENVIRONMENT*

DANIEL SWINEHART, GENE McDANIEL
AND DAVID BOGGS

(1979)

WFS is a shared file server available to a large network community. WFS responds to a carefully limited repertoire of commands that client progams transmit over the network. The system does not utilize connections, but instead behaves like a remote disk and reacts to page-level requests. The design emphasizes reliance upon client programs to implement the traditional facilities (stream IO, a directory system, etc.) of a file system. The use of atomic commands and connectionless protocols nearly eliminates the need for WFS to maintain transitory state information from request to request. Various uses of the system are discussed and extensions are proposed to provide security and protcction without violating the dcsign principles.

1 Introduction

Existing file systems implement different levels of service for their clients, and correspondingly leave different amounts of work for the clients to do. Traditionally, file systems have evolved to provide more and more functionality from simple file access to complicated arrangements which provide sharing, security, and distributed data storage.

---

*D. Swinehart, G. McDaniel and D. Boggs, WFS: a simple shared file system for a distributed environment. *ACM Symposium on Operating Systems Principles*, Pacific Grove, CA, (December 1979), 9–17.

This paper describes WFS, a file system that provides a concise set of file operations for use in a distributed computing environment. Designed by the authors in 1975, and built by one of us (Boggs) in under two months, WFS has successfully supported a number of interactive applications.

The filing needs of *Woodstock*, an early office system prototype, dictated the functional and performance criteria of WFS. Woodstock provided facilities for creating, filing, and retrieving simple office documents, and a rudimentary facility for exchanging these documents as electronic messages.

Woodstock's hardware environment was a network of minicomputers, each providing specialized functions (terminal control, editing, filing, message services, etc.) in support of the overall application. WFS was designed as the shared filing component, storing Woodstock documents on high-capacity disks attached to one of these processors.

During development, Woodstock used small local disks on each editing processor. The software that supported the editing application had to provide facilities for transforming access to physical disk pages into higher-level functions. These included character and word I/O, file positioning, and functions for opening and closing files. The application also implemented its own hierarchical document directory structure.

WFS was designed after the rest of the system was operational. Consequently, it was easy to define its functional specification, since Woodstock already provided the higher-level functions. The local file access was to be replaced by network access to a shared file system running on another machine. A file system based upon page-level access to randomly addressable files would be adequate, and a small amount of file sharing needed by the application could be accommodated by a simple locking mechanism at the file level. A two month limit on implementation time, combined with a conviction that a very simple file system organization could achieve the same purposes as existing more complex designs, led to the system described here.

2 System Description

2.1 The Client's File System Model

In this paper, a *server* is a program that supplies a well-defined service over a computer network to *client* programs, which use the service to implement some application. A client program may or may not be operating in direct response to the actions of a human *user*.

WFS is a server that provides its clients with a collection of files. It is currently implemented on a dedicated Xerox Alto research minicomputer [Thacker *et al*] augmented by one or more disk drives, each with a transfer rate of around 7 megabits per second and a capacity of from 80 to 300 megabytes. A WFS file contains up to 60,516 data pages, each 246 16-bit words long. Clients may write pages in any order, and WFS waits to allocate space for a page until it is first written. A file is denoted by a 32-bit unsigned integer, its *file identifer (FID)*. WFS allocates FIDs for new files, on request, from a single name space. There is no additional naming or directory structure within the system. For this reason, and because of the carefully limited repertoire of operations, an application programmer might well choose to view each FID as a handle on a "virtual disk", interfaced through a moderately intelligent controller.

2.2 WFS Operations

The complete set of WFS operations is shown in Table 1. Each operation involves an exchange of network packets using the protocol described in the next section. The operations partition into four groups, used for:

- Reading and writing pages of files
- Allocating and deallocating FIDs and pages of files
- Obtaining and modifying file properties
- Performing system maintenance activities

The most commonly executed operations are those used for reading and writing a selected file page, given its FID and page number. A number of *page properties* are returned along with each page that is read (see below), and client modifications to some page properties may be specified during each write operation.

The second group of operations allows one to create a file (with no assigned pages) and obtain its FID, to expunge a FID (illegal if any pages remain), and to deallocate the storage for a page. In addition, there is an operation that allows a client to create a file with an explicitly specified FID value. WFS reserves a range of FID values for this purpose when it creates a new file system.

The third group allows the client to find out what file pages are allocated, and to examine a FID's current *file properties.* One of the operations allows the client to modify those file properties that are under its control.

Operation	Description
Page Transfer	
ReadPage(fid,pageNum) WritePage(fid,pageNum,lock,page properties)	Read or write page properties and page data
File Management	
GetFID()	Allocates a new file and returns its fid
ExpFID(fid)	If fid has no pages allocated, expunges (deletes) the file
DeallocatePage(fid,lock, pageNum)	Releases storage for page and removes page from page map
Status Query/Modification	
GetFIDStatus(fid)	Return file status values
SetFIDStatus(fid,mask,value)	Set client status values, ignore attempt to affect system values
ReadPageMap(fid,lock, pageMapNumber)	Return page map information to determine which pages are allocated
Lock(fid)	Return key, required in subsequent operations until file is unlocked
UnLock(fid)	Unlock file (set lock to zero)
Maintenance	
ReallocFID(fid) ResetLastFID(newFid) ReadRealPage(realAddress) GetVMap()	These operations allow examination of the system at the disk logical and physical page level. In addition, the FID allocation routines can be used to restore the file system using backup information.
WFSPing()	WFS merely acknowledges this operation. It allows one to check the basic communications path.

Table 1 WFS operations

The fourth group provides maintenance facilities. Utility client programs use them to copy WFS files to a backup store, restore selected files, rebuild WFS volumes from backup, and repair client-level file structures.

2.3 Properties

WFS associates with each data page a set of *page properties*, some of which are of interest to the client (see Figure 1). WFS reads and writes the page propertics along with the data. The first few felds provide a safety check since they duplicate the FID and page number, and the system checks them on each page access. They may also be used by low-level crash recovery routines to reconstruct damaged file structures. The *client* fields are assigned and interpreted by the client. The client may ask WFS to compare a page's client properties against the ones supplied in a command, and to abort the command if they fail to match. This allows the system to validate client assertions about the page in question.

Similarly, each file has a set of *file properties* (see Figure 2). The system uses some of this space to record the status of the file directory entry (free, allocated, deleted, expunged). The client cannot change these. Other properties are cooperatively maintained by the system and its clients. Whenever a file is dirtied, WFS sets the file's *dirty* bit. A client that desires higher

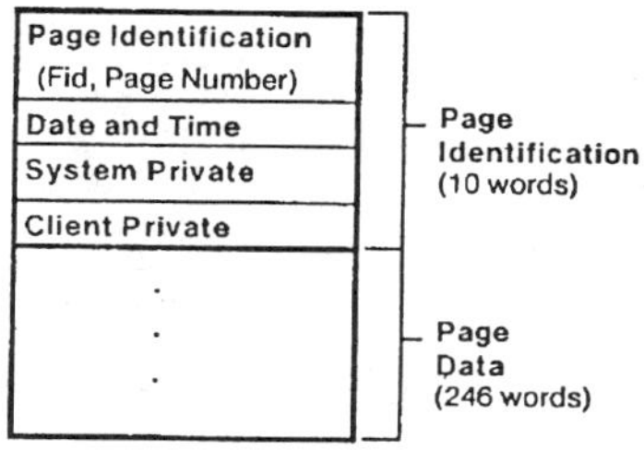

Figure 1 WFS disk page format

reliability may backup dirty files and then ciear this bit. Finally, some space is reserved for client-private uses; WFS does not touch these properties.

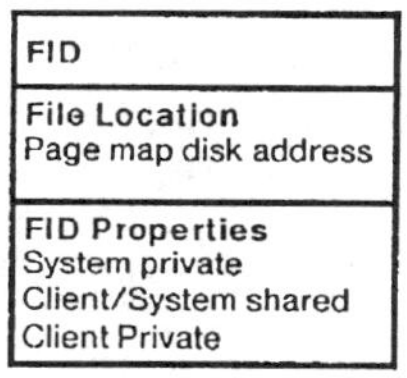

Figure 2 FID directory entry

2.4 File locks

A client may lock a file, preventing access by anyone without the proper key. The lock operation returns a key that must be supplied with all subsequent operations on the file, until either the client issues an unlock operation or the lock breaks. WFS will break a file's lock if no operation has been performed on the file for a minute or so. A system restart breaks all locks. A key of zero fits an unlocked file. A client can detect a broken lock because the non-zero key will not fit the lock on an unlocked file.

key	lock	access	file state
0	0	allowed	unlocked
0	X	denied	locked
X	X	allowed	locked
X	Y	denied	locked
X	0	denied	unlocked

These locking operations provide primitives that are adequate to implement completely safe sharing mechanisms (see section 4.2.)

2.5 Communications Protocol

Within the Xerox research community, the foundation for process-to-process communication is an internetwork packet (or *datagram*), as opposed to a stream (or *virtual circuit*) [Boggs *et al.*] However, many of the applications that use the Xerox internetwork choose to hide the packet boundaries and to assure reliable transmission by means of a stream facility constructed from the packet protocols. A stream is an example of a connection-based protocol: a substantial amount of state must be correctly maintained at both ends for the duration of the connection.

The WFS protocol, on the other hand, is based on the direct transmission of internetwork packets, and does not rely on the reliable delivery of every packet. WFS provides an example of a connectionless protocol: the server maintains no state between packets, and the client maintains very little—often none.

To perform a WFS operation, a client constructs a *request* packet containing the operation code and any necessary parameters, and sends it to the selected WFS host (see Figure 3). WSF processes commands in the order in which they arrive and then returns a *response* packet to the sender. The response contains the requested data or a failure code. The server is entirely passive: it never initiates activity, but only responds to requests.

Since the reliable delivery of request packets and their responses is not guaranteed, the client must take the appropriate steps to assure robust performance. It usually suffices to retransmit a request if a reasonable interval has elapsed without receiving its response. The operations are designed so that any write action will have the same effect if it is repeated. In addition, it must not be possible for packets to be delayed for so long that write and read operations can occur out of order without detection. This behavior is not difficult to arrange in our environment, but would have to be dealt with if the methods were generalized.

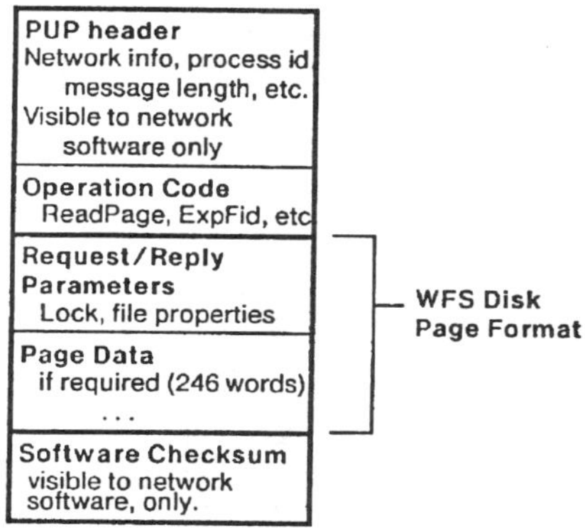

Figure 3 Request/Acknowledgement packet

2.6 File System Implementation

WFS is written in BCPL [Richards], supported by a simple custom-tailored operating system and communications package.

For each file, WFS maintains a *page map* that translates client page numbers into physical disk addresses and identifies unallocated pages. Depending on the current length of the file, the page map is either one or two levels deep (see Figure 4).

The FID directory is a hash table implemented as a contiguous, fixed-size file at a known disk address. Entries in the directory associate FIDs with their corresponding file properties and top-level page map locations.

A single process interprets client operations in the WFS server. This process sequentially extracts request packets from the network input queue, checks them for validity, and dispatches to the indicated operation. When the operation completes, the process returns a response packet to the requesting client. By using this simple, sequential scheme, lockup behavior is impossible, and starvation (unfair treatment of a particular client) is very unlikely.

During a write operation, WFS reads the specified data page (and in some cases auxiliary pages) before writing it, in order to validate its FID, page number, and other page properties. If a discrepancy is found, the operation is rejected (see section 2.5). The system writes the data into its assigned disk page immediately, before returning the acknowledgment packet.

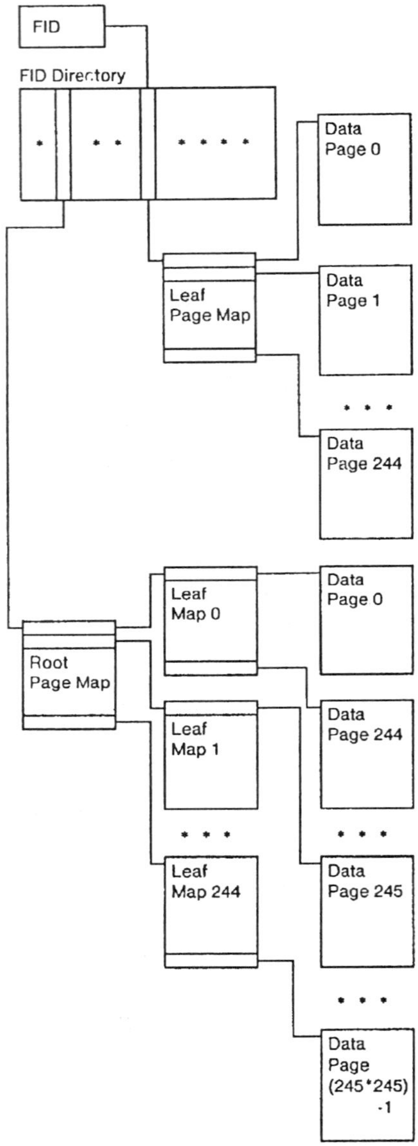

Figure 4 WFS File Structure. Small files use a single page map level, while larger files use a two level map. Empty data pages are not allocated on the disk.

Although a WFS application will occasionally make closely spaced references to the same data page, such references are not frequent enough to warrant special treatment. However, multiple references to auxiliary disk pages (page maps, directories, and allocation bit tables) predominate. For this reason, WFS uses a substantial percentage of main memory as a write-through cache of recently referenced disk pages. Discarding the least recently referenced page whenever cache space is needed favors retention of the auxiliary pages, while accommodating the infrequent case of closely spaced accesses to the same data page.

Since pages to be changed are always written immediately, the cache is entirely redundant and is maintained for efficiency only; any page of it, or all of it, can be discarded for any reason (including a system crash) without affecting the integrity of the file system.

2.7 Performance

WFS has never been used in an environment subject to a high volume of concurrent accesses by a large number of hosts. However, we did measure its performance under a heavy load generated by one to three hosts running the *Woodstock* application. Table 2 provides the performance figures obtained from these tests (see [McDaniel] regarding the network-based instrumentation tool). The table compares both reading and writing times of WFS with times obtained by performing the same activities using the local disk. The WFS times include the cost of the client's service routines that provide packet composition, transmission and response interpretation activities as well as the actual WFS software and disk access times. In each case, one or more Woodstock users manually produced a very high request rate. While the table doesn't detail this observation, we found that the network transmission times through the high-bandwidth Ethernet local network [Metcalfe-Boggs] were negligible. Measurements of subsequent server/client configurations have produced comparable results.

Write operations yielded poorer results than read operations in the tests because WFS reads data pages to validate them before writing new contents (see section 2.6).

In the single-user (lightly loaded) case, WFS improved Woodstock's average input response time over the local disk's time for several reasons: WFS's disks were faster than Woodstock's local disks, requested pages were sometimes still in the WFS main memory cache, and the amount of arm motion on the local disk was reduced because it no longer had to seek between a

Read Page	AVG	MIN	MAX
Using Local Disk	60	30	90
WFS with one user	48	20	260
with two users	76	20	330
with three users	100	20	330

All times in milliseconds

Write Page	AVG	MIN	MAX
Using Local Disk	47	10	110
WFS with one user	73	30	260
with two users	109	30	350
with three users	150	40	420

Table 2 WFS performance observations. In multiple-user experiments, system users manually produced extremely demanding loads. Maximum load for the same number of users could be somewhat greater.

code swap-area and the user data area.

In general, performance has been adequate for a number of nontrivial applications. Notice that the measurements exhibit nearly linear degradation with increasing load. A system implementing more sophisticated scheduling methods could improve this performance.

3 Design Philosophy

The principle theme of the WFS design is that client programs must provide the higher-level abstractions usually associated with file systems, while WFS implements a simple, low-level abstraction with relatively few operations and with high reliability. Low-level, reliable file service in WFS stems from its passive, *atomic* operations which are characterized by the following properties:

- Each operation may access at most one data page, and no more than a few auxiliary disk pages.
- Each operation runs to completion before WFS acknowledges it. A write operation is not complete until the data is on the disk. Between

operations WFS retains no state information that cannot be regenerated from the contents of the disk.

- Command and protocol boundaries are the same—each command and response comprises a single internet packet.

- Clients access the server through connectionless protocols—each packet proceeds independently over the network.

The receipt of a command acknowledgment is an assurance that the overall integrity of the file system is correct at the "virtual disk" level. This means that a subsequent crash recovery or other reinitialization in either the client or the server will be invisible except for a possible time delay. Although this approach places additional burdens on the client and ultimately limits the efficiency of deletion and copy operations, it simplifies the protocol design by limiting operations and responses to single packets. It also improves the ease with which a reasonable and fair response to client requests can be guaranteed. We believe this property was crucial to meeting our time constraints for implementing Woodstock.

The connectionless protocol frees WFS from the requirements of maintaining communication state information during client interactions, and reduces the work clients must do to communicate with WFS. Since we have found that the size and computing overhead of high-level communication code often exceeds that needed to provide the higher-level abstractions, this reduction becomes more important when client programs are implemented on personal computers which may not be particularly powerful.

If the client receives an acknowledgment for a write request, then the write operation has clearly occurred. The write algorithms are also constructed to reduce the possibility that the state of the file system can become inconsistent at the file and page level. Therefore, our atomic property provides a high probability, but not an absolute guarantee, that an unacknowledged write request has been performed either in its entirety or not at all. The WFS system and protocol have no facilities for assuring that higher-level transactions involving changes to multiple data pages have this property, although a client-based algorithm can achieve this goal [Paxton].

4 Functional Capabilities and Implications

This section examines the extent to which the WFS design can support generally useful file system activities. We first look at uses that do not involve the sharing of files, then extend the discussion to shared applications. Finally, we consider the comparative cost to the client of using WFS instead of a more functionally rich system.

4.1 Single User Applications

We contend that, for uses that do not involve sharing, WFS is functionally sufficient, since a more traditional system (e.g., character-level I/O and directory functions) can be built using the "virtual disk" provided by the page access operations. A single implementation of these facilities might well satisfy the needs of a number of applications. Our application was Woodstock; other applications are described elsewhere [Paxton], [Shoch-Weyer].

Clients must provide their own naming and file directory structures. If an application creates a file and forgets the FID returned by WFS, the file is lost, although client programs can be written to scan the FID directory and find it again. The Woodstock application implements a directory by keeping FIDs "hidden" in text files where document names are referenced. Since the FID is a sufficient handle to access the file, Woodstock can easily and efficiently find a file regardless of the context of its reference. Other applications have made quite different arrangements, all of which are of no concern to WFS.

We have found that it is straightforward to rewrite device drivers using network communications rather than driving the disk directly. Since WFS makes no assumptions about the structure of application files except that they are a sequence of pages, specific file structures are conventions enforced only by the application. For example, the conversion of Woodstock to WFS instead of a local disk required no file structure modifications.

As indicated in section 2.5, some network configurations can lead to the arrival of so-called *delayed duplicate* packets, which can cause write and read operations to occur out of order. The rather primitive communication protocols in WFS would need to be augmented for the system to be usable in an environment where this behavior was possible. One approach would be to retain sufficient mutual state information between client and scrver hosts (i.e., a simple connection) that packets arriving out of ordcr could be detected and discarded. The packet sequence numbers used to detect delayed or fraudulent packets would be allowed to repeat only over extremely long intervals (months or years.) See [Lampson-Sturgis] for an example of this approach.

4.2 Shared Applications

In examining WFS's ability to support shared access to files, it is useful to consider the following three categories of file system state:

> Long-term information endures throughout a file's lifetime or longer. Examples are the data files themselves, the system allocation tables, and the FID directory.
>
> Medium-term information is retained across atomic operations. The timeout lock that enables the sharing of data is the only medium-term state WFS keeps, whereas traditional file servers also maintain medium-term information associated with communication connections, open files, and the like.
>
> Short-term information is the state that must be kept during the execution of an atomic operation. In WFS, though there may be large amounts of such information, all that state may be discarded after an operation completes without sacrificing the integrity of the file system.

Clearly, the maintenance of medium-term information is necessary for any reasonable set of file system facilities. We believe that the client can maintain all such information, except for that required to enable the locking of data when shared access is possible. The goal is an overall improvement in the size and cleanliness of the total system.

WFS's medium-term lock information must also be augmented by client activities to obtain file sharing with behavior that can be guaranteed. While Woodstock's approach to sharing is quite primitive, Paxton discusses the design of a file system that uses WFS as its base and that provides reliable shared access to user files [Paxton]. Clark describes time limit locks in a shared resource system. In his system, IO device routines implemented on top of a virtual memory facility must implement reliable service, in the presence of memory locks which will break after their time limits expire [Clark]. The DFS [Israel *et al.*] system uses time limit locks as part of its approach to sharing, although DFS itself handles lock timeouts.

4.3 Cost Considerations

Implementing the higher abstractions on client machines costs them code space and execution time, although much of this expense is recovered because the interface to the server is simpler. Correspondingly, WFS saves code space which it may use for disk buffers, and saves execution time which it may provide to more users.

Our insistence upon the atomic operations property has led to some objectionable inefficiencies. An obvious example is the requirement that clients deallocate files, one page at a time, in order to delete them. Another drawback is that there is no provision for high-speed access to consecutive pages. In section 5.2 we suggest some simple extensions to handle these kinds of operatiors.

5 Possible Extensions

5.1 Privacy and Security

Any host that can communicate with WFS has full access to all operations on all WFS files. Thus, security cannot be guaranteed, and privacy can be guaranteed only if the application encrypts everything. In this area alone WFS is not adequate to meet the functional needs of a generally useful file server (see [Birrell-Needham] for a discussion about the attributes of a universal file server).

For our experimental applications, the absence of server-enforced security was reasonable, because security and privacy were supplied by application programs. Again, we were willing to impose more responsibility on the client, in return for the flexibility to experiment with different user-level protection schemes, or to defer protection issues altogether.

Methods for communications privacy and for access control would have to be added to WFS to achieve acceptable security in a more hostile environment. By applying recent work in both these areas, this could be accomplished without affecting the simplicity or robustrless of the current design.

Communications privacy (see [Kent] for a general discussion) can be supplied by a number of encryption approaches, and can be compatible with the atomic, connectionless design of WFS. The methods developed in [Needham-Schroeder] and [Rivest *et al.*] are particularly relevant to this application.

Flexible use of a file server causes more problems than an encryption system can handle easily, but they are problems that a capability-based access mechanism can solve [Birrell-Needham]. One reasonable approach for WFS would adapt a method, described in [Needham], for adding capability access to a conventional file server that has login authentication. To perform an operation, a client would now have to present an unforgeable capability for a file instead of the file's FID). The file system would create and return such a capability in response to a file creation request from an authenticated user. This initial capability would allow the possessor arbitrary access to the file. Additional operations would allow the client to request different capabilities for the same file, with restricted access rights (e.g., read-only). Such capabilities could be passed safely to other users. Clients would use these capability facilities to produce applications exhibiting the desired user-level protection.

WFS would implement these capabilities as records encrypted with a private key. The records would include the FID and the file access rights associated with the capability. The capability generated at file creation time would grant full rights to the creator. This approach would allow WFS to locate the relevant FID, check access, etc., by merely decoding the incoming capability, without the need for additional information. The required user authentication could be handled by supplying an operation that would return a "user identification capability" when presented with a user name and correct password.

In this section we have discussed minor extensions to WFS that would increase the privacy and security of its transactions without sacrificing the partitioning of client and server responsibilities. However, to build into the server the additional transaction-based interface that Paxton produced in the client machine [Paxton] would require a fundamental redesign. Systems that provide capability or transaction-based facilities at the server level are reported in [Needham-Birlell], [Israel *et al.*], and [Birrell-Needham].

5.2 Changes for Efficiency

The performance of WFS is ultimately limited by one of its strengths: the independence of each page-level request. When it is known that an application will require the successive use of a substantial number of contiguous file pages, much better performance would be possible if this knowledge could be used to optimize their transfer to and from the disk. One way to do this would involve extending the command set to include an explicit statement that a range of pages will be needed, counting on the server's page caching methods to transfer them efficiently into its main memory in advance of their use. Another method would not involve any new commands, but would require the elaboration of the command interpreter to allow the processing of more than one incoming operation at a time. Information about sequential disk access could be passed on to the disk-management level, where the same efficient transfer scheduling decisions could be made.

Although the network software and hardware delays are smaller than disk access time, they are not negligible. The latter method above, allowing multiple outstanding requests, could also result in an average increase in network throughput.

If the basic page transfer performance were improved, one major source of inefficiency would remain: the absence of operations for deleting entire files, copying their contents, etc. These operations were omitted in order to guarantee the client response times and file integrity properties discussed at length above. It would be straightforward to spawn a process within WFS to submit successive page-level requests (at the same priority as client requests) until the task was complete. System integrity at the virtual disk level would not be impaired, although a server crash could prevent the file-level task from completing (see [Lampson-Sturgis] for a more robust approach to the system crash problem). The server could acknowledge the operation either on receipt of the request or on final temination; both approaches are problematical, since they violate the atomic property in one way or another. An alternative would be for the client to retain the burden of sequencing these activities, but to speed them up using one of the bulk-transfer methods proposed above.

While none of the methods discussed in this section have been tried, we are confident that their application would result in a shared page-level file system with very impressive overall performance.

6 WFS Applications

In addition to the Woodstock system, now defunct, whose requirements drove the development of WFS, a number of applications have been built that continue to use WFS for their files. Two of them are described in separate articles (see [Paxton] and [Shoch-Weyer].)

A final example of an application with a set of higher-level characteristics different from Woodstock is an implementation of an experimental telephone directory data base. This application uses entirely different naming structures and access methods than Woodstock does, but can coexist with other WFS-based applications.

The telephone directory application runs on personal computers in the Xerox internetwork, providing access to approximately 40,000 entries. Each entry associates a name with a telephone number and other public information. All the entries are stored within a single WFS file with a fixed, known

FID. The user supplies a key, and the application responds with one or more entries whose names match the key (the key is an initial substring). A typical single-entry query can be completed in approximately one-half second, reading an average of three WFS data pages.

For this simple application, a data base method using B-Trees [McCreight] was an obvious candidate. An available B-Tree package (which runs in the client machine) and WFS made an ideal combination: the former implements a particular high-level data structure, given operations that can read and write numbered data pages of any fixed size; the latter implements just these operations without in any way interpreting the contents of the pages.

7 Conclusion

We have demonstrated empirically that a very simple central file server, teamed with appropriate file system elaborations in the client host, can meet or exceed many of the capabilities of more comprehensive central facilities at acceptable cost to the client. Clients benefit from the flexibility and file system robustness resulting from this approach. Extensions to meet more stringent performance requirements and to provide adequate security seem possible without major modification to the design. Although this approach has been quite successful, it remains to be seen which of the possible partitionings of server-client functions will prove to be the most powerful and convenient.

References

1. A. Birrell and R. Needham, A Universal File Server, to appear in *Communications of the ACM.*
2. D. Boggs, J. Shoch, E. Taft, and R. Metcalfe, Pup: An Internetwork Architecture, to appear in *IEEE Transactions on Communication.*
3. D. Clark, *An Input/Output Architecture for Virtual Memory Computer Systems*, MIT MAC TR-117, January 1974.
4. J. Israel, J. Mitchell, and H. Sturgis, Separating Data from Function in a Distributed File System, *Proc. Second International Symposium on Operating Systems*, IRIA, Rocquencourt, France, October 1978; to appear D. Lanciaux, ed., *Operating Systems*, North Holland.
5. S. Kent, *Encryption-based Protection for Interactive User-Computer Communication*, MIT MAC TR-162, May 1976.
6. B. Lampson and H. Sturgis, Crash Recovery in a Distributed Data Storage System, to appear in *Communications of the ACM.*

7. E. McCreight, Pagination of B*-Trees with Variable-Length Records, *Communications of the ACM*, 20 (9):670–674, September 1977.

8. G. McDaniel, METRIC: A Kernel Instrumentation System for Distributed Environments, *Operating Systems Review* 11 (5):93–99, November 1977.

9. R. Metcalfe and D. Boggs, ETHERNET: Distributed Packet Switching for Local Computer Networks, *Communications of the ACM*, 19 (7):395–404, July 1976.

10. R. Needham, Adding Capability Access to Conventional File Servers, *Operating Systems Review*, 13 (1):3–4, January 1979.

11. R. Needham and A. Birrell, The CAP Filing System, *Operating Systems Review* 11 (5):11–16, November 1977.

12. R. Needham and M. Schroeder, Using Encryption for Authentication in Large Networks of Computers, *Communications of the ACM*, 21 (12):993–999, December 1978.

13. W. Paxton, Client-Based Transactions to Maintain Data Integrity, *Proceedings of the Seventh Symposium on Operating System Principles*, 1979.

14. M. Richards, BCPL: A Tool for Compiler Writing and System Programming, *AFIPS Conference Proceedings* (SJCC) 35:557–566, 1969.

15. R. Rivest, A. Shamir, and L. Adelman, A Method for Obtaining Digital Signatures and Public-key Cryptosystems, *Communications of the ACM*, 21 (2):120–126, February 1978.

16. J. Shoch and S. Weyer, Page Level Access to a Network File Server from Smalltalk, to appear.

17. C. Thacker, E. McCreight, B. Lampson, R. Sproull, and D. Boggs, Alto: A Personal Computer, *Computer Structures: Readings and Examples* (Siewiorek, Bell, and Newell, eds.), 1979, to appear.

22

THE DESIGN OF A RELIABLE REMOTE PROCEDURE CALL MECHANISM*

SANTOSH SHRIVASTAVA AND FABIO PANZIERI

(1982)

In this correspondence we describe tbe design of a reliable Remote Procedure Call mechanism intended for use in local area networks. Starting from the hardware level that provides primitive facilities for data transmission we describe how such a mechanism can be constructed. We discuss various design issues involved, including the choice of a message passing system over which the remote call mechanism is to be constructed and the treatment of various abnormal situations such as lost messages and node crashes. We also investigate what the reliability requirements of the Remote Procedure Call mechanism should be with respect to both the application programs using and the message passing system on which it itself is based.

I INTRODUCTION

In this correspondence we describe the design of a reliable Remote Procedure Call (RPC) mechanism which we have been investigating within the context of programming reliable distributed applications. In the following we consider a distributed system as composed of a number of interacting "client" and "server" processes running on possibly distinct nodes of the system; the interactions between a client and a server are made possible by the suitable use of the RPC mechanism. Essentially, in this scheme a client's remote call is transformed into an appropriate message to the named server which

*S. K. Shrivastava and F. Panzieri, The design of a reliable remote procedure call mechanism. *IEEE Transactions on Computers 31*, 7 (July 1982), 692–697.

performs the requested work and sends the result back to the client and so terminating the call. The RPC mechanism is thus implemented on top of a message passing interface. Some of the interesting problems that need to be faced are: 1) the selection of appropriate semantics and reliability features of the RPC mechanism, 2) the design of an appropriate message passing interface over which the RPC is to be implemented, and 3) the treatment of abnormal situations such as node crashes. These problems and their solutions are discussed in this correspondence. We shall concentrate primarily on the relevant reliability issues involved, so other directly or indirectly related issues such as type checking, authentication, and naming will not be addressed here.

The RPC mechanism described in the following has been designed for a local area network composed of a number of PDP 11/45 and LS 11/23 computers (nodes) interconnected by the Cambridge Ring [1]; each node runs the UNIX (V7) operating system. However, most of the ideas presented in this correspondence are, we believe, sufficiently general to be applicable to any other local area network system.

II AN OVERVIEW OF RELIABILITY ISSUES IN DISTRIBUTED PROGRAMMING

In this section we briefly review the main reliability problems in distributed programming and discuss which of these problems need closer attention during the design of an RPC mechanism.

In this discussion we shall concentrate upon a distributed system consisting of a number of autonomous nodes connected by a local area network. A node in such a network will typically contain one or more processes providing services (e.g., data retention) that can be used by local or remote processes. We shall refer to such processes as "servers" and "clients," respectively. So an execution of a typical application program will give rise to a computation consisting of a client making various service requests to servers. These service requests take the form of procedure calls—if a server is remote then the calls to it will be remote procedure calls. In the rest of the correspondence we will assume the general and more difficult case of remote calls (note, however, that it is possible to hide the "remoteness" of servers by providing a uniform interface for all service calls). It can be seen that we have adopted a "procedure based" model of computation rather than a "message based" model. It has been pointed out that these two models appear to be duals of each other [2]. Bearing this in mind, we have chosen to support the first model because this allows us to directly apply the existing knowledge on the design and development of programs to distributed systems.

Let us ignore, for the time being, any reliability problems in the mechanization of a suitable RPC facility and concentrate upon the reliability problems at the application program level. The most vexing problems is to do with guaranteeing a clean termination of a program despite breakdowns (crashes) of nodes and communication subsystems. It is now well known that this can be achieved by structuring a program as an *atomic action* with the following "all or nothing" property: either all of the client's requested services are performed or none are [3, 4, 5]. Thus, a program terminates either producing the intended results or none at all. In a distributed system the implementation of atomic actions requires the provision of a special protocol, such as the *two phase commit* protocol [3, 4] to coordinate the activities of clients and servers. In addition, some recovery capability is also needed at each node to "undo" any results produced at that node by an ongoing atomic action that is subsequently to be terminated with null results. We shall not discuss here the details of how the various facilities needed for the provision of atomic actions can be constructed—they are well documented in the already cited references—but draw the reader's attention to Fig. 1 which shows a typical hierarchy of software interfaces. The point to note is that the atomic action software that supports $L3$ contains major reliability measures for application programs (undo capability, two phase commit). This has important consequences on the design of RPC—in particular in choosing its semantics and reliability capability.

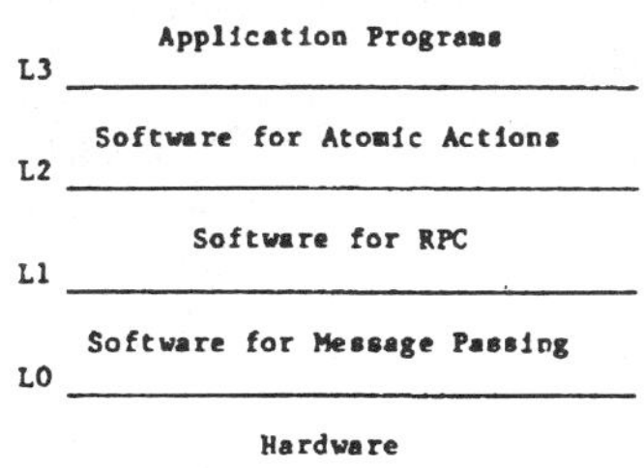

Figure 1 Hierarchy of software interfaces.

The algorithm below, which shows the bare essentials of an RPC mechanism will be used to illustrate the reliability problems. The send and receive primitives provide a message handling facility (the precise semantics of which are not relevant in the following discussion). Suppose that the message handling facility is such that messages occasionally get lost. Then a client would be well justified by resending a message when it "suspects" a loss. This could sometimes result in more than one execution at the server. To take another case, suppose that the client's node crashes immediately after the server starts to perform the requested work. Suppose now that the the client's "comes up" again and the client reissues the remote call: this again gives rise to the possibility of repeated executions at the server (the above situation can occur even if messages never get lost). If a client is not aware of the fact that repeated executions have taken place, then many of a server's executions will be in vain, with no client to receive the sent responses. Such executions have been termed *orphans* by Lampson and many ingenious schemes have been deviced for detecting and treating orphans [6, 7]. The above mentioned problems have led Nelson to classify the semantics of remote procedure calls as follows [7].

```
Client                  Server
                        cycle
send (···);      →        receive (···);
 - - -                    - -
                          "work"
                          - -
receive (···);   ←        send (···);
                        end
```

1) *"Exactly Once" Semantics:* If a client's call succeeds (i.e., the call does not return abnormally), then this implies that exactly one execution has taken place at the server; this is, of course, the meaning associated with conventional procedure calls.

2) *"At Least Once" Semantics:* If a client's call succeeds, then this implies that at least one execution has taken place at the server. Further subclassification is also possible (e.g., first one or last one) indicating which execution is responsible for the termination of a call.

To start with, it should be clear that out of the two, 1) has the more desirable semantics but is also the more difficult of the two to achieve. An approach that has been widely used (see, for example, [3]) is to adopt—for the sake of simplicity at the RPC level—the "at least once" semantics and to make all of the services of servers idempotent (that is, repeated executions are equivalent to a single execution). Thus the problems of repeated executions and orphans can be more or less ignored. The major shortcoming of this approach is that it is relatively difficult to provide servers with arbitrary services (e.g., a server cannot easily provide services that include increment operations); for this reason we have rejected this option in our RPC design and have chosen instead the "exactly once" semantics. This has been achieved by introducing sufficient measures at the RPC level to enable processes to reject unwanted messages arising during a call. This capability is not enough to cope with orphans, however, since as stated before, a client's crash can result in more than one remote call directed at a server when only one call was intended. We treat orphans at the next level (in the software supporting $L3$, see Fig. 1) by insisting that all programs that run over $L3$ be atomic actions with the "all or nothing" property. In particular, this means that any executions at servers be atomic as well. This atomicity criteria implies that repeated executions at a server are performed in a logically serial order with orphan actions terminating without producing any results. This is the basis of the work presented in [5] where the techniques needed for the construction of level $L3$, given the existence of $L2$, are described (a broadly similar approach has, we understand, been independently developed by Liskov's group at the Massachusetts Institute of Technology [8]).

To sum up this section: 1) we have chosen the exactly once semantics for our RPC, 2) the main reliability feature needed at the RPC level is that necessary to discard any unwanted messages, and 3) any other reliability features necessary for ensuring proper executions of application programs are added not at the RPC level but at the next level concerned with the provision of atomic actions. In the design of the RPC mechanism to be presented we have followed the rule of keeping each level as simple as possible; this has been achieved by making reliability mechanisms application specific rather than general as argued in [9].

III COMMUNICATIONS SUPPORT FOR RPC: DATAGRAM VERSUS TRANSPORT SERVICE

The implementation of RPC requires that the underlying level support some kind of Interprocess Communication (IPC) facility. On the one hand, this facility could be quite sophisticated with features such as guaranteed, undamaged and unduplicated delivery of a message, flow control, and end to end acknowledgment. An interface supporting such features is usually said to provide a *transport service* for messages. On the other hand, the IPC facility could be rather primitive, lacking most of the above desirable properties. An interface supporting such an IPC mechanism is said to provide a *datagram service* [10].

Transport services are designed in order to provide fully reliable communication between processes exchanging data (messages) over unreliable media—they are particularly suitable for wide area packet switching networks which are liable to damage, lose, or duplicate packets. The implementation of a "transport layer" tends to be quite expensive in terms of resources needed since a significant amount of state information needs to be maintained about any data transfer in progress. The initialization and maintenance of this state information, is required to support the abstraction of a "connection" between processes. To establish, maintain, and terminate a connection reliably is rather complex and a significant number of messages are needed just for connection purposes [11].

On the other hand, a datagram service provides the facility of the transmission of a finite size block of data (a message known as a datagram) from an origin address to a destination address. In its simplest form, the datagram service does not provide any means for flow control or end to end acknowledgments; the datagram is simply delivered on a "best effort" basis. If any of the features of the transport service are required, then the user must implement them specifically using the datagram service.

At a superficial level, it would seem that a good way to construct a reliable RPC would be to start with a reliable message service, i.e., a transport service. However, we reject this viewpoint and adopt the datagram service as the more desirable alternative. The argument for this decision is as follows. To start with, it must be noted that in the distributed system previously mentioned, the users are not given the abstraction of sending or receiving messages; rather only a very specific piece of software—that needed to implement RPC—is the sole user of messages. As such the full generality of the transport service is not needed. The provision of the transport service entails a considerable reduction of the available communication bandwidth (this is because of the overheads of connection management and the need for end to end acknowledgment). We may be able to utilize this bandwidth more effectively by reducing the need for connection management and acknowledgments as much as possible. This is indeed feasible in typical local area networks since the underlying hardware—the Cambridge Ring in our case—provides a reliable means of data transmission. So a fairly reliable datagram service (whereby every datagram is delivered with a high probability to its destination address) can certainly be built on top of the hardware interface. Any additional facilities needed are then specifically implemented making the implementation of the RPC a bit more complex but highly efficient. Hence, we conclude that it is appropriate to give the software of the RPC mechanism the responsibility of coping with any unreliabilities of a datagram service. In the next section we will describe the specific datagram service to be implemented over the Cambridge Ring hardware in order to support our RPC mechanism.

IV THE HARDWARE AND THE DATAGRAM SERVICE

The Cambridge Ring hardware [12] provides its users with the ability to transmit and receive packets of a fixed size between nodes connected to the Ring—each transmitted packet is individually acknowledged. At the Ring level each node is identified by a unique station address. The following two primitive operations are available.

1) *transmit-packet(destination, pkt,* **var** *status)*

where the acknowledgement is encoded as

status = *(OK, unselected, busy, ignored, transmission-error).*

The meaning of "status" is as follows:

status = *OK:* The destination station has received the packet.

status = *unselected:* The packet was not accepted by the destination station because that station was "listening" to some other source station.

status = *busy:* The packet was not accepted by the destination station because that station was "deaf" (not listening to anyone). Note that either of the above two status conditions implies that the destination station is most likely to become available shortly.

status = *ignored:* The packet was not accepted because the destination station was not on-line. This indication can be taken to mean that there is little chance of packets being accepted by that station or a while.

status = *transmission-error:* The packet got corrupted somewhere during its passage through the Ring. This is the only case where the response of the destination station is not known.

It is worth mentioning here that the transmit primitive does not have a time-out response associated with it. As a consequence, the execution of this primitive will not return if the packet is not acknowledged due to a fault in the Ring hardware.

2) *receive-packet(***var** *source,* **var** *pkt).*

The receive primitive allows for the reception of packets either from any source station on the Ring or from a specific source (a special operation is provided by the Ring for setting up a station in either of the modes). In either case, "source" will contain the identity of the sender with "pkt" containing the received packet. A curious aspect of the Ring is that each node has a parity error detection logic, but neither the sender nor the receiver of a packet get any indication when a parity error is detected in a packet (this does not matter all that much in reality as the probability of a packet getting corrupted has been shown to be very low).

We shall assume that all of the hardware components (e.g., Ring. processors, clocks) either perform exactly as specified or a component simply does not work (so, for example, for the Ring. a "send" or "receive" operation will not terminate). If this assumption were realistic, then the design to follow has some very nice reliability properties. However, unpredictable behavior of the hardware interface (i.e., a behavior that does not meet the specification) is likely to result in the same at the RPC/user interface to the extent that guaranteed behaviour cannot be promised.

The proposed datagram service will provide its users (processes) with the ability of: 1) sending a block of data to a named destination process, and 2) receiving a block of data from a specific or any process. We shall ignore here the fine details of how this may be implemented using the Ring operations described earlier; only the properties of the datagram service primitives will be described.

1) *send_msg (destination, message,* **var** *status).*

where *status = (OK, absent, not-done, unable).*

The message is broken into packets and transmitted to the home station of the destination process. If all these packets are accepted by the station, then "status = OK" will hold. Note that this *only* means that the message has reached the station, and *not* that it has been accepted by the destination process. If a packet is not accepted (possibly even after a few retries) by the station (packet level response is "unselected" or "busy"), then "status = not-done" will hold. A packet level response of "ignored" is translated as "status = absent" indicating that the destination process is just not available. The last two responses indicate that the message was not delivered. A time-out mechanism will be needed to cope with Ring malfunctions during the transmission of a message. The "unable" status holds either if the time out expires or if a packet level "transmission-error" response is obtained.

The "unable" response indicates inability of the datagram layer to deliver a message properly (the message may or may not have reached the destination station).

2) *receive_msg (source,* **var** *msg).*

The above primitive is to receive a message from a specified "source" process. This primitive is implemented by repeatedly making use of the receive-packet(...) primitive. A time-out mechanism will be needed to detect an incomplete message transmission and Ring failures. Any corruption of the sent message can be detected if the sender includes a checksum in the message and appropriate computation is performed at the receiver; corrupted messages are simply discarded. So the receive_msg(...) primitive only delivers a "good" message (if any).

The receive_msg(...) primitive can also be used for receiving messages from any source by simply specifying "source" parameter as "any."

The datagram service described above is based on the Basic Block Protocol designed at Cambridge [13].

V RPC MECHANISM

A client invokes the following primitive to obtain a service from a server (where the "time-out" parameter specifies how long the client is willing to wait for a response to his request):

remote_call(server, service, **var** *result,* **var** *status, time-out)*

where *status = (OK, not-done, absent, unable)* and parameters and results are passed by value.

The meaning of the call under various responses is given below.

status = OK: The service specified has been performed (*exactly once*) by the server and the answers are encoded in "result."

status = not-done: The server has not performed the service because it is currently busy (so the client can certainly reissue the call in the hope of getting an "OK" response).

status = absent: The server is not available (so it is pointless for the client to retry).

status = unable: The parameter "result" does not contain the answers; whether the server performed the service is not known. The action of the client under this situation will depend typically on the property of the requested service. If the service required has the idempotency property, then the client can retry without any harm; otherwise backward recovery should be invoked to maintain consistency. How this is achieved is not relevant here; it is sufficient to observe, as noted in the section on reliability issues, that the consistency and recovery problems could be handled within the framework of the two phase commit protocol and atomic actions.

We believe that these responses are meaningful, simply understood and quite adequate for robust programming. We shall show next that is possible to design RPC with the above properties based on our datagram service despite numerous fault manifestations in the distributed system (including node crashes). A skeleton program showing only the essential details of the RPC implementation is depicted below which should be self-explanatory. The following two assumptions will be made in the ensuing discussion: 1) some means exists for a receiver process to reject unwanted (i.e., spurious, duplicated) messages; the next section contains a proposal for achieving this goal; 2) node crashes amount to that station being not on line. We now consider the treatment of various responses obtained during message handling.

```
                Client                                        Server
remote-call (···) corresponds               cycle
to the following code:
      - - -                                        - - -
                                                   repeat "get work"
   send_ msg ( );                   →              receive_ msg (any, ···);
 "send service request"                            until msg = valid;
                                                   - - -
                                                   "perform work"
set(time-out);                                     - - -
repeat
                                                   "send result"
   receive_ msg ( );                ←              send_ msg ( );
until msg = valid;                                 - - -
      - - -                                 end;
```

1) *The Client Sends a Service Request:* Recall that a send_msg(...) can return the response "OK," "absent," "not done," or "unable." If the response is "OK," the control goes to the "set(time-out)" statement. If the response is "absent," then the execution of remote_call(...) terminates with "status = absent." If the response is "not-done," then the message is sent again. If after a few retries the same response is obtained, then the execution of remote_call(...) terminates with "status = not-done." A few retries can also be made if the send_msg(...) results in an "unable" response. If this

response still holds after retries, then the execution of remote-call(...) terminates with "status = unable." Note that it is all right to send a message repeatedly. The server is in a position to discard any duplicates.

2) *The Client Waits for a Message:* The client prepares to wait for a response from the server. A time-out is set to stop the client from waiting forever; the maximum duration of the waiting is as specified in the last parameter of the remote_call(...). All the unwanted messages are discarded. A client may get such messages, for example, as a result of the actions performed by that node before it crashed and came up again. If a valid message is received, then the execution of remote_call(...) terminates with "status = OK" and "result" containing the answer. If the time-out expires, then the execution of the remote_call(...) terminates with "status = unable." Note that "unable" response can be obtained for several reasons: server did not receive the message, server node crashed, or server's message not received because of a Ring fault.

3) *Server Waits for a Service Request:* Any spurious, in particular duplicated, messages are rejected. This guarantees that despite the possibility of repeated requests being sent by a client, only one service execution will take place.

4) *Server Sends the Reply:* If the execution of send_msg(...) results in an "OK" response, then the server is ready for the next request—it goes to the beginning of its cycle. Note that it is not guaranteed that the client will receive the reply, rather it implies that most probably the reply has reached the client. If the "send" operation gives rise to the "absent" response, then "unable" is signaled to the server. If the "send" operation gives rise to either a "not-done" or an "unable" response, then the message can be resent a few times before accepting defeat by signaling "unable" to the server. The reason for mapping all the three abnormal responses of send_msg(...) onto a single "unable" response is based on the belief that it is of little interest to a server as to why he was not able to deliver the result satisfactorily (this response means that most probably the client did not receive the reply). As before, any recovery actions of the server will be handled within the framework of atomic actions and the two phase commit protocol.

We conclude that the level concerned with RPC implementation provides three operations: 1) remote_call(...)—this is the client half of the program with the semantics discussed earlier; 2) get_work(...)—this corresponds to the repeat loop code of the server, and 3) send_result(..., status)—this corresponds to the code concerned with sending of the results, with status =

(OK, unable), where the "absent," "not-done," and "unable" responses of send_msg(...) are all mapped onto "unable" response of send-result.

It should be noted that if fault manifestations are rare and messages are delivered with a high probability, then *almost always, only two messages are required* for RPC. This is not possible if the transport service is used for message passing.

VI GENERATION OF SEQUENCE NUMBERS

In the previous section it was assumed that a receiver is always in a position to reject unwanted messages; this can be arranged by appropriately assigning sequence numbers (SN's) to messages. The problem of sequence numbering of messages is fairly complex if tolerance to node crashes is required. For example, it is necessary for a process of a node that has "come up" after a crash to be able to distinguish those incoming messages that have originated as a result of any actions performed before the crash. This typically requires maintaining relevant state information on a "crash proof," storage. This is a complicated and expensive process, so a scheme that has minimum crash proof storage requrements is to be preferred. A transport level is designed to cope with sequence numbering problems and users are not concerned with them; however, in our case they need to be generated explicitly within the RPC level. There can be three approaches to the generation and assignment of SN's.

1) SN's are unique over a given client-server interaction: this would be the approach implicitly taken by a transport level supported RPC. This is a fairly complex approach requiring the maintenance of a relatively large amount of state information that has to survive crashes [11].

2) SN's are unique over node to node interactions: rather than maintaining state information on a process to process basis, it is possible to maintain information on a node to node basis only. Clearly, it is less demanding than 1) above, in its requirements for crash proof storage.

3) SN's are unique over the entire system: if SN's are made unique over the entire network, then a very simple scheme suggests itself. A server need only maintain "the last largest SN received" in a crash proof storage (and as we shall see, even this requirement can be dispensed with). Further, all the retry messages are sent by a sender with the same SN as the original message. If a server accepts only those messages whose SN is greater than the current value of "last largest SN," then it is easy to see now that we have the server property assumed in the previous section (that of rejecting

unwanted messages). A similar approach is necessary at the client's end.

We have chosen to incorporate the third method in our design because, as indicated above, coping with node crashes is comparatively easier in such a technique. Two of the best known techniques for the generation of network wide unique sequence numbers are based on: 1) the circulating token method of Le Lann [14], and 2) the loosely synchronized clock approach of Lamport [15]. In the former all of the nodes are logically connected in a ring configuration and an integer valued "token" circulates round the ring in a fixed direction. A node that wants to send a message waits for the token to arrive, then it copies its value, increments the value of the token, and passes it on to the next node. The copied value can be used for sequence numbering. In the latter method each node is equipped with a clock and each node is also assigned a unique "node number." A sequence number at any node is the current clock value concatenated with the node number. For "acceptable behavior" (see later) it is necessary that the clock values at various nodes be approximately the same at any given time. This is achieved as follows. Whenever a process at say node n_i receives a message, it checks the SN of that message with the current SN of n_i; if SN(received) is greater or equal to SN(n_i), then the clock of n_i is advanced by enough ticks to make SN(n_i) greater than SN(received).

Out of the above two methods, we have adopted the second in our system for the following two reason: 1) because of the kind of message facility we are using, it will not be easy for a node to find out whether its sent token has been received by the next node or not; as a result the detection of the lost token is not a straightforward process; and 2) the algorithm for the reinsertion of the token—which must ensure that only one token gets inserted—is rather complex. In comparison, as we shall see, Lamport's technique can be made to tolerate lost messages and node crashes in a straightforward manner. We shall next describe how we have incorporated Lamport's technique into our design.

The SN at a node at any time is constructed out of the time of day and calendar clock of the node and the Ring station number.

SN =

time and data	station number

The SN of a node is maintained by a monitor [16] that provides the following two procedures:

get_SN(**var** *s_number*)

this procedure returns the SN

update_SN(s_number)

The SN at the monitor is compared with passed sequence number and the clock of the node adjusted as described earlier. The SN's are used in the RPC algorithm as depicted below.

Client		Server
		begin
		llsn := get_ SN (···);
...		*"llsn = last largest seq. no."*
		cycle
i := get_ SN (···);		...
		repeat *"get work"*
send_ msg (···);	→	*receive_ msg (any, ···)*
"message includes i"		**until** *msg · SN > llsn;*
		llsn := msg · SN;
		...
		"perform work"
set (time-out);		...
repeat		
receive_ msg (···);	←	*send_ msg (···);*
until *msg · SN = i;*		*"msg sent with SN = llsn"*
...		...
		end;
		end;

Strictly speaking, in our system there is no logical requirement that the various clocks be "approximately the same." However, in the absence of such a situation, a client with a slower clock will have difficulty in obtaining services since his requests will stand a higher chance of rejection by servers. Hence, it is necessary that each node regularly receives messages from other nodes so that it can keep its clock value nearer to those of others. For this purpose we maintain two processes at each node (see below).

Broadcaster	Clock Synchronizer
cycle	**cycle**
delay(t);	*receive_ msg (···);*
i := get_ SN(···);	*update_ SN (msg · SN);*
for *all remote nodes*	**end;**
do	
send_ msg (···);	
"send message with SN = i to a clock synchronizer"	
end;	

The "broadcaster" process of a node regularly (say once every few minutes) sends its sequence number to all of the remote clock-synchronizer processes. A few retries can be made if a send operation returns a "not-done" or an "unable" response. If these responses persist or an "absent" response is obtained, then no further attempt is made to send the message to that clock-synchronizer in that cycle (at this level, a crashed node in no way affects the noncrashed nodes). We shall now discuss how our sequence numbering scheme can be made to tolerate node crashes economically. We can avoid the need for any crash proof storage for our scheme by being careful during the start up phase of a node after a crash. In a centralized system. when the computer system is started up, the operator inputs the time and date to the system clock. This is not desirable in our system since careless clock updates can introduce problems. For example entering "future time and date" will eventually affect the rest of the system in that all clocks will become "inaccurate" in the sense that they will not represent physical time (logically this is irrelevant). Also, entering a "past time and date" can result in the acceptance of wrong messages. We simply insist that the "clock-synchronizer" process be the only process (with one exception, see below) that can update the clock. So when a node comes up, eventually (within a few minutes) it will be able to get an appropriate clock value. An important requirement is that a node, when it comes up, should have its clock initialized to zero. The only drawback of the above scheme is that if all the other nodes are down (presumably a rare event), then our node will never get a clock value. This problem can be solved by giving some privileged user the authority for clock updates.

We conclude this section by summarizing the net effect of our sequence number assignment and generation scheme on the fault-tolerant behavior of our RPC mechanism: 1) since none of the state information of a call is maintained on a crash proof storage, a call does not survive a crash; 2) the clock management scheme ensures that any messages belonging to a "crashed call" are ignored.

VII CONCLUDING REMARKS

The design presented here is currently being implemented on our UNIX systems. At a superficial level it would seem that to design a program that provides a remote procedure call abstraction would be a straightforward exercise. Surprisingly, this is not so. We have found the problem of the design of the RPC to be rather intricate. To the best of our ability we have checked that all of the possible normal and abnormal situations properly map onto the responses of the "remote_call(...)," "get_work(...)," and "send_result(...)." Clearly, a formal validation exercise and experience with the completed implementation should expose any inadequacies in our design.

Note Added in Proof: The RPC is now operational; its implementation is described in a report available from the authors.

Acknowledgements

The authors' understanding of the subject matter reported here has been improved as a result of discussions with their colleagues at Newcastle; in addition, they have also benefited from informal contacts with other groups, most notably those at Cambridge, MIT, and Xerox.

References

1. M. V. Wilkes and D. J. Wheeler, "The Cambridge communication ring," in *Proc. Local Area Network Symp.*, Boston, MA, Nat. Bureau of Standards, May 1979.
2. H. C. Lauer and R. M. Needham, "On the duality of operating system structures," in *Proc. 2nd Int. Symp. on Operating Syst.*, IRIA, Oct. 1978; also in *Oper. Syst. Rev.*, vol. 13. pp. 3–19, Apr. 1979.
3. B. Lampson and H. Sturgis, "Atomic transactions," in *Lecture Notes in Computer Science*, Vol. 105. New York: Springer-Verlag, 1981, pp. 246–265.
4. J. N. Gray, "Notes on data base operating systems," in *Lecture Notes in Computer Science*, Vol. 60. New York: Springer-Verlag, 1978, pp. 398–481.
5. S. K. Shrivastava, "Structuring distributed systems for recoverability and crash resistance," *IEEE Trans. Software Eng.*, vol. SE-7, pp. 436–447, July 1981.
6. B. Lampson, "Remote procedure calls," in *Lecture Notes in Computer Science*, Vol. 105. New York: Springer-Verlag, 1981, pp. 365–370.
7. B. J. Nelson, "Remote procedure call," Ph.D. dissertation, Dep. Comput. Sci., Carnegie-Mellon Univ.. Pittsburgh, PA, CMU-CS-81-119, 1981.
8. B. Liskov, "On linguistic support for distributed programs," in *Proc. Symp. Reliable Distributed Software and Database Syst.*, Pittsburgh, PA, July 1981, pp. 53–60.
9. J. H. Saltzer, D. P. Reed, and D. D. Clark, "End to end argument in system design," in *Proc. 2nd Int. Conf. on Distributed Syst.*, Paris, France, Apr. 1981, pp. 509–512.
10. R. W. Watson, "Hierarchy," in *Lecture Notes in Computer Science*, Vol. 105. New York: Springer-Verlag, 1981, pp. 109–118.
11. C. A. Sunshine and Y. K. Dalal, "Connection management in transport protocols," in *Computer Networks*, vol. 2, Amsterdam, The Netherlands: North-Holland, 1978, pp. 454–473.
12. Science and Engineering Research Council (U.K.), "Cambridge data ring," Tech. Note, Sept. 1980.
13. R. M. Needham, "System aspects of the Cambridge ring," in *Proc. 7th Oper. Syst. Symp.*, Dec. 1979, pp. 82–85.

14. G. Le Lann, "Distributed systems: Towards a formal approach," in *Information Processing 77*. Amsterdam, The Netherlands: North-Holland, 1977, pp. 155–160.

15. L. Lamport, "Time, clocks and the ordering of events in a distributed system," *Commun. Ass. Comput. Mach*, vol. 21. pp. 558–565, July 1978.

16. C. A. R. Hoare, "Monitors: An operating system structuring concept," *Commun. Ass. Comput. Mach.*, vol. 17, Oct. 1974.

23

THE NEWCASTLE CONNECTION OR UNIXES OF THE WORLD UNITE*

DAVID R. BROWNBRIDGE, LINDSAY F. MARSHALL AND BRIAN RANDELL

(1982)

In this paper we describe a software subsystem that can be added to each of a set of physically interconnected UNIX or UNIX look-alike systems, so as to construct a distributed system which is functionally indistinguishable at both the user and the program level from a conventional single-processor UNIX system. The techniques used are applicable to a variety and multiplicity of both local and wide area networks, and enable all issues of inter-processor communication, network protocols, etc., to be hidden. A brief account is given of experience with such a distributed system, which is currently operational on a set of PDP11s connected by a Cambridge Ring. The final sections compare our scheme to various precursor schemes and discuss its potential relevance to other operating systems.

1 INTRODUCTION

The Newcastle Connection is the name that we could not resist giving to a software subsystem that we have added to a set of standard UNIX systems in order to connect them together, initially using just a single Cambridge Ring. The resulting distributed system (which in fact can use a variety and multiplicity of both local and wide area networks) is functionally indistinguishable, at both 'shell' command language level and at system call level,

---

*D. R. Brownbridge, L. F. Marshall and B. Randell, The Newcastle Connection or UNIXes of the World Unite! *Software—Practice and Experience 12*, 12 (December 1982), 1147–1162. Copyright © 1982, John Wiley & Sons, Ltd. Reprinted by permission.

from a conventional centralized UNIX system [1]: Thus all issues concerning network protocols and inter-processor communications are completeIy hidden. Instead, all the standard UNIX conventions, e.g. for protecting, naming and accessing files and devices, for inter-process communications, for input/output redirection, etc., are made applicable, without apparent change, to the distributed system as a whole.

This is done, without any modification to any existing source code, of either the UNIX operating svstem, or any user programs. The technique is therefore not specific to any particular implementation of UNIX, but instead is applicable to any UNIX look-alike system that claims, and achieves, compatibility with the original at the system call level.

In subsequent sections we discuss the structure of this distributed system, (which for the purposes of this paper we will term UNIX United), the internal design of the Newcastle Connection, the networking and internetworking issues involved, some interesting extensions to the basic scheme, our operational experience with it to date, its relationship to prior work and its potential relevance to other operating systems.

2 UNIX UNITED

A UNIX United system is composed out of a (possibly large) set of interlinked standard UNIX systems, each with its own storage and peripheral devices, accredited set of users, system administrator, etc. The naming structures (for files, devices, commands and directories) of each component UNIX system are joined together in UNIX United into a single naming structure, in which each UNIX system is to all intents and purposes just a directory. Ignoring for the moment questions of accreditation and access control, the result is that each user, on each UNIX system, can read or write any file, use any device, execute any command, or inspect any directory, regardless of which system it belongs to. The simplest possible case of such a structure, incorporating just two UNIX systems, is shown in Figure 1.

With the root directory (/) as shown, one could copy the file a into the corresponding directory on the other machine with the shell command

```
cp /user/brian/a /../unix2/user/brian/a
```

(For those unfamiliar with UNIX, the initial '/' symbol indicates that a path name starts at the root directory, and the '..' symbol is used to indicate the parent directory.)

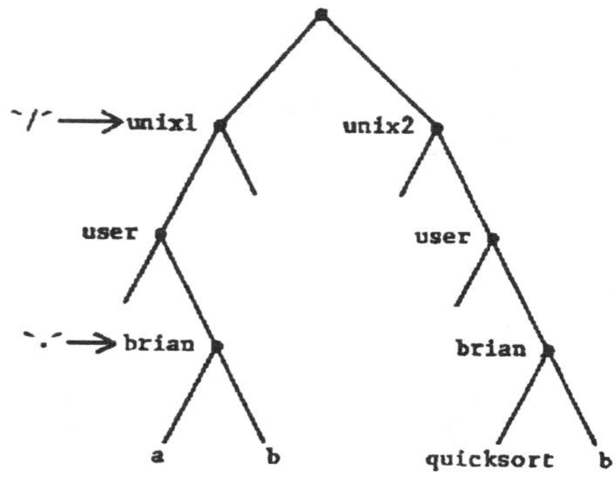

Figure 1

Making use of the current working directory ('.') as shown, this command could be abbreviated to

```
cp a /../unix2/user/brian/a
```

If the user has set up the shell variable `U2` as follows

```
U2 = /../unix2/user/brian
```

it could be called forth, using the $ convention, so as to permit the further abbreviation

```
cp a $U2/a
```

All the above commands are in fact conventional uses of the standard 'shell' command interpreter, and would have exactly the same effect if the naming structure shown had been set up on a single machine, with `unix1` and `unix2` actually being conventional directories.

All the various standard UNIX facilities (whether invoked via shell commands, or by system calls within user programs) concerned with the naming structure carry over unchanged in form and meaning to UNIX United, causing inter-machine communication to take place as necessary. It is therefore possible, for example, for a user to specify a directory on a remote machine as being his current working directory, to request execution of a program held in a file on a remote machine, to redirect input and/or output, to use files and peripheral devices on a remote machine, etc. Thus, using the same naming structure as before, the further commands

```
cd /../unix2/user/brian
quicksort a > /../unix1/user/brian/b
```

have the effect of applying the quicksort program on `unix2` to the file `a` which had been copied across to it, and of sending the resulting sorted file back to file `b` on `unix1`. (The command line

```
/../unix2/user/brian/quicksort /../unix2/user/brian/a > b
```

would have had the same effect, without changing the current working directory.)

It is worth reiterating that these facilities are completely standard UNIX facilities, and so can be used without conscious concern for the fact that several machines are involved, or any knovledge of what data flows when or between which machines, and of which processor actually executes any particular programs. (In fact, in our existing implementation, programs are executed by the processor in whose file store the program is held, and data is transferred between machines in response to normal UNIX read and write commands.)

2.1 User accreditation and access control

UNIX United allows each constituent UNIX system to have its own named set of users, user groups and user password file, its own system administrator (super-user), etc. Each constituent system has the responsibility for authenticating (by user identifier and password) any user who attempts to log in to that system.

It is possible to unite UNIX systems in which the same user identifier has already been allocated (possibly to different people). Therefore when a request, say for file access, is made from system 'A', of system 'B', on behalf of user 'u', the request arrives at 'B' as being from, in effect user 'A/u'—a user identifier which would not be confused with a local user identifier 'u'. It will be, in effect, this user identifier 'A/u' which governs the uses by 'u' of files, commands, etc., on machine 'B'.

Just as the system administrator for each machine has responsibility for allocating ordinary user identifiers, so he also has responsibility for maintaining a table of recognized remote user identifiers, such as 'A/u'. If the system administrator so wishes, rather than refuse all access, he can allow default authentication for unrecognized remote users, who might for example be given 'guest' status—i.e. treated as if they had logged in as 'guest', presumably a user with very limited access privileges.

From an individual user's point of view therefore, though he might have needed to negotiate not just with one but with several system administrators for usage rights beforehand, access to the whole UNIX United system is via a single conventional log in. Subject to the rights given to him by the various system administrators, he will then be governed by, and able to make normal use of, the standard UNIX file protection control mechanisms in his accessing of the entire distributed file system. In particular there is no need for him to log in, or provide passwords, to any of the remote systems that his commands or programs happen to use. This approach therefore preserves the appearance of a totally unified system, without abrogating the rights and responsibilities of individual system adrninistrators.

2.2 The structure tree

The naming structure of the UNIX United system represents the way in which the component UNIX system are inter-related, as regards naming issues. When a large number of systems are united, it will often be convenient to set up the overall naming tree so as to reflect relevant aspects of the environment in which the UNIX systems exist. For example, a UNIX United system set up within a university might have a naming structure which matches the departmental structure. with the naming structure as shown in Figure 2, files in the system `U1` in the Computing Science Department could be named using the prefix `/../../CS/U1` from within the Electrical Engineering Department's UNIX systems.

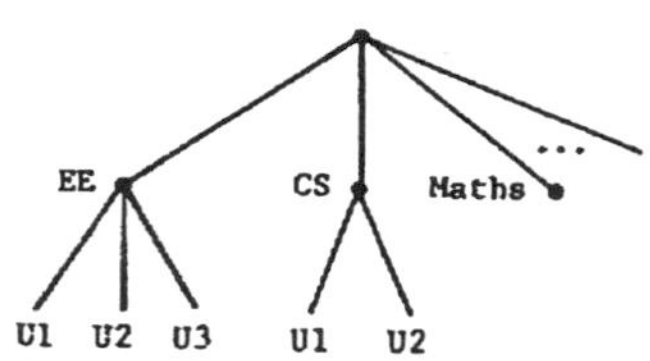

Figure 2

Such a naming structure has to be one that can be agreed to by all the system administrators, and which does not require frequent major modification—such modification of the UNIX United naming structure can be as disruptive as a major modification of the structure inside a single UNIX system would be, owing to the fact that stored path names (e.g. incorporated in files and programs) could be invalidated.

The naming structure could, but does not necessarily, reflect the topology of the underlying communications network. It certainly is not intended to be changed in response to temporary breaks in communication paths, or of service from particular UNIX systems. (An analogy is to the international telephone directory—the U.K. country code (44) continues to exist whether or not the transatlantic telephone service is operational.) This issue is pursued further in Section 4 below.

One final point: UNIX systems can appear in the naming structure in positions subservient to other UNIX systems. For example, in the previous figure, CS might denote a UNIX system, not just an ordinary directory. This has obvious implications with respect to the respective responsibilities and authority of the various system administrators. If the structure reflects the structure of communication paths, it indicates that all traffic to and from the CS department flows via this particular UNIX system, which is in effect therefore fulfilling a gateway role.

3 THE NEWCASTLE CONNECTION

The UNIX United scheme whose external characteristics were described above is provided by means of communication links, and the incorporation of an additional layer of software—the Newcastle Connection—in each of the component UNIX systems. This layer of software sits on top of the resident UNIX kernel, i.e. between the UNIX kernel and the rest of the operating system (e.g. shell and the various command programs) and the user programs. From above, the layer is functionally indistinguishable from the kernel. From below, it appears to be a normal user process. Its role is to filter out system calls that have to be re-directed to another UNIX system, and to accept system calls that have been directed to it from other systems. Communication between the Connection layers on the various systems is based on the use of a remote procedure call (RPC) protocol [2], and is shown schematically in Figure 3.

In fact a slightly more detailed picture of the structure of the system would of course reveal that communications actually occur at hardware level, and that the kernel includes means for handling low level communications protocols.

The Connection layer has to disguise from the processes above it the fact that some of their system calls are handled remotely (e.g. those concerned with accessing remote files). It similarly has to disguise from the kernel below it that the requests for the kernel's services, and the responses it provides,

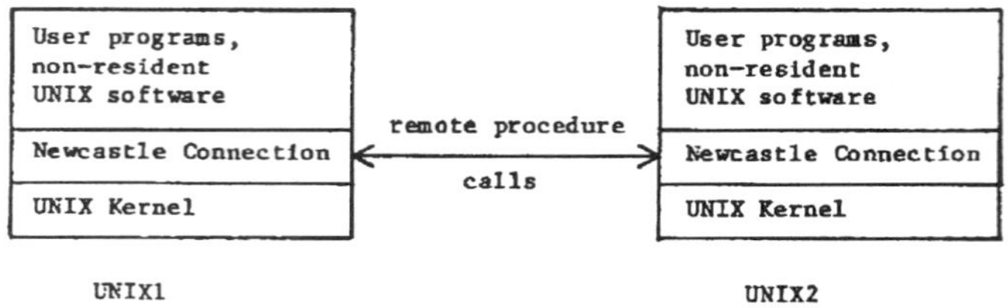

Figure 3

can be coming from and going to, remote processes. This has to be done without in any way changing the means by which system calls (apparently direct to the UNIX kernel) identify any real or abstract objects that are involved.

The kernel in fact uses various different means of identification for the various different types of object. For example, open files (and devices) are identified by an integer (usually in the range 0 to 19), logged on users by what is effectively an index into the password file, etc. Such name spaces are of course inherently local. The Connection layer therefore has to accept such an apparently local name and use mapping tables to determine whether the object really is local, or instead belongs to some other system (where it may well be known by some quite different local name). The various mapping tables will have been set up previously—for example when a file is opened—and for non-local objects will indicate how to communicate with the machine on which the object is located The selection of actual communication paths, the management of alternative routing strategies, etc., are thus all performed by the Connection layer, and completely hidden from the user and his programs.

Such mapping does not however apply to the single most visible name space used by UNIX, i.e. the naming structure used at shell level, and at the program level in the *open* and *exec* system calls, for identifying files and commands, respectively. Rather, the Connection layer can be viewed as performing the role of glueing together the parts of this naming structure that are stored on different UNIX machines, to form what appears to be a single structure. A given UNIX system will itself store only a part of the overall structure. Taking the example given above in Figure 1, `unix1` will store all of the overall structure except those elements that are below `unix2`, and vice versa. Thus, copies of some parts of the structure will be held on several systems, and must of course remain consistent—a problem which would become severe if changes to these parts of the structure were a frequent occurrence.

It is essential for the mapping layer to be able to distinguish local and remote file accesses. The Newcastle Connection layer intercepts all system calls that use files and determines whether the access is local or remote. Local calls are passed unaltered to the underlying local kernel for service, remote calls are packaged with some extra information, such as the current user-id, and passed to a remote machine for service. The Connection uses its own local fragment of the UNIX United naming tree to resolve file names. Names are interpreted as a route through the tree, each element specifying the next branch to be taken. If the name can be fully interpreted locally, only a local access is involved. If a leaf corresponding to a remote system is reached, then execution must be continued remotely by making a remote procedure call to the appropriate system. Such leaves are specially marked with the address of the appropriate remote station. This address is given to the RPC as routing information. In some cases (examined in more detail in the next section) a request may be passed on through a number of Connections before being satisfied.

As well as accessing files using a name, a UNIX program can *open* a file and access it using the file descriptor returned from the *open* system call. When a file is opened the Connection makes an entry in a per-process table indicating whether or not the file descriptor refers to a local or a remote file. The table also holds remote station addresses for remote file descriptors. Subsequent accesses using the descriptor refer to this table using the information there to route remote accesses without further delay.

The actual remote file access is carried out for the user by a file server process that runs in the remote machine. Each user has their own file server, and the initial allocation of these is carried out by a 'spawner' process that runs continuously. This latter process is callable (using a standard name) by any external user and, upon request, will spawn a file server (after carrying out some user/group mapping), returning its external name to the user that initiated the request. The user then communicates directly with this file server, which is capable of carrying out the full range of UNIX file operations. The user/group mapping is carried out to ensure that the access rights of the file server are in accord with those allowed to the external user by the local system manager, and consists of converting external names into valid local names. Nevertheless, a file server is still an extension of the environment of a user on a remote machine, and any relevant changes in the environment seen by a user must be mirrored by it. The most important of these is that when a user process 'forks' (that is, creates a duplicate of itself), all the remote file servers that it is connected with must also fork. This greatly simplifies the implementation of remote execution and signalling, as each user process only ever has to deal with a single remote file server.

Communication with the 'spawner' and the file servers always takes the form of a remote procedure call, the first parameter of all calls being a sequence number. This is used by the servers to detect retry attempts—if the received sequence number is the same as that of the last call, then it is a retry (the RPC scheme precludes calls being lost, so there is no need to check for continuity in the sequence).

4 NETWORKING AND INTER-NETWORKING ISSUES

The various kernels provide mappings between the user-visible name spaces and the hardware name spaces—in particular between the names of what appear to be directories, and the hardware names of distant UNIX systems. It is important that this latter mapping be such that:

(i) The file naming hierarchy need bear no relationship to the inter-system communications topology.

(ii) Modifications to the communications topology should be easy, as well as having no effect on the way in which any user or user program accesses anything.

File naming does, however, have some implications concerning protection and authentication—thus when a path is specified in an *open* command, checks are made against the permissions associated with each directory or file entry named explicitly or implicitly in the path, an activity that can require access to one or more distant UNIX systems. However it may not be necessary to repeat the same inter-system route when a file has been successfully opened, if some shorter route is available. For example, opening the file identified by the path

```
/../Unix1/a/Unix1.3/b
```

would involve accessing both `Unix1` and `Unix1.3`, though subsequent reads and writes might not involve accessing `Unix1`, depending on the underlying communications topology.

Our approach to providing these facilities takes advantage of the fact that the UNIX and hence the UNIX United file (and device, etc.) naming hierarchy constitutes a set of stable system-wide distinct identifiers. Only one such set is needed, so given that we already have this set available at user level, we are not using the Xerox Ethernet approach, which we understand requires the different stations on a set of interconnected Ethernets to have built-in uniquely assigned identification numbers. Rather, when a UNIX system is introduced into, or physically moved within, a UNIX United system, it will have to be identified to the system using an identifier such as

`UK/NEWCASTLE/DAYSH/REL/U5`

This identification will remain valid no matter the geographical location of the machine.

Our approach also involves arranging that hardware names related to one machine do not permeate to other machines in the system. At the hardware level, each machine identifies the machines it is directly connected to simply by identifying the means of connection, i.e. by I/O device number, and has no means of identifying any other machines. The I/O device numbers remain private to each machine, though presumably all machines on a given network will use the same ring port or modem numbers for a given machine.

In Figure 4, the kernel on machine `U1` will make use of hardware addresses for accessing `P1` (identifying the hardwired connection to be used) and `U2`, `U3`, `U4`, `U5` and `CRS` (identifying the ring and the port number to be used). It will not have knowledge of any hardware addresses relevant to `P2` or `N`. Similarly, if it is `U2` that gets connected to a wide area network, say, then only this machine, of the ones shown, will contain any wide area network telephone numbers for other UNIX systems. (Questions of routing through the wide area network will of course not concern the kernel, which only has to deal with routing between UNIX systems, not network nodes.)

Each kernel therefore routes accesses to distant machines to an appropriate one of its adjacent neighbouring machines, which can then pass the request on further, through another wide or local area network, or a direct hard-wired connection, if necessary. (The routing information used is that held in the various special files which of course are accessed by means of the paths or the file descriptors specified by users and user programs.

Means must be provided for modifying this routing information appropriately when a system is unplugged from one place in the overall netvork, and replugged into another—or indeed when any changes are made to the communications topology visible at the Newcastle Connection level. (Changes

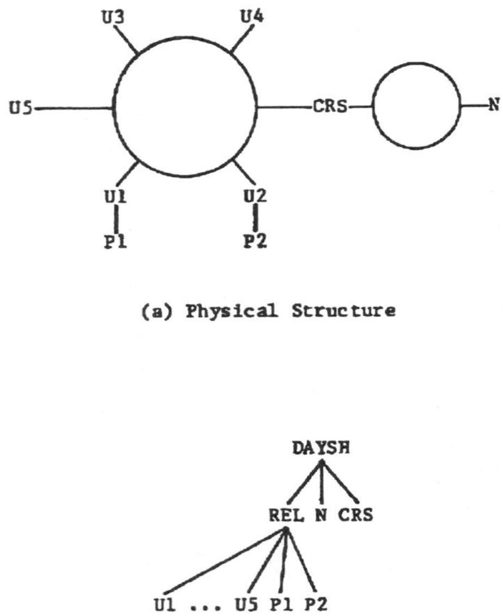

(a) Physical Structure

(b) Naming Structure

Figure 4

within any of the networks are of no concern, rather the Newcastle Connection has to deal just with changes concerning hardwired machine links and inter-networking.)

We choose to separate the question of updating topological information from that of performance-oriented dynamic routing, and plan to ignore the latter issue (which in any case seems more suitable for networking than inter-networking). In fact some dynamic routing schemes do, almost as a by-product, cope vith topological changes, but typically respond rather slowly to such changes [3]. A scheme such as that described by Chu [4], which arranges the immediate broadcasting of updates to routing tables when a topological change is notified (or perhaps discovered) seems much more appropriate to our needs, and is to be investigated. (Such a distributed approach can be contrasted, for example, with Cambridge's scheme of using a special machine on a ring as a name server, which has to be interrogated whenever an actual ring port number is needed, but thereby simplifies the table updating required when moving a machine from one port to another.)

As a message is passed from one machine to the next, the addressing information it contains (which will be described in terms of paths) will sometimes have to be adjusted, to allow for the fact that movement around the physical structure causes movement around the naming structure. Thus in Figure 4, a message emanating from `P1`, intended for `P2`, will not have its addressing information changed as it travels through `U1` and `U2`, since from both systems, as from `P1`, `P2` would in effect be identified by the path `/../P2`. In contrast a message from `U4` to `N` would have its addressing information in effect changed from `/../../N` to `/../N` as it passed through `CRS`. If system `N` had been made subservient to directory `REL` instead of `DAYSH` then `U4`, having a common parent directory with `N`, would in effect use the path `/../N`; to send a message to it. En route through `CRS`, this message would need this path to be changed to `/../REL/N`, because `CRS` though physically closer to `N` is in fact more distant from it in naming terms. (In practice, file descriptors rather than paths would be used as addressing information—though the principle of changing the addressing information en route still applies.)

5 EXTENSIONS TO THE BASIC UNIX UNITED SCHEME

We have found that the conceptual simplifications to the task of implementing a UNIX-based distributed computing system that the Newcastle Connection approach has provided have spurred us to produce a variety of extensions of, or variations on, the basic theme, some of which we have already started to implement.

The Connection layer can be regarded as isolating and solving the problems associated just with distribution—and, it turns out, is applicable to the case of distributed systems made from components other than complete UNIX systems. For example, one could connect together some systems which have little or no file storage with other systems that have a great deal—i.e. construct a UNIX United system out of workstations and file servers. Almost all that is necessary is to set up the naming tree properly.

Moreover since the Connection layer is independent of the internals of the UNIX kernel, it is not even necessary for the Connection layer to have a complete kernel underneath it—all that is needed is a kernel that can respond properly (even if only with exception messages) to the various sorts of system call that will penetrate down through, or are needed to support, the Connection layer. In fact the Connection layer itself can be economized on, if for example it is mounted on a workstation that serves as little more than a screen editor, say, and so has only a very limited variety of interactions with the rest of the UNIX United system. All that is necessary is adherence to the general format of the inter-machine system call protocol used by the Newcastle Connection, even if most types of call are responded to only by exception reports.

Thus the syntax and semantics of this protocol assume a considerable significance, since it can be used as the unifying factor in a very general yet extremely simple scheme for putting together sophisticated distributed systems out of a variety of size and type of component—an analogy we like to make is that the protocol operates like the scheme of standard-size dimples that allow a variety of shapes of LEGO children's building blocks to be connected together into a coherent whole.

In addition to the problem of distribution, we also have taken what are, we believe, several other equally separable problems, in particular those of (i) providing error recovery (for example in response to input errors or unmaskable hardware faults), (ii) using redundant hardware provided in the hope of masking hardware faults, (iii) the enforcement of multi-level security policies and (iv) load balancing between the component systems, and plan to embody their solutions in other separate layers of software. Indeed, two significant extensions of UNIX United are already operational, albeit in prototype form. The first of these provides multi-level security, using encryption to enforce security barriers and to control permissible security reclassifications. The second uses file and process replication and majority voting to mask hardware faults—application programs are unchanged, though in fact running in synchronization on several machines with hidden voting. Further details of these and other extensions of the UNIX United scheme are the subject of separate papers.

6 OPERATIONAL EXPERIENCE

At the time of writing (July 1982) the basic UNIX United system is in regular use at Newcastle on a set of three PDP11/23s and two PDP11/45s, connected by a Cambridge ring. The most heavily used facilities have been those concerned with file transfer and I/O redirection, for example in order to make use of the line printer and magnetic tape unit that are attached to one machine. The system is now also relied on for network mail, and for solving the problems of overnight file-dumping (of all machines, onto the one tape unit) and of software maintenance and distribution. As mentioned earlier, two prototype extensions of the system, concerned with security and hardware fault tolerance, respectively, are already operational, and work is under way on facilities for replicated files and on a distributed version of MASCOT [5].

A pre-release version of the Newcastle Connection has been provided to the University of Kent, where work has started on the (it is believed comparatively simple) modifications needed in order to use it to unite several computers, running Berkeley UNIX, also over a Cambridge Ring. The incorporation of X25 network links, and the actual implementation of the mechanisms we have designed for inter-networking, have been delayed by problems beyond our control concerned with the provision of network connections, which it is hoped will be resolved soon.

A first analysis of the performance of the remote procedure call protocol [6] used by the Connection layer indicates that, subjectively, terminal users of the Newcastle system in general notice little performance difference between local and remote accesses and execution. This is despite the fact that the Cambridge Ring stations used are quite slow, being interrupt-driven devices, and perhaps indicates that such stations are reasonably well matched to the rather modest performance that UNIX itself can achieve on a small PDP11/23 used as a personal workstation, or on a PDP11/45 that is usually being used by a number of demanding terminal jobs. However a further and more extensive programme of performance monitoring and evaluation is planned, which would also include experiments with the DMA ring stations that we have recently obtained and, it is hoped, with more powerful computers than our current set of PDP11s.

The modest size of the Newcastle Connection reflects the need we had to make the system work on our small PDP11/23s, which provided a strong incentive to find simple well-structured solutions to the various implementation problems. (In our view an overabundance of program storage space can have almost as bad an effect on the quality of a software system as does inadequate space—it is surely no coincidence that UNIX was first designed for quite modestly sized machines.) A program that made use of every facility provided by the Newcastle Connection would be increased in size by slightly more than 7K however, it is very unlikely that this would ever be the case and a more usual figure would be an increase of 4.5K, the absolute minimum being 3K (including the code for the RPC interface).

7 RELATED EARLIER WORK

The Newcastle Connection, and the UNIX United scheme that it makes possible, have many precursors, and not just within the UNIX world.

The idea of providing a layer of software which aims to shield users of a set of interconnected computers from the need to concern themselves with networking protocols, or even the fact of there being several computers involved, is well-established. It is, for example, what the IBM CICS System [7] does for users of various transaction processing programs, and what the National Software Works project [8] aimed to do for the users of various software development tools, running on a variety of different operating systems. Such layers of software are intended for somewhat specialized use, and run on top of specific sets of application programs. At the other end of the spectrum, such location- or network-transparency is also one of the aims of the Accent kernel [9], on which operating systems can be constructed which use its 'port' concept as a means of unifying inter-process communication, inter-computer message passing, and operating system calls.

The dawning realization that the 'shell' job control language and the program-level facilities (i.e. system calls) of the UNIX multiprogramming system could suffice, and indeed would be highly appropriate, to control a distributed computing system can be traced in a whole series of distributed UNIX projects. The global file naming technique used in the early 'uucp' facilities [10] for interconnecting UNIX systems via standard telephone circuits can be seen as a special, but rather *ad hoc*, extension of the individual file system naming hierarchies, and had been copied by us in our Distributed Recoverable File System [11]. (The technique provides what is in effect a set of named hierarchies, rather than a single enlarged hierarchy.)

Rather better integrated with the standard UNIX file naming hierarchy are the facilities provided in the Network UNIX System [12]. This modification of standard UNIX provides a series of Arpanet protocols, which are invoked by means of some additional system commands, using what appear to be ordinary file names as the means of identifying which Arpanet host is to be communicated with. (The paper describing this system also speculates on the possibility of redesigning the shell interpreter so as to provide network transparency for commands and files at the shell command language level.) The Purdue Engineering Computer Network [13] is conceptually similar to the Network UNIX System, though based on hard-wired high speed duplex connections. It provides additional commands which invoke the services of special protocols for virtual terminal access and remote execution at the shell level, and also a means of load balancing through a scheduling program which takes responsibility for deciding which processor should execute certain selected commands.

The distributed system of interconnected S-UNIX personal workstations and F-UNIX file servers [14] goes further by providing each workstation user with an ordinary UNIX interface, without any additional non-standard commands, yet incorporating a distributed version of the UNIX hierarchical file store containing just his own local files plus all the files held on the file servers. This system is one of several built at Bell Labs using the Datakit virtual circuit switch—others are RIDE [15] and D/UNIX [16]. The RIDE system provides complete remote file access and remote program execution, but is based on a 'uucp'-like, rather than standard, UNIX naming hierarchy—it is however implemented merely by adding a software layer on top of the UNIX kernel, an approach which is highly similar to that we have since used with our Newcastle Connection technique. D/UNIX is a distributed system based on modified versions of UNIX which provide virtual circuits between processes, and a transparent file sharing scheme covering all the files on all the component systems.

A fully symmetrical means of linking computer systems together so as to give the appearance of a single UNIX-like hierarchical file store, and the standard shell command language, is also provided by the LOCUS system—the paper [17] describing this system also discusses its intended extension to provide remote program execution as well as remote file access. However, for all its external similarity to UNIX, the LOCUS system involves a completely redesigned operating system rather than a modification of an existing UNIX system, albeit an operating system which is also designed to have extensive fault tolerance facilities.

The penultimate stage in the evolution can be seen in the COCANET local network operating system [18], a system which has been built using the standard UNIX system, and which comes very close indeed to our aim of combining a set of standard UNIX systems into a single unified system, and which certainly supports network-transparent remote execution as well as file access. However the COCANET designers have allowed themselves to make a number of changes to the UNIX kernel and would appear, from the description they give, not to have coped fully with user-id mapping. It would also appear that COCANET is designed specifically around the idea of having a relatively small number of machines linked by a single high-speed ring, and hence has a rather restrictive structure tree, which is viewed slightly differently from each machine. However many of the mechanisms incorporated in UNIX United are very similar to those used in COCANET.

It is thus but a comparatively small step from COCANET to UNIX

United, and to the idea of the Connection layer resting on top of an unchanged UNIX kernel, replicating all its facilities exactly in a network-transparent fashion, and capable of making a distributed system involving large numbers of computers, connected by a variety of local and wide area networks. Incidentally, one can draw an interesting parallel between the Connection layer and what is sometimes called a 'hyperviso", the best-known example of which is VM/370 [19]. Each is a self-contained layer of software, which makes no changes to the functional appearance of the system beneath it (the IBM/370 architecture in the case of VM/370, which fits under rather than on top of the operating system kernel). However, whereas a hypervisor's function is to make a single system act as a set of separate systems, the Newcastle Connection (a 'hypovisor'?) makes a set of separate (though of course linked) systems act like a single system!

However, to our embarrassment, we have to admit that the idea of the Connection layer, of the basic UNIX United scheme, and of most of the extensions of the scheme, did not arise from careful study and analysis of these precursors. (Indeed it is clear that what was presented above as a more-or-less orderly evolutionary development path often involved parallel activity by several groups, and much accidental reinvention.) In fact we were not consciously aware of any of these systems (other than 'uucp' and of course DRFS) while the work that led to the Newcastle Connection was in progress. Indeed, by the time we learnt of LOCUS and COCANET, alI thesic ideas and strategies to be incorporated in the Newcastle Connection had been worked out, though not all in full detail, and much of the system was already operational and in daily use. Rather we can trace the origins of our scheme to the existence of the plans for our remote procedure call protocol, and the idea, which we now know has occurred to many groups independently, of extending the UNIX 'mount' facilty from that of mounting replaceable disk packs to that of mounting one UNIX system on another.

This idea arose at Newcastle in early December 1981—within a week or so much of the UNIX United concept had been thought up and even roughly documented. A hesitant start at what was initially intended as just an experimental and partial implementation was made after Christmas, but within a month many facilities related to accessing and operating on files remotely over the Cambridge Ring were in active use. Work proceeded rapidly, both on extending the range of UNIX kernel features that the Newcastle Connection mapped correctly, and on discovering, mainly via experimentation, some of the more arcane features of the kernel interface as implemented and used in V7 UNIX. At about this stage we found out about first the S-UNIX/F-UNIX and LOCUS systems, and shortly afterwards the COCANET and then the RIDE systems. These various papers were a considerable encouragement to us to continue our efforts, and also provided us with a useful perspective on our approach. In particular they strengthened our growing belief in the viability of an alternative, UNIX-based, approach to distributed computing to that based on the use of a variety of explicit servers, each with its own specialized service protocol [20, 21].

Returning to the layered ('level of abstraction') aspect of UNIX United and its various extensions, this of course can be seen as being directly in the tradition pioneered by Dijkstra's seminal THE operating system [22]—a system which it now seems to be as unfashionable to reference as it was once fashionable. However, if only through our extensive work on multi-level structuring for purposes of fault tolerance [23], we remain convinced that this approach to designing (and describing) systems is of great merit. It leads to designs which work well and which seem to us to be much easier to comprehend, and therefore have faith in, than those where little explicit thought has apparently been given to achieving any sort of separation of logical concerns, such as those of naming, communications routing, load balancing, recoverability, etc.

8 WHY JUST UNIX?

It is interesting to analyse just what it is about UNIX, and the linguistic interfaces it provides at shell and system call level, that make it so suitable for use as the model and basis for a network operating system. There seem to be six principle factors involved.

First, there is the hierarchical file (and device and command) naming system. This makes it easy to combine systems, because the various hierarchical name spaces just become component name spaces in a larger hierarchy, without any problems due to name clashes. The standard UNIX mechanisms for file protection and controlled sharing of files then earry over directly, once the problem of possible clashes of user identifiers is handled properly.

Second, there are the UNIX facilities for dynamically selecting the current working directory and root directory. In particular the ability to select the root directory—normally thought of as one of the more exotic and little needed of the UNIX system commands—seems to have been designed especially for UNIX United, since it provides a perfect way of hiding the extra levels of the directory tree that have to be introduced.

Third, and obviously vital, is the fact that UNIX allows its users, and their programs, to initiate asynchronous processes. This is used inside the Newcastle Connection, and also provides the means whereby even a single user can make use via the Newcastle Connection of several or indeed all of the computers that are involved in the UNIX United system. It also provides the means whereby slow file transfers (via low bandwidth wide area networks) can be relegated to background processing, and so still be organized using remote procedure calls.

Fourth, there is the fact that the UNIX system call interface is (relatively) clean and simple, and can easily be regarded as providing a small number of well defined abstract types. The task of virtualizing these types, so as to give network transparency, therefore remains manageable.

Fifth, there is the fact, even in this day and age still regrettably worthy of mention, that the original UNIX system, and all of its derivatives known to us, are written in a reasonably satisfactory high level language. Our method of incorporating the Newcastle Connection layer therefore merely involved recompiling relevant parts of the system, using a different subroutine library.

Finally, there is the well-established set of exception reporting conventions that are used in UNIX, for example, to indicate the reasons why particular system call requests cannot be honoured. When such a call has, via the Newcastle Connection, involved attempted communication with another UNIX system there are various other (quite likely) reasons, but they can be mapped onto the exceptions that the caller is already supposed to be able to deal with.

However it is unlikely that the idea could not be carried across to at least some other systems. Indeed a report by Goldstein *et al.* [24] implies that something similar is being bravely contemplated for IBM's MVS operating system, and some aspects of the idea are we understand commercially available as additions to the RSX/11 operating system—no doubt other examples exist. The one other system whose suitability for the Newcastle Connection approach has been considered at all seriously by us is DEC's VAX/VMS system. It would appear that it has many of the necessary characteristics though there could be problems with the way that devices are involved with its system of file naming.

This section would not be complete without any mention of what we regard as some shortcomings of the UNIX V7 specifications (at system call level): Firstly, the system of *signals* for asynchronous communication between processes could be improved. Allied to this, a general synchronous inter-process communication mechanism would be useful, allowing communication between numbers of unrelated processes. Some awkward features in the file protection scheme were encountered when constructing the file server. These were associated with the notions of *super-user* and *effective user-id.* Lastly, we found that the ability to have many directory entries (*links*), each naming the same physical file, was elegant in concept but severely limited in generality by the actual UNIX V7 implementation.

With respect to the programs that are provided with the UNIX system, very few difficulties were encountered in connecting them, except, that is, for the Shell. This program makes use of system facilities in non-standard ways, and its internal design is obscure to say the least. However, it has proved to be an excellent testbed for the system—if the Shell works you can be pretty sure that most other programs will!

9 CONCLUSION

The first of our internal memoranda on what we later came to call the Newcastle Connection described the idea as 'so simple and obvious that it surely cannot be novel'. And, as described above, it did turn out to have a number of precursors—in fact probably many more than we yet realize. However we take this as confirmation of the merits of the twin ideas of network transparency and of its provision by a single separate mapping layer, an approach whose ramifications we feel we have barely begun to explore. Certainly our present plan is to continue our programme of experimental implementations and applications, and to determine how well the Newcastle Connection (and UNIX) can withstand the weight of additional software layers containing the various reliability and security-related mechanisms that we have developed, hitherto in a rather fragmented fashion for various systems and languages.

One other point is worth stressing. It has for some years been well accepted that the structure and mechanisms of a multiprocessing operating system are very similar to those of a (good) multiprogramming system. What has now become clear to us, as a result of our work on UNIX United, is that this similarity can usefully extend also to distributed systems. The additional problems and opportunitles that face the designer of homogeneous distributed systems should not be allowed to obscure the continued relevance on much established practice regarding the design of multprogramming systems.

Acknowledgements

Many of our colleagues at Newcastle have had a part in the often apparently furious, yet always enjoyable, discussions out of which the Newcastle Connection scheme, and its internal design, evolved. Two colleagues in particular, Fabio Panzieri and Santosh Shrivastava, also deserve acknowledgements as designers and implementors of the Remote Procedure Call protocol on which we have relied so heavily. The X25 protocol software that we are planning to use was provided by Keith Ruttle of the University of York, who is being most co-operative with our efforts at burying his software in a way that he could hardly have been foreseen or intended.

A special acknowledgement is obviously due to the creators of that famous Registered Footnote of Bell Laboratories, UNIX, much of whose external characteristics, if not detailed internal design, deserve the highest praise. Last but not least, we are pleased to acknowledge that our work has been supported by research contracts from the U.K. Science and Engineering Research Council, and the Royal Radar and Signals Establishment.

References

1. D. M. Ritchie and K. Thompson, 'The UNIX time-sharing system', *Comm. ACM*, 17 (7), 365-375 (1974).
2. S. K. Shrivastava and F. Panzieri, 'The design of a reliable remote procedure call mechanism', *IEEE Trans. Computers*, **C-31**, (7), 692-697 (1982).
3. A. S. Tanenbaum, *Computer Networks*, Prentice-Hall, Englewood Cliffs, N. J. (1981).
4. K. Chu, 'A distributed protocol for updating network topology information', *Report RC 7235*, IBM T. J. Watson Research Center, Yorktown Heights, New York (27 July 1978).
5. *The Official Handoook of MASCOT*, MASCOT Suppliers Association (5 December 1980).
6. F. Panzieri and S. K. Shrivastava, 'Reliable remote calls for distributed UNIX: an implementation study', *Report 177*, Computing Laboratory, University of Newcastle upon Tyne (June 1982).
7. J. Gray, 'IBM's customer information control system (CICS)', Operating System Review, **15** (3), 11–12, (1981).
8. R. E. Millstein, 'The national software works: a distributed processing system', *Proc. ACM 1977 Annual Conference*, Seattle, Washington, 44–52 (1977).
9. R. Rashid, 'Accent: a communication oriented network operating system kernel', *Operating Systems Review*, **15** (5), 64–75 (1981).
10. D. A. Nowitz, 'Uucp implementation description', Sect. 37 in *UNIX Programmer's Manual, Seventh Edition, Vol. 2* (January 1979).

11. M. Jegado, 'Recoverability aspects of a distributed file system', *Technical Report*, Computing Laboratory, University of Newcastle upon Tyne (February 1981).

12. G. L. Chesson, 'The network UNIX system', *Operating Systems Review*, **9** (5), 60–66 (1975). Also in *Proc. 5th Symp. on Operating Systems Principles.*

13. K. Hwang, W. J. Croft, G. H. Goble, B. W. Wah, F. A. Briggs, W. R. Simmons and C. L. Coates, 'A UNIX-based local computer network with load balancing', *Computer*, **15**, (4), 55–66 (1982).

14. G. W. R. Luderer, H. Che, J. P. Haggerty, P. A. Kirslis and W. T. Marshall, 'A distributed Unix system based on a virtual circuit switch', *Operating Systems Review*, **15**, (5), 160–168 (1981). (*Proc. ACM 8th Conf. Operating System Principles*, Asilomar, Calif.).

15. P. M. Lu, 'A system for resource sharing in a distributed environment—RIDE', *Proc. IEEE Computer Society 3rd COMPSAC*, IEEE, New York, 1979.

16. J. C. Kaufeld and D. L. Russell, 'Distributed UNIX system', in *Workshop on Fundamental Issues in Distributed Computing*, ACM SIGOPS and SIGPLAN (15–17 December 1980).

17. G. Popek, B. Walker, J. Chow, D. Edwards, C. Kline, G. Rudisin and G. Thiel, 'LOCUS: a network transparent, high reliability distributed system', *Operating Systems Review*, **15** (5), 169–177 (1981) (*Proc. ACM 8th Conf. Operating System Principles*, Asilomar, Calif.).

18. L. A. Rowe and K. P. Birman, 'A local network based on the UNIX operating system', *IEEE Trans. Software Eng.*, **SE-8** (2), 137–146 (1982).

19. L. H. Seawright *et al.*, 'Papers on virtual machine facility/370', *IBM Systems J.*, **18** (1), 4–180 (1979).

20. M. V. Wilkes and R. M. Needham, 'The Cambridge model distributed system', *Operating System Review*, **14** (1), 21–28 (1980).

21. E. Lazowska, H. Levy, G. Almes, M. Fischer, R. Fowler and S. Vestal, 'The architecture of the EDEN system', *Operating Systems Review*, **15** (5), 148–159 (1981) (*Proc. ACM 8th Conf. Operating System Principles*, Asilomar, Calif.).

22. E. W. Dijkstra, 'The structure of the "THE" multiprogramming system, *Comm. ACM*, **11** (5), 683–696 (1968).

23. T. Anderson, P. A. Lee and S. K. Shrivastava, 'A model of recoverability in multilevel systems', *IEEE Transactions on Software Engineering*, **SE-4** (6), 486–494 (1978) (also *Report 115*, Computing Laboratory, University of Newcastle upon Tyne).

24. B. Goldstein, G. Trivett and I. Wladavsky-Berger, 'Distributed computing in the large systems environment', *Report RC 9027*, IBM T. J. Watson Research Center, Yorktown Heights, New York (9 September 1981).

24

EXPERIENCES WITH THE AMOEBA DISTRIBUTED OPERATING SYSTEM*

ANDREW S. TANENBAUM, ROBBERT VAN RENESSE, HANS VAN STAVEREN, GREGORY J. SHARP, SAPE J. MULLENDER, JACK JANSEN AND GUIDO VAN ROSSUM

(1990)

The Amoeba distributed operating system has been in development and use for over eight years now. In this paper we describe the present system and our experience with it—what we did right, but also what we did wrong. Among the things done right were basing the system on objects, using a single uniform mechanism (capabilities) for naming and protecting them in a location independent way, and designing a completely new, and very fast file system. Among the things done wrong were having threads not be pre-emptable, initially building our own homebrew window system, and not having a multicast facility at the outset.

INTRODUCTION

The Amoeba project is a research effort aimed at understanding how to connect multiple computers together in a seamless way [15, 16, 26, 28, 32]. The basic idea is to provide the users with the illusion of a single powerful time-sharing system, when, in fact, the system is implemented on a collection of machines, potentially distributed among several countries. This research has

*A. S. Tanenbaum, R. van Renesse, H. van Staveren, G. J. Sharp, S. J. Mullender, J. Jansen and G. van Rossum, Experiences with the Amoeba distributed operating system. *Communications of the ACM 33*, 12 (December 1990), 46–63.

led to the design and implementation of the Amoeba distributed operating system, which is being used as a prototype and vehicle for further research. In this paper we will describe the current state of the system (Amoeba 4.0), and tell some of the lessons we have learned designing and using it over the past eight years. We will also discuss how this experience has influenced our plans for the next version, Amoeba 5.0.

Amoeba was originally designed and implemented at the Vrije Universiteit in Amsterdam, and is now being jointly developed there and at the Centre for Mathematics and Computer Science, also in Amsterdam. The chief goal of this work is to build a distributed system that is *transparent* to the users. This concept can best be illustrated by contrasting it with a network operating system, in which each machine retains its own identity. With a network operating system, each user logs into one specific machine, his home machine. When a program is started, it executes on the home machine, unless the user gives an explicit command to run it elsewhere. Similarly, files are local unless a remote file system is explicitly mounted or files are explicitly copied. In short, the user is clearly aware that multiple independent computers exist, and must deal with them explicitly.

In a transparent distributed system, in contrast, users effectively log into the system as a whole, and not to any specific machine. When a program is run, the system, not the user, decides the best place to run it. The user is not even aware of this choice. Finally, there is a single, system wide file system. The files in a single directory may be located on different machines possibly in different countries. There is no concept of file transfer, uploading or downloading from servers, or mounting remote file systems. A file's position in the directory hierarchy has no relation to its location.

The remainder of this paper will describe Amoeba and the lessons we have learned from building it. In the next section, we will give a technical overview of Amoeba as it currently stands. Since Amoeba uses the client-server model, we will then describe some of the more important servers that have been implemented so far. This is followed by a description of how wide-area networks are handled. Then we will discuss a number of applications that run on Amoeba. Measurements have shown Amoeba to be fast, so we will present some of our data. After that, we will discuss the successes and failures that we have encountered, so that others may profit from those ideas that have worked out well and avoid those that have not. Finally we conclude with a very brief comparision between Amoeba and other systems.

TECHNICAL OVERVIEW OF AMOEBA

Before describing the software, it is worth saying something about the system architecture on which Amoeba runs.

System Architecture

The Amoeba architecture consists of four principal components, as shown in Fig. 1. First are the workstations, one per user, on which users can carry out editing and other tasks that require fast interactive response. The workstations are all diskless, and are primarily used as intelligent terminals that do window management, rather than as computers for running complex user programs. We are currently using Sun-3s and VAXstations as workstations. In the next generation of hardware we may also use X-terminals.

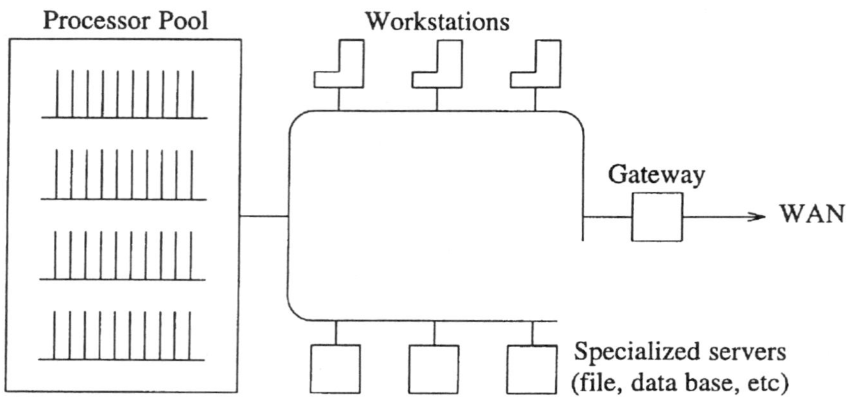

Figure 1 The Amoeba architecture.

Second are the pool processors, a group of CPUs that can be dynamically allocated as needed, used, and then returned to the pool. For example, the *make* command might need to do six compilations, so six processors could be taken out of the pool for the time necessary to do the compilation and then returned. Alternatively, with a five-pass compiler, $5 \times 6 = 30$ processors could be allocated for the six compilations, gaining even more speedup. Many applications, such as heuristic search in AI applications (e.g., playing chess), use large numbers of pool processors to do their computing. We currently have 48 single board VME-based computers using the 68020 and

68030 CPUs. We also have 10 VAX CPUs forming an additional processor pool.

Third are the specialized servers, such as directory servers, file servers, data base servers, boot servers, and various other servers with specialized functions. Each server is dedicated to performing a specific function. In some cases, there are multiple servers that provide the same function, for example, as part of the replicated file system.

Fourth are the gateways, which are used to link Amoeba systems at different sites and different countries into a single, uniform system. The gateways isolate Amoeba from the peculiarities of the protocols that must be used over the wide-area networks. All the Amoeba machines run the same kernel, which primarily provides multithreaded processes, communication services, I/O, and little else. The basic idea behind the kernel was to keep it small, to enhance its reliability, and to allow as much as possible of the operating system to run as user processes (i.e., outside the kernel), providing for flexibility and experimentation.

Objects and Capabilities

Amoeba is an object-based system. The system can be viewed as a collection of objects, on each of which there is a set of operations that can be performed. For a file object, for example, typical operations are reading, writing, appending, and deleting. The list of allowed operations is defined by the person who designs the object and who writes the code to implement it. Both hardware and software objects exist.

Associated with each object is a *capability* [8] a kind of ticket or key that allows the holder of the capability to perform some (not necessarily all) operations on that object. A user process might, for example, have a capability for a file that permitted it to read the file, but not to modify it. Capabilities are protected cryptographically to prevent users from tampering with them.

Each user process owns some collection of capabilities, which together define the set of objects it may access and the type of operations he may perform on each. Thus capabilities provide a unified mechanism for naming, accessing, and protecting objects. From the user's perspective, the function of the operating system is to create an environment in which objects can be created and manipulated in a protected way.

This object-based model visible to the users is *implemented* using remote procedure call [5]. Associated with each object is a *server* process that manages the object. When a user process wants to perform an operation on an object, it sends a request message to the server that manages the object. The message contains the capability for the object, a specification of the operation to be performed, and any parameters the operation requires. The user, known as the *client*, then blocks. After the server has performed the operation, it sends back a reply message that unblocks the client. The combination of sending a request message, blocking, and accepting a reply message forms the remote procedure call, which can be encapsulated using stub routines, to make the entire remote operation look like a local procedure call (although see [27]).

The structure of a capability is shown in Fig. 2. It is 128 bits long and contains four fields. The first field is the *server port*, and is used to identify the (server) process that manages the object. It is in effect a 48-bit random number chosen by the server.

48	24	8	48
Server port	Object number	Rights	Check field

Figure 2 A capability. The numbers are the current sizes in bits.

The second field is the *object number*, which is used by the server to identify which of its objects is being addressed. Together, the server port and object number uniquely identify the object on which the operation is to be performed.

The third field is the *rights* field, which contains a bit map telling which operations the holder of the capability may perform. If all the bits are 1s, all operations are allowed. However, if some of the bits are 0s, the holder of the capability may not perform the corresponding operations. Since the operations are usually coarse grained, 8 bits is sufficient.

To prevent users from just turning all the 0 bits in the rights field into 1 bits, a crypto-graphic protection scheme is used. When a server is asked to create an object, it picks an available slot in its internal tables, puts the information about the object in there along with a newly generated 48-bit random number. The index into the table is put into the object number field of the capability, the rights bits are all set to 1, and the newly-generated random number is put into the *check field* of the capability. This is an *owner capability*, and can be used to perform all operations on the object.

The owner can construct a new capability with a subset of the rights by turning off some of the rights bits and then XOR-ing the rights field with the random number in the check field. The result of this operation is then run through a (publicly-known) *one-way function* to produce a new 48-bit number that is put in the check field of the new capability.

The key property required of the one-way function, f, is that given the original 48-bit number, N (from the owner capability) and the unencrypted rights field, R, it is easy to compute $C = f(N \text{ XOR } R)$, but given only C it is nearly impossible to find an argument to f that produces the given C. Such functions are known [9].

When a capability arrives at a server, the server uses the object field to index into its tables to locate the information about the object. It then checks to see if all the rights bits are on.

If so, the server knows that the capability is (or is claimed to be) an owner capability, so it just compares the original random number in its table with the contents of the check field. If they agree, the capability is considered valid and the desired operation is performed.

If some of the rights bits are 0, the server knows that it is dealing with a derived capability, so it performs an XOR of the original random number in its table with the rights field of the capability. This number is then run through the one-way function. If the output of the one-way function agrees with the contents of the check field, the capability is deemed valid, and the requested operation is performed if its rights bit is set to 1. Due to the fact that the one-way function cannot be inverted, it is not possible for a user to "decrypt" a capability to get the original random number in order to generate a false capability with more rights.

Remote Operations

The combination of a request from a client to a server and a reply from a server to a client is called a *remote operation*. The request and reply messages consist of a header and a buffer. Headers are 32 bytes, and buffers can be up to 30 kilobytes. A request header contains the capability of the object to be operated on, the operation code, and a limited area (8 bytes) for parameters to the operation. For example, in a write operation on a file, the capability identifies the file, the operation code is *write*, and the parameters specify the size of the data to be written, and the offset in the file. The request buffer contains the data to be written. A reply header contains an error code, a limited area for the result of the operation (8 bytes), and a capability field that can be used to return a capability (e.g., as the result of the creation of an object, or of a directory search operation).

The primitives for doing remote operations are listed below:

get_request(req-header, req-buffer, req-size)
put_reply(rep-header, rep-buffer, rep-size)
do_operation(req-header, req-buffer, req-size, rep-header, rep-buffer, rep-size)

When a server is prepared to accept requests from clients, it executes a *get_request* primitive, which causes it to block. When a request message arrives, the server is unblocked and the formal parameters of the call to *get_request* are filled in with information from the incoming request. The server than performs the work and sends a reply using *put_reply*.

On the client side, to invoke a remote operation, a process uses *do_operation*. This action causes the request message to be sent to the server. The request header contains the capability of the object to be manipulated and various parameters relating to the operation. The caller is blocked until the reply is received, at which time the three rep- parameters are filled in and a status returned. The return status of *do_operation* can be one of three possibilities:

1. The request was delivered and has been executed.
2. The request was not delivered or executed (e.g., server was down).
3. The status is unknown.

The third case can arise when the request was sent (and possibly even acknowledged), but no reply was forthcoming. This situation can arise if a server crashes part way through the remote operation. Under all conditions of lost messages and crashed servers, Amoeba guarantees that messages are delivered at most once. If status 3 is returned, it is up to the application or run time system to do its own fault recovery.

Remote Procedure Calls

A remote procedure call actually consists of more than just the request/reply exchange described above. The client has to place the capability, operation code, and parameters in the request buffer, and on receiving the reply it has to unpack the results. The server has to check the capability, extract the operation code and parameters from the request, and call the appropriate procedure. The result of the procedure has to be placed in the reply buffer. Placing parameters or results in a message buffer is called *marshalling*, and has a non-trivial cost. Different data representations in client and server also have to be handled. All of these steps must be carefully designed and coded, lest they introduce unacceptable overhead.

To hide the marshalling and message passing from the users, Amoeba uses *stub routines* [5]. For example, one of the file system stubs might start with:

```
int read_file(file_cap, offset, nbytes, buffer, bytes_read)
    capability_t *file_cap;
    long offset;
    long *nbytes;
    char *buffer;
    long *bytes_read;
```

This call reads *nbytes* starting at *offset* from the file identified by *file_cap* into *buffer*. It returns the number of bytes actually read in *bytes_read*. The function itself returns 0 if it executed correctly or an error code otherwise. A hand-written stub for this code is simple to construct: it will produce a request header containing *file_cap*, the operation code for *read_file*, *offset*, and *nbytes*, and invoke the remote operation:

```
do_operation(req_hdr, req_buf, req_bytes, rep_hdr, buf, rep_bytes);
```

Automatic generation of such a stub from the procedure header above is impossible. Some essential information is missing. The author of the handwritten stub uses several pieces of derived information to do the job.

1. The buffer is used only to receive information from the file server; it is an output parameter, and should not be sent to the server.

2. The maximum length of the buffer is given in the *nbytes* parameter. The actual length of the buffer is the returned value if there is no error and zero otherwise.

3. *File_cap* is special; it defines the service that must carry out the remote operation.

4. The stub generator does not know what the servers operation code for *read_file* is. This requires extra information. But, to be fair, the human stub writer needs this extra information too.

In order to be able to do automatic stub generation, the interfaces between client and servers have to contain the information listed above, plus information about type representation for all language/machine combinations used. In addition, the interface specifications have to have an *inheritance* mechanism which allows a lower-level interface to be shared by several other interfaces. The *read_file* operation, for instance, will be defined in a low-level interface which is then inherited by all file-server interfaces, the terminal-server interface, and the segment-server interface.

AIL (Amoeba Interface Language) is a language in which the extra information for the generation of efficient stubs can be specified, so that the AIL compiler can produce stub routines automatically [33]. The *read_file* operation could be part of an interface (called *class* in AIL) whose definition could look something like this:

```
class simple_file_server [1000..1999] {
    read_file(*, in unsigned offset, in out unsigned nbytes,
        out char buffer[nbytes:NBYTES]);
    write_file(*,. . . );
};
```

From this specification, AIL can generate the client stub of the example above with the correct marshalling code. It can also generate the server main loop, containing the marshalling code corresponding to the client stubs. The AIL specification tells AIL that the operation codes for the simple_file_server can be allocated in the range 1000 to 1999; it tells which parameters are input parameters to the server and which are output parameters from the server, and it tells that the length of buffer is at most *NBYTES* (which must be a constant) and that the actual length is *nbytes*.

The Bullet File Server, one of the file servers operational in Amoeba, *inherits* this interface, making it part of the Bullet File Server interface:

```
class bullet_server[2000..2999] {
    inherit simple_file_server;
    creat_file(*, . . .);
};
```

AIL supports *multiple inheritance* so the Bullet server interface can inherit both the simple file interface and, for instance, a *capability management* interface for restricting rights on capabilities.

Currently, AIL generates stubs in C, but Modula stubs and stubs in other languages are planned. AIL stubs have been designed to deal with different data representations—such as byte order and floating-point representation—on client and server machines.

Threads

A process in Amoeba consists of one or more threads that run in parallel. All the threads of a process share the same address space, but each one has a dedicated portion of that address space for use as its private stack, and each one has its own program counter. From the programmer's point of view, each thread is like a traditional sequential process, except that the threads of a process can communicate using shared memory. In addition, the threads can (optionally) synchronize with each other using mutexes or semaphores.

The purpose of having multiple threads in a process is to increase performance through parallelism, and still provide a reasonable semantic model to the programmer. For example, a file server could be programmed as a process with multiple threads. When a request comes in, it can be given to some thread to handle. That thread first checks an internal (software) cache to see if the needed data are present. If not, it performs an RPC with a remote disk server to acquire the data.

While waiting for the reply from the disk, the thread is blocked and will not be able to handle any other requests. However, new requests can be given to other threads in the same process to work on while the first thread is blocked. In this way, multiple requests can be handled simultaneously, while allowing each thread to work in a sequential way. The point of having all the threads share a common address space is to make it possible for all of them to have direct access to a common cache, something that is not possible if each thread is its own address space.

The scheduling of threads within a process is done by code within the process itself. When a thread blocks, either because it has no work to do (i.e., on a *get_request*) or because it is waiting for a remote reply (i.e., on a *do_operation*), the internal scheduler is called, the thread is blocked, and a new thread can be run. Threads are thus effectively co-routines. Threads are not pre-empted, that is, the currently running thread will not be stopped because it has run too long. This decision was made to avoid race conditions. A thread need not worry that when it is halfway through updating some critical shared table it will be suddenly stopped and some other thread will start up and try to use the table. It is assumed that the threads in a process were all written by the same programmer and are actively co-operating. That is why they are in the same process. Thus the interaction between two threads in the same process is quite different from the interaction between two threads in different processes, which may be hostile to one another and for which hardware memory protection is required and used. Our evaluation of this approach is discussed later.

SERVERS

The Amoeba kernel, as described above, essentially handles communication and some process management, and little else. The kernel takes care of sending and receiving messages, scheduling processes, and some low-level memory management. Everything else is done by user processes. Even capability management is done entirely in user space, since the crypto-graphic technique discussed earlier makes it virtually impossible for users to generate counterfeit capabilities.

All of the remaining functions that are normally associated with a modern operating system environment are performed by servers, which are just ordinary user processes. The file system, for example, consists of a collection of user processes. Users who are not happy with the standard file system are free to write and use their own. This situation can be contrasted with a system like UNIX[1], in which there is a single file system that all applications must use, no matter how inappropriate it may be. In [24] for example, the numerous problems that UNIX creates for database systems are described at great length.

In the following sections we will discuss the Amoeba memory server, process server, file server, and directory server, as examples of typical Amoeba servers. Many others exist as well.

The Memory and Process Server

In many applications, processes need a way to create subprocesses. In UNIX, a subprocess is created by the *fork* primitive, in which an exact copy of the original process is made. This process can then run for a while, attending to housekeeping activities, and then issue an *exec* primitive to overwrite its core image with a new program.

In a distributed system, this model is not attractive. The idea of first building an exact copy of the process, possibly remotely, and then throwing it away again shortly thereafter is inefficient. Consequently, Amoeba uses a different strategy. The key concepts are segments and process descriptors, as described below.

A *segment* is a contiguous chunk of memory that can contain code or data. Each segment has a capability that permits its holder to perform

[1]UNIX is a Registered Trademark of AT&T Bell Laboratories

operations on it, such as reading and writing. A segment is somewhat like an in-core file, with similar properties.

A *process descriptor* is a data structure that provides information about a stunned process, that is, a process not yet started or one being debugged or migrated. It has four components. The first describes the requirements for the system where the process must run: the class of machines, which instruction set, minimum available memory, use of special instructions such as floating point, and several more. The second component describes the layout of the address space: number of segments and, for each segment, the size, the virtual address, how it is mapped (e.g., read only, read-write, code/data space), and the capability of a file or segment containing the contents of the segment. The third component describes the state of each thread of control: stack pointer, stack top and bottom, program counter, processor status word, and registers. Threads can be blocked on certain system calls (e.g., get_request); this can also be described. The fourth component is a list of ports for which the process is a server. This list is helpful to the kernel when it comes to buffering incoming requests and replying to port-locate operations.

A process is created by executing the following steps.

1. Get the process descriptor for the binary from the file system.

2. Create a local segment or a file and initialize it to the initial environment of the new process. The environment consists of a set of named capabilities (a primitive directory, as it were), and the arguments to the process (in Unix terms, *argc* and *argv*).

3. Modify the process descriptor to make the first segment the environment segment just created.

4. Send the process descriptor to the machine where it will be executed.

When the processor descriptor arrives at the machine where the process will run, the memory server there extracts the capabilities for the remote segments from it, and fetches the code and data segments from wherever they reside by using the capabilities to perform READ operations in the usual way. In this manner, the physical locations of all the machines involved are irrelevant.

Once all the segments have been filled in, the process can be constructed and the process started. A capability for the process is returned to the initiator. This capability can be used to kill the process, or it can be passed to a debugger to stun (suspend) it, read and write its memory, and so on.

The File Server

As far as the system is concerned, a file server is just another user process. Consequently, a variety of file servers have been written for Amoeba in the course of its existence. The first one, *FUSS* (*Free University Storage System*) [17] was designed as an experiment in managing concurrent access using optimistic concurrency control. The current one, the *bullet server* was designed for extremely high performance [29, 31, 32]. It is this one that we will describe below.

The decrease in the cost of disk and RAM memories over the past decade has allowed us to use a radically different design from that used in UNIX and most other operating systems. In particular, we have abandoned the idea of storing files as a collection of fixed size disk blocks. All files are stored contiguously, both on the disk and in the servers main memory. While this design wastes some disk space and memory due to fragmentation overhead, we feel that the enormous gain in performance (described below) more than offsets the small extra cost of having to buy, say, an 800 MB disk instead of a 500 MB disk in order to store 500 MB worth of files.

The bullet server is an immutable file store, with as principal operations *read-file* and *create-file*. (For garbage collection purposes there is also a *delete-file* operation.) When a process issues a *read-file* request, the bullet server can transfer the entire file to the client in a single RPC, unless it is larger than the maximum size (30,000 bytes), in which case multiple RPCs are needed. The client can then edit or otherwise modify the file locally. When it is finished, the client issues a *create-file* RPC to make a new version. The old version remains intact until explicitly deleted or garbage collected. Note that different versions of a file have different capabilities, so they can co-exist, making it straightforward to implement source code control systems.

The files are stored contiguously on disk, and are cached in the file servers memory (currently 12 Mbytes). When a requested file is not available in this memory, it is loaded from disk in a single large DMA operation and stored contiguously in the cache. (Unlike conventional file systems, there are no "blocks" used anywhere in the file system.) In the *create-file* operation one can request the reply before the file is written to disk (for speed), or afterwards (to know that it has been successfully written).

When the bullet server is booted, the entire "i-node table" is read into memory in a single disk operation and kept there while the server is running. When a file operation is requested, the object number field in the capability is extracted, which is an index into this table. The entry thus located gives the disk address as well as the cache address of the contiguous file (if present). No disk access is needed to fetch the "i-node" and at most one disk access is needed to fetch the file itself, if it is not in the cache. The simplicity of this design trades off some space for high performance.

The Directory Server

The bullet server does not provide any naming services. To access a file, a process must provide the relevant capability. Since working with 128-bit binary numbers is not convenient for people, we have designed and implemented a directory server to manage names and capabilities.

The directory server manages multiple directories, each of which is a normal object. Stripped down to its barest essentials, a directory maps ASCII strings onto capabilities. A process can present a string, such as a file name, to the directory server, and the directory server returns the capability for that file. Using this capability, the process can then access the file.

In UNIX terms, when a file is opened, the capability is retrieved from the directory server for use in subsequent read and write operations. After the capability has been fetched from the directory server, subsequent RPCs go directly to the server that manages the object. The directory server is no longer involved.

It is important to realize that the directory server simply provides a mapping function. The client provides a capability for a directory (in order to specify which directory to search) and a string, and the directory server looks up the string in the specified directory and returns the capability associated with the string. The directory server has no knowledge of the kind of object that the capability controls.

In particular, it can be a capability for another directory on the same or a different directory server, a file, a mailbox, a database, a process capability, a segment capability, a capability for a piece of hardware, or anything else. Furthermore, the capability may be for an object located on the same machine, a different machine on the local network, or a capability for an object in a foreign country. The nature and location of the object is completely arbitrary. Thus the objects in a directory need not all be on the same disk, for example, as is the case in many systems that support "remote mount" operations.

Since a directory may contain entries for other directories, it is possible to build up arbitrary directory structures, including trees and graphs. As an optimization, it is possible to give the directory server a complete path, and have it follow it as far as it can, returning a single capability at the end.

Actually, directories are slightly more general than just simple mappings. It is commonly the case that the owner of a file may want to have the right to perform all operations on it, but may want to permit others read-only access. The directory server supports this idea by structuring directories as a series of rows, one per object, as shown in Fig. 3.

Object name	Capability	Owner	Group	Other
	cap1	11111	11000	10000
games_dir	cap2	11111	10000	10000
paper.t	cap3	11111	00000	00000
prog.c	cap4	11111	11100	10000

Figure 3 A directory with three user classes, four entries and five rights.

The first column gives the string (e.g., the file name). The second column gives the capability that goes with that string. The remaining columns each apply to one user class. For example, one could set up a directory with different access rights for the owner, the owners group, and others, as in UNIX, but other combinations are also possible.

The capability for a directory specifies the columns to which the holder has access as a bit map in part of the rights field (e.g., 3 bits). Thus in the above example, the bits 001 might specify access to only the *Other* column. Earlier we discussed how the rights bits are protected from tampering by use of the check field.

To see how how multiple columns are used, consider a typical access. The client provides a capability for a directory (implying a column) and a string. The string is looked up in the directory to find the proper row. Next, the column is checked against the (singleton) bit map in the rights field, to see which column should be used. Remember that the cryptographic scheme described in Sec. 2.2 prevents users from modifying the bit map, hence accessing a forbidden column.

Then the entry in the selected row and column is extracted. Conceptually this is just a capability, with the proper rights bits turned on. However, to avoid having to store many capabilities, few of which are ever used, an optimization is made, and the entry is just a bit map, b. The directory server can then ask the server that manages the object to return a new capability with only those rights in *b*. This new capability is returned to the user and also cached for future use, to reduce calls to the server.

The directory server supports a number of operations on directory objects. These including looking up capabilities, adding new rows to a directory, removing rows from directories, listing directories, inquiring about the status of directories and objects, and deleting directories. There is also provision for performing multiple operations in a single atomic action, to provide for fault tolerance.

Furthermore, there is also support for handling replicated objects. The capability field in Fig. 3 can actually hold a set of capabilities for multiple copies of each object. Thus when a process looks up an object, it can retrieve the entire set of capabilities for all the copies. If one of the objects is unavailable, the other ones can be tried. The technique is similar to the one Eden used [20]. In addition, when a new object is installed in a directory, an option is available to have the directory server itself request copies to be made, and then store all the capabilities, thus freeing the user from this administration.

In addition to supporting replication of user objects, the directory server is itself duplicated. Among other properties, it is possible to install new versions of it by killing off one instance of it, installing a new version as the replacement, killing off the other (original) instance, and installing a second replacement also running the new code. In this way bugs can be repaired without interrupting service.

WIDE-AREA AMOEBA

Amoeba was designed with the idea that a collection of machines on a LAN would be able to communicate over a wide-area network with a similar collection of remote machines. The key problem here is that wide-area networks are slow and unreliable, and furthermore use protocols such as X.25, TCP/IP, and OSI, in any event, not RPC. The primary goal of the wide-area networking in Amoeba has been to achieve transparency without sacrificing performance [30]. In particular, it is undesirable that the fast local RPC be slowed down due to the existence of wide-area communication. We believe this goal has been achieved.

The Amoeba world is divided up into *domains*, each domain being an interconnected collection of local area networks. The key aspect of a domain (e.g., a campus), is that broadcasts done from any machine in the domain are received by all other machines in the domain, but not by machines outside the domain.

The importance of broadcasting has to do with how ports are *located* in Amoeba. When a process does an RPC with a port not previously used, the kernel broadcasts a *locate* message. The server responds to this broadcast with its address, which is then used and also cached for future RPCs.

This strategy is undesirable with a wide-area network. Although broadcast can be simulated using a minimum spanning tree [7] it is expensive and inefficient. Furthermore, not every service should be available worldwide. For example, a laser printer server in the physics building at a university in California may not be of much use to clients in New York.

Both of these problems are dealt with by introducing the concept of *publishing.* When a service wishes to be known and accessible outside its own domain, it contacts the *Service for Wide-Area Networks* (SWAN) and asks that its port be published in some set of domains. The SWAN publishes the port by doing RPCs with SWAN processes in each of those domains.

When a port is published in a domain, a new process called a *server agent* is created in that domain. The process typically runs on the gateway machine, and does a *get_request* using the remote server's port. It is quiescent until its server is needed, at which time it comes to life and performs an RPC with the server.

Now let us consider what happens when a process tries to locate a remote server whose port has been published. The process' kernel broadcasts a *locate*, which is received by the server agent. The server agent then builds a message and hands it to a *link* process on the gateway machine. The link process forwards it over the wide-area network to the servers domain, where it arrives at the gateway, causing a *client agent* process to be created. This client agent then makes a normal RPC to the server. The set of processes involved here is shown in Fig. 4.

The beauty of this scheme is that it is completely transparent. Neither user processes nor the kernel know which processes are local and which are remote. The communication between the client and the server agent is completely local, using the normal RPC. Similarly, the communication between the client agent and the server is also completely normal. Neither the client nor the server knows that it is talking to a distant process.

Of course, the two agents are well aware of what is going on, but they are automatically generated as needed, and are not visible to users. The link processes are the only ones that know about the details of the wide-

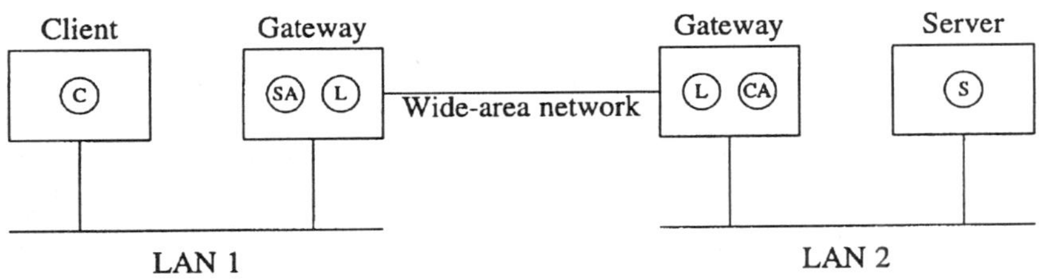

Figure 4 Wide-area communication in Amoeba involves six processes.

area network. They talk to the agents using RPC, but to each other using whatever protocol the wide-area network requires. The point of splitting off the agents from the link processes is to completely isolate the technical details of the wide-area network in one kind of process, and to make it easier to have multiway gateways, which would have one type of link process for each wide-area network type to which the gateway is attached.

It is important to note that this design causes no performance degradation whatsoever for local communication. An RPC between a client and a server on the same LAN proceeds at full speed, with no relaying of any kind. Clearly there is some performance loss when a client is talking to a server located on a distant network, but the limiting factor is normally the bandwidth of the wide-area network, so the extra overhead of having messages being relayed several times is negligible.

Another useful aspect of this design is its management. To start with, services can only be published with the help of the SWAN server, which can check to see if the system administration wants the port be to published. Another important control is the ability to prevent certain processes (e.g., those owned by students) from accessing wide-area services, since all such traffic must pass through the gateways, and various checks can be made there. Finally, the gateways can do accounting, statistics gathering, and monitoring of the wide-area network.

APPLICATIONS

Amoeba has been used to program a variety of applications. In this section we will describe several of them, including UNIX emulation, parallel make, traveling salesman, and alpha-beta search.

UNIX Emulation

One of the goals of Amoeba was to make it useful as a program development environment. For such an environment, one needs editors, compilers, and numerous other standard software. It was decided that the easiest way to obtain this software was to emulate UNIX and then to run UNIX and MINIX [25] compilers and other utilities on top of it.

Using a special set of library procedures that do RPCs with the Amoeba servers, it has been possible to construct an emulation of the UNIX system call interface—which was dubbed *Ajax*—that is good enough that about 100 of the most common utility programs have been ported to Amoeba. The Amoeba user can now use most of the standard editors, compilers, file utilities and other programs in a way that looks very much like UNIX, although in fact it is really Amoeba. A *session server* has been provided to handle state information and do *fork* and *exec* in a UNIX-like way.

Parallel Make

As shown in Figure 1, the hardware on which Amoeba runs contains a processor pool with several dozen 68020 and 68030 processors. One obvious application for these processors in a UNIX environment is a parallel version of *make* [10]. The idea here is that when *make* discovers that multiple compilations are needed, they are run in parallel on different processors.

Although this idea sounds simple, there are several potential problems. For one, to make a single target file, a sequence of several commands may have to be executed, and some of these may use files created by earlier ones. The solution chosen is to let each command execute in parallel, but block when it needs a file being made but not yet fully generated.

Other problems relate to technical limitations of the *make* program. For example, since it expects commands to be run sequentially, rather than in parallel, it does not keep track of how many processes it has forked off, which may exceed various system limits.

Finally, there are programs, such as *yacc* [11] that write their output on fixed name files, such as *y.tab.c*. When multiple *yacc*s are running in the same directory, they all write to the same file, thus producing gibberish. All of these problems have been dealt with by one means or another, as described in [2].

The parallel compilations are directed by a new version of *make*, called *amake*. *Amake* does not use traditional *makefiles*. Instead, the user tells it which source files are needed, but not their dependencies. The compilers have been modified to keep track of the observed dependencies (e.g., which files they in fact included). After a compilation, this information goes into a kind of mini-database that replaces the traditional *makefile*. It also keeps track of which flags were used, which version of the compiler was used, and other information. Not having to even think about *makefiles*, not even automatically generated ones, has been popular with the users. The overhead due to managing the data base is negligible, but the speedup due to parallelization depends strongly on the input. When making a program consisting of many medium-sized files, considerable speedup can be achieved. However, when a program has one large source file and many small ones, the total time can never be smaller than the compilation time of the large one.

The Traveling Salesman Problem

In addition to various experiments with the UNIX software, we have also tried programming some applications in parallel. Typical applications are the traveling salesman problem [13] and alpha-beta search [14] We briefly describe these below. More details can be found in [3].

In the traveling salesman problem, the computer is given a starting location and a list of cities to be visited. The idea is to find the shortest path that visits each city exactly once, and then return to the starting place. Using Amoeba we have programmed this application in parallel by having one pool processor act as coordinator, and the rest as slaves.

Suppose, for example, that the starting place is London, and the cities to be visited include New York, Sydney, Nairobi, and Tokyo. The coordinator might tell the first slave to investigate all paths starting with London-New York, the second slave to investigate all paths starting with London-Sydney, the third slave to investigate all paths starting with London-Nairobi, and so on. All of these searches go on in parallel. When a slave is finished, it reports back to the coordinator and gets a new assignment.

The algorithm can be applied recursively. For example, the first slave could allocate a processor to investigate paths starting with London-New York-Sydney, another processor to investigate London-New York-Nairobi, and so forth. At some point, of course, a cutoff is needed at which a slave actually does the calculation itself and does not try to farm it out to other processors.

The performance of the algorithm can be greatly improved by keeping track of the best total path found so far. A good initial path can be found by using the "closest city next" heuristic. Whenever a slave is started up, it is given the length of the best total path so far. If it ever finds itself working on a partial path that is longer than the best-known total path, it immediately stops what it is doing, reports back failure, and asks for more work. Initial experiments have shown that 75 percent of the theoretical maximum speedup can be achieved using this algorithm. The rest is lost to communication overhead.

Alpha-Beta Search

Another application that we have programmed in parallel using Amoeba is game playing using the alpha-beta heuristic for pruning the search tree. The general idea is the same as for the traveling salesman. When a processor is given a board to evaluate, it generates all the legal moves possible starting at that board, and hands them off to others to evaluate in parallel.

The alpha-beta heuristic is commonly used in two-person, zero-sum games to prune the search tree. A window of values is established, and positions that fall outside this window are not examined because better moves are known to exist. In contrast to the traveling salesman problem, in which much of the tree has to be searched, alpha-beta allows a much greater prun-ing if the positions are evaluated in a well chosen order.

For example, on a single machine, we might have three legal moves A, B, and C at some point. As a result of evaluating A we might discover that looking at its siblings in the tree, B and C was pointless. In a parallel implementation, we would do all at once, and ultimately waste the computing power devoted to B and C. The result is that much parallel searching is wasted, and the net result is not that much better than a sequential algorithm on a single processor. Our experiments running Othello (Reversi) on Amoeba have shown that we were unable to utilize more than 40 percent of the total processor capacity available, compared to 75 percent for the traveling salesman problem.

PERFORMANCE

Amoeba was designed to be fast. Measurements show that this goal has been achieved. In this section, we will present the results of some timing experiments we have done. These measurements were performed on Sun 3/60s (20 MHz 68020s) using a 10 Mbps Ethernet. We measured the performance for three different configurations:

1. Two user processes running on Amoeba.
2. Two user processes running on Sun OS 4.0.3 but using the Amoeba primitives.
3. Two user processes running on Sun OS 4.0.3 and using Sun RPC.

The latter two were for comparison purposes only. We ran tests for the local case (both processes on the same machine) and for the remote case (each process on a separate machine, with communication over the Ethernet). In all cases communication was from process to process, all of which were running in user mode outside the kernel. The measurements represent the average values of 100,000 trials and are highly reproducible.

For each configuration (pure Amoeba, Amoeba primitives on UNIX, Sun RPC on UNIX), we tried to run three test cases: a 4-byte message (1 integer), an 8 Kbyte message, and a 30 Kbyte message. The 4-byte message test is typical for short control messages, the 8-Kbyte message is typical for reading a medium-sized file from a remote file, and the 30-Kbyte test is the maximum the current implementation of Amoeba can handle. Thus, in total we should have 9 cases (3 configurations and 3 sizes). However, the standard Sun RPC is limited to 8K, so we have measurements for only eight of them. It should also be noted that the standard Amoeba header has room for 8 bytes of data, so in the test for 4 bytes, a only a header was sent and no data buffer. On the other hand, on the Sun, a special optimization is available for the local case, which we used.

In Fig. 5 we give the delay and the bandwidth of these eight cases, both for local processes (two distinct processes on the same machine) and remote processes (processes on different machines). The delay is the time as seen from the client, running as a user process, between the calling of and returning from the RPC primitive. The bandwidth is the number of data bytes per second that the client receives from the server, excluding headers. The measurements were done for both local RPCs, where the client and server processes were running on the same processor, and for remote RPCs over the Ethernet.

The interesting comparisons in these tables are the comparisons of pure Amoeba RPC and pure Sun OS RPC both for short communications, where delay is critical, and long ones, where bandwidth is the issue. A 4-byte Amoeba RPC takes 1.1 msec, vs. 6.7 msec for Sun RPC. Similarly, for 8 Kbyte RPCs, the Amoeba bandwidth is 721 Kbytes/sec, vs. only 325 Kbytes

	Delay (msec)			Bandwidth (Kbytes/sec)		
	case 1 (4 bytes)	case 2 (8 Kb)	case 3 (30 Kb)	case 1 (4 bytes)	case 2 (8 Kb)	case 3 (30 Kb)
pure Amoeba local	0.5	2.0	5.6	7.4	4000	5232
pure Amoeba remote	1.1	11.1	37.4	3.5	721	783
UNIX driver local	4.2	7.7	17.0	0.9	1039	1723
UNIX driver remote	5.1	26.7	88.6	0.8	300	331
Sun RPC local	5.7	12.8	imposs.	0.7	625	imposs.
Sun RPC remote	6.7	24.6	imposs.	0.6	325	imposs.
		(a)			(b)	

Figure 5 RPC between user processes in three common cases for three different systems. Local RPCs are RPCs where the client and server are running on the same processor. (a) Delay in msec. (b) Bandwidth in Kbytes/sec. The UNIX driver implements Amoeba RPCs and Amoeba protocol under Sun UNIX.

for the Sun RPC. The conclusion is that Amoebas delay is 6 times better and its throughput is twice as good.

While the Sun is obviously not the only system of interest, its widespread use makes it a convenient benchmark. We have looked in the literature for performance figures from other distributed systems and have shown the null-RPC latency and maximum throughput in Fig. 6.

The RPC numbers for the other systems listed in Fig. 6 are taken from the following publications: Cedar [5], x-Kernel [19], Sprite [18], V [6], Topaz [22], and Mach [19].

The numbers shown here cannot be compared without knowing about the systems from which they were taken, as the speed of the hardware on which the tests were made varies by about a factor of 3. On all distributed systems of this type running on fast LANs, the protocols are largely CPU bound. Running the system on a faster CPU (but the same network) definitely improves performance, although not linearly with CPU MIPS because at some point the network saturates (although none of the systems quoted here even come close to saturating it). As an example, in an earlier paper [32] we reported a null RPC time of 1.4 msec, but this was for Sun 3/50s. The current figure of 1.1 msec is for the faster Sun 3/60s.

System	*Hardware*	*Null RPC in msec.*	*Throughput in kbytes/s*	*Estimated CPU MIPS*	*Implementation Notes*
Amoeba	Sun 3/60	1.1	783	3.0	Measured user-to-user
Cedar	Dorado	1.1	250	4.0	Custom microcode
x-Kernel	Sun 3/75	1.7	860	2.0	Measured kernel-to-kernel
V	Sun 3/75	2.5	546	2.0	Measured user-to-user
Topaz	Firefly	2.7	587	5.0	Consists of 5 VAX CPUs
Sprite	Sun 3/75	2.8	720	2.0	Measured kernel-to-kernel
Mach	Sun 3/60	11.0	?	3.0	Throughput not reported

Figure 6 Latency and throughput for some systems reported in the literature.

In Fig. 6 we have not corrected for machine speed, but we have at least made a rough estimate of the raw total computing power of each system, given in the fifth column of the table in MIPS (Millions of Instructions Per Second). While we realize that this is only a crude measure at best, we see no other way to compensate for the fact that a system running on a 4 MIPS machine (Dorado) or on a 5 CPU multiprocessor (Firefly) has a significant advantage over slower workstations. As an aside, the Sun 3/60 is indeed faster than the Sun 3/75; this is not a misprint.

Cedar's RPC is about the same as Amoeba's although it was implemented on hardware that is 33 percent faster. Its throughput is only 30% of Amoeba's, but this is partly due to the fact that it used an early version of the Ethernet running at 3 megabits/sec. Still, it does not even manage to use the full 3 megabits/sec.

The x-Kernel has a 10% better throughput than Amoeba, but the published measurements are kernel-to-kernel, whereas Amoeba was measured from user process to user process. If the extra overhead of context switches from kernel to user and copying from kernel buffers to user buffers are considered, to make them comparable to the Amoeba numbers, the x-kernel performance figures would be reduced to 2.3 msec for the null RPC with a throughput of 748 kbytes/sec when mapping incoming data from kernel to user and 575 kbytes/sec when copying it (L. Peterson, private communication).

Similarly, the published Sprite figures are also kernel-to-kernel. Sprite does not support RPC at the user level, but a close equivalent is the time to send a null message from one user process to another and get a reply, which is 4.3 msec. The user-to-user bandwidth is 170 kbytes/sec [34].

V uses a clever technique to improve the performance for short RPCs: the entire message is put in the CPU registers by the user process and taken out by the kernel for transmission. Since the 68020 processor has eight 4-byte data registers, up to 32 bytes can transferred this way.

Topaz RPC was obtained on Fireflies, which are VAX-based multiprocessors. The performance obtained in Fig. 6 can only be obtained using several CPUs at each end. When only a single CPU is used at each end, the null RPC time increases to 4.8 msec and the throughput drops to 313 kbytes/sec.

The null RPC time for Mach was obtained from a paper published in May 1990 [19] and applies to Mach 2.5, in which the networking code is in the kernel. The Mach RPC performance is worse than any of the other systems by more than a factor of 3 and is ten times slower than Amoeba. A more recent measurement on an improved version of Mach gives an RPC time of 9.6 msec and a throughput of 250K bytes/sec (R. Draves, private communication).

Like Amoeba itself, the bullet server was designed with fast performance as a major objective. Below we present some measurements of what has been achieved. The measurements were made between a Sun 3/60 client talking to a remote Sun 3/60 file server equipped with a SCSI disk. Figure 7 gives the performance of the bullet server for tests made with files of 1 Kbyte, 16 Kbytes, and 1 Mbyte. In the first column the delay and bandwidth for read operations is shown. Note that the test file will be completely in memory, and no disk access is necessary. In the second column a create and a delete operation together is measured. In this case, the file is written to disk. Note that both the create and the delete operations involve disk requests.

The careful reader may have noticed that a user process can pull 813 kbytes/sec from the bullet server (from Fig. 7), even though the user-to-user bandwidth is only 783 kbytes/sec (from Fig. 5). The reason for this apparent descrepancy is as follows. As far as the clients are concerned, the bullet server is just a black box. It accepts requests and gives replies. No user processes run on its machine. Under these circumstances, we decided to move the bullet server code into the kernel, since the users could not tell the difference anyway, and protection is not an issue on a free-standing file server with only 1 process. Thus the 813 kbyte/sec figure is user-to-kernel for access to the file cache, whereas the 783 kbyte/sec one is user-to-user, from

File Size	Delay (msec) READ	Delay (msec) CREATE+DEL
1 Kbyte	2	50
16 Kbyte	20	84
1 Mbyte	1260	3210

(a)

File Size	Bandwidth (Kbytes/sec) READ	Bandwidth (Kbytes/sec) CREATE+DEL
1 Kbyte	427	20
16 Kbyte	788	191
1 Mbyte	813	319

(b)

Figure 7 Performance of the Bullet file server for read operations, and create and delete operations together. (a) Delay in msec. (b) Bandwidth in Kbytes/sec.

memory-to-memory without involving any files. The pure user-to-kernel bandwidth is certainly higher than 813 kbytes/sec, but some of it is lost to file server overhead.

To compare the Amoeba results with the Sun NFS file system, we have measured reading and creating files on a Sun 3/60 using a remote Sun 3/60 file server with a 16 Mbyte of memory running Sun OS 4.0.3. The file server had the same type of disk as the bullet server, so the hardware configurations were, with the exception of extra memory for NFS, identical to those used to measure Amoeba. The measurements were made at night under a light load. To disable local caching on the Sun 3/60 we locked the file using the Sun UNIX *lockf* primitive while doing the read test. The timing of the read test consisted of repeated measurement of an *lseek* followed by a *read* system call. The write test consisted of consecutively executing *creat*, *write* and *close*. (The *creat* has the effect of deleting the previous version of the file.) The results are depicted in Fig. 8.

Observe that reading and creating 1 Mbyte files results in lower bandwidths than for reading and creating 16 Kbyte files. The Bullet file server's performance for read operations is two to three times better than the Sun NFS file server. For create operations, the Bullet file server has a constant overhead for producing capabilities, which gives it a relatively better performance for large files.

EVALUATION

In this section we will take a critical look at Amoeba and its evolution and point out some aspects that we consider successful and others that we con-

File Size	Delay (msec) READ	Delay (msec) CREATE
1 Kbyte	20	101
16 Kbyte	47	186
1 Mbyte	2030	13350

(a)

File Size	Bandwidth (Kbytes/sec) READ	Bandwidth (Kbytes/sec) CREATE
1 Kbyte	50	10
16 Kbyte	340	86
1 Mbyte	504	77

(b)

Figure 8 Performance of the Sun NFS file server for read and create and operations. (a) Delay in msec. (b) Bandwidth in Kbytes/sec.

sider less successful. In areas where Amoeba 4.0 was found wanting, we will make improvements in Amoeba 5.0, which is currently under development. These improvements are discussed below.

One area where little improvement is needed is portability. Amoeba started out on the 680x0 CPUs, and has been easily moved to the VAX, NS 32016 and Intel 80386. The Amoeba RPC protocol has also been implemented as part of MINIX [25] and as such is in widespread use around the world.

Objects and Capabilities

On the whole, the basic ideas of an object-based system has worked well. It has given us a framework which makes it easy to think about the system. When new objects or services are proposed, we have a clear model to deal with and specific questions to answer. In particular, for each new service, we must decide what objects will be supported and what operations will be permitted on these objects. This structuring technique has been valuable on many occasions.

The use of capabilities for naming and protecting objects has also been a success. By using cryptographically protected capabilities, we have a unique system-wide fixed length name for each object, yielding a high degree of transparency. Thus it is simple to implement a basic directory as a set of (ASCII string, capability) pairs. As a result, a directory may contain names for many kinds of objects, located all over the world and windows can be written on by any process holding the appropriate capability, no matter where it is. We feel this model is conceptually both simpler and more flexible than models using remote mounting and symbolic links such as Suns NFS. Furthermore, it can be implemented just as efficiently. We have no experience with capabilities on huge systems (thousands of simultaneous users). On one hand, with such a large system, some capabilities are bound to leak out, compromising security. On the other hand, capabilities provide a kind of firewall, since a compromised capability only affects the security of one object. Whether such fine-grained protection is better or worse in practice than more conventional schemes for huge systems is hard to say at this point.

We are also satisfied with the low-level user primitives. In effect there are only three principal system calls, *get_request*, *put_reply*, and *do_operation*, each easy to understand. All communication is based on these primitives, which are much simpler than, for example, the socket interface in Berkeley UNIX, with its myriad of system calls, parameters, and options.

Amoeba 5.0 will use 256-bit capabilites, rather than the 128-bit capabilities of Amoeba 4.0. The larger Check field will be more secure against attack. Other security aspects will also be tightened, including the addition of secure, encrypted communication between client and server. Also, the larger capabilities will have room for a *location hint* which can be exploited by the SWAN servers for locating objects in the wide-area network. Third, all the fields of the new 256-bit capability will be aligned at 32-bit boundaries, which potentially may give better performance.

Remote Procedure Call

For the most part, RPC communication is satisfactory, but sometimes it gives problems [27]. In particular, RPC is inherently master-slave and point-to-point. Sometimes both of these issues lead to problems. In a UNIX pipeline, such as:

pic file | eqn | tbl | troff >outfile

for example, there is no inherent master-slave relationship, and it is not at all obvious if data movement between the elements of the pipeline should be read driven or write driven.

In Amoeba 4.0, when an RPC transfers a long message it is actually sent as a sequence of packets, each of which is individually acknowledged at the driver level (stop-and-wait protocol). Although this scheme is simple, it slows the system down. In Amoeba 5.0 we will only acknowledge whole messages, which will allow us to achieve higher bandwidths than shown in

Fig. 6.

Because RPC is inherently point-to-point, problems arise in parallel applications like the traveling salesman problem. When a process discovers a path that is better than the best known current path, what it really wants to do is send a multicast message to a large number of processes to inform all of them immediately. At present this is impossible, and must either be simulated with multiple RPCs or finessed.

Amoeba 5.0 will fully support group communication using multicast. A message sent to a group will be delivered to all members, or at least an attempt will be made. A higher-level protocol has been devised to implement 100% reliable multicasting on unreliable networks at essentially the same price as RPC (two messages per reliable broadcast). This protocol is described in [12]. There are many applications (e.g., replicated data bases of various kinds) for which reliable broadcasting makes life much simpler. Amoeba 5.0 will use this replication facility to support fault tolerance.

Although not every LAN supports broadcasting and multicasting in hardware, when it is available (e.g., Ethernet), it can provide an enormous performance gain for many applications. For example, a simple way to update a replicated data base is to send a reliable multicast to all the machines holding copies of the data base. This idea is obvious and we should have realized it earlier and put it in from the start.

Although it has long since been corrected, in Amoeba 2.0 we made a truly dreadful decision to have asynchronous RPC. In that system the sender transmitted a message to the receiver and then continued executing. When the reply came in, the sender was interrupted. This scheme allowed considerable parallelism, but it was impossible to program correctly. Our advice to future designers is to avoid asynchronous messages like the plague.

Memory and Process Management

Probably the worst mistake in the design of the Amoeba 4.0 process management mechanisms was the decision to have threads run to completion, that is, not be pre-emptable. The idea was that once a thread starting using some critical table, it would not be interrupted by another thread in the same process until it logically blocked. This scheme seemed simple to understand, and it was certainly easy to program.

Problems arose because programmers did not have a very good concept of when a process blocked. For example, to debug some code in a critical region, a programmer might add some print statements in the middle of the critical region code. These print statements might call library procedures that performed RPCs with a remote terminal server. While blocked waiting for the acknowledgement, a thread could be interrupted, and another thread could access the critical region, wreaking havoc. Thus the sanctity of the critical region could be destroyed by putting in print statements. Needless to say, this property was very confusing to naive programmers.

The run-to-completion semantics of thread scheduling in Amoeba 4.0 also prevents a multiprocessor implementation from exploiting parallelism and shared memory by allocating different threads in one process to different processors. Amoeba 5.0 threads will be able to run in parallel. No promises are made by the scheduler about allowing a thread to run until it blocks before another thread is scheduled. Threads sharing resources must explicitly synchronize using semaphores or mutexes.

Another problem concerns the lack of timeouts on the duration of remote operations.

When the memory server is starting up a process, it uses the capabilities in the process descriptor to download the code and data. It is perfectly legal for these capabilities to be for somebody's private file server, rather than for the bullet server. However, if this server is malicious and simply does not respond at all, a thread in the memory server will just hang forever. We probably should have included service timeouts, although doing so would introduce race conditions.

Finally, Amoeba does not support virtual memory. It has been our working assumption that memory is getting so cheap that the added complexity of virtual memory is not worth it. Most workstations have at least 4M RAM these days, and will have 32M within a couple of years. Simplicity of design and implementation and high speed have always been our goals, so we really have not decided yet whether to implement virtual memory in Amoeba 5.0.

In a similar vein, we do not support process migration at present, even though the mechanisms needed for supporting it already exist. Whether process migration for load balancing is an essential feature or just another frill is still under discussion.

File System

One area of the system which we think has been eminently successful is the design of the file server and directory server. We have separated out two distinct parts, the bullet server, which just handles storage, and the directory server, which handles naming and protection. The bullet server design allows it to be extremely fast, while the directory server design gives a flexible protection scheme and also supports file replication in a simple and easy to understand way. The key element here is the fact that files are immutable, so they can be replicated at will, and copies regenerated if necessary.

The entire replication process takes place in the background (lazy replication), and is entirely automatic, thus not bothering the user at all. We regard the file system as the most innovative part of the Amoeba 4.0 design, combining high performance with reliability, robustness, and ease of use.

An issue that we are becoming interested in is how one could handle databases in this environment. We envision an Amoeba-based database system that would have a very large memory for an essentially "in-core" database. Updates would be done in memory. The only function of the disk would be to make checkpoints periodically. In this way, the immutability of files would not pose any problems.

A problem that has not arisen yet, but might arise if Amoeba were scaled to thousands of users is caused by the splitting of the directory server and file server. Creating a file and then entering its capability into a directory are two separate operations. If the client should crash between them, the file exists but is inaccessible. Our current strategy is to have the directory server access each file it knows about once every k days, and have the bullet server automatically garbage collect all files not accessed by anyone in n days ($n \gg k$). With our current setup and reliable hardware, this is not a problem, but in a huge, international Amoeba system it might become one.

Internetworking

We are also happy with the way wide-area networking has been handled, using server agents, client agents, and the SWAN. In particular, the fact that the existence of wide-area networking does not affect the protocols or performance of local RPCs at all is crucial. Many other designs (e.g., TCP/IP, OSI) start out with the wide-area case, and then use this locally as well. This choice results in significantly lower performance on a LAN than the Amoeba design, and no better performance over wide-area networks.

One configuration that was not adequately dealt with in Amoeba 4.0 is a system consisting of a large number of local area networks interconnected by many bridges and gateways. Although Amoeba 4.0 works on these systems, its performance is poor, partly due to the way port location and message handling is done. In Amoeba 5.0, we have designed and implemented a completely new low-level protocol called the *Fast Local Internet Protocol* (FLIP), that will greatly improve the performance in complex internets. Among other features, entire messages will be acknowledged instead of individual packets, greatly reducing the number of interrupts that must be processed. Port location is also done more efficiently, and a single server agent can now listen to an arbitrary number of ports, enormously reducing the number of quiescent server agents required in the gateways for large systems.

One unexpected problem that we had was the poor quality of the wide-area networks that we had to use, especially the public X.25 ones. Also, to access some machines we often had to traverse multiple networks, each with their own problems and idiosyncracies. Our only insight to future researchers is not to blindly assume that public wide-area networks will actually function correctly until this has been experimentally verified.

UNIX Emulation

The Amoeba 4.0 UNIX emulation consists of a library and a session server. It was written with the idea of getting most of the UNIX software to work without too much effort on our part. The price we pay for this approach is that we will never be able to provide 100% compatibility. For example, the whole concept of user-ids and group-ids is very hard to get right in a capability-based system. Our view of protection is totally different.

Furthermore, Amoeba is essentially a stateless system. This means that various subtle properties of UNIX relating to how files are shared between parent and child are virtually impossible to get right. In practice we can live with this, but for someone who demanded binary compatibility, our approach has some shortcomings.

Parallel Applications

Although Amoeba was originally conceived as a system for *distributed* computing, the existence of the processor pool with 48 680x0 CPUs close together has made it quite suitable for *parallel* computing as well. That is, we have become much more interested in using the processor pool to achieve large speedups on a single problem. To program these parallel applications, we are currently engaged in implementing a language called Orca [4].

Orca is based on the concept of globally shared objects. Programmers can define operations on shared objects, and the compiler and run time system take care of all the details of making sure they are carried out correctly.

This scheme gives the programmer the ability to atomically read and write shared objects that are physically distributed among a collection of machines without having to deal with any of the complexity of the physical distribution. All the details of the physical distribution are completely hidden from the programmer. Initial results indicate that almost linear speedup can be achieved on some problems involving branch and bound, successive overrelaxation, and graph algorithms. For example, we have redone the traveling salesman problem in Orca and achieved a ten-fold speedup with 10 processors (compared to 7.5 using the non-Orca version described earlier). Alpha-beta search in Orca achieves a factor of 6 speedup with 10 processors (compared to 4 without Orca). It appears that using Orca reduces the communication overhead, but it remains true that for problems with many processes and a high interaction rate (i.e., small grain size), there will always be a problem.

Performance

Performance, in general, has been a major success story. The minimum RPC time for Amoeba is 1.3 msec between two user-space processes on Sun 3/60s, and interprocess throughput is nearly 800 kbytes/sec. The file system lets us read and write files at about the same rate.

User Interface

Amoeba originally had a homebrew window system. It was faster than X-windows, and in our view cleaner. It was also much smaller and easier to understand. For these reasons we thought it would be easy to get people to accept it. We were wrong. Technical factors sometimes play second fiddle to political and marketing ones. We have abandoned our window server and switched to X windows.

Security

An intruder capable of tapping the network on which Amoeba runs can discover capabilities and do considerable damage. In a production environment some form of link encryption is needed to guarantee better security. Although some thought has been given to a security mechanism [26] it was not implemented in Amoeba 4.0.

Two potential security systems have been designed for Amoeba 5.0. The first version can only be used in friendly environments where the network and operating system kernels can be assumed secure. This version uses one-way ciphers and, with caching of argument/result pairs, can be made to run virtually as fast as the current Amoeba. The other version makes no assumptions about the security of the underlying network or the operating system. Like MITs Kerberos [23] it uses a trusted authentication server for key establishement and encrypts all network traffic.

We intend to install both versions and investigate the effects on performance of the system. We are researching the problems of authentication in very large systems spanning multiple organizations and national boundaries.

COMPARISON WITH OTHER SYSTEMS

Amoeba is not the only distributed system in the world. Other well-known ones include Mach [1], Chorus [21], V [6], and Sprite [18]. Although a comprehensive comparison of Amoeba with these would no doubt be very interesting, it is beyond the scope of this paper. Nevertheless, we would like to make a few general remarks.

The main goal of the Amoeba project differs somewhat from the goals of most of the other systems. It was our intention to develop a new operating system from scratch, using the best ideas currently available, without regard for backward compatibility with systems designed 20 years ago. In particular, while we have written a library and server that provide enough UNIX compatibility that over 100 UNIX utilities run on Amoeba (after relinking with a special library), 100% compatibility has never been a goal. Although from a marketing standpoint, not aiming for complete compatibility with the latest version of UNIX may scare off potential customers with large existing software bases, from a research point of view, having the freedom to selectively use ideas from UNIX is a plus. Some other systems take a different viewpoint.

Another difference with other systems is our emphasis on Amoeba as a *distributed* system. It was intended from the start to run on a large number of machines. One comparison with Mach is instructive on this point. Mach uses a clever optimization to pass messages between processes running on the same machine. The page containing the message is mapped from the senders address space to the receivers address space, thus avoiding copying. Amoeba does not do this because we consider the key issue in a distributed system the communication speed between processes running on different machines. That is the normal case. Only rarely will two processes happen to be on the same physical processor in a true distributed system, especially if there are hundreds of processors, so we have put a lot of effort into optimizing the distributed case, not the local case. This is clearly a philosophical difference.

CONCLUSION

The Amoeba project has clearly demonstrated that it is possible to build an efficient, high-performance distributed operating system on current hardware. The object-based nature of the system, and the use of capabilities provides a unifying theme that holds the various pieces together. By making the kernel as small as possible, most of the key features are implemented as user processes, which means that the system can evolve gradually as needs change and we learn more about distributed computing.

Amoeba has been operating satisfactorily for several years now, both locally and to a limited extent over a wide-area network. Its design is clean and its performance is excellent. By and large we are satisfied with the results. Nevertheless, no operating system is ever finished, so we are continually working to improve it. Amoeba is now available. For information on how to obtain it, please contact the first author (Tanenbaum), preferably by electronic mail.

References

1. Accetta, M., Baron, R., Bolosky W., Golub, D., Rashid, R., Tevanian, A., and Young, M. Mach: A New Kernel Foundation for UNIX Development. *Proceedings of the Summer Usenix Conference*, Atlanta, GA, July 1986.
2. Baalbergen, E.H, Verstoep, K., and Tanenbaum, A.S. On the Design of the Amoeba Configuration Manager. *Proc. 2nd Int'l Workshop on Software Config. Mgmt.*, ACM, 1989.
3. Bal, H.E., Van Renesse, R., and Tanenbaum, A.S. Implementing Distributed Algorithms using Remote Procedure Call. *Proc. Nat. Comp. Conf.*, AFIPS, 1987. pp. 499–505.
4. Bal, H.E., and Tanenbaum, A.S. Distributed Programming with Shared Data, *IEEE Conf. on Computer Languages*, IEEE, 1988, pp. 82–91.
5. Birrell, A.D., and Nelson, B.J. Implementing Remote Procedure Calls, *ACM Trans. Comput. Systems* 2, (Feb. 1984) pp. 39–59.
6. Cheriton, D.R. The V Distributed System. *Comm. ACM* 31, (March 1988), pp. 314–333.
7. Dalal, Y.K. Broadcast Protocols in Packet Switched Computer Networks. Ph.D. Thesis, Stanford Univ., 1977.
8. Dennis, J., and Van Horn, E. Programming Semantics for Multiprogrammed Computation. *Comm. ACM* 9, (March 1966), pp. 143–155.

9. Evans, A., Kantrowitz, W., and Weiss, E. A User Authentication Scheme Not Requiring Secrecy in the Computer. *Comm. ACM* 17, (Aug. 974), pp. 437–442.

10. Feldman, S.I. Make—A Program for Maintaining Computer Programs. *Software—Practice and Experience* 9, (April 1979) pp. 255–265.

11. Johnson, S.C. Yacc Yet Another Compiler Compiler. Bell Labs Technical Report, Bell Labs, Murray Hill, NJ, 1978.

12. Kaashoek, M.F., Tanenbaum, A.S., Flynn Hummel, S., and Bal, H.E. An Efficient Reliable Broadcast Protocol. *Operating Systems Review*, vol. 23, (Oct. 1989), pp. 5–19.

13. Lawler, E.L., and Wood, D.E. Branch and Bound Methods A Survey. *Operations Research* 14, (July 1966), pp. 699–719.

14. Marsland, T.A., and Campbell, M. Parallel Search of Strongly Ordered Game Trees. *Computing Surveys* 14, (Dec. 1982), pp. 533–551.

15. Mullender, S.J., van Rossum, G., Tanenbaum, A.S., van Renesse, R., van Staveren, J.M. Amoeba—A Distributed Operating System for the 1990s. *IEEE Computer* 23, (May 1990), pp. 44–53.

16. Mullender, S.J., and Tanenbaum, A.S. The Design of a Capability-Based Distributed Operating System. *Computer Journal* 29, (Aug. 1986), pp. 289–299.

17. Mullender, S.J., and Tanenbaum, A.S. A Distributed File Service Based on Optimistic Concurrency Control. *Proc. Tenth Symp. Operating System Principles*, (Dec. 1985), pp. 51–62.

18. Ousterhout, J.K., Cherenson, A.R., Douglis, F., Nelson, M.N., and Welch, B.B. The Sprite Network Operating System. *IEEE Computer* 21, (Feb. 1988), pp. 23–26.

19. Peterson, L., Hutchinson, N., O'Malley, S., and Rao, H. The x-kernel: A Platform for Accessing Internet Resources. *IEEE Computer* 23 (May 1990), pp. 23–33.

20. Pu, C., Noe, J.D., Proudfoot, A. Regeneration of Replicated Objects: A Technique and its Eden Implementation. *Proc. 2nd Int'l Conf. on Data Eng.*, (Feb. 1986), pp. 175–187.

21. Rozier. M, Abrossimov. V, Armand. F, Boule. I, Gien. M, Guillemont. M, Hermann. F, Kaiser. C, Langlois. S, Leonard, P., and Neuhauser. W. CHORUS Distributed Operating System. *Computing Systems* 1 (Fall 1988), pp. 299–328.

22. Schroeder, M.D., and, Burrows, M. Performance of the Firefly RPC. *Proc. Twelfth ACM Symp. on Oper. Syst. Prin.*, ACM, (Dec. 1989), pp. 83–90.

23. Steiner, J.G., Neuman, C., and Schiller, J.I. Kerberos An Authentication Service for Open Network Systems. *Proceedings of the Usenix Winter Conference*, USENIX Assoc., (1988), pp. 191–201.

24. Stonebraker, M. Operating System Support for Database Management. *Comm. ACM* 24, (July 1981), pp. 412–418.

25. Tanenbaum, A.S. A UNIX Clone with Source Code for Operating Systems Courses. *Operating Syst. Rev.* 21, (Jan. 1987), pp. 20–29.

26. Tanenbaum, A.S., Mullender, S.J., and Van Renesse, R. Using Sparse Capabilities in a Distributed Operating System. *Proc. Sixth International Conf. on Distr. Computer Systems*, IEEE, 1986.

27. Tanenbaum, A.S., and Van Renesse, R. A Critique of the Remote Procedure Call Paradigm. *Proc. Euteco '88*, (1988), pp. 775–783.

28. Tanenbaum, A.S., and Van Renesse, R. Distributed Operating Systems. *Computing Surveys* 17, (Dec. 1985), pp. 419–470.

29. Van Renesse, R., Tanenbaum, A.S., and Wilschut, A. The Design of a High-Performance File Server. *Proc. Ninth Int'l Conf. on Distr. Comp. Systems*, IEEE, (1989a), pp. 22–27.

30. Van Renesse, R., Tanenbaum, A.S., Van Staveren, H., and Hall, J. Connecting RPC-Based Distributed Systems Using Wide-Area Networks. *Proc. Seventh Int'l Conf. on Distr. Comp. Systems*, IEEE, (1987), pp. 28–34.

31. Van Renesse, R., Van Staveren, H., and Tanenbaum, A.S. Performance of the Amoeba Distributed Operating System. *Software—Practice and Experience* 19, (March 1989b) pp. 223–234.

32. Van Renesse, R., Van Staveren, H., and Tanenbaum, A.S. Performance of the World's Fastest Distributed Operating System. *Operating Systems Review* 22, (Oct. 1988), pp. 25–34.

33. Van Rossum, G. AIL—A Class-Oriented Stub Generator for Amoeba. *Proc. of the Workshop on Experience with Distributed Systems*, (J. Nehmer, ed.), Springer Verlag, 1990 (in preparation).

34. Welch, B.B. and Ousterhout, J.K. Pseudo Devices: User-Level Extensions to the Sprite File System. *Proc. Summer USENIX Conf.*, pp. 37–49, June 1988.

BIBLIOGRAPHY

This is an alphabetic list of all operating systems considered for inclusion in this book. The selected systems are marked with a bullet, for example, •*Amoeba System.* For each system there is a chronological list of literature. These lists include cross-references to the selected articles, such as *Article 24.*

Accent Kernel (1981)

R. F. Rashid and G. G. Robertson 1981. Accent: a communication oriented network operating system kernel. *ACM Symposium on Operating Systems Principles 8*, 64–75.

• Alto System (1979–88)

B. W. Lampson and R. F. Sproull 1979. An open operating system for a single-user machine. *Operating Systems Review 13*, 5 (December), 98–105. *Article 18.*

A. Z. Spector 1982. Performing remote operations efficiently on a local computer network. *Communications of the ACM 25*, 4 (April), 246–260.

B. W. Lampson 1988. Personal distributed computing: the Alto and Ethernet software. In *A History of Personal Workstations*, A. Goldberg Ed., Addison-Wesley, Reading, MA, 291–344.

• Amoeba System (1981–90)

A. S. Tanenbaum and S. Mullender 1981. An overview of the Amoeba distributed operating system. *Operating Systems Review 15*, 3 (July), 51–64.

A. S. Tanenbaum and R. van Renesse 1988. A critique of the remote procedure call paradigm. *Research into Networks and Distributed Applications*, R. Speth Ed., North-Holland, Amsterdam, The Netherlands, 775–783.

S. J. Mullender, G. van Rossum, A. S. Tanenbaum, R. van Renesse and H. van Staveren 1990. Amoeba: a distributed operating system for the 1990s. *IEEE Computer 23*, 5 (May), 44–53.

A. S. Tanenbaum, R. van Renesse, H. van Staveren, G. J. Sharp, S. J. Mullenden, J. Jansen and G. van Rossum 1990. Experiences with the Amoeba distributed operating system. *Communications of the ACM 33*, 12 (December), 46–63. *Article 24.*

Andrew System (1985–90)

M. Satyanarayanan, J. H. Howard, D. A. Nichols, R. N. Sidebotham, A. Z. Spector and M. J. West 1985. The ITC distributed file system: principles and design. *ACM Symposium on Operating Systems Principles*, (December), 35–50.

J. H. Morris, M. Satyanarayanan, M. H. Conner, J. H. Howard, D. S. H. Rosenthal and F. D. Smith 1986. Andrew: a distributed personal computing environment. *Communications of the ACM 29*, 3 (March), 184–201.

J. H. Howard, M. J. Kazar, S. G. Menees, D. A. Nichols, M. Satyanarayanan, R. N. Sidebotham and M. J. West 1988. Scale and performance in a distributed file system. *ACM Transactions on Computer Systems 6*, 1 (February), 55–81.

M. Satyanarayanan 1990. Scalable, secure and highly available distributed file access. *IEEE Computer 23*, 5 (May), 9–21.

Apollo Domain (1983)

P. J. Leach, P. H. Levine, B. P. Douros, J. A. Hamilton, D. L. Nelson and B. L. Stumpf 1983. The architecture of an integrated local network. *IEEE Journal on Selected Areas in Communications 1*, 5, 842–856.

Athena System (1985–90)

E. Balkovich, S. R. Lerman and R. P. Parmelee 1985. Computing in higher education: the Athena experience. *Communications of the ACM 28*, 11 (November), 1214–1224.

G. W. Treese 1988. Berkeley Unix on 1000 workstations: Athena changes to 4.3BSD. *Usenix Conference*, (February), 175–182.

G. A. Champine, D. E. Geer, Jr. and W. N. Ruh 1990. Project Athena as a distributed computer system. *IEEE Computer 23*, (September), 40–51.

• Atlas System (1961–72)

T. Kilburn, R. B. Payne and D. J. Howarth 1961a. The Atlas supervisor. *AFIPS Computer Conference 20*, 279–294. *Article 3.*

T. Kilburn, D. J. Howarth, R. B. Payne and F. H. Sumner 1961b. The Manchester University Atlas operating system. Part I: Internal organization. *The Computer Journal 4*, 1 (April), 222–225.

D. J. Howarth, R. B. Payne and F. H. Sumner 1961. The Manchester University Atlas operating system. Part II: User's description. *The Computer Journal 4*, 3 (October), 226–229.

J. Fotheringham 1961. Dynamic storage allocation in the Atlas computer including an automatic use of a backing store. *Communications of the ACM 4*, 10 (October), 435–436.

D. Morris, F. H. Sumner and M. T. Wyld 1967. An appraisal of the Atlas supervisor. *ACM National Meeting*, (August), 67–75.

M. H. J. Baylis, D. G. Fletcher and D. J. Howarth 1968. Paging studies made on the ICT Atlas computer. *IFIP Congress*, (August), 831–836.

D. J. Howarth 1972. A re-appraisal of certain features of the Atlas I supervisory system. In *Operating Systems Techniques*, C. A. R. Hoare and R. H. Perrott Eds., Academic Press, New York, 371–377.

BBN System (1963)

J. McCarthy, S. Boilen, E. Fredkin and J. C. R. Licklider 1963. A time-sharing debugging system for a small computer. *Spring Joint Computer Conference 23*, 51–57.

• BKS System (1961)

R. B. Smith 1961. The BKS system for the Philco-2000. *Communications of the ACM 4*, 2 (February), 104 and 109. *Article 2.*

• Boss-2 System (1975)

S. Lauesen 1975. A large semaphore based operating system. *Communications of the ACM 18*, 7 (July), 377–389. *Article 14.*

• Burroughs B5000 System (1961–87)

R. S. Barton 1961. A new approach to the functional design of a digital computer. *Joint Conference Proceedings 19*, 393–396.

W. Lonergan and P. King 1961. Design of the B 5000 system. *Datamation 7*, 5 (May), 28–32.

C. Oliphint 1964. Operating system for the B 5000. *Datamation 10*, 5 (May), 42–54. *Article 4.*

F. B. MacKenzie 1965. Automated secondary storage management. *Datamation 11*, 11 (November), 24–28.

D. J. Roche 1972. Burroughs B5500 MCP and time-sharing MCP. In *Operating Systems Techniques*, C. A. R. Hoare and R. H. Perrott Eds. Academic Press, New York, 307–320.

D. P. Fenton 1972. B6700 "working set" memory allocation. In *Operating Systems Techniques*, C. A. R. Hoare and R. H. Perrott Eds. Academic Press, New York, 321–327.

E. I. Organick 1973. *Computer System Organization: The B5700/B6700 Series.* Academic Press, New York.

R. M. McKeag 1976. Burroughs B5500 Master Control Program. In *Studies in Operating Systems*, R. M. McKeag and R. Wilson Eds., Academic Press, New York, 1–66.

R. F. Rosin, Ed. 1987. Prologue: the Burroughs B 5000. *Annals of the History of Computing 9*, 1, 6–7.

CAL System (1976)

B. W. Lampson and H. E. Sturgis 1976. Reflections on an operating system design. *Communications of the ACM 19*, 5 (May), 251–265.

Cambridge Distributed System (1980–82)

M. V. Wilkes and R. M. Needham 1980. The Cambridge Model Distributed System. *Operating Systems Review 14*, 1 (January), 21–29.

A. D. Birrell and R. M. Needham 1980. A universal file server. *IEEE Transactions on Software Engineering 6*, 5 (September), 450–453.

C. Dellar 1980. Removing backing store administration from the CAP operating system. *Operating Systems Review 14*, 4 (October), 41–49.

J. Dion 1980. The Cambridge file server. *Operating Systems Review 14*, 4 (October), 26–35.

R. M. Needham and A. J. Herbert 1982. *The Cambridge Distributed Computing System.* Addison-Wesley, Reading, MA.

J. G. Mitchell and J. Dion 1982. A comparison of two network-based file servers. *Communications of the ACM 25*, 4 (April), 233–245.

CDC 6600 Systems (1967–76)

M. C. Harrison and J. T. Schwartz 1967. Sharer, a time sharing system for the CDC 6600. *Communications of the ACM 10*, 10 (October), 659–665.

D. F. Stevens 1968. On overcoming high-priority paralysis in multiprogramming systems: a case history. *Communications of the ACM 11*, 8 (August), 539–541.

V. A. Abell, S. Rosen and R. E. Wagner 1970. Scheduling in a general purpose operating system. *Fall Joint Computer Conference*, 89–96.

H. Lipps 1972. Batch processing with 6600-series Scope. In *Operating Systems Techniques*, C. A. R. Hoare and R. H. Perrott Eds., Academic Press, New York, 291–297.

R. Wilson 1976. CDC Scope 3.2. In *Studies in Operating Systems*, R. M. McKeag and R. Wilson Eds., Academic Press, New York, 67–144.

Cedar System (1984–88)

W. Teitelman 1984. A tour through Cedar. *IEEE Software 1*, 2, 44–73.

A. D. Birrell and B. J. Nelson 1984. Implementing remote procedure calls. *ACM Transactions on Computer Systems 2*, 1 (February), 39–59.

D. C. Swinehart, P. T. Zellweger and R. B. Hagmann 1985. The structure of Cedar. *SIGPLAN Notices 20*, 7 (July), 230–244.

M. R. Brown, K. N. Kolling and E. A. Taft 1985. The Alpine file system. *Transactions on Computer Systems 3*, 4 (November), 261–293.

D. K. Gifford, R. M. Needham and M. D. Schroeder 1988. The Cedar file system. *Communications of the ACM 31*, 3 (March), 288–298.

Chorus System (1988)

M. Rozier, V. Abrossimov, F. Armand, I. Boule, M. Gien, M. Guillemont, F. Hermann, C. Kaiser, S. Langlois, P. Leonard and W. Neuhauser 1988. Chorus distributed operating system. *Computing Systems 1*, (October), 305–379.

M. Rozier, V. Abrossimov, F. Armand, I. Boule, M. Gien, M. Guillemont, F. Hermann, C. Kaiser, S. Langlois, P. Leonard and W. Neuhauser 1992. Overview of the Chorus distributed operating system. *Usenix Workshop on Microkernels and other Kernel Architectures*, (April), 39–70.

CP/M (1978–81)

J. F. Stewart 1978. CP/M primer—a most sophisticated operating system. *Kilobaud*, (April), 30–34.

G. Kildall 1981. CP/M: a family of 8- and 16-bit operating systems. *Byte 6*, 6 (June), 216–232.

• CTSS System (1962–66)

F. J. Corbató, M. Merwin-Daggett and R. C. Daley 1962. An experimental time-sharing system. *Spring Joint Computer Conference 21*, 335–344. *Article 7.*

P. A. Crisman Ed. 1965. *The Compatible Time-Sharing System: A Programmer's Guide.* Second Edition, The MIT Press, Cambridge, MA.

Jack Dennis' System (1964)

J. B. Dennis 1964. A multiuser computation facility for education and research. *Communications of the ACM 7*, 9 (September), 521–529.

• Egdon System (1966)

D. Burns, E. N. Hawkins, D. R. Judd and J. L. Venn 1966. The Egdon system for the KDF9. *The Computer Journal 8*, 4 (January), 297–302. *Article 6.*

• Exec II System (1966–72)

W. C. Lynch 1966. Description of a high capacity fast turnaround university computing center. *Communications of the ACM 9*, 2 (February), 117–123. *Article 5.*

W. C. Lynch 1972. An operating system designed for the computer utility environment. In *Operating Systems Techniques*, C. A. R. Hoare and R. H. Perrott Eds. Academic Press, New York, 341–350.

Grapevine System (1982–84)

A. D. Birrell, R. Levin, R. M. Needham and M. D. Schroeder 1982. Grapevine: an exercise in distributed computing. *Communications of the ACM 25*, 4 (April), 260–273.

M. D. Schroeder, A. D. Birrell and R. M. Needham 1984. Experience with Grapevine: the growth of a distributed system. *ACM Transactions on Computer Systems 2*, (1), 3–23.

Hydra System (1974–75)

W. A. Wulf, E. S. Cohen, W. M. Corwin, A. K. Jones. R. Levin, C. Pierson and F. J. Pollack 1974. Hydra: the kernel of a multiprocessor operating system. *Communications of the ACM 17*, 6 (June), 337–345.

W. A. Wulf, R. Levin and C. Pierson 1975. Overview of the Hydra operating system development. *ACM Symposium on Operating Systems Principles*, (November), 122–131.

E. Cohen and D. Jefferson 1975. Protection in the Hydra operating system. *ACM Symposium on Operating Systems Principles*, (November), 141–160.

• IBM 701 Open Shop (1983)

G. F. Ryckman 1983. The IBM 701 computer at the General Motors Research Laboratories. *Annals of the History of Computing 5*, 2 (April), 210–212. *Article 1.*

Edgar Irons' System (1965)

E. T. Irons 1965. A rapid turnaround multiprogramming system. *Communications of the ACM 8*, 3 (March), 152–157.

JOSS (1964)

J. C. Shaw 1964. JOSS: a designer's view of an experimental online computing system. *Fall Joint Computer Conference 26*, 454–464.

Locus System (1981–83)

G. J. Popek, B. J. Walker, J. Chow, D. Edwards, C. Kline, G. Rudison and G. Thiel 1981. Locus: a network transparent, high reliability distributed system. *ACM Symposium on Operating Systems Principles*, Pacific Grove, CA, 169–177.

B. J. Walker, G. J. Popek, R. M. English, C. Kline and G. Thiel 1983. The Locus distributed operating system. *ACM Symposium on Operating Systems Principles*, (December), 49–70.

E. T. Mueller, J. D. Moore and G.J. Popek 1983. A nested transaction system for Locus. *Operating Systems Review 17*, 5, 71–89.

Mac System (1984)

L. Poole 1984. A tour of the Mac desktop. *Macworld 1*, (May–June), 19–26.

Mach System (1986)

M. Accetta, R. Baron, W. Bolosky, D. Golub, R. Rashid, A. Tevanian and M. Young 1986. Mach: a new kernel foundation for Unix development. *Usenix Conference*, (July), 93–112.

• Multics System (1965–72)

F. J. Córbato and V. A. Vyssotsky 1965. Introduction and overview of the Multics system. *Fall Joint Computer Conference 27*, 185–196.

V. A. Vyssotsky, F. J. Córbato and R. M. Graham 1965. Structure of the Multics supervisor. *Fall Joint Computer Conference 27*, 203–212.

R. C. Daley and P. G. Neumann 1965. A general purpose file system for secondary storage. *Fall Joint Computer Conference 27*, 213–229. *Article 8.*

R. C. Daley and J. B. Dennis 1968. Virtual memory, processes and sharing in Multics. *Communications of the ACM 11*, 5 (May), 306–312.

F. J. Córbato, J. H. Saltzer and C. T. Clingen 1972. Multics—the first seven years. *Spring Joint Computer Conference 40*, 571–583.

E. I. Organick 1972, *The Multics System: An Examination of Its Structure.* The MIT Press, Cambridge, MA.

Oberon System (1989)

N. Wirth and J. Gutknecht 1989. The Oberon System. *Software—Practice and Experience 19*, 9 (September), 857–893.

• OS 6 (1972)

J. E. Stoy and C. Strachey 1972. OS6—an experimental operating system for a small computer. *The Computer Journal 15*, 2 & 3, 117–124 & 195–203. *Article 17.*

• Pilot System (1980)

D. D. Redell, Y. K. Dalal, T. R. Horsley, H. C. Lauer, W. C. Lynch, P. R. McJones, H. G. Murray and S. C. Purcell 1980. Pilot: an operating system for a personal computer. *Communications of the ACM 23*, 2 (February), 81–92. *Article 19.*

Plan 9 System (1995)

R. Pike, D. Presotto, S. Dorward, B. Flandrena, K. Thompson, H. Trickey and P. Winterbottom 1995. *Plan 9 from Bell Labs.* Lucent Technologies.

• RC 4000 System (1969–73)

P. Brinch Hansen 1969. *RC 4000 Software: Multiprogramming System.* Regnecentralen, Copenhagen, Denmark, (April). *Article 12.*

P. Brinch Hansen 1970. The nucleus of a multiprogramming system. *Communications of the ACM 13*, 4 (April), 238–241, 250.

P. Brinch Hansen 1973a. *Operating System Principles*, Chapter 8. A Case Study: RC 4000. Prentice-Hall, Englewood Cliffs, NJ, 237–286.

P. Brinch Hansen 1973b. Testing a multiprogramming system. *Software—Practice and Experience 3*, 2 (April–June), 145–150.

Roscoe System (1979)

M. H. Solomon and R. A. Finkel 1979. The Roscoe distributed operating system. *ACM Symposium on Operating Systems Principles*, (December), 108–114.

SAGE System (1957–83)

R. R. Everett, C. A. Zraket and H. D. Benington 1957. SAGE—a data processing system for air defense. *Eastern Joint Computer Conference*, 148–155.

M. Astrahan and J. F. Jacobs 1983. History of the design of the SAGE computer—the AN/FSQ-7. *Annals of the History of Computing 5*, 4, 340–349.

SDC Q-32 System (1964–67)

J. I. Schwartz, E. G. Coffman and C. Weissman 1964. A general-purpose time-sharing system. *Conference Proceedings 25*, 397–411.

J. I. Schwartz and C. Weissman 1967. The SDC time-sharing system revisited. *ACM National Meeting*, (August), 263–271.

SDS 940 System (1966)

B. W. Lampson, W. W. Lichtenberger and M. W. Pirtle 1966. A user machine in a time-sharing system. *Proceedings of the IEEE 54*, 12 (December), 1766–1774.

SHARE 709 System (1959)

D. L. Shell 1959. The SHARE 709 system: a cooperative effort. *Journal of the ACM 6*, 2 (April), 123–127.

O. Mock and C. J. Swift 1959. The SHARE 709 system: programmed input-output buffering. *Journal of the ACM 6*, 2 (April), 145–151.

H. Bratman and I. V. Boldt, Jr. 1959. The SHARE 709 system: supervisory control. *Journal of the ACM 6*, 2 (April), 152–155.

K. V. Hanford 1960. The SHARE operating system for the IBM 709. *Annual Review in Automatic Programming 3*, Pergamon Press, New York, 169–177.

• Solo System (1976–93)

P. Brinch Hansen 1976a. The Solo operating system: a Concurrent Pascal program. *Software—Practice and Experience 6*, 2 (April–June), 141–149. *Article 15.*

P. Brinch Hansen 1976b. The Solo operating system: job interface. *Software—Practice and Experience 6*, 2 (April–June), 151–164.

P. Brinch Hansen 1976c. The Solo operating system: processes, monitors and classes. *Software—Practice and Experience 6*, 2 (April–June), 165–200. *Article 16.*

P. Brinch Hansen 1976d. Disk scheduling at compile time. *Software—Practice and Experience 6*, 2 (April–June), 201–205.

P. Brinch Hansen 1977a. Experience with modular concurrent programming. *IEEE Transactions on Software Engineering 3*, 2 (March), 156–159.

P. Brinch Hansen 1977b. *The Architecture of Concurrent Programs.* Prentice-Hall, Englewood Cliffs, NJ, July.

P. Brinch Hansen 1993. Monitors and Concurrent Pascal: a personal history. *SIGPLAN Notices 28*, 3 (March), 1–35.

Sprite System (1988)

J. K. Ousterhout, A. R. Cherenson, F. Douglis, M. N. Nelson and B. B. Welch 1988. The Sprite network operating system. *IEEE Computer 21*, 2 (February), 23–36.

• Star System (1982)

D. C. Smith, C. Irby, R. Kimball, B. Verplank and E. Harslem 1982. Designing the Star user interace. *Byte*, (April), 242–282.

D. C. Smith, C. Irby, R. Kimball and E. Harslem 1982. The Star user interface: an overview. *National Computer Conference*, 515–528. *Article 20.*

J. A. Johnson, T. L. Roberts, W. Verplank, D. C. Smith, C. H. Irby, M. Beard, K. Mackey 1989. The Xerox Star: a retrospective. *IEEE Computer 22*, (September) 11–29.

SUN Network File System (1985)

R. Sandberg, D. Goldberg, S. Kleiman, D. Walsh and B. Lyon 1985. Design and implementation of the Sun Network Filesystem. *Usenix Conference*, (June), 119–130.

Taos System (1990)

B. N. Bershad, T. E. Anderson, E. D. Lazowska and H. M. Levy 1990. Lightweight remote procedure call. *ACM Transactions on Computer Systems 8*, 1 (February), 37–55.

Tenex System (1972)

D. G. Bobrow, J. D. Burchfiel, D. L. Murphy and R. S. Tomlinson 1972. Tenex, a paged time sharing system for the PDP-10. *Communications of the ACM 15*, 3 (March), 135–143.

• THE System (1968–76)

E. W. Dijkstra 1968. The structure of the THE multiprogramming system. *Communications of the ACM 11*, 5 (May), 341–346. *Article 11.*

C. Bron 1972. Allocation of virtual store in the THE multiprogramming system. In *Operating Systems Techniques*, C. A. R. Hoare and R. H. Perrott Eds., Academic Press, New York, 168–184.

R. M. McKeag 1976. THE multiprogramming system. In *Studies in Operating Systems*, R. M. McKeag and R. Wilson Eds., Academic Press, New York, 145–184.

• Titan System (1967–76)

D. W. Barron, A. G. Fraser, D. F. Hartley, B. Landy and R. M. Needham 1967. File handling at Cambridge University. *Spring Joint Computer Conference 30*, 163–167.

A. G. Fraser 1968. User control in a multi-access system. *The Computer Journal 11*, 1, 12–16.

D. F. Hartley, B. Landy and R. M. Needham 1968. The structure of a multiprogramming supervisor. *The Computer Journal 11*, 3 (November), 247–255.

A. G. Fraser 1969. Integrity of a mass storage filing system. *The Computer Journal 12*, 1 (February), 1–5.

B. Landy 1971. Development of scheduling strategies in the Titan operating system. *Software—Practice and Experience 1*, 279–297.

D. F. Hartley 1972. Techniques in the Titan supervisor. In *Operating Systems Techniques*, C. A. R. Hoare and R. H. Perrott Eds., Academic Press, New York, 271–276.

A. G. Fraser 1972. File integrity in a disc-based multi-access system. In *Operating Systems Techniques*, C. A. R. Hoare and R. H. Perrott Eds., Academic Press, New York, 227–248. *Article 9.*

R. M. Needham 1972. Tuning the Titan operating system. In *Operating Systems Techniques*, C. A. R. Hoare and R. H. Perrott Eds., Academic Press, New York, 277–281.

M. V. Wilkes 1973. The Cambridge multi-access system in retrospect. *Software—Practice and Experience 3*, 323–332.

R. Wilson 1976. The Titan supervisor. In *Studies in Operating Systems*, R. M. McKeag and R. Wilson Eds., Academic Press, New York, 185–263.

Tripos System (1979)

M. Richards, A. R. Aylward, P. Bond, R. D. Evans and B. J. Knight 1979. Tripos—a portable operating system for minicomputers. *Software—Practice and Experience 9*, 7 (July), 513–526.

• Unix System (1974–79)

D. M. Ritchie and K. Thompson 1974. The Unix time-sharing system. *Communications of the ACM 17*, 7 (July), 365–375. *Article 10.*

J. Lions 1977. *Lions' Commentary on Unix 6th Edition with Source Code.* Peer-to-Peer Communications, San Jose, CA.

B. W. Kernighan and J. R. Mashey, J. 1979. The Unix programming environment. *Software—Practice and Experience 9*, 1 (January), 1–15.

• Unix United (1982)

S. K. Shrivastava and F. Panzieri 1982. The design of a reliable remote procedure call mechanism. *IEEE Transactions on Computers 31*, 7 (July), 692–697. *Article 22.*

D. R. Brownbridge, L. F. Marshall and B. Randell 1982. The Newcastle Connection or Unixes of the World Unite! *Software—Practice and Experience 12*, 12 (December), 1147–1162. *Article 23.*

• Venus System (1972)

B. H. Liskov 1972. The design of the Venus operating system. *Communications of the ACM 15*, 3 (March), 144–149. *Article 13.*

V Kernel (1984–88)

D. R. Cheriton 1984. The V kernel: a software base for a distributed system. *IEEE Software 1*, 2 (April), 19–42.

D. R. Cheriton 1988. The V distributed system. *Communications of the ACM 31*, 3 (March), 314–333.

• WFS File System (1979)

D. Swinehart, G. McDaniel and D. R. Boggs 1979. WFS: a simple shared file system for a distributed environment. *ACM Symposium on Operating Systems Principles*, Pacific Grove, CA, (December), 9–17. *Article 21.*

Xerox Distributed File System (1978–82)

J. E. Israel, J. G. Mitchell and H. E. Sturgis 1978. Separating data from function in a distributed file system. In *Operating Systems: Theory and Practice*, D. Lanciaux Ed., North-Holland, Amsterdam, The Netherlands, 17–27.

J. G. Mitchell and J. Dion 1982. A comparison of two network-based file servers. *Communications of the ACM 25*, 4 (April), 233–245.

X-Kernel (1989)

N. C. Hutchinson, L. L. Peterson, M. B. Abbott and S. O'Malley 1989. RPC in the x-kernel: evaluating new design techniques. *Operating Systems Review 23*, 5, 91–101.